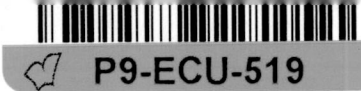

THE ART OF SHEN KU

BY ZEEK

"THE ULTIMATE TRAVELER'S GUIDE OF THIS PLANET"

THE FIRST INTERGALACTIC ARTFORM OF THE ENTIRE UNIVERSE

HEALTH is a Princess in this Artform because responsibility is an honor, most missed if it goes.

HUMOR is a Prince in this Artform because happiness is more valuable than gold.

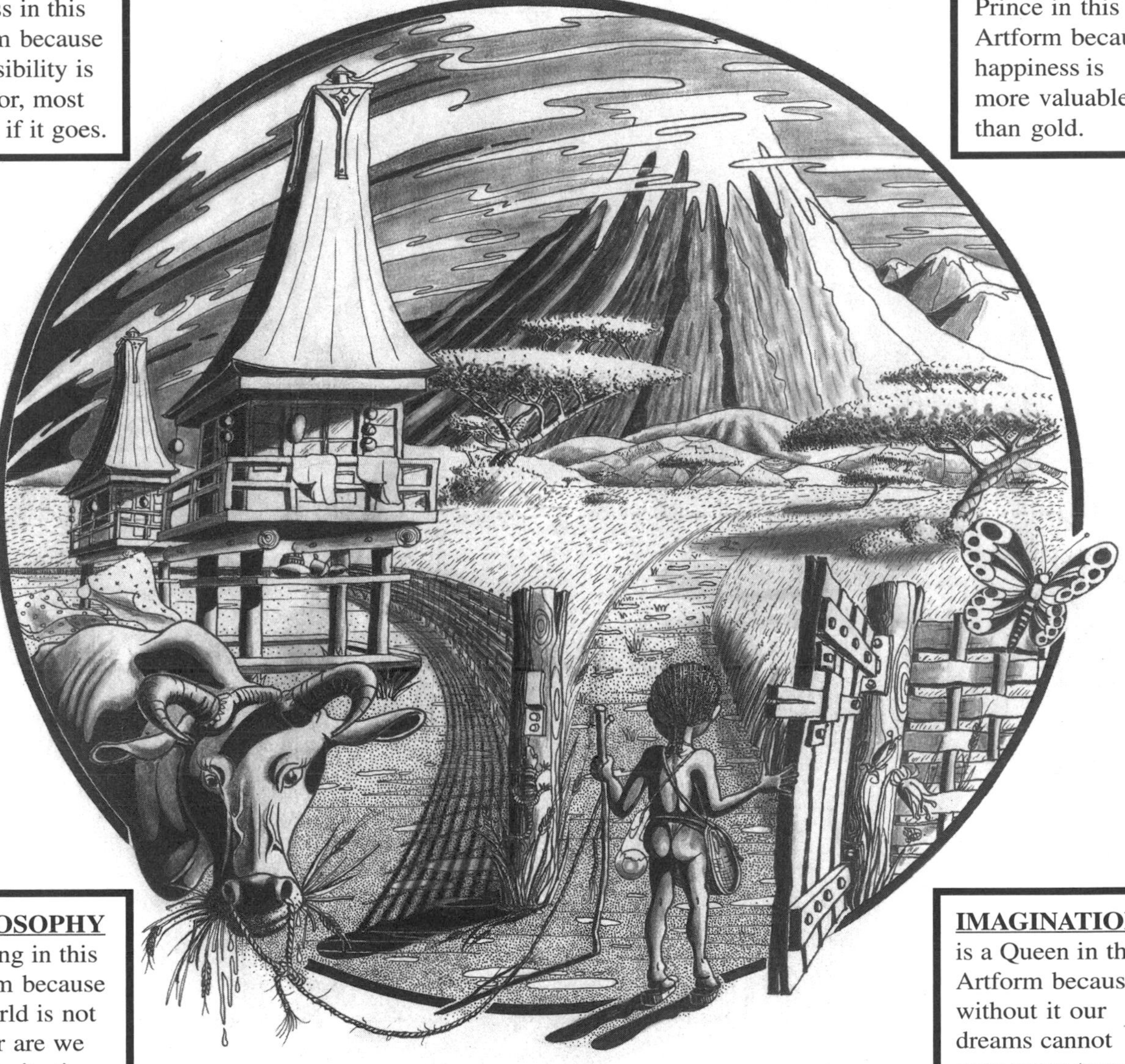

PHILOSOPHY is a King in this Artform because the world is not flat nor are we alone in its time.

IMAGINATION is a Queen in this Artform because without it our dreams cannot ever come true.

A PERIGEE BOOK

DEDICATED TO ALL LIFE IN ANY GALAXY, suffering from illness, persecution, circumstance or despair - This Work is for you - ......DON'T GIVE UP.

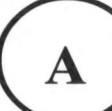

DEDICATED TO ALL LIFE IN ANY GALAXY,

SUFFERING FROM ILLNESS, PERSECUTION, CIRCUMSTANCE, OR DESPAIR. THIS WORK IS FOR YOU . . . DON'T GIVE UP.

The ART OF SHEN KU is....

....an intergalactic form, & as such will in time be (& actually already is) exchanged across the ultimate boundaries of time & space (which it transcends). Its logics govern all conscious progress & are profoundly applicable & totally diversifiable to any "intelligent" life or species on or off any celestial body absolutely anywhere.
It is (& always was) both logically & culturally...............

THE FIRST INTERGALACTIC ARTFORM
OF THE ENTIRE UNIVERSE

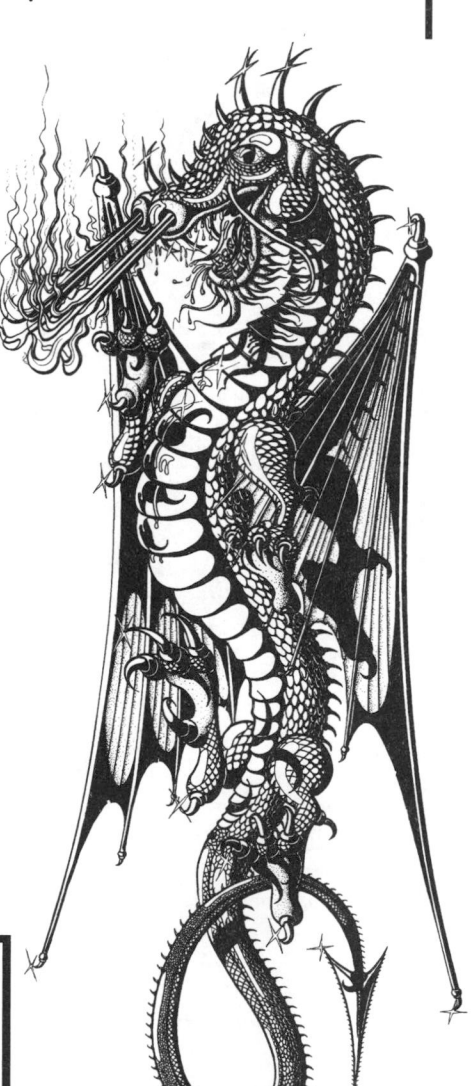

A Perigee Book
Published by The Berkley Publishing Group
A division of Penguin Putnam Inc.
375 Hudson Street
New York, New York 10014

Copyright © 1999 by Zeek
Illustrations copyright © by Zeek

Previously published in the UK by Shen Ku
First Perigee edition: September 2001
Published simultaneously in Canada.

Visit our website at
www.penguinputnam.com

Library of Congress Cataloging-in-Publication Data

Zeek.
   The art of Shen Ku : "the ultimate traveler's guide" : the first intergalactic artform of the entire universe / by Zeek.
       p. cm.
   ISBN 0-399-52725-7
   1. Travel—Safety measures. 2. Travel—Health aspects. 3. Fantasy in art. I. Title.

G155.A1 Z44 2001
910'.2'020207—dc21

                                                              2001036109

DISCLAIMER

THIS BOOK IS DESIGNED TO PROVIDE ACCURATE AND AUTHORI-TATIVE INFORMATION. THE INFORMATION PROVIDED IN THIS BOOK IS NOT INTENDED AS A SUBSTITUTE FOR MEDICAL OR OTHER EXPERT ADVICE. THE PUBLISHER AND THE AUTHOR EXPRESSLY DISCLAIM RESPONSIBILITY FOR ANY UNFORSEEN CONSE-QUENCES ARISING FROM THE INFORMATION CONTAINED HEREIN.

Printed in the United States of America
10 9 8 7 6 5 4 3 2

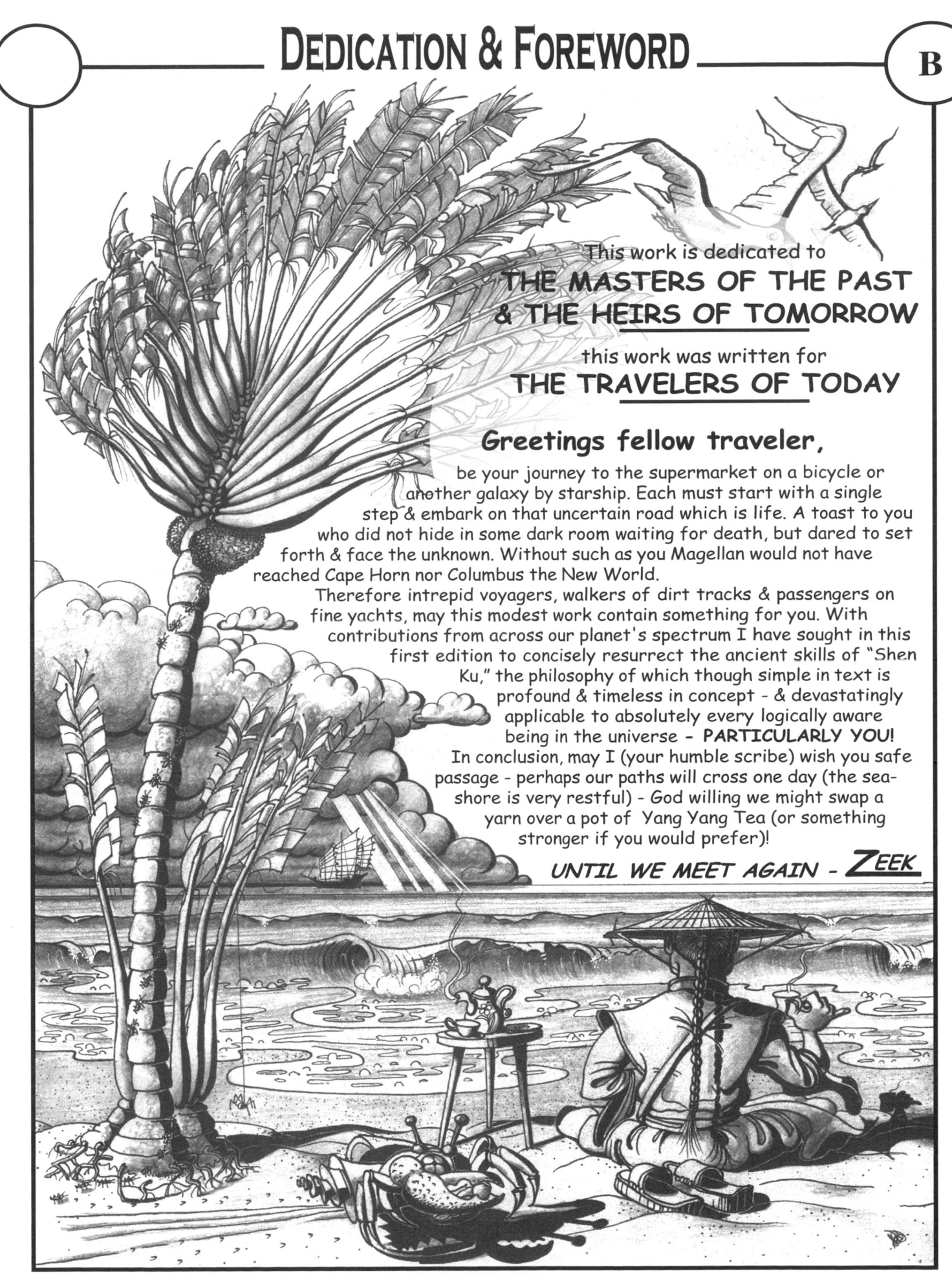

This work is dedicated to

THE MASTERS OF THE PAST & THE HEIRS OF TOMORROW

this work was written for

THE TRAVELERS OF TODAY

Greetings fellow traveler,

be your journey to the supermarket on a bicycle or another galaxy by starship. Each must start with a single step & embark on that uncertain road which is life. A toast to you who did not hide in some dark room waiting for death, but dared to set forth & face the unknown. Without such as you Magellan would not have reached Cape Horn nor Columbus the New World.

Therefore intrepid voyagers, walkers of dirt tracks & passengers on fine yachts, may this modest work contain something for you. With contributions from across our planet's spectrum I have sought in this first edition to concisely resurrect the ancient skills of "Shen Ku," the philosophy of which though simple in text is profound & timeless in concept - & devastatingly applicable to absolutely every logically aware being in the universe - **PARTICULARLY YOU!**

In conclusion, may I (your humble scribe) wish you safe passage - perhaps our paths will cross one day (the seashore is very restful) - God willing we might swap a yarn over a pot of Yang Yang Tea (or something stronger if you would prefer)!

UNTIL WE MEET AGAIN - ZEEK

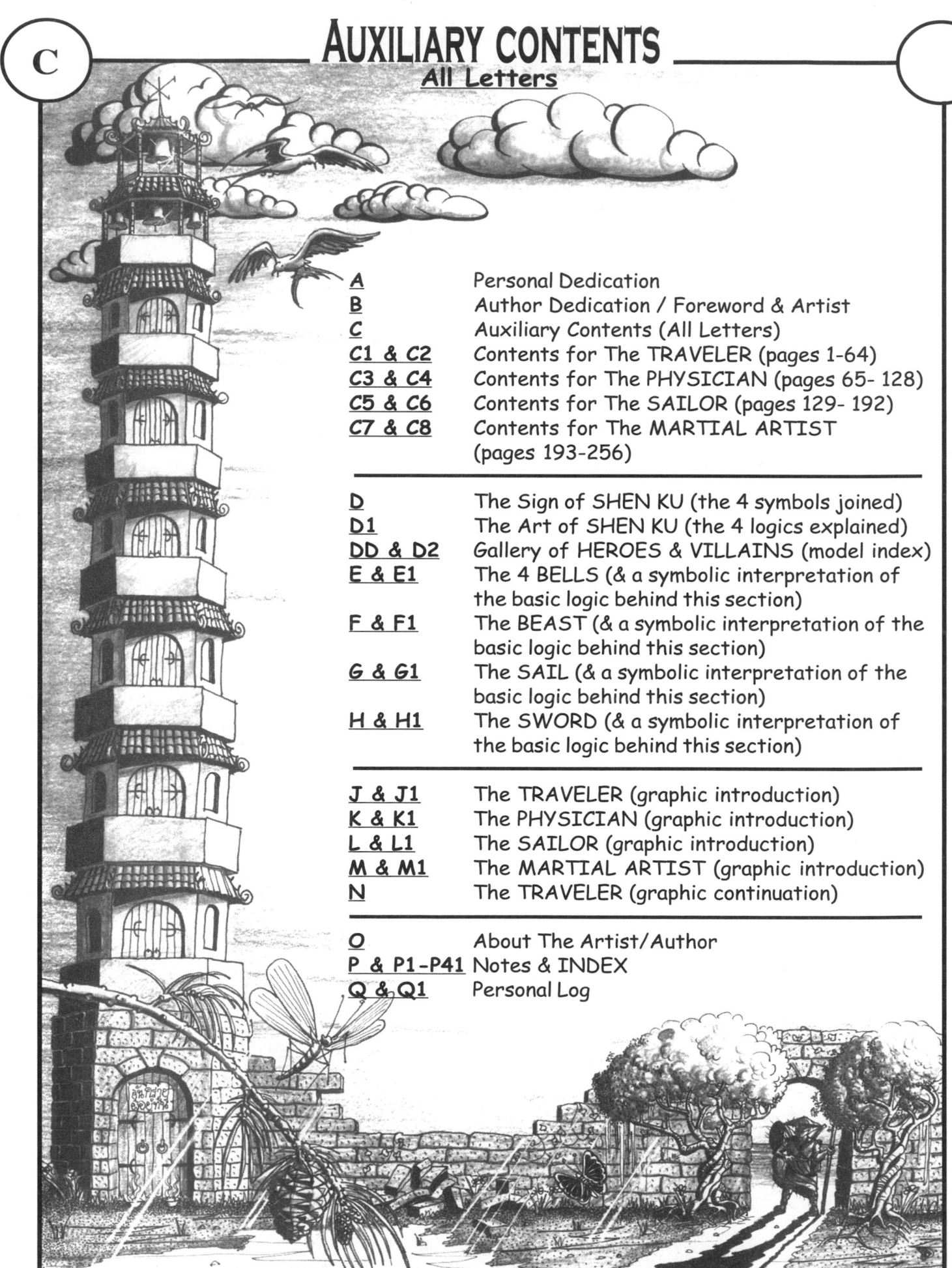

AUXILIARY CONTENTS
All Letters

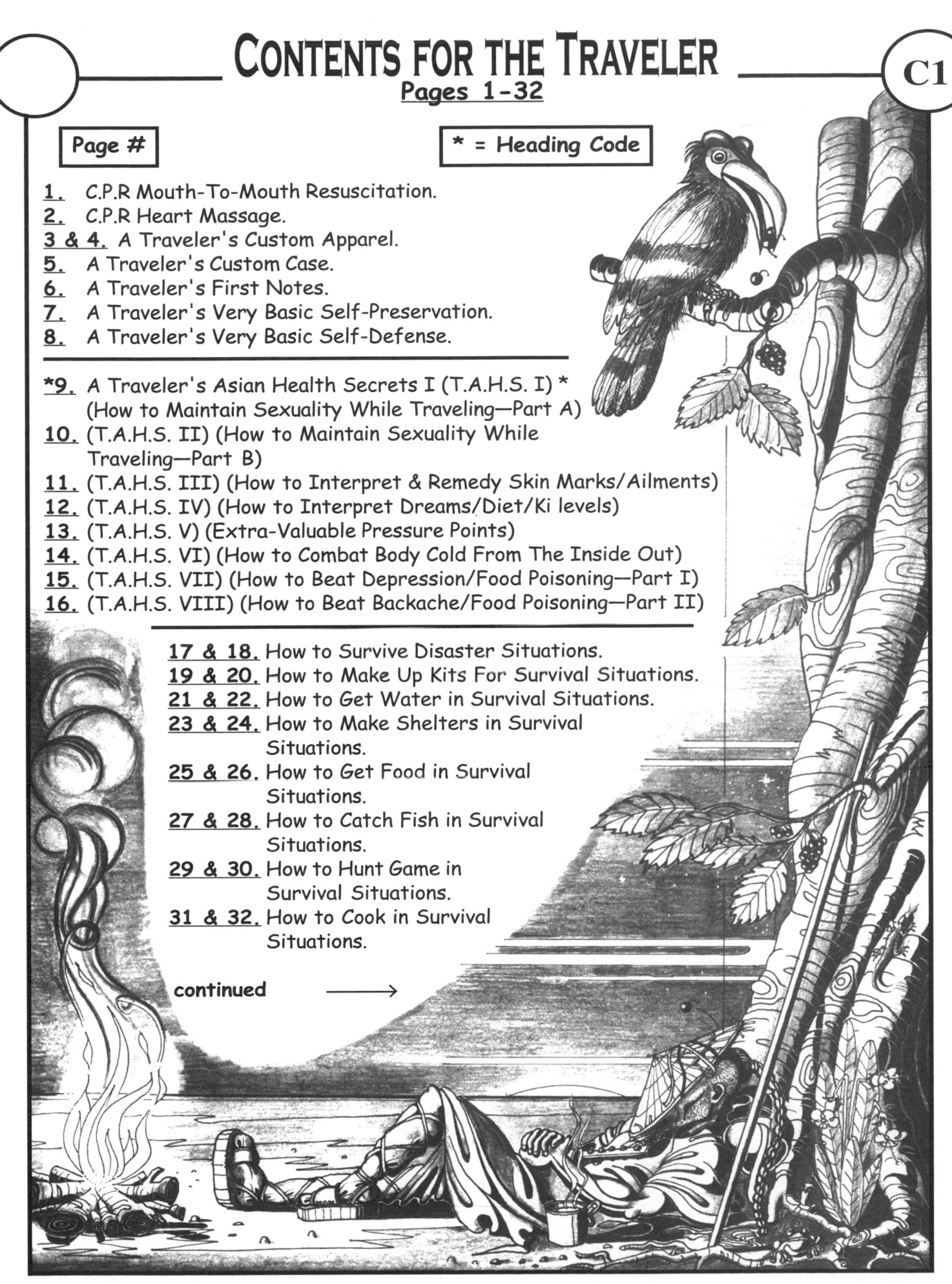

CONTENTS FOR THE TRAVELER
Pages 1-32

Page #   * = Heading Code

continued ⟶

CONTENTS FOR THE TRAVELER

pages 33-64

Page #

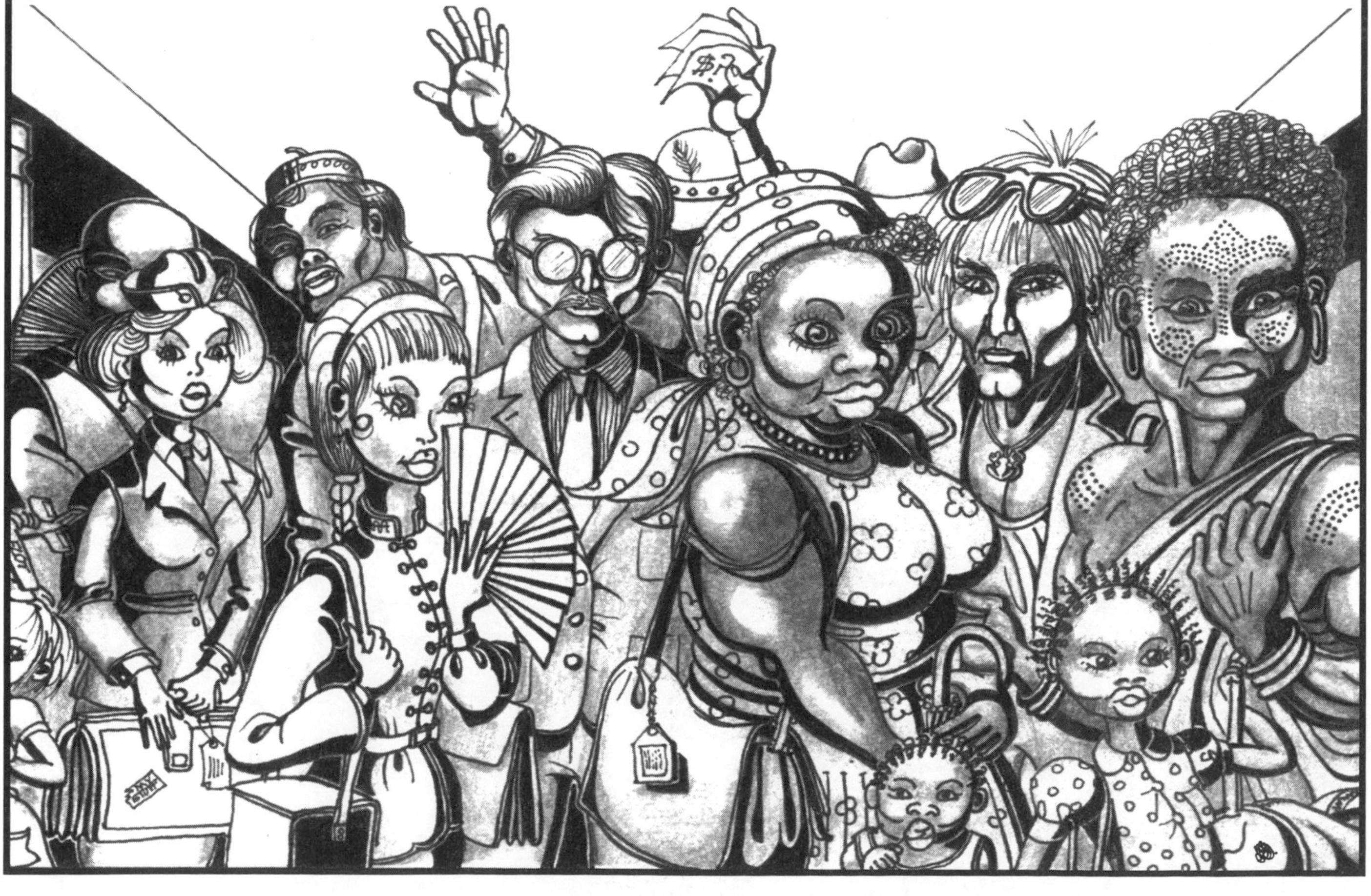

CONTENTS FOR THE PHYSICIAN
pages 65-94

C3

continued over ⟶

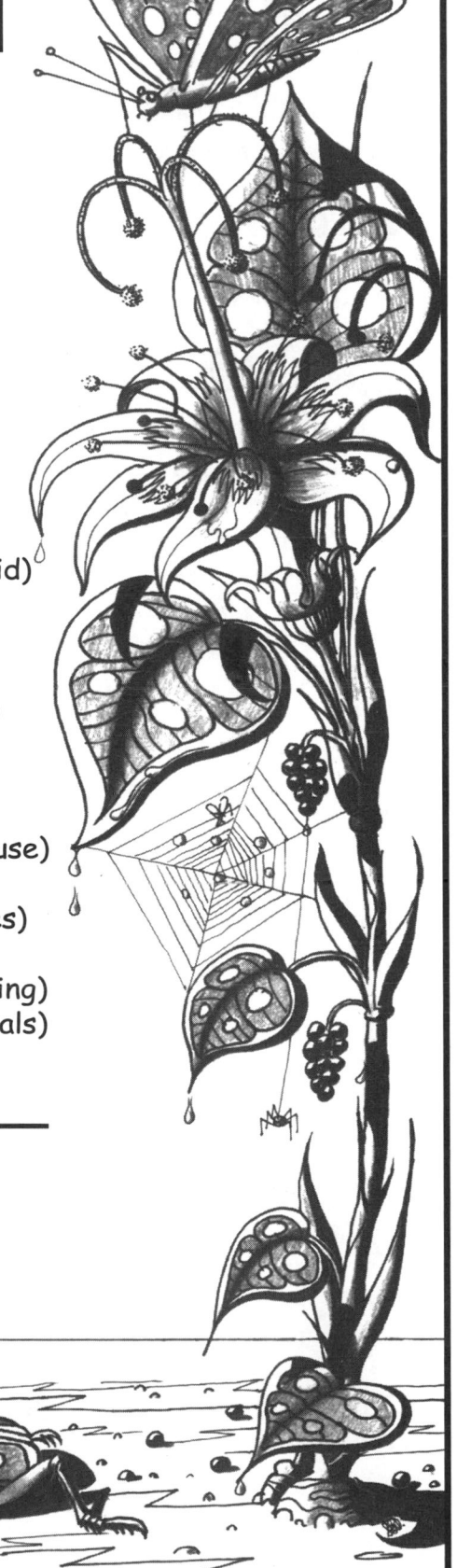

CONTENTS FOR THE PHYSICIAN

pages 95-128

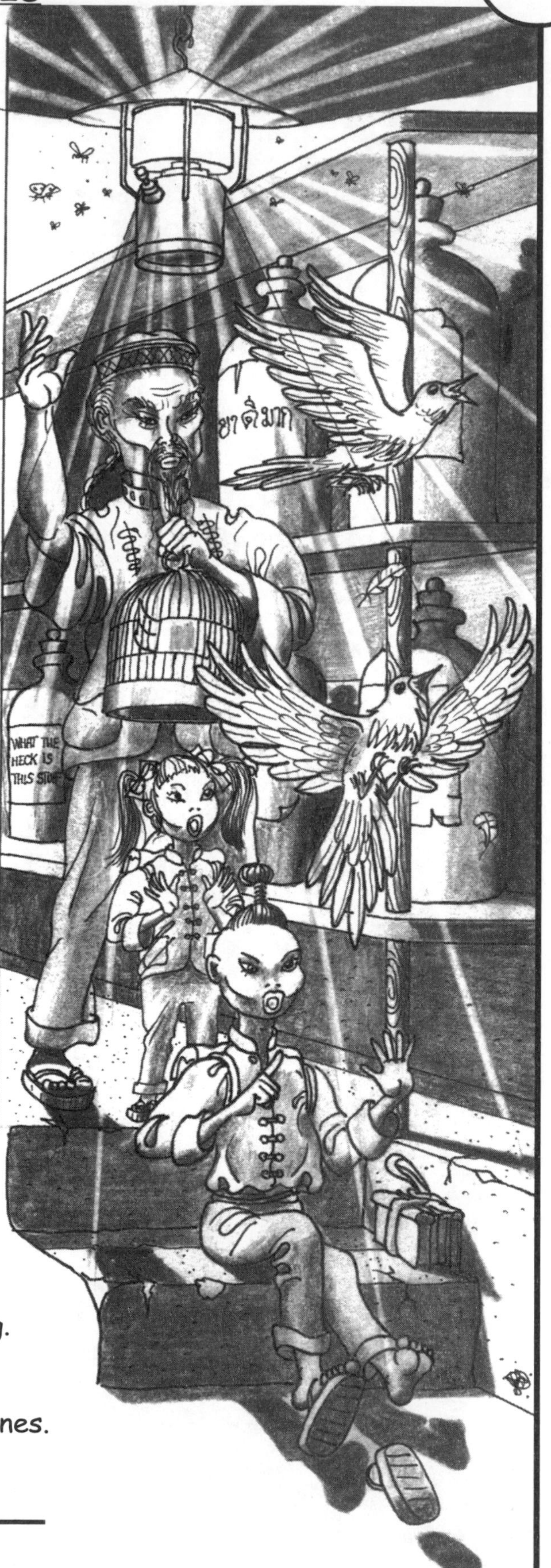

Page # *** = Heading Code**

CONTENTS FOR THE SAILOR

pages 129-156

C5

Page #

* = Heading Code

continued over ⟶

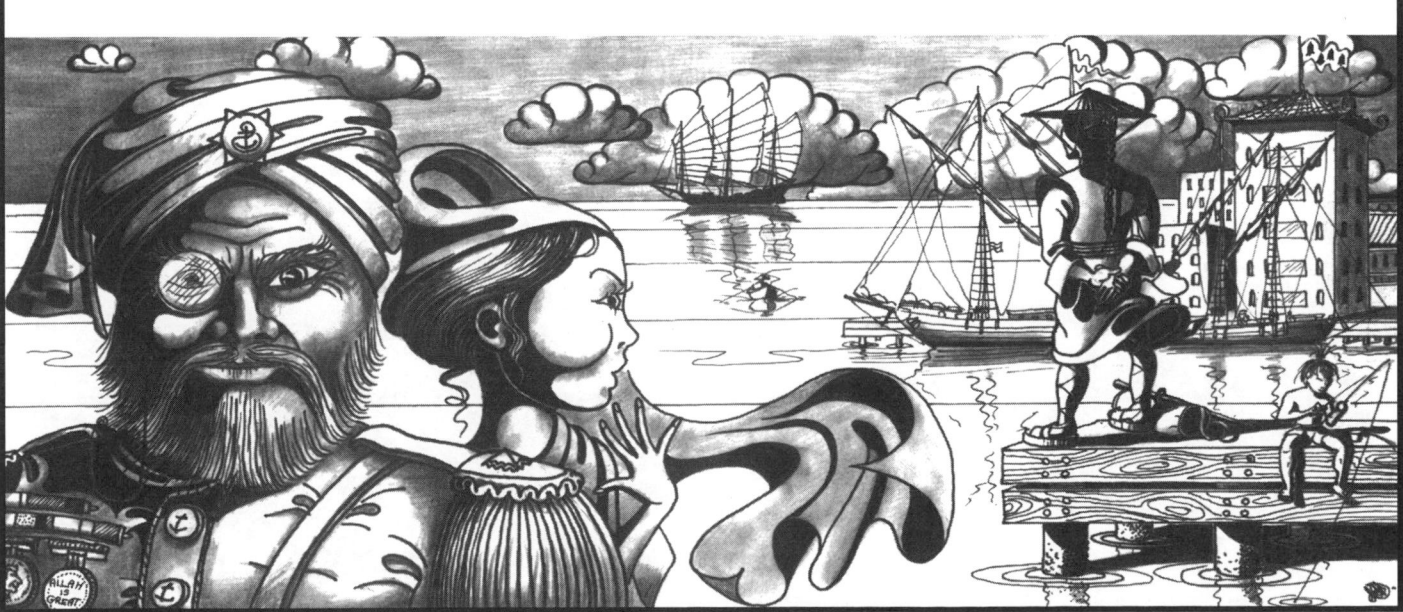

CONTENTS FOR THE SAILOR
pages 157-192

C6

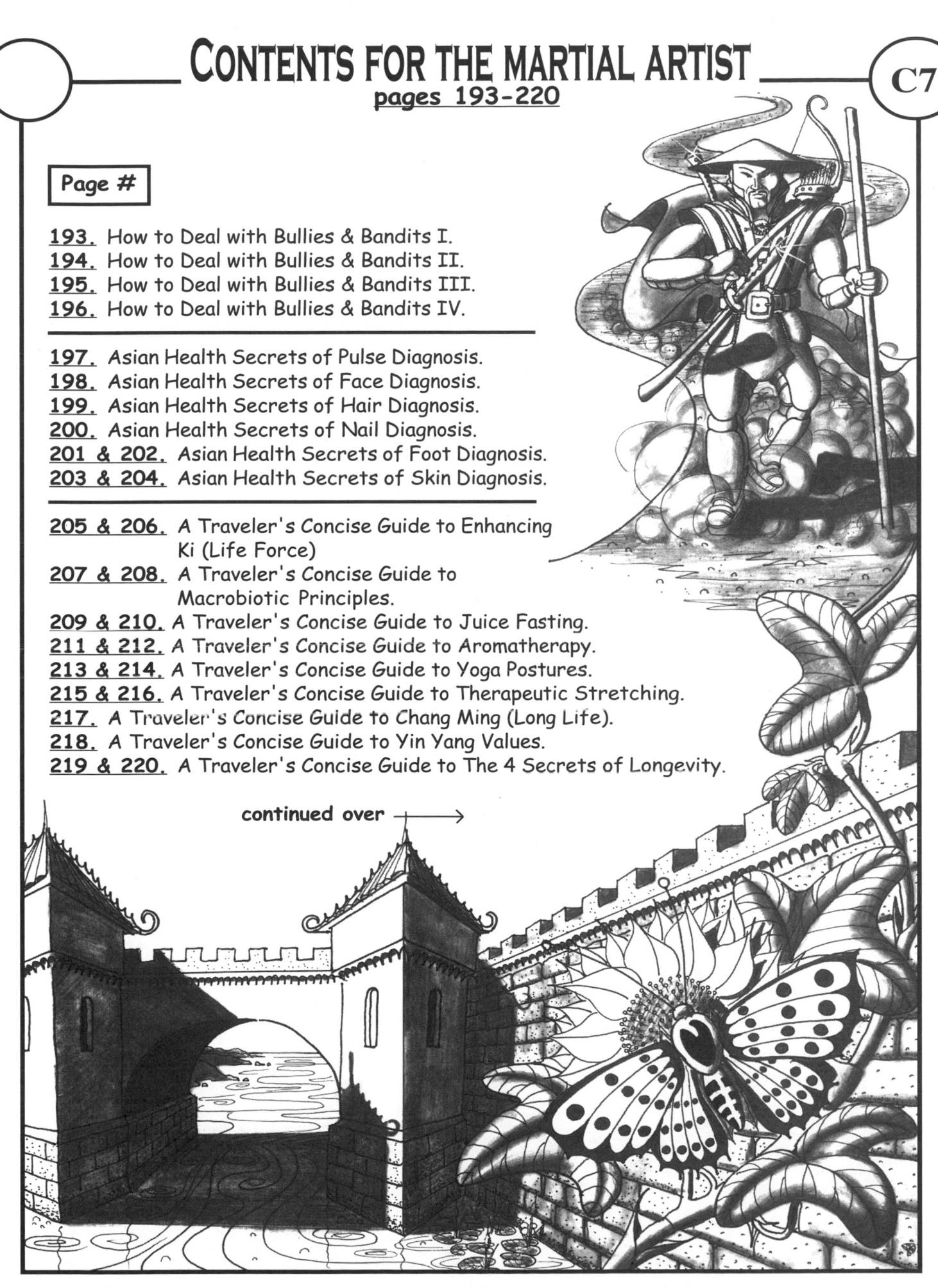

CONTENTS FOR THE MARTIAL ARTIST

pages 193-220

C7

continued over ———→

CONTENTS FOR THE MARTIAL ARTIST
pages 221-256

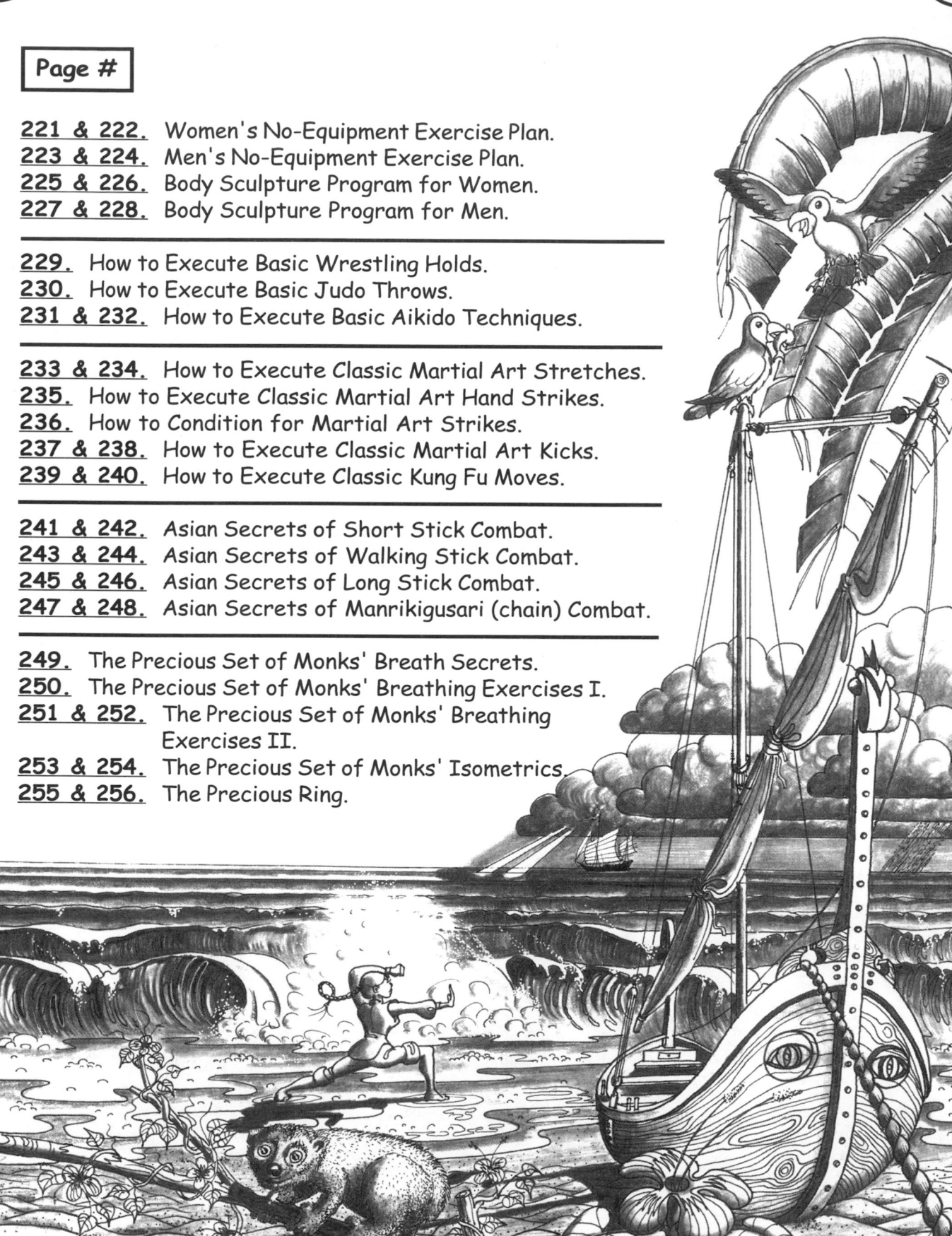

THE MARK OF SHEN KU

D

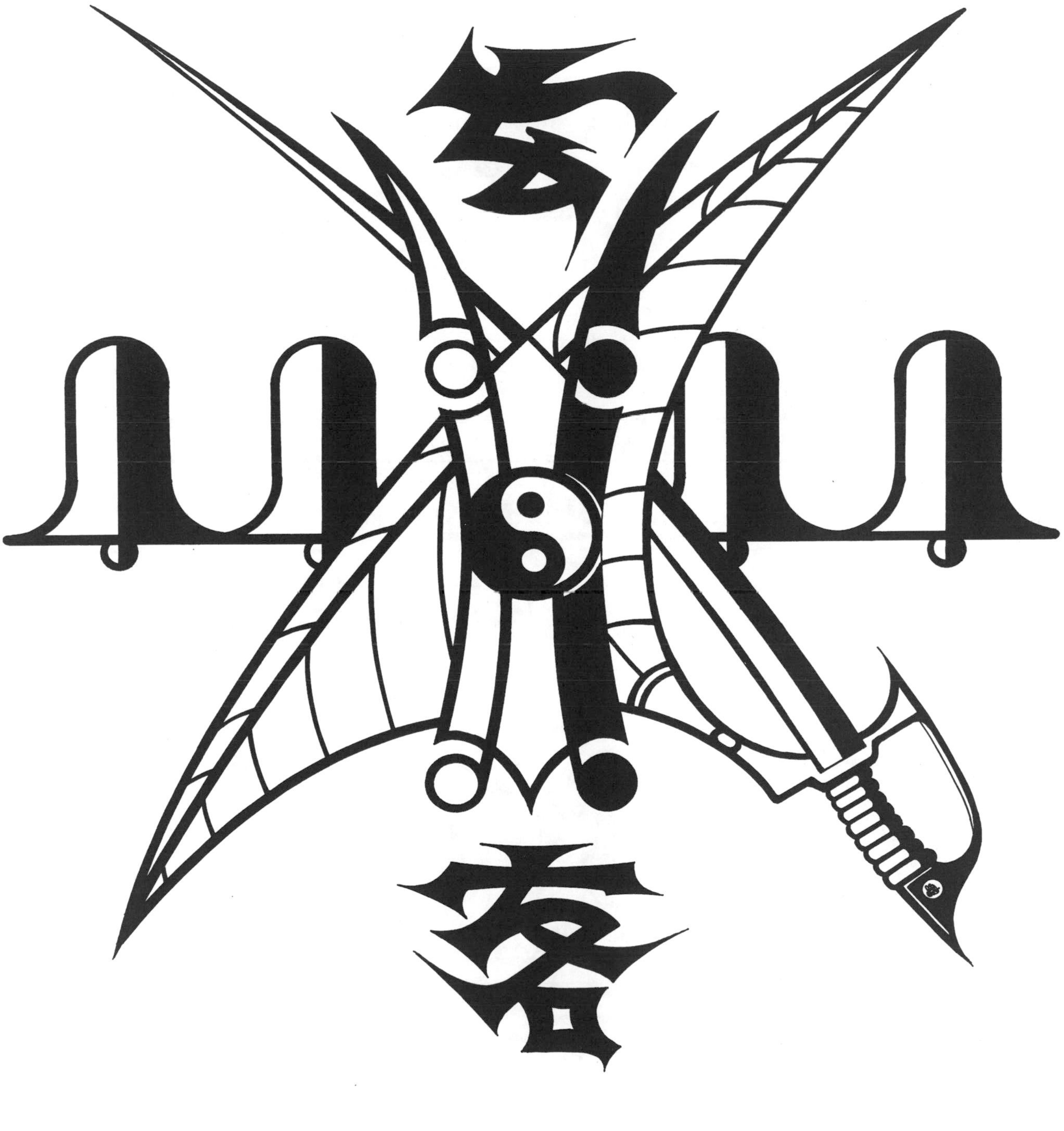

SHEN KU....

TRANSLATES INTO ENGLISH according to context & area variously e.g., "Pure Traveler," "Secret Stranger," "Dark Visitor" or "Phantom Passenger" . . . The Art encompasses <u>by far</u> the widest diversity of skills & knowledge from <u>by far</u> the widest spectrum of cultures & locations **EVER** (you will see why later), although this first formal contribution from our planet was mainly researched in Asia. An exact definition of the Art is elusive, a state of mind, a spiritual elevation, a conditioning of the body or an evolving study of life, it is what you make it, **BUT** its four basic philosophies remain the same for all situations. They are simple but disturbing **& GOVERN ALL CONSCIOUS PROGRESS IN LIFE.**

MOST SPECIFICALLY however this Art is that of the Traveler on &/or preparing for a journey....

It is applicable to any journey, anywhere, anyhow, anytime.... & to <u>every</u> logically aware being in existence. This ancient skill will (& actually already has, in these few seconds) change your life & you by being different have already changed the circumstances of the entire universe, perhaps a bit, perhaps a lot, **BUT FOREVER**.... Don't laugh because soon you may cry, (the logic is deep).... Just remain calm.

"O.K, BUT I DON'T quite understand it yet.... Where did this art come from?".... First answer where did F = MA come from?.... The formula bears Isaac Newton's name & is a law of physics **BUT** Force = Mass x Acceleration is a principle that existed long before this planet did!

SO IT WAS THAT the Art of Shen Ku came to us on our speck in space.... perhaps in a Cambodian Jungle, the Pacific Islands, the Andes mountains or the deserts of Egypt, tens of thousands of years ago. **BUT** it surely came to others long before us somewhere, because its applicability is directly (& devastatingly) proportional to the degree of advancement we (or they) achieve.

THERE HAVE BEEN students (& masters) of Shen Ku way beyond our short historical record. Buddha & Jesus Christ were its holy ambassadors, as were in their own vein the great explorers of yesteryear. Shen Nung (1800 BC), Marco Polo, Christopher Columbus, Vasco Da Gamma.... All knew & used this powerful Art to great effect.

TODAY, THE SPIRITUAL & physical travelers of our age are its unwitting exponents. We all to a lesser or greater degree are its followers, for who among us has not dreamed of, planned, or embarked on many journeys in their lifetime & who among us will not take that most uncertain of voyages at its end?

HOWEVER MOST INCREDIBLY, as it applies totally & indiscriminately & timelessly to <u>all</u> intelligent life <u>anywhere</u>, it is therefore <u>universally</u> exchangeable & thus we appear to have, on our 2000th birthday, recognized at last what logically always was ***THE FIRST INTERGALACTIC ARTFORM***

the mark of **SHEN KU** symbolizes.

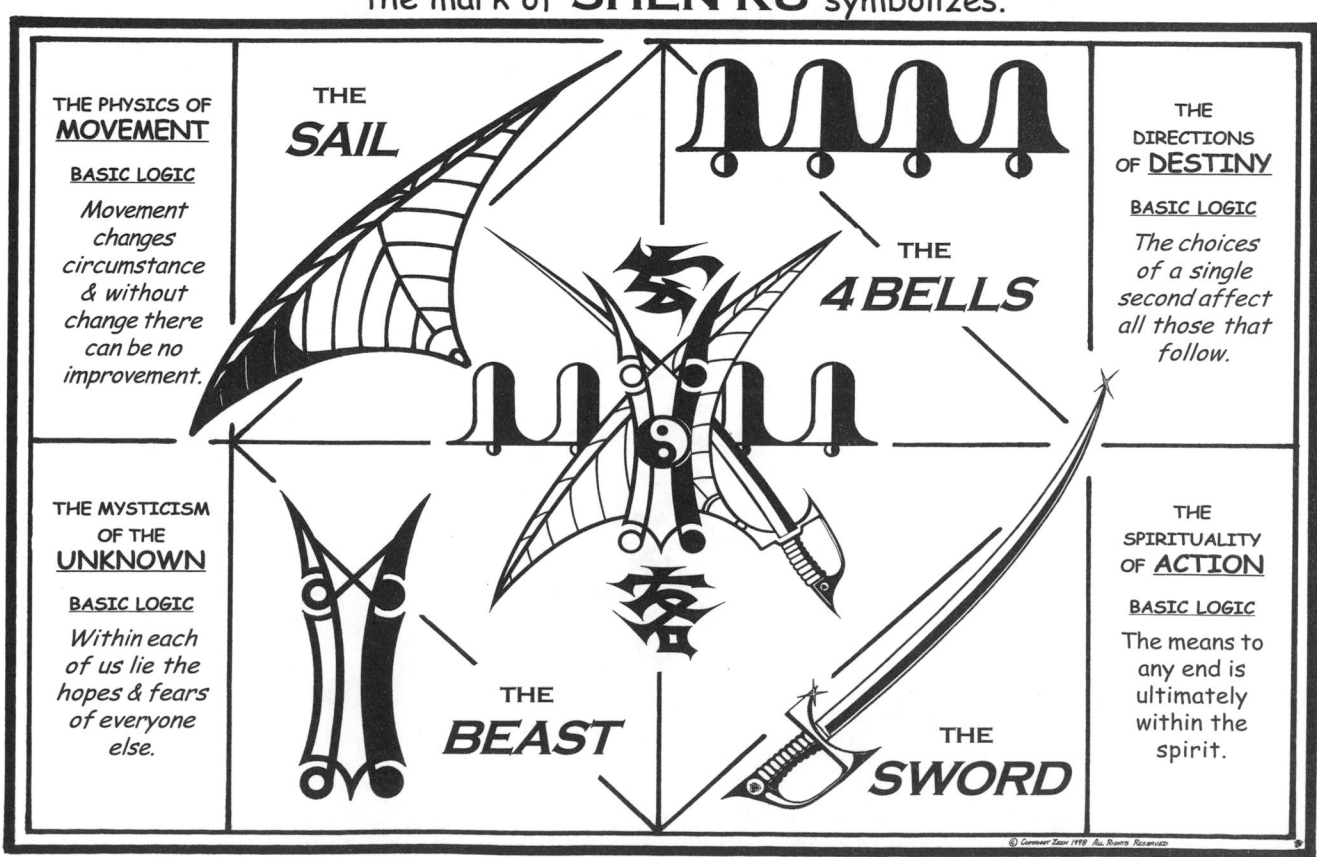

THE PHYSICS OF **MOVEMENT**

BASIC LOGIC

Movement changes circumstance & without change there can be no improvement.

THE *SAIL*

THE *4 BELLS*

THE **DIRECTIONS** OF **DESTINY**

BASIC LOGIC

The choices of a single second affect all those that follow.

THE MYSTICISM OF THE **UNKNOWN**

BASIC LOGIC

Within each of us lie the hopes & fears of everyone else.

THE *BEAST*

THE *SWORD*

THE **SPIRITUALITY** OF **ACTION**

BASIC LOGIC

The means to any end is ultimately within the spirit.

GALLERY OF HEROES & VILLAINS

Demonstrating the Artform for this Planet in this Edition are:

LOM PING

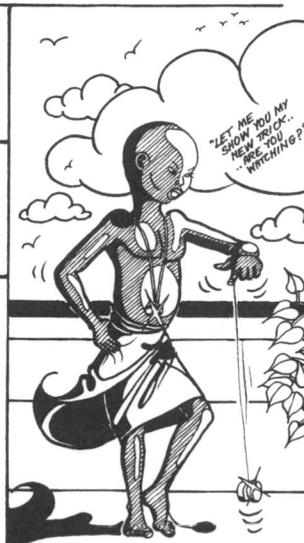

ORIGIN
Thailand. (Great grand-father fled Red Guard).

HISTORY
Broken family led to stress & slow growth.

REMARKS
Originally nicknamed Slow Ant at school but then met the weird old man & soon surprised everyone.

"LET ME SHOW MY NEW TRICK... ARE YOU WATCHING?"

THE BLACK MONK

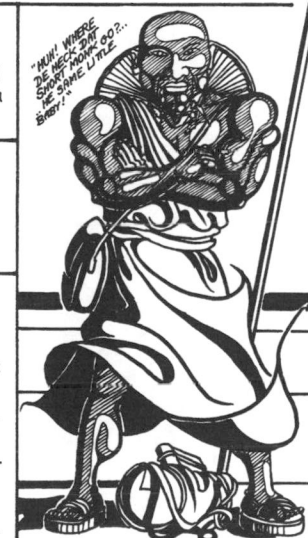

ORIGIN
Reputed to have walked from Africa to E. Asia.

HISTORY
Joined a Buddhist Monastery in N. China.

REMARKS
Studied Martial & Therapeutic exercise for 8 years. Friend of Short Monk. Reputed Mercenary in S. Japan.

"HUH! WHERE DE NECK DNT SHORT MONK GO?... HE SAME LITTLE BABY!"

HOO CHIN

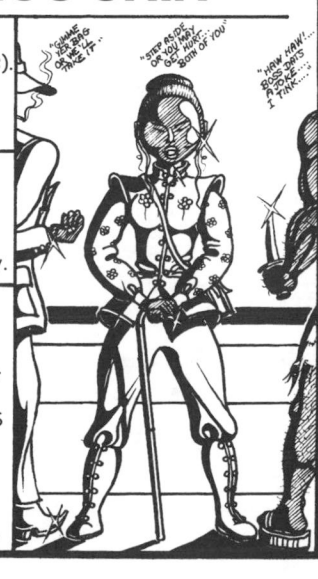

ORIGIN
1 of 2 (twins). Orphan of peasant farmers.

HISTORY
State took kids after murder of whole family.

REMARKS
Separated from sister Woo at 2. At 10 adopted by Asian/US family. At 26 expert in Artistic & Martial Stick Forms.

"GIMME ISS BAG OR YOU MAY TAKE IT?"
"STEP ASIDE OR YOU MAY GO BANG ON YOU."
"HAW HAW! ISS BOSS DAYS I SAKE I TINK!..."

Zeek would like to thank the many powerful characters & beautiful models (young & old) who have contributed hereto....

SHEN KU

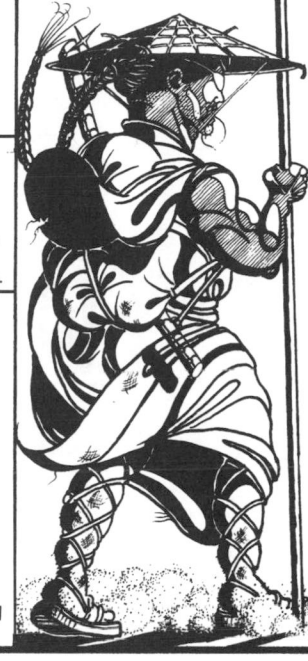

ORIGIN
Unknown but reported sightings in many far countries is mystery.

HISTORY
Different Translations of name over centuries can not refer to the same man.

REMARKS
Mystic Master of the Shen Ku Artform. Advanced exponent of multiple techniques. Often effects disguises — particularly that of one-eyed Chinese peasant. Transient in nature. Frugal in speech.

....Including the Captain & Crew of the Oceangoing Junk "Nok Ye Oh Dam" (Black Hawk) e.g.: "Big Joe Fung" (Engineer) & "Kwai" (Buffalo) (Deckhand) &........

ROBBERS FOUR

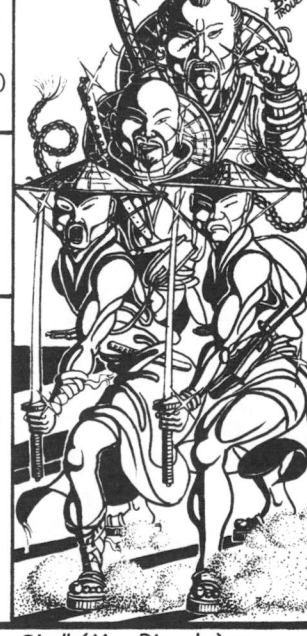

ORIGIN
Nationalities unknown but believed from island(s) in S.E. Asia.

HISTORY
Extremely dangerous leaders of Cutthroat gang of 50-100 thugs.

REMARKS
Took names from bad deeds L. to R. Bling (Leech) Ngoo (Snake) Mee (Bear) Tacap (C.Pede). Currently believed in jungle hide-out (Golden Triangle Area).

"YOU IN BIG TROUBLE"

....& "Koon Siw" (Mr. Pimple) (ships doctor) & "Old Yung" (Mosquito) (Sail Maker) & "Cha" (Slow) (Deckhand) & "Moo" (Pig) (Cook) & Passengers (like me).

LUCY (HIT)

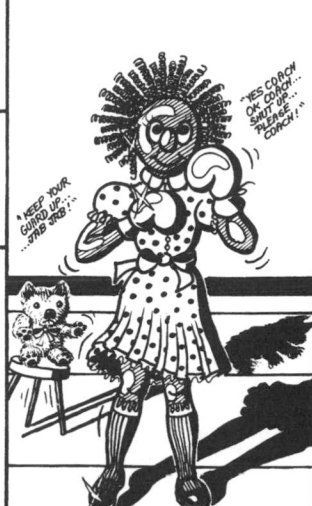

ORIGIN
Mixed race child of multinational parents.

HISTORY
Traveled a lot. Attended far too many schools.

REMARKS
Real name withheld. Real face withheld. Nicknamed "Lucy Hit" because of hard punch & tough character.

"YES COACH... OK COACH... SHUT UP... PLEASE...!"
"KEEP YOUR GUARD UP... JAB JAB!"

THE SHORT MONK

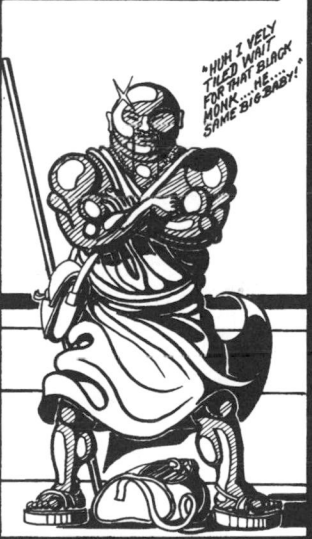

ORIGIN
Nationality uncertain, but from Mongolia.

HISTORY
Old friend of Black Monk from Afghan War.

REMARKS
Studied 8 years Herbal Medicine & Breathing Secrets in Buddhist Monastery. Last seen buying gold bars in Osaka

"HUH I VELY TILED WAT FROM THAT BLACK MONK... HE SAME BIG BABY!"

ALOE VERA

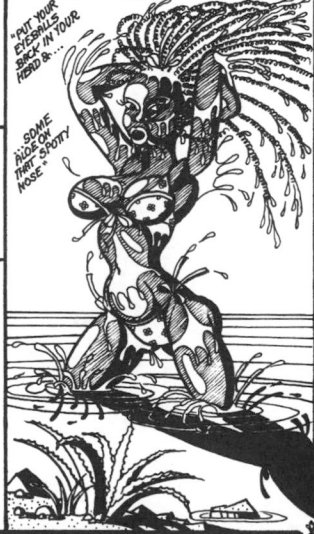

ORIGIN
Born in Wind Ward islands of Caribbean.

HISTORY
Academic dropout. Physically outstanding.

REMARKS
Refused to study at school. Numerous sporting (& beauty) qualities. Loves to grow & use Aloe Vera.

"PUT YOUR EYEBALLS BACK IN TOUR HEAD &..."
"SOME ALOE ON THAT SNOTTY NOSE"

LITTLE NOO (RAT)

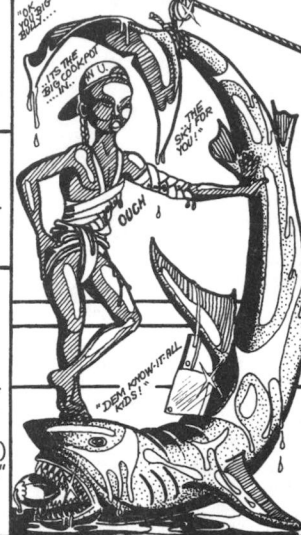

ORIGIN
Ran away to sea at 10. Unknown parentage.

HISTORY
Child of broken home. Will not talk about it.

REMARKS
Quiet but brave kid. Survivor of shark attack. Signed at 12 by captain (pirates shot) of "Black Hk" when both in hospital.

CARL?.....SKI

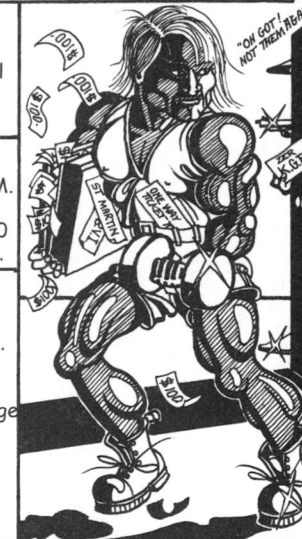

ORIGIN
Former U.S.S.R. jail escapee via China.

HISTORY
Sold I.C.B.M. plans to W. for U.S. $10 million cash.

REMARKS
$ beleived hidden B.V.I. K.G.B. squad sent to get. Effects image of bit silly bodybuilder. Last seen on Muscle Beach, Cal.

ABDUL & ANITA

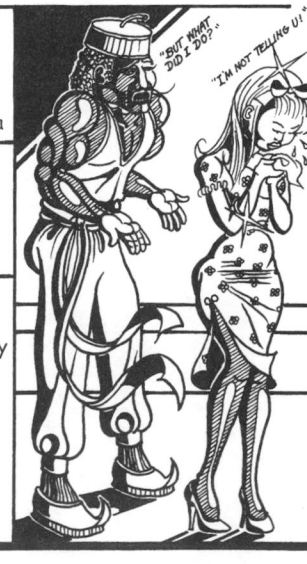

ORIGIN
Middle East & E. Europe— Scandinavia

HISTORY
Aerobics instructor. Glamour model.

REMARKS
Tough guy Abdul is very religious.... & nervous wreck from flirting impatient waiting for love Anita. (lucky guy).

ZEEK would also like to thank "Dog Mai" (Flower) for being a good mother & "Fat Aunt Ho" for being a good friend....

WOO CHIN

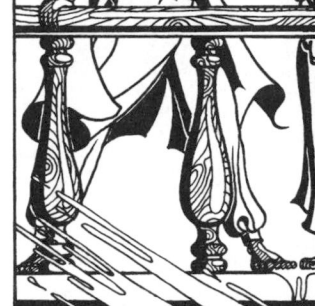

ORIGIN
Born 1 of 5 kids on farm burnt by extremists.

HISTORY
Sent by state to live with evil aunt, ran away.

REMARKS
Worked on fake Junk 7 years (then owned).... smuggling immigrants to Hong Kong. Was imprisoned & escaped 3 times. Quite rich. Skilled Martial Arts. Unaware of Sister Hoo.

....& Tom & Samantha for being us before we grew old & "Small Joe Fung" & "Delicia" (Penn) for showing us how to live life well....

YO YO (BRAIN)

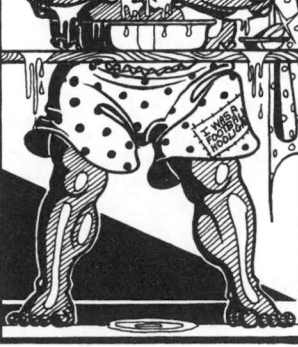

ORIGIN
Unknown but served warlord in Shantung.

HISTORY
Fickle loyalties vary with remuneration.

REMARKS
Extensive Martial Arts training depleted by greed & lazinees. Grovelling. oppotunist. Bully by nature but coward if hard pressed.

...& Finally Zeek would like to thank you (**yes you**) the reader for being in this book on some page, in some way, at some time.
Until We Meet Again.

THE OLD MYSTIC

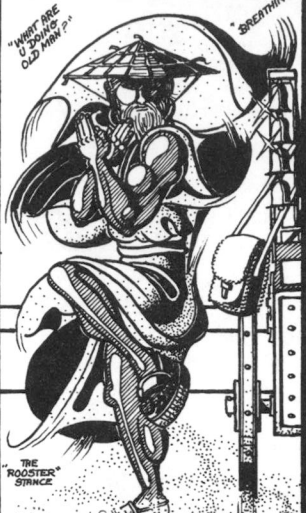

ORIGIN
Unknown family. Unknown nationallity.

HISTORY
Reported encounters across Asia over centuries.

REMARKS
Mysterious traveler with carved wood cart associated with Shen Ku. Saviour of distressed by bizarre techniques.

THE BOSUN

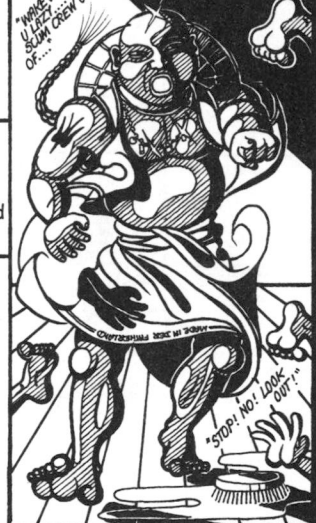

ORIGIN
Probabbly German. Grew up in Asia.

HISTORY
Kidnapped from Mom at 3. Ransom paid but stolen.

REMARKS
Lived on Sampan in Hong Kong. Worked as body guard. Signed by Captain of "Black Hk." Very mean.... but honorable.

THE NINGPO CAT "NING"

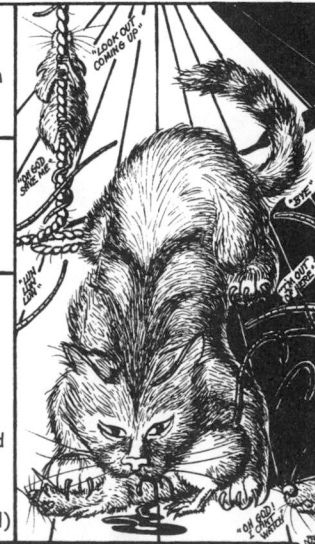

ORIGIN
Stowaway on ship from Liverpool to Bangkok.

HISTORY
Hid in a cargo on "Black Hk" To Ningpo.

REMARKS
Discovered in Hangchow. Had killed & eaten (not bones) 64 rats & 2 snakes. Signed by captain at 1/fish/day + rat bonus. (Ning is a girl)

THE 4 BELLS

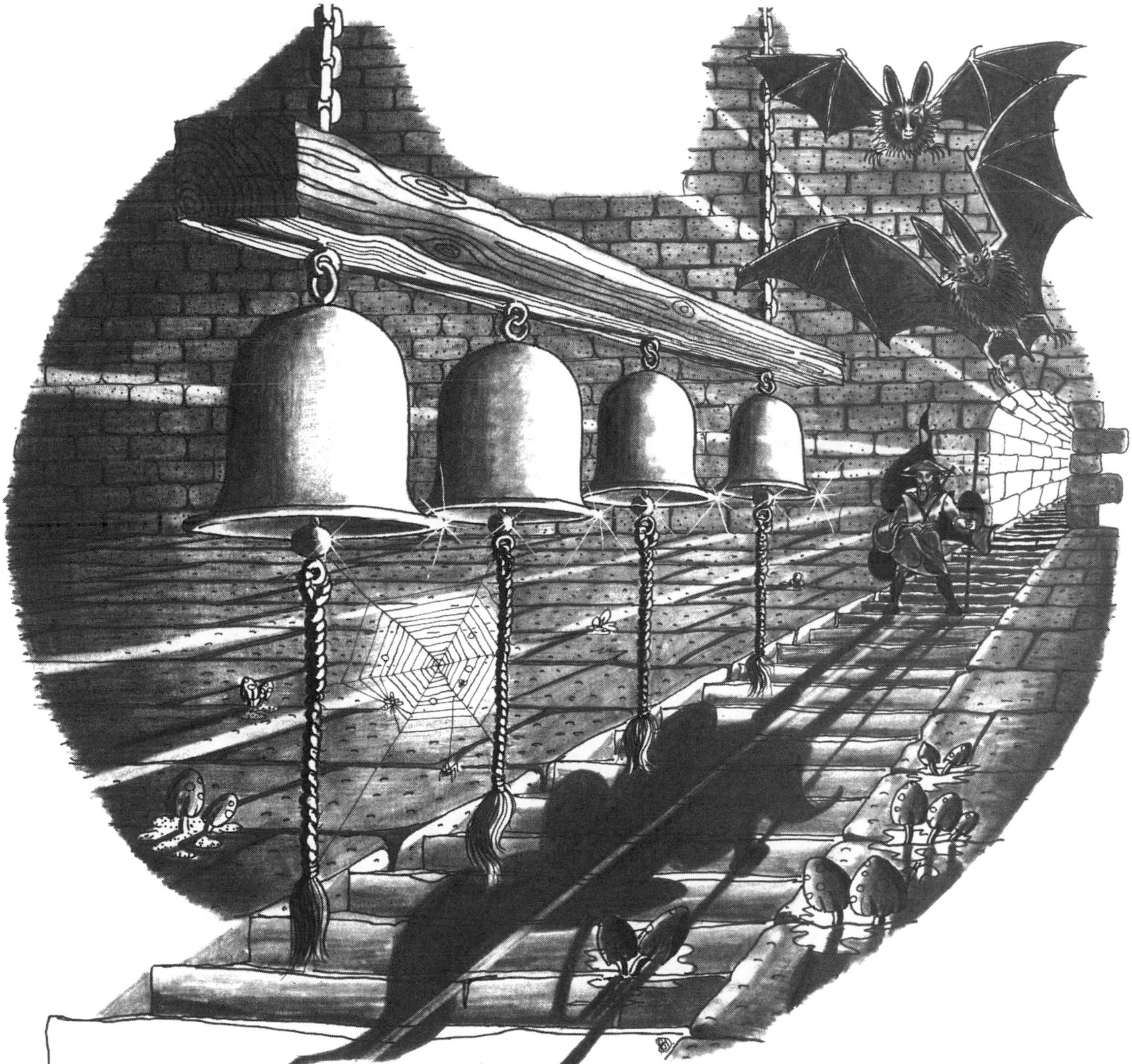

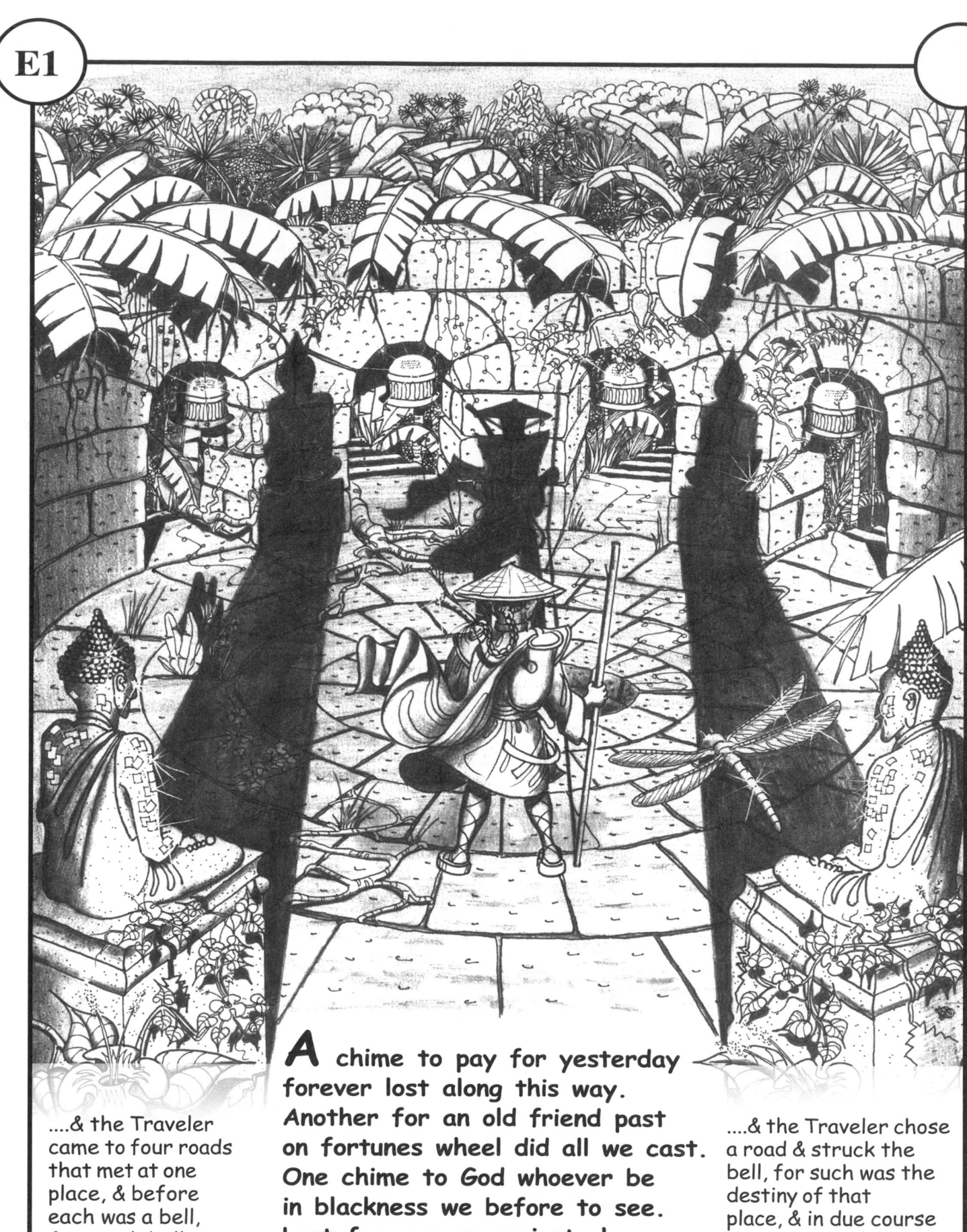

....& the Traveler
came to four roads
that met at one
place, & before
each was a bell,
& on each bell
was a rhyme....

A chime to pay for yesterday
forever lost along this way.
Another for an old friend past
on fortunes wheel did all we cast.
One chime to God whoever be
in blackness we before to see.
Last for you an ancient rhyme
cut in a bell on the edge of time.

....& the Traveler chose
a road & struck the
bell, for such was the
destiny of that
place, & in due course
the Traveler came
to four roads that
met at one place....

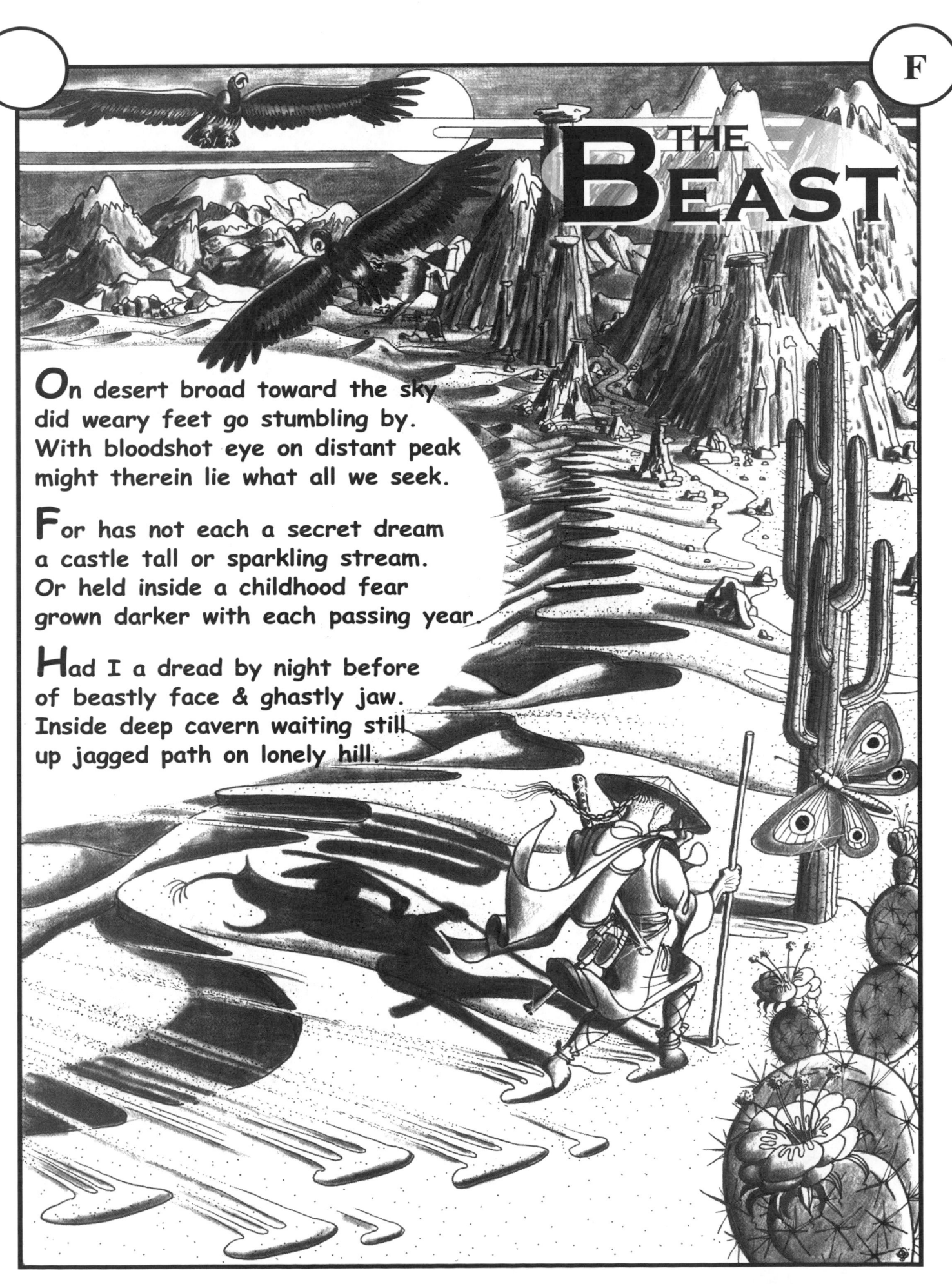

THE BEAST

On desert broad toward the sky
did weary feet go stumbling by.
With bloodshot eye on distant peak
might therein lie what all we seek.

For has not each a secret dream
a castle tall or sparkling stream.
Or held inside a childhood fear
grown darker with each passing year.

Had I a dread by night before
of beastly face & ghastly jaw.
Inside deep cavern waiting still
up jagged path on lonely hill.

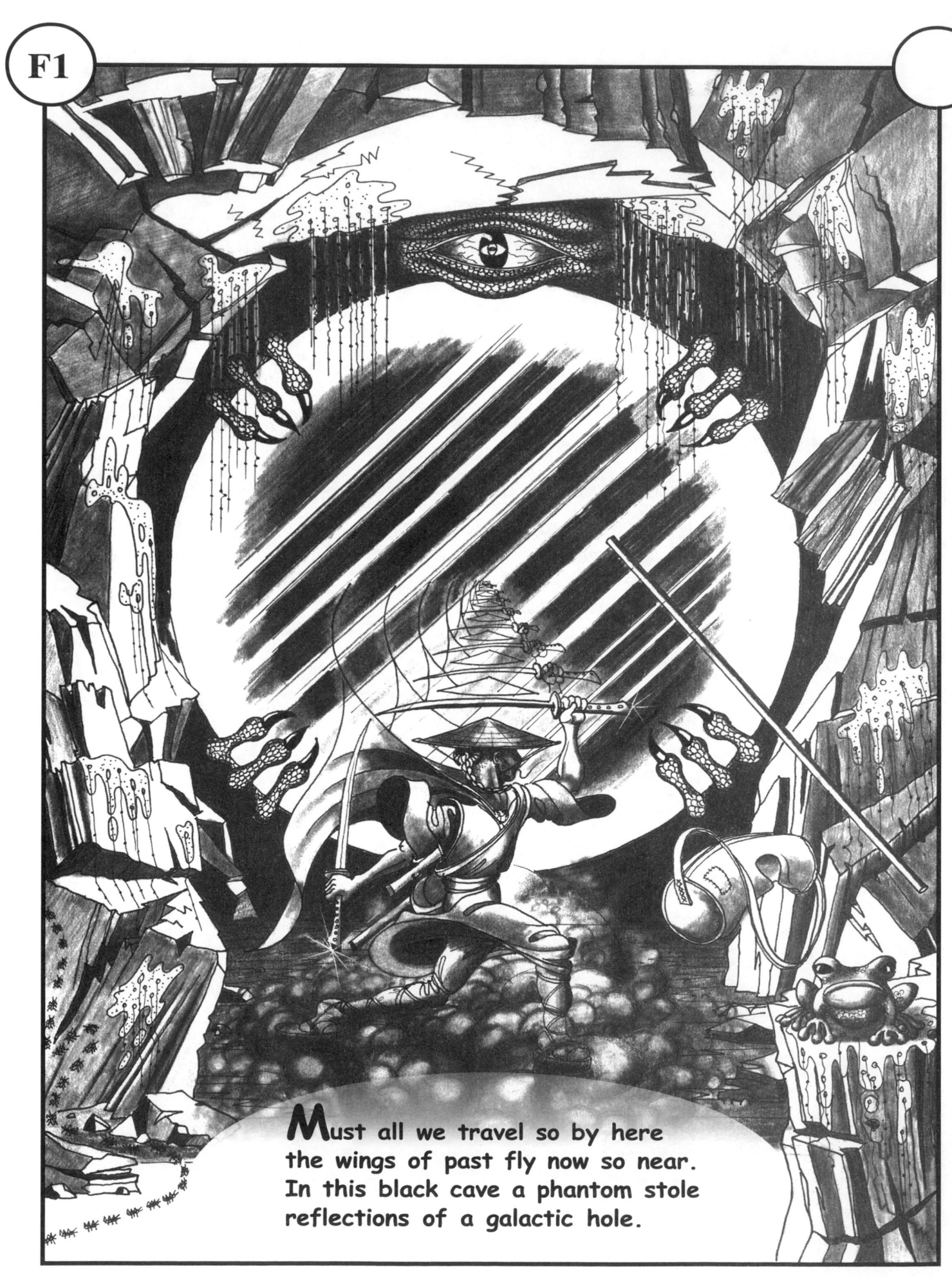

Must all we travel so by here
the wings of past fly now so near.
In this black cave a phantom stole
reflections of a galactic hole.

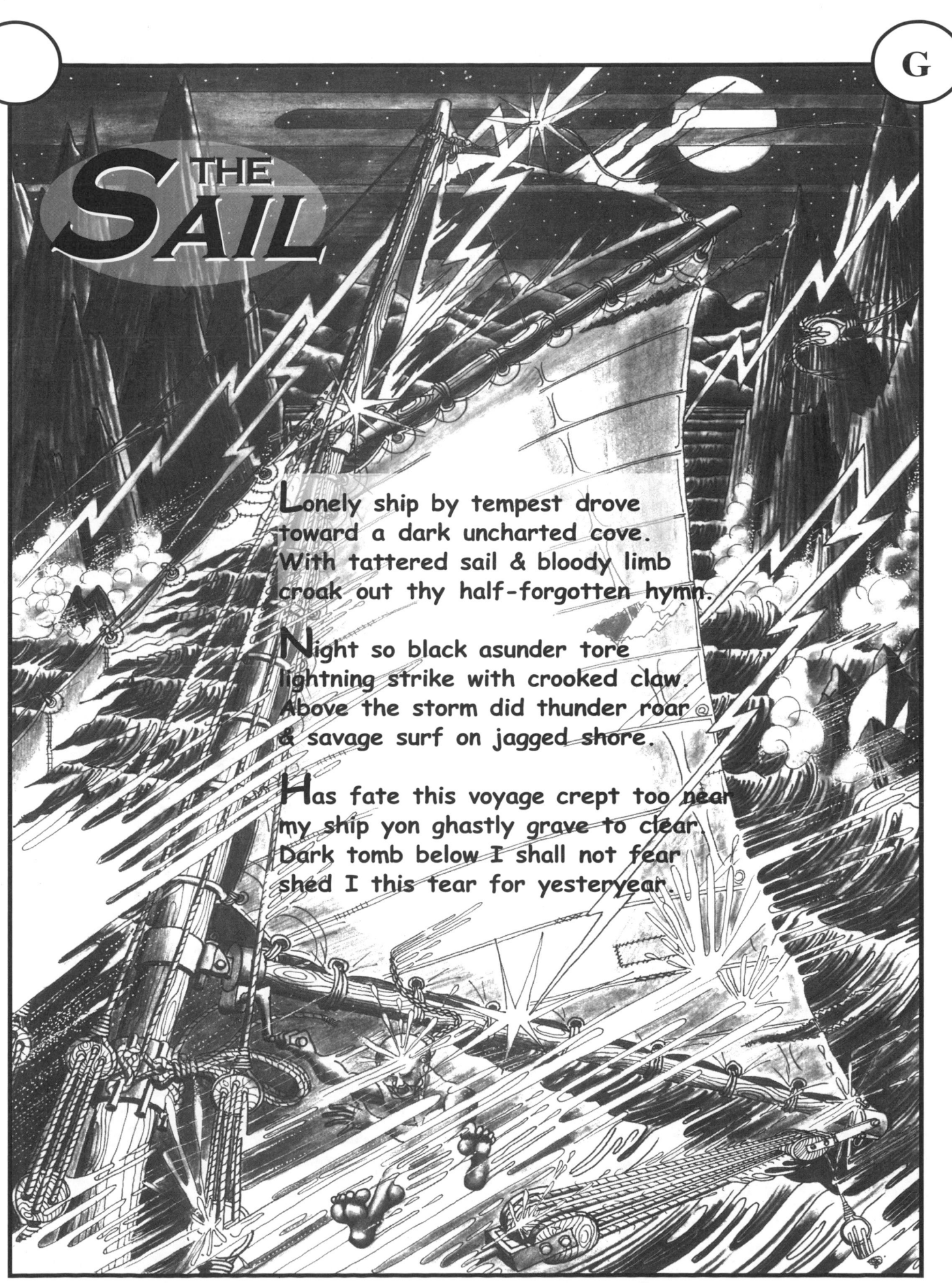

THE SAIL

Lonely ship by tempest drove
toward a dark uncharted cove.
With tattered sail & bloody limb
croak out thy half-forgotten hymn.

Night so black asunder tore
lightning strike with crooked claw.
Above the storm did thunder roar
& savage surf on jagged shore.

Has fate this voyage crept too near
my ship yon ghastly grave to clear
Dark tomb below I shall not fear
shed I this tear for yesteryear.

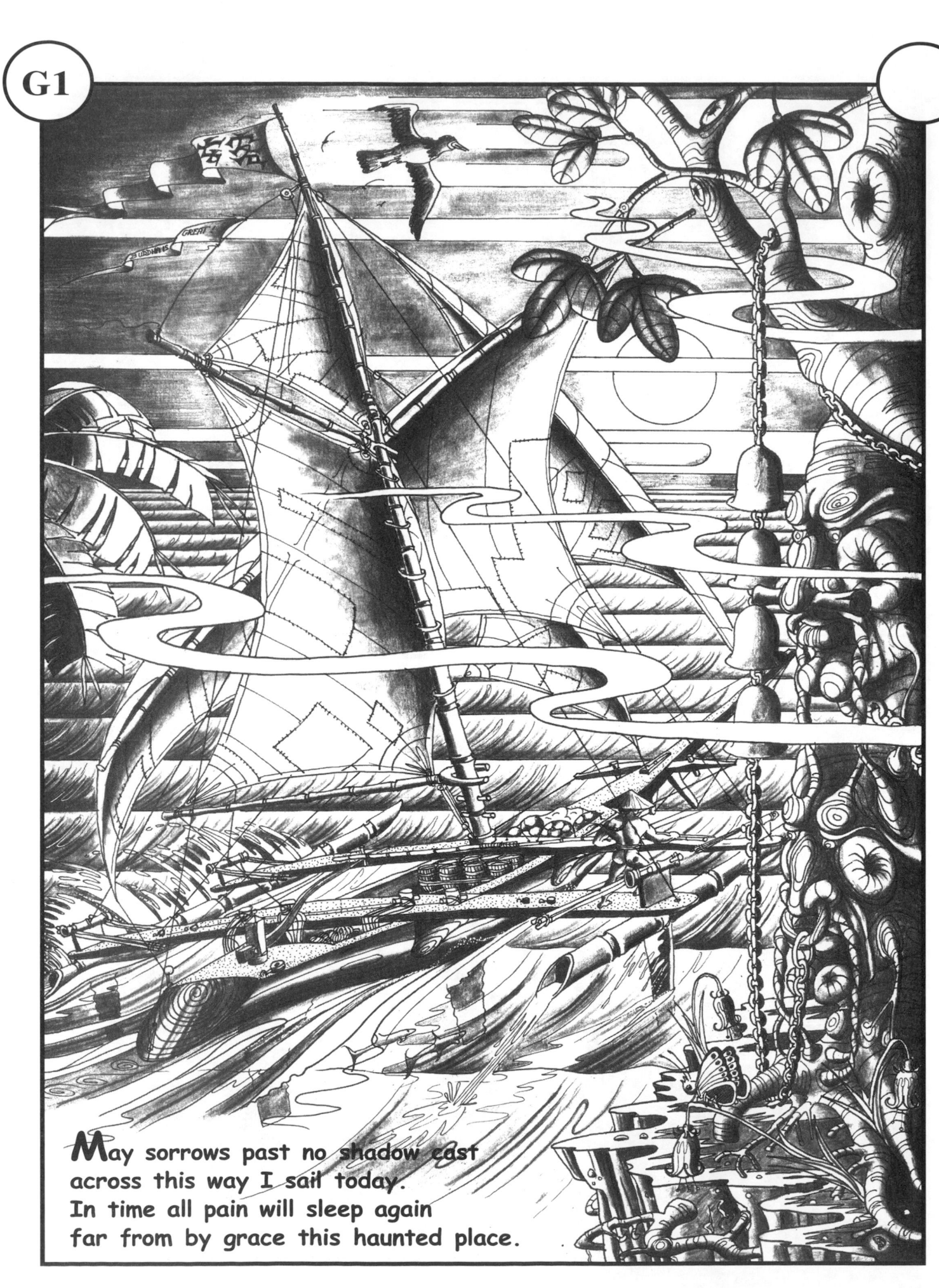

May sorrows past no shadow cast
across this way I sail today.
In time all pain will sleep again
far from by grace this haunted place.

THE SWORD

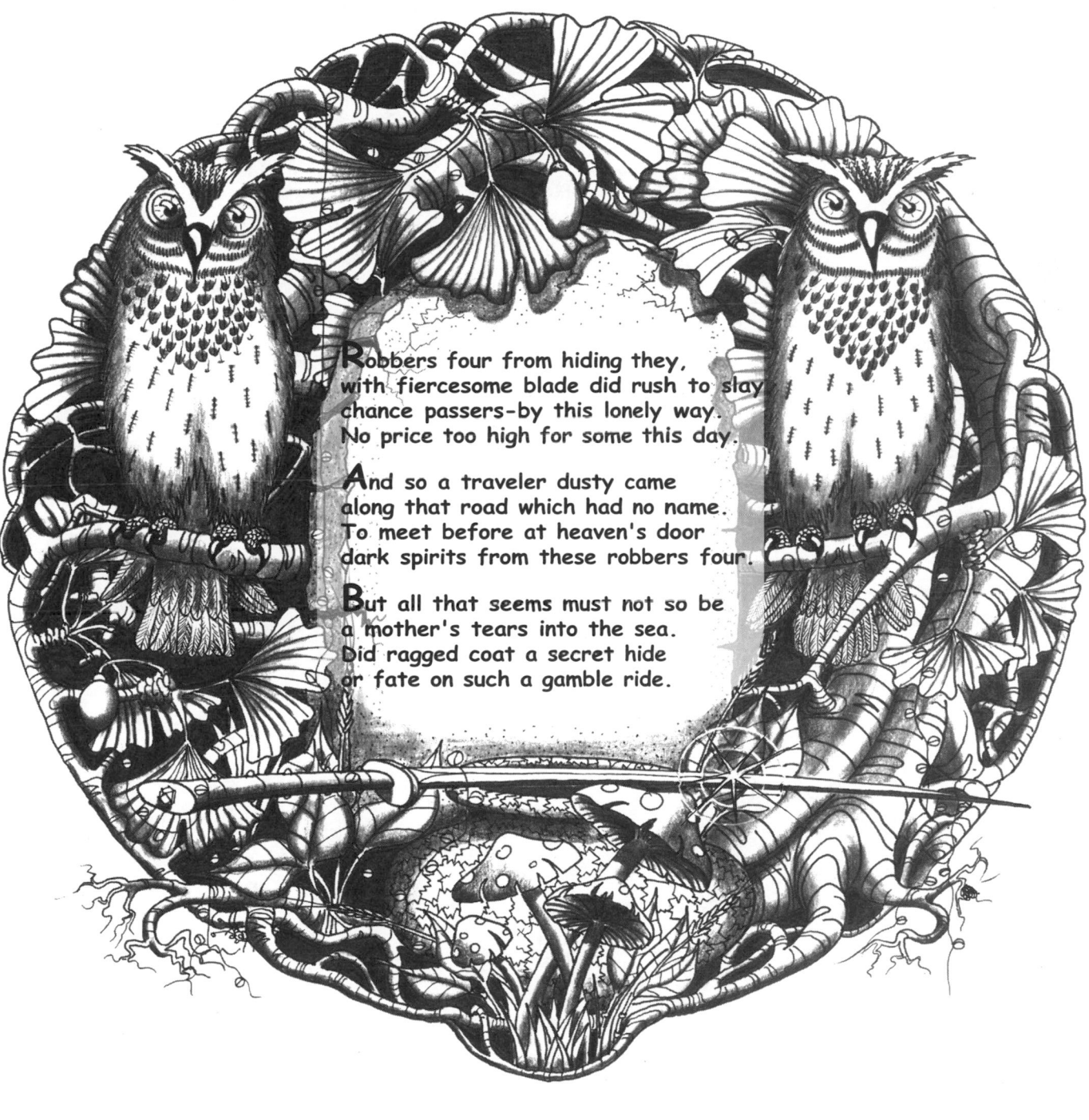

Robbers four from hiding they,
with fiercesome blade did rush to slay
chance passers-by this lonely way.
No price too high for some this day.

And so a traveler dusty came
along that road which had no name.
To meet before at heaven's door
dark spirits from these robbers four.

But all that seems must not so be
a mother's tears into the sea.
Did ragged coat a secret hide
or fate on such a gamble ride.

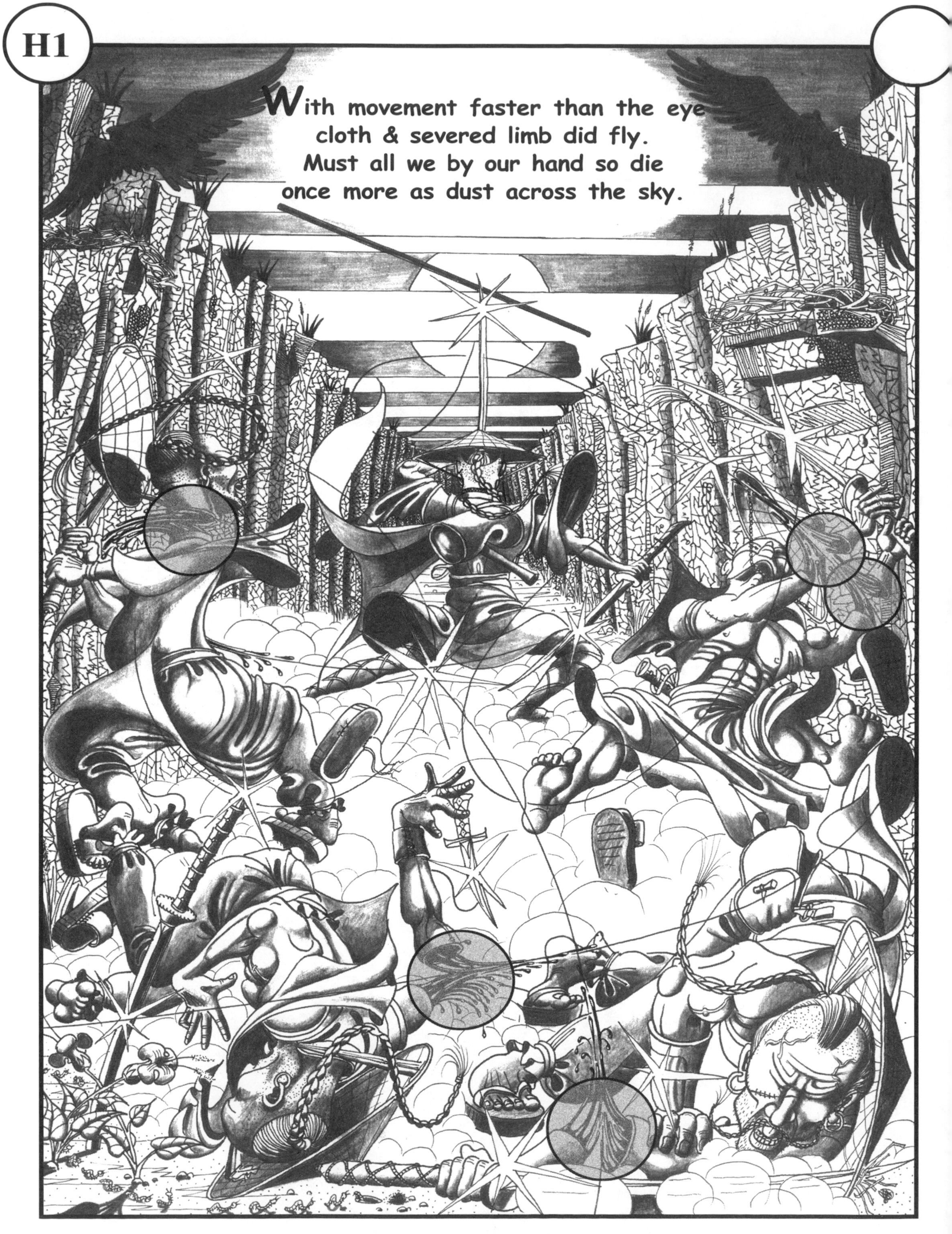
H1
With movement faster than the eye
cloth & severed limb did fly.
Must all we by our hand so die
once more as dust across the sky.

THE TRAVELER

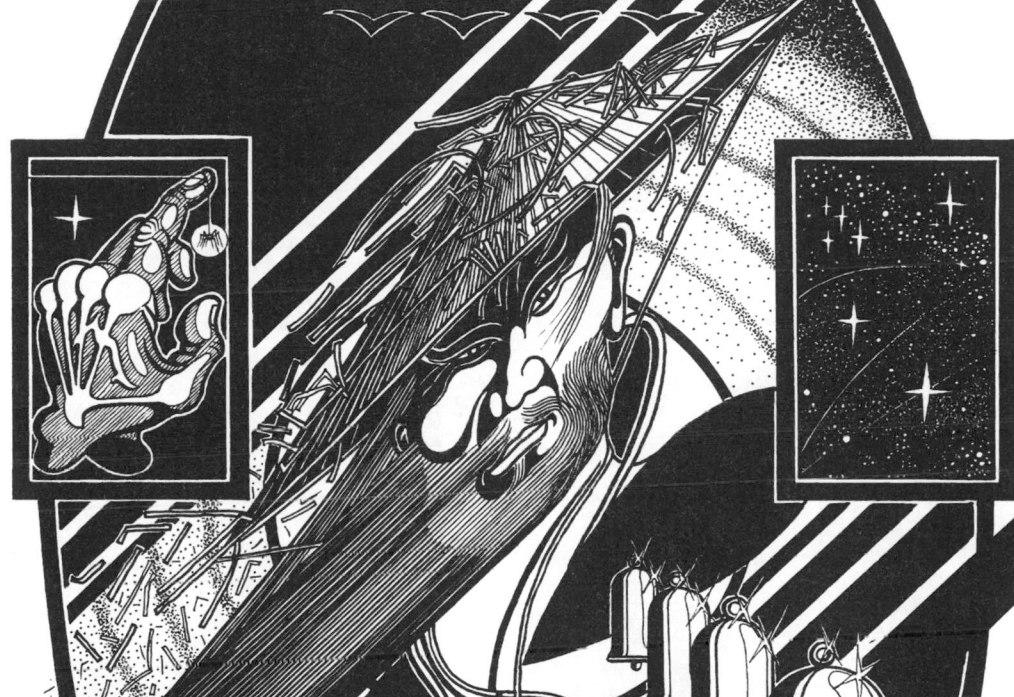

* THE CHOICES OF A SINGLE SECOND AFFECT ALL THOSE THAT FOLLOW.

*<u>NOTE</u>

<u>The 4 logics of SHEN KU</u> are jointly relevant & inextricably interlinked. Together and with devastating applicability proportional to species advancement they govern

ALL conscious progress in **ALL** situations throughout **ALL** of time, transcending **ALL** frontiers..............

...*INTERGALACTICALLY*

THE OLD MYSTIC

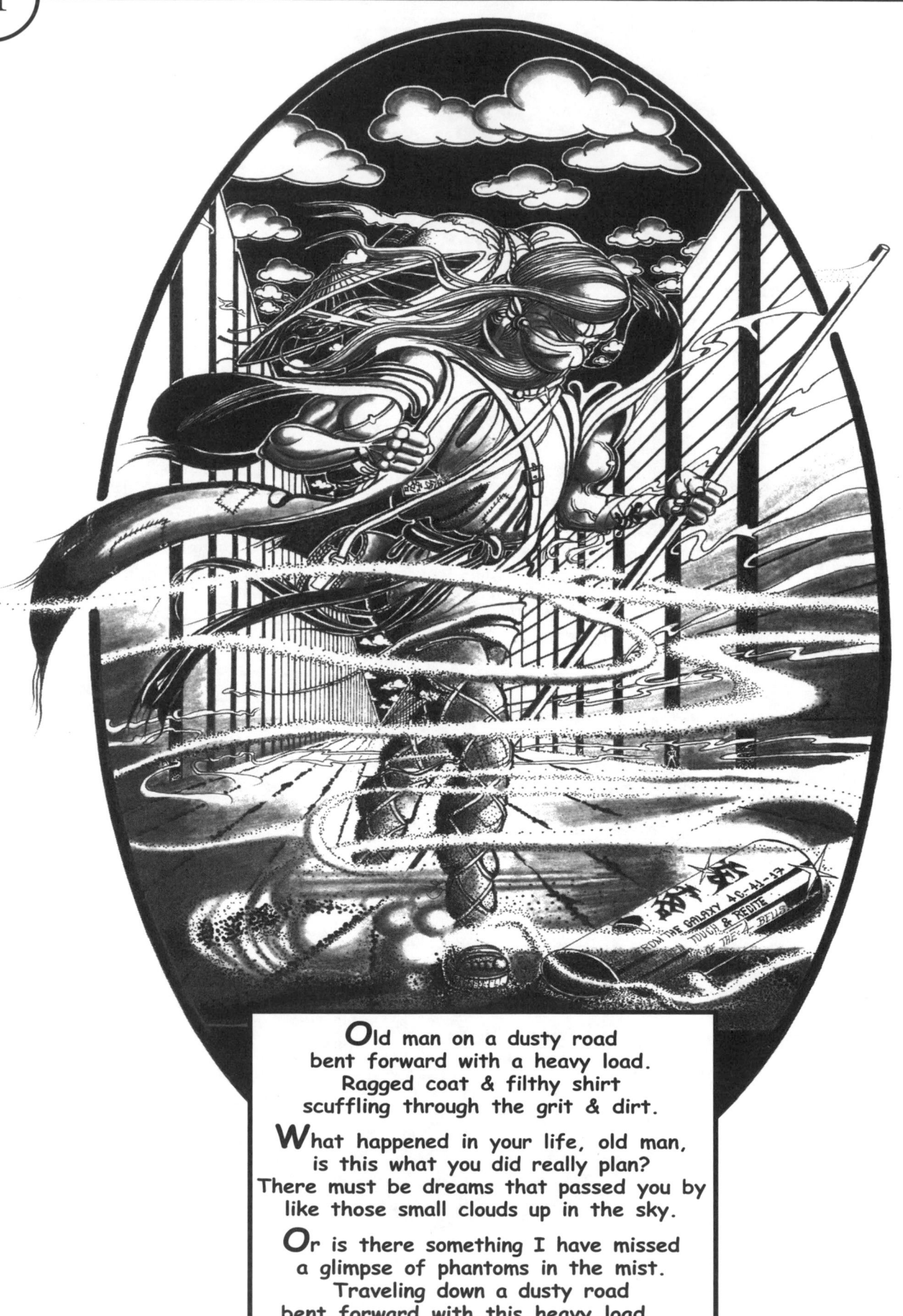

*O*ld man on a dusty road
bent forward with a heavy load.
Ragged coat & filthy shirt
scuffling through the grit & dirt.

*W*hat happened in your life, old man,
is this what you did really plan?
There must be dreams that passed you by
like those small clouds up in the sky.

*O*r is there something I have missed
a glimpse of phantoms in the mist.
Traveling down a dusty road
bent forward with this heavy load....

MOUTH-TO-MOUTH RESUSCITATION

Emergency Breathing For Victim With Failed Respiration

1 — **UNCONSCIOUS OR NOT?**

Jiggle/Shout/Slap

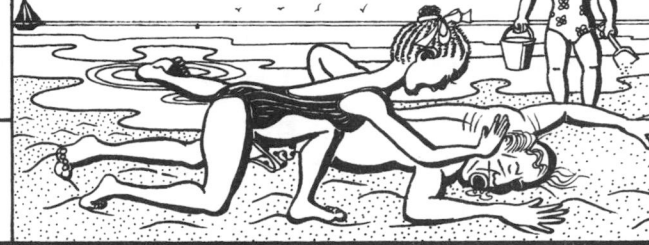

2 — **SHOUT FOR HELP**

Send bystander (if any) for ambulance

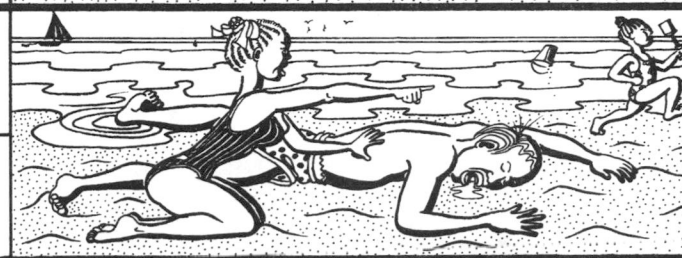

3 — **ROLL VICTIM ONTO BACK**

Note victim must be on hard surface for heart massage

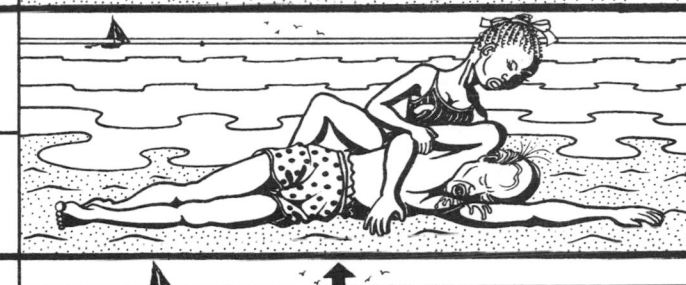

4 — **OPEN AIRWAY**

Lift back of neck, tilt head back, pull chin up, check throat, clear

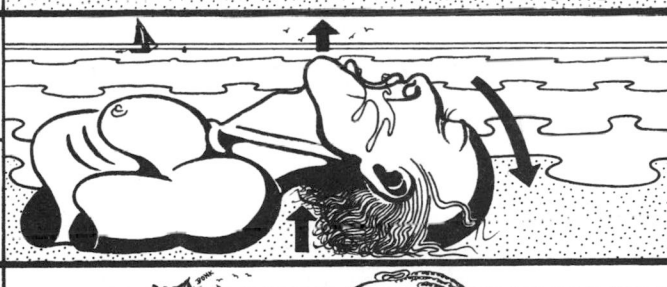

5 — **BREATHING OR NOT?**

Listen close, feel for breath on your cheek, watch for chest move

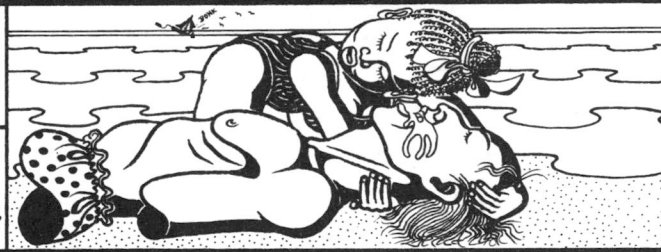

6 — **GIVE 4 QUICK BREATHS (WATCH CHEST RISE)**

Adult: mouth to mouth, pinch nose with fingers

Child: mouth to nose & mouth & gently

Adult **Child**

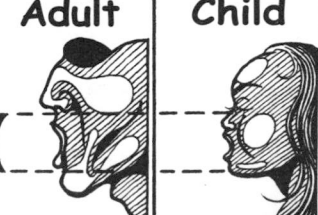

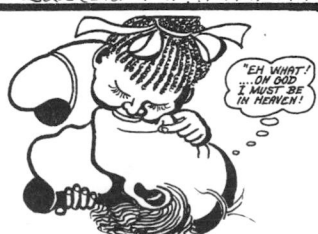

7 — **PULSE BEAT OR NOT?**

Check with fingers here whilst continuing mouth-to-mouth at normal rate.

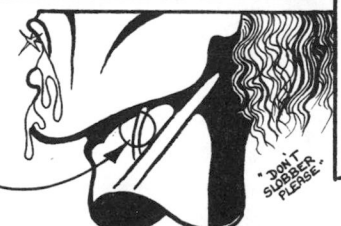

IF NOT, TURN OVER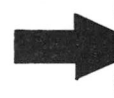

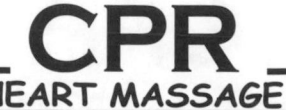

Emergency Stimulation For Victim With No Heartbeat

8 ## KNEEL CLOSE TO VICTIM'S CHEST

With victim on back, on hard surface, kneel facing chest. Here or here

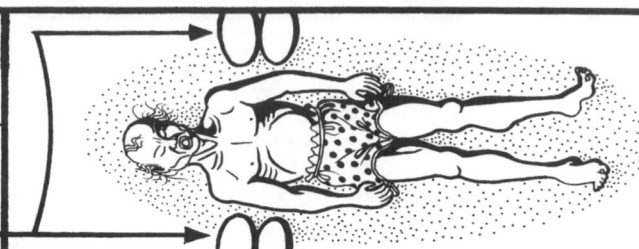

9 ## QUICKLY LOCATE COMPRESSION POINT

Pull clothes up. Locate bottom of center of rib cage & come up 3 inches (adult) less on child.

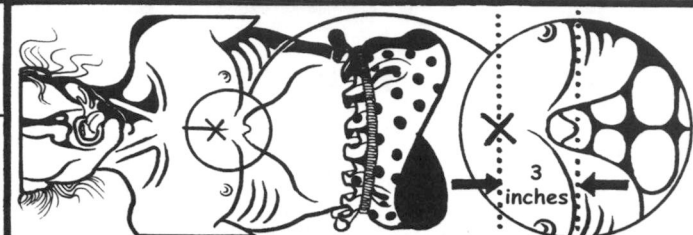

10 ## WITH BALL OF HAND ON POINT (OTHER HAND ON TOP OF IT) - COMPRESS CHEST (ADULT) 1.5 INCHES 75 TIMES PER MINUTE

11 ## - IMPORTANT -
2 QUICK FULL MOUTH-TO-MOUTH BREATHS ARE REQUIRED EVERY 15 CHEST COMPRESSIONS

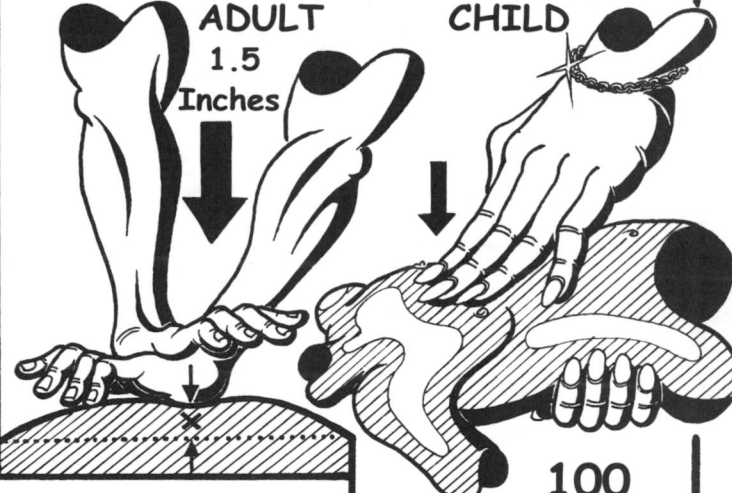

ADULT 1.5 Inches   CHILD

12 ## DO NOT STOP FOR MORE THAN 5 SECS.

13 ## 15 COMPRESSIONS, 2 BREATHS ETC.

14 ## CHECK FOR A PULSE OCCASIONALLY

100 Times/Minute

With 1 breath every 5 compressions. Do not stop either

— NOTES —

- Before starting heart massage, a single hard blow with the ball of the hand to the victim's compression point (careful with children) may stimulate the heart to restart pumping immediately.
- Number of heart beats/minute is higher in young victims.
- An infant's pulse is best checked on inside of upper arm.
- A child's compression point is about midway between nipples.
- The first breaths of mouth-to-mouth resuscitation are given as fast as possible to saturate the blood with oxygen.
- If two rescuers are present #1 may do chest compression's at 60/minute & #2 give a mouth-to-mouth breath every 5th compression & check the pulse (swap jobs periodically).

WARNING: NEVER PRACTICE HEART MASSAGE ON A LIVING PERSON

Unisex Travelers' Shirt & Trousers Tailoring Design

Versatile & highly functional—Commonly worn open with vest, with shorts or longs, in or out at waist, even with tie.

THE SHIRT (with 6 secret pockets)

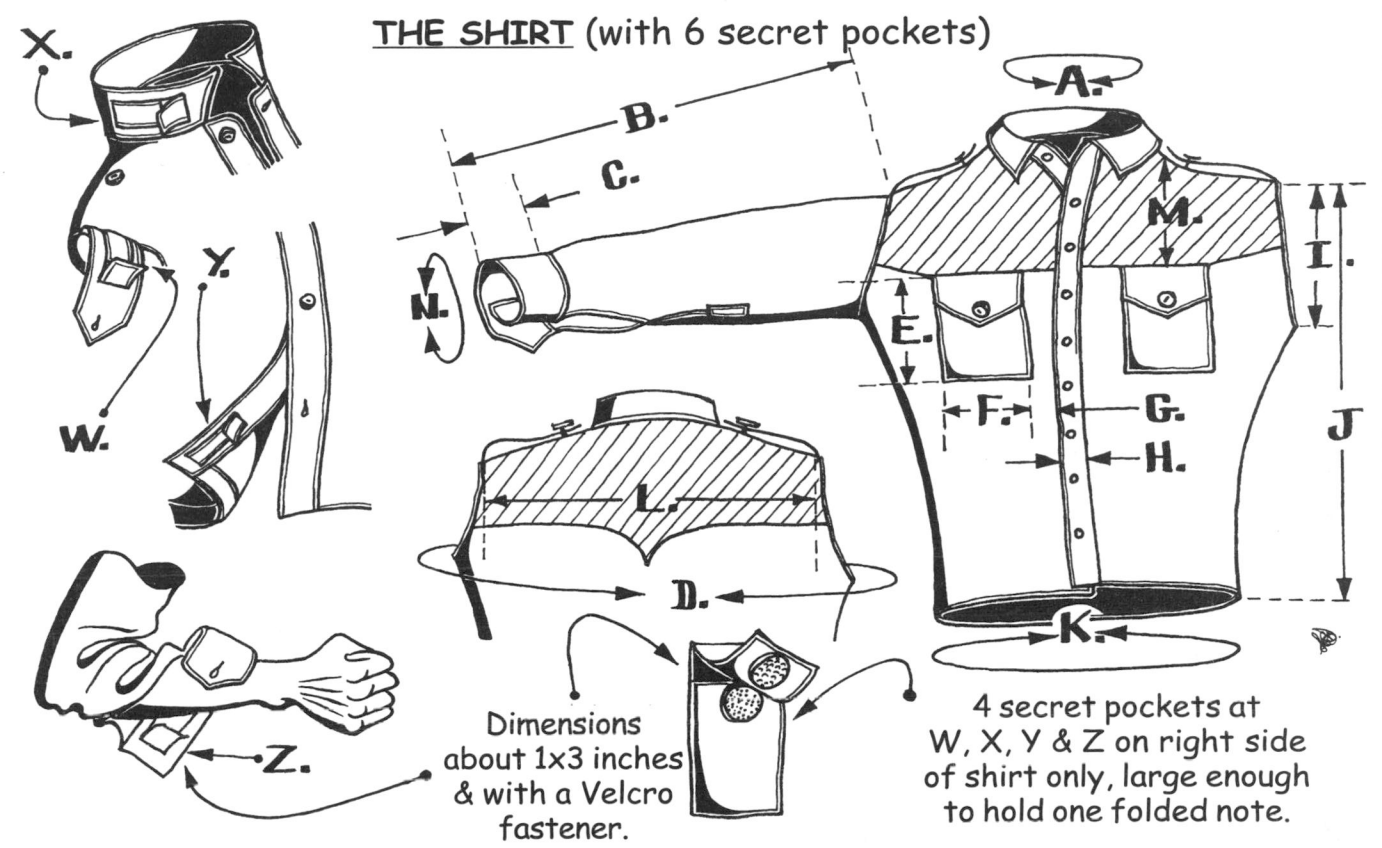

Dimensions about 1x3 inches & with a Velcro fastener.

4 secret pockets at W, X, Y & Z on right side of shirt only, large enough to hold one folded note.

IMPORTANT NOTES

● This shirt has double chest pockets (i.e.: outside pockets are exactly duplicated on inside, except with Velcro fasteners).

● The shaded areas (front & back) over the shoulders is double cloth thickness (2 layers of cloth) (sun protection & wear).

● Use a cloth of about 60% synthetic (ease of washing & crease resistance) & 40% cotton (comfort, sweat absorption, & sun protection).

● Use a synthetic thread which is ultra-violet (sun) resistant (i.e.: Dacron or terylene - not nylon).

● With each shirt please provide four spare buttons, thread, & about half a square foot of spare cloth.

CODE	YOUR MEASUREMENTS	INCHES
A	**C**ollar (buttoned)	
B	**S**leeve (total)	
C	**C**uff Only	3
D	**C**hest	
E	**P**ocket Height	6
F	**P**ocket Width	4.5
G	**P**ocket Side Gap	1
H	**B**utton Strip Width	1.5
I	**S**leeve Depth At Top	
J	**S**houlder To Bottom	
K	**B**ottom	
L	**S**houlder Width	
M	**S**houlder To Pocket Top	
N	**C**uff (buttoned)	
O	**S**pare	

Note : For your own use take this publication to your tailor with your own personal measurements filled in the inches column.

A TRAVELER'S CUSTOM APPAREL
Unisex Travelers' Shirt & Trousers Tailoring Design

*Versatile & highly functional, wear with belt or braces,
dress shoes or trainers, matching shirt or string vest.*

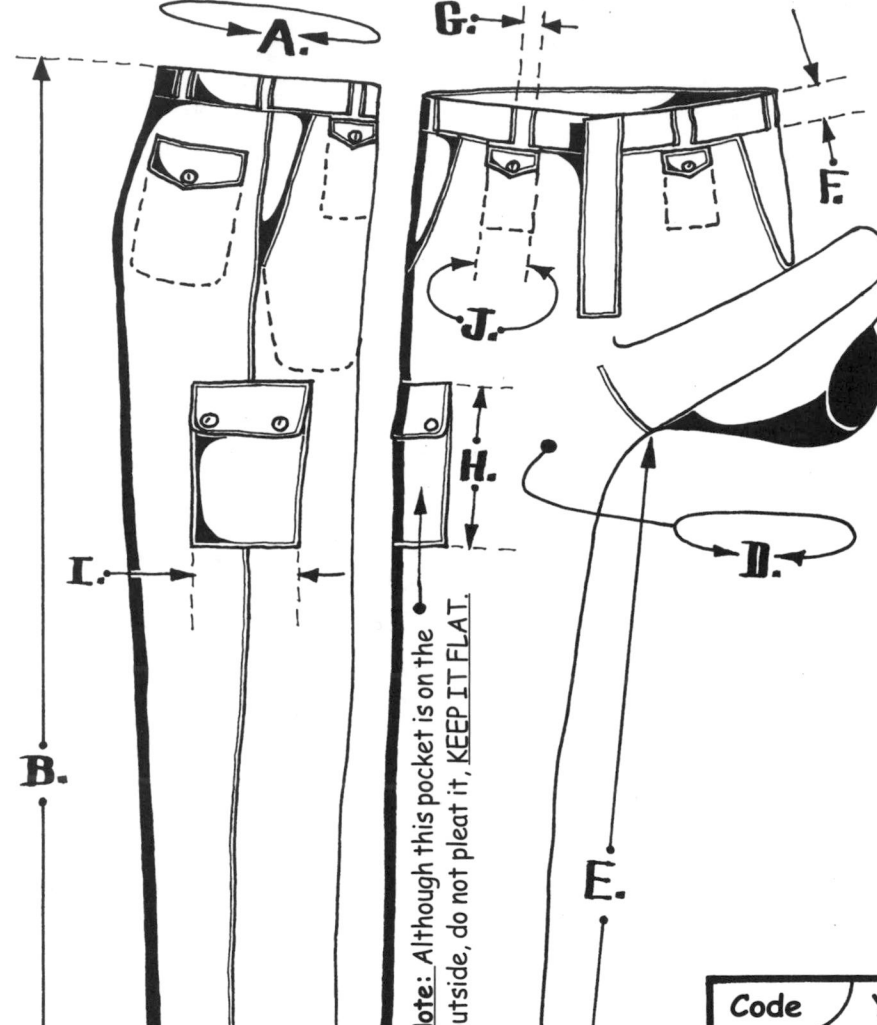

Note: Although this pocket is on the outside, do not pleat it, KEEP IT FLAT.

IMPORTANT NOTES

● **All pockets** (rear, side, front, & thigh) are on both left & right sides.

● **The two thigh pockets** (left & right) are duplicated inside (except the flaps are secured with Velcro whilst the outside is secured with buttons).

● **Be sure the crotch** is cut with enough material TO PERMIT KICKS.

● **Use a cloth** of about 60% synthetic (ease of washing & crease resistance) & 40% cotton (comfort, sweat absorption **& sun protection**).

● **Use synthetic thread** which is ultraviolet (sun) resistant (ie: Dacron or Terylene - NOT NYLON).

● **Fly to be strong** zip with button at top (inside).

● **With each pair of trousers** please provide one spare zip, 2 spare buttons, thread, **& about one square foot of cloth.**

SECRET POCKETS

● **There are two** secret pockets (besides the two inside thigh ones) as per diagram, located inside the inside turnup on the inside of each leg (big enough to take **one folded banknote each**).

Code	Your Measurements	Inches
A	Waist	
B	Total Height	
C	Around Trouser Bottom	
D	Around Trouser Thigh	
E	Inside Leg	
F	Belt Loop Height	1.5
G	Belt Loop Width	1
H	Thigh Pocket Height	9
I	Thigh Pocket Width	5.5
J	Front Pocket Width	3
K	Spare	

Note: For your own use take this publication to your tailor with your own personal measurements filled in the inches column.

A TRAVELER'S CUSTOM CASE

Practical Hints & Ideas To Help Make Your Trip A Success

__The Three Golden Rules:__

TRAVEL LIGHT - TRAVEL PREPARED - TRAVEL SECURE

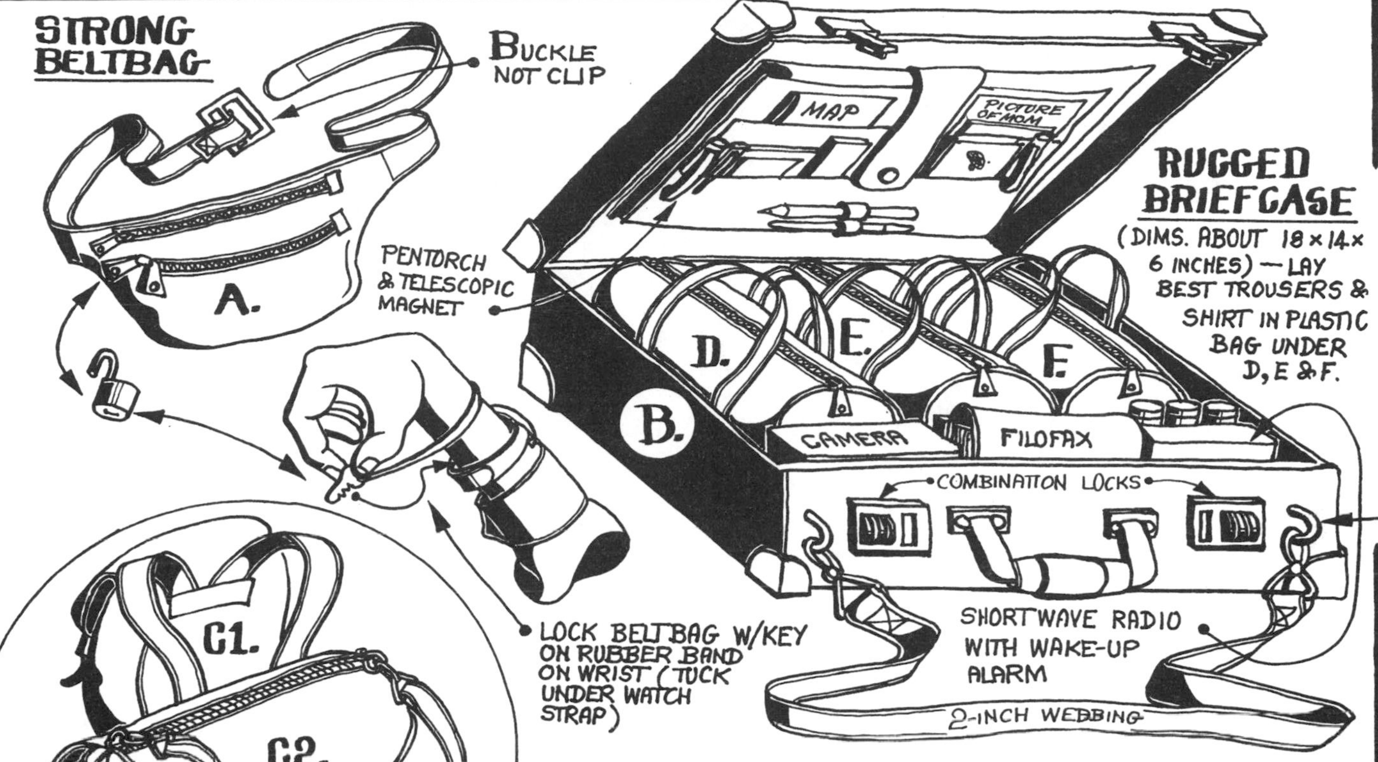

STRONG BELTBAG
BUCKLE NOT CLIP
A.
PENTORCH & TELESCOPIC MAGNET
MAP
PICTURE OF MOM
RUGGED BRIEFCASE
(DIMS. ABOUT 18 x 14 x 6 INCHES) — LAY BEST TROUSERS & SHIRT IN PLASTIC BAG UNDER D, E & F.
D.
E.
F.
B.
CAMERA
FILOFAX
COMBINATION LOCKS
LOCK BELTBAG W/KEY ON RUBBER BAND ON WRIST (TUCK UNDER WATCH STRAP)
SHORTWAVE RADIO WITH WAKE-UP ALARM
2-INCH WEBBING

C1.
C2.
LIGHT FOLDING BAG
(WITH LOCK TAGS)

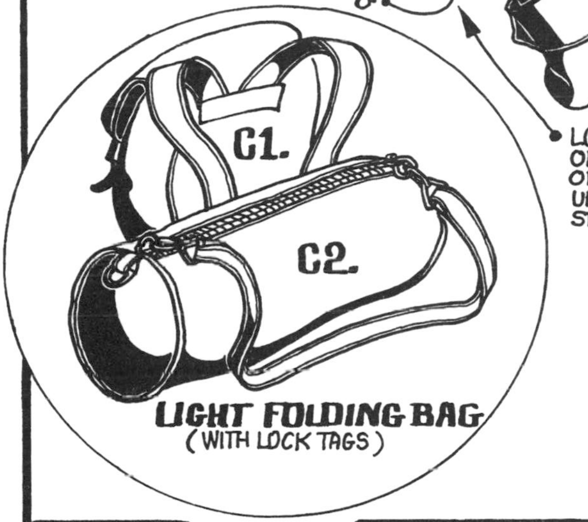

- **GENERAL PLAN** is to travel with only belt bag (A) to hold documents & a little cash (main cash reseve to hide on body) & breifcase (B) (see contents list) - This is also a seat (on end) & a footrest to raise feet on long journeys.

SUGGESTED CONTENTS LIST

BAG D
- Sew repair kit
- Spare batteries
- Rubber bands
- Fork & spoon
- Zip plastic bags
- Safety pins
- Sunglasses
- Electronic phrasebook
- Small lighter
- Nylon cord
- Swiss army knife
- Secret container
- Passport photos
- Bag C1 or C2

BAG E
- Underwear
- Socks
- Swimwear
- Folding hat
- Shorts
- Plastic rain cape
- Handkerchief
- Sports vest

BAG F
- Toothbrush
- Toothpaste
- Soap in box
- Shampoo
- Suntan Cream
- Vitamins
- Comb/Brush
- Scissors
- Tweezers
- Mirror
- Band-Aids
- Razor etc.
- Medicinals

- **BAGS D, E, F** are cloth with a zip top (about 6" dia. x 10" long).

EXTRA HINTS

- **DIRTY CLOTHES:** stow them in a plastic zip bag & try to wash them every night (try shampoo).
- **TOWELS** are bulky to carry - if none available - use face flannel.

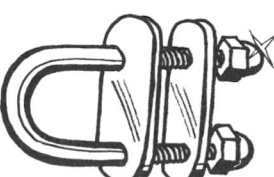

- **U BOLTS** for attaching a shoulder strap to a briefcase can be purchased at a boat shop.
- **WATCHES:** the best ones (even if you don't like them) are quartz digital divers watches (200m) because they are strong, accurate & **don't attract thieves.**

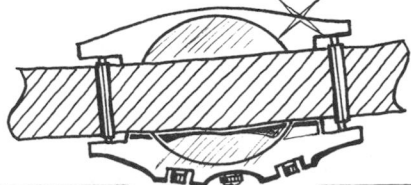

- Choose a strap (Velcro is best) **that goes thru** (not on to) **__both pins.__**

Nowhere is the Boy Scouts' motto of "Be Prepared" more applicable than when traveling - Plan to survive your journey!

CLEAR NAIL POLISH...

...is very useful, carry some.

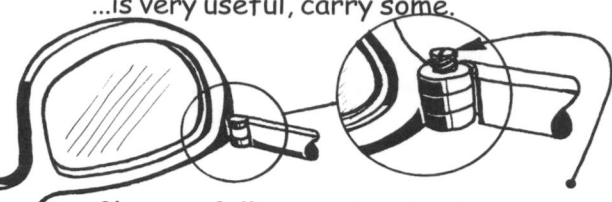

- **Glasses falling to bits?** - Put a dab here & solve the problem.

- **Before setting out** on your journey put a dab here & **keep your buttons on** for at least twice as long.

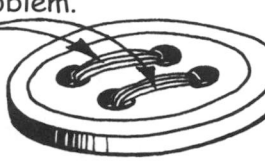

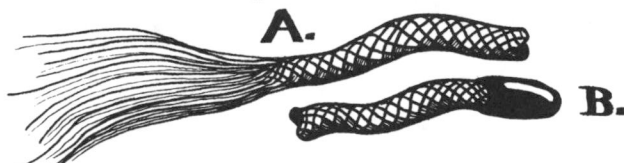

A.

B.

- Natural fiber shoe **laces or drawstrings frayed?** - Change them from "A" to "B" by cutting off & dipping or "painting" the end.
- There are lots more uses.

RAPID ROUGH CONVERSION FORMULAE

	From	How	To
WEIGHT	* ozs	× 30 - 1/20 =	gms
	*gms	+1/20 div. by 30 =	ozs
	lbs	div. by 2 - 1/10 =	kgs
	kgs	+ 1/10 × 2 =	lbs

	From	How	To
LENGTH	ins	× 10 div. by 4 =	cms
	cms	div. by 10 × 4 =	ins
	feet	div. by 3 - 1/10 =	mtrs
	mtrs	× 3 + 1/10 =	feet
	yds	- 1/10 =	mtrs
	mtrs	+ 1/10 =	yds
	miles	× 8 div. by 5 =	k.mtrs
	k.mtrs	div. by 8 × 5 =	miles

	From	How	To
VOLUME	imp gls	× 9 div. by 2 =	lts
	lts	× 2 div. by 9 =	imp gls
	U.S. gls	× 15 div. by 4 =	lts
	lts	× 4 div. by 15 =	U.S. gls

* Same for fluids ozs ⇄ millilitres.

NEEDLE AND THREAD

Stow yours like this -

buy long thin spool of your favorite color. Stick a scrap of foam up one end - the threaded needle down the other - secure in place with rubber band.

EMERGENCY   ZIP REPAIR

Zip gone at a bad time? Don't Panic.

Put the zip back **together** & sew over the break tightly - it should still work (break under).

SMELLS

- **SHOES:** Sprinkle baking soda in at bedtime & brush out before wearing.
- **GARLIC BREATH:** Can be neutralized by chewing fresh parsley (or a coffee bean).
- **TOBACCO ODOR:** On clothes (& in rooms) will be absorbed by vinegar or weak ammonia solution in a bowl left overnight in room or closet.
- **OPEN FIRES:** Are a good excuse to throw your orange or lemon peel in & enjoy the fragrance.

- **BATHROOMS:** Can have embarrassing smells - strike a match for quick results.
- **BLEACH:** Smells on hands, neutralize by a dash of vinegar rubbed on & rinsed off.

- **TRAVEL BAGS:** & their contents will stay fresh & sweet smelling if you include a sachet or two of lavender.

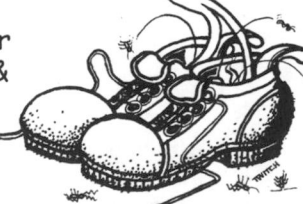

A TRAVELER'S VERY BASIC SELF-PRESERVATION

Simple Counterattacks & Possession Safeguards

If prevention is better than cure then make a habit of taking these simple precautions & reduce your vulnerability.

• **DISPLAYING VALUABLES** is like **<u>begging to be robbed</u>** (or worse) - Keep most of your assets OUT OF SIGHT.

• **TRAVEL <u>with 2 wallets</u>** (or more) - one with a few $ in (keep in convenient place & use to pay all small costs [drinks, fares, in the market etc.]) The other wallet with your main bankroll <u>keep in a hidden place</u> & **DO NOT GET IT OUT IN PUBLIC.**

• Even an elderly lady can **PACK A PUNCH**, ... with a little help from her purse, keys or a coin roll (clenched in the fist) **<u>can be quite deadly.</u>**

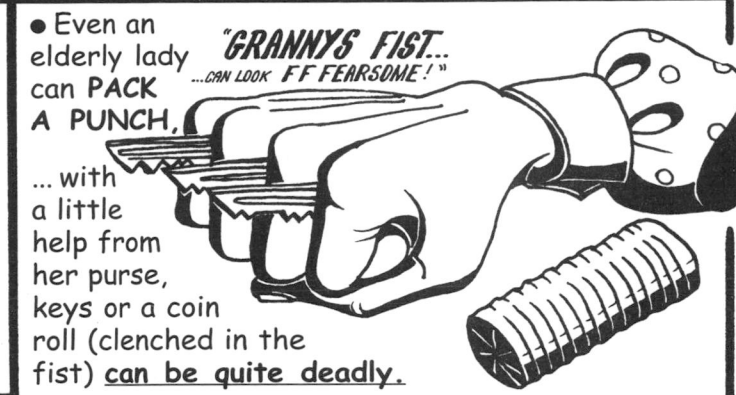

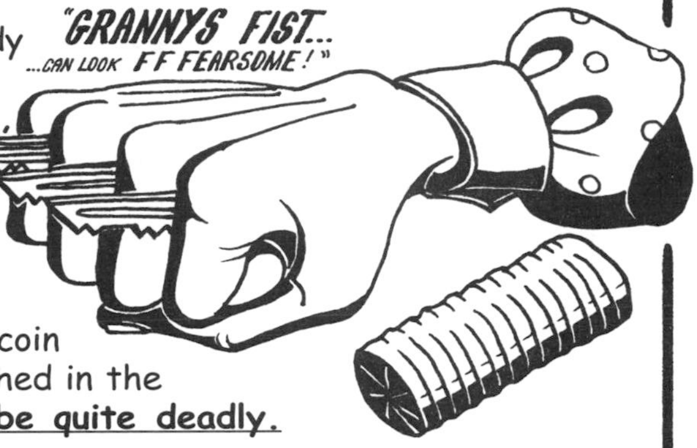
"GRANNYS FIST...
...CAN LOOK FF FEARSOME!"

• **DON'T WEAR <u>expensive looking jewelery,</u>** (necklaces are a prime - target for **<u>"Grab & Run Thieves"</u>**)

TRAVEL LIGHT - **<u>Too much luggage</u>** is a loss (& a crime) waiting to happen - It is also a burden on you & can <u>SERIOUSLY CRAMP YOUR STYLE.</u>

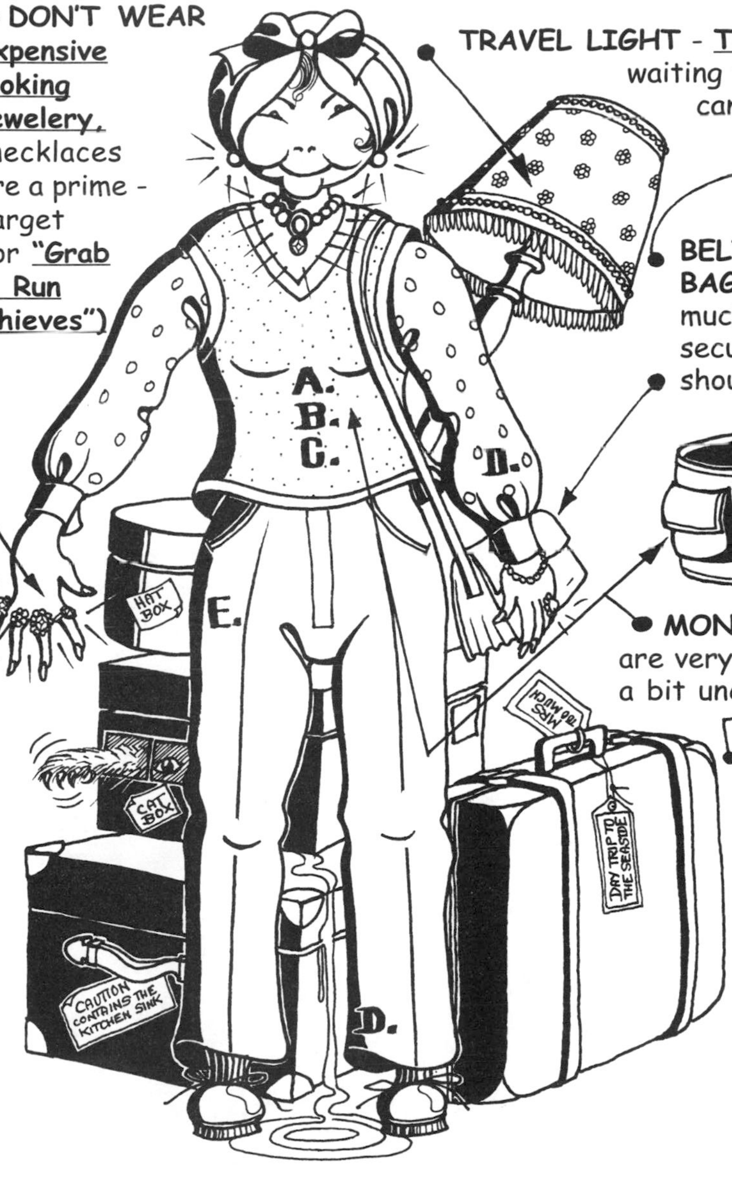
A.
B.
C.
D.
E.
HAT BOX
CAT BOX
CAUTION CONTAINS THE KITCHEN SINK
DAY TRIP TO THE SEASIDE
D.

• **BELT BAGS** are much more secure than shoulder purses.

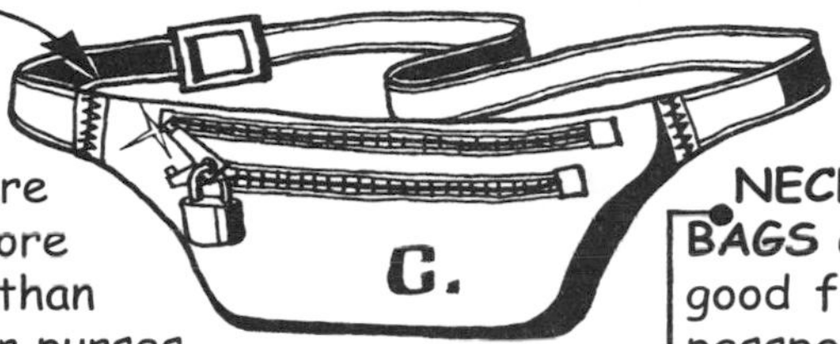
C.

NECK BAGS are good for passports & money, keep it all out of sight

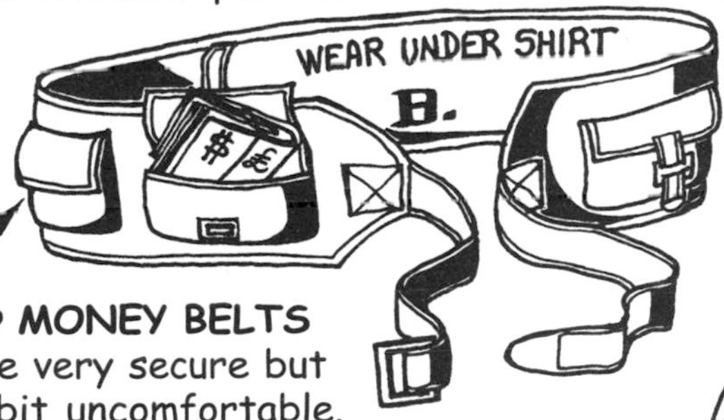
WEAR UNDER SHIRT
B.

• **MONEY BELTS** are very secure but a bit uncomfortable.

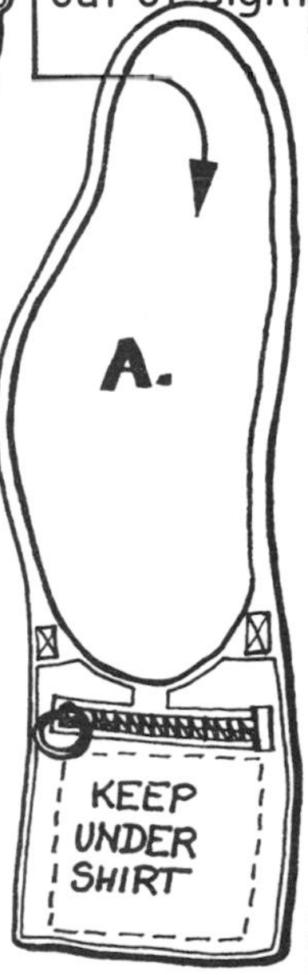
A.
KEEP UNDER SHIRT

• **WRIST POUCH:** good for a secret bank note, etc. (keep it out of sight).

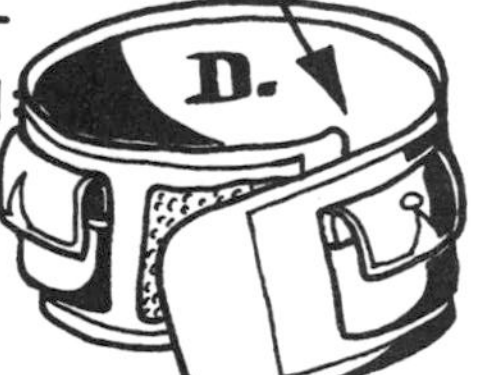
D.

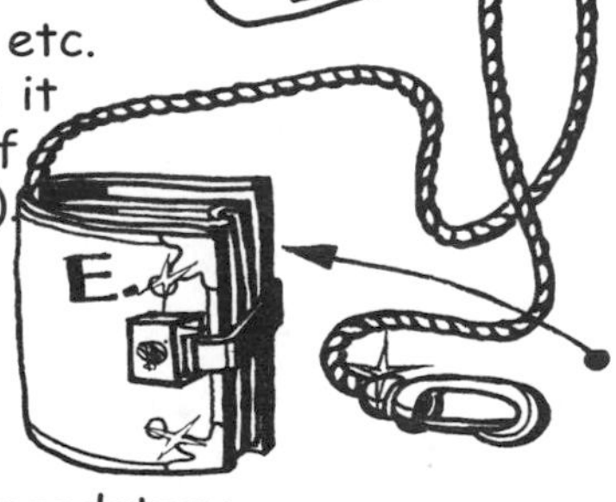
E.

• **WALLET** on a cord (or wire)—clip around waist & put in pocket.

• **SELF-CONFIDENCE** (or fear) are auras detectable by predatory animals, thieves & muggers - Even if you don't feel confident, practice looking like you do - **IT COULD SAVE YOU A LOT OF GRIEF.**

These simple defenses will be even more effective if you can find a friend or relative to practice them on!

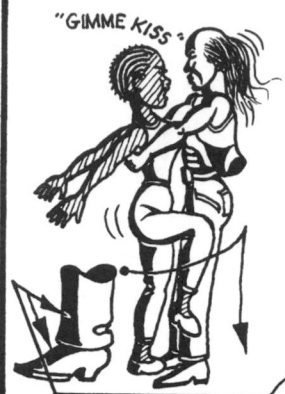

INSTEP STAMP

Easily executed & potentially very painful escape technique from hug from front or back - (instep, toes & shin-bone all useful targets).

Stamp with heel here.

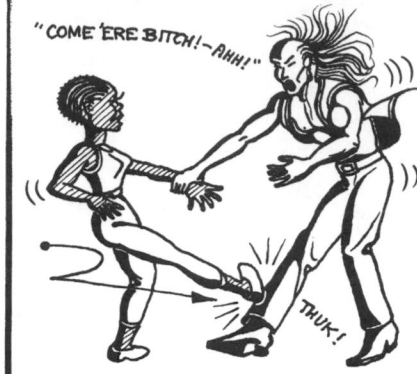

SHIN KICK

Excellent reach & minor damage potential. Useful as a distraction to effect an escape for woman or even child (kick, run & scream).

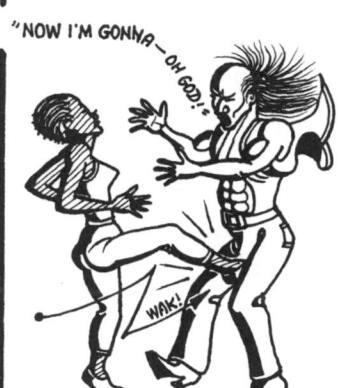

CROTCH KICK

An old favorite relied on perhaps too much by ladies.
- Like any move it needs practice.
- Stand in front of a mirror & kick out fast & hard
- (& dont forget to practice using the knee also).

DIGIT BEND

Grasp the upper outer **small** finger & bend back &/or grasp genitals & twist/pull.

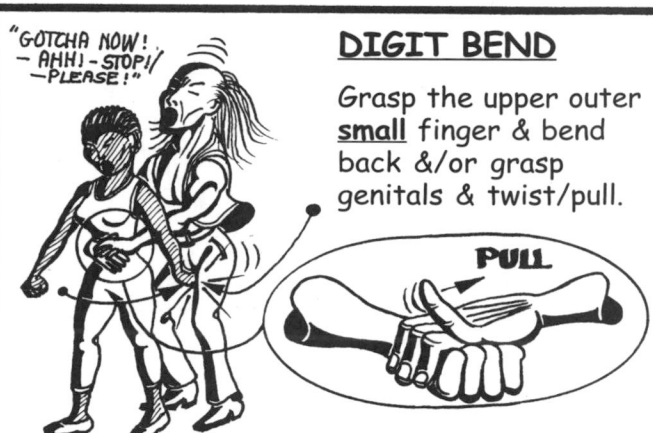

PULL

HAIR-PULL RELEASE

Grasp attackers hand very hard with both hands, ducking & twisting **toward** attacker - which will force attackers fingers open, & pitch him or her forward. **In a serious attack** this would be followed by a kick to the face.

1.

"HEY!"

2.

"OK NOW I'M GETTING MAD!"

"NOW EAT GRAVEL YOU JERK!"

3.

"OH GOD! MEAN BITCH! AAAAH! BAD DAY! OOOO!"

FOOT TWIST

Grasp attackers foot with both hands (**one on heel & one on toe**) & push & twist violently in direction of other foot.

"HAW HAW! GOTCHA NOW!"

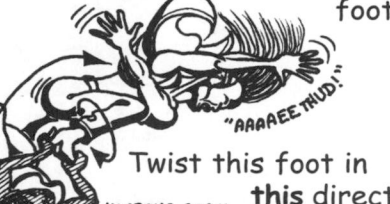

"AAAAEE THUD!"

Twist this foot in **this** direction.

"WRONG AGAIN PINHEAD"

ONE-HAND STRANGLE-HOLD BREAK

In the case at right: The victim strikes violently with her right hand the right wrist of the attacker - followed by a kick or knee (right leg) to the groin of attacker.

"GGHH"

How to maintain sexuality while traveling

REJUVENATING SEXUALITY WITH MASSAGE.

● **CIRCULATION OF KI**: via the meridians is direct-ly related to well-being & tsubo stimulation (by pressure 3 to 10 seconds &/or by massage 4 to 16 minutes) will benefit travel-weary sexuality of male or female.

● **TUMMY**: Place fist on belly button & open palm on top of it, push in & massage (actual points are 2 fingers widths N,S,E, & W of belly button).

● **GENITALS**: Press the old favourite tsubo half-way between genitals & anus (on centerline).

● **ANKLE**: Press two points 1) one palm width above inner ankle bone (in hollow behind shin) & 2) just behind & below inner ankle bone(s).

● **SHIN**: Press hard with both thunbs a point 1 palm width down from bottom of kneecap & one finger outside of shinbone.

● **SOLE OF FOOT**: Put bare or stockinged foot on a big marble or round corner & press/massage a point 1/3 from mid toe tip to heel on centerline (just behind balls of foot).

● **KNEE**: With thumb(s) press & massage center of hollows at back of knees.

● **LOW BACK**: For self massage 1) curl into fetal position & roll back & forth (on back) on double towel on floor & 2) lie on back with clenched fists knuckle up under low back & move around.

● **LOW BELLY**: Deep knead with 4 fingers of both hands from groin to belly button.

REJUVENATING SEXUALITY WITH HERBS

● **MIX** 3 units each of True Unicorn Root, Damiana Leaves, Yohimbe Bark, Muira Bark & one unit of Cassia Bark. Mix together, grind up & load in gelatin capsules. Take one capsule 3 times/day when traveling.

● **OTHER ENHANCERS Of Sexuality:**

chickweed, gold-enseal, fenugreek saw palmetto, safflower, eryngo root, nettle seeds, red pepper, gotu kola, myrtle tree leaves, false unicorn, rose hips, jasmine, nutmeg, lovage, saffron, savory, mint.

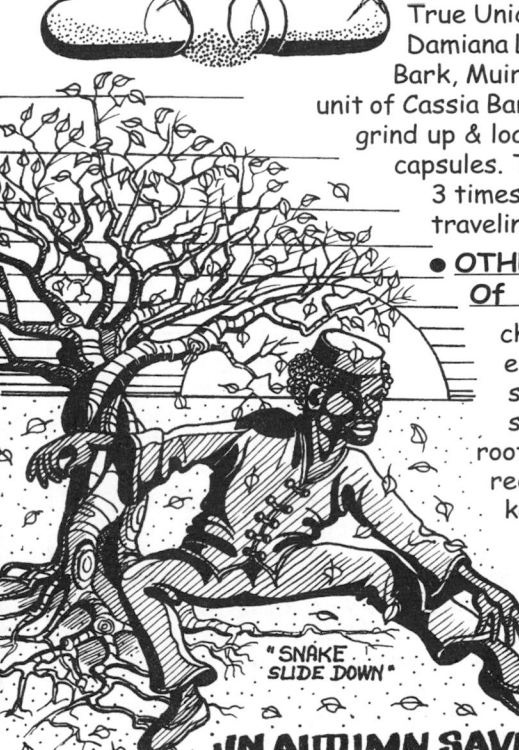

"SNAKE SLIDE DOWN"

-IN AUTUMN SAVE KI-

LACK OF SUN

● **It has been variously demon-strated** that a lack of full spectrum unfiltered (by glass) sunlight entering the eye adversely affects the pituitary gland and thus levels of testosterone (sex hormone).

"TIGER CREEP FORWARD"

-IN SUMMER GROW KI-

EXERCISE

● **Particularly that which raises the heartbeat** improves circulation, energy, metabo-lism & sexuality (particularly in men) - So after that long plane trip choose the stairs to your hotel room & be stronger (in more ways than one) tommorow.

● **DIET WHEN TRAVELING is often very poor** due to unavailibility &/or inconvenience & what is available may be extremely yin (ie: sweets, soft drinks, processed junk food etc.) therefore be prepared & take basic yang staples (eg: raw carrots, apples, almonds [alkaline], rice cakes [neutral] & ginseng tea) & attempt yin/yang balance during sometimes tiring & stressful journeys.

● **SEXUALITY EXTRAS for maintaining levels of testosterone** & metabolic virality include : Raise low fat protein intake (white fish/turkey etc. two meals/day), caviar, mussels, plantain, fig, mandrake root, parsley, parsnips, fertilized eggs, bran cereals, avocado, onion, cayenne pepper, mushrooms, celery, pumpkin seeds, sassafras, walnuts, a little sea salt & tuber of orchid (eg: Orchis Mascula), also sprouted wheat & adzuki beans.

GENITAL CONTRACTONS
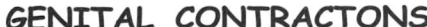

● **SOUNDS RUDE but is actually a yoga tech-nique** for enhancing sexuality & general well-being which is particularly applicable to travelers because it **can be done almost anywhere:** If possible sit cross-legged with straight back & breathe completely in (thru nose) & hold (total usually 10 - 20 seconds but even for men & odd for women). **During "hold" time only, tense & contract** genital/groin/anus area - then while brea-thing out thru mouth slowly to same count re-lax tensed area. **During "in" time "feel" the Ki** building & storing.

How to maintain sexuality while traveling

● LIFE FORCE (energy) (Chi in Chinese & Ki in Japan) is vital for sexual & reproductive well-being & as **all body functions vary with the seasons** (e.g.: warm = yang, cold = yin) it follows that to avoid fatigue, illness & loss of sexuality seek harmonious balance with the time of year. This awareness is thus most important for travelers, who may experience many & rapid changes such as diet, sleeping, time, culture etc. **all of which affect Ki.**

SPRING	Plant & Nurture
SUMMER	Strengthen & Fill
AUTUMN	Gather & Store
WINTER	Conserve & Protect

THE KIDNEYS & SEX

● ORIENTAL MEDICINE holds that the health of the kidney meridian (sole of foot to inside ankle, calf, thigh, groin & 2 finger widths either side of center up tummy & chest) is **vital to sexuality with anything ailing one also harming the other.**

● TOO MUCH SUGAR, fructose (fruit), lactose (milk), molasses, glucose etc. even honey **but particularly white sugar** are all considered very Yin & also seriously burden the adrenal glands & kidneys. - Sweets, soft drinks, cream cakes, even fruit juices are most harmful.

● TOO MUCH FLUID in any dietary form (including "flushing" with lots of water) but particularly caffeine, alcohol & soft (sugar) drinks overburden the kidneys filtration function & by association **interfere with sexual well-being.**

● TOO MUCH COLD from (a) external extremes (either continuos long-term mild cold or brief severe cold or cold/iced drinks or ice cream etc. **all damage the kidneys** & their meridian & associated functions including reproduction/sexuality.

● TOO MUCH LOW BACKACHE often causes reproductive difficulties & vice versa. This is because of the strong effect one has on the other. Thus particularly when traveling it is vital to **stretch & exercise the lower back** (see back sec.) **3-7 times/week.**

· IN WINTER GUARD KI ·

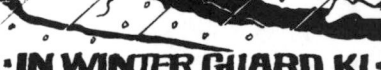
FATIGUE & SEX

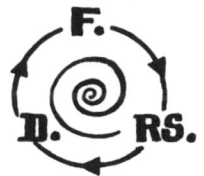

F = fatigue
D = depression
RS = reduced sexuality

● **STRESS/anxiety/worry/loss** etc. (often experienced while traveling) can easily result in depression which in turn almost always leads to fatigue (& reproductive decline). Therefore attack this downward spiral at its weakest point - depression.

FIX IT BY

● **BREATHING: Slowly & deeply** (abdomen & rib cage) all day supplying more oxygen to blood & tissues (& removing more toxins) dramatically improving outlook & metabolism.

● **CIRCULATION degenerates without regular exercise** leaving blood & tissues short of nutrients & full of stagnate toxins leading to a rapid decline in optimism & metabolism : Exercise More.

● **DIET if poor or imbalanced** with nutritional shortages &/or alcohol etc. excesses inevitably leads to fatigue & sexual ailments: Study yin/yang & adopt macrobiotic diet or similar.

● **A SEASONAL PERSPECTIVE:** is also an invaluable skill in combating fatigue.

WOMEN-ONLY SECTION

● MENSTRUATION DIFFICULTIES: **(When traveling you don't need)** so here are three main problems & what to do about them.

● AMENORRHEA: (No menstruation/egg) **Possible causes:** Stress, upset, too low (under 20%) or too high body fat, sickness (e.g. anemia) or malnutrition (particularly B-complex shortages) : Take high-potency time-release multi vit/min + extra B6, B12 & Vit E (100 IU/3 times a day), take hot baths followed by brief cold, take Aloe Vera & avoid constipation.

● MENORRHAGIA: (Excess Blood) **Possible causes:** Stress, uterus injury/infection, underactive thyroid: Take extra Vit A, B12, C, E, folic acid, iron & zinc. Eat more whole grains, leafy greens, & chicken liver, also aduki beans, comfrey root & lemon.

● DYSMENORRHEA: (Excess pain) **Possible causes:** Hormones too high or low with associated muscle cramps : Take 400mg magnesium, 800mg calcium, 300 IU Vit E & 2000 mg evening primrose oil - all daily for the week before period. Put ice pack on low back 10 mins then hot pack on low tummy 30 mins.

"WHITE CRANE SPREAD WINGS"

· IN SPRING SOW KI ·

Ancient Far Eastern Techniques For Combating Common Travelers Ailments

Do Peculiar Body MARKS & SIGNS Worry You En Route?

HANDS

- **SWOLLEN END JOINTS =** Possible osteoarthritis.
- **SWOLLEN KNUCKLES =** Possible rheumatoid arthritis.
- **EMACIATED MUSCLE** between thumb & index finger = Possible tendency to diabetes.

PALM SIGNS

- **WARM, THIN SKIN** & moist = Excess dietary liquid & sugar, probable hair loss & rheumatoid arthritis.
- **DRY, ROUGH & SPONGY** = Excess dietary oil/fat & possible underactive thyroid gland & impaired sexuality & circulation.
- **OVERLY SMOOTH, WARM OR EVEN SHINY** = Possible overactive thyroid gland.

PALM COLORS

- **WHITE:** Poor circulation/cold/anemia.
- **YELLOW:** Bile overflow into blood.
- **BLUE:** Poor circulation &/or heart problems.
- **RED:** Possible stress, arthritis, cirrhosis (liver), high blood pressure, diabetes, gout.

EXTRA NAIL SIGNS

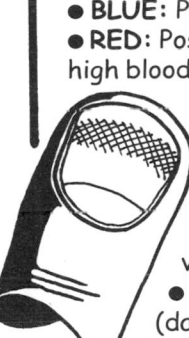

- **YELLOW NAILS** (often thick & with stunted growth) = Possible impaired lymph system function &/or vitamin E shortage.
- **PALE & DARK NAILS** (dark at tip) can be an indication of kidney malfunction.
- **RIDGED/BRITTLE/**flattened nails often indicate long-term stress &/or cold, poor circulation &/or iron deficiency.

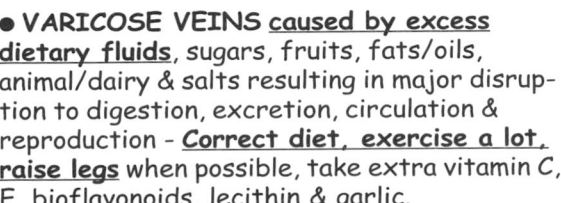

- **VARICOSE VEINS caused by excess dietary fluids,** sugars, fruits, fats/oils, animal/dairy & salts resulting in major disruption to digestion, excretion, circulation & reproduction - **Correct diet, exercise a lot, raise legs** when possible, take extra vitamin C, E, bioflavonoids, lecithin & garlic.
- **WARTS caused by overeating** & in particular fat, protein & sugar, resulting in metabolic disorders including viral vulnerability. (thru cuts etc.). Correct diet & apply pure vitamin A oil (from fish) twice daily up to 6 months.

BEFORE BIRTH

- **BIRTHMARKS** are acquired because of **mothers exposure during pregnancy** to disease, fever, drugs, medication, radiation, toxins etc.

AFTER BIRTH

- **FRECKLES caused by yang sunlight** attracting internal usually dietary yin such as sugar, too much fruit (fructose), milk (lactose), honey, soft drinks, sweets etc. & often appear on the meridian being overburdened (e.g.: large & small intestine on hand, back, arms & shoulders). **Correct diet = freckles fade.**
- **"BEAUTY SPOTS"** (flat, black, roundish) appear mainly along meridians after a fever or disease & **indicate an overburdened organ** attempting to eliminate carbon residues from overeating particularly of animal fats/proteins & processed carbohydrates.
- **WHITE PATCHES caused mainly by excess dietary dairy products** including milk, cheese, butter, yogurt etc. Mucus & fat progressively deteriorate hormonal respiratory & reproductive functions with a tendency to cyst & tumor formation. Long-term elimination of animal/dairy fats also excess vegetable oils required.
- **MOLES caused by overeating** (particularly of protein, fat & carbohydrate). Appearing on the skin site of the most adversely affected organs meridian & its related muscles. Correct long-term dietary practices may shrink & even remove them.
- **EASY BRUISING** (blue marks) **caused by excess dietary yin** (sugar, soft drinks, fruit juices, chemicals, drugs etc.) also usually affected are emotions, circulation (including blood quality & pulse) & bladder. Correct diet & take a vitamin K supplement.
- **ECZEMA caused by excess dietary fats/oils** mainly of animal/dairy origin e.g.: meat, eggs, milk, cheese, butter etc. resulting in serious overload of major organs & systems e.g.: heart/circulation, digestion & elimination. Danger of toxic buildup, cysts & tumors.
- **ACNE (& PIMPLES) caused by hormonal changes** &/or excess dietary sugar, animal & particularly dairy products, fruits, fats, oils & refined carbohydrates, resulting in fat &/or mucus buildup along the meridian affected worst. **Correct diet & supplement with extra vitamins** A, B, C, E & F, also zinc, potassium & sulphur.

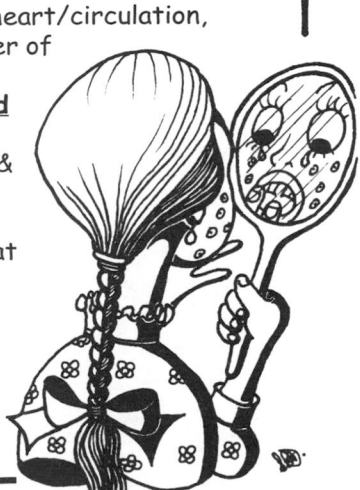

How to relate DREAMS to ki levels

Whole Body Picture

DREAMS OF	INDICATES
Flying & floating	Upper pulse too strong
Falling down	Lower pulse too strong
Wading thru rivers	Yin is too strong
Caught in a fire	Yang is too strong
Violent fighting	Yin & Yang both strong.

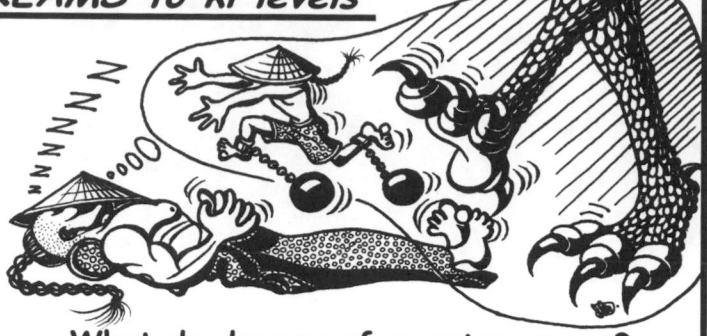

What do dreams of monsters mean?

SPECIFIC ORGAN DIAGNOSIS

DREAMS OF	MERIDIAN STATUS	ASSOCIATED VULNERABILITY
Happiness/sex	Excess Ki in heart	Backache, gleeful, dry mouth.
Sadness/worry	Excess Ki in lungs	Chest & respiratory pain & ailments.
Monsters/ghosts	Excess Ki in liver	Dizzy, ear/eye ailments, pessimistic.
Worms/wounds	Excess Ki in kidneys	Quiet, bloated/heavy feeling, sweat.
Slavery/bullying	Spleen / stomach	Argues, bowel ailments, legs stiff.

● **Imbalance Of Yin & Yang In Any Organ (Or Body) Will Cause Illness.** ●

Salvation/success	Too little Ki in heart	Depressed, backache, face pale/tense.
Whiteness/conflict	Too little Ki in lungs	Coughing blood, thin, breathless.
Paralysis/vegetation	Too little Ki in liver	Joint pain, brittle nails, worrying.
Drowning/wrecks	Too little Ki in kidneys	Vague, low sexuality, tired legs.
Building/starving	Spleen / stomach	Abdominal cramps, vomit, diarrhea.

DIET-RELATED AILMENT VULNERABILITY

	Food Group Eaten Most	Typical Personality.	Typical Health Problems
	Honey, syrup, **SUGARS**, sweets, molasses etc.	Schizophrenic, emotional, nervous, cyclic moodiness.	Obesity, reduced sexual desire, indigestion, bowel, kidney & sensory problems.
	Excess salt, **SPICES**, curry, peppers etc.	Volatile, erratic, insecure, suicidal, argumentative.	Reproduction, circulation, heart, skin, bowels, kidneys, blood pressure.
	Butter, cheese, **DAIRY**, yogurt, cream, milk etc.	Passive, restrained, not easily angered, delayed responses.	Mucus, allergies, heart, circulation, skin, liver, sexual, spleen, cancer.
	Fresh, frozen **FRUITS**, juices, preserves etc.	Discerning, critical outlook, sensitive, sentimental, nervous.	Reduced sexual desire, prone to digestive & intestinal complaints, spots, skeletal.
	Beef, pork, **RED MEATS**, eggs, sausages etc.	Aggressive outlook, opinion-ated, quick, tempered, materialistic.	Blood pressure, circulation, heart, digestive & intestinal problems, tumors & cancer.
	Shellfish, **FISH**, poultry, white meat etc.	Calculating outlook, deter-mined, choosy, controlled desires.	Similar problems to "meat" category but to a lesser degree (fat content critical).
	Lightly cooked, **VEGETA-RIAN**, raw salads etc.	Quiet, composed, non-violent outlook, suspicious, cautious.	Chronic digestive troubles, possible bone, teeth, intestine, skin, lung & bowel problems.
	Bread, cereal, **GRAINS**, cooked vegetables etc.	Usually well-balanced temperament, calm, reason-able, intuitive.	Usually physically robust consti-tution with good resistance to most diseases.

EXTRA VALUABLE PRESSURE POINTS

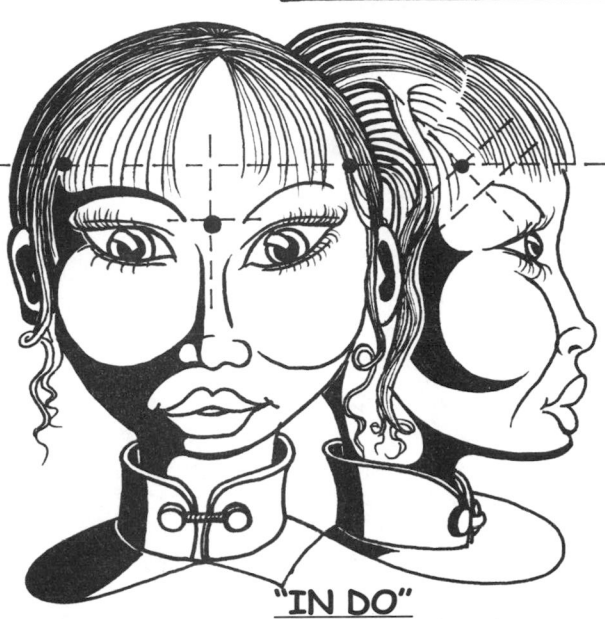

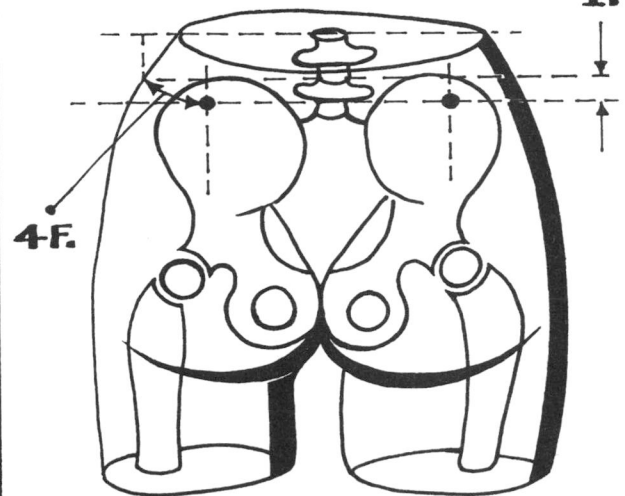

"IN DO"
- **Where:** Between inner corners of eyebrows
- **For:** Headaches, nasal congestion ● **How:** Press in hard with 2 thumbs for 10 seconds 3 times.

"TAI YO"
- **Where:** 1 1/2 fingers up & back from outer eyebrow tips ● **For:** Headaches, insomnia, dizzy, red/swollen eyes, worry/stress ● **How:** Press with thumb 10 seconds 3 times.

"TEN SHI"
- **Where:** On back of upper hip bone, 1 finger width from top & about (depends on fat) 4 finger widths around from body side
- **For:** Low back ache, sexual strength, bed wetting, numb legs, sciatica
- **How:** Press in hard with one thumb on point for 10 seconds 3 times.

NOTE: Press one finger above "TEN SHI" for constipation.

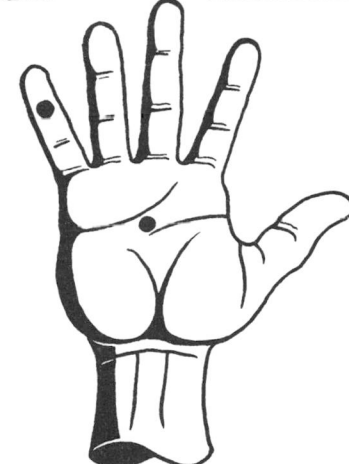

"POLYHYDROSIS POINT"
- **Where:** Mid palm
- **For:** Sweating too much
- **How:** Press 10 seconds 3 times

"NOCTURIA POINT"
- **Where:** End joint little finger on palm side.
- **For:** Bed wetting
- **How:** Press 10 seconds 3 times.

NOTE: In Japan; bed wetters are tickled (4 minutes) pre bed.

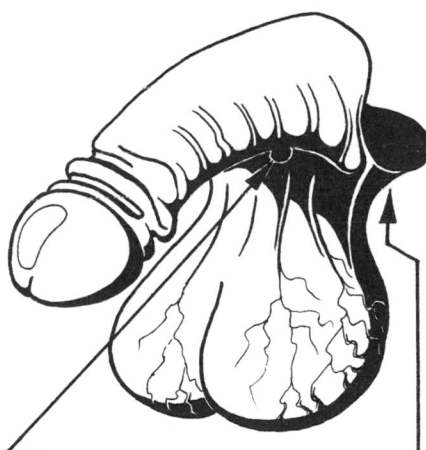

"TRIGGER POINT" + CV.1
- **Where:** Underside midline of penis at top of balls bag.
- **For:** Improved sexuality.
- **How:** Press 10 seconds 3 times

NOTES: For most sexual ailments (inc. impotence, fridgity [ladies], low sperm count etc) treat CV - 1 (on midline between genitals & anus).

EXTRA: Keep balls cool & squeeze daily (once for every year of life).

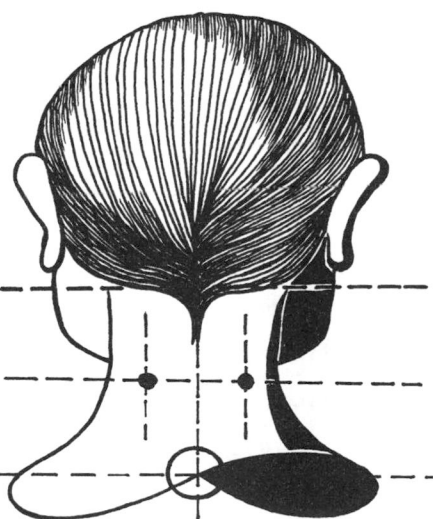

"TRIGGER POINT"
- **Where:** 2 fingers either side on neck center & halfway between base of skull & prominent spine/neck bone.
- **For:** Headaches, loss of voice, throat ailments & tension &/or pain in neck, shoulders & arms.
- **How:** Find points of tension & press 10 - 15 seconds with thumbs/fingers 3 times.

How to stay warm in THE COLD without that extra coat.

FOOD

● **It all provides calories** & thus warmth BUT as from the oriental viewpoint cold is a yin condition, then consumption of yin foods (sugar, sweets, drugs etc.) make the adverse <u>effects of cold on the body worse</u> & conversely consumption of yang foods (e.g. fish, whole grains, onion, carrots, poultry etc.) increases resistance & blood circulation.

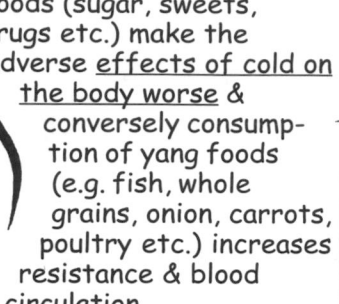

EXERCISE

● **When physical** exercise moves the body, the heart beats faster, driving warm blood, oxygen & nutrients to the furthest ends (toe & fingertips) of the body & removing from the stagnant tissues toxins & cold blood for reprocessing. **Harder Exercise = Faster Heart Beat = Quicker Warming = Stronger Muscles, Bones & Increased Flexibility.**

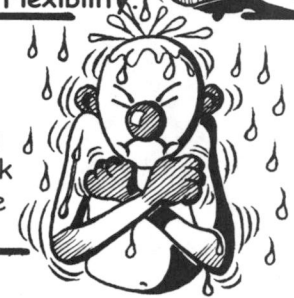

TENSION

● **Muscular tension** (tensing muscles in cold/stress etc.) actually physically constricts the flow of warming blood to & thru arteries, veins & capillaries, partially blocking the supply of oxygen & nutrients to the tissues & preventing the return of toxin-laden colder blood back to the body center for warming & cleaning. **Thus it is vital to relax** as well as use the muscles to achieve efficient circulation.

CHOLESTEROL

● **Excess dietary** animal/dairy fats <u>(also palm & coconut oils)</u> cause hardening & internal size reduction of the arteries, veins & capillaries with reduced blood flow, nutrients, oxygen & warmth to the body tissues, particularly the extremities. **Result:** Sluggish circulation & toxin removal, higher risk of heart diasese & faster metabolic decline plus <u>unjustifiably cold hands & feet.</u>

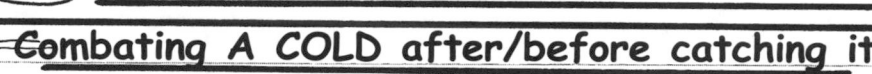

Combating A COLD after/before catching it

● **ORIENTAL MEDICINE** considers a cold not so much an acquired virus but <u>an opportunity taken deliberately by the body</u> (lowering its defences) to expel accumulations of toxins (in the form of mucus) from ingested chemicals, sugars, processed foods, stress, anger, etc.

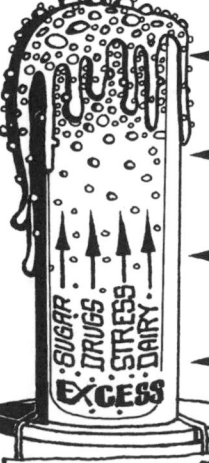

● **DIET:** <u>Mucus is very yin</u>, thus its formation is encouraged by too much yin food (cold soft/fruit drinks, ice cream, potato, etc.) & discouraged by yang foods (rice, grain, carrot, fish etc.). Balance of yin/yang is vital for health & excess either way (particularly yin) will cause illness.

EXTREME YIN: Get sick now
HIGH YIN: Body not very well.
MED. YIN: Correct diet now.

BODY YIN LEVELS (too high = get sick)

● **RECOVERY:** During any fever (including colds) do not eat unless hungry (& choose carefully what you eat) <u>because digestion removes body resources from fighting the fever</u>, which can cause a relapse.

● **GETTING IT BEFORE IT GETS YOU:** Combat the onset of illness (such as a cold) by using the Indian yoga trick of swinging a heavy club (or log) around at arms length. This stretches & loosens the area either side of the spine (just off & below the inner tips of shoulder blades) <u>where tension accumulates just prior to an illness</u> (if you don't have a log handy, apply pressure [3 x 10 seconds] or massage with thumbs - **area may be tender/ hard**).

● **ALSO: 1)** Cut out all refined/ canned etc. foods **2)** Reduce meal size **3)** Simplify menu (i.e. whole rice with veg or salad with fish or whole bread with veg soup).

● **ALSO:** Take extra fresh garlic (4 cloves/day), vit C (1 - 3g/4 hours), (vit A* 20,000 IU/day) & taper all off slowly after recovery.

*pregnancy caution

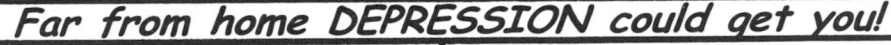

Far from home DEPRESSION could get you!

WILD MOOD SWINGS

can result from changes in blood sugar levels, from "highs" (sugar, sweets, fruit juices, soft drinks etc.) all rated extremely yin by oriental values, which produce temporary feelings of well-being & energy, UNTIL the pancreas in compensation overproduces insulin. **Result: depression, fatigue, bad temper etc.**

SOLUTION

Cut out sugars & balance diet (study yin/yang) for long-lasting energy & stable disposition.

NATURAL ANTIDEPRESSANTS

● **SUNLIGHT**, daylight & light in that order raise spirits.
● **EXERCISE**, particularly that which raises the heart beat.
● **CREATIVE ACTIVITY**, ideally make, paint, etc. something.

MERIDIAN STIMULATION

● **By massage** & tsubo pressure (see accupressure section).
● **By cold water** on face, neck, ears, hands, feet & ankles.

The above techniques work in various ways **to energise mind & body & to dispel negativity.**

RAPID ANTIDEPRESSANT

● A major cause of depression (& many other ailments, too) is insufficient oxygen in the blood supply, but this negative frame of mind can be reversed virtually anytime, anywhere in minutes by concentrating on deep breathing **(& if convenient simple self-hypnosis).**

"THE TECHNIQUE"

Below is the ideal, but not necessary scenario, as deep breathing works almost any which way.
● **Select a quiet place & sit with a straight back.**
● Breathe all the way in (tummy then lungs full) & all the way out completely each time (pick a sequence below but don't count).

IN SECONDS	EASY	MID	HARD
In (nose)	2	4	8
Hold	8	16	32
Out (mth).	4	8	16
Hold	1	2	4

● During each "in breath" visualize that **everything good is coming in your body.**
● During each "out breath" visualize that **everything bad is going out of your body.**
● If you have concentrated, the change in mental & physical well-being **will be quite dramatic.**

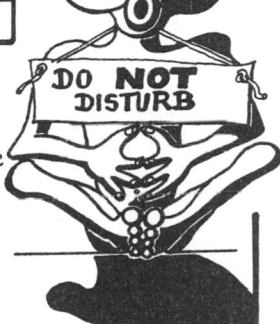

Traveler beware—FOOD POISONING—it can kill you (Part I)

1. VULNERABILITY is higher during & up to 5 days after travel because changes can & do affect your immune system in transit, e.g. stress, diet, time & sleep changes, culture shock & climate differences. **Therefore take extra care of your health until "settled in."**

2. IN ASIA, FOR EXAMPLE, don't eat fresh salads or unpeeled fruit (which may be fertilized with feces). Don't drink tap water (or ice cubes). Don't eat half warm/cold meat, eggs & dairy (including ice cream).

3. BUT DO be scrupulously hygienic. Do eat well boiled (or fried) rice, veg, fish, etc. Do drink bottled water, beer, etc. Do patronise clean high turnover suppliers (restaurants, hotels, etc).

4. IF ALL FAILS & you get sick (starting 1 hour to 3 days after eating) (& lasting 1 - 7 days) often with diarrhoea, vomiting, fever, cramps, fatigue, depression, blood in stools, headaches, etc. & **affecting very young, old, or infirm worse.**

5. COMBAT IT BY consulting a local doctor (if any) &/or **stop all solid foods & dairy products for 24 hours minimum.** Drink lots of liquids (babies every half hour) (for example thin, warm vegetable & garlic broth). Avoid cold & citrus drinks. Stimulate the spleen meridian (starts inner foot side of big toenail) with accupressure.

6. RECOVERING: When diarrhoea subsides, introduce high-nutrition mashed foods (e.g.: boiled whole rice & carrots. Next meal, mashed banana. Next meal, wholemeal toast & hard-boiled egg).

7. TAKE EXTRA POTASSIUM, MAGNESIUM, vitamins B complex (in brewers yeast) & C, pectin (in apples), fiber &/or bran & acidophilus (in yogurt) & sea salt.

ANTI-DIARRHEA

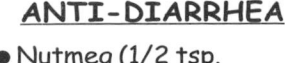

● Nutmeg (1/2 tsp. 3 times/day) ● Garlic ● Red Raspberry ● Cloves ● Ginger ● Peppermint ● Basil ● Sage ● Fast 24 + hours.

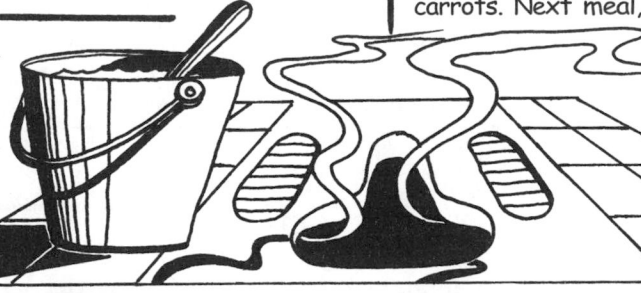

"THE TRAVELERS NIGHTMARE": BACKACHE

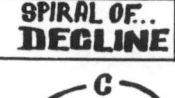
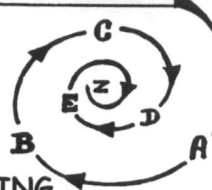

SPIRAL OF...
DECLINE

● **From whatever cause** (lack of exercise, poor posture, stress, injury, etc.), the spiral of decline is vicious (e.g.: Backache = Reduced flexibility = Reduced muscle tone = Reduced circulation = Reduced clearance of toxins = Reduced stimulation to the meridians which run along & around the spine = More backache = Etc. Etc.).

USING "YU POINTS"

"FIXING IT"
Is vital to avoid progressive decline to the whole body.

USING EXERCISE

....**Which relate to organs** &/ or functions in the body . . .

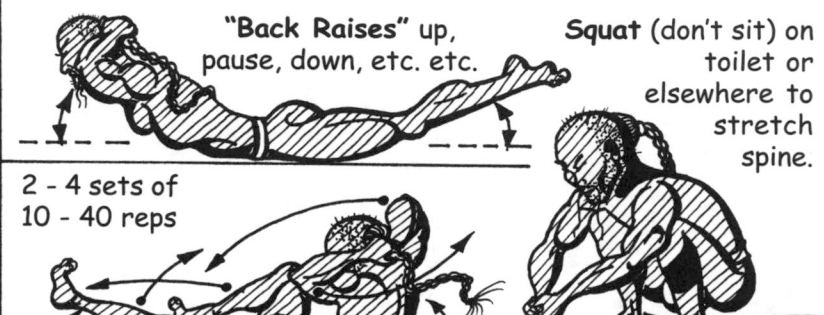

Relates to lungs, heart, circulation, stress, sadness, overwork, grief.	**UPPER**
Liver, gallbladder, stomach, spleen, overeating (particularly animal/dairy/sugar.)	**MIDDLE**
Kidneys, bladder, large intestines, too much sex, salt or liquids, apprehension or fear.	**LOWER**

...And thus a problem in the organ can affect the Yu Point or vice versa.

Most common cause of backache is unbalanced or poor muscle tone. Just 10 minutes/day will fix this.

"Back Raises" up, pause, down, etc. etc.

Squat (don't sit) on toilet or elsewhere to stretch spine.

2 - 4 sets of 10 - 40 reps

"Sit-Up Crunches" (alternate knee/elbow) 2 - 4 sets (2 minutes rest) 10 - 40 repetitions.

Sleep on a firm flat bed on back (or on side in fetal position with sufficient pillows), avoid sleeping on stomach.

TRAVELER BEWARE—FOOD POISONING—IT CAN KILL YOU (Part II)
READ THIS MAIN CHARACTERISTICS CHART, IT'S BORING BUT IT COULD SAVE YOU.

Latin Name	Caught From	Incu. Time	Symptoms	Duration	Notes
Bacillus Cereus	Warm cereals particularly rice & corn.	1 - 16 hours	Violent vomiting, possibility of diarrhea.	under 24 hours	Particular danger from low turnover carryout restaurants.
Campylobacter	Undercooked poultry & bad human hygiene.	2 - 5 days	Fever, violent diarrhea & stomach cramps.	1 - 7+ days	Often with bile/blood in motions & serious wall inflammation of stomach.
Clostridium Botulinium	Usually from contaminated tins & bottles.	18 - 96 hours	Fatigue, headache, dizzy, bowels, senses, coma, dead.	up to 6 months	Attacks central nervous system with paralysis, must survive 1st 8 days to live.
Clostridium Perfringens	Ground (soil), poorly cooked food, dirty nails.	8 - 22 hours	Stomach pain, diarrhea but not usual to vomit.	12 - 24 hours	Common in excreta, raw meat, dehydrated foods, can survive heat.
Listeria Monocytogenes	Ground (soil), dirty water, animal gut/dung.	up to 21 days	Dizziness, fever & flulike symptoms.	difficult to establish	Also from unwashed vegetables, affects very young/old/low immunity badly.
Salmonella	Animal/human excreta/water (poultry is bad.)	6 - 48 hours	Diarrhea, fever, headache, vomiting, aching limbs.	up to 7 days	Can be fatal in vulnerable groups, easy to spread by dirty kitchen habits.
Staphylococus Aureus	Low-heat meat, dairy, mucus (nose), cuts, spots.	2 - 6 hours	Vomiting, diarrhea, stomach pains.	usually 24 hours	Can survive even in salted meats, also passed by sneezing.
Vibro Para-haemolyticus	Seafood, particularly shellfish.	2 - 48 hours	Violent vomiting & diarrhea also fever.	2 - 5+ days	Symptoms similar to cholera & dysentery can be in frozen fish.

IMPORTANT NOTE
After an infection of food poisoning the victim(s) may still be a carrier or the bacteria (which can be transmitted by poor hygiene) for over 12 months after recovery.

TORNADO - WATERSPOUT

● **GENERAL:** Very violent upwardly spiralling columns of air rushing to fill a pocket of extremely low pressure - Although quite small at ground/sea level (less than 200 feet diameter) THEY CAN ROTATE AT OVER 300 MPH, sucking almost everything under them up - Their speed over the land/sea depends on the movements of the cumulonimbus storm clouds to which their top ends are attached.

● **ACTIONS:** In the cases of both tornados & waterspouts the one cardinal rule is "GET OUT OF THE WAY" because they can usually be seen (& heard) some distance away. If you have a compass take a bearing of it (if not, compare its position with skyline) - <u>If bearing does not change it is coming directly at you</u> - Travel sideways to get out of its way - If you get caught, get in a cellar (outside, lie in ditch) & squat against a solid side wall - Doors, windows, roofs & even walls may explode out - Cars, wood houses, **people may be sucked up.**

NUCLEAR BOMB/LEAK

● **RADIATION** surrounds us, from above (outer space), below (ground) & many other sources (luminous paint, x-rays etc.) - <u>but too much of the wrong type</u> can sicken &/or kill almost instantly or many years after.

● **EXPLOSIONS** not only spread deadly radiation far & wide but also create a vast heat blast which destroys all life near it.

● **ACTIONS** (before): Get away (<u>upwind</u>) from targets before explosions or be prepared with purpose-built shelters.

● **ACTIONS** (if caught): Seek immediate shelter (3 feet or more underground best) - **Take iodine & calcium orally to fill thyroid gland & skeleton** before radiation does - Dispose of dust-contaminated clothes - Wash body to remove dust - Cover body with clean clothes - Wear damp cloth over nose/mouth - Stockpile water/food (it gets contaminated) - Do not leave underground shelter for 3 days (<u>or if wind comes from bomb site</u>) - After that go out only 10 minutes/day extending by 5 minutes each day - **Do not eat or drink anything exposed to fallout for years after.**

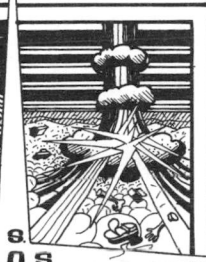

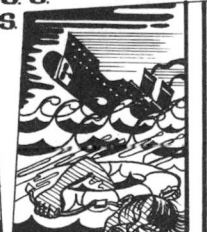

EARTHQUAKE

● **GENERAL:** Most activity along & close to fault lines which cover the earth like seams of a patchwork quilt - Caused by magma (molten rock) pressures moving the earth's crust.

● **DANGERS:** Mainly from collapsing buildings & falling parts thereof - Fissures may open unexpectedly in ground - <u>Gas, water, electricity & sewerage may rupture with explosion, fire & hygiene risks.</u>

● **ACTIONS (BEFORE):** Stockpile; food & water & ensure sufficient batteries, candles & alternative cooking facilities - Plan where all family members will go & what to do if quake occurs.

● **ACTIONS (IF CAUGHT):** The safest situation is lying down in an open space away from tall buildings/trees/cliffs - If inside, the safest places are lower floors, against walls, under strong furniture (e.g.: table) - Don't use elevators - Don't (unless obliged to) transit in/out of buildings during a quake as showers of masonry/glass are likely - But if there is a pause, do go out to an open space - TURN OFF ALL SERVICES UNTIL LEAKS HAVE BEEN CHECKED FOR.

HURRICANE

● **GENERAL:** Also known as cyclones/typhoons - Deep low-pressure systems developing over the ocean (rotate counterclockwise in N. Hemisphere & clockwise in S. Hemisphere) - Winds of 70-200 mph with a calm center, 5-30 miles diameter - Overall diameter 100-300 miles - **Move usually west then curve away from equator (0-30 mph) but can loop.**

● **DANGERS:** Very destructive winds, torrential rain, giant seas & on coasts RISING SEA LEVELS (0-20 FT).

● **ACTIONS** (land): Shutter windows - Stockpile supplies - Remove outside loose items - Retreat to lower/cellar rooms - Prepare for flooding, cut mains services & flying missiles - DON'T BE DECEIVED BY EYE OF STORM.

● **ACTIONS** (vessel at sea): **Get out of way** - If coming straight for you on a westerly track make all speed away diagonally toward the equator.

● **ACTIONS** (vessel in port): Depending on circumstances either; Put to sea (as above) or Seek a "Hurricane Hole" (land-locked harbor) & lay down all ground tackle. Run lines to shore with double chafe guards. Strip spars of sails & running rigging. Double lash all deck gear. Batten down hatches & GET A BIG POT OF HOT SPICY SOUP ON THE STOVE.

(BUILDING) FIRE (FOREST)

● **GENERAL:** Fires require heat, oxygen & fuel - TAKE AWAY ANY ONE & IT WILL GO OUT.

● **BUILDINGS:** First warning usually smoke - In smoke-filled room <u>cover nose with cloth & stay low</u> - TEST DOORS BY TOUCHING HANDLES - If hot, don't open - If forced into burning room, cover body with wet blanket - Tie sheets together with a reef knot - **If forced to jump, wrap head in towel**, aim for soil/grass & roll to side on landing.

● **FORESTS:** First warnings, smell, sound, wildlife, visual - <u>Think before acting, wind direction & strength critical</u> - Escape via roads, fire breaks, ravines, river banks - **Go down not up hills** - Travel diagonally away from not directly before advancing fires - **Seek sanctuary in rivers/lakes, open spaces & rocky outcrops** - In a thin fire line situation (grass fire) consider a dash thru to the burnt side (use protection).

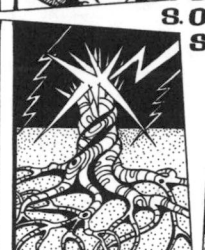

(WAVE/SURGE) FLOOD (OTHER)

● **LOW GROUND** flood from heavy rain &/or failed defenses should provide ample warning to remove furniture etc. from low rooms, sandbag doorways, block off vent bricks - **If ingress of dirty flood water is unavoidable then deliberately flood cellars etc. with tap/roof water to minimise damage** - Keep emergency supplies (dinghy, food, water, batteries etc.).

● **STORM SURGE** from combinations of wind (on shore & strong) & tide (high) &/or extreme low pressure (sucks sea/lake levels up) - <u>Sea levels can rise as much as 20 ft</u> causing massive destruction - BE PREPARED TO EVACUATE.

● **TIDAL WAVE (Tsunami)** Mainly, but not exclusively in Pacific (but possible as a result of any submarine earthquake anywhere in the world) - Wave height, shape & onshore penetration vary with seabed & coastal configuration - **But Doomsday heights of 100 ft are possible** - <u>If you live on the coast be ready to evacuate to high ground after any earthquake.</u>

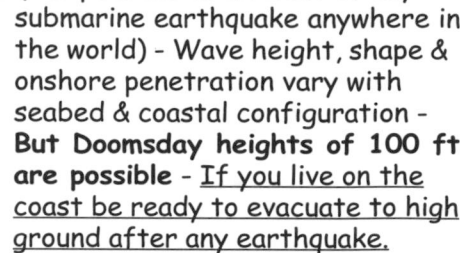

S.
S.O.S.
S.

LIGHTNING

● **GENERAL:** Accumulation of electrical energy at cloud level seeking to neutralise itself by the easiest (least resistance) & shortest route available to ground.

● **DANGERS: (In humans):** Burns, heart failure, asphyxiation, death. (In electrics), & particularly electronics: - Extensive burnout **even if switched off & located some distance from strike.** (Trees/buildings): fire & actual physical damage.

● **ACTIONS: (Humans indoors)** Stay dry, wear rubber-sole shoes, KEEP AWAY FROM WINDOWS & EXTERNALLY CONNECTED METAL (pipes, wires, railings etc.). Retreat to inner lower room if storm very bad. **(Humans Outside):** Stay away from all tall/high objects particularly metal ones. Leave high ground but avoid crossing open spaces. Seek low dry ground, if none squat & hug knees with head down - IN THE EVENT OF PRE-STRIKE SENSATIONS <u>(HAIR ON END)</u> - INSTANTLY DROP PRONE TOUCHING HANDS FIRST. (Electrical): Unplug appliances, phones, aerials etc.

VOLCANO

● **GENERAL:** Locations closely associated with earthquake acivity, in that crust faults in the earth permit magma (molten rock) under pressure to penetrate the surface.

● **DANGERS:** As lava flow rarely moves at more than 10 mph it is not as dangerous as - **Red hot gas/dust balls which can roll downhill at 100 mph** & engulf & kill in seconds before passing - <u>Mud slide walls (lahars) which can move at 50 mph down valleys</u> (caused by melting ice & snow) (can engulf whole towns) - Missiles of rock & lava exploding from the crater can impact miles away - Ash clouds of corrosive dust can fall in vast quantities, burying roads, collapsing roofs, cutting off light over large areas & MAY DRIFT AS A CLOUD THOUSANDS OF MILES.

● **ACTIONS:** Evacuate on signs of coming eruption (steam/gas & sulphur smell with rumbling). **IF TOO LATE, wear head protection & cloth over nose, avoid valley routes (lahars) & travel upwind if possible.**

Assembling Basic Equipment For Emergency Circumstances

Being prepared is the basis of life, as is staying alive,
(the definition of survival) - Don't be paranoid, but do be ready.

THE PLAN

● **USING THESE LISTS:** Select the category of terrain thru/over which you plan to travel & read off its code letter (if in doubt select "U") - Read down the "codes" column, listing those items with your code letter opposite to it.

A = Arctic (or cold).   **D** = Desert (or hot/dry).   **S** = Sea.

J = Jungle (tropical/forest).   **U** = Unknown.

● **IDEALLY** items should be sealed in small zip-type plastic bags (medicines in square, opaque, screw-top plastic bottles), which are all inside a small (say 6" x 4" x 1 1/2") stainless steel mess tin (with lid) which along with neatly folded bulkier items (such as plastic survival bags, mosquito/fish nets etc.) should all fit into a convenient pouch-style bag for belt or shoulder.

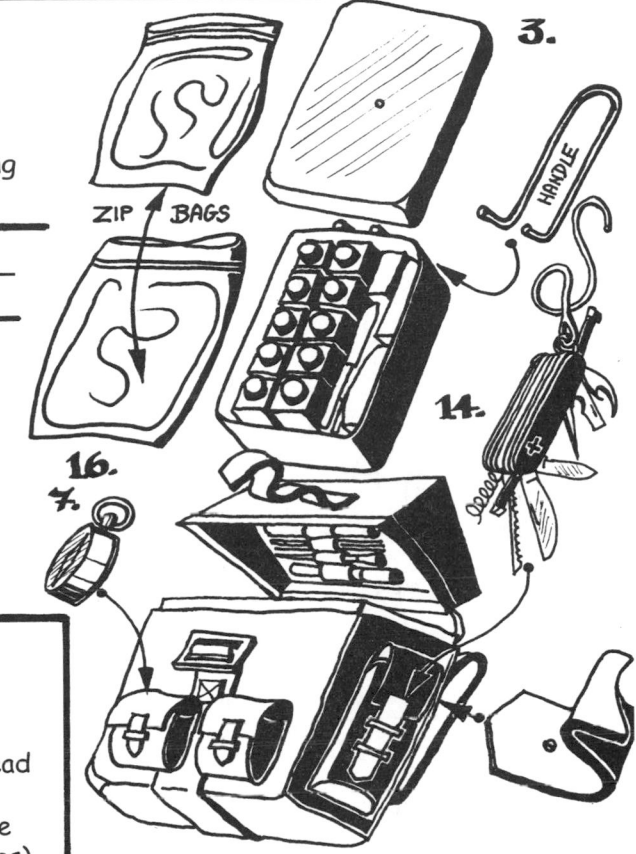

ZIP BAGS

CLOTHING....

....Although not detailed, remember these important items - **VERY COLD** climates: Complete head covering including ears & nose, sunglasses & goggles, also gloves & mittens (one to go inside other), socks (heavy outer & thinner inner ones), + one-piece plastic exposure suit. **VERY HOT** climates: Wide hat, long sleeve & long leg cotton apparel, changes of cotton socks & underwear. **VERY WET** climates: Because of versatility a "poncho" style cape & sou'wester hat with plastic trousers + changes of cotton socks. (One-piece exposure suit better for emergency use at sea.)

THE LIST

ITEM DESCRIPTION	CODES	VISUAL NOTES
● **CANDLES** (the small type in metal dish, lasts longer & can be refilled with oil).	ALL 1	
● **SNARE WIRE:** Stainless steel multistrand with copper swages to suit wire (about 1/16" diameter).	ALL 2	
● **HELIOGRAPH:** Buy a stainless mess tin with flat lid (drill a 1/8-inch hole in the middle & mirror polish it).	ALL 3	
● **MAGNIFYING GLASS** (powerful, compact [about 1 1/2 inches dia.] with cloth cover to protect).	J-D-U 4	
● **WATERPROOF MATCHES** (cut in half to save space & stored in square plastic sealing bottle).	ALL 5	
● **MINI FISH NET** with wire rim to fit exactly in mess tin bottom (used to catch tiddlers under dinghy).	S 6	

Assembling Basic Equipment's For Emergency Circumstances

ITEM DESCRIPTION	CODE	VISUAL NOTES
● COMPASS (Liquid filled, about 1 1/2 in dia. with folding prism & luminous card).	ALL 7	
● MAPS/CHARTS (Xerox copy those applicable on light weight paper, spray them with a moisture protector, fold & fit in plastic zip bag).	ALL 8	
● PLASTIC BODY BAG (Use for survival, rain collection, protection & distillation etc).	ALL 9	
● CONDOMS (Use as emergency water containers [about 1 liter] & hot water bottles in Arctic).	ALL 10	
● FISHING KIT (Nylon line, trace wire, hooks, lures - [more for sea]).	S. A. J. U. 11	
● DRUG KIT (To contain: Analgesic [pain relief], broad spectrum antibiotic [bacterial infections], antihistamine [stings & allergies],intestinal sedative [diarrhea etc.], water sterilization tablets).	ALL 12	
● FIRST AID KIT (Band-aids [inc. butterfly] scalpel blade, curved surgical needle & thread, high-factor sun block, antiseptic cream).	ALL 13	
● MULTIBLADE KNIFE (Such as Swiss Army type with wood saw, tweezers, pliers etc).	ALL 14	
● NEEDLES & THREAD (Sailmakers best with Dacron thread wrapped around needles).	ALL 15	
● MARKER DYE (Distress situations).	S. A.	
● MOSQUITO NET (Just enough to cover exposed body parts) & small tube insect repellent.	J 16	
● MINI SOLID FUEL STOVE & tablets.	ALL 17	
● BREW UP KIT (Tea, Sugar, Milk in sachets in plastic zip bags).	ALL 18	
● FLINT & STRIKER STEEL.	A.J.U. 19	
● FLEXIBLE SAW (Coils like string).	J 20	
● PENLIGHT torch (Waterproof).	ALL	
● SHARPENING STONE (Pencil size)	ALL 21	

	ITEM DESCRIPTION	CODE	
LUXURY BULKY ITEMS	● MACHETE (Blade only)	J 22	
	● SNOW SAW ([Blade only] used for building snow shelters).	A 23	
	● TRANSISTOR A.M. RADIO (Use for morale, weather & direction finding etc).	ALL	
	● SOLAR SURVIVAL STILL ([Book size] fresh from salt).	S	
	● MINI PYROTECHNIC KIT ([Spectacle case size] but airlines will refuse to carry).	ALL 24	

REMEMBER, KEEP IT SIMPLE, KEEP IT SMALL & KEEP IT WITH YOU.

Obtaining The Basic Essentials Of Life From Nature

If absolutely necessary most of us can live for (literally) months without food but only a few days without water.

HOW MUCH TO LIVE?

....From as much as 1+ gallons per day, on the move in the desert to as little as a few ozs per day in a temperate marine environment (supplemented by soaking body in sea water) - **A normal subsistence amount is about 1 pint per day.**

● **DESERT TRAVEL:** By resting in a cool place during the day (wearing loose clothes conserves water usage) & walking at night, **about 20 miles can be covered consuming 1 gallon of water** (daytime walking would require 2+ gallons to cover the same distance).

NATURAL DISTILLATION

....Using solar energy (particularly effective in climates with big day/night temperature changes [i.e.: Desert]).
1) Dig a round hole 3 - 4 ft across & 2 ft deep & put a container in the bottom of it.
2) Cover with a clear plastic sheet - put stones on corners to hold, & 1 in the middle to make an inverted cone about 18 inches deep.
3) Build soil/sand ridge round edge to seal rim.

● **WHY DO ARABS** dress like this when they live in a very hot country?

NOTES: a) Put tube in container to suck water out, b) Roughen underside of cone to hasten dribbles of condensing water, c) **Put some cut vegetation in hole to add extra moisture.**
CAN COLLECT 1 - 4 PINTS IN 24 HOURS.

ARTIFICIAL DISTILLATION

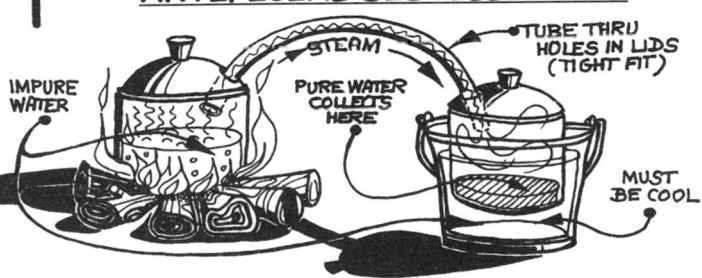

IMPURE WATER

STEAM

PURE WATER COLLECTS HERE

TUBE THRU HOLES IN LIDS (TIGHT FIT)

MUST BE COOL

● **THIS SYSTEM** can be used to obtain drinking water from polluted or suspect sources such as ponds - even urine or sea water etc.

● **DANGER,** pools with animal bones around &/or without vegetation of some kind may be dangerously polluted (in any case it is best to distill all such standing pool waters).

● **BACTERIOLOGICAL PURIFICATION**
- Boil for 4 minutes & let settle.
- Add 9 drops iodine/quart.
- Add chlorine tablets (such as halazone) until faint smell of chlorine comes from water.

ICE AT SEA

● **ICEBERGS** can provide fresh water, but capsize risk is directly proportional to distance from the poles they have drifted from, as erosion occurs faster underwater.

● **NEW SEA ICE** has a rough shape & is milky gray in color - It is salty & **not suitable for consumption.**

● **OLD SEA ICE** is smoother & bluish in colour - After about a year it looses most of its salt content & **is almost fresh if melted.**

WATER FROM SNOW/ICE

....Melting snow uses about twice as much heat as melting ice - Chip off a small piece, melt it in the pot & slowly add more. **Don't melt either in the mouth,** as this lowers the body temperature & discourages blood circulation.

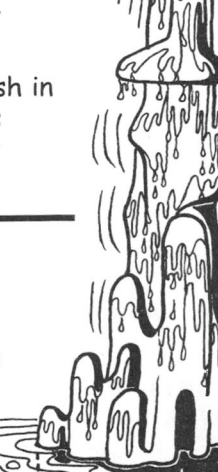

WARMER SEA

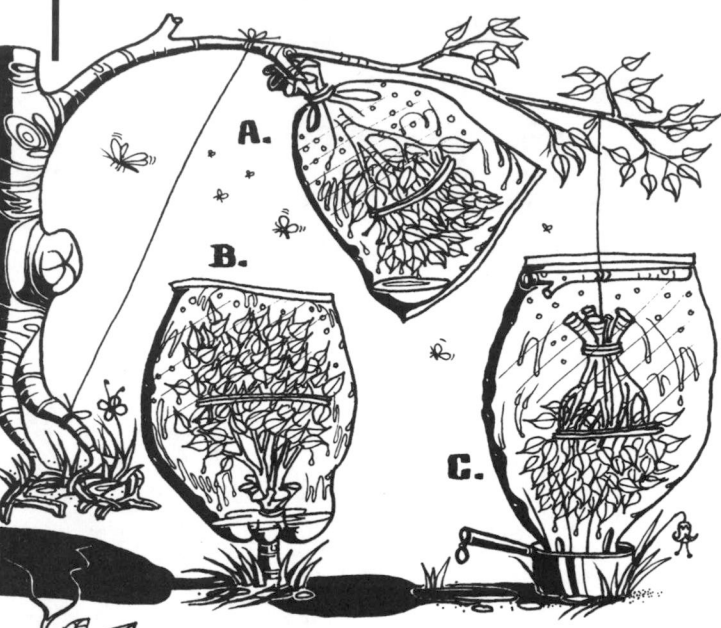

CONDENSATION TECHNIQUES

....In **A, B & C** examples, enclose nontoxic, green healthy foliage, in a clear plastic bag tied at the neck. Lightly bind the leaves to try & keep them off the sides.
- In "**A**" keep one corner down.
- In "**B**" invert the neck of bag.
- In "**C**" the foliage is already cut.
- **Big day/night temperature changes produce the best results.**

SIGNS OF WATER

- **ANIMALS** which graze (on grass & foliage) require water dawn & dusk - <u>Follow their tracks (usually downhill)</u>.
- **BIRDS** which eat grains require water dawn & dusk **(they usually fly low & straight [no rests] to the water)** - Then indirectly (stops to rest & search for food) after drinking.
- **INSECTS** require water & <u>many do not travel far from it</u> (e.g.: follow a column of ants from the nest [even up trees]).

WATER FROM PLANTS

....can often be collected from suitably shaped foliage & branches as provided by nature.

- **INSIDE** various plants are drinkable juices or water **but some are poisonous** - Use distillation if in doubt.
- **VINES** (not those with milky saps) can provide water - Pick a large stem & cut a notch (air vent) high up then progressively cut off the same stem from ground level up, & drain each time.
- **BAMBOO** (older better) can hold drinkable water **(shake the stems & listen for sloshing).**

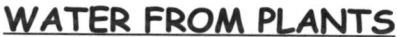

FIELD TEST FOR PLANT TOXICITY

- **ONE PERSON ONLY TEST** - <u>No to milky or bitter fluids</u> - Apply to inner forearm & wait - Apply to lip & wait - Apply to tongue tip & wait - Taste in mouth & wait - Swallow small amount & **WAIT FOR 4 HOURS.**
  - If at any stage adverse reactions (stinging, burning, gastric upset) occur then stop immediately.
  - If necessary induce vomiting by putting finger down throat.
- **EXTREME** thirst followed by rapid drinking causes vomiting.

YOU & WATER

- **BODY TEMPERATURE** should be 98.6 degrees Fahrenheit - to maintain this in a hot climate you sweat, **so stay cool & save water.**
- **DEHYDRATION:** <u>If you sweat & don't replace the water you dehydrate & eventually die.</u> Progressive **SYMPTOMS** are: Thirst - Flushed - Sleepy - Fast Pulse - Nausea - Headache - Dizzy - Slurred Speech - Numb & Shrivelled Skin - Swollen Tongue - Sight & Hearing Fade.

CONSERVING BODY WATER

- **DON'T EAT** (<u>particularly fats & protein</u>) unless water is also available - Wear some clothes (even in a hot climate) - Stay cool (i.e. don't lie on hot ground) - Don't smoke - Don't talk - Don't Drink Alcohol - Don't Exercise & BREATHE THRU NOSE.
- **DIGGING** behind beaches usually reaches a layer of fresh water first.
- **DON'T** drink alcohol, urine or add sea to fresh water.
- **OXYGENATE** boiled water by shaking it after.

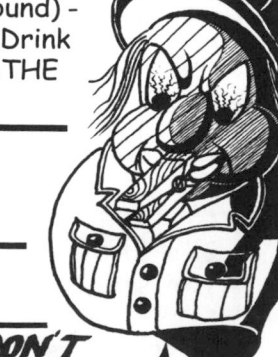
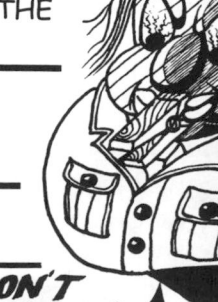
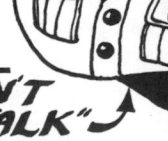

"DON'T TALK"

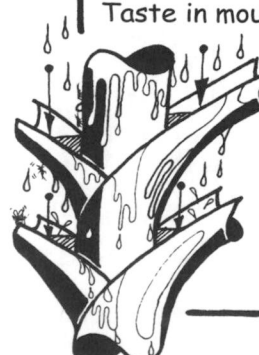

Obtaining The Basic Essentials Of Life From Nature

You may survive without it, but shelter (however modest) will help body & soul stay together in difficult times.

BEFORE STARTING

(<u>Location is very important,</u> before choosing consider)

● SECURITY (are you near or exposed to danger from wild animals, insects, flooding, high winds etc.).

● WATER (proximity to a source is critical to the success of a base.).

● NATURAL PROTECTION from prevailing winds, sun, cold etc-as formed by cliffs, trees, hollows etc.

● FUEL (wood for fire to cook, keep warm, scare off wildlife etc.)

● FOOD (proximity to game, fishing, edible vegetation).

● RESCUE (try & stay close to prominent features e.g.: crashed plane, beached vessel, unusual geography).

● TIME (how long do you intend (or have to) stay there)

VERY COLD CLIMATES

● AIRHOLES (2 or more) are essential in igloos & snow caves to prevent asphyxiation (see L,N,O,Q,R,)

● SMALL shelters are easier to keep warm.

● SPADE or improvised tool must be kept IN snow shelters in case of burial.

● WIND (prevailing) build shelter facing away from.

● <u>ENTRANCES</u> of snow shelters to be marked with flag or stick as <u>VERY EASY TO LOSE.</u>

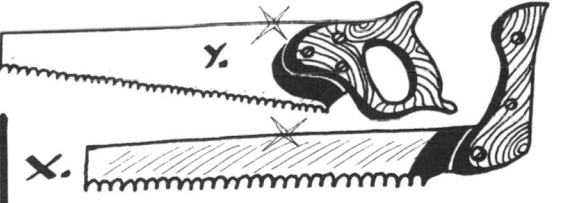

● ROOF thickness of snow shelters to be 6-36 inches thick (depends on snow density.)

● SNOW SAW (X) or wood saw (Y) is needed to cut igloo blocks (about 18 x 18 x 6 inches) from compact snow (in emergency use knife or notched hardwood)

● ROOF (build it with a slope/curve to direct drips down walls.

IGLOO SIZE

INSIDE DIA. IN FEET.	NUMBER OF PERSONS.
7	1
9	2
11	3
12	4
13	5
14	6
15	7

THE ULTIMATE SURVIVAL TOOL....

<u>Is probably a polythene sheet</u> - use it to - catch rain - shelter from elements - wrap up in & keep warm - make solar still (ground or foliage) - use as a sail in dinghy - protect maps, food & electronics - catch small fish from dinghy.

● ONE CANDLE will raise the temperature of a small snow house by about 6 degrees fahrenheit (Eskimos use a wick in a bowl of fat or oil)

FIRE HINTS

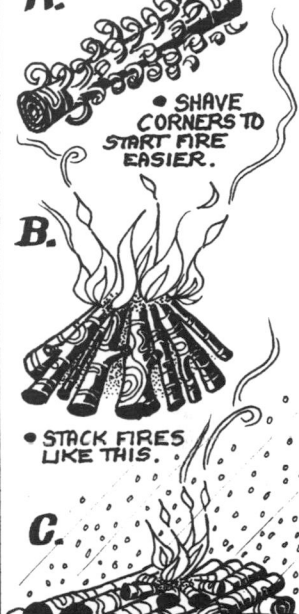

A. ● SHAVE CORNERS TO START FIRE EASIER.

B. ● STACK FIRES LIKE THIS.

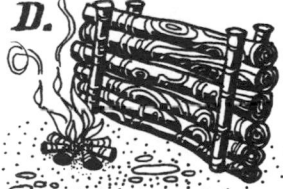

C. ● ON SNOW PUT GREEN LOGS UNDER.

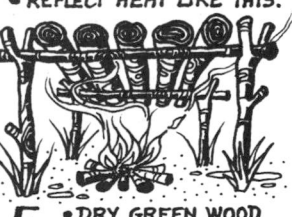

D. ● REFLECT HEAT LIKE THIS.

E. ● DRY GREEN WOOD LIKE THIS.

WARM CLIMATE ROOF & WALLS FROM LEAVES

NOTE with all types put top of leaf facing UP.

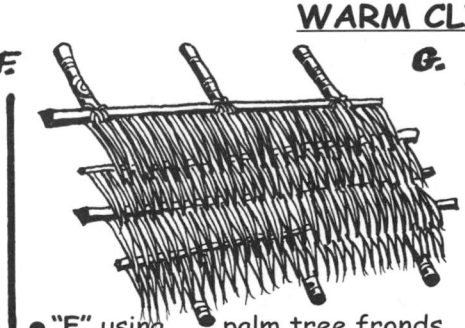

● "F" using palm tree fronds split down center & start from bottom alternating direction.

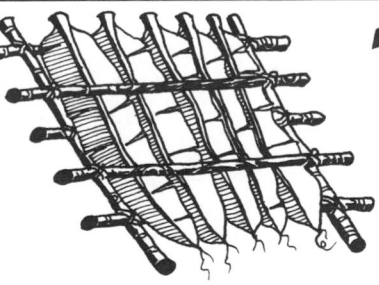

● "G" (flexible leaf) overlapped sideways & interwoven.

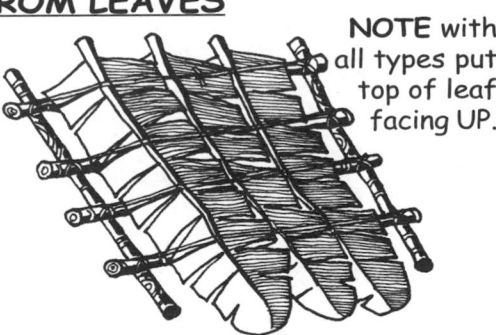

● "H" banana type leaf overlapped.

HOW TO MAKE SHELTERS IN SURVIVAL SITUATIONS
Obtaining The Basic Essentials Of Life From Nature

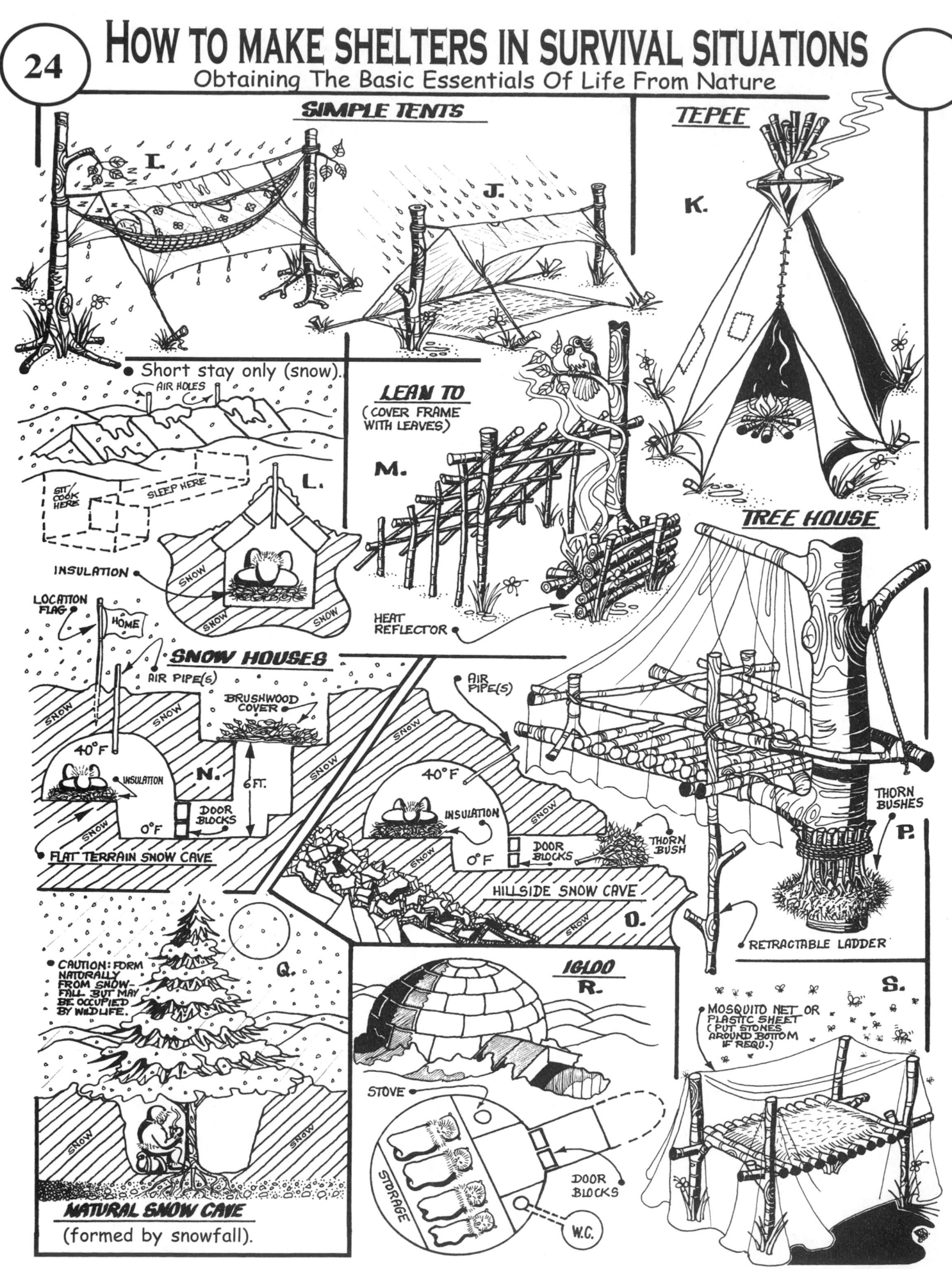

SIMPLE TENTS

I.

J.

TEPEE

K.

• Short stay only (snow).

AIR HOLES

SIT COOK HERE

SLEEP HERE

INSULATION

SNOW SNOW SNOW

L.

LEAN TO
(COVER FRAME WITH LEAVES)

M.

HEAT REFLECTOR

TREE HOUSE

LOCATION FLAG

HOME

SNOW HOUSES

AIR PIPE(S)

BRUSHWOOD COVER

SNOW SNOW

40°F

INSULATION

N.

6 FT.

DOOR BLOCKS

0°F

SNOW

• FLAT TERRAIN SNOW CAVE

AIR PIPE(S)

SNOW

40°F

INSULATION

SNOW

0°F

DOOR BLOCKS

THORN BUSH

HILLSIDE SNOW CAVE

O.

THORN BUSHES

P.

RETRACTABLE LADDER

• CAUTION: FORM NATURALLY FROM SNOW-FALL BUT MAY BE OCCUPIED BY WILDLIFE.

Q.

IGLOO

R.

STOVE

STORAGE

DOOR BLOCKS

W.C.

S.

MOSQUITO NET OR PLASTIC SHEET (PUT STONES AROUND BOTTOM IF REQU.)

SNOW SNOW

NATURAL SNOW CAVE
(formed by snowfall).

Obtaining The Basic Essentials Of Life From Nature

Nowhere is knowledge more important than when survival is in question - These few words could save a life for another day.

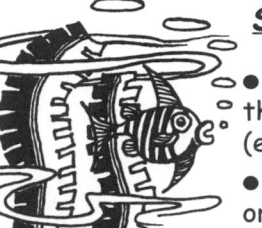
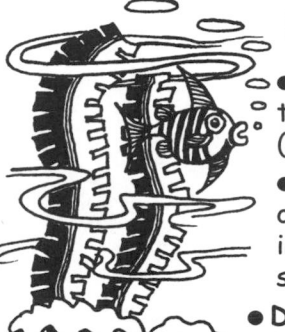

SEA LIFE

SEAWEED

- **WHERE?** More plentiful inshore than off - **Most types are edible** (either cooked or raw).
- **DON'T EAT (TYPES):** Thread or branch types, which if crushed in air will **smell within 10 minutes** strongly.
- **DON'T EAT (CONDITION):** any which are **slimy, stale, smelly** or have broken surfaces.
- **CLEAN** any intended seaweed meal carefully **of any resident bugs**/crabs etc. before dining.

FRESH WATER FISH

....Caught in non-polluted situations should all be edible (unlike many sea water species) but <u>must be cooked as many have parasites.</u>

PLANKTON

....**Has a number of toxic varieties** which result in symptoms from gastric upsets to paralysis & death, so unless you know the differences....!

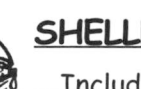

SHELLFISH

....Including clams, crabs, mussels, limpets etc, providing they are alive & in an unpolluted environment are **all believed edible** (this includes starfish & sea cucumbers) but <u>all fresh water or land species must be cooked because of parasites.</u>

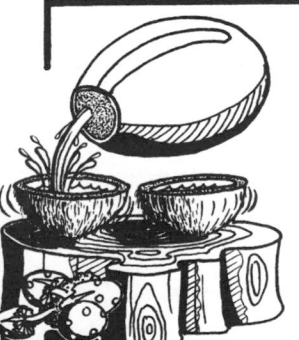

- **WATER** (liquid) is essential for digestion, <u>so don't eat unless you have sufficient to drink.</u>
- **PROTEINS & FATS** (e.g.: fish, birds [also seaweeds]) **require about 2 - 1 (water to food) or 30 oz/day.**
- **CARBOHYDRATES** (sugar & starches) such as fruits require least.

FISH

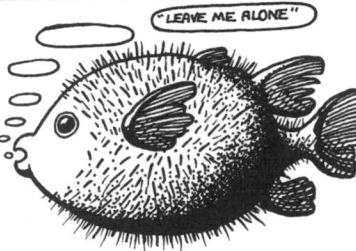

"LEAVE ME ALONE"

PUFFER FISH

- **WHERE?** Most fish caught offshore (out of sight of land) can be eaten, but other locations in order of suspicion are: Ponds/lagoons, harbors, rivers, reefs & coastal - **Eat only with caution.**
- **DON'T EAT (TYPES)** <u>or handle</u> fish with no scales, or none/small belly fin, or bony boxlike body, or spines over body, or small parrot mouth, or small gills.
- **DON'T EAT (CONDITION)** fish with sunken/dull eyes, or slimy gills, or flabby flesh (press thumb in - **If depression stays then throw fish away).**

SYMPTOMS OF FISH POISONING

....**Typical example** (Puffer Fish): Numb tongue, lips, fingers, toes - Erratic body temperatures & severe itching - dizzy - vomiting - not able to speak - **creeping body paralysis.**

- <u>COOKING</u> does not decrease ingested fish toxicity.

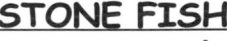

STONE FISH

CLIMBING PALM TREES

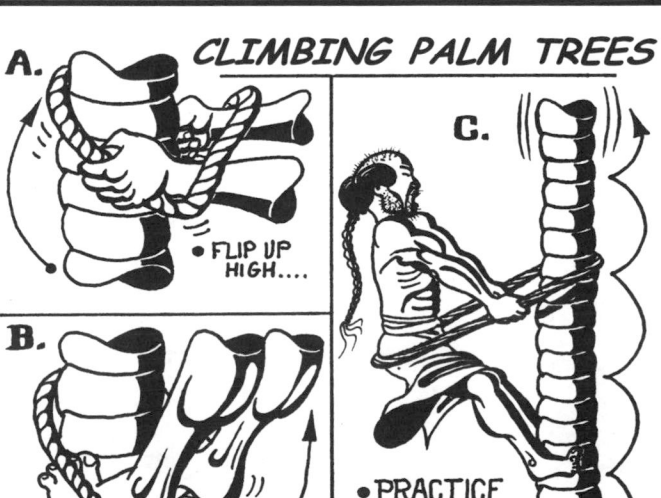

A. • FLIP UP HIGH....

B. ....THEN LIFT FEET.

C. • PRACTICE LOW ONES FIRST!!!!

- **POISONOUS** (to eat) reef fish are common in the tropics (Pacific bad).

- **SEA BIRDS:** Catch with floating, trailing, baited hook or gorger.

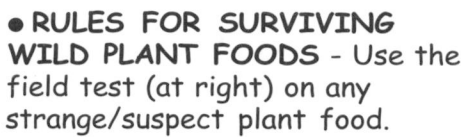

LAND LIFE

- **RULES FOR SURVIVING WILD PLANT FOODS** - Use the field test (at right) on any strange/suspect plant food.

- **DON'T EAT (TASTE)** any plant with a bitter or burning/stinging taste/smell/feel.

- **DON'T EAT (CONDITION)** any plant with wilted/old leaves or mutated grains/fruit <u>even if the plant is known.</u>

- **DON'T EAT (TYPE)** any plant with a milky sap, tiny hook hairs on, with 5 section fruits on or with red colors on foliage etc.

FIELD TEST

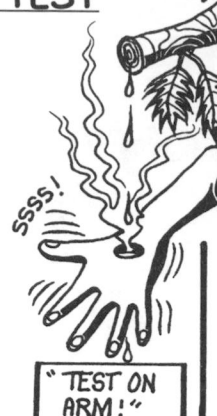

- **FOR PLANT TOXICITY** - <u>One person only test</u> - No milky sap or bitter plants - Apply to inner forearm & wait - Apply to lip & wait - Apply to tongue tip & wait - Taste in mouth & wait - Swallow a bit & wait 8 hours. If at any time adverse reactions (e.g.: burning, gastric upset, pain) occurs - **STOP**, drink plenty of hot water & <u>IF NECESSARY</u> <u>**INDUCE VOMITING** by putting finger down throat.</u>

SSSS!

" TEST ON ARM!"

PLANTS

- **BARK** (inside white layer) of many ever-green trees in temperate climates (e.g. pine) is edible raw or roasted, it is best when new (in spring).

- **CACTUS** leaves (the flat types) & ripe fruits (edible stems also) have water **(avoid any with milky sap).**

- **PALMS** offer a variety of edible parts (apart from the nuts). There are the flowers, stems & the inside of young branches.

- **COCONUTS** (apart from the food) boil or dry heat out the oil & **use it to repel insects & as a skin oil.**

- **FERNS**, most are edible but choose the very young (still opening) leaves & shoots & <u>avoid bitter types</u> - Clean by rubbing together in water then cook by boiling.

PRICKLY PEAR

- **GRASS** (grains) **all known edible** (if healthy) but disgard any attacked by insects &/or fungus, or with a bitter taste, <u>or mutated</u> - Gather ripe grains & beat over a cloth, then rub together to remove husks. Boil or dry heat.

- **WATER LILIES:** All species & parts believed edible, **but boil first and test a sample.**

- **PIPS & STONES** in fruits should not be eaten even if fruit is edible as pips may contain toxins.

FERN

WILDLIFE
SIGNS OF MAMMALS

- **DROPPINGS:** Big droppings = Big animals - Soft/smelly droppings = Recent - (examine contents for species clues).

- **FEEDING:** Look for stripped bark - Damaged foliage & fruit - Look for carcasses, bones & other remnants.

- **TRACKS:** Big imprint = Big animal - Clear imprint = Recent - Heavy traffic = Water.

BIRDS

....**All believed edible.** Set passive and/or spring snares, deadfalls or cage traps & bait with meat, fruit, water, berries, grain or nuts.

BE HUMANE

REPTILES

....**All believed edible** (<u>but some with poison-ous bites</u>) - Pick on small ones. Pin with a forked stick & kill before touching at all (snake meat like chicken).

INSECTS

....**Many edible species** including ants, termites, grasshoppers, caterpillars, **BUT don't eat/touch** a) those feeding on droppings or carrion or garbage, b) those brightly colored or slimy or on underside of leaves. **TO COOK:** Remove wings, stings & legs & boil or roast (5 minutes).

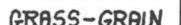

GRASS-GRAIN

Special Survival Fishing Techniques For Desperate Times

Even when hungry, tired, perhaps frightened - Try to avoid unnecessary suffering and pointless killing of other living creatures.

AVOIDING INJURY	AVOIDING DETECTION

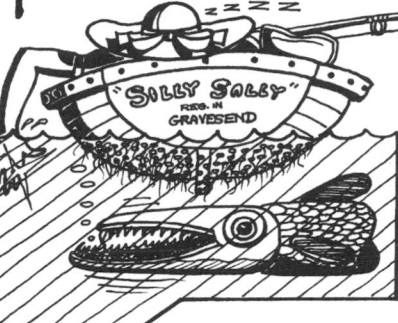

DON'T....

- **Dangle fingers** over the side of dinghies.
- **Clean fish** in the water by hand.
- **Continue to fish** from small boats if sharks are around.

- **FRESH WATER FISH** all believed edible - But may contain parasites so <u>cook before eating.</u>

- **SALTWATER FISH** have various poisonous species particularly in tropical reefs - Avoid all saltwater fish with a) <u>No scales</u> b) <u>Small parrot-like mouths</u> c) <u>small or no belly fin</u> d) <u>Bony box-like bodies.</u>

TIME & PLACE

- **WHERE?** - **In hot climates** fish in cool places (under boats, rocks, deep holes, in the shade etc.). **In cold climates** fish in warm places (in the sun &/or the shallows). **In fast flowing rivers** fish in tributaries, on the outside of bends or in sheltered corners. - Wherever you see shoals of small fish, lots of insects/birds.

- **WHEN?** - Usually not in the middle of the day - **Try dusk, dawn &/or nighttime.**

EEL BAGS

- Loosely fill a cloth bag or burlap sack (best) with straw (or similar) & put bait (entrails are good) in the middle. Tie off neck & leave overnight on bottom near rocks or weed - **Eels bite their way in & can't get out quick enough** when you pull it up in the morning.

- **BAIT** - For best results take yours from the immediate area (e.g. insects, sprats, berries etc.)

- **GROUND BAIT** your fishing patch preferably with the same bait used on your hook.

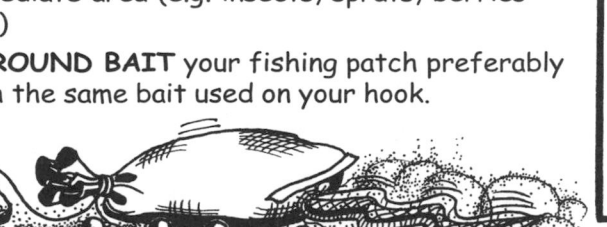

DON'T....

- **Cast your shadow** on water you are fishing in.
- **Stand** (as opposed to sit) close to the edge of river/lake banks when fishing.
- **Make noise** while fishing.

NO HOOK?
DON'T PANIC!

- An elongated diamond shaped piece of metal, bone, wood, plastic sharpened at both ends & tied in the middle, then hidden in a bait lengthwise will jam crossways in the gullet when swallowed (can also be used on sea birds).

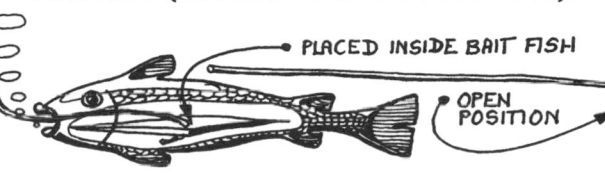

PLACED INSIDE BAIT FISH

OPEN POSITION

- **NO HOOK AGAIN!** - Certain crustaceans, eels, catfish etc. will either swallow a bait whole or **hold on to it so tightly** that in either case they can quickly be pulled in and landed without the use of any hooks).

- **NO BAIT? DON'T PANIC!**

- **JIGGING:** - To hook fish in the body anywhere Dangle multi hook line (with something shiny above) amongst fish (curious). **Then jerk hooks up.**

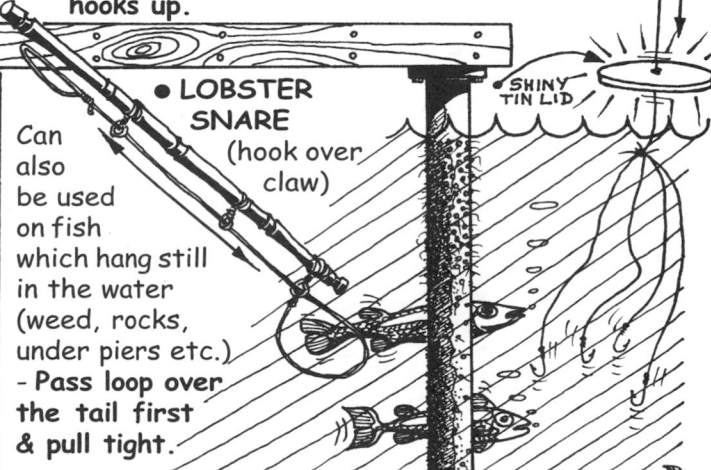

- **LOBSTER SNARE** (hook over claw)

Can also be used on fish which hang still in the water (weed, rocks, under piers etc.) - Pass loop over **the tail first & pull tight.**

SHINY TIN LID

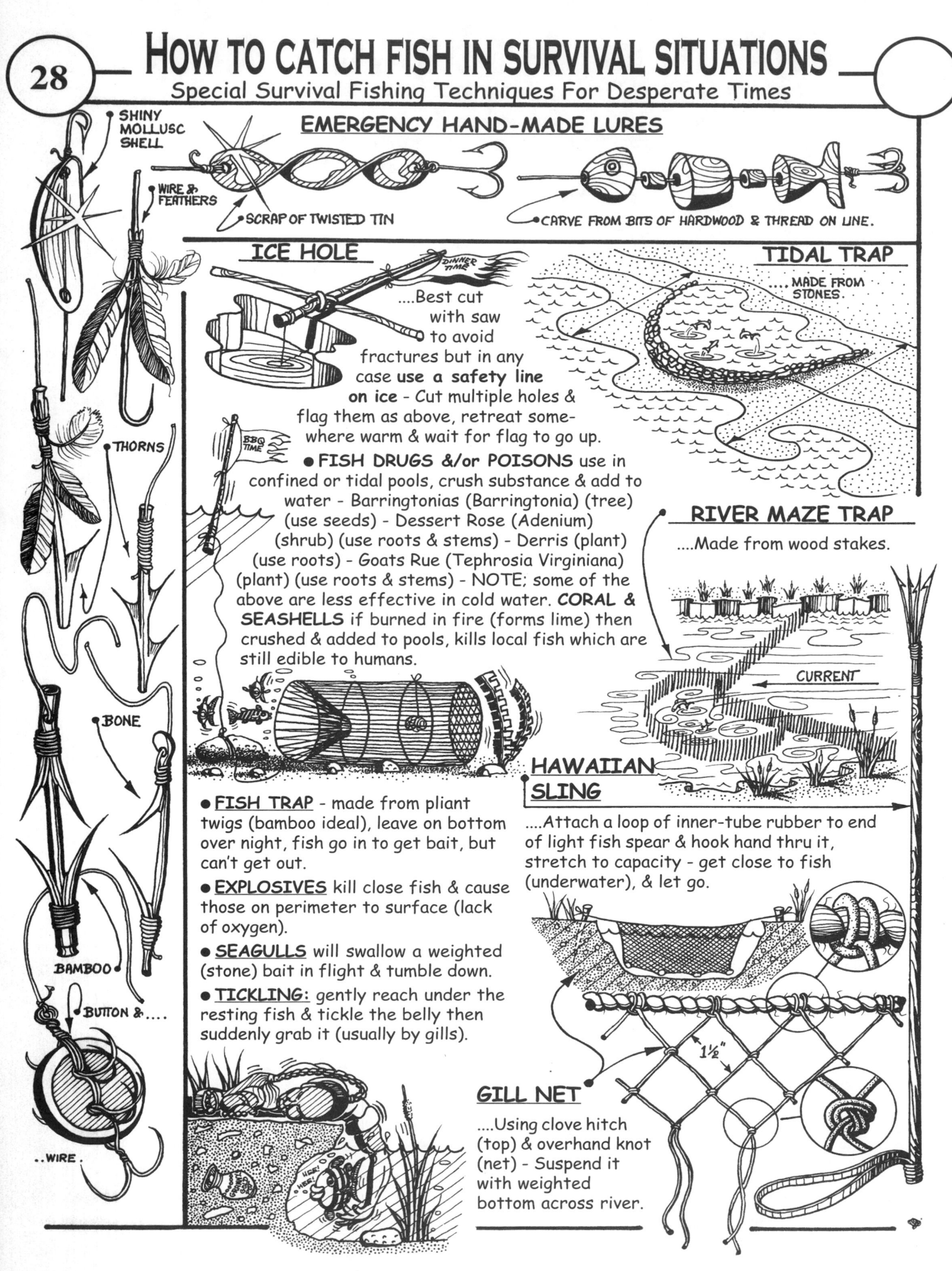

SHINY MOLLUSC SHELL

WIRE & FEATHERS

THORNS

BONE

BAMBOO

BUTTON &....

..WIRE.

EMERGENCY HAND-MADE LURES

• SCRAP OF TWISTED TIN

• CARVE FROM BITS OF HARDWOOD & THREAD ON LINE.

ICE HOLE

DINNER TIME

....Best cut with saw to avoid fractures but in any case **use a safety line on ice** - Cut multiple holes & flag them as above, retreat somewhere warm & wait for flag to go up.

BBQ TIME

• **FISH DRUGS &/or POISONS** use in confined or tidal pools, crush substance & add to water - Barringtonias (Barringtonia) (tree) (use seeds) - Dessert Rose (Adenium) (shrub) (use roots & stems) - Derris (plant) (use roots) - Goats Rue (Tephrosia Virginiana) (plant) (use roots & stems) - NOTE; some of the above are less effective in cold water. **CORAL & SEASHELLS** if burned in fire (forms lime) then crushed & added to pools, kills local fish which are still edible to humans.

• **FISH TRAP** - made from pliant twigs (bamboo ideal), leave on bottom over night, fish go in to get bait, but can't get out.

• **EXPLOSIVES** kill close fish & cause those on perimeter to surface (lack of oxygen).

• **SEAGULLS** will swallow a weighted (stone) bait in flight & tumble down.

• **TICKLING:** gently reach under the resting fish & tickle the belly then suddenly grab it (usually by gills).

HER! HER!

TIDAL TRAP

... MADE FROM STONES.

RIVER MAZE TRAP

....Made from wood stakes.

CURRENT

HAWAIIAN SLING

....Attach a loop of inner-tube rubber to end of light fish spear & hook hand thru it, stretch to capacity - get close to fish (underwater), & let go.

1½"

GILL NET

....Using clove hitch (top) & overhand knot (net) - Suspend it with weighted bottom across river.

To live we must eat, to eat we must get food, to get food in some cases, you must first catch it. Here's how:

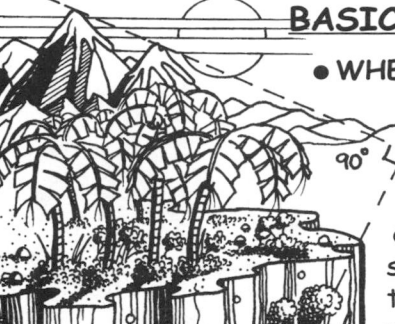

BASIC HUNTING RULES

- **WHERE?** - Orientate yourself with a prominent landmark & **know its position in relation to your base camp.**

- **SET TRAPS** if you are staying in one place, as they work day & night whilst you do other things.

- **MOVE QUIETLY** - Don't crack twigs, kick stones, cough etc. - **Stop frequently, listen & look hard.**

- **STUDY SIGNS** - droppings & tracks (size, age & direction), birds, broken foliage, carcasses etc.

- <u>BE PREPARED for the unexpected</u>. - Carry weapons, avoid skylines, stay downwind of game & keep the sun behind you.

MAKING WEAPONS

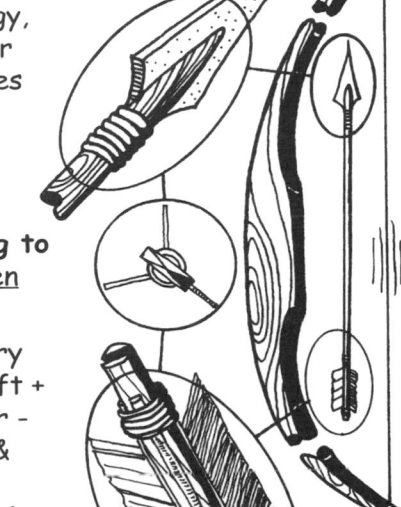

- **BOW** - Select a springy, hardwood branch & taper both ends on back & sides only (as shown) - Part season the wood over a fire then rub with oil or fat. - **Only string the bow when you are going to use it**, & <u>unstring it when finished.</u>

- **ARROWS** - Select very straight wood shoots 2 ft + long & 3/8 inch diameter - Part harden above fire & attach 3 x 1/2 feather flights. Split & whip end to take tip of metal, flint, bone.

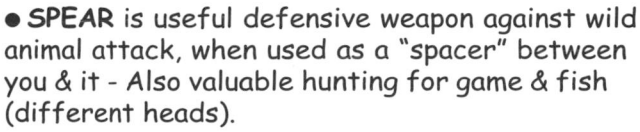

DANGEROUS ANIMALS

Bears, big cats, crocodiles, buffalo etc. - What to do if you meet one unarmed.

- **FREEZE!** Look it in the eyes & back slowly off, **don't run, <u>yet</u>.**

- **IF IT CHARGES** (particularly on a track) - get out of the way, to the side **(don't run ahead of it).**

- **AGILE** lighter animals if they corner you are best kept at bay with <u>one long & one short spear.</u>

- **CLUMSY** heavier animals <u>usually charge in a straight line</u> - so zigzag off to the side thru trees (if any).

- **CORNERING wild animals is asking for trouble.** - <u>Leave an escape route open in any confrontation.</u>

- **LOUD NOISES** (e.g. shouting) may, **(or may not)** frighten animals. As may gesticulating &/or illusions of height by you.

- **SPEAR** is useful defensive weapon against wild animal attack, when used as a "spacer" between you & it - Also valuable hunting for game & fish (different heads).

- **THROWER** is made less than half length of spear, & is used **(with practice)** to propel spear from end at increased velocity.

- **SLING** - a length of leather (or cord) with a pouch & a marble sized stone. Swing it fast & let go one end **(practice)** - (Good in flocks of birds).

SIMPLE DEADFALL TRAP

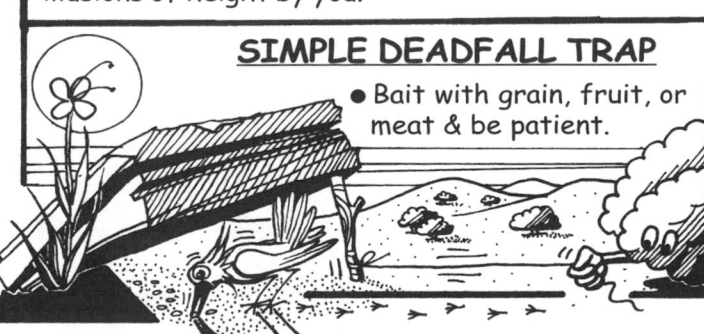

- Bait with grain, fruit, or meat & be patient.

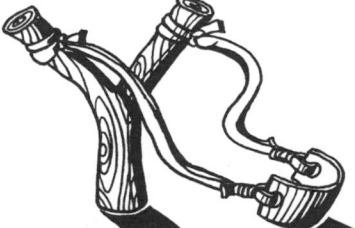

- **CATAPULT** - A length of inner-tube rubber & leather pouch attached to a forked stick.

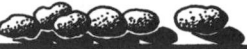

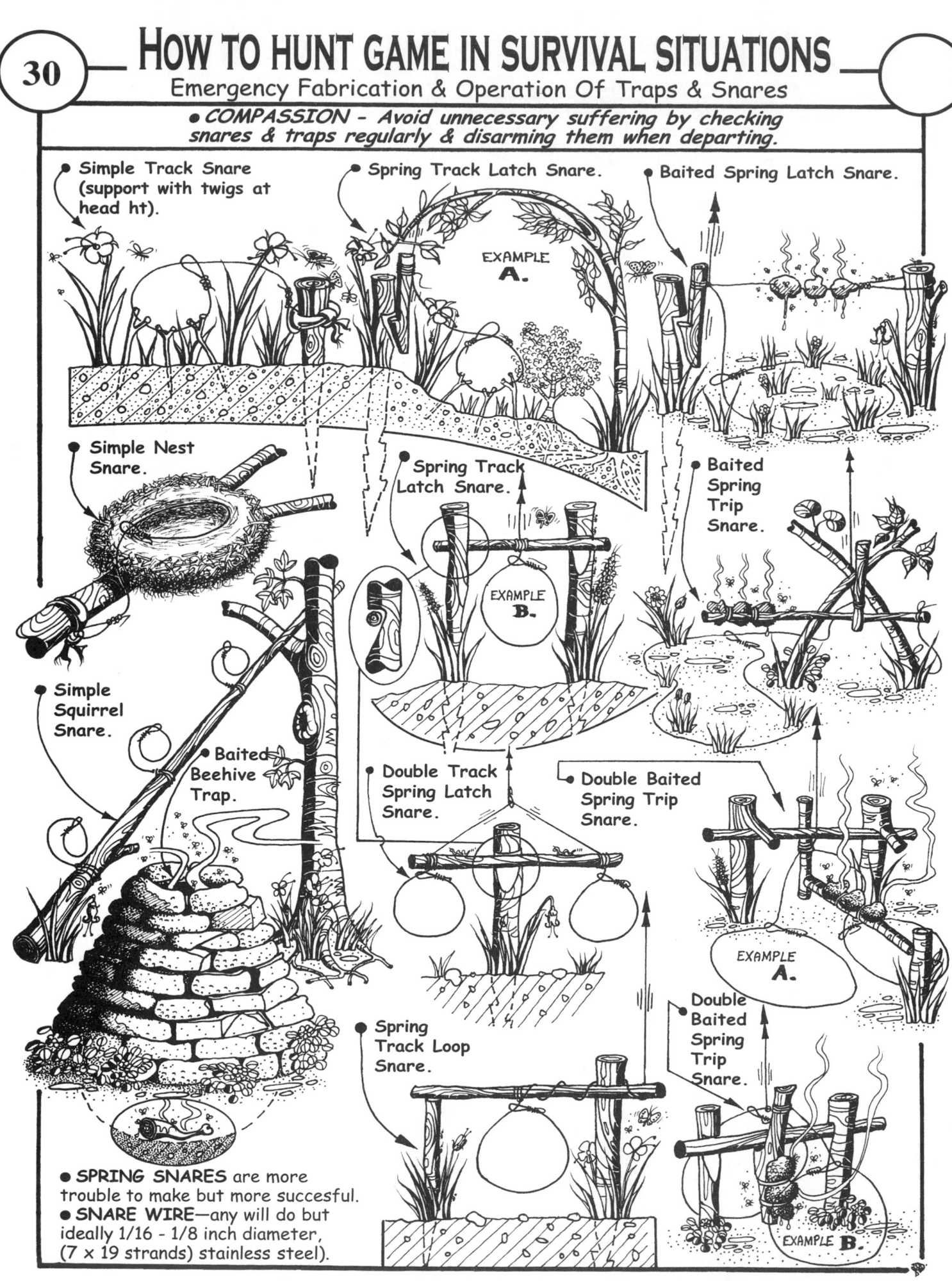

● COMPASSION - Avoid unnecessary suffering by checking snares & traps regularly & disarming them when departing.

● Simple Track Snare (support with twigs at head ht).

● Spring Track Latch Snare.

● Baited Spring Latch Snare.

EXAMPLE A.

● Simple Nest Snare.

● Spring Track Latch Snare.

EXAMPLE B.

● Baited Spring Trip Snare.

● Simple Squirrel Snare.

● Baited Beehive Trap.

● Double Track Spring Latch Snare.

● Double Baited Spring Trip Snare.

EXAMPLE A.

● Spring Track Loop Snare.

● Double Baited Spring Trip Snare.

EXAMPLE B

● **SPRING SNARES** are more trouble to make but more succesful.
● **SNARE WIRE**—any will do but ideally 1/16 - 1/8 inch diameter, (7 x 19 strands) stainless steel).

Preparing Food With Limited Resources In Emergencies

WARNING: Some stones if used around or in the fire may explode (particularly if they have been in the water) - Bang together hard to test.

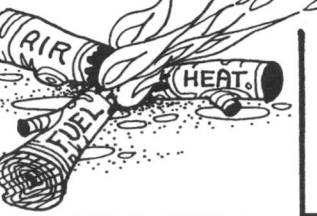

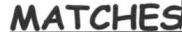

FIRST FIRE.... without it long-term survival (& cooking) **will be very difficult** - Use it for: - Cooking otherwise indigestible foods - Providing warmth - Frightening off wild animals - Discouraging insects (smoke) - Baking clay pots - Fashioning metal tools/ weapons - Drying clothes & bodies - Raising the sprits.

● **FIRE NEEDS** all three of above <u>take away any one & the fire will go out</u>. Reduce the air & it will burn more slowly (saving fuel).

STARTING A FIRE WITHOUT MATCHES

● **Get everything ready first, you need;**

● **TINDER**, which needs to be fine in texture <u>& very dry</u> (e.g.: wood dust, feathers, birds nest down, shredded bandage, clothes fibers (a few drops of liquid fuel [if available] will speed up ignition).

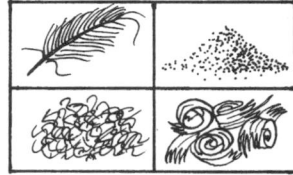

● **KINDLING** consisting of dry twigs, grasses etc. used to get the fire hot enough to burn larger fuels (e.g. logs)

● **FUEL** if available pick dry hardwoods (which give more prolonged heat - dry green woods around established fire).

MATCHES

● **SPLIT** into 2 or more if supplies are short.
● **STRIKE** split matches by pressing your finger on the head while striking **(cool it fast if you burn yourself.)**
● **DAMP** matches - Coat tip with nail varnish - Dry it - Strike.
● **WATER PROOF** matches by dipping heads in molten wax (pick it off when required).

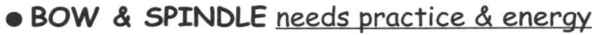

● **BOW & SPINDLE** <u>needs practice & energy</u>

● **Pliant bow** (loop string round spindle & pull back & forth quickly),

Something smooth & hard with a hollow end to push hard on,

● **Hard wood spindle** with a point on it.
● **Soft wood base** with a hollow under it.
● **Tinder** onto which the red hot tip of the spindle will eventually drop.

● **SUN &** magnifying glass (take your camera, telescope etc. to bits).

● **FLINT & STEEL:** Use any hard stone & strike obliquely with steel object - When sparks fall on tinder, Blow.

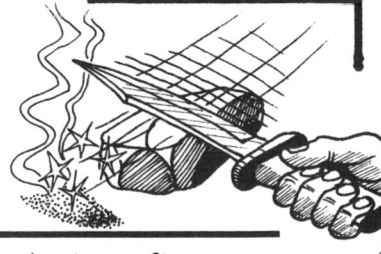

● **CHEMICALS:**
-Sodium Chlorate & sugar (3 to 1 mix).
-Potassium Chlorate & sugar (3 to 1 mix).
-Potassium Permanganate & sugar (9 to 1 mix).
(be careful with all above).

● **CANDLES** will save matches & get obstinate fires started by a few drops of wax on tinder & kindling.
● **VENTILATION** - Be sure your shelter has at least one top & bottom if you have a fire inside to avoid asphyxiation &/or air poisoning.
● **DYING FIRES** come to life with sugar.
● **HYPOTHERMIA** occurs when body temperature (usually 98.6 degrees Fahrenheit) drops below 90 degrees (32 degrees centegrade).
● **BOILING** food uses least fuel yet conserves the most nutrients.
● **STRONG WINDS** in open spaces - Dig a hole for your fire &/or surround it with stones or logs.
● **TRAPS & SNARES** for wild game work better if set in a bottle neck, camouflaged & not contaminated with the hunters scent & sign.
● **CANDLES** burn more slowly if salt is added.

● **BATTERY** terminals when brought nearly together close to tinder will use a lot of energy but may get your fire going.

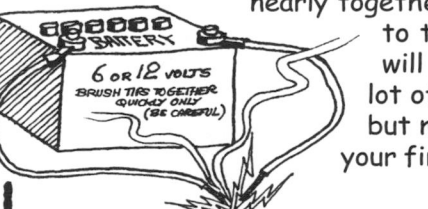

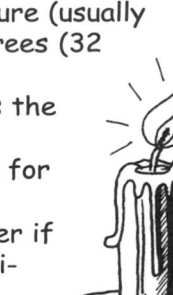

IMPROVISED STOVE

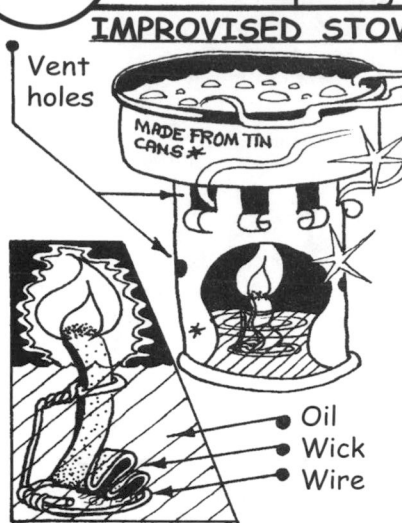

Vent holes

MADE FROM TIN CANS *

- Oil
- Wick
- Wire

- Can also be used with candle - If used with volatile fuel (eg: petrol) **put an inch of sand in bottom** & saturate it before lighting **(don't add fuel while stove is lit).**

- **BREAD** will sun dry (2 hours per side per slice) & keep for months.
- **POTATOES & ONIONS** will keep for 3 months if dry, dark, & sprouts are removed.
- **EGGS (less than 24 hours old)** will keep 3 months if coated in petroleum jelly or grease - Or put in boiling water for a few seconds only.

WET GROUND OR SNOW

- Raise fire on stones (or earth) & green logs, on a platform.

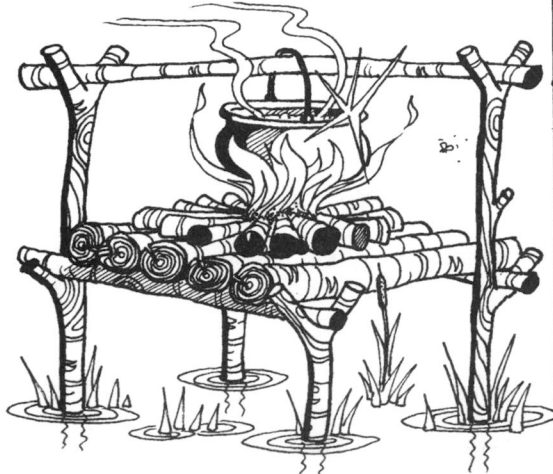

BAKING

- 2 inch layer of soil
- Hot coals
- Food
- Clay
- Stones to hold heat

- **Dig hole.** Line with stones. Build fire in it. Encase food in clay/mud. Cover with hot coals & earth.

ROASTING

- Log to reflect heat.
- Pan to collect drips.
- Fork to keep fish up.
- Spit to turn it.
- Stone to keep end down.
- Turn every 5 minutes.

PRESERVING FOOD IN EMERGENCIES

- **SALTING** a) Brine solution (1 part salt to 1 part water) to preserve previously boiled chunk-sized foods. b) Dried foods can be prepared between layers of dry salt.

- **SUN DRY** - Fillet meat into 1/4 inch (or less) thick strips & spread on twig racks in hot sun to dry until brittle (avoid insects & **in any case boil before eating).**

- **PICKLING** can be acheived by cutting meat/fish small (1 inch pieces) & soaking in 2 parts lime/lemon juice & 1 part water.

- **SMOKING:** a) Seals the outside surfaces. b) Dehydrates at same time. c) Keeps insects away. d) Can be done in any weather. e) Is quite fast (18 - 24 hours).

- **To promote smoke** put green leaves from non-oily type plants on hot embers of fire (keep tepee completely full of smoke but leave a small hole at the top to encourage flow.

- **Cut meat/fish** into 1/4-inch-thick strips & hang or lay **without any touching.**

- Small hole
- Tepee covered with cloth or leaves.
- Racks
- Earth bank.
- Logs

STEAMING IN BAMBOO

- Loose cap
- Food (chunks)
- Small holes in sections.
- Steam
- Stone
- Water

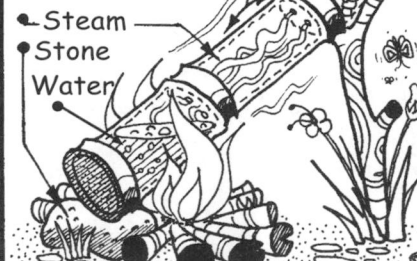

PREPARING FISH

- **Under 2 inches long:** cook whole. - **Over 2 inches:** Cut throat & bleed (to delay spoiling). Slit belly & gut (keep roe [hard in females & soft in males]) — (use other intestines for bait). - Descale if required & cook.

Navigation is as old as man's existence - We have moved from caves to the stars but are no closer to understanding infinity!

N/S LINE FROM A SHADOW

A) Drive a vertical stick in ground about an hour before noon.

B) Mark the tip of the shadow every 5 - 10 minutes with a pebble or small peg until the exact position of the shortest shadow is marked. -

NORTH/SOUTH LINE

Continue marking the shadow tip for a short while after noon to be sure it is lengthening.

C) Draw a line where the shortest shadow fell & this marks the North/South line.

HOW TO FIND LAND
(From the ocean)

● **CUMULUS CLOUDS:** often indicate a land mass under.

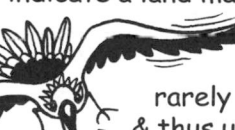

● **SEA BIRDS** rarely sleep at sea & thus usually fly from land in the AM & to land in the PM.

● **SMELL** of land can often be detected well before it is sighted. Note the wind direction.

● **REFLECTION** of land &/or shallow water colors can often be seen on the underside of clouds.

ON LAND

● **VEGETATION** (flowers, buds, leaves, branches) are all more prolific on the side which the sun usually is (**useful at night**).

SUN MOVEMENT FACTS

● No matter where you are the sun **RISES** from the eastern side & sets on the western side.

● If you are **NORTH** of 23 1/2 Degrees N. latitude the sun will always pass south of you.

● If you are **SOUTH** of 23 1/2 Degrees S. latitude the sun will always pass north of you.

● For **LATITUDES** between 23,1/2 Degrees N. & S. The sun's path varies (lines of lat. run E - W).

● lines of **LONGITUDE** run N - S & converge at the poles.

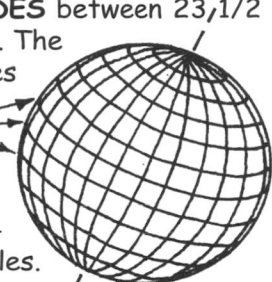

IMPROVISING A COMPASS

You require:

● An elongated piece of **FERROUS** (iron/steel) material (e.g. nail, wire, needle, razor blade)

● A method of inducing **MAGNETISM** in the object (e.g. stroking with a magnet or on silk in one direction only, or wrapping a coil of wire [insulated] around the object & putting a DC current (3 volts or more) thru it for 5 minutes).

● A method of permitting the object to **SWING** (e.g.. suspended from the middle by a thread or float on a circle of paper (or leaf in liquid).

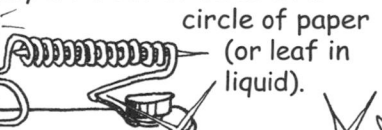

OVER 3V. DC BATTERY

BEARINGS FROM THE SUNRISE

(of top of sun in Degrees east of north for dates & latitudes as shown below.

DATES	0°	20°	40°	60°
6 Jan	112	114	120	140
21 Jan	110	111	117	133
6 Feb	106	107	111	123
21 Feb	101	101	104	112
6 Mar	96	96	98	102
21 Mar	90	90	90	90
6 Apr	84	83	82	77
21 Apr	78	78	75	66
6 May	74	73	68	56
21 May	70	69	63	47
6 Jun	67	66	60	40
21 Jun	67	65	59	39
6 Jul	67	66	60	40
21 Jul	69	68	63	45
6 Aug	73	72	68	54
21 Aug	78	77	74	65
6 Sep	83	83	81	77
21 Sep	89	89	89	88
6 Oct	95	95	97	100
21 Oct	101	101	104	112
6 Nov	106	107	111	123
21 Nov	110	111	116	133
6 Dec	112	114	120	140
21 Dec	113	115	121	141

TRAIL BLAZING

....In survival situations has these advantages
● Aids in finding return routes if required
● Aids in relocating desirable features (e.g. water, food, tracks etc.)
● Aids in avoiding undesirable features (e.g. bogs, crevasses, impassable paths etc.)
● Aids others (perhaps rescue) to find you

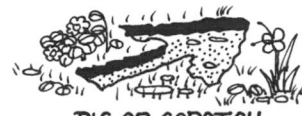

DIG OR SCRATCH

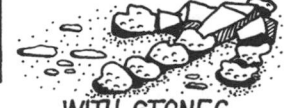

WITH STONES

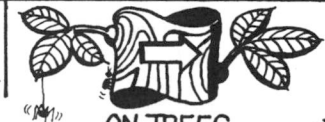

ON TREES

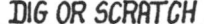

SIMPLIFIED STELLAR NAVIGATION

NORTHERN HEM.

- **BIG DIPPER (or Plough):** A group of 7 bright stars in the **Great Bear Constellation** which appears to rotate around the northern sky.
- **CASSIOPEIA:** A group of 5 bright stars (shaped like a flat "W"), also appears to rotate round the northern sky
- **POLARIS:** A single bright star (one of a small group) which sits stationary above the **north pole.**

BOTH HEMISPHERES

- **MILKY WAY:** Orientate yourself by finding this band of millions of hazy stars which stretch across the sky.
- **ORION:** A group of 7 bright stars (3 of which form a "belt"), rises (on its side) due east & sets due west.

SOUTHERN HEM.

- **SOUTHERN CROSS (Crux):** A group of 4 bright stars (plus 2 identification stars [pointers] close by). - Beware of confusing the **Southern Cross** with another larger (but fainter) group known as the **"False Cross."**

BIG DIPPER

ROTATES

POLARIS

CASSIOPEIA

POINTERS
SOUTHERN CROSS
FALSE CROSS

- Constellations rotate in this direction.

- 4 1/2 times **"The Cross"** then straight down is due south.

HORIZON

S

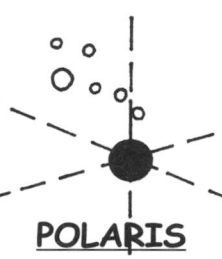

NOTE ORION is aligned N/S with **Polaris** as shown, but is not this close.

Celestial Equator.

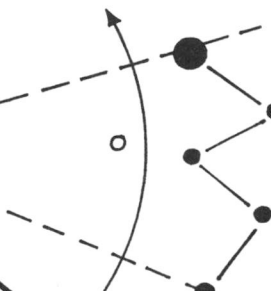

ORION

RADIO BEARINGS

(Using any M.W. radio)
- Tune to nearest station. - Rotate radio for minimum signal. - End of radio is now pointing at (or 180 degrees opposite to) the station broadcasting.

ROUGH NIGHTIME ORIENTATION

STARS SEEM TO MOVE	YOU ARE FACING
←	N
↖	NE
↑	E
↗	SE
↔	S
↘	SW
↓	W
↙	NW

STARS

- **DRIVE 2 STICKS** into the ground at different heights (about 2 ft apart) so they line up on any bright star & compare its movement as at left.

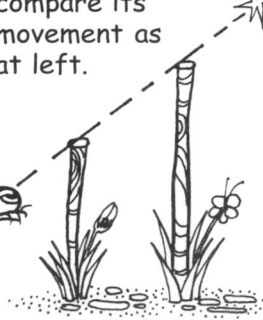

MOON

- **If the moon rises before the sun has set, the bright side of the moon will be to the west.**
- **If the moon rises after midnight the bright side will be to the east.**

READING MAPS & CHARTS

- **SCALE** (land) e.g.: 1:10,000 means 1 cm on the map = 10,000 cms on the ground.
- **SCALE** (sea) 1' of latitude (side only of chart) = 1 nautical mile (60' = 1 degree).
- **CONTOUR** (&/or depth) indicates height (or depth) on that line.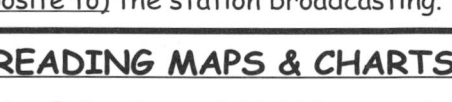
- **MAGNETIC VARIATION:** Compass & true bearings are very rarely the same. - So remember **"Error East, Compass Least, Error West, Compass Best"** (e.g.: 20 degree East variation means, 340 degrees on your compass = true north).

Simplified Use Of Non-Electric International Signals

International distress signals in code, speech, or letters: SOS (Save Our Souls), or "MAYDAY" (m'aidez) - or 3 evenly spaced lights or noises.

- Note spot of sunshine from hole in middle on cheek.

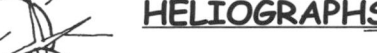

HELIOGRAPHS

- **DEFINITION:** A heliograph is a shiny surface used to reflect the sun's rays in another direction for the purpose of signalling.

- **CUSTOM MADE:** Heliograph is mirrored on both sides & has a hole in the middle.

- **LIGHT LAW:** The angle of incidence "A" = the angle of reflection "B".

- **USING IT: 1)** Wait until target (plane, boat, person) is in same quadrant as sun. **2)** Sight thru center hole at target. **3)** Note location of "spot" of sunlight which falls on your face/cheek etc. **4)** Adjust angle of mirror so that reflection of this sun spot (as seen in the back of the mirror) coincides with the hole in the centre. **5)** Flick minutely on & off this position according to signal (usually Morse code).

- **IMPROVISE** a heliograph using any shiny surface (tin, vanity mirror etc.).

INTERNATIONAL GROUND TO AIR EMERGENCY SIGNALS

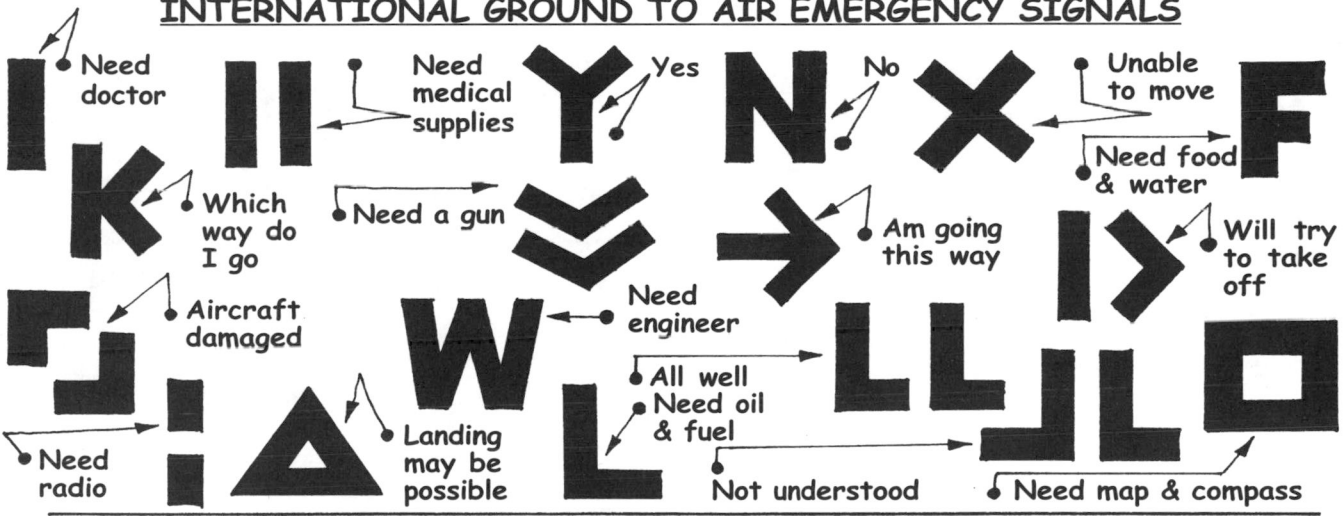

- Need doctor
- Need medical supplies
- Yes
- No
- Unable to move
- Need food & water
- Which way do I go
- Need a gun
- Am going this way
- Will try to take off
- Aircraft damaged
- Need engineer
- Need radio
- Landing may be possible
- All well
- Need oil & fuel
- Not understood
- Need map & compass

- **SIZE:** Figures should be about 40 ft long (10 ft gap between pairs).
- **LOCATION:** Open space on flat ground, near signal fire.
- **MATERIAL:** Anything contrasting with terrain background.
- **— DESTROY SIGNALS WHEN LEAVING —**

SIGNAL FIRES

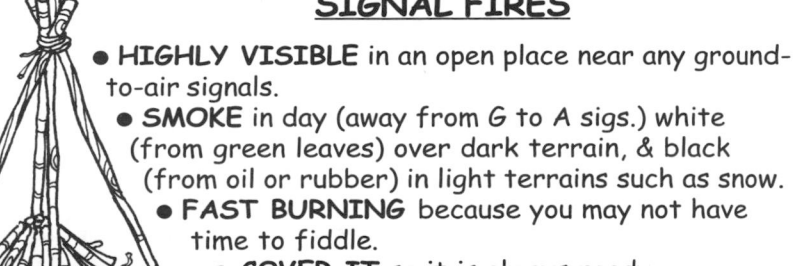

- **HIGHLY VISIBLE** in an open place near any ground-to-air signals.
- **SMOKE** in day (away from G to A sigs.) white (from green leaves) over dark terrain, & black (from oil or rubber) in light terrains such as snow.
- **FAST BURNING** because you may not have time to fiddle.
- **COVER IT** so it is always ready.
- **3 EVENLY SPACED** fires is a well known distress sign.

SEARCH PATTERNS

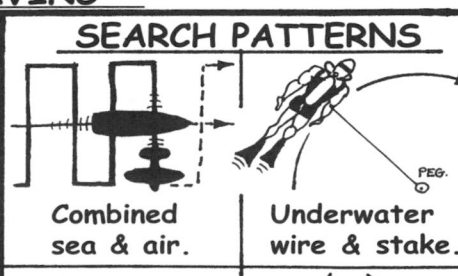

Combined sea & air.

Underwater wire & stake.

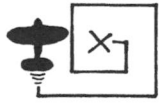

Last known position.

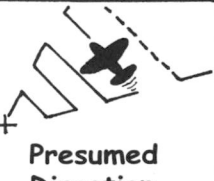

Presumed Direction.

MORSE CODE

A	·—	N	—·
B	—···	O	———
C	—·—·	P	·——·
D	—··	Q	——·—
E	·	R	·—·
F	··—·	S	···
G	——·	T	—
H	····	U	··—
I	··	V	···—
J	·———	W	·——
K	—·—	X	—··—
L	·—··	Y	—·——
M	——	Z	——··
1	·————	6	—····
2	··———	7	——···
3	···——	8	———··
4	····—	9	————·
5	·····	0	—————

SENDING CODES

AAAAA = I am calling you.
EEEEE = Error.
AR = Message ends.

RECEIVING CODES

TTTTT = I am receiving you.
IMI = Please repeat.
R = Message received.

PHONETICS

Alfa	November
Bravo	Oscar
Charlie	Papa
Delta	Quebec
Echo	Romeo
Fox-trot	Sierra
Golf	Tango
Hotel	Unicorn
India	Victor
Juliet	Whiskey
Kilo	X - Ray
Lima	Yankee
Mike	Zulu

SEMAPHORE

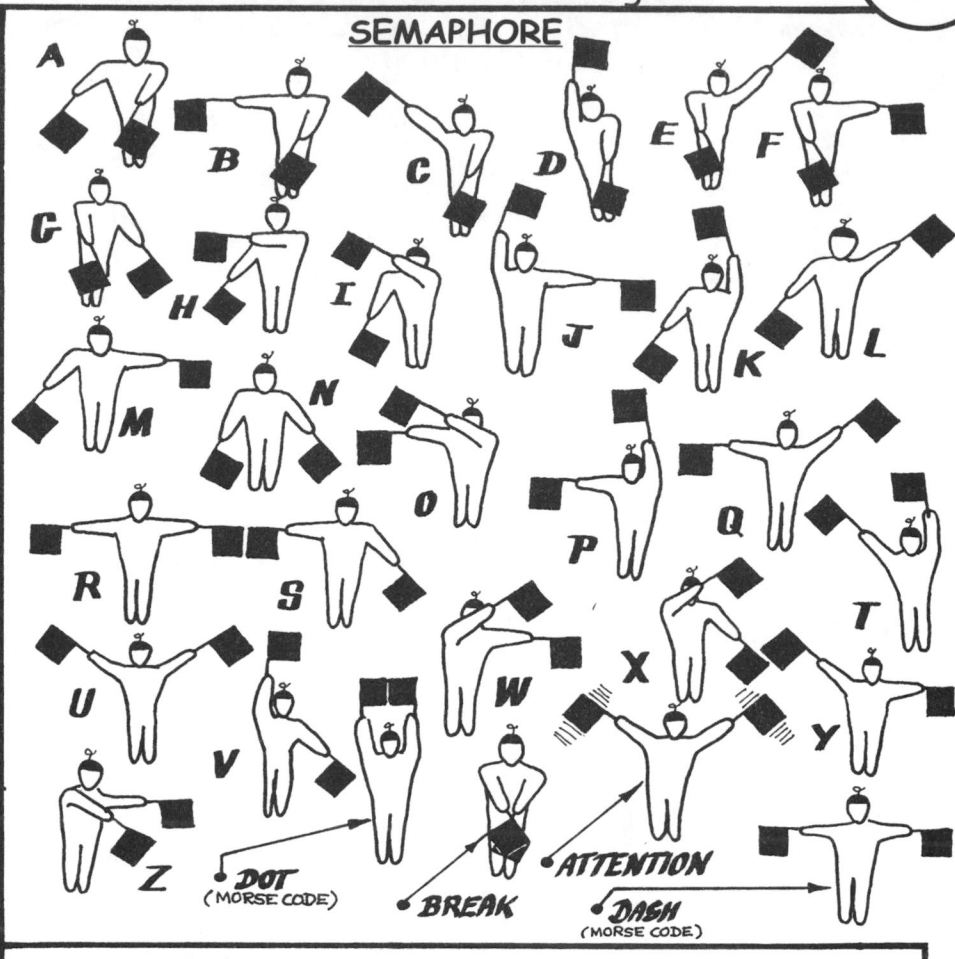

INTERNATIONAL MARINE SIGNAL FLAGS

BLACK ■ WHITE □ ORANGE ▧ BLUE ▨ YELLOW ▨

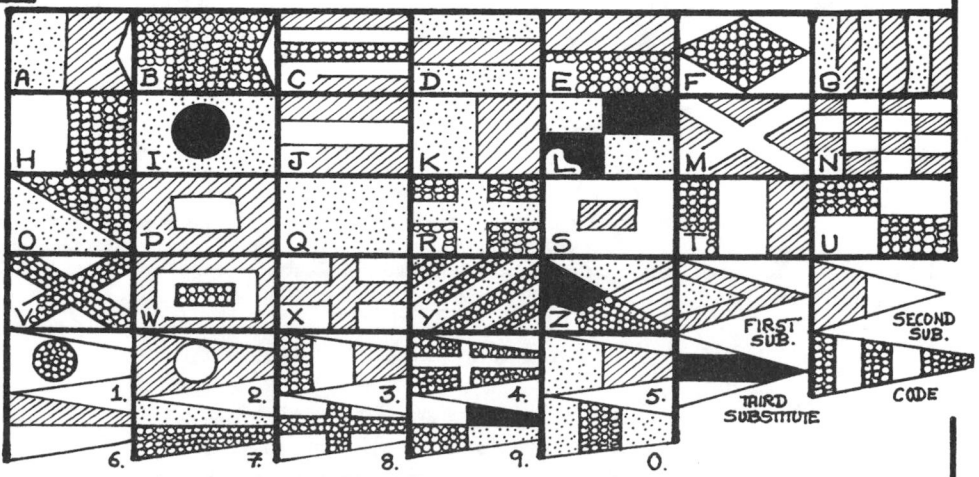

FLAGS FLOWN SINGLY ALSO MEAN

A = Diver down. B = Dangerous cargo. C = Yes. D = Keep away.
E = Steering starboard. F = I am disabled. G = I need pilot or
hauling net. H = Pilot on board. I = Steering port. J = Dangerous
fire - keep away. K = I wish to communicate L = Stop your vessel. M = I am stopped. N = No.
O = Man overboard. P = Vessel departing or nets stuck. Q = Request practique. R = Not allocated
yet. S = My engine going astern. T = Trawling - stay away. U = You in danger. V = I need help.
W = I need medical help. X = Stop what you are doing. Y = My anchor dragging. Z = I need a tug.

Avocado Masque

- **PURPOSE**: Remove dead skin cells (enzyme action) - Deep cleanse - Moisturize - Stimulate blood circulation.

- **INGREDIENTS**: 1 ripe avocado. ● **HOW TO USE**: Cleanse area to be treated (face/neck) - Peel avocado - Remove & retain stone - Mash (or liquidize flesh) - Apply to face & leave for 15 - 30 minutes - Rinse with warm then cool water. ● **VARIATIONS**: Massage face with stone.

Oat Milk Hand Lotion

- **PURPOSE**: Nourish & soften work- or weather-roughened hands.
- **INGREDIENTS**: 1/2 cup oat flour & 3 cups of water. ● **HOW TO USE**: Mix ingredients - Simmer for half an hour - Strain - Massage into clean hands & leave to dry (don't wash off). ● **VARIATIONS**: Add half a cup of clear honey after mixture cools (store excess in fridge).

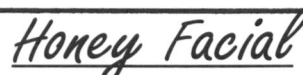

Sea Salt Body Scrub

- **PURPOSE**: Removes dead skin cells - Stimulates circulation - Draws out body wastes & toxins. -
- **INGREDIENTS**: 1 or 2 cups of coarse sea salt (not table salt). ● **HOW TO USE**: Wet body with warm water to open the pores - Working against hair growth & from feet up, massage salt into wet skin - Leave to dry before rinsing. ● **VARIATIONS**: Mix oil with salt for tender skin.

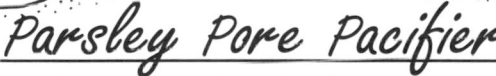

Honey Facial

- **PURPOSE**: Rejuvenation of skin texture & appearance.
- **INGREDIENTS**: Raw, natural untreated honey.
- **HOW TO USE**: Wash face well & rinse in warm water - While still moist apply honey in up & out strokes of the fingers - After about 20 minutes rinse away with warm water.
- **VARIATIONS**: Final rinse with apple cider & water (equal parts for oily skin - less for dry).

Parsley Pore Pacifier

- **PURPOSE**: Cleanser for oily skin problems (blackheads, big pores, inflammation).
- **INGREDIENTS**: 1 cup of fresh chopped parsley & 2 cups of water. -
- **HOW TO USE**: Boil parsley in glass or stainless steel for 2 minutes, & let stand till only warm - Strain - Apply to clean face as compress for 10 - 20 minutes each day till better.
- **VARIATIONS**: Add a spoon of sage to the brew.

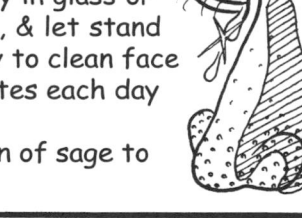

Eau De Lavender

- **PURPOSE**: Simple perfumed toner - Ladies we (men) love you to wear this, on clothes, body or pillow, it drives us wild.
- **INGREDIENTS**: 1/4 oz oil of lavender & 1 pint ethyl alcohol.
- **HOW TO USE**: Mix very well - Mature for 60 days & shake daily before use (glass container best).
- **VARIATIONS**: Add oil of cloves to above - Or for quick usage, mix 4 drops pure oil with half teaspoon water & apply.

Eye Bags

- **PURPOSE**: Reduce dark puffy areas under eyes.
- **INGREDIENTS**: Slice of raw potato.
- **HOW TO USE**: Grate potato into two gauze bags - Lie down with feet raised & apply bags to closed eye problem area for 30 minutes - Rinse away & apply a dab of light nut oil.
- **VARIATIONS**: Instead of potato, substitute grated cucumber or 2 used tea bags (not hot).

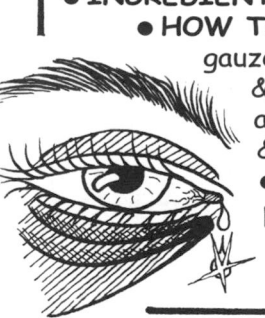

Shower/Bath Massage Oils

- **PURPOSE**: Lubricate & stimulate skin & underlying tissues.
- **INGREDIENTS**: 1/2 cup of vegetable/nut oil (Oily skin: sesame, sunflower, corn - Dry skin: olive, almond, peanut). ● **HOW TO USE**: Right after (or during warm shower/bath, massage oil well in skin from feet up. ● **VARIATIONS**: Add 2 teaspoons of exotic essential oil to your bottle of nut/vegetable oil & mix well.

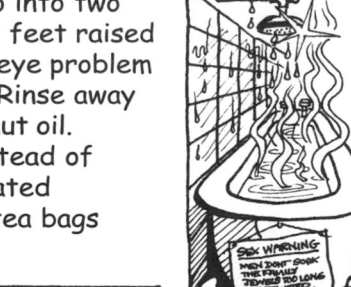

Many commercially manufactured cosmetics contain preservatives, chemical colors & scents, which can actually do more harm than good.

Almond Scrub

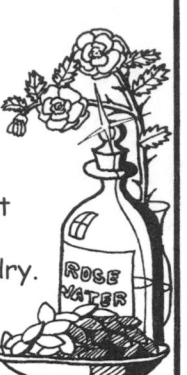

- **PURPOSE:** Deep cleanse & remove dead skin cells.
- **INGREDIENTS:** 1 cup of almonds.
- **HOW TO USE:** Grind to powder in blender (store in an airtight jar) - Wet face & gently rub in a small handful - Rinse in warm water, then cool & dab dry.
- **VARIATIONS:** Add Rose Water & either egg white or almond oil & lemon juice to condition skin at same time.

Tea & Sesame Sunscreen

- **PURPOSE:** Ultraviolet blocker.
- **INGREDIENTS:** 1 cup sesame oil & 1 cup very (six tea bags) strong tea.
- **HOW TO USE:** Brew tea & leave to cool - Extract bags & squeeze dry - Add oil to tea & shake well.
- **NOTES:** Both tannin (in tea) & sesame oil have natural UV screening properties.
- **VARIATIONS:** Add few drops of exotic perfume oil to mixture (shake well).

Wrinkle Eraser

- **PURPOSE:** Tighten fine creases & pores + nutrition. **INGREDIENTS:** Raw egg white.
- **HOW TO USE:** Don't waste that bit of raw egg white in the shell at breakfast - Apply to nose, neck, forehead etc. - Leave to dry - Rinse off later & apply a few drops of vegetable oil if skin dry. **VARIATIONS:** Add few drops of honey to leftover white & mix in shell.

Vitamin A Skin Food Cream

- **PURPOSE:** Nourish, lubricate & ease out fine lines. **INGREDIENTS:** 1 spoon of soft sweet butter & 1 spoon of either lemon, cucumber or strawberry juice or pulp. **HOW TO USE:** Beat butter & other ingredient very well together - Apply to clean face/neck - Leave for 15 - 30 minutes - Rinse with water, then astringent - Dab dry.
- **VARIATIONS:** Use 1 teaspoon egg yolk instead of veg.

Papaya Enzyme Treat

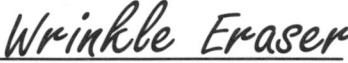

- **PURPOSE:** Remove dead skin cells (enzyme action) & deep cleanse pores. **INGREDIENTS:** Fresh papaya. **HOW TO USE:** Cleanse face - Rub face & neck & with small sections of papaya - Reapply as required - Leave juice on for 30 minutes Rinse off & dab dry. **NOTE:** Although beneficial to prewash face with warm water to open pores, do not heat papaya (over 125 degrees F.) as this destroys its enzymes.

Milk Lubricating Cleanser

- **PURPOSE:** To remove grime & make-up whilst moisturising.
- **INGREDIENTS:** 1 tablespoon fresh milk, 2 - 10 drops vegetable/nut oil.
- **HOW TO USE:** Mix oil & milk well Massage into face - Rinse or blot off.
- **VARIATIONS:** For dry skin use full cream milk & up to 10 drops of oil - For oily skin use skimmed milk & down to 2 drops of oil - A few drops of liquid honey can be added.

Protein Egg Rinse

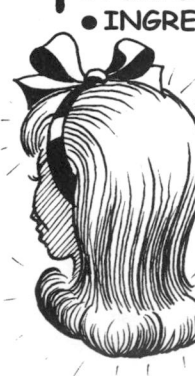

- **PURPOSE:** Cleans, conditions & feeds the hair.
- **INGREDIENTS:** 1 - 3 egg yolks & 1/2 - 1 1/2 cups of warm water.
- **HOW TO USE:** Do not shampoo before or after - Mix yolk & water well & massage into hair & scalp for 5 minutes - Cover with towel or plastic bag for 25 minutes more - Rinse very well in warm then cool water.
- **VARIATIONS:** Also used to treat dandruff, dullness, limpness & weak hair.

A Natural Wash Routine

- **PURPOSE:** Simple cleansing (also before treatments such as oil &/or skin food).
- **INGREDIENTS:** PH balanced pure vegetable soap & apple cider vinegar.
- **HOW TO USE:** Lather well with small circular strokes of a natural fiber complexion brush - Soap & warm water - Warm rinse - Final rinse with 1 teaspoon of apple cider vinegar in 1 cup of water to restore acid skin mantle **VARIATIONS:** Add a cup of vinegar to bath to soothe skin & muscles.

Don't reduce calorie intake too much too fast as this is a considerable shock to the body with possible serious side effects.

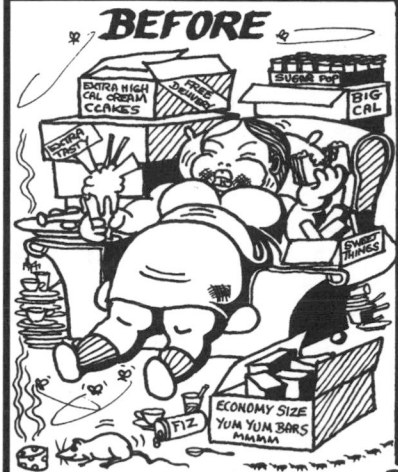

STARTING: Although most overweight problems are from overeating - There are other causes:

- **FLUID RETENTION:** Can be caused by various drugs, stress, even slow metabolism (body does not burn food quickly enough - Toxins build up - Body overheats - Fluid retained to cool).
- **EATING TOO MANY PROCESSED** foods with high levels of preservatives, colorings etc. discourages digestion & metabolism as above.
- **EATING TOO MUCH PROTEIN** can result in the body being inefficient in breaking down excess which can turn to fat.
- **EATING TOO MANY CARBOHYDRATES** can hinder the efficient breaking down of proteins & fats.
- **IF THE CAUSE OF YOUR OBESITY IS OVEREATING** ....

BASIC PRINCIPLES & HOW TO DO IT

1. **CALORIES** are units of energy (or heat) - <u>1 calorie is the amount of energy needed to raise the temperature of 1,000 grams of water by 1 degree centigrade.</u> Different foods (& quantities thereof) contain different numbers of calories, which if eaten in excess are stored on the body as fat.

2. **METABOLIC NEEDS:** The adult human (according to size) <u>requires about 1,500 calories per 24 hours</u> just to maintain the requirements of breathing, circulation etc. - <u>This does not allow for any physical activity at all.</u>

3. **MINIMUM ACTIVITY NEEDS** vary according to lifestyle, weight, sex etc. (a 200 lb builders' laborer obviously requires more calories to get through his working day than does a 100 lb VDU programmer) but as an approximate guide <u>a woman requires 1,700 - 2,300 calories per 24 hours & a man 2,500 - 3,500.</u>

4. **OVEREATING WEIGHT GAINS** are easily estimated by the simple process of converting excess calories eaten to ounces (or grams) of body fat at the rate of <u>250 cals. = 1oz (or 28 gms) of body fat</u> - For example if Miss X requires 1,500 cals. for her metabolism & 500 cals. for her daily activities (total 2,000 cals.) but actually eats 3,000 cals. during the day she has an excess of 1,000 cals, <u>or a potential of 4 oz (or 112 gms) of extra body fat acquired during the 24-hour period!</u>

5. **WEIGHT LOSS** by calorie control is achieved by a) Estimating the approximate calories your body requires to cover metabolism & activities (in Miss X's case 2,000 cals.) then b) Reducing the number of calories actually eaten by a controlled (NOT EXCESSIVE) amount (500 CALS. IS SUFFICIENT) below this figure c) Thus in Miss X's case she limits her calorie intake (food & drink) to 1,500 cals. per 24 hours & with a calorie deficit of 500 cals. per day <u>should lose about 2 ozs (or 56 gms) of body fat per day or about 1 lb per week or 50 lbs per year!</u>

NOTES

- **WEIGH ONCE PER WEEK** (say Sunday morning after going to the bathroom but before breakfast) because of <u>daily variations.</u>
- **ENTER WEEKLY RATE** readings <u>on a graph</u> (to compare progress).
- **FIRST WEEK** may show greater reductions because of <u>fluid loss.</u>
- **MORE FREQUENT SMALL MEALS** are better than less frequent large ones (of the <u>same total calories</u>) for the purpose of weight loss.
- **LARGE MEALS AT NIGHT** result in more weight gain than larger meals during the day because <u>CALORIES ARE HARDLY USED WHILE ASLEEP.</u>

GOOD LUCK

over ——→

CALORIFIC VALUES OF COMMON FOODS

FOODS	per oz	per 100 g	FOODS	per oz	per 100 g	FOODS	per oz	per 100 g
All bran (cereal)	80	280	Flour	100	350	Rice (boiled)	35	122
Almonds	170	595	Ham	120	420	Salmon	40	140
Apples	10	35	Hard Candy	94	330	Sausage (pork)	92	322
Apricots in syrup*	30	105	Honey	80	280	Soya flour	95	332
Bacon (fried)	170	595	Ice cream	70	245	Strawberries	7	24
Bananas	13	45	Jam	75	262	Sugar	115	402
Beans (baked)*	25	88	Kidney	50	175	Tomatoes	4	14
Beans (runner)	2	7	Lard (fat)	265	927	Tomato ketchup	29	100
Beef (corned)*	65	230	Lobster	12	42	Trout	25	87
Beef steak	80	280	Macaroni	35	122	Turkey (roast)	34	119
Biscuits (digestive)	137	480	Margarine	225	787	White bait (fried)	150	525
Boiled Sweets	94	330	Mars bars	125	437	Yogurt (low fat)	15	52
Bread	70	245	Melon	4	14			
Butter	225	787	Milk (whole)	20	70			

DRINKS	per fluid oz	per 100 ml
Cabbage			Milk (low fat)	10	35	Coca cola	12	42

FOODS	per oz	per 100 g	FOODS	per oz	per 100 g	DRINKS	per fluid oz	per 100 ml
Cabbage	3	10	Milk (low fat)	10	35	Coca cola	12	42
Carrots	6	21	Mushrooms	2	7	Lucozade	21	75
Cashew nuts	175	612	Oats	110	385	Ginger ale	11	38
Catfish	29	100	Olive oil	265	927	Soda water	-	-
Cheese (cheddar)	120	420	Onion	7	24	Draft beer	10	35
Chicken	38	133	Onion (fried)	100	350	Strong ale	21	75
Chocolate	160	560	Pastry	160	560	Dry cider	10	35
Coconut	105	367	Peaches	10	35	Strong cider	28	98
Cod (fish)	20	70	Peanuts	170	595	Port	45	157
Cod-liver oil	260	910	Peanut butter	180	630	Wine	20	70
Cornflakes	105	367	Pilchards*	55	192	Alcohol	70	245
Dates	65	227	Popcorn	135	472	Pilehards*	55	192
Egg white	11	38	Pork	130	455			
Egg yolk	100	350	Potatoes	24	84			
Fish fingers	50	175	Potato chips	70	245			
			Rice	100	350			

codes * = canned.

SIMPLIFIED CONCLUSION
- LESS FAT, OIL & SUGAR, MORE EXERCISE & GREEN VEGETABLES

ACTIVITIES & APPROXIMATE CALORIES USED

ACTIVITY	cals/hr.	ACTIVITY	cals/hr.
Sitting/reading	70	Fast walking	350
Eating	80	Jogging	400
Ironing	110	Cycling	400
Cooking	120	Active tennis	400
Driving	150	Fast jogging	550
House cleaning	200	Digging a hole	550
Slow walking	200	Active swimming	600
Active golf	250	Active rowing	800
Dancing	300	Circuit training	1,000

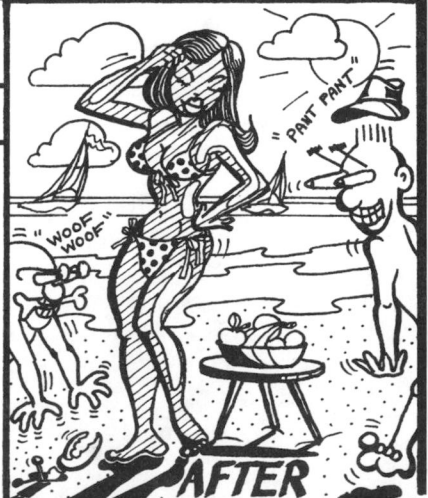

AFTER

● **ACID:** <u>Flush immediately with cold running water</u> & neutralize with BICARBONATE OF SODA or BORAX (mix 1 teaspoon with 1 pint water).

● **ADHESIVE:** (CONTACT/CLEAR) Use ACETONE or non-oily nail polish remover - (EPOXY RESIN) Use METHYLATED SPIRITS before the glue sets - (TAPE & STICKY LABELS) Use WHITE SPIRITS - (ANIMAL & FISH GLUES) Use a little vinegar in hot water (soak it) - (SUPER GLUE) Immediately immerse in cold water. ● **ALCOHOL:** (BEER) Either dab with white vinegar or wash using biological soap powder - (SPIRITS) Dish washing liquid & warm water - (WINE) Pour salt on first then soak in cold water or weak BORAX solution. ● **BALLPOINT PEN:** Soak with METHYLATED SPIRITS then biological soap powder solution then rinse.

● **BLOOD:** Immediately immerse in cold water with a strong salt content - If it "colors," change water - If still there then rub with salt paste - If still there soak in biological soap powder solution overnight - For old stains try a few drops of diluted AMMONIA then wash - Other techniques are spittle, diluted HYDROGEN PEROXIDE, lemon juice & salt. ● **BUTTER:** Wash at highest possible temperature. ● **CANDLE WAX:** Freeze or pack with ice then break off - If some left, put stain between two sheets of brown paper & iron (medium heat). ● **CHEWING GUM:** Treat as for wax but any trace remaining will dissolve with WHITE SPIRITS or METHYLATED SPIRITS. ● **CHOCOLATE, COCOA, COFFEE:** Rinse in cold soapy water - If still there soak in warm BORAX solution (1 oz to 1 pint). ● **COLAS:** Cold water with dishwashing liquid from back - If still there try diluted white vinegar or METHYLATED SPIRITS. ● **CRAYONS, FELT TIP PENS:** (Even indelible) Use METHYLATED SPIRITS then launder. ● **CREOSOTE:** Use EUCALYPTUS OIL then wash. ● **GRASS:** Use METHYLATED SPIRITS then wash or apply paste of salt or CREAM OF TARTAR, let it dry & brush off.

● **GREASE:** Scrape off excess with blunt knife, apply talcum powder or cornflour, pat in & brush off - If stain remains apply WHITE SPIRITS from back of fabric then wash in hot soapy water.

● **IODINE:** Dissolve 1 tablespoon of HYPO CRYSTALS (photographic) in half pint of water & soak for 5 - 10 minutes then rinse & wash.

● **IRON:** (RUST) First try lemon juice & salt left on the stain for an hour - If still there use *OXALIC ACID solution (half teaspoon to 1 pint of water) *<u>poisonous & do not use on silk or wool.</u> ● **LIPSTICK, MAKEUP:** Sponge from back with METHYLATED SPIRITS then dab with neat dishwashing liquid, then wash. ●

● **MILDEW:** Try soaking in 1 teaspoon white vinegar, 2 teaspoons bleach & 1 pint water - For nonwashables (e.g. books) wipe with weak ANTISEPTIC SOLUTION to kill fungi.

● **MILK:** Don't use very hot water (which will set the stain) - rinse, then soak/wash with a biological powder in warm water - For fast results use BORAX solution (1 oz to 1 pint water).

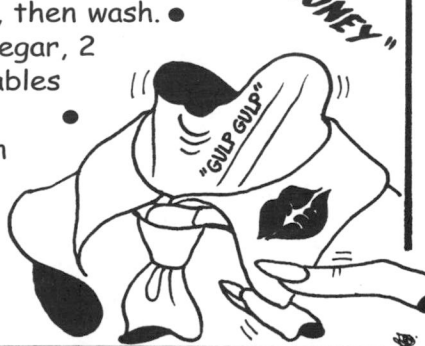

continued ——————→

Continued→ ● **METAL STAINS:** (TIN, COPPER, BRASS etc.) Use white vinegar, lemon juice or ACETIC ACID then rinse in cold water (do not use bleach).
● **MUSTARD:** Rinse or sponge with water, soak in dish washing solution - If still there soak in a solution 1 teaspoon of AMMONIA to 1 pint water. ● **NEWSPRINT:** Sponge with METHYLATED SPIRITS then wash. ● **NAIL POLISH:** (Working from back of fabric) Sponge with non-oily nail polish remover (or ACETONE), then WHITE SPIRITS, then METHYLATED SPIRITS, then wash. ● **ORANGE/ PINEAPPLE ETC:** Flush first with cold water - If still there stretch fabric over bucket top & pour hot water thru it. ● **PAINT (ACRYLIC):** Wash immediately with soap & water - (METHYLATED SPIRITS may help but not when paint is hard).

● **PAINT (CELLULOSE):** CELLULOSE THINNERS then launder.
● **PAINT (OIL GLOSS)** remove excess, sponge with WHITE SPIRITS on throwaway rags, apply dishwashing liquid neat then wash.
● **PAINT (2 PART PLASTICS):** Scrape of excess, swab with ACETONE & throwaway rags (before hard), then apply neat dishwashing liquid, work in, then launder.
● **PARAFFIN:** Apply talcum powder or cornflour & pat in, brush off & iron between two sheets of brown paper, apply dish washing liquid neat, work in & launder.
● **PENCIL:** Try soft rubber, then apply dishwashing liquid & rub in & rinse - If still there apply diluted AMMONIA & launder. ● **PERSPIRATION:** Soak in biological soap powder & water - If still there try a couple of ASPIRIN in a pint of water or a weak AMMONIA solution.

● **SCORCH MARKS:** First soak fabric in cold milk - If still there treat with soap & BORAX solution or on natural linens or cotton a bleach solution. ● **TAR:** Scrape off excess, soften with WHITE SPIRITS or GLYCERINE (work from back of fabric), finish with EUCALYPTUS OIL or DRY CLEANING FLUID - Finally hottest wash possible with fabric. ● **TOBACCO:** METHYLATED SPIRITS on most fabrics (BENZENE on acetates) - If still there a solution of HYDROGEN PEROXIDE & water. ● **URINE:** Rinse in cold water, soak in biological powder solution, launder - If still there try (on old stains) HYDROGEN PEROXIDE solution or white vinegar (1 part) to 3 parts water - If color of fabric changes then neutralize with AMMONIA (1 part) to 20 parts water.

IMPORTANT CLEANING NOTES.

● **WOOL** may deteriorate physically if treated with neat detergent.
● **BLOODSTAINS** may become "set" if any heat is applied to them.
● **SILK & WOOL** should not be soaked in biological powder solutions.
● **NATURAL FIBERS** respond best when treated with METHYLATED SPIRITS, WHITE SPIRITS, CELLULOSE THINNERS or ACETONE.
● **SYNTHETIC FIBERS** respond best when treated with WHITE SPIRITS or LIGHTER FUEL - Particularly don't use ACETONE (or nail polish remover) on any synthetic - Or METHYLATED SPIRITS on acetates.
● **APPLICATION** of cleaning fluids & solvents is preferably applied from the back of the fabric as this tends to flood the stain out again.

Be Prepared For Radiation Risks With These Simple Steps

One rad of X-RAYS produces about 2 million ionization events (destructive occurrences) in human tissues.

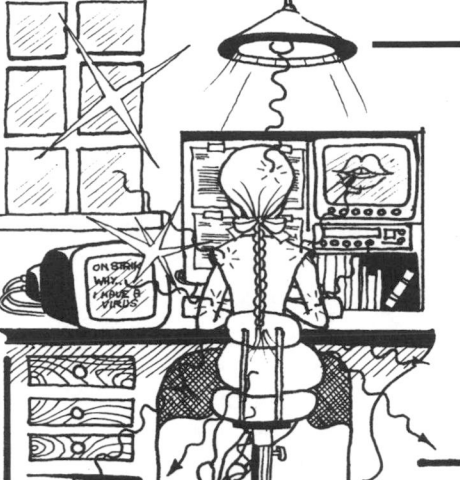

UNDERSTANDING IT

● **MATTER TO ENERGY:** All matter (solid, liquid & gas) is composed of molecules. Each molecule is made up of atoms arranged in varying structures with gaps between & moving so fast (thru 3 dimensions) that they appear to be solid (like this piece of paper) - **Thus all matter is actually energy** (Einstein's Formula: $E = MC^2$ [Energy = Mass X Light Speed squared]).

● **ENERGY TO RADIATION:** **Radiation is an energy flow** of atomic or subatomic particles (such as electrons) &/or electromagnetic energy waves (light, heat, T.V & radio signals etc.).

WHAT DOES IT DO TO ME ?

● **HARMFUL OR NOT?** The problem with radiation is that it either a) bounces off any matter it encounters or b) passes right thru it, or c) does a combination of both - but whatever case it is, when radiation strikes, say your body, (& as both are forms of energy) **an interaction takes place resulting in cellular changes in your body!** - (more later) but first:

● **"SAFE" LEVELS:** **Radioactivity at any level is harmful to living tissues.** Our governments in their "wisdom" give us conflicting (**& ever reducing**) maximum levels which vary between .25 & 5 msv - However people are not the same & **VULNERABILITY VARIES WITH LIFESTYLE, AGE & DIET ETC.**

MEASURING RADIATION

Unit	What It Measures
RAD (100 rad = 1 gray)	Measurement of radiation absorbed by living tissues.
REM	Measurement of effect of radiation on living tissues.
10 Millisievert (MSV) = 1 REM, 100 REM = **1 SIEVERT** (SV)	
BEC-QUEREL	Measurement of radioactive disintergrations per second.
CURIE	Measurement of radioactive emission.

HARMFUL RADIATION

● **NUCLEAR BOMBS/LEAKS** (such as Chernobyl) where unstable radioactive atoms are introduced to the atmosphere & carried by winds (perhaps thousands of miles), to fall in rain, contaminating water supplies, vegetation, crops, livestock & all life for years (**perhaps hundreds to come**). **Some Chernobyl victims received massive (& fatal) doses of 800 REMs!**

● **GROUND RADIOACTIVITY** varies greatly according to location - But exposures are roughly (from average terrain) of .02 RAD TO ALMOST 3 RAD in parts of India.

● **SOLAR & STELLA** radiation (in the form of particles & cosmetic rays) vary erratically with location & time - Average sea level readings are about .03 RAD/YEAR (**this doubles at 5,000 ft**).

● **AIR** (including the gas Radon 222), of which levels inhaled vary greatly according to under house ventilation, but also including naturally occurring Carbon 14 - Total average exposure about .08 RAD/YEAR.

● **FOOD & DRINK:** Because of atmospheric fall out & soil contamination our water, produce, fish & livestock contribute a further average ingested exposure of about .06 RAD/YEAR.

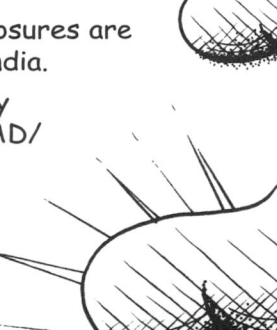

Continued Over ⟶

Continued →

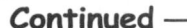

"DON'T WORRY, IT'S QUITE HARMLESS!"

SOLID LEAD

OTHER DANGEROUS SOURCES

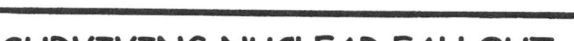

- **X-RAYS** (which some doctors and dentists love to bombard us with) - A "still" X-ray can expose you to as much as 1 rad of radiation - & a "movie" sequence X-ray exam **a massive 25 rad dose.**
- **TELEVISION**, computer screens, radio signals, microwaves, electric cables, transformers, pylons etc. transmissions are everywhere & to a degree are unavoid-able - But they are reducible by avoidance of close proximity with same. **Stay away.** Average (but widely differing) exposures vary from .3 RAD /YEAR in cities to .05 RAD/YEAR in rural areas.

SURVIVING NUCLEAR FALLOUT

- **MILK** is highly susceptible to contamination because cattle feed on grass which may have had radioactive **RAIN** fall on it from an explosion or leak thousands of miles away, **WATER** supplies, **FRUIT & VEGETABLES** even **LIVESTOCK & FISH** can all be contaminated from rainfall & wind-borne debris.

RADIATION EXPOSURE CHART

Levels in rads	Time to appear	Symptoms & results of exposure
100	Varies with physical condition.	**Serious damage to cells** & DNA etc. free radicals release.
200	Within a few hours.	**Massive ionization of cells**, very high risk of cancer (initially dizzy, nausea, headache)
500	Within 30 minutes.	**Death probable** in a few months.
1,000	5 minutes.	**Death almost certain** within a few weeks.
5,000	Instant.	**Death within days.**

COMBATING ITS EFFECTS (A)

- **RADIOACTIVE IODINE** 131 is a highly dangerous isotope which is absorbed thru the skin & lungs then **lodges in the thyroid gland** - To prevent this (in the event of fallout) nutritional iodine is taken to fill the gland (**gets there in 6 hours & stays for months**).

- **HEAVY METALS** again in the form of radioactive isotopes accumulate & **lodge in living tissues, particularly bones** - Thus oral calcium is taken to minimize space in the skeleton for contaminants.

COMBATING ITS EFFECTS (B):

- **RADIATION** results in the release of free radicals & electrons within living tissues cells, resulting in progressive, destructive degeneration.

- **CERTAIN VITAMINS**, minerals & other nutritional aids can combat & absorb destructive elements, among these are vits. **A, C, E & B Complex & Zinc, Selenium, Lecithin, Germanium, Royal Jelly, Ginseng, Pectin, Rutin & Seaweed.**

- **THERAPEUTIC DOSES** (in the event of exposure to high levels of radioactivity) are high (e.g.: Vit A* up to 150,000 units/day [six days/wk.] Vit E up to 1,000 IU/day, Vit C 5,000+/day. (*pregnancy caution)

- **EXTRA PROTECTION** & therapy have been proven from (amongst others): POSITIVE OUTLOOK, HYPNOSIS, MACROBIOTIC DIETS, YOGA, EXERCISE ETC.

- **PENETRATION:** Earth's atmosphere stops as much ionising radiation as **3 ft. of solid lead,** but particles from outer space have been detected penetrating **A MILE UNDER GROUND.**

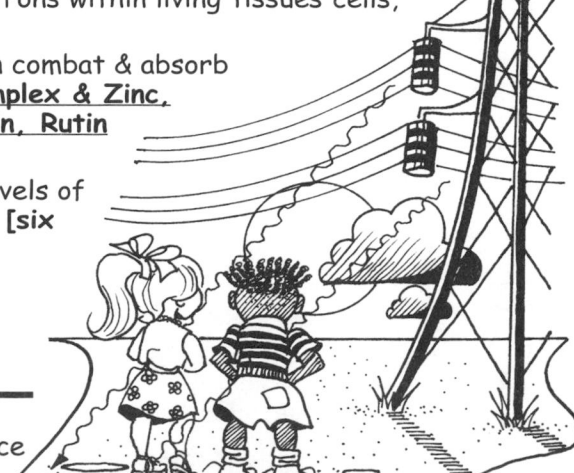

Quick Reference Guide To Common Health Problems For Kids

NAME	SYMPTOM	REMARKS
ALLERGY	• Various including eczema, asthma, dermatitis etc.	• Isolate (by elimination) the problem item. Common problems: Cows milk, wheat, house dust etc.
APPENDICITIS	• Pain mid to lower right tummy. Nausea.	• Difficult to diagnose, Surgery is common.
ASTHMA	• Wheezing & coughing.	• Often heard/wheezing with a cold. Keep away from irritants: Dust, smoke etc.
ATHLETE'S FOOT	• Cracking & peeling between toes with raw patches under.	• **Highly contagious** fungal infection. Keep feet dry & powder. Boil socks & towels daily.
BRONCHITIS	• Similar to chest cold which does not go. Phlegm.	• **Infectious.** Maintain even temp. In recovery, drink plenty. Clean air & good diet help.
BALANITIS	• Inflammation on end of penis.	• Caused by poor hygiene, pull foreskin back and wash daily.
BED WETTING	• Common problem, restrict drinking in P.M., get child up at say 10 pm, 12 pm & 3 am, keep stress for child low. Leave small light on.	
CONSTIPATION	• Usually caused by shortage of liquid &/or fruit/juice/fiber. Massage anus with Vaseline.	
CHICKEN POX	• Feel unwell. Raised pink spots mainly on face & trunk, then watery blisters, then itchy scabs (Also fever & appetite loss).	• Incubation: 1 -2 weeks. **Infectious.** Drink plenty. Don't scratch. Use calamine lotion.
CRADLE CAP	• Scaly crust on scalp & forehead.	• Mainly affects infants. Apply oil, leave to soften, shampoo.
CROUP	• Difficult breathing with croaking wheeze.	• Humidity & warmth help - Steam from kettle. Keep child calm.
CYSTITIS	• Frequent passing of water which hurts. Girls more than boys.	• Keep clean. Girls wipe front to back.
DEFIANCE	• Talking infants worse. Want to test parents. With important things be firm. Use psychology.	
DIAPER RASH	• Change often. Leave open to air when possible. Use a barrier cream, (thrush is a fungal rash).	
EARACHE	• Caution: may be "referred" pain from elsewhere, otherwise hold warmth to ear & give aspirin.	
ECZEMA	• Rash, itching, dry, red patches. Sometimes blisters & weeps.	• Caused by allergy - Find irritant (perhaps cows milk). Don't use soap. Cut nails short. Warm bath. Apply lotion.
EYES — CONJUNCTIVITIS	• Red eye(s). Irritation.	• **Contagious.** Bathe from center out with warm water. Sunglasses.
EYES — STYES	• Eyelid sore with developing spot.	• Bring to head with warm water. Ointment/drops.
FEBRILE CONVULSIONS	• Fit with red face. Rigid twitching.	• **Don't panic.** Don't interfere- Caused by high temp in child - Cool after.
FEVER	• Children more prone to but recover faster. Take temp often (infants in bottom). Should be 98.6 degrees F: (37 degrees C). Temps over 103 degrees F: Strip & tepid sponge down till 100 Degrees F.	
GERMAN MEASLES	• Spreading rash of small pink raised spots from top down. Incubation 2 -3 weeks. Neck glands may swell. Rash lasts 1 - 2 days.	• **Infectious. In pregnancy dangerous.**

"MMUMMY TTUMMY...."

A TRAVELER'S VERY BASIC GUIDE TO KIDS' AILMENTS
Kids Turn Up With An Amazing Variety Of Bugs - Check This List First

NAME	SYMPTOM	REMARKS
GASTRO-ENTERITIS	● Nausea, stomachache, temperature, diarrhoea, (bacterial infection).	● **Infectious.** Give lots of liquid but no food till nausea/diarrhoea stop. **Dangerous in babies.**
HEAD LICE	● Itchy minute white eggs stuck on hair.	● **Easily spread to others** by contact/use of combs/towels etc. - Treat all family with suitable insecticide & use nit comb.
HEAT — RASH	● Multiple pinhead eruptions on pores (pink or red). Itchy.	● Tepid bath. Calamine lotion. No wool or nylon.
HEAT — STROKE	● Red face. Very high temp. (102 - 108 degrees F). Fast pulse.	● **Dangerous.** Strip & cool down (ideally in tepid bath).
HERNIA	● Protruding lump on tummy or groin.	● If lump in groin or different color get help soon. Correctable by surgery.
IMPETIGO	● Red spots to weeping yellow crusts which heal from center out on face, scalp, hands.	● **Very infectious** bacteria. Usually requires antibiotic ointment/capsules.
MEASLES	● Starts like a cold. White spots inside mouth. Red sore eyes. Blistering red rash lasting 3 - 4 days. High temp.	● As rash appears (head to upper body) temp up (tepid sponge if necessary). Plenty to drink. Aspirin (or similar).
MUMPS	● Fever, earache, swollen glands under ear, sore throat. Incubation 7 - 14 days.	● **Viral infection.** Drink plenty of liquids & eat mushy foods. Aspirin.
NOSEBLEED	● Sit at table with head slightly forward. Pinch nose closed 10 minutes (don't blow nose). Dry nose inside can cause nosebleed. Use Vaseline.	
PYLORIC STENOSIS	● Construction in tummy causing projectile vomit. Victim hungry.	● Consult physician.
RINGWORM	● Rash of round patches of dry skin healing from center out (on head bald rings) (also athlete's foot).	● **Very contagious** from people & animals. See doctor.
SCABIES	● Rash of small blisters & zigzag lines usually on hands, arms, waist.	● **A mite easily caught from people,** pets, bedding. Very itchy. See doc. Wash clothes/linens.
SCARLET FEVER	● Very sore throat. Fever. Headache. Flushed face. Peeling rash (also tongue).	● **Contagious throat condition.** Plenty of liquids. Rest. Usually requires antibiotics.
THREAD WORMS	● 1/2 inch thread size intestine worms. See in motions. Come out of anus at night. Very itchy. Stomachache.	● **Spread by touch, seats, toys,** bedclothes etc. Egg can live 3 weeks. Take suitable oral purge.
TONSILITIS	● Temp. Swollen neck glands. Red tonsils with spots on. Can be viral or bacterial. May last a week or more.	● **Infectious.** Liquids & soft food. Aspirin. Take temp. often & if over 102 degrees give tepid sponge down.
TOOTHACHE	● Pain from teeth coming thru gum is most common. ● Put covered hot water bottle on cheek. Aspirin. Oil of cloves in missing filling hole.	
TRAVEL SICKNESS	● Psychology important: Don't mention it before & treat casually if it occurs. No greasy food. Fresh air. Look at horizon. Sleep. Dry crackers. Don't read.	
URINE INFECTION	● Varied symptoms from: Nothing, pain, frequent urinating, dark, smelly, dribbling, fever etc.	● Take urine sample for laboratory testing.
WHOOPING COUGH	● Persistent dry cough (whoop at end) & vomit. Fever. Can last for weeks	● Easily spread by air. **Dangerous in infants,** (food & drink after coughing).

THE SCHOLAR RETURNS.. ..VIA THE POND!

Don't Smack. Motivate & Discipline With This Simple System

We all want the best for "our" children - Let us try to set a good example, & hope they will do better than our poor efforts.

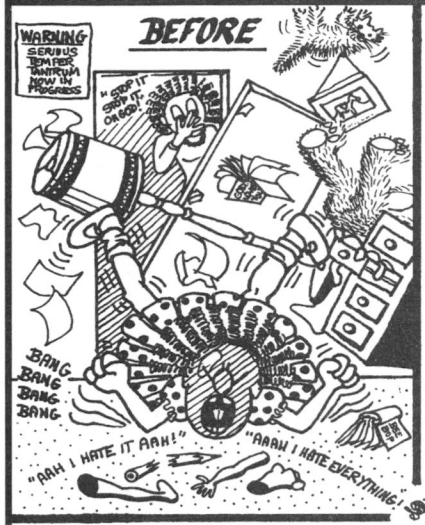

HISTORY. <u>THIS SYSTEM WAS DEVISED</u> (*& TORTURE TESTED*) by a harassed parent (me) who though not against corporal punishment as such, preferred not to use it if other means of discipline were possible.

LOGIC. <u>AS ADULTS WE SHOULD</u> be able to mentally out-maneuver children & maintain reasonable order, without resorting to violence. **This is a test of our own ingenuity & self-control** & is perhaps **OUR MOST IMPORTANT LESSON** to the children we look after.

BASICS. <u>IN ORDER TO INITIATE THE SYSTEM</u> we must first determine what each child wants. Is it ice cream, T.V. programs, visit friends, a doll, pocket money etc. It doesn't matter (**we all want something**) the list is as varied as are people....As we must all work, or pay (in some form) our way thru life to hopefully achieve our desires, <u>THEN WE PRESENT THIS PRINCIPLE OF LIFE TO OUR CHARGES IN A MANNER THEY CAN UNDERSTAND</u>, & with a goal they can attain by efforts proportional to their abilities.

EXAMPLE 1. <u>IN ITS SIMPLEST FORM</u> (with a very young child) it might be "Eat your vegetables & you can have some ice cream after - If you don't, sorry you won't!" - *THIS MAY INITIALLY INVOKE A TEMPER TANTRUM*, but if you "stick to your guns" will achieve results perhaps the next day.

EXAMPLE 2. "<u>SON, IF YOU WANT A T.V.</u> in your room then you will have to work for it as I did when buying this house." However, I will help by paying you a certain number of points for jobs (such as wash and put away breakfast dishes = 5 plus points) or school achievements (such as grade A on Friday math tests = 50 plus points) etc. - "<u>THESE POINTS YOU CAN EITHER CONVERT TO POCKET MONEY</u> on Saturday, at 1 plus point = 1 cent, <u>OR YOU CAN SAVE THEM UP</u> until you get 500 when I will put a T.V. in your room."

DOING IT. <u>THE ONLY MATERIALS YOU NEED</u> are a pocket-size notebook, pen & a little perseverance. - Tom (7 yrs) & sister Lucy (9 yrs) on a school day wake up at 6:30, read some comics, get up, dress, make beds & report to Dad at 7:15 (or get I minus point/min for being late) (Tom by the way has a problem with wee wee in bed which costs him 50 minus points if he does it, but gets 50 plus points if dry for 7 nights in a row) . At 7:15 they all do breathing exercises (for which the children get 4 plus points each (less [even minus] if not done well). At 7:30 Lucy who is on duty at breakfast (7 plus points/meal) lays the table. During the first part of the meal the children test each other with 20 questions on the times tables (for which they get 4 plus points for no mistakes). After math, if they have no minus points, they can watch T.V. but must finish all their meal by 8:00 or get minus points at 1/min). Lucy dries dishes & cleans up, prior to departing for school at 8:45. They must clean teeth (2 plus) & read out loud for 5 mins (max. 3 plus).

THE CHILDREN know all their jobs & keep track of how many plus points they have accumulated & are always asking to have them entered in the book (the adult enters minus pts. in the book when incurred but only enters plus points at certain times (usually at a meal or bedtime).

SAMPLE REWARD & PENALTY VALUES FOR 6 - 10 YEARS OLD.
(Change to suit age & circumstances)

PLUS POINTS (+)							MINUS POINTS (-)						
Number of points		1/2	1	10	20	100	Number of points		1/2	1	10	20	100
Write in book as		1	+	'1'	'2'	'10'	Write in book as		•	–	1̂	2̂	1̂0
● **Return** from school before 3:15						4	● **Wasting** toilet paper (per sheet)						1
● **Ready** for school first						1	● **Reporting** late per min						1
● **Per** glass of milk						2	● **Crying** per min						1
● **Eat** vitamins first						2	● **Bad** manners at table						2
● **Do** exercises properly						1-4	● **Bad** tempered						3
● **Tidy** bedroom (each night)						1-4	● **Answering** back						3
● **Good** posture (per day)						1-4	● **Not** doing what told quickly						4
● **Vacuum** clean one room						3	● **Lifting** girls' skirts up (Tom)						5
● **Go** to local shop to buy milk						5	● **Fiddling** with things in shops						5
● **Wash** dishes & clean up						7	● **Hitting** first						7
● **Add** up cost of shopping right						2-10	● **Crossing** road without looking						9
● **Water** garden properly						6	● **Being** selfish or greedy						3
● **Top** of class (any subject)						100	● **Leaving** light on (empty room)						3
● **2nd** in class (any subject)						50	● **Writing** in reading books						15
● **3rd** in class (any subject)						25	● **Writing** on walls/cupboards						10-30
● **Win** school race						100	● **Hitting** (people) with things						20
● **2nd** in school race						50	● **Playing** with electricity						30
● **3rd** in school race						25	● **Wee** wee in bed						30
● **No** wee wee in bed (7 nights)						50	● **Lying**						100
● **Saturday** bonus (7 days over zero+)						25	● **Stealing**						100

NOTES

● *Make your own list of rewards & penalties to suit the child.*

● **TRY TO KEEP** the level of plus or minus reasonable (i.e.. try not to go over a couple of hundred as they can get **bigheaded** [too many pluses] **or discouraged** [too many minuses]).

● **LINK THE FACT** of their total being plus (above zero) or minus (below) deciding if they are eligible to do some favorite daily pastime (i.e.. watch T.V., play with friends, stay up later etc.).

● **WHEN SETTING UP** the system discuss the number of + or - for each item with the child (treat them as a grown-up). **Explain that you want them to have the things they want but like everyone else they must earn them.**

● **POCKET MONEY** should be paid on Saturday according to how many plus points the child has (i.e. 43 plus points = 43 cents) the total then goes to zero.

● *P.S. in real life Tom & Lucy are now both top of their classes in math.*

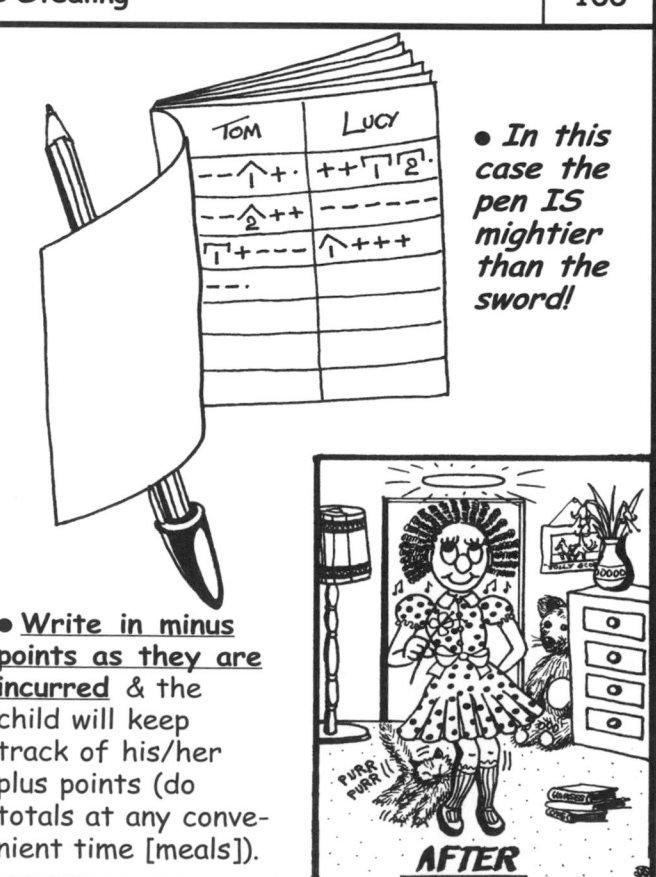

● *In this case the pen IS mightier than the sword!*

● **Write in minus points as they are incurred** & the child will keep track of his/her plus points (do totals at any convenient time [meals]).

AFTER

CAUTION: Only use in desperate situations - Such as ....

Famous Books

- <u>Repairing Toilets</u> by Justin Time.
- <u>Growing Rice</u> by I. Flung Dung.
- <u>Wine Tasting</u> by M. T. Bottle.
- <u>Slim with Hypnosis</u> by U. R. Thinner.
- <u>Survive at Sea</u> by M. M. Mayday.
- <u>Caribbean Church Buses</u> by Rev. D. Engin.
- <u>Caribbean Shipwrecks</u> by Mandy Lifeboats
- <u>The 39 Steps</u> by Legs. R. A. Kin.
- <u>Dodgey Dynamite</u> by B. Igbang.

☐ Doctor Doctor....

.... people keep ignoring me!".
— *"Next please."*
.... I've lost my memory!" — *"When did it happen?"* — "When did what happen?"
.... I think I'm a $100 bank note!".
— *"Go shopping, the change will do you good."*
.... will these pills cure me?" — *"Well, no one ever returned for more."*
.... how much do you charge for teaching a split personality?" — *"$20 each."*
...... I think I'm going deaf!" — *"What makes you say that?"* — "No thank you"

Rude Irish Jokes

- "How do you sink an Irish submarine?
  — *Knock on the door while it's under water."*
- "How do you burn an Irishman's ear?
  — *Ring him up while he's ironing."*
- "How do you get a one armed Irish man out of a tree?
  — *Wave to him."*

Rude Scottish Jokes

- "How do you make a Scotsman run a mile?
  — *Roll a penny down a steep hill."*
- "How do you get a Scotsman to leave a party?
  — *Put a hole in a can & start collecting for charity."*
- "Why did the Scotsman drive his car to Iraq?
  — *To fill up his tank with cheap gas."*

Sick Jokes

- "What goes Peck, Peck, Boom?
  — *A chicken in a mine field."*
- "Did you hear about the dog's skeleton?
  — *It kept burying itself."*
- "A blind man was swinging his dog in a circle — when asked what he was doing, he replied, *"Having a look around!"*
- "What goes Ho, Ho, Plop?
  — *Santa laughing his head off."*
- "Did you hear about the karate expert that joined the army?
  — *The first time he saluted he killed himself."*
- "What's worse than finding a worm in your apple?
  — *Finding half a worm."*

Rude English Jokes

- "Why did the English bank robber get caught?
  — *He left his umbrella in the bank, then went to the police station to claim it."*
- On a hot summer's day, 2 Dorset yokels were slowly

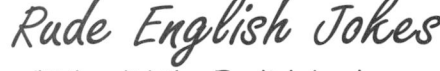

nailing planks on the side of a barn, when one started throwing some nails away — *"Ar!"* said the other, *"Why be you doin' that?"* — *"Aar!"* said the nail thrower. *"The point be on the wrong end."* — *"Aaar!"* said the clever one (swatting a blue-assed fly) *"You be gettin' stupid, we can use them wrong nails on the other side of this 'ere barn."* — The nail throwers brow furrowed, as his brain struggled with this plan — *"Aaaar!"* he mumbled sheepishly & taking off his grubby cap started putting the wrong-end nails in it.

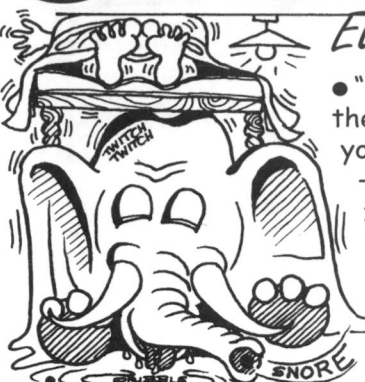

Elephant Jokes

● "How do you know when there's an elephant under your bed?
— *Your nose is touching the ceiling.*"

● "Why is it dangerous to go in the jungle between 11 & 12 o'clock at night?
— *Because the elephants are having parachute practice.*"

● "Why are alligators flat on top?
— *Because they went in the jungle between 11 & 12 o'clock at night.*"

● "What do you do if an elephant sneezes?
— *Get out of the way.*"

● "What has 16 wheels & is a traffic policeman's worst nightmare?
— *An elephant on roller skates.*"

How Jokes

● "How do you know if a hippo sits next to you at school?
— *He has an "H" on his pencil case.*"

● "How do you stop a kid jumping on the bed?
— *Put glue on the ceiling.*"

● "How do you know if your teacher loves you?
— *She puts kisses next to your sums.*"

● "How do you stop a dog barking in the kitchen?
— *Put it in the hall.*"

Kids' Choices

● "What did the robot say to the gas pump? — *Take your finger out of your ear when I'm talking to you.*"

● "What's slimy & hangs from trees?
— *Giraffe snot.*" †

● "What's the difference between a letterbox & a cow's bottom?"
— "Don't know" — *"Well then I wouldn't let you post my letters.*" †

● "What do you call a 10-foot monster with long claws? — *Sir.*"

● "Did you hear about the dentist that got hiccups?
— *His drill slipped & he became a brain surgeon.*"

What Jokes

● "What's the first thing a monster eats after it had a tooth out?
— *The dentist.*"

● "What's green & wobbles? — *A lizard on a tightrope.*"

● "What did one flea on Robinson Crusoe say to the other flea? — *Bye for now, see you on Friday.*"

● "What's black & white & bounces?
— *A penguin on a pogo stick.*"

● "What time is it when a ghost comes to dinner?
— *Time to go.*"

● "What is black & white & noisy?
— *A zebra with a drum.*"

● "What has one horn & gives milk?
— *A milk delivery van.*"

● "What begins with "P" & has hundreds of letters?
— *A postman.*"

● "What do you say to a two-headed monster?
— *Hello hello.*"

Why Jokes

● "Why are Siberian dogs such fast runners?
— *Because the trees are so far apart.*"

● "Why was the Egyptian confused?
— *Because his daddy was a mummy!*"

● "Why is "6" scared of "7"? — *Because 7, 8, 9.*"

● "Why do some elephants paint their toenails yellow?
— *So that they can hide upside-down in bowls of custard.*"

● "Why did the rooster cross the road?
— *To show he wasn't chicken.*"

☐ Knock Knock....☐

● "Who's there?" — *"Wendy-"* — "Wendy who?" — *"Wendy heck you gonna open de door?*"

● "Who's there?" — *"Madam."* — "Madam who?" — *"Madam finger is stuck in de keyhole.*"

● "Who's there?" — *"Stan."* — "Stan who?" — *"Stan back I got a battering ram.*"

† kids only

— OUTDOOR THINGS —

- "WHY DID EINSTEIN'S DAD always wear sunglasses? - *Because his kid was too bright!*"

"HOPSCOTCH"

- <u>Draw with chalk or crayon</u> your court as shown.
- <u>Players take turns</u> to hop on one foot.
- <u>If any player hops</u> to the highest number & back without a mistake (i.e. step on a line or put other foot down) they can claim any space by writing an initial in it which means <u>that player can put both feet in it</u> but all other players must hop over it.
- <u>When a player makes a mistake</u>, or writes their initial, it is the next players turn.
- <u>When all spaces have initials</u> in, then anyone making a mistake is out, & THE LAST IS THE WINNER.

"SUM CAN RUN"

- <u>All players (except fastest,</u> who is the Caller) stand behind a line at one end of game area.
- <u>A math sum is called out,</u> & if correct, everyone (except the Caller) runs to a line at the other end (last to arrive becomes the Caller).
- <u>If the sum is wrong,</u> no one must move, & if they do, the player who moved the furthest becomes the Caller.
- <u>A player is out</u> when they have been a Caller 3 times.
- <u>Winner is</u> last player remaining.
- <u>This game</u> can also be played with other subjects.

INDOOR THINGS

- "2 MEN FELL OFF THE PIER into the sea but only 1 got his hair wet, why didn't the other? - *Because he was bald!*"

"RUBBER GUN FIGHT"

- <u>Get a supply of rubber bands</u> & a row of match boxes lined up about 1 meter away & arrange your own championship
- <u>You need bands</u> about 1 1/2 times the length of your index finger - The little finger is the trigger.

"THE WORLD MEMORY CHAMPION"

- <u>For any number of players.</u>
- <u>Spread all cards facedown</u> on the table (not touching).
- <u>First player</u> turns over any 2 - If they match (i.e. 2 queens, 2 tens, 2 twos etc.) then he/she keeps them & has another go - If not then he/she turns them back facedown (in the same place) & the next player tries.
- <u>When all cards</u> have been claimed as pairs then the player with the most *wins.*

"WIN YOUR LUCKY DAY NOW!"

- <u>Play this by yourself</u> (but friends can watch & play it after).
- <u>Take all tens out</u> (not needed).
- <u>Shuffle</u> the other 48 cards & layout 16 cards in 4 rows of 4 faceup.
- <u>Then throw out</u> either a) J, Q, K (same suit) or b) any others which add up to 15 (e.g. 6 & 9 or ace [1], 3, 4 & 7 [same suit] which are showing & replace them with others from the pack. • <u>The idea</u> is to throw out all cards in this manner, & if you do *you win your*........

LUCKY DAY

ANYWHERE THINGS

"SQUARK!" "LEGO CAT" "SQUARK"

"MEOW HISS LEGO BIRD HISS!"

● **"What did your father say** when you were first sent to jail?" said the vicar — "Hello, Son!" said the crook.

"HOW TO ... WIN A BET EVEN WITH DAD"

"OK PAY UP" "NO NO" "NO NO"

● **You need a BIG sheet** of paper (try newspaper) & you say: *"Hey Dad, how many times do you think you could fold this sheet of newspaper in half?"*

● **He will almost certainly say** *"Well, Ha Ha, something like 15 maybe 20 times."*

● **But you being** EXTREMELY **smart** & clever know that there is no way that he is going to fold it more than ten times so - **MAKE YOUR BET NOW.**

"HOW TO MAKE YOUR AUNT FAINT"

● **WHEN TO DO IT**....Very useful when your Aunt is not giving you enough ice cream - So you move close & holding your nose as shown say, *"I may break my nose"* .... "CLICK" .... & you go ...."AHHHH!" as she goes "AHHEEEE!"

● VERY SMALL & MEAN PORTION!
● VERY LARGE & GREEDY PORTION!

ZONK!   CLICK!

● **HOW TO DO IT**.... Hook thumbnail behind front tooth & flick forward (move hands so it looks real).

How To Play "JACK OF HEARTS" And Win.

1.
2.
3.
4.
5. A. B. C.

● **Decide what you are going to play for** (say 1 marble each or 2 football cards each), winner takes all.

● **Get 5 pebbles** (not round) or similar.

1. First player puts all 5 in palm & flips them up ......
2. ...... then turn your hand over & try to catch them on the back ......
3. ...... then flip those you caught up again & ......
4. ...... turn your hand to catch them in the palm, & the number you caught is your score ...... unless, if you dropped any, you can (but don't have to), have up to that many extra tries to pick the fallen ones up by ......
5a. ..... flipping those already on your hand up in the air, & while they are still in the air ......
5b. ...... turn your hand & try to pick up 1 (at a time) of those on the floor, before quickly ......
5c. ...... turning your hand back (with the one you picked up) palm up, to catch the ones in the air!

● **Then it is the next players turn** & highest score **WINS.**

Are You "KING OF THE CASTLE" ??

"YEAH! WANNA MAKE SOMETHING OF IT?"

● **Shoot like this.**
● **Draw** (or tape) **a line** (to shoot from), & 5 ft away a circle (2 ft in dia.) (the moat).

● **Pick a King**, who piles 4 marbles (the castle) in the center of the circle.

● **Each player** shoots 4 marbles at the castle, & keeps any knocked outside the moat.

● **After 4 shots** the King has to rebuild the castle but keeps all marbles inside the moat area.

● **If a shooter does not hit the castle** in 4 shots, he/she must pay the King one marble.

● Players take turns being *King.*

"HOW TO SETTLE ANY ....ARGUMENT"

● **Don't fight**, punch, kick or shout "Warty Pigface" — Instead:

● **Settle it in pairs.** Each "Warty Pigface" puts 1 hand behind their backs, & both count to three together.

● **On 3 both bring their hands out**, as Rock, Scissors or Paper, & see who wins.

● **If both** are the same, do it again.

ROCK   "BASH!"

ROCK BLUNTS SCISSORS.

SCISSORS   "CUT!"

SCISSORS CUT PAPER.

PAPER   "WRAP!"

PAPER COVERS ROCK.

"OINK SNIFF OINK!"

Invaluable for: Transforming traumatized children, communicating without speaking, entertaining old friends and winning one-sided bets.

BEFORE YOU START

- **SECRECY:** <u>Don't reveal how your tricks are done to anyone</u> (except another magician - who you can swap tricks with). • **PRACTICE** <u>all your tricks alone</u> in front of a mirror, with the "patter" (talk) that goes with each. • **TALK** <u>when you want to divert your audiences</u> attention away from your hands as they will usually look at your face.
- **LOOK** <u>only where you want your audience to look</u>, as they tend to follow your eyes.
- **PROPS** (<u>Things you need for tricks</u>) - keep yours in a locked bag or box. • **MAGIC WAND** (<u>Make it black</u> with white or silver ends, about 15 inches long)
- **MAGIC HANDKERCHIEF** (<u>Every magician needs one</u>) - Make it shiny, colored & with seamed edges.
- **MAGIC WORD** (<u>Think of your own</u>) - Try taking the first one or two letters from the front of your name & put a "Z" - & add an "A" at the end - So Tom becomes *"Zoma."*

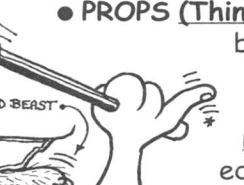

"ZOMA!"

WILD BEAST

* IMPORTANT NOTE: OBSERVE POSITION OF LITTLE FINGER.

BOING!

"MADAME X"

" HOUDINI'S LOOP"

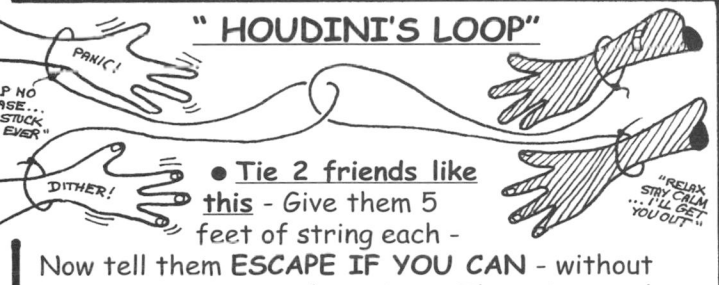

PANIC!

"HELP NO PLEASE... I'M STUCK FOR EVER"

DITHER!

"RELAX STAY CALM ...I'LL GET YOU OUT"

- **Tie 2 friends like this** - Give them 5 feet of string each -
Now tell them **ESCAPE IF YOU CAN** - without untying the wrists - There is a way!
- **If, (when) they give up**, it is done like this.

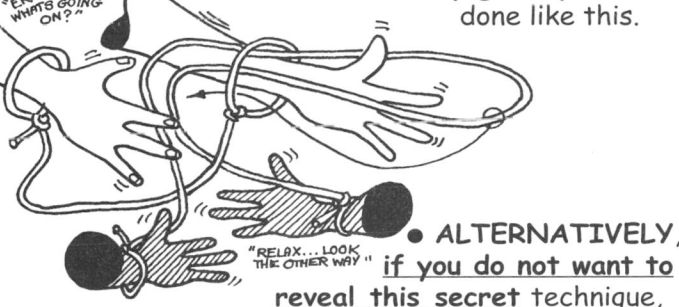

"ER WAIT... WHATS GOING ON?"

"RELAX... LOOK THE OTHER WAY"

- **ALTERNATIVELY,** <u>if you do not want to reveal this secret</u> technique, you can do it as an escape trick - Tie yourself to any pair of solid objects (as if they were the wrists of another person) then turn your back on the audience for a moment *to escape.*

"MERLIN'S BOX"

- **Take an empty box** and glue a partition in the middle, & put a dot at one end - A quarter open the box & show it is empty, then ask a spectator to drop in a small object (button, ring etc.) -
- **Close box**, cover it with magic handkerchief and say magic word. - Whisk handkerchief away & carefully open box from other end! - *gone!*

MATCH CO

"ALADDINS BOX"

- **Take an empty box** & insert the stick end of several matches between the cover and top of tray
- **With box half open** show spectator the inside & hold upsidedown & shake
- **Then close box carefully**, put on table & cover with magic handkerchief - Say magic word, whisk handkerchief away & *open box slowly! - Matches!*

LOOKS EMPTY

HAPPY, SMART, COOL

"WRONG WRONG WRONG!"

ANGRY, MIXED UP, BAFFLED

DAD

- **Take 4 match boxes** & half fill 2 with matches - Secretly attach one of those (with matches in) under your sleeve - Put the other 3 on the table & show audience that 2 are empty & one has matches in - Shuffle them around & pick up one (<u>without matches in</u>) & shake it (with the arm having the 4th box on) - it will rattle - Tell audience to watch it carefully - & move them around on the table (<u>this time not too fast</u>) - Ask a volunteer to choose the one with matches in - They will of course get it wrong because *they have followed an empty box!*

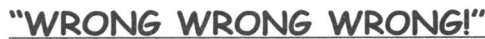

LAST COIN

"MISS X"

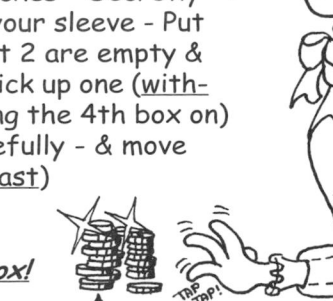

TAP TAP!

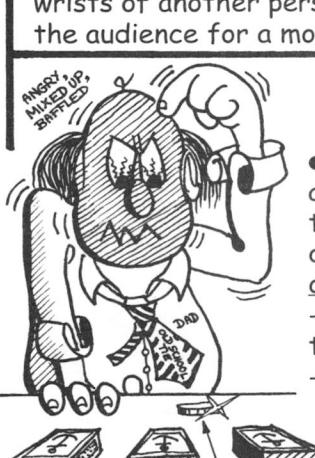

↳ ALL THIS WON FROM DAD.

"MIND READER"

● TAKE ANY 15 CARDS from the pack & deal face up in 3 piles of 5 each (but deal 1, 2, 3 & 1, 2, 3 etc. - or trick won't work). ● Ask a volunteer to pick any card but only tell you what pile it was in. ● Gather up the cards with the chosen pile in the middle of the other two. ● Repeat this process twice more (3 times in all), BUT on the last time pick up only the chosen pile & put it behind your back. ● Now ask volunteer to think hard of chosen card. You utter the magic word & extract the center card from the 5 behind your back. - Hold it up - DA DAAR!

"GAMBLERS GOLD"

● ASK VOLUNTEER to shuffle cards. ● When you take them back SNEAK a look at the bottom card. ● Spread cards on the table face down & ask volunteer to pick one up & memorize it. ● As they pick up the card you gather the pack (then all in one smooth motion) ask volunteer to put their card on top of pack, then cut. ● YOU then put the bottom of pack (with your memorized card) on top of volunteers card. ● Then you dramatically start to turn over cards from the top of the pack until you come to your card (the volunteer's card is the next one). ● BEWARE: It is common practise amongst tricksters to keep turning over cards after that of the volunteer is reached (but to say nothing) & then to BET MONEY that the next card turned will be the volunteer's! ● Then go back several cards & pick out & turn the volunteers card.

"MATH MYSTERY"

● WRITE THE NUMBER 4 on a paper, fold it small & give to volunteer. ● Ask them to think of any number under 20. ● Add 5. ● Double it. ● Take away 2. ● Half it. ● Take away the number they first thought of. Ask the volunteer to say their answer out loud. ● Unfold piece of paper!

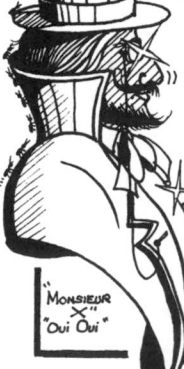

"THE GHOUL'S GOLD"

● CASUALLY DROP a few (say 4 -8) coins on the table & remember how many heads are up (odd or even number). ● Turn your back & ask a volunteer to turn the coins over as many times as they want. BUT it must always be 2 at a time (or the spell is broken). ● Now ask volunteer to choose any coin & cover it with their hand. ● Turn round & MYSTICALLY EXAMINE the coins (wave your hand over them) - If the number of heads now showing is even & was odd before - or was even before & is now odd - The hidden coin is a head. ● HOWEVER If the number of heads now showing is odd (& was odd before) or is even (& was even before) then the hidden coin is a tail.

"BALLOON BRAIN"

● SECRETLY WRITE the number 1089 on a slip of paper, roll it up, put in balloon & blow it up. ● Place balloon in full view & ask someone for any 3 different digits 1 - 9 & write them on a blackboard (e.g. 1, 5, 2). ● Reverse the digits & take the smaller number from the larger. ● Reverse the answer & add that figure to the answer. ● Pick up the balloon & with your magic wand write 1089 in the air & say your magic word.

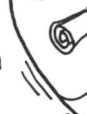
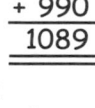

```
  251
- 152
-----
  099
+ 990
-----
 1089
```

● GIVE A PIN to the volunteer & ask them to pop the balloon & read the slip of paper inside. ● NOTE: do this trick only once per audience as the answer is always the same.

"BANANA SPLIT"

● HOW DO YOU SLICE a banana without peeling it? ● Everyone will probably say impossible. ● Take a ripe banana (with brown spots) into another room & push a toothpick thru the skin at regular intervals & move it from side to side as shown. ● Smooth off the marks & take the banana back into the other room & ask someone to peel it - SURPRISE!

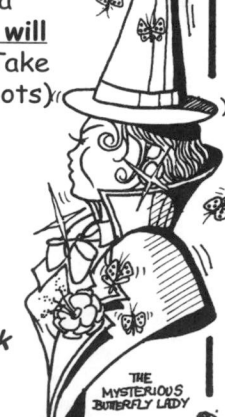

The Simplified Interpretation Of Personality From Hand Features

Palmistry requires the accumulation of all possible clues (contradictory & collaboratory) before reaching a conclusion.

FEATURE NAMES

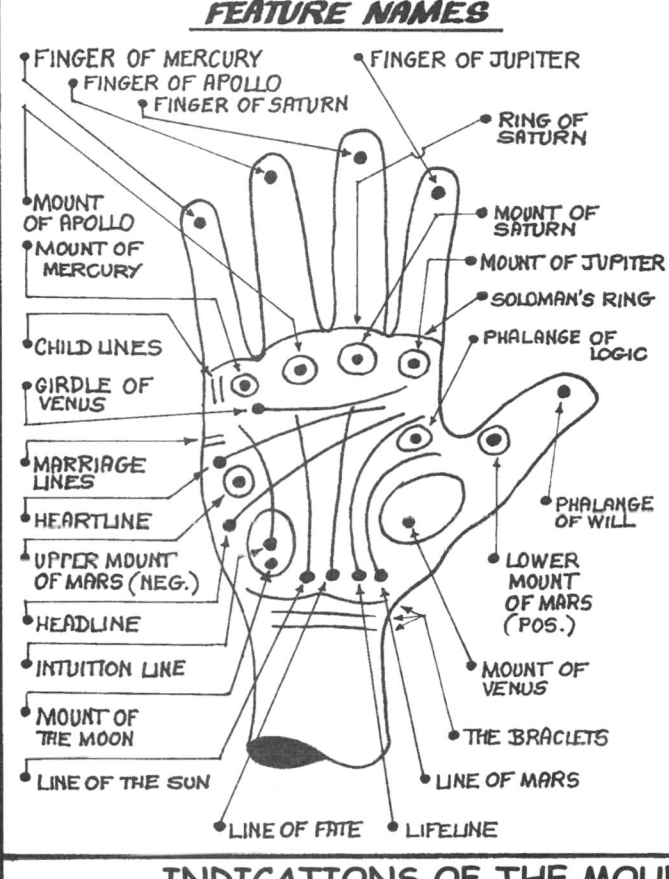

- FINGER OF MERCURY
- FINGER OF APOLLO
- FINGER OF SATURN
- FINGER OF JUPITER
- RING OF SATURN
- MOUNT OF APOLLO
- MOUNT OF MERCURY
- MOUNT OF SATURN
- MOUNT OF JUPITER
- SOLOMAN'S RING
- PHALANGE OF LOGIC
- CHILD LINES
- GIRDLE OF VENUS
- MARRIAGE LINES
- HEARTLINE
- PHALANGE OF WILL
- UPPER MOUNT OF MARS (NEG.)
- LOWER MOUNT OF MARS (POS.)
- HEADLINE
- INTUITION LINE
- MOUNT OF VENUS
- MOUNT OF THE MOON
- THE BRACLETS
- LINE OF THE SUN
- LINE OF MARS
- LINE OF FATE
- LIFELINE

HAND TYPES

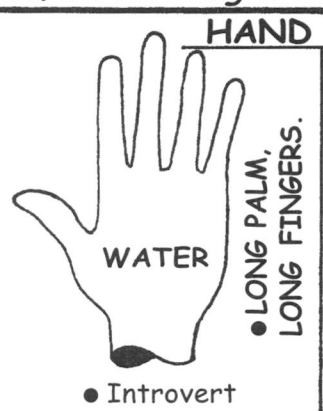

WATER — LONG PALM, LONG FINGERS.
- Introvert - Inventive - Emotional.

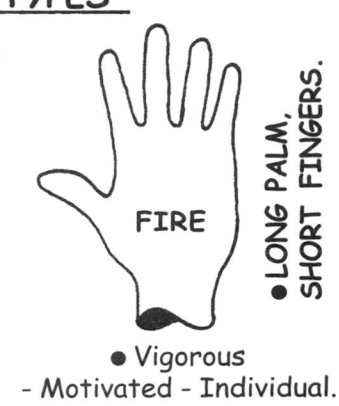

FIRE — LONG PALM, SHORT FINGERS.
- Vigorous - Motivated - Individual.

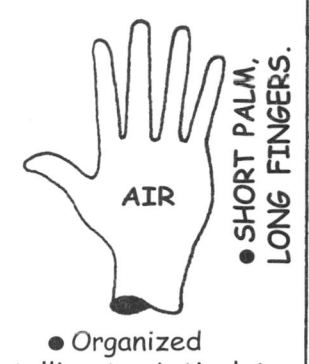

AIR — SHORT PALM, LONG FINGERS.
- Organized - Intelligent - Articulate.

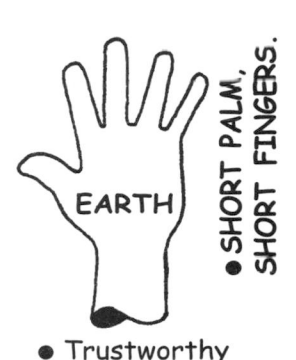

EARTH — SHORT PALM, SHORT FINGERS.
- Trustworthy - Practical - Reliable.

INDICATIONS OF THE MOUNTS (By Size)

Mount	Small	Medium	Large	Very Large
Venus	Introverted	Warm-hearted	Energetic	Hyperactive
L. Mars	Timid	Brave	Argumentative	Aggressive
Jupiter	Inconsiderate	Considerate	Selfish	Arrogant
Saturn	Ineffectual	Balanced	Gloomy	Suicidal
Apollo	Aimless	Fashionable	Pretentious	Egotistical
Mercury	Dull	Gregarious	Humorous	Trickster
U. Mars	Passive	Moralistic	Cantankerous	Sadistic
Moon	Unimaginative	Romantic	Dreamer	Irrational

NAIL SHAPES

SHORT & SQUARE Demanding, Physical, Opinionated.

BIG & SQUARE Introvert, Calm, Inflexible.

SMALL & ROUND Energetic, Creative, Curious.

WEDGE SHAPE Emotional, Romantic, Impulsive.

LONG & OVAL Intellectual, Sensitive, Affable.

INDICATIONS OF MARKS

#	Mark	Indication	Diagram
1	Break	Interruption	
2	Bar	Barrier	
3	Chain	Uncertainty	
4	Cross	Shock	
5	Double	Extra	
6	Fork	Diversion	
7	Thatch	Confusion	
8	Triangle	Good Luck	
9	Box	Protection	

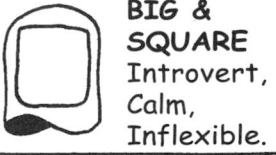
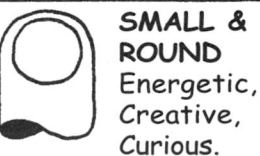
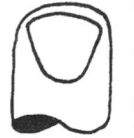
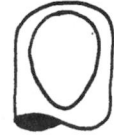

NAIL COLOURS

White	Anemia
Pink	Good Health
Red	Excess Protein
Yellow	Jaundice

HANDED

- If **right-handed:** Read left as what born with & right what have become.
- If **left-handed:** Reverse above.

♀ VENUS	♂ MARS	♃ JUPITER	♄ SATURN	☉ SUN	☿ MERCURY	☽ MOON

CORRESPONDING SYSTEMS

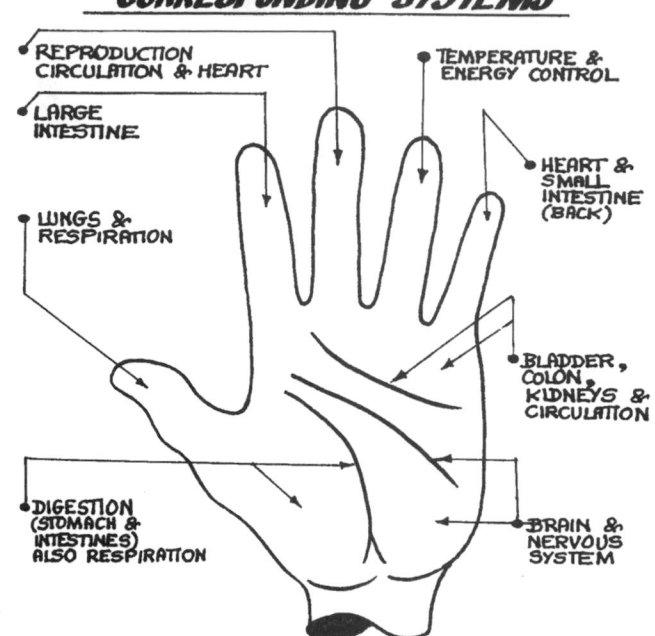

- REPRODUCTION CIRCULATION & HEART
- LARGE INTESTINE
- LUNGS & RESPIRATION
- DIGESTION (STOMACH & INTESTINES) ALSO RESPIRATION
- TEMPERATURE & ENERGY CONTROL
- HEART & SMALL INTESTINE (BACK)
- BLADDER, COLON, KIDNEYS & CIRCULATION
- BRAIN & NERVOUS SYSTEM

PALM COLORS

COLOR	POSSIBLE CAUSE
White - Pale	Anemia - Circulation
Yellow	Jaundice - Liver - Spleen
Purple	Too much sugar/fruit
Red	Circulation - Diet change

FINGERPRINTS

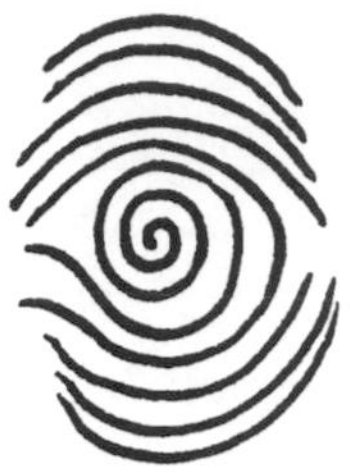

WHIRL
Solitary, Independent, Resourceful, Intelligent.

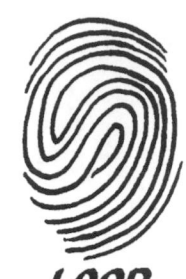

LOOP
Clever, Diplomatic, Reasonable, Logical.

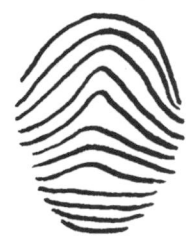

ARCH
Materialistic, Unromantic, Suspicious, Unflappable.

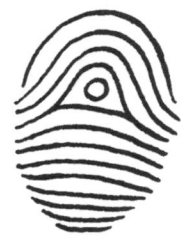

TENT
Creative, Nervous, Opinionated, Impulsive.

INDICATIONS OF THE LINES

HEART LINE
● Straight = Restrained ● Curved = Warm ● Breaks = Multiple Relationships ● Fork to Headline = Love & Business together ● Break Under 2nd or 3rd Finger = Rejected Love.

FATE LINE
● Straight = Good Life ● Breaks = Troubles ● No Line = No trouble ● Fork to Mercury = Money ● Wavy = Erratic Life ● Curve to Jupiter = Effort Pays Rewards ● Start From Moon = Travel.

HEAD LINE
● Long = Intelligent ● Straight = Judgement ● Distinct = Concentration ● Breaks = Traumas ● Fork to Apollo = Talent ● Fork to Mercury = Career ● Fork to Saturn = Ambitious ● Fork to Jupiter = Success.

LIFE LINE
● Long = Long Life ● Clear = Healthy ● Breaks (one hand) = Ill but well soon ● Breaks (two hands) = Worse Illness ● Fork to Sun = Talent ● Fork to Moon = Search for Change ● Fork to Saturn = Difficult Life.

LINE OF SUN (APOLLO)
● Straight & Clear = Luck & Charm ● Start from Moon = Magnetic Charm ● Start from Venus = Artistic ● No Line = Many Troubles ● Start at Heart Line = Contented Retirement.

SOLOMON'S RING (Round Base Of Index Finger)
● Can indicate outstanding potential.

INTUITION LINE
● Associated with the paranormal & can indicate considerable psychic ability.

BRACELETS
● Well defined & parallel lines indicate & long, healthy & prosperous life.

GIRDLE OF VENUS
● Clear = Emotion & Excitement ● Runs off Hand = Indecision ● None = Calm.

MARRIAGE LINES
● Clear & Long = Happy & Long Relationship ● End in Fork = Separation.

CHILD LINES
● Clear Lines = Male Offspring. ● Faint Lines = Female (add both hands & div. by two).

No two samples of handwriting are exactly the same - Each has a unique message - But add all parts before reaching a total.

LETTER SECTIONS

● **Handwriting analysis is initially divided into 3 (top, middle & bottom)** each section covering a group of indications as below.

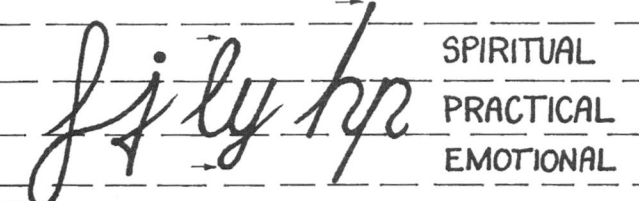

SPIRITUAL

PRACTICAL

EMOTIONAL

EXAMPLES

● **The lower loop of "f" is long & rounded,** indicating either a romantic or egotistical personality.

● **In the "J" the lower section is angular** & short, indicating an unhappy mental situation (perhaps sexual or love).

● **The "LY" is mainly in the middle section,** indicating a strong aspect of realism/family/home.

● **The high "h" indicates an idealistic** perhaps religious aspect.

● **The loopless "HP" shows single minded-ness** & fatalism, perhaps scientific abilities.

WRITING ANGLE

● The angle of writing is a good initial guide to personality.

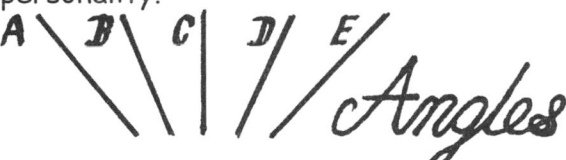

A = RECLUSIVE.   B = INTROVERT.
C = CONTROLLED.   D = SOCIABLE.
E = LOQUACIOUS.

● **Varied angles in one persons writing** indicates an erratic & impulsive personality.

PEN PRESSURE

A : LIGHT   **B** : MEDIUM   **C** : HEAVY

A = Sensitive, Particular, Frail.
B = Reasonable, Balanced.
C = Opinionated, Forceful.

● **Look at back of paper** for heavy pressure on certain words = Emotion.

SPACINGS

	WHAT	POSSIBLE MEANING
MARGINS	Big top.	Formal. Reserved.
	Small top.	Familiar. Careful with advance expenditure.
	Big bottom.	Apprehension of deep relationships (love, sex or business).
	Small left &/or bottom	Forward personality. Material hoarder.
	Wide left.	Educated. Aesthetical.
LINES	Big space between.	Organized but often generous spender.
	Small space Between.	Lack of forward planning &/or possible meanness.
WORDS	Big space Between.	Socially cautious. Discrimina-tory but not mean.
	Small space between.	Gregarious. Talkative. Possibly frugal.

WRITING SIZE

Small script	Educated. Rational. Organized. Investigative.
Medium script	Normal. Reasonable. Moderate characteristics.
Large script	Possible overbearing & egotistical personality.
Varied sizes	Erratic. Impulsive &/or short attention span.

WRITING SLOPE

The rain in Spain...... A

B falls mainly....

.. on the plain.. C

● **Unruled writing paper** is an excellent indication of the writer's frame of mind.

● A = **Indicates** a pessimistic & gloomy outlook on life.

● B = **Indicates** an optimistic & cheerful outlook on life.

● C = **Indicates** the writer is uncertain, impulsive, moody.

TEN SIGNATURE POINTS

- **Signature close to rest of text** = Involvement. Participation.
- **Signature far from text** = Individualistic. Independent.
- **Underlined Signature** = Individual. Egotistic (often driving personality).
- **Fancy with many flourishes** = Big ego. Perhaps loud & overbearing.
- **Encircled Signature** can indicate a pessimistic out look on life(even a suicidal urge).
- **Clearly written signatures** = Open. Usually honest. Conventional outlook on life.
- **Signatures written at a pronounced angle** = Pronounced, even aggressively, individualistic.
- **Lines/Flourishes thru the signature** & tiny signatures with small capitals indicate low self esteem, inferiority.
- **Closely grouped letters** indicate a limited perspective on life & an unwillingness to accept others' views.
- **Light pen pressure** indicates possible physical frailty. Illegible final letters = Short cuts to an end. (possibly unethical) &/or poor attention to detail.

LETTER CONNECTING LINES

- **Spidery & poorly formed** = Rapid thought, Wheeler-dealer (with limited attention to fine details).
- **Connecting lines that don't quite connect** = Easygoing but possibly lazy.
- **Connecting lines that form a peak** = Aesthetical. Formal. Suspicious. Private.
- **Connecting lines that are direct & firm** = Decisive. Opinionated. Persistent.
- **No connecting lines** = Individualistic. Opinionated. Introverted.

START & FINISH LINES

- **Starting line on words** = An element of living in the past.
- **Finishing lines on words** = Possibly lonely or socially dependent. (Does not want to go.)

IMPORTANT NOTE

- **Before concluding a character summary** decide if (for example) flourishes are egotistical or artistic? - & tiny figures (for example) are an inferiority complex or math training.

EXAMPLES OF SMALL LETTERS

Long dot on " i "		Critical
High faint dot on " i "		Sensitive
Heavy dot on " i "		Temper
Closed top on " o " & " a "		Discreet
Open top on " o " & " a "		Gossip
Firm long " t " bar		Confidence
Faint short " t " bar		Insecurity
Very long " t " bar		Egotistical

EXAMPLES OF CAPITAL LETTERS

Vertical line "I"		Capable
Printed "I"		Well Read
Very small "I"		Insecure
Big flourishing "I"		Egotistical
Very large "I"		Selfish
Loop at start "M"		Jealous
Low start "M"		Easy Going
Higher start "M"		Confidence
Pointed "M"		Aggressive
Rounded "M"		Passive

Zodiac	Dates	Hexagram	Hexagram	Hexagram	Hexagram	Animal
♈ ARIES	Mar 21 - Apr 20	Chien (Creative)	Kun (Receptive)	Ken (Immobile)	Sun (Gentle)	**TIGER** ev. Feb & 1902 (& ev. 12 yrs.)
♉ TAURUS	APR 21 - May 21	Chen (Arousing)	Kan (Terrible)	Li (Clinging)	Tui (Joyful)	**HARE** ev. Mar & 1903 (& ev. 12 yrs.)
♊ GEMINI	May 22 - Jun 21					**DRAGON** ev. Apr & 1904 (& ev. 12 yrs.)
♋ CANCER	Jun 22 - Jul 23					**SNAKE** ev. May & 1905 (& ev. 12 yrs.)
♌ LEO	Jul 24 - Aug 23					**HORSE** ev. Jun & 1906 (& ev.12 yrs)
♍ VIRGO	Aug 24 - Sep 23					**SHEEP** ev. Jul. & 1907 (& ev. 12 yrs)
♎ LIBRA	Sep 24 - Oct 23					**MONKEY** ev. Aug. & 1908 (& ev.12 yrs)
♏ SCORPIO	Oct 24 - Nov 22					**ROOSTER** ev. Sep. & 1909 (& ev.12 yrs)
♐ SAGITTARIUS	Nov 23 - Dec 21					**DOG** ev. Oct. & 1910 (& ev.12 yrs)
♑ CAPRICORN	Dec 22 - Jan 20					**PIG** ev. Nov. & 1911 (& ev. 12 yrs)
♒ AQUARIUS	Jan 21 - Feb 19					**RAT** ev. Dec. & 1900 (& ev.12 yrs)
♓ PISCES	Feb 20 - Mar 20					**OX** ev. Jan. & 1901 (& ev.12 yrs)

UNDERSTANDING IT

● **HISTORY** & origins of this ancient art are lost in the distant pasts of North Africa (Egypt), Asia and pre-Roman Europe. <u>It is one the of oldest occult lores in existence</u> and closely related to other systems, e.g. Western astrology (left), Eastern astrology (right), I - Ching (top) and Runes (bottom - A Rune set will also have a blank [unknown]).

● **WHAT IS IT?** - It is simple & quite specific (unlike most other techniques) on a wide variety of topics from inherited character & ability probabilities, to specific guidance on future courses of action on any subject - <u>All that you need is a person's birth details</u>, names & nicknames, & for any other event, action, place or thing, all you need is a name or a number.

HOW TO DO IT

I. All dates, names, places etc. have to first be converted to a primary (1 - 9) number.
II. <u>Your birth number is by far the most important.</u> Let us say your name was Samantha & you were born 25 March 1985 so this is written: 2 + 5 + 3 + 1 + 9 + 8 + 5 = 33 = 3 + 3 = 6 which is Samantha's birth number & of course unchangeable (see details over).
III. By the same process of addition (but using the table below to convert letters to numbers first). We arrive at: 1 + 1 + 4 + 1 + 5 + 2 + 8 + 1 = 23 = 2 + 3 = 5 which is Samantha's name number.

IV. <u>Harmony between a person's birth number</u> & other numbers in their lives such as names, nicknames, initials, house/telephone numbers, dates for travel, moves, investments etc. are considered very critical.
V. Thus Samantha (name number 5) would have a more harmonious life if she used the nick name Sam (1 + 1 + 4 = 6) which exactly matches her birth number (see II opposite) - However if she wanted to develop some characteristics from the number 5 profile she would continue to use the name Samantha.
IV. <u>So, influence of the future</u> is possible thru planning, for example, don't name your baby until his/her birth number is known - & <u>*don't fall in love until you have worked out your "intendeds" likely character thru numerology.*</u>

1	2	3	4	5	6	7	8	9
A	B	C	D	E	F	G	H	I
J	K	L	M	N	O	P	Q	R
S	T	U	V	W	X	Y	Z	

Rune	Meaning	Rune	Meaning	Rune	Meaning	Rune	Meaning
◇	BEORC - New Birth - Begin	B	ING - Energy before start	⋈	WYN - Happy - Joy - Balance	S	PEORTH - Gain - Secret - Test
◇	ODAL - Duty - Inheritance	↗	GER - Sow to harvest.	S	SIGEL - Life force - Whole	∩	UR - Patience in strength
I	EH - Journey - Big change	M	MAN - Right relationships	⋈	KEN - Physical/mental light	<	ELOH - Weapon - Defend - Heal
I	IS - Patience - Energy - Wait	F	FEOH - Money - Success etc.	▷	THORN - Test - Protect - Pain	F	OS - Sacrifice - Create - Know
X	LAGU - Flow - Understand	M	EOH - Eternal evolvement	↑	RAD - Travel - Change - Force	R	TYR - Courage - Power - Male
X	GYFU - Peace - Gift - Share	M	DAEG - Total change - Dawn	↓	NYD - Limits - Inner energy	↑	HAEGL - Force - Unknown change

Primary number	Ruled by	Sign of planet	Your day	PRINCIPAL POSITIVE CHARACTERISTICS	PRINCIPAL NEGATIVE CHARACTERISTICS	OTHER NOTES RELEVANT.
1	SUN	☉	SUNDAY	**Decisive**. Confident. Courageous. Creative. Possibly artistic. Determined. Active. Ambitious. Energetic. Innovative. Loyal.	**Ruthless**. Dominant. Intolerant. Stubborn. Self-centred. Bossy. Arrogant. Aggressive. Inflexible. Possibly complacent in love.	**Usually have strong personalities** & seek to be leaders of their group, family or work situation at almost any cost.
2	MOON	☽	MONDAY	**Considerate**. Kind. Co-operative. Self-sacrificing. Artistic. Inventive. Gentle. Caring. Peaceful. Make good healers.	**Insecure**. Erratic. Over passive. Timid. Possibly deceitful. Over-sensitive. Shy. Possibly suicidal. Emotional. Changeable.	**Tend to get on well with stronger spirits** - Good in home & family (& deputy at work) situations. Tenacious in love.
3	JUPITER	♃	THURSDAY	**Conscientious**. Jovial. Independent. Lucky. Energetic. Spiritual. Often successful. Disciplined. Zealous. Talented. Eloquent.	**Boastful**. Lonely. Attention seeking. Envious. Conceited. Intolerant. Greedy. Proud. Hypocritical. Extravagant. Bossy.	**Often compulsive travellers** seeking to expand all aspects of their lives. Like to be in control but also get on with 6 & 9's
4	URANUS MERCURY	♅	SUNDAY	**Trustworthy**. Stable. Hard-working. Loyal. Dependable. Cautious. Highly organized. Purposeful. Tenacious. Honorable. Tidy.	**Troublesome**. Rigid. Unconventional. Shy. Rebellious. Isolated. Tunnel visioned. Reclusive. Intense. Often argumentative.	**Often take opposite views** of situations & despite being expert developers of systems are rarely materialistic.
5	MERCURY	☿	WEDNESDAY	**Gregarious**. Quick-witted. Versatile. Inquisitive. Alert. Enterprising & usually honest. Sensual. Friendly.	**Quick tempered**. Nervous. Impulsive. Restless. Sloppy. Pleasure seeking. Get bored easily. Dislike responsibility.	**Can get on with any other number** but probably best with other 5's. Good at making money in risk situations.
6	NEPTUNE VENUS	♀	FRIDAY	**Peaceful**. Loving. Friendly. Artistic. Attractive. Popular. Charming. Reliable. Romantic. Creative. Financially capable.	**Obstinate**. Self-indulgent. Plucky. Possessive. Greedy. Intolerant. Selfish. Materialistic. Lazy. Cynical. Careless.	**Good at making friends** & often money but very unforgiving romantically, avoids arguments. Family & harmony important.
7	NEPTUNE	♆	MONDAY	**Spiritual**. Mystical. Sensitive. Visionary. Possibly psychic. Make good teachers. Philosophical. Kind. Compassionate. Quiet.	**Reclusive**. Escapist. Idealistic. Aloof. Romantically inept. Restless. Deceptive. Self delusionary. Private. Bookish.	**Occult associations** — also close to moon. Gets on well with 4's. Drawn to water & travel. True love can be hard to find.
8	SATURN	♄	SATURDAY	**Strong will**. Loyal. Confident. Energetic. Individual. Persistent. Ambitious. Practical. Responsible. Careful. Usually hard working.	**Rebellious**. Envious. Lonely. Intolerant. Status conscious. Demanding. Tense. Resentful. Picky. Materialistic. Biased.	**Because of a strong inner drive** often have very successful careers but may end up lonely because of being misunderstood.
9	MARS	♂	TUESDAY	**Tenacious**. Energetic. Competitive. Inventive. Resourceful. Bold. Honest. Determined. Organized. Astute. Curious. Dextrous.	**Quarrelsome**. Rash. Aggressive. Impatient. Critical. Unreliable. Outspoken. Restless. Blunt. Nit-picking. Rarely listen to advice.	**Once won (difficult) make good friends**. Tend to be accident prone. Magnetic drive inspires in sport & competition.

SECONDARY NUMBERS: Are those above 9. Some are considered relevant & are either interpreted as such or borne in mind (& further reduced to a primary number). Principle examples are 12 & 40 (complete numbers), 13 (Black arts indicator), 11 (indicates mystical balance, inner strength, faith, innovation, idealism, courage, loyalty), 22 (indicates outstanding potential, deep insight & ability in life, but if not used can result in laziness & complacency).

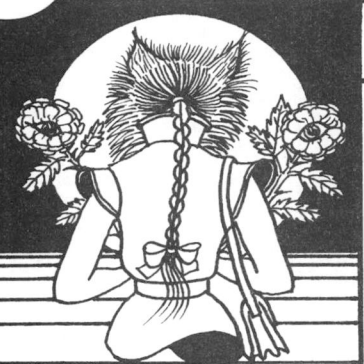

DARE YOU OPEN THIS DOOR? - *& reckon your fate by the principles of a thousand years of study*

- HOW TO DO IT -

1. <u>Consult table "A" & find the dates between which you were born</u> - Read off your primary animal influence & element.
2. <u>Consult tables "B" & "C" & read off (for your month & time of birth)</u> your secondary animal influences.
3. <u>Consult the animal & element interpretation lists</u> to find the astrological influences on your personality.
4. <u>Perform the same procedure on lovers, friends, family & business contacts</u> - then enter the compatibility chart to check relationships.

● Don't fall in love with a female tiger — they are *TROUBLE*

ANIMAL INTERPRETATION

RAT: <u>Charming, crafty, clever with numbers,</u> bargain hunter, hoarder, critical, adaptable, name dropper, erratic, sociable.

OX: <u>Patient, conservative, placid, sensible,</u> methodical, loyal, unimaginative, possessive, hard worker, idealistic, trustworthy.

TIGER: <u>Stubborn, vibrant, rash, competitive,</u> brave, hothead, emotional, magnetic leader, quarrelsome, passionate, trouble.

HARE: <u>Gregarious, meek (but not a coward),</u> warm, peace-loving, good judge of character, proud, healer, cautious, industrious.

DRAGON: <u>Fashionable, energetic, imaginative</u> dreamer, generous, healthy, perfectionist, honest, determined (but erratic), tactless.

SNAKE: <u>Elegant, philosophical, subtle, analytical,</u> sensual, sentimental, flirtatious, lazy, lucky with money (but bad loser).

HORSE: <u>Extrovert, sociable, born politician,</u> cunning, insecure, sporty, opinionated, egotistical, quick-witted, team orientated.

GOAT: <u>Inoffensive, caring, yin, irresponsible</u> (but diplomatic), creative (but uninventive), worrier, gregarious, passive (but democratic).

MONKEY: <u>Inventive, scheming, curious, vocal,</u> unscrupulous, good with money (but easily bored), friendly (but vain), versatile.

COCK: <u>Independent and potentially aggressive,</u> dreamer, creative, perfectionist, intolerant, shrewd, determined, proud, rude.

DOG: <u>Friendly, trustworthy, loyal, inflexible,</u> sporty, occasionally violent, pessimistic, no good with money, shy, stubborn, worrier.

PIG: <u>Intellectual, honest, gallant, industrious,</u> home-loving, kind, gullible, unpretentious, sad, sensitive, loyal.

OPPOSITE PAIRS

	BUILD	EXPAND	MYSTERY	SEX	CAREER	FAMILY
YIN	Ox	Hare	Snake	Goat	Cock	Pig
YANG	Rat	Tiger	Dragon	Horse	Monkey	Dog

ELEMENT INTERPRETATION

NAME & INFLUENCE (Low to High)

WOOD: <u>Observant, handy, creative, literary,</u> imaginative, inventive, highly artistic, visionary.

FIRE: <u>Observant, alert, active, motivated,</u> vigorous, spirited, highly energetic, dynamic.

EARTH: <u>Stable, reliable, practical, steadfast,</u> trustworthy, highly responsible, circumspect.

METAL: <u>Alert, sporting, brave, competitive,</u> entrepreneurial, assertive, aggressive, hard.

WATER: <u>Open, talkative, outgoing,</u> communicative, articulate, eloquent, adventurous, loquacious.

COMPATIBILITY CHART

Codes
- • = Business better
- ■ = Love better
- 1 = Very bad
- 2 = Bad
- 3 = Mixed
- 4 = Good
- 5 = Very good

	Rat	Ox	Tiger	Hare	Dragon	Snake	Horse	Goat	Monkey	Cock	Dog	Pig
Rat	4											
Ox	5	3										
Tiger	3.	1	2									
Hare	1	3.	•3	•3								
Dragon	5	2	5	2	3.							
Snake	4	4	1	•3	5	4						
Horse	1	•2	5	3	3	3	4					
Goat	2	1	4	•5	4	2	•4	4				
Monkey	5	3	2	2	4	2	3.	3.	3			
Cock	4.	5	3	2.	3	4.	5.	3	3.	2		
Dog	4	2	5	4	2	3	5	2	4	3	4	
Pig	•4	4	2.	•5	4	3	3	5	1	4	4	5

TABLE A. YEAR & ELEMENT CHART

BORN BETWEEN		OF THE ELEMENT	IN THE YEAR	BORN BETWEEN		OF THE ELEMENT	IN THE YEAR
19 Feb 1901	7 Feb 1902	Metal	Ox	7 Feb 1951	26 Jan 1952	Metal	Hare
8 Feb 1902	28 Jan 1903	Water	Tiger	27 Jan 1952	14 Feb 1953	Water	Dragon
29 Jan 1903	15 Feb 1904	Water	Hare	15 Feb 1953	3 Feb 1954	Water	Snake
16 Feb 1904	3 Feb 1905	Wood	Dragon	4 Feb 1954	23 Jan 1955	Wood	Horse
4 Feb 1905	24 Jan 1906	Wood	Snake	24 Jan 1955	11 Feb 1956	Wood	Goat
25 Jan 1906	12 Feb 1907	Fire	Horse	12 Feb 1956	30 Feb 1957	Fire	Monkey
13 Feb 1907	1 Feb 1908	Fire	Goat	31 Jan 1957	18 Feb 1958	Fire	Cock
2 Feb 1908	21 Jan 1909	Earth	Monkey	19 Feb 1958	7 Feb 1959	Earth	Dog
22 Jan 1909	9 Feb 1910	Earth	Cock	8 Feb 1959	28 Jan 1960	Earth	Pig
10 Feb 1910	29 Jan 1911	Metal	Dog	29 Jan 1960	14 Feb 1961	Metal	Rat
30 Jan 1911	17 Feb 1912	Metal	Pig	15 Feb 1961	4 Feb 1962	Metal	Ox
18 Feb 1912	5 Feb 1913	Water	Rat	5 Feb 1962	25 Jan 1963	Water	Tiger
6 Feb 1913	25 Jan 1914	Water	Ox	26 Jan 1963	12 Feb 1964	Water	Hare
26 Jan 1914	13 Feb 1915	Wood	Tiger	13 Feb 1964	1 Feb 1965	Wood	Dragon
14 Feb 1915	2 Feb 1916	Wood	Hare	2 Feb 1965	20 Jan 1966	Wood	Snake
3 Feb 1916	22 Jan 1917	Fire	Dragon	21 Jan 1966	8 Feb 1967	Fire	Horse
23 Jan 1917	10 Feb 1918	Fire	Snake	9 Feb 1967	29 Jan 1968	Fire	Goat
11 Feb 1918	31 Jan 1919	Earth	Horse	30 Jan 1968	16 Feb 1969	Earth	Monkey
1 Feb 1919	19 Feb 1920	Earth	Goat	17 Feb 1969	5 Feb 1970	Earth	Cock
20 Feb 1920	7 Feb 1921	Metal	Monkey	6 Feb 1970	26 Jan 1971	Metal	Dog
8 Feb 1921	27 Jan 1922	Metal	Cock	27 Jan 1971	14 Feb 1972	Metal	Pig
28 Jan 1922	15 Feb 1923	Water	Dog	15 Feb 1972	2 Feb 1973	Water	Rat
16 Feb 1923	4 Feb 1924	Water	Pig	3 Feb 1973	23 Jan 1974	Water	Ox
5 Feb 1924	24 Jan 1925	Wood	Rat	24 Jan 1974	10 Feb 1975	Wood	Tiger
25 Jan 1925	13 Feb 1926	Wood	Ox	11 Feb 1975	30 Jan 1976	Wood	Hare
14 Feb 1926	2 Feb 1927	Fire	Tiger	31 Jan 1976	17 Feb 1977	Fire	Dragon
3 Feb 1927	22 Jan 1928	Fire	Hare	18 Feb 1977	6 Feb 1978	Fire	Snake
23 Jan 1928	10 Feb 1929	Earth	Dragon	7 Feb 1978	27 Jan 1979	Earth	Horse
11 Feb 1929	30 Jan 1930	Earth	Snake	28 Jan 1979	15 Feb 1980	Earth	Goat
31 Jan 1930	17 Feb 1931	Metal	Horse	16 Feb 1980	4 Feb 1981	Metal	Monkey
18 Feb 1931	6 Feb 1932	Metal	Goat	5 Feb 1981	24 Jan 1982	Metal	Cock
7 Feb 1932	25 Jan 1933	Water	Monkey	25 Jan 1982	12 Feb 1983	Water	Dog
26 Jan 1933	13 Feb 1934	Water	Cock	13 Feb 1983	1 Feb 1984	Water	Pig
14 Feb 1934	4 Feb 1935	Wood	Dog	2 Feb 1984	19 Feb 1985	Wood	Rat
5 Feb 1935	23 Jan 1936	Wood	Pig	20 Feb 1985	8 Feb 1986	Wood	Ox
24 Jan 1936	11 Feb 1937	Fire	Rat	9 Feb 1986	28 Jan 1987	Fire	Tiger
12 Feb 1937	31 Jan 1938	Fire	Ox	29 Jan 1987	16 Feb 1988	Fire	Hare
1 Feb 1938	18 Feb 1939	Earth	Tiger	17 Feb 1988	5 Feb 1989	Earth	Dragon
19 Feb 1939	7 Feb 1940	Earth	Hare	6 Feb 1989	26 Jan 1990	Earth	Snake
8 Feb 1940	27 Jan 1941	Metal	Dragon	27 Jan 1990	14 Feb 1991	Metal	Horse
28 Jan 1941	15 Feb 1942	Metal	Snake	15 Feb 1991	3 Feb 1992	Metal	Goat
16 Feb 1942	4 Feb 1943	Water	Horse	4 Feb 1992	22 Jan 1993	Water	Monkey
5 Feb 1943	25 Jan 1944	Water	Goat	23 Jan 1993	9 Feb 1994	Water	Cock
26 Jan 1944	12 Feb 1945	Wood	Monkey	10 Feb 1994	30 Jan 1995	Wood	Dog
13 Feb 1945	1 Feb 1946	Wood	Cock	31 Jan 1995	18 Feb 1996	Wood	Pig
2 Feb 1946	21 Jan 1947	Fire	Dog	19 Feb 1996	6 Feb 1997	Fire	Rat
22 Jan 1947	9 Feb 1948	Fire	Pig	7 Feb 1997	27 Jan 1998	Fire	Ox
10 Feb 1948	29 Jan 1949	Earth	Rat	28 Jan 1998	15 Feb 1999	Earth	Tiger
30 Jan 1949	17 Feb 1950	Earth	Ox	16 Feb 1999	4 Feb 2000	Earth	Hare
18 Feb 1950	6 Feb 1951	Metal	Tiger	5 Feb 2000	24 Jan 2001	Metal	Dragon

TABLE B — MONTHLY CHART		TABLE C — HOUR CHART	
January	Ox	11 pm - 1 am	Rat
February	Tiger	1 - 3 am	Ox
March	Hare	3 - 5 am	Tiger
April	Dragon	5 - 7 am	Hare
May	Snake	7 - 9 am	Dragon
June	Horse	9 - 11 am	Snake
July	Sheep	11 am - 1 pm	Horse
August	Monkey	1 - 3 pm	Sheep
September	Cock	3 - 5 pm	Monkey
October	Dog	5 - 7 pm	Cock
November	Pig	7 - 9 pm	Dog
December	Rat	9 - 11 pm	Pig

USED FOR OVER 7,000 YEARS in lands near & far to answer a range of questions as diverse as the universe we live in.

UNDERSTAND IT....

.... is a kind of communication system, <u>a medium between the conscious & subconscious mind</u> - & external energy patterns (which surround both inanimate objects & living organisms). In many cases <u>these energy patterns are not even detectable without the involvement of a psychic aspect.</u> This is where your subconscious mind & a pendulum come in.

WHAT KIND OF PENDULUM WILL WORK?..

....Almost any kind of small weight (on a short thread) will work....

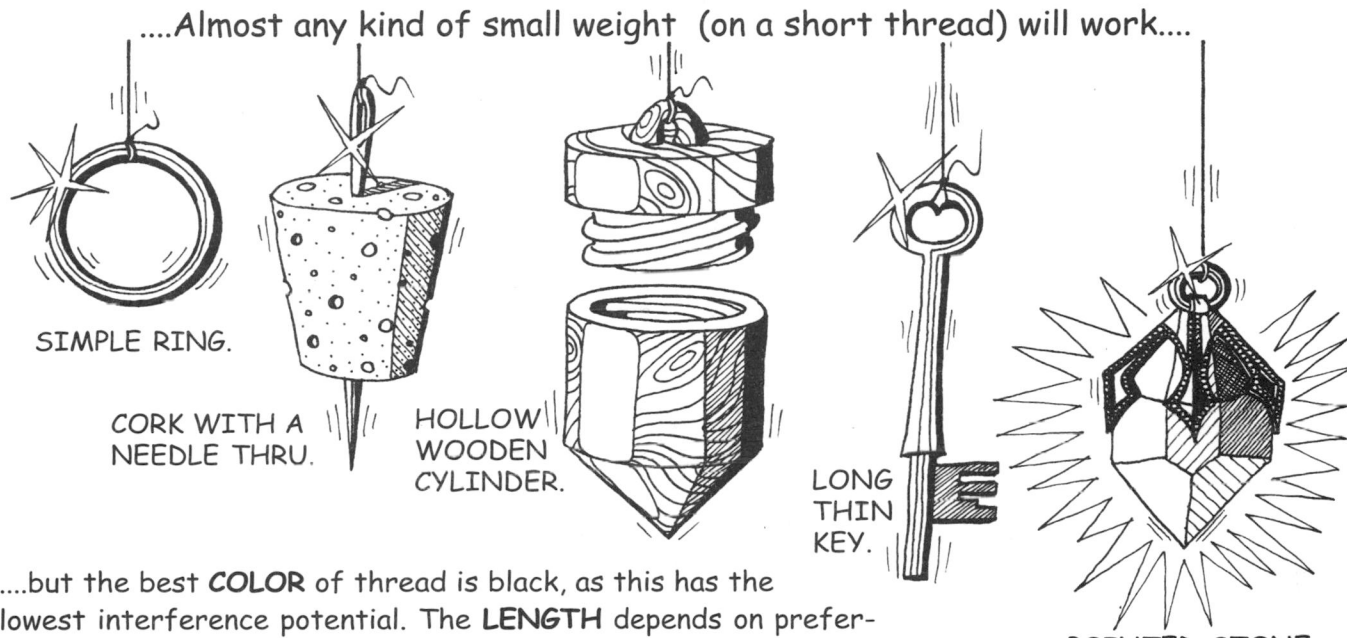

SIMPLE RING.

CORK WITH A NEEDLE THRU.

HOLLOW WOODEN CYLINDER.

LONG THIN KEY.

POINTED STONE.

....but the best **COLOR** of thread is black, as this has the lowest interference potential. The **LENGTH** depends on preference & experience .... it can be a few inches (start with about 4) to 2 feet or more. **HOLD** thread <u>in dominant hand between thumb & forefinger with other fingers extended (facing down)</u> .... & *HOLD VERY STILL.*

HOLLOW CYLINDERS are used to contain a sample of the substance (e.g. gold) being sought - <u>However gold sample may impair a find of another substance.</u>

THE USES....

.... of a pendulum in the hands of an experienced operator are almost infinite. For example:

- **LOCATING FROM A MAP** (minerals, people, ships, missing objects).
- **LOCATION OF DISEASE** (in the body).
- **DETERMINING DOSAGES** (& types of medicinals which are most suited to a particular problem).
- **LOCATING LOST OBJECTS** & people in say a house or town.
- **DETERMINING THE TIME** & nature of future (& past) events.

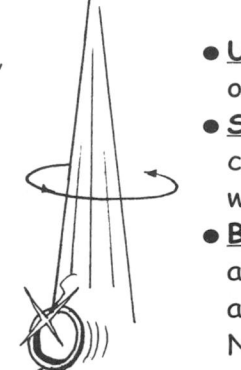

IMPORTANT

- <u>**Understand**</u> the meaning of our own questions.
- <u>**Stay away**</u> from electrical & electronic items when using a pendulum.
- <u>**Be sure all**</u> questions asked can be simply answered with "Yes or No."

● **ON 4 SHEETS** (postcard size is O.K.) of white paper draw one of these figures clearly on each.

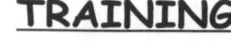

TRAINING

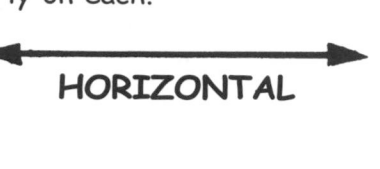

HORIZONTAL

VERTICAL

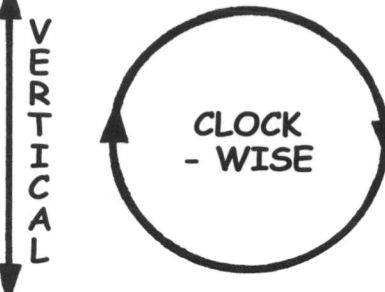

CLOCK - WISE

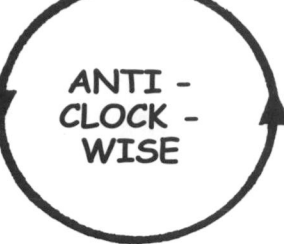

ANTI - CLOCK - WISE

● **HOLDING YOUR PENDULUM** as explained overleaf **POSITION** yourself comfortably at a table without touching or crossing either hands or feet - Hold the pendulum over one of the symbols & with a **CALM** mind, "will" it to swing in the directions of the arrows **(don't move your hand)** - **IT WILL MOVE BY WILLPOWER** but you may or may not need practice &/or perhaps another time &/or place to first gain your confidence.

● **When you have achieved** the **CLOCKWISE** rotation by willpower, tell your subconscious mind **(in a commanding voice)** that if you ask it a question, to which the answer is **YES**, then *IT WILL ROTATE* in this direction.

● **When you have achieved** the **ANTI-CLOCKWISE** rotation by willpower, tell your subconscious mind **(in a commanding voice)** that if you ask it a question to which the answer is **NO** then *IT WILL ROTATE* in this direction.

● **Repeat the above daily** until the subconscious is **TRAINED** (perhaps a week) - You are now **READY** to ask "yes or no" questions of the pendulum, **BUT** first ensure your conscious mind is **UNBIASED** as to the answer (as this can influence the swing) - **Empty your mind** of all feelings & emotions, & *THINK ONLY OF THE QUESTION & THE PENDULUM.*

● Using similar principles **DOWSING** is an ancient technique used mainly to locate subterranean minerals, oil, water, ruins - even pipes & cables. Authenticated over 7,000 years - **ABOUT 75% OF US HAVE A DORMANT ABILITY TO DOWSE.**

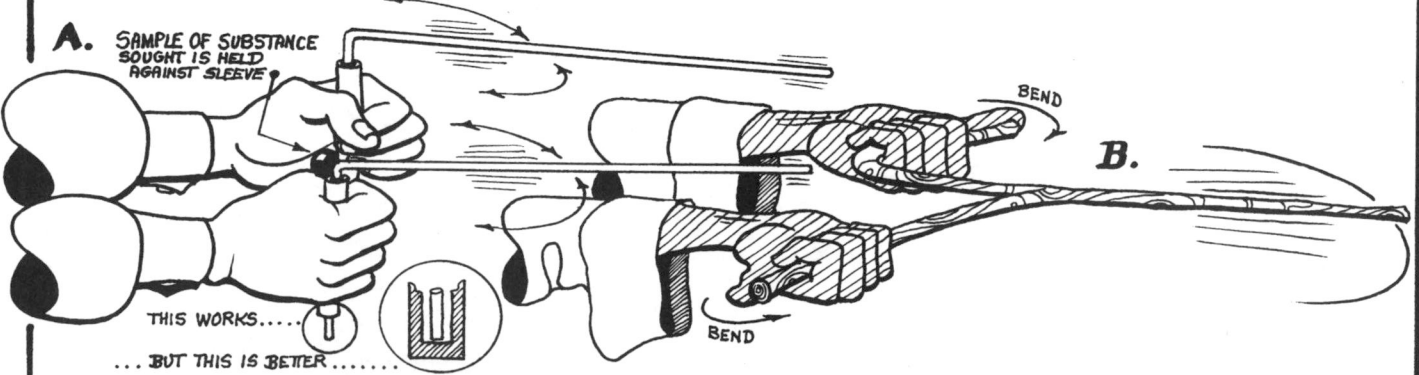

A. SAMPLE OF SUBSTANCE SOUGHT IS HELD AGAINST SLEEVE

BEND

B.

BEND

THIS WORKS.....

... BUT THIS IS BETTER ....

● **FOCUS YOUR MIND ON THE MATERIAL YOU ARE SEEKING** & if possible carry a sample with you (which is in contact with both the rod(s) & your skin.

A. **Made from** stiff wire, bent & put thru a tube to hold (e.g. pen casing)

B. **Made from** 3/8 inch thick pliable sapling twig e.g.: Willow, Hedge, Apple, Hazel.

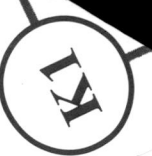

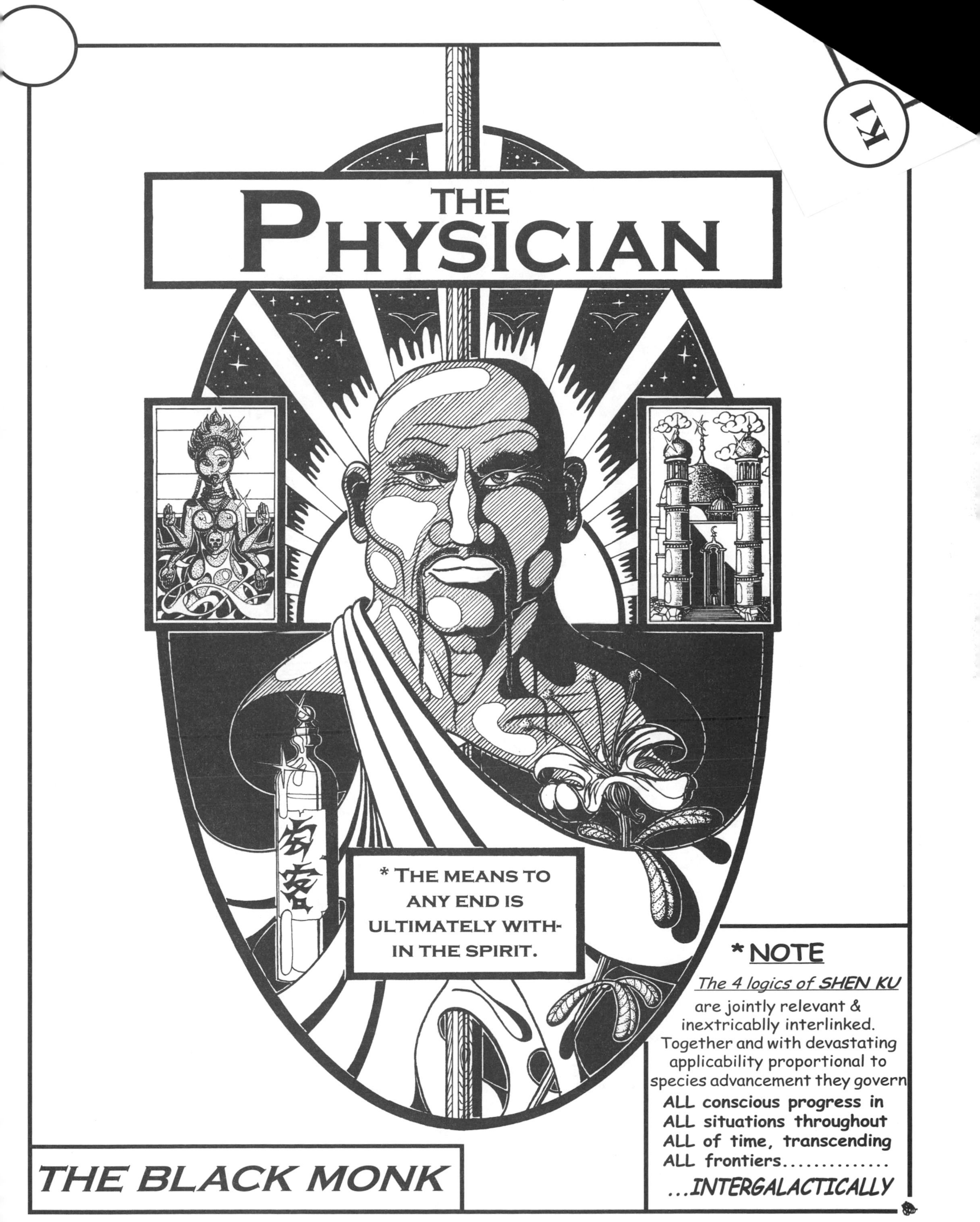
K1
THE
PHYSICIAN
* THE MEANS TO ANY END IS ULTIMATELY WITH-IN THE SPIRIT.
* NOTE
The 4 logics of SHEN KU are jointly relevant & inextricablly interlinked. Together and with devastating applicability proportional to species advancement they govern ALL conscious progress in ALL situations throughout ALL of time, transcending ALL frontiers.............
...INTERGALACTICALLY
THE BLACK MONK

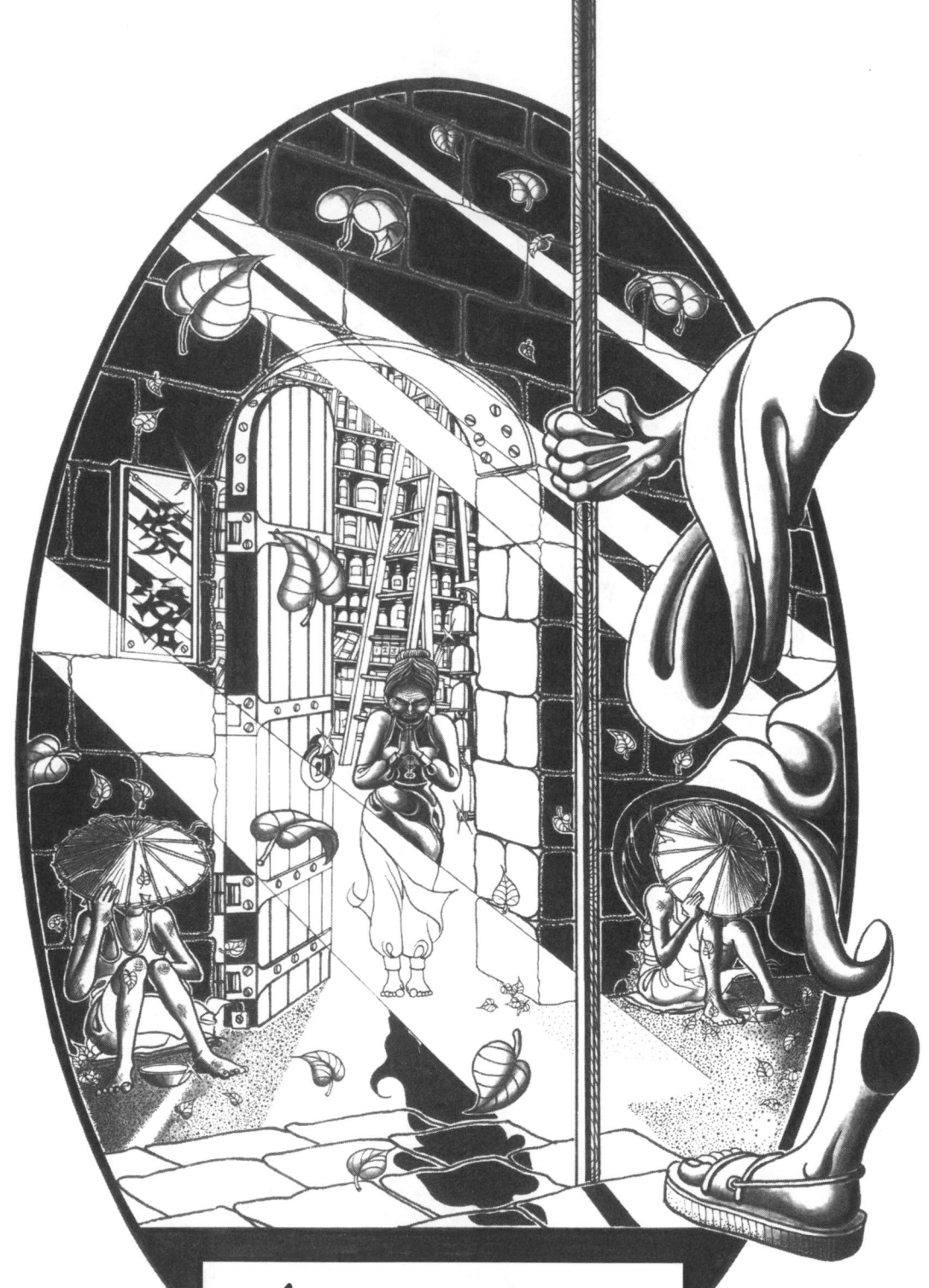

Aged sage I beg you hear,
this sad tale of yesteryear.
In foreign parts with ailments rife,
without a care came I through life.

Until this day that I must pay,
for indiscretions which dormant lay.
Sins & tears I bring you here,
in search of wisdom's breath so near.

How To Give (& Receive) Acupressure Therapy

Acupuncture/shiatzu/accupressure, all branches of the same ancient tree.
ONCE SCORNED IN THE WEST, NOW RESPECTED INTERNATIONALLY.

HOW DOES IT WORK?

....*ACCORDING TO THE 5,000 YEAR OLD PRINCIPLES OF ORIENTAL MEDICINE* the energy/life force (Ki) of the human body flows thru 14 major meridian channels, each named after an organ or bodily function. Along each of these meridians at specific positions are critical sites (tsubos), which affect the flow of Ki - *IF WE ARE IN GOOD HEALTH* the Ki flows well - *IF WE ARE ILL* then the flow of Ki to a particular organ or function may be "stuck" at one or more tsubos & require stimulation to clear the blockage - Conversely certain tsubos may be encouraging too much Ki to pass with equally unpleasant results (such as aggression, hyperactivity, glandular excesses, temper etc.) & thus benefit from sedation.

BALL OF THUMB

....Versatile technique used widely on chest, low back, shoulders, limbs, feet, hands.

I

STACKED FINGERS

....Use as an alternative to "I"

II

MULTIPLE FINGERS

....Used to simultaneously stimulate several sites.

III

KNUCKLES

....Roll them slowly across scalp.

IV

MERIDIANS	Codes
Large Intestine	LI
Stomach	St
Small Intestine	SI
Bladder	B
Gall Bladder	GB
Triple Warmer	TW
Governing Vessel	GV
Pericardium	P
Lung	Lu
Spleen	Sp
Heart	H
Kidney	K
Liver	Liv
Conception Vessel	CV

YIN & YANG

The Yin/Yang identity of a meridian is considered by oriental masters to be important (Yang [positive] meridians run down from head or raised finger tips, & Yin [negative] meridians run up from toes or body center). <u>There are 3 Yin & 3 Yang meridians in each arm & leg & one controlling vessel meridian in the front & back of the body.</u> - The direction of flow dictates the direction of manipulation of the tsubos according to whether an increase or decrease in that energy flow is sought.

AM I YIN OR YANG?

....*THE ANSWER IS BOTH*, but in what proportions, organs & functions is the diagnostic question. - Modern living (junk food, chemicals etc.) usually lead to serious imbalances with complex combinations, but typical excess <u>Yin traits are: thin/flabby, listless/tired, passive/non-ambitious, chronic ailments etc.</u>

HOW TO TREAT EXCESS YANG

<u>Work against the energy flow</u> of appropriate meridian (i.e. from high to low tsubo numbers) with strong pressure.

HOW TO TREAT EXCESS YIN

<u>Work with the energy flow</u> of appropriate meridian (i.e. from low to high tsubo numbers) with softer pressure.

PALM DOWN

....For softest body parts e.g. eyes, tummy & massage.

VI

SIDE BY SIDE

....(Fingers) for soft body parts e.g. neck, groin, kidney area etc.

V

LOOSEN MUSCLES BEFORE ACUPRESSURE

.....*FOR SEVERAL MINUTES* (by massage &/or manipulation [IX to XII]) **to reduce muscle tension & encourage better contact** with the tsubos for therapy.

STIMULATION TECHNIQUES

....*OF THE TSUBOS CAN BE VARIOUSLY DONE* with fingers/ thumb (I to VIII) acupressure, with needles (acupuncture), or by heat (Moxa) where a fleck of herb (usually Mugwort) is burned on the tsubo site, or by suction (a partial vacuum is induced under a glass cup over the tsubo [usually by burning something in it]). Electrical charges may also sometimes be used.

HOW LONG TO STIMULATE?

....**Duration of pressure** with thumb/finger etc. usually 4+ secs. (7+ secs. on back) up to 10 secs. (or up to 60 secs. of palm pressure on soft areas [e.g. tummy]) - If a repeat round is called for wait 10+ seconds.

FINGER IN EAR

.... vibrate digit slowly one ear at a time for stress &/or fa-tigue. *"JIGGLE JIGGLE!"*

XIII

ABOUT TSUBOS

● **HOW MANY?** - In total about 361 - but the frequently used number about 80.
● **HOW BIG?** - About one centimeter in diameter.
● **HOW DEEP?** - Varies from just under skin to several inches.

"DON'T" SITUATIONS

....*IT IS NOT RECOMMENDED* to give/ receive acupressure when in late pregnancy/under bad stress/very tired, just eaten/very hungry or seriously ill. Unless by a qualified therapist as diagnosis, symptoms & reactions are complicated by such conditions.

MEASUREMENTS

....Expressed in finger or thumb or palm widths (always refers to patient's own digits etc.)

BREATHING

....Acupressure works better if patient **exhales** during treatment.

DON'T FORGET

● *APPLY WEAK PRESSURE* to a tsubo when an organ is underfunctioning **(to stimulate it)**.
● *APPLY STRONG PRESSURE* to a tsubo when an organ is overactive or the tsubo itself is painful **(to sedate it)**

BOTTOM OF FISTS

....Use loosely clenched on bottom, thighs, back etc. *"BAM! BAM! BAM BAM!"*

XII

CORNER OF THUMB

....Rotary pres-sure sometimes used after initial vertical therapy.

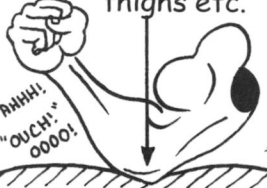

VII

ELBOW

....For deep pressure on back, bottom, hips, thighs etc.

"AHHH!" "OUCH!" "OOOO!"

VIII

APPLY THIS TECHNIQUE CAUTIOUSLY

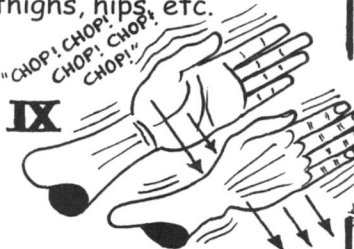

CHOPPING WITH EDGE OF HANDS

....Use on back, bottom, thighs, hips, etc.

"CHOP! CHOP! CHOP! CHOP! CHOP!"

IX

CUPPED HANDS

....Slap quickly on back, hips, chest, thighs etc.

"PLOP PLOP! PLOP PLOP!"

X

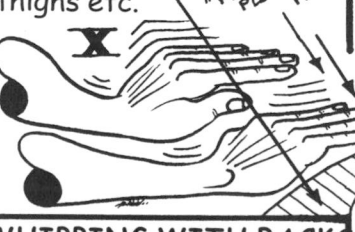

WHIPPING WITH BACKS OF LOOSE FINGERS

Use like whips on back, neck, chest, limbs etc.

"FLAP! FLAP! FLAP! FLAP! FLAP!"

XI

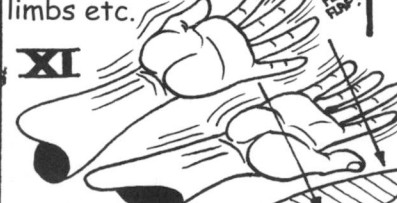

● **DON'T GET DISCOURAGED** - *Start with simple single tsubo sites (e.g. GV 26 stops sneezing) from the Shen Ku ailment sheets.*

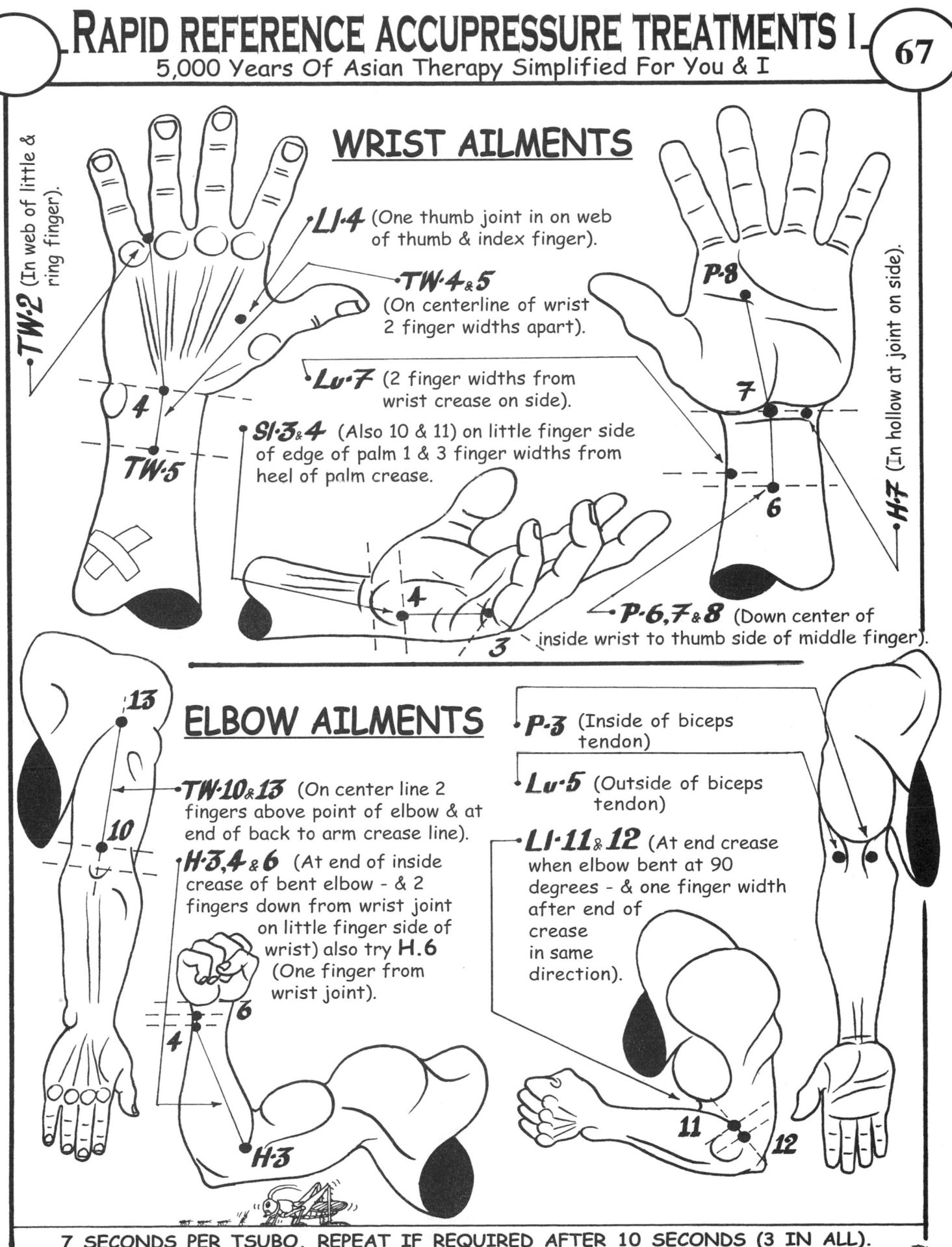

WRIST AILMENTS

TW·2 (In web of little & ring finger).

LI·4 (One thumb joint in on web of thumb & index finger).

TW·4 & 5 (On centerline of wrist 2 finger widths apart).

Lu·7 (2 finger widths from wrist crease on side).

SI·3 & 4 (Also 10 & 11) on little finger side of edge of palm 1 & 3 finger widths from heel of palm crease.

P·8

H·7 (In hollow at joint on side).

P·6, 7 & 8 (Down center of inside wrist to thumb side of middle finger).

ELBOW AILMENTS

TW·10 & 13 (On center line 2 fingers above point of elbow & at end of back to arm crease line).

H·3, 4 & 6 (At end of inside crease of bent elbow - & 2 fingers down from wrist joint on little finger side of wrist) also try **H.6** (One finger from wrist joint).

P·3 (Inside of biceps tendon)

Lu·5 (Outside of biceps tendon)

LI·11 & 12 (At end crease when elbow bent at 90 degrees - & one finger width after end of crease in same direction).

7 SECONDS PER TSUBO. REPEAT IF REQUIRED AFTER 10 SECONDS (3 IN ALL).

ANKLE AILMENTS

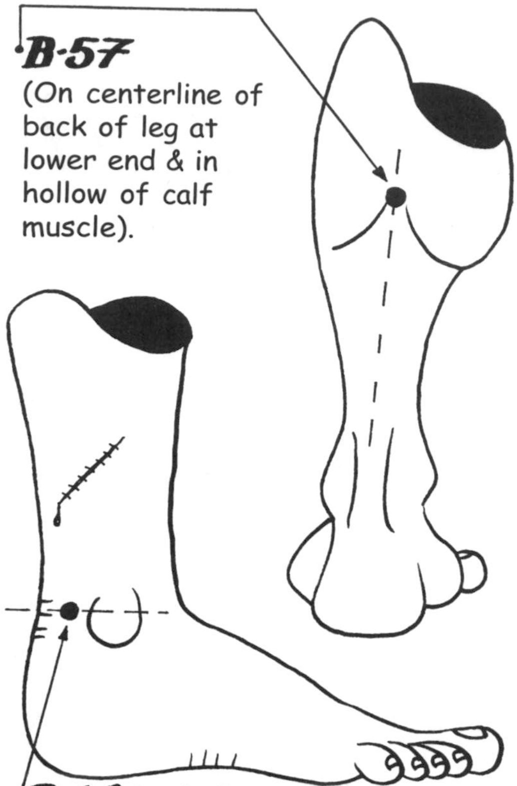

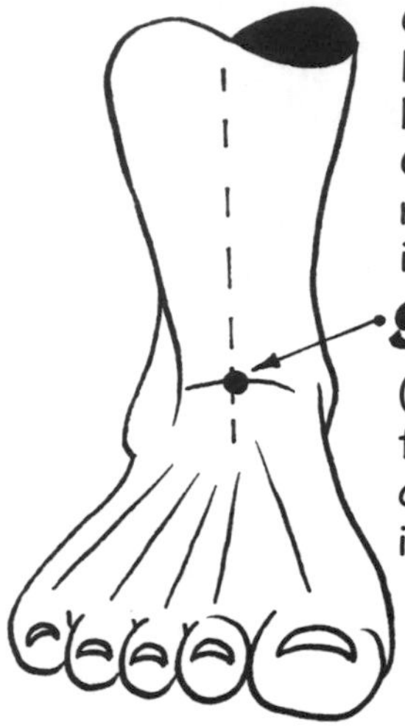

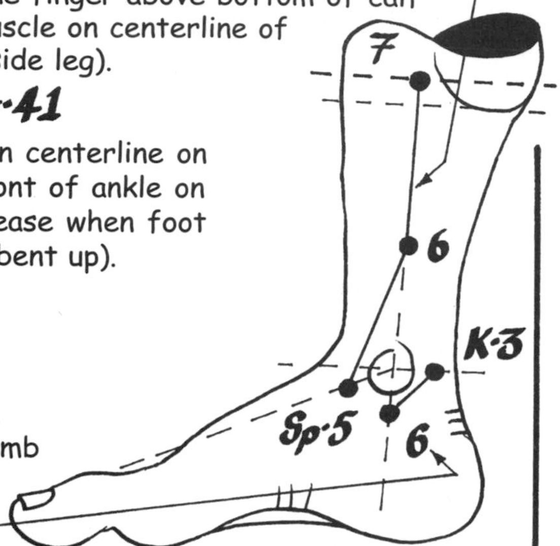

B·57 (On centerline of back of leg at lower end & in hollow of calf muscle).

Sp·5,6 & 7 (Sp. 5: One finger out from ankle bone on line towards big toe, Sp. 6: Double height of inside ankle bone, Sp. 7: One finger above bottom of calf muscle on centerline of inside leg).

St·41 (On centerline on front of ankle on crease when foot is bent up).

NOTE: Press **B.60 & K.3** together (with thumb & index finger).

B·60 (In hollow to rear of ankle bone on outside of foot).

K·3 & 6 (One finger out from inside ankle bone to rear & down).

KNEE AILMENTS

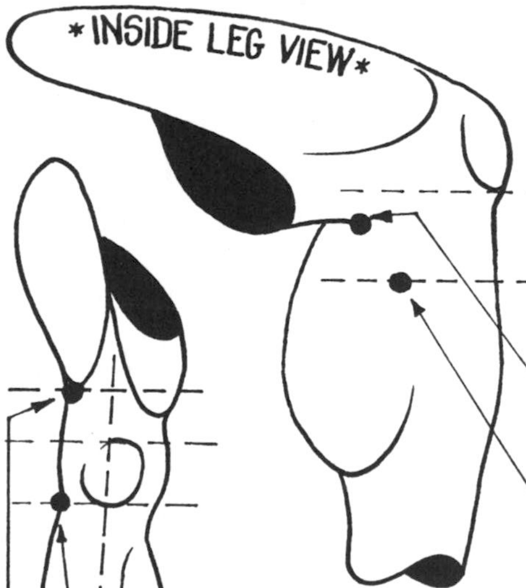

* INSIDE LEG VIEW *

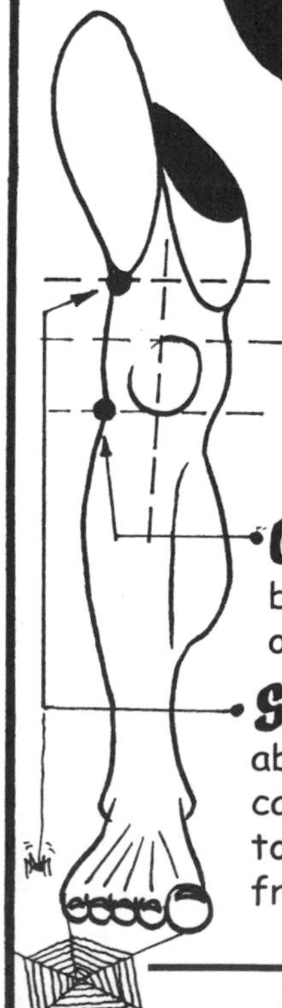

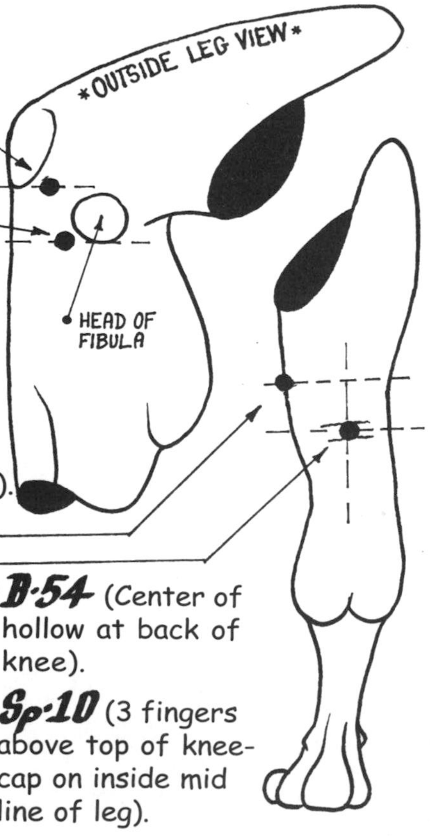

* OUTSIDE LEG VIEW *

St·35 (In hollow at lower outside edge of kneecap).

GB·34 (2 fingers below bottom of kneecap on outside).

HEAD OF FIBULA

Liv·8 (At end of crease line of bent knee on inside leg).

Sp·9 (3 fingers down from bottom of kneecap on inside leg).

GB·33 (Level with bottom of kneecap on outside).

St·34 (3 fingers above top of kneecap & 3 fingers toward outside from center).

B·60 (See ankle section) Is also used for pain in knee joints &/or arthritis.

B·57 (See ankle section) Is also used for swollen knee joints.

B·54 (Center of hollow at back of knee).

Sp·10 (3 fingers above top of kneecap on inside mid line of leg).

PRESS SOFTER TO STIMULATE - PRESS HARDER TO SEDATE.

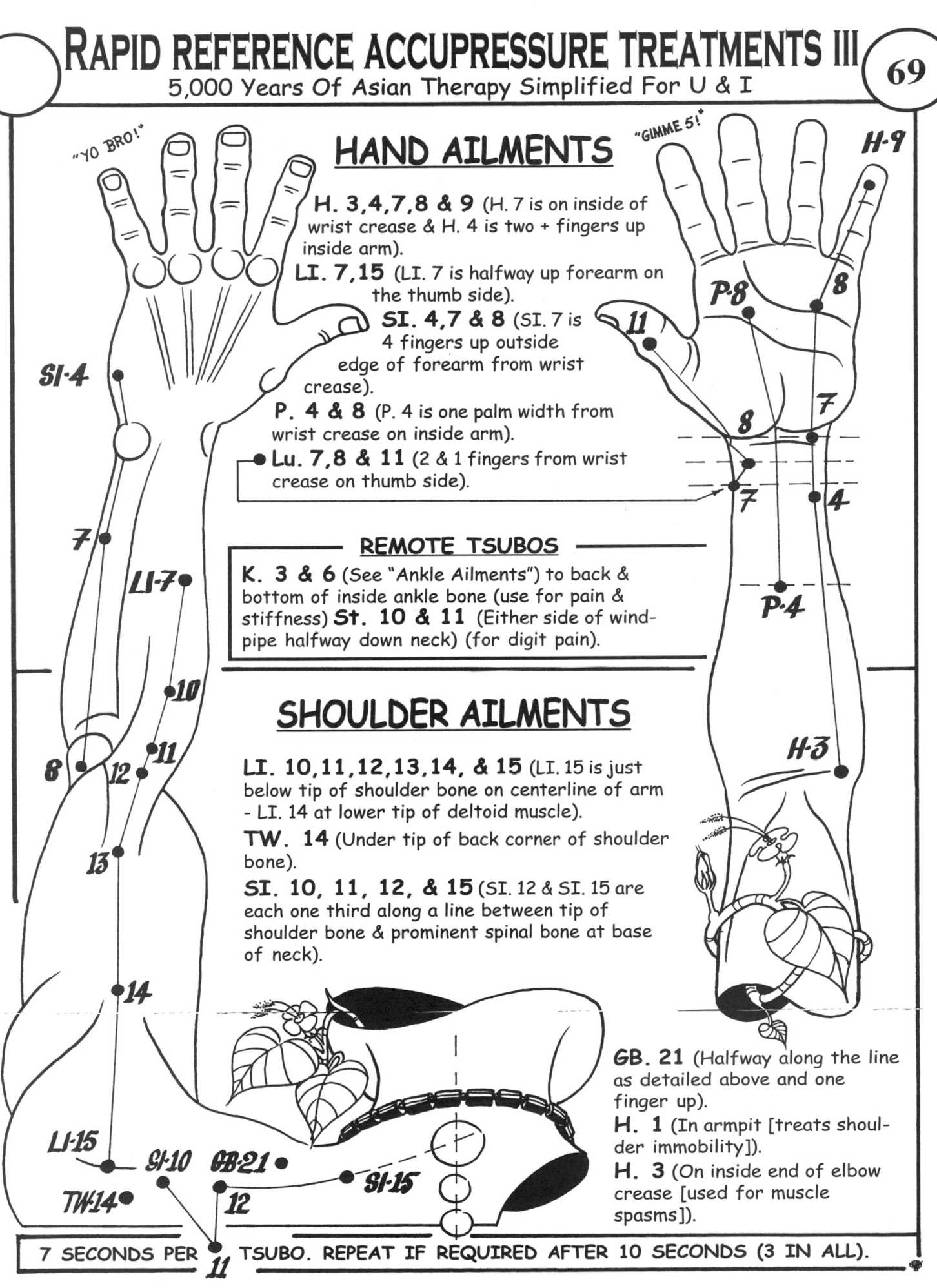

"YO BRO!"

"GIMME 5!"

H-9

HAND AILMENTS

H. 3,4,7,8 & 9 (H. 7 is on inside of wrist crease & H. 4 is two + fingers up inside arm).

LI. 7,15 (LI. 7 is halfway up forearm on the thumb side).

SI. 4,7 & 8 (SI. 7 is 4 fingers up outside edge of forearm from wrist crease).

P. 4 & 8 (P. 4 is one palm width from wrist crease on inside arm).

Lu. 7,8 & 11 (2 & 1 fingers from wrist crease on thumb side).

— REMOTE TSUBOS —

K. 3 & 6 (See "Ankle Ailments") to back & bottom of inside ankle bone (use for pain & stiffness) **St. 10 & 11** (Either side of wind-pipe halfway down neck) (for digit pain).

SHOULDER AILMENTS

LI. 10,11,12,13,14, & 15 (LI. 15 is just below tip of shoulder bone on centerline of arm - LI. 14 at lower tip of deltoid muscle).

TW. 14 (Under tip of back corner of shoulder bone).

SI. 10, 11, 12, & 15 (SI. 12 & SI. 15 are each one third along a line between tip of shoulder bone & prominent spinal bone at base of neck).

GB. 21 (Halfway along the line as detailed above and one finger up).

H. 1 (In armpit [treats shoulder immobility]).

H. 3 (On inside end of elbow crease [used for muscle spasms]).

7 SECONDS PER TSUBO. REPEAT IF REQUIRED AFTER 10 SECONDS (3 IN ALL).

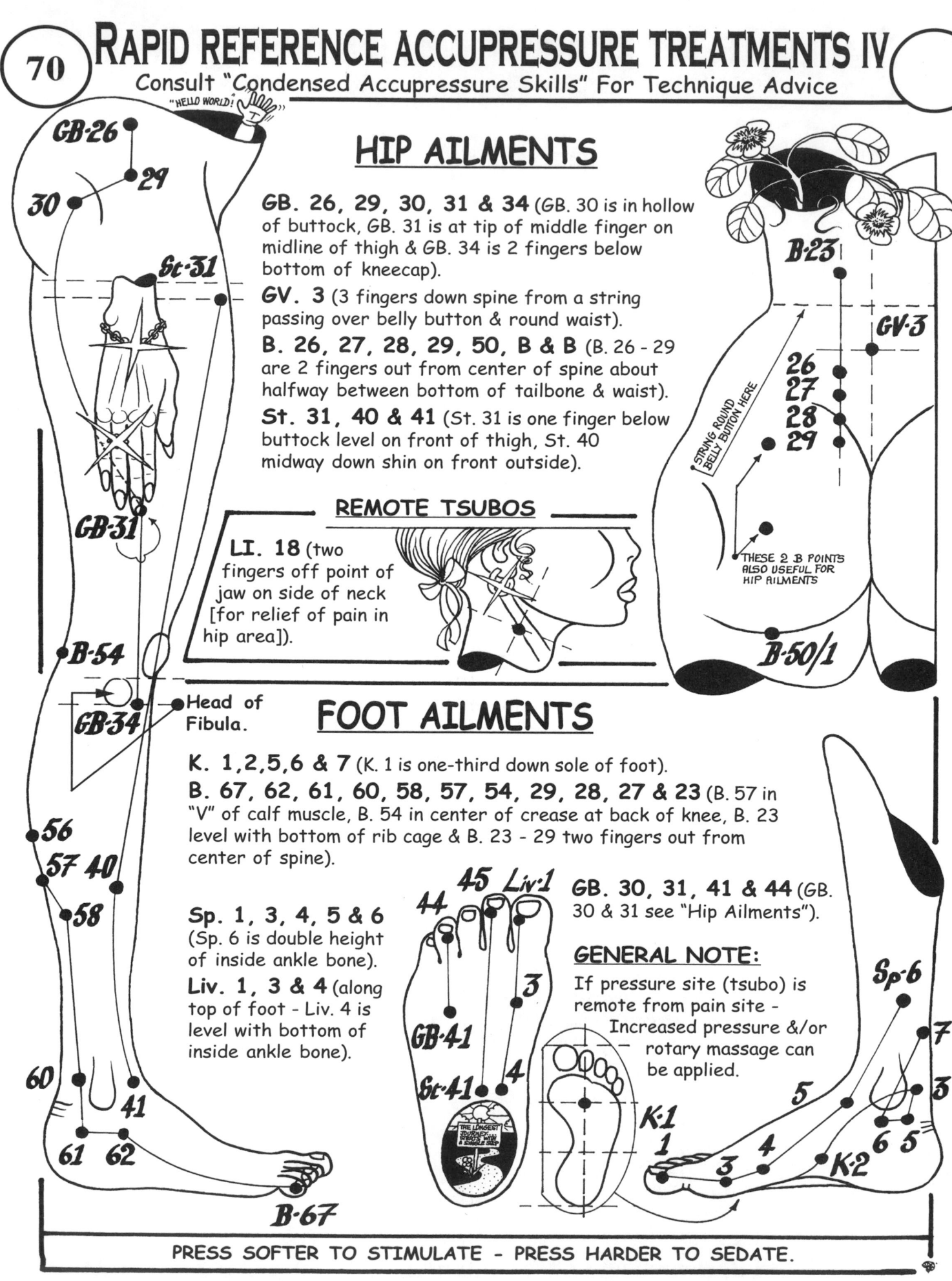

"HELLO WORLD!"

GB·26

29

30

St·31

GB·31

B·54

GB·34   Head of Fibula.

56

57 40

58

60

41

61 62

B·67

HIP AILMENTS

GB. 26, 29, 30, 31 & 34 (GB. 30 is in hollow of buttock, GB. 31 is at tip of middle finger on midline of thigh & GB. 34 is 2 fingers below bottom of kneecap).

GV. 3 (3 fingers down spine from a string passing over belly button & round waist).

B. 26, 27, 28, 29, 50, B & B (B. 26 - 29 are 2 fingers out from center of spine about halfway between bottom of tailbone & waist).

St. 31, 40 & 41 (St. 31 is one finger below buttock level on front of thigh, St. 40 midway down shin on front outside).

REMOTE TSUBOS

LI. 18 (two fingers off point of jaw on side of neck [for relief of pain in hip area]).

B·23

GV·3

26
27
28
29

STRING ROUND BELLY BUTTON HERE

THESE 2 B POINTS ALSO USEFUL FOR HIP AILMENTS

B·50/1

FOOT AILMENTS

K. 1, 2, 5, 6 & 7 (K. 1 is one-third down sole of foot).

B. 67, 62, 61, 60, 58, 57, 54, 29, 28, 27 & 23 (B. 57 in "V" of calf muscle, B. 54 in center of crease at back of knee, B. 23 level with bottom of rib cage & B. 23 - 29 two fingers out from center of spine).

Sp. 1, 3, 4, 5 & 6 (Sp. 6 is double height of inside ankle bone).

Liv. 1, 3 & 4 (along top of foot - Liv. 4 is level with bottom of inside ankle bone).

44 45 Liv·1

3

GB·41

St·41

THE LONGEST JOURNEY...

GB. 30, 31, 41 & 44 (GB. 30 & 31 see "Hip Ailments").

GENERAL NOTE:

If pressure site (tsubo) is remote from pain site - Increased pressure &/or rotary massage can be applied.

Sp·6

7

5

3

4

K·1
1

3 4 K·2

6 5

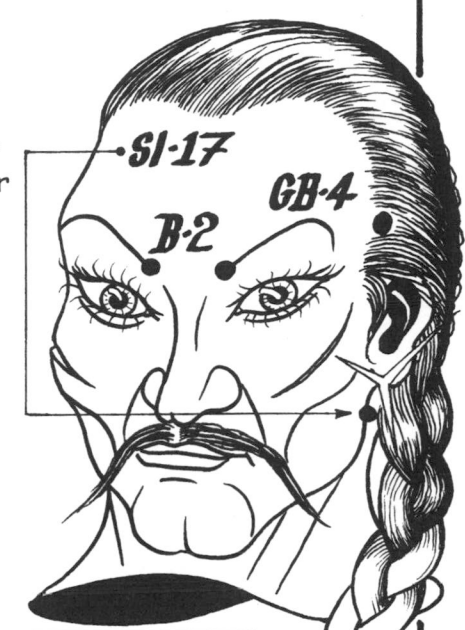

NECK AILMENTS

GB. 4, 20, 21 (GB.4 is one finger above & forward of top of ear, GB.21 is on top of shoulder halfway between prominent spinal bone & shoulder tip).

GV. 14 & 16 (GV.14 between prominent spinal bone & next one down, GV.16 in hollow at base of skull).

B. 10 (one finger down from skull bone about 3 fingers apart on base of neck).

SI. 15 & 17 (SI. 15 is two-thirds along a line from tip of shoulder bone to prominent spinal bone, SI.17 is one finger down from ear lobe on back of jaw bone).

"A THORNY PROBLEM"

IMPORTANT NOTE

Don't forget to treat all acupressure points (tsubos) except "GV" (Governing Vessel) & "CV" (Conception Vessel) **on both sides** (left & right) **of the body.**

GV.16 · GB.20 · 21 · SI·15 · B·10 · GV·14 · TRIGGER POINT · SHOULDER BLADE · RIB CAGE · 23 · GV·4 · 26 · B·27 · 2 · GB·30 · GV·1 · B·50/1 · 54 · 57 · B·60

LOW BACK AILMENTS

GB. 30 (in hollow of buttock muscle).

GV. 1, 2 & 4 (GV.1 & 2 on tailbone, GV.4 is opposite the belly button but on the spine - Use a string round waist).

B. 23, 26, 27, 50/1, 54, 57 & 60 (B.23 level with bottom of ribcage, B.23, 26 & 27 are two fingers out from center of spine, B.50/1, 54 & 57 on centerline of back of leg at buttock crease, knee crease & "V" of calf muscle, B. 60 on outside of leg just to rear of anklebone).

TRIGGER POINTS....

....**for low back ailments** are on the upper back, 2 fingers out from the centerline of spine & on a line between 5th & 6th spinal bone down (as shown).

NUMBERING....

....**of tsubos may vary across cultural boundaries** (particularly "B" [Bladder Meridian]) but the effects of pressure on a given site remain basically the same.

FOR LOW BACK ACHE
- LIE ON FLOOR · PULL KNEES (BENT) TOGETHER (& LATER SINGLY) UP TOWARD CHIN WITH (& LATER WITHOUT) HELP FROM HANDS
- ALSO DO DAILY BENT LEG SIT UPS, BACK RAISES & MAINTAIN GOOD POSTURE · TAKE EXTRA B COMPLEX, CALCIUM & DRINK SLIPPERY ELM TEA.

SI-17 · B·2 · GB-4

7 SECONDS PER TSUBO. IF REQUIRED REPEAT AFTER 10 SECS (3 IN ALL).

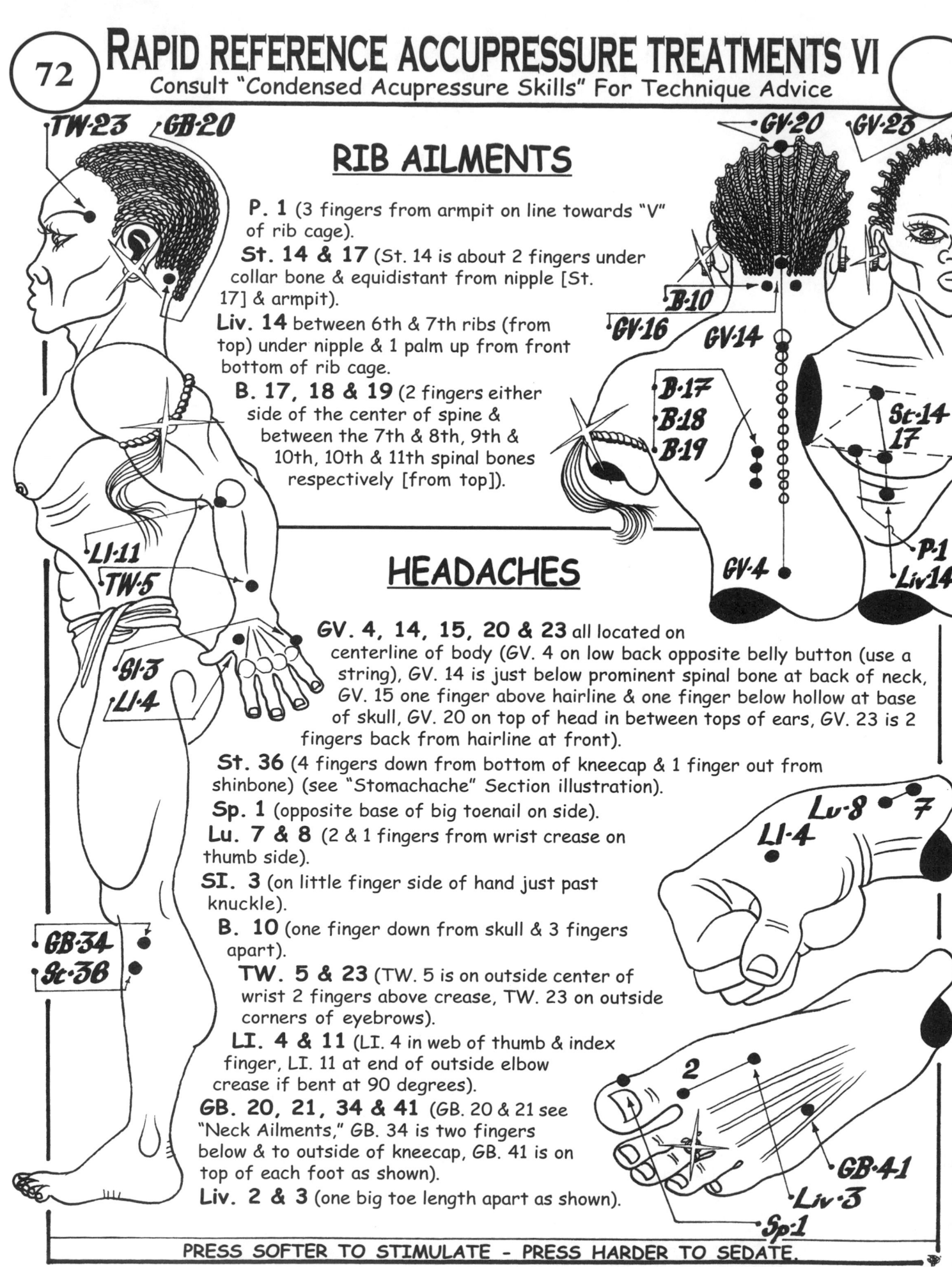

RIB AILMENTS

P. 1 (3 fingers from armpit on line towards "V" of rib cage).

St. 14 & 17 (St. 14 is about 2 fingers under collar bone & equidistant from nipple [St. 17] & armpit).

Liv. 14 between 6th & 7th ribs (from top) under nipple & 1 palm up from front bottom of rib cage.

B. 17, 18 & 19 (2 fingers either side of the center of spine & between the 7th & 8th, 9th & 10th, 10th & 11th spinal bones respectively [from top]).

HEADACHES

GV. 4, 14, 15, 20 & 23 all located on centerline of body (GV. 4 on low back opposite belly button (use a string), GV. 14 is just below prominent spinal bone at back of neck, GV. 15 one finger above hairline & one finger below hollow at base of skull, GV. 20 on top of head in between tops of ears, GV. 23 is 2 fingers back from hairline at front).

St. 36 (4 fingers down from bottom of kneecap & 1 finger out from shinbone) (see "Stomachache" Section illustration).

Sp. 1 (opposite base of big toenail on side).

Lu. 7 & 8 (2 & 1 fingers from wrist crease on thumb side).

SI. 3 (on little finger side of hand just past knuckle).

B. 10 (one finger down from skull & 3 fingers apart).

TW. 5 & 23 (TW. 5 is on outside center of wrist 2 fingers above crease, TW. 23 on outside corners of eyebrows).

LI. 4 & 11 (LI. 4 in web of thumb & index finger, LI. 11 at end of outside elbow crease if bent at 90 degrees).

GB. 20, 21, 34 & 41 (GB. 20 & 21 see "Neck Ailments," GB. 34 is two fingers below & to outside of kneecap, GB. 41 is on top of each foot as shown).

Liv. 2 & 3 (one big toe length apart as shown).

PRESS SOFTER TO STIMULATE - PRESS HARDER TO SEDATE.

NAUSEA

GV. 16 (in hollow at base of skull).

Liv. 13 (just below front of rib cage).

P. 4 & 6 (on center of inside wrist 2 & 4 fingers from wrist crease).

Lu. 3 (on front outer upper arm 3 fingers down from armpit level).

GB. 14 (1 finger above eyebrow directly above pupil [in hollow]).

H. 1 (in armpit just under pectoral muscle).

St. 21 (4 fingers up from belly button & 3 fingers out from centerline on lower ribcage edge).

B.18 & 41 (mid back [9th spinal vertebrae] 2 & 4 fingers out from centerline of spine).

> **TRAVEL SICKNESS** can also be treated by the above points (particularly B. 18).

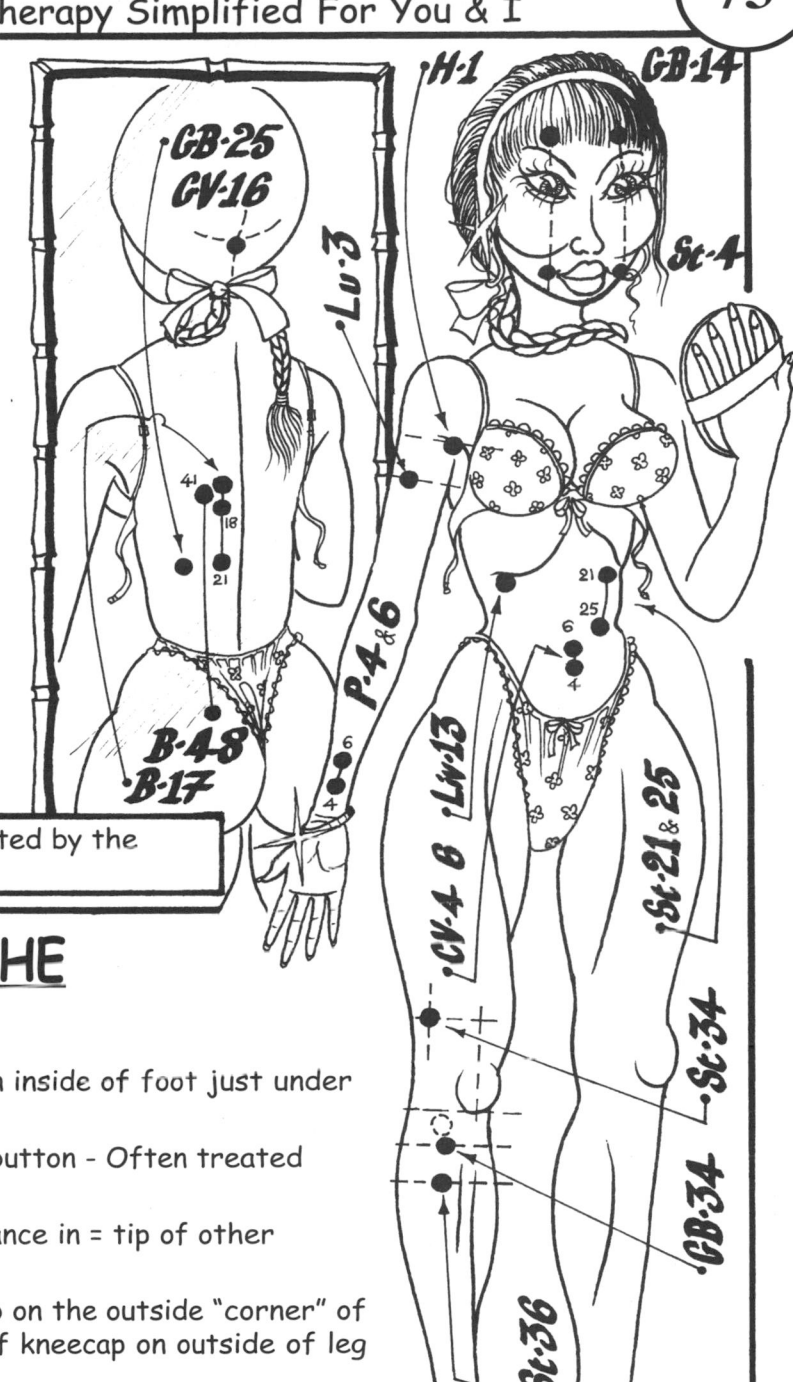

STOMACHACHE

Liv. 13 (just below front of rib cage).

Sp. 4 (one palm back from end of big toe on inside of foot just under bone (press up & in).

CV. 4 & 6 (4 & 2 fingers down from belly button - Often treated with palm pressure).

LI. 4 (in web of thumb & index finger [distance in = tip of other thumb to first joint]).

GB.25 & 34 (GB. 25 just below twelfth rib on the outside "corner" of the back, GB. 34 is 2 fingers below bottom of kneecap on outside of leg just below head of fibula).

St. 4, 25, 34, 36 & 44 (St. 4 in line with mouth & below pupil, St. 25 is 3 fingers to the sides of belly button, St. 34 is 3 fingers above & to outside of center of top of kneecap, St. 36 is 4 fingers below bottom of kneecap & 1 finger out from shinbone, St. 44 is between 2nd & 3rd toes on top [press in]).

B. 17 & 21. (B. 17 is between 7th & 8th spinal bone & 2 fingers out from center, B. 21 is 3 fingers above bottom of ribcage & 2 fingers out from spinal center).

LI·4
(IN DISTANCE x = y)

RAPID REFERENCE ACCUPRESSURE TREATMENTS VIII

Consult "Condensed Acupressure Skills" For Technique Advice

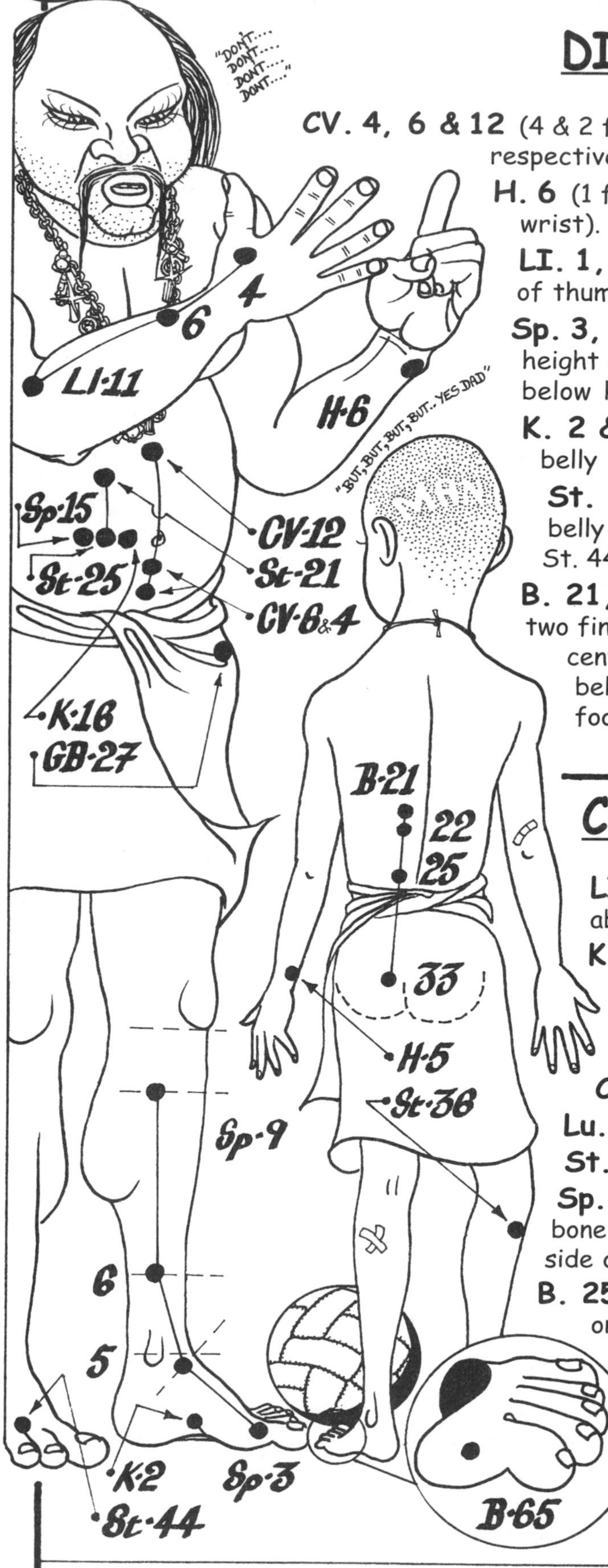
"DON'T....
DONT....
DONT....
DONT...."
"BUT, BUT, BUT, BUT.. YES DAD"
4
6
LI·11
H·6
Sp·15
St·25
CV·12
St·21
CV·6&4
K·16
GB·27
B·21
22
25
33
H·5
St·36
Sp·9
6
5
K·2
Sp·3
St·44
B·65

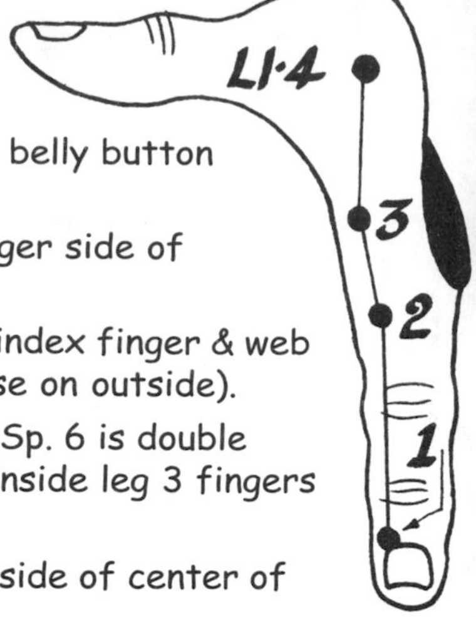
LI·4
3
2
1

DIARRHEA

CV. 4, 6 & 12 (4 & 2 fingers below & one palm above belly button respectively).

H. 6 (1 finger from crease on little finger side of wrist).

LI. 1, 2, 3, 4 & 11 (LI . 1 - 4 on index finger & web of thumb, LI. 11 at end of elbow crease on outside).

Sp. 3, 6 & 9 (all on inside foot/leg, Sp. 6 is double height of ankle bone, Sp. 9 is center inside leg 3 fingers below kneecap).

K. 2 & 16 (K. 16 is 2 fingers either side of center of belly button).

St. 21, 25 & 44 (St. 21 & 25 both 3 fingers to side of belly button, but 4 fingers up, & level with respectively, St. 44 is at base of 2nd & 3rd toes on top).

B. 21, 22, 25 & 65 (B. 21 see "Stomachache," B. 22 is two fingers below B. 21, B. 25 is 2 fingers either side of center of 5th lumber vertebra - (or about 2 fingers below belly button level), B. 65 is on the outside of the foot just past base of little toe).

CONSTIPATION

LI. 4 is the key point & will often be tender

LI. 4 & 6 (LI. 4 see "Diarrhea," LI. 6 is 3 fingers above wrist on thumb side).

K. 1 & 16 (K. 1 is one-third along sole of foot, K. 16 [see "Diarrhea" Section]).

H. 5 (one thumb width up from wrist crease on little finger side of wrist).

CV. 6 (see "Diarrhea" Section).

Lu. 3 (see "Nausea" Section).

St. 36 (see "Stomachache" Section).

Sp. 5 & 15 (Sp. 5 is one finger from ankle bone toward big toe, Sp. 15 is 4 fingers either side of belly button).

B. 25 & 33 (B. 25 see "Diarrhea" Section, B. 33 one finger either side of center of tailbone).

GB. 27 & 34 (GB. 27 on front side of each hip, GB. 34 see "Stomachache " Section).

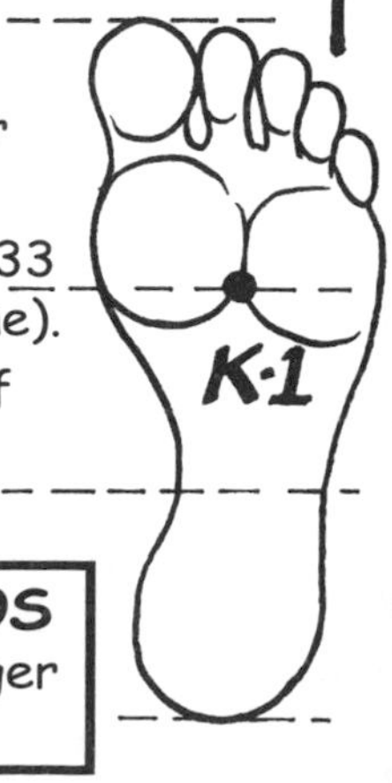
K·1

Don't forget **STOMACH TSUBOS** are often treated with multiple finger or palm pressure.

PRESS SOFTER TO STIMULATE - PRESS HARDER TO SEDATE.

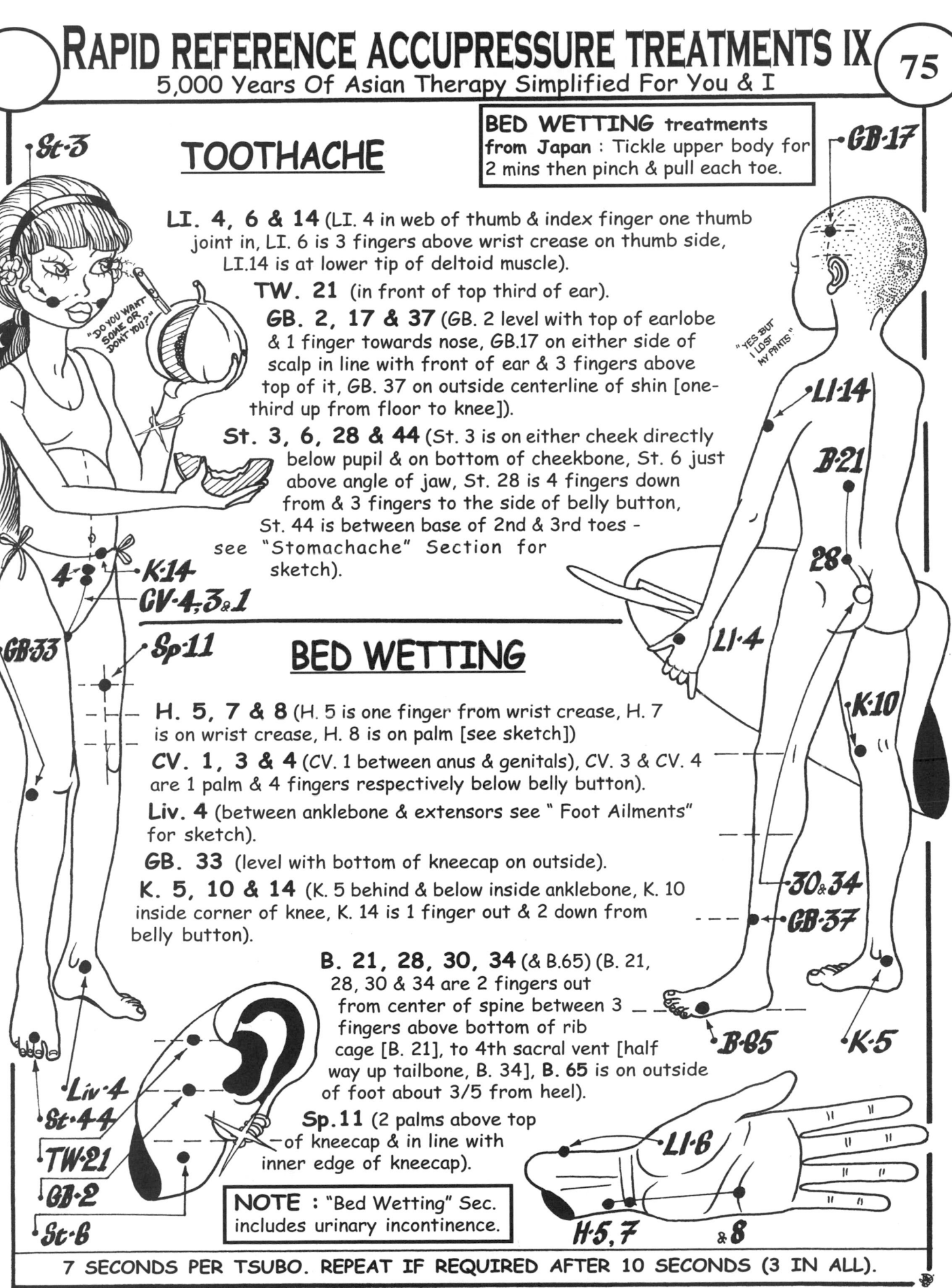

BED WETTING treatments from **Japan** : Tickle upper body for 2 mins then pinch & pull each toe.

TOOTHACHE

LI. 4, 6 & 14 (LI. 4 in web of thumb & index finger one thumb joint in, LI. 6 is 3 fingers above wrist crease on thumb side, LI.14 is at lower tip of deltoid muscle).

TW. 21 (in front of top third of ear).

GB. 2, 17 & 37 (GB. 2 level with top of earlobe & 1 finger towards nose, GB.17 on either side of scalp in line with front of ear & 3 fingers above top of it, GB. 37 on outside centerline of shin [one-third up from floor to knee]).

St. 3, 6, 28 & 44 (St. 3 is on either cheek directly below pupil & on bottom of cheekbone, St. 6 just above angle of jaw, St. 28 is 4 fingers down from & 3 fingers to the side of belly button, St. 44 is between base of 2nd & 3rd toes - see "Stomachache" Section for sketch).

BED WETTING

H. 5, 7 & 8 (H. 5 is one finger from wrist crease, H. 7 is on wrist crease, H. 8 is on palm [see sketch])

CV. 1, 3 & 4 (CV. 1 between anus & genitals), CV. 3 & CV. 4 are 1 palm & 4 fingers respectively below belly button).

Liv. 4 (between anklebone & extensors see " Foot Ailments" for sketch).

GB. 33 (level with bottom of kneecap on outside).

K. 5, 10 & 14 (K. 5 behind & below inside anklebone, K. 10 inside corner of knee, K. 14 is 1 finger out & 2 down from belly button).

B. 21, 28, 30, 34 (& B.65) (B. 21, 28, 30 & 34 are 2 fingers out from center of spine between 3 fingers above bottom of rib cage [B. 21], to 4th sacral vent [half way up tailbone, B. 34], **B. 65** is on outside of foot about 3/5 from heel).

Sp.11 (2 palms above top of kneecap & in line with inner edge of kneecap).

NOTE : "Bed Wetting" Sec. includes urinary incontinence.

7 SECONDS PER TSUBO. REPEAT IF REQUIRED AFTER 10 SECONDS (3 IN ALL).

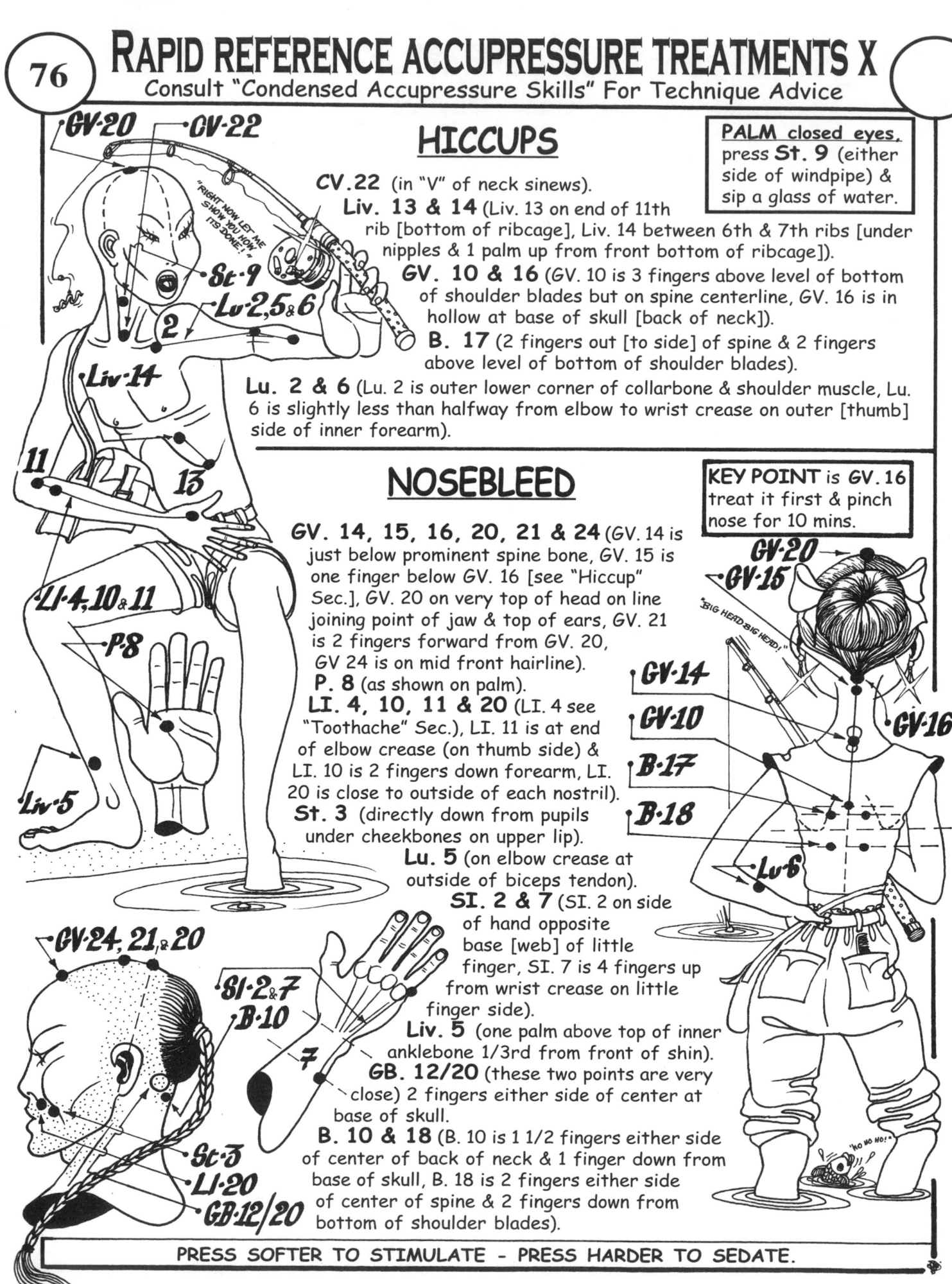

HICCUPS

CV.22 (in "V" of neck sinews).

Liv. 13 & 14 (Liv. 13 on end of 11th rib [bottom of ribcage], Liv. 14 between 6th & 7th ribs [under nipples & 1 palm up from front bottom of ribcage]).

GV. 10 & 16 (GV. 10 is 3 fingers above level of bottom of shoulder blades but on spine centerline, GV. 16 is in hollow at base of skull [back of neck]).

B. 17 (2 fingers out [to side] of spine & 2 fingers above level of bottom of shoulder blades).

Lu. 2 & 6 (Lu. 2 is outer lower corner of collarbone & shoulder muscle, Lu. 6 is slightly less than halfway from elbow to wrist crease on outer [thumb] side of inner forearm).

PALM closed eyes, press **St. 9** (either side of windpipe) & sip a glass of water.

NOSEBLEED

GV. 14, 15, 16, 20, 21 & 24 (GV. 14 is just below prominent spine bone, GV. 15 is one finger below GV. 16 [see "Hiccup" Sec.], GV. 20 on very top of head on line joining point of jaw & top of ears, GV. 21 is 2 fingers forward from GV. 20, GV 24 is on mid front hairline).

P. 8 (as shown on palm).

LI. 4, 10, 11 & 20 (LI. 4 see "Toothache" Sec.), LI. 11 is at end of elbow crease (on thumb side) & LI. 10 is 2 fingers down forearm, LI. 20 is close to outside of each nostril).

St. 3 (directly down from pupils under cheekbones on upper lip).

Lu. 5 (on elbow crease at outside of biceps tendon).

SI. 2 & 7 (SI. 2 on side of hand opposite base [web] of little finger, SI. 7 is 4 fingers up from wrist crease on little finger side).

Liv. 5 (one palm above top of inner anklebone 1/3rd from front of shin).

GB. 12/20 (these two points are very close) 2 fingers either side of center at base of skull.

B. 10 & 18 (B. 10 is 1 1/2 fingers either side of center of back of neck & 1 finger down from base of skull, B. 18 is 2 fingers either side of center of spine & 2 fingers down from bottom of shoulder blades).

KEY POINT is GV. 16 treat it first & pinch nose for 10 mins.

PRESS SOFTER TO STIMULATE - PRESS HARDER TO SEDATE.

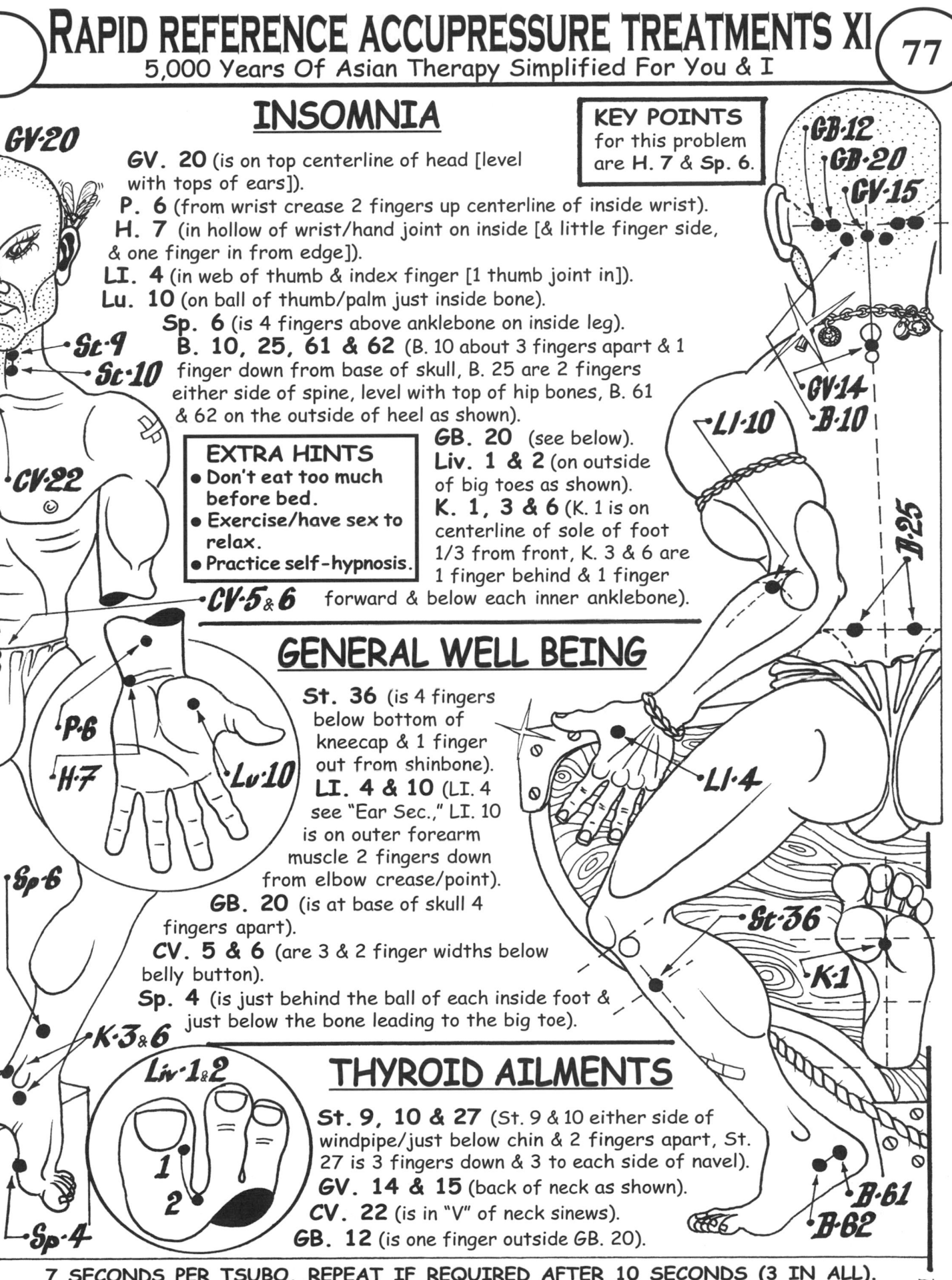

INSOMNIA

GV. 20 (is on top centerline of head [level with tops of ears]).

P. 6 (from wrist crease 2 fingers up centerline of inside wrist).

H. 7 (in hollow of wrist/hand joint on inside [& little finger side, & one finger in from edge]).

LI. 4 (in web of thumb & index finger [1 thumb joint in]).

Lu. 10 (on ball of thumb/palm just inside bone).

Sp. 6 (is 4 fingers above anklebone on inside leg).

B. 10, 25, 61 & 62 (B. 10 about 3 fingers apart & 1 finger down from base of skull, B. 25 are 2 fingers either side of spine, level with top of hip bones, B. 61 & 62 on the outside of heel as shown).

GB. 20 (see below).

Liv. 1 & 2 (on outside of big toes as shown).

K. 1, 3 & 6 (K. 1 is on centerline of sole of foot 1/3 from front, K. 3 & 6 are 1 finger behind & 1 finger forward & below each inner anklebone).

KEY POINTS for this problem are H. 7 & Sp. 6.

EXTRA HINTS
- Don't eat too much before bed.
- Exercise/have sex to relax.
- Practice self-hypnosis.

GENERAL WELL BEING

St. 36 (is 4 fingers below bottom of kneecap & 1 finger out from shinbone).

LI. 4 & 10 (LI. 4 see "Ear Sec.," LI. 10 is on outer forearm muscle 2 fingers down from elbow crease/point).

GB. 20 (is at base of skull 4 fingers apart).

CV. 5 & 6 (are 3 & 2 finger widths below belly button).

Sp. 4 (is just behind the ball of each inside foot & just below the bone leading to the big toe).

THYROID AILMENTS

St. 9, 10 & 27 (St. 9 & 10 either side of windpipe/just below chin & 2 fingers apart, St. 27 is 3 fingers down & 3 to each side of navel).

GV. 14 & 15 (back of neck as shown).

CV. 22 (is in "V" of neck sinews).

GB. 12 (is one finger outside GB. 20).

7 SECONDS PER TSUBO. REPEAT IF REQUIRED AFTER 10 SECONDS (3 IN ALL).

RAPID REFERENCE ACCUPRESSURE TREATMENTS XII

Consult "Condensed Acupressure Skills" For Technique Advice

EAR/HEARING AILMENTS

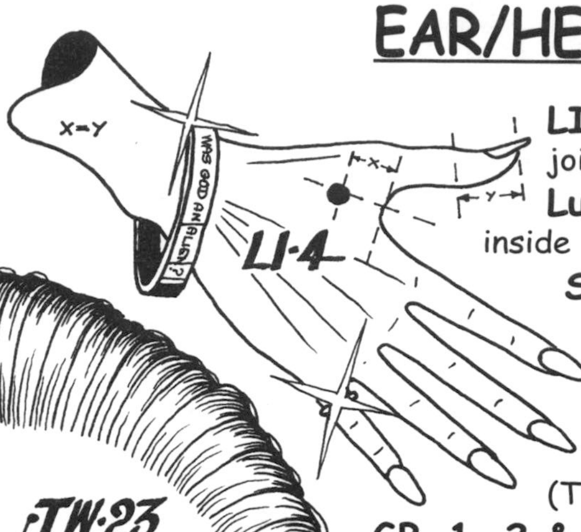
X=Y
WAS GOOD AN RUSH ?
LI·4

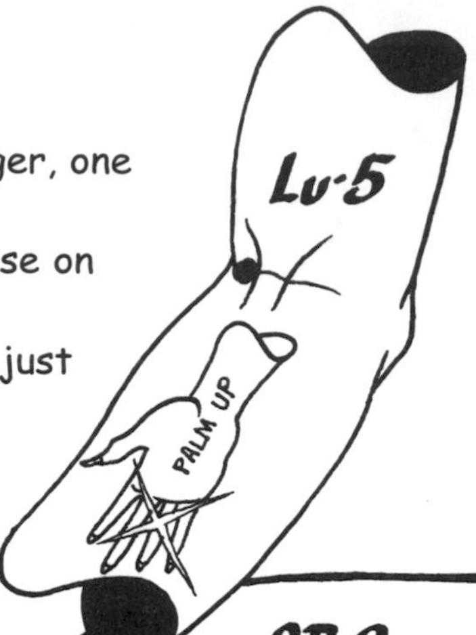
Lu·5
PALM UP

LI. 4 (in web of thumb & index finger, one joint in).
Lu. 5 (on outside of tendon at crease on inside of elbow).
SI. 19 (open mouth & feel hollow just in front of middle of ear lobe).
St. 3 (on line down from pupil & on bottom of cheekbone).
TW. 17, 18, 19 & 20 (TW. 17 is under ear lobe).
GB. 1, 2 & 3 (GB. 1 is one small finger out from outer eye corner).
K. 5 & 8 (K. 5 is 1 finger out from inside anklebone toward corner of heel, K. 8 is 2 fingers above inner ankle-bone & 1 finger to rear).

USE **SI·19** FOR RINGING OR WHISTLING NOISES IN EARS

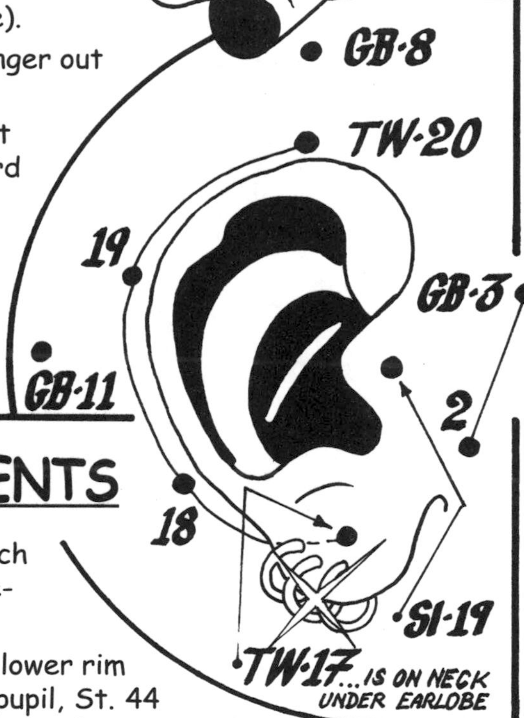
GB·8
TW·20
19
GB·3
GB·11
2
18
SI·19
TW·17...IS ON NECK UNDER EARLOBE

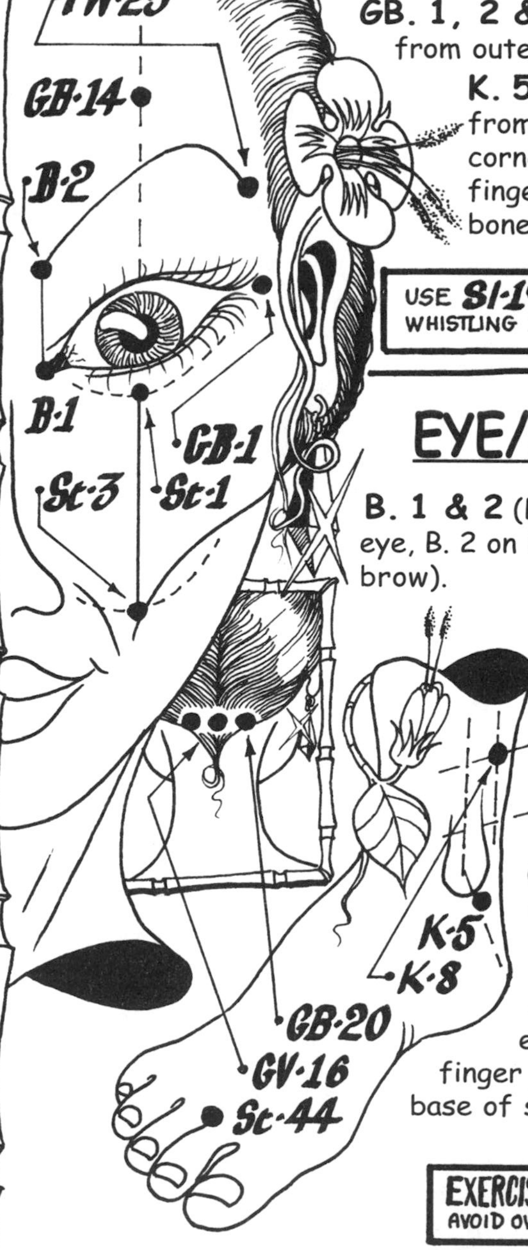
TW·23
GB·14
B·2
B·1
GB·1
St·3
St·1
K·5
K·8
GB·20
GV·16
St·44

EYE/SIGHT AILMENTS

B. 1 & 2 (B. 1 in inner corner of each eye, B. 2 on inner corner of each eye-brow).
St. 1 & 44 (St. 1 on lower rim of eye sockets below pupil, St. 44 between 2nd & 3rd toes at base on top).
TW. 10 & 23 (TW. 10 is on centerline of back of elbow 2 fingers above point, TW. 23 on outside corners of each eye-brow).
GB. 1, 3, 8, 11, 14 & 20 (GB. 1 & 3 as in "Ear Ailments," GB. 8 is one finger above top of ear, GB. 11 is one finger behind middle of ear, GB. 14 on forehead (above eye pupil) in hollow about 1 finger above eyebrow, GB. 20 at base of skull 4 fingers apart).

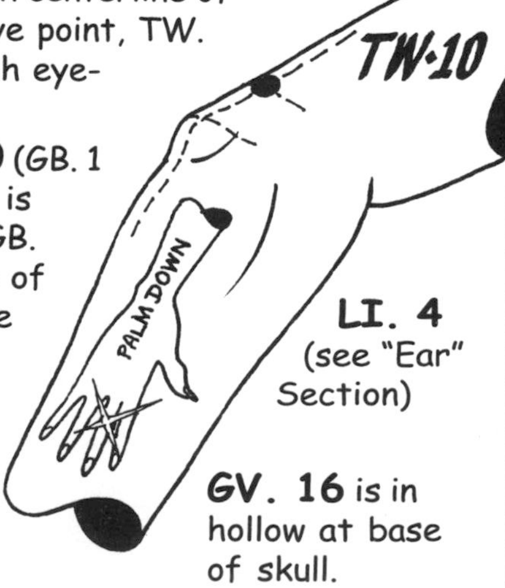
TW·10
PALM DOWN

LI. 4 (see "Ear" Section)

GV. 16 is in hollow at base of skull.

EXERCISE EYES DAILY (READ W/OUT GLASSES) AVOID OVEREATING & EXCESS OIL/FAT.

PRESS SOFTER TO STIMULATE - PRESS HARDER TO SEDATE

5,000 Years Of Asian Therapy Simplified For You & I

GV·16 & 15 (LOWER)
TW·17
St·6
LI·20
B·2

COLDS/SINUS

KEY POINT for this page (top & bottom) is Lu. 1

LI. 4, 16 & 20 (LI. 4 in web of thumb & index finger, LI. 16 is in hollow just above shoulder, LI. 20 is either side of bottom of nose in hollows).

B. 2 (inner corner of each eyebrow [also use B. 12]).

Lu. 1 & 7 (Lu. 1 is one finger down from collarbone & 4 from inside corner, Lu. 7 on thumb side of wrist, 2 fingers from crease).

TW. 5 & 17 (TW. 5 is 2 fingers above wrist on back, TW. 17 under earlobe).

CV. 14 (3 fingers below chest bone on centerline).

SI. 3 (at base of little finger on side of hand).

St. 1, 3, 6, 9 & 10 (St. 1 mid lower eye socket rim, St. 3 under pupil at bottom of cheekbone, St. 6 just above angle of jaw, St. 9 & 10 on windpipe 2 fingers either side of center & level with bottom of chin & 2 fingers down respectively).

GB. 14 & 20 (GB. 14 is 1 finger above eyebrow above pupil, GB. 20 either side of GV. 16 [2 fingers]).

GV. 12, 13, 14, 15 & 16 (all on spinal center - GV. 16 at base of skull, GV. 15 one small finger above hairline, GV. 14 just below prominent spine bone).

K. 22 (4 fingers toward armpit from tip of breast bone).

Sp. 16 (at bottom of 10th ribs).

"COME HERE DEAR"

12
B·13
LI·16
SI·3
GV·14
13
12

NOTE: THESE POINTS WHEN "WRAPPED AROUND" ARE CLOSE TO THE WINDPIPE.

FLATVIEW OF POINTS:
St·10
St·9

FRONT THROAT VIEW

EXTRA HINTS ON SINUS: DONT OVEREAT BEFORE BED · AVOID SUGAR & DAIRY · DO DRINK FENUGREEK TEA · ALSO TRY POINTS St·2, B·7, LI·19 · DO EAT GARLIC.

GB·14
"NO"
Lu·1
K·22

TW·5

COUGHS

11
9
7

St. 36 (1 finger out from shinbone & 4 down from bottom of kneecap).

GV. 14 (see "Colds" Sec.).

LI. 1 & 4 (LI.1 on thumb side & end of index finger nail, LI. 4 see above).

Lu. 1, 5, 7, 9 & 11 (Lu. 1 & 7 as in "Colds," Lu. 5 on outside of biceps tendon).

CV. 6 & 12. (CV. 6 is 2 fingers below belly button, CV. 12 is 4 fingers below breastbone).

B. 12 & 13 (between 2nd, 3rd & 4th spinal bone down from prominent one, but 2 fingers either side).

BELLY BUTTON
6

Lu·5

OTHER POINTS exist for coughs 4 fingers from spine between shoulder blades (middle to top).

St·36
Sp·16
St·1 & 3 (LOWER)   CV·6, 12 & 14   LI·4

7 SECONDS PER TSUBO. REPEAT IF REQUIRED AFTER 10 SECONDS (3 IN ALL).

THROAT AILMENTS

KEY POINT for all this page is **Lu. 1.**

LI. 1, 4, 9, 14 & 20 (LI. 1, 14 & 20 see "Colds" Section), LI. 9 is 4 fingers from elbow crease on muscle of outside forearm, LI. 14 is on the centerline of bottom of deltoid muscle (one third down upper arm).

GV. 13 (between 2nd & 3rd spinal bone down from prominent one at base of neck [see "Colds" Section]).

TW. 10 (on centerline of back of upper arm [2 finger widths above elbow tip]).

K. 1 & 5 (K. 1 on sole of foot one-third along centerline, K. 5 one finger down & to rear of inside anklebone).

St. 6 & 40 (St. 6 see "Colds" Section, St. 40 midway down shin on front outside of bone).

SI. 17 & 18 (SI. 17 is one finger down from ear lobe on back of jawbone, SI. 18 is 2 fingers from ear lobe towards nostril).

CV. 22 (between "V" shaped neck sinews).

Lu. 1, 6, 8, 10 & 11 (Lu. 1 & 11 see "Coughs" Section, Lu. 6 is slightly less than halfway from elbow to wrist crease on outer side of inner forearm, Lu. 8 is one finger up from wrist crease).

GB. 21, 38 & 40 (GB. 21 is one finger up from halfway along a line from shoulder bone tip to prominent spinal bone at base of neck - [treat gently] GB. 38 is one palm width above outside anklebone, GB. 40 is just in front of outside anklebone on line toward little toe).

BREATHING AILMENTS

LI. 4 & 14 (see "Colds" & "Throat" Sections).

CV. 17 (between nipples, 2 fingers above chest bone on centerline).

GV. 12 & 14 (see "Colds" Section).

P. 2, 3 & 6 (P. 2 is 3 fingers down from armpit on front of biceps, P. 3 on inside of biceps tendon, P. 6 is 2 fingers from wrist crease).

B. 12 & 13 (between 2nd & 3rd, & 3rd & 4th spinal bones down from prominent one at neck, & 2 fingers out from spine).

Liv. 2 (in between big & next toe).

Sp. 8 & 9 (Sp. 9 is 3 fingers below bottom of kneecap on center of inside leg, Sp. 8 is 1 palm below Sp. 9).

Lu. 1, 5, 7 & 9 (see "Colds/Coughs" Sec.)

St. 4, 13 & 16 (St. 4 at corners of mouth, St. 13 is halfway along & under collarbone, St. 16 is between 3rd & 4th rib down & under St. 13 but above nipple).

Labels on illustrations: K-1, K-5, CV-22, St-13, LI-14, St-4, SI-18, P-2, P-3, 16, TW-10, GV-13, GB-21, B-12 & 13 (Bottom), Sp-9, 17, 9, 11, 10, 8, Lu-6, P-6, CV-17, Liv-2, 8, St-40, GB-38 & 40 (Lower)

Speech bubbles: "YES GRANDAD YES GRANDAD YES..." "AND DON'T FORGET THE ANCHOR & STAY AWAY FROM THE REEF & DON'T SHOW OFF &..."

PRESS SOFTER TO STIMULATE - PRESS HARDER TO SEDATE.

HEART ATTACKS & STROKES

K. 1 (on centerline of sole of foot 1/3 from front).
B. 15 (on back, 2 fingers out from center opposite nipples).
Lu. 9 (on palm side of wrist to thumb base line).
H. 7 & 9 (H. 7 on little finger tip [squeeze hard], H. 9 in hollow at little finger side of wrist crease [just in from edge]).
GV. 11, 16 & 26 (GV. 11 on spine between B. 15 points, GV. 16 in hollow at base of skull, GV. 26 below nose on center of upper lip).

BAD CIRCULATION

Sp. 4 (in the hollow behind the ball of the inside foot).
K. 1 (on sole of foot [see at top]).
GB. 31 (on midline of outer thigh, level with tip of middle finger).
B. 43 & 57 (B. 43 just off inner edges of shoulder blades [just above armpit level], B. 57 in "V" of calf muscle).

HIGH BLOOD PRESSURE

K. 1 (mid sole of foot one-third from front).
St. 9 & 36 (St. 9 either side of windpipe just below chin level, St. 36 is 4 fingers below bottom of kneecap & 1 finger outside of shinbone).
P. 9 (on palm side tip of middle finger).
SI. 10 (on back just below arm/shoulder joint).
LI. 11 & 15 (LI. 11 at end of crease when elbow bent at 90 degrees, LI. 15 just below tip of shoulder bone [hang arm by side]).
GB. 21 (one finger up from halfway along a line from shoulder blade tip to prominent spine bone [back of neck] do with arm down).
CV. 4 & 17 (CV. 4 is 4 fingers below belly button and CV. 17 on center chest between nipples.
TW. 5 (on back of wrist 2 fingers up from crease).
GV. 16 (in hollow at base of skull [back of neck]).

Liv. 13 (just below front lower tips of rib cage).

B. 15, 54 & 62 ([B. 15 see at top], B. 54 in hollow at back of knee, B. 62 outside foot 2 fingers below and forward of anklebone).

KEY POINTS for this problem St. 9, K. 1 & LI. 11.

TIP: Squeeze/pull ends of middle and little fingers.

Labels on illustrations: GV-26, "COOL IT ROMEO", "YO BABY! HOW'S ABOUT A DATE?", St-9, P-9, 9, 8, Lu-9, H-7, GV-16, CV-17, B-43, B-15, GV-11, CV-4, SI-10, Liv-13, K-1, 54, B-57, GB-31, St-36, Sp-4, B-62, TW-5, 90°, LI-15 *(LOCATE WITH ARM DOWN)*, GB-21, GV-16, LI-11

7 SECONDS PER TSUBO. REPEAT IF REQUIRED AFTER 10 SECONDS (3 IN ALL).

Consult "Condensed Acupressure Skills" For Technique Advice

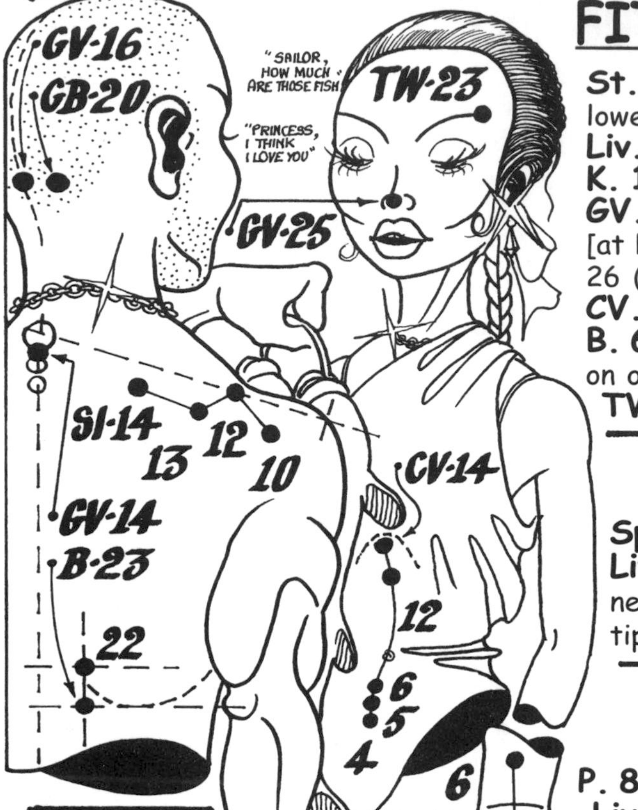
GV-16
GB-20
"SAILOR, HOW MUCH ARE THOSE FISH"
"PRINCESS, I THINK I LOVE YOU"
TW-23
GV-25
SI-14
13
12
10
CV-14
GV-14
B-23
22
12
6
5
4
6
Lu-10
LI-4
P-8

FITS/FAINTING/UNCONSCIOUS

St. 41 & 42 (St. 41 on instep of foot, St. 42 is 2 fingers lower down).
Liv. 1 & 2 (on outside of big toe [see sketch]).
K. 1 (see "Heart Attack" Sec.).
GV. 14, 25 & 26 (GV. 14 between prominent spinal bone [at back of neck] & next down, GV. 25 is on nose tip), GV. 26 (see "Heart Attack").
CV. 12 (one palm width above belly button).
B. 60 (in hollow to rear of anklebone on outside of foot).
TW. 23 (on outside tips of eyebrows).

KEY POINTS are: **K. 1 & GV. 26**

CRAMPS/MUSCLE SPASMS

Sp. 4 (in hollow behind ball of inside foot).
Liv. 3 (on foot top between big & next toe tendons 2/5 way from toe tip to ankle).

TIP: Press **Liv. 3** at same time as cramp site.

EXHAUSTION/FATIGUE

P. 8 (on palm as shown).
Liv. 1 & 2 (on outside of big toe [see below]).
GV. 14 & 16 ([GV. 14 see at top], GV. 16 in the hollow at base of skull [back of neck]).
St. 43 (on foot top halfway between toe tip and ankle [between 2nd & 3rd tendons]).
SI. 10,12,13 & 14 (scattered as shown below a line between shoulder bone tip & prominent spine bone at base of neck).
CV. 4,5,6 & 14 (4,3 & 2 fingers below belly button, CV. 14 is just below chest bone [centerline of abdomen]).
GB. 20, 21, 34 & 41 (GB.20 are 4 fingers apart on base of skull line, GB. 21 [see over], GB. 34 is 2 fingers below bottom of kneecap on outside, GB. 41 [see below]).
B. 22, 23, 59 & 60 (B.23 level with bottom of ribcage & 2 fingers out from spine center, B. 22 [2 fingers above B . 23], B. 59 & 60 behind outer ankle-bone as shown).
K. 1–7 (scattered around inner ankle-bone as shown).

KEY POINTS: GB. 21, K. 1 & K. 7

DIZZY

KEY POINTS: GB. 20, Liv. 3, K. 1 & P. 6

OTHERS: LI. 4 ([outer web on thumb], **Lu. 10** palm side outer ball of thumb, **B. 66 & 67** outside of little toe).

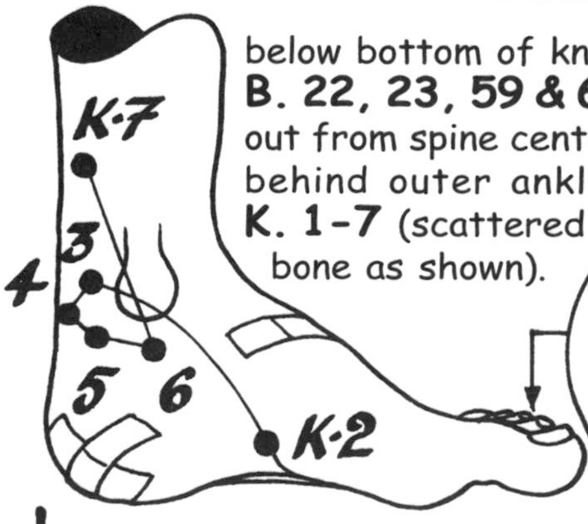
K-7
3
4
5
6
K-2

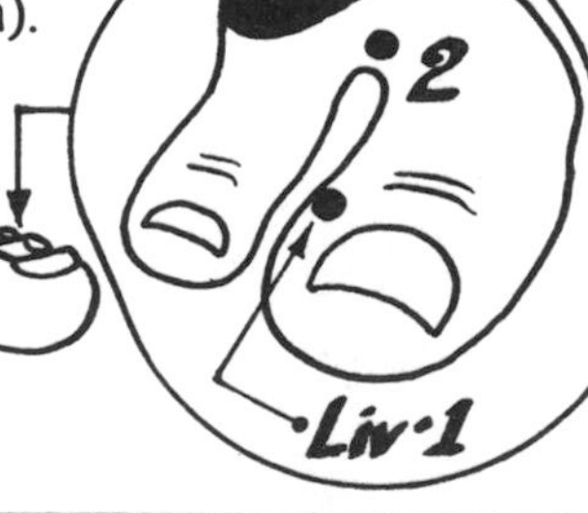
2
Liv-1

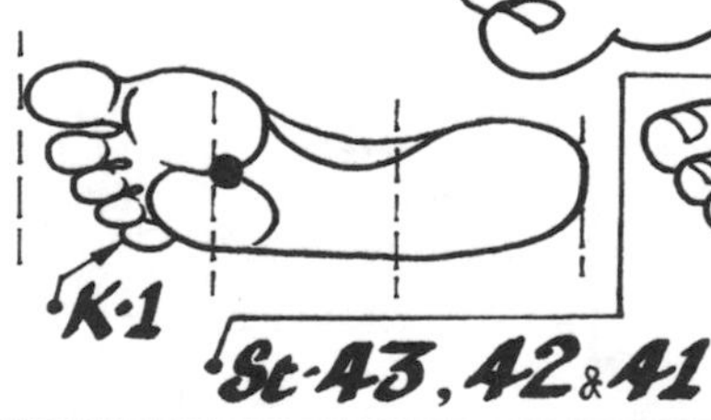
K-1
St-43, 42 & 41

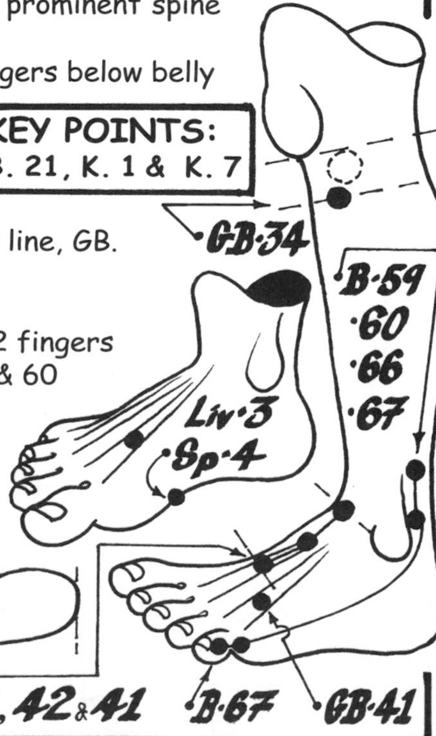
GB-34
B-59
60
66
67
Liv-3
Sp-4
B-67
GB-41

PRESS SOFTER TO STIMULATE - PRESS HARDER TO SEDATE.

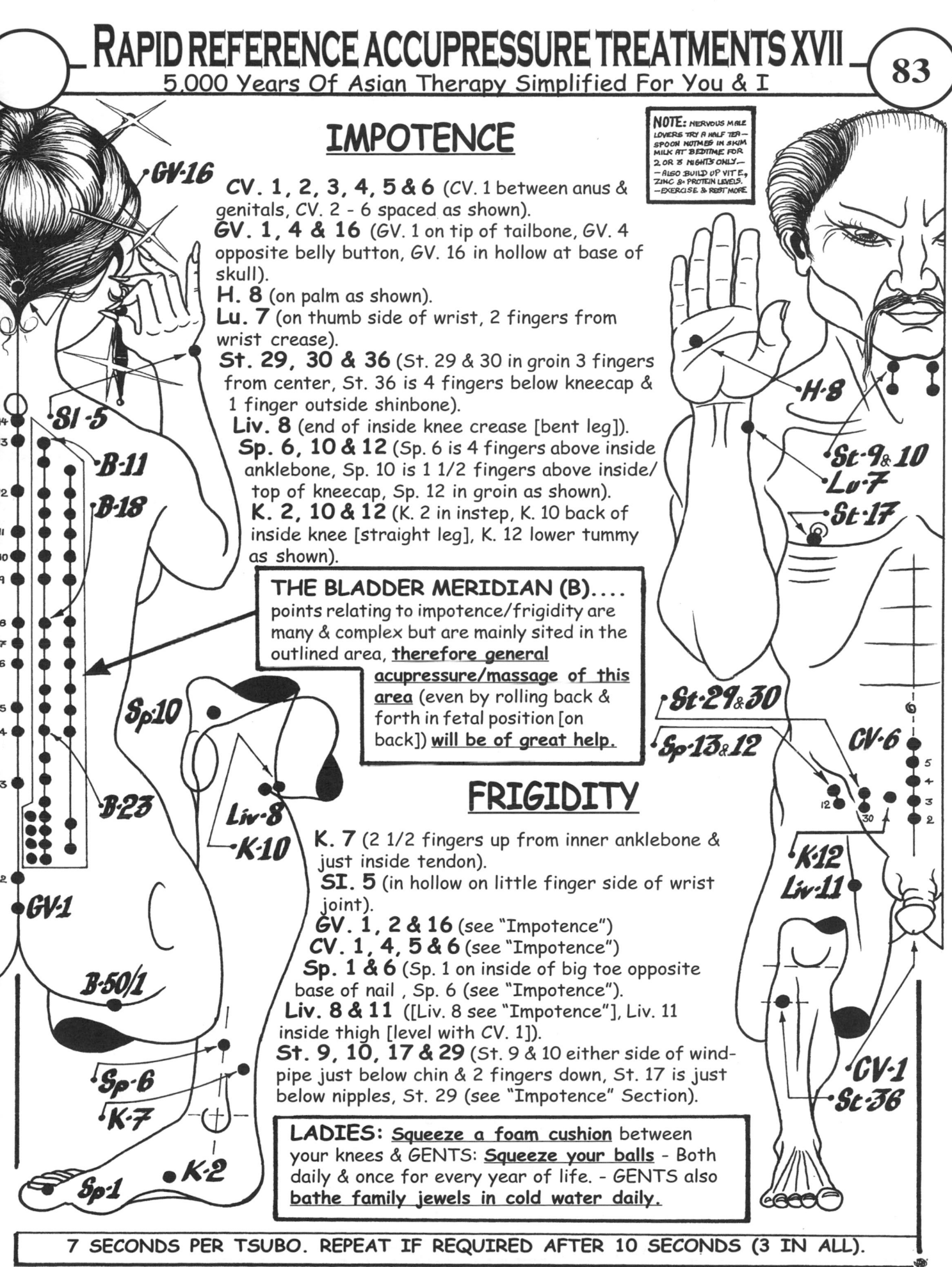

IMPOTENCE

NOTE: NERVOUS MALE LOVERS TRY A HALF TEA-SPOON NUTMEG IN SKIM MILK AT BEDTIME FOR 2 OR 3 NIGHTS ONLY.— —ALSO BUILD UP VIT E, ZINC & PROTEIN LEVELS. —EXERCISE & REST MORE.

CV. 1, 2, 3, 4, 5 & 6 (CV. 1 between anus & genitals, CV. 2 - 6 spaced as shown).

GV. 1, 4 & 16 (GV. 1 on tip of tailbone, GV. 4 opposite belly button, GV. 16 in hollow at base of skull).

H. 8 (on palm as shown).

Lu. 7 (on thumb side of wrist, 2 fingers from wrist crease).

St. 29, 30 & 36 (St. 29 & 30 in groin 3 fingers from center, St. 36 is 4 fingers below kneecap & 1 finger outside shinbone).

Liv. 8 (end of inside knee crease [bent leg]).

Sp. 6, 10 & 12 (Sp. 6 is 4 fingers above inside anklebone, Sp. 10 is 1 1/2 fingers above inside/top of kneecap, Sp. 12 in groin as shown).

K. 2, 10 & 12 (K. 2 in instep, K. 10 back of inside knee [straight leg], K. 12 lower tummy as shown).

THE BLADDER MERIDIAN (B).... points relating to impotence/frigidity are many & complex but are mainly sited in the outlined area, **therefore general acupressure/massage of this area** (even by rolling back & forth in fetal position [on back]) **will be of great help.**

FRIGIDITY

K. 7 (2 1/2 fingers up from inner anklebone & just inside tendon).

SI. 5 (in hollow on little finger side of wrist joint).

GV. 1, 2 & 16 (see "Impotence")

CV. 1, 4, 5 & 6 (see "Impotence")

Sp. 1 & 6 (Sp. 1 on inside of big toe opposite base of nail , Sp. 6 (see "Impotence").

Liv. 8 & 11 ([Liv. 8 see "Impotence"], Liv. 11 inside thigh [level with CV. 1]).

St. 9, 10, 17 & 29 (St. 9 & 10 either side of wind-pipe just below chin & 2 fingers down, St. 17 is just below nipples, St. 29 (see "Impotence" Section).

LADIES: Squeeze a foam cushion between your knees & GENTS: **Squeeze your balls** - Both daily & once for every year of life. - GENTS also **bathe family jewels in cold water daily.**

7 SECONDS PER TSUBO. REPEAT IF REQUIRED AFTER 10 SECONDS (3 IN ALL).

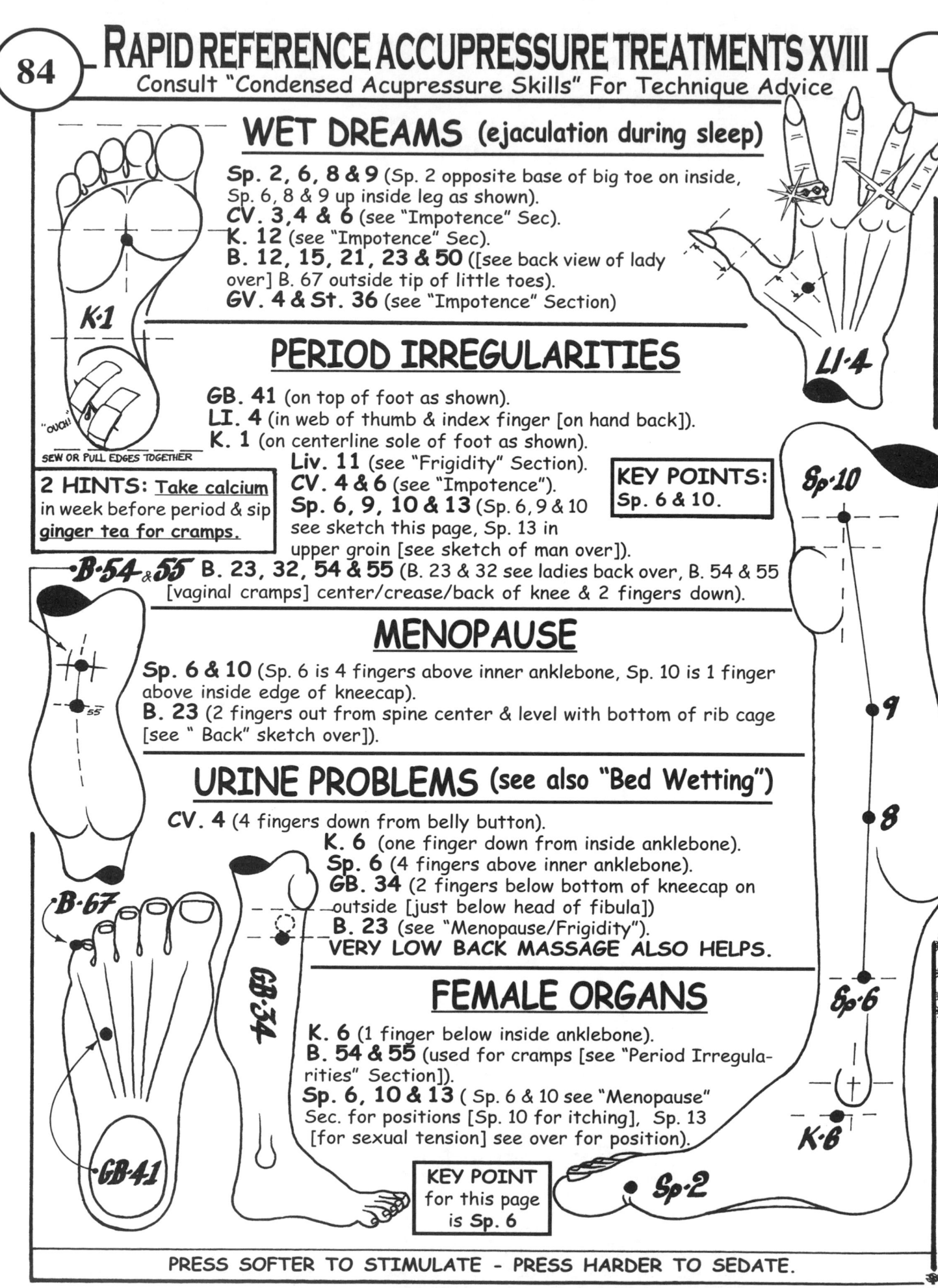

WET DREAMS (ejaculation during sleep)

Sp. 2, 6, 8 & 9 (Sp. 2 opposite base of big toe on inside,
Sp. 6, 8 & 9 up inside leg as shown).
CV. 3, 4 & 6 (see "Impotence" Sec).
K. 12 (see "Impotence" Sec).
B. 12, 15, 21, 23 & 50 ([see back view of lady
over] B. 67 outside tip of little toes).
GV. 4 & St. 36 (see "Impotence" Section)

PERIOD IRREGULARITIES

GB. 41 (on top of foot as shown).
LI. 4 (in web of thumb & index finger [on hand back]).
K. 1 (on centerline sole of foot as shown).
Liv. 11 (see "Frigidity" Section).
CV. 4 & 6 (see "Impotence").
Sp. 6, 9, 10 & 13 (Sp. 6, 9 & 10
see sketch this page, Sp. 13 in
upper groin [see sketch of man over]).

KEY POINTS:
Sp. 6 & 10.

B. 23, 32, 54 & 55 (B. 23 & 32 see ladies back over, B. 54 & 55
[vaginal cramps] center/crease/back of knee & 2 fingers down).

2 HINTS: Take calcium
in week before period & sip
ginger tea for cramps.

"OUCH!"
SEW OR PULL EDGES TOGETHER

MENOPAUSE

Sp. 6 & 10 (Sp. 6 is 4 fingers above inner anklebone, Sp. 10 is 1 finger
above inside edge of kneecap).
B. 23 (2 fingers out from spine center & level with bottom of rib cage
[see " Back" sketch over]).

URINE PROBLEMS (see also "Bed Wetting")

CV. 4 (4 fingers down from belly button).
K. 6 (one finger down from inside anklebone).
Sp. 6 (4 fingers above inner anklebone).
GB. 34 (2 fingers below bottom of kneecap on
outside [just below head of fibula])
B. 23 (see "Menopause/Frigidity").
VERY LOW BACK MASSAGE ALSO HELPS.

FEMALE ORGANS

K. 6 (1 finger below inside anklebone).
B. 54 & 55 (used for cramps [see "Period Irregula-
rities" Section]).
Sp. 6, 10 & 13 (Sp. 6 & 10 see "Menopause"
Sec. for positions [Sp. 10 for itching], Sp. 13
[for sexual tension] see over for position).

KEY POINT
for this page
is Sp. 6

PRESS SOFTER TO STIMULATE - PRESS HARDER TO SEDATE.

5,000 Years Of Asian Therapy Simplified For You & I

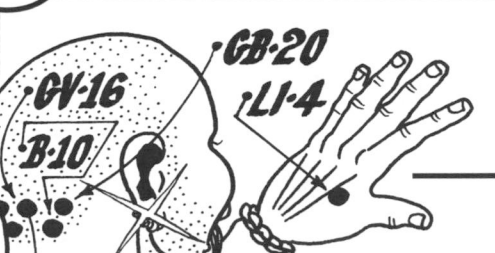

NERVOUSNESS

GV. 5, 6, 7, 8, 9, 10, 11 & 12 (along spine from bottom of rib cage level to just above armpit level).

WORRY/STRESS

LI. 4 (in web of thumb & index finger [hand back]).
H. 7 (on palm/little finger side of wrist crease [in hollow]).
B. 10 (one finger down from base of skull & 3 fingers apart).
TW. 15 (just above inner/upper corners of shoulder blades [may be tense/sensitive like a marble]).
GB. 20 & 21 (GB. 20 just below bottom of skull 4 fingers apart, GB. 21 is 1 finger above halfway between prominent spine bone & point of shoulder).

BAD TEMPER

B. 15 (either side of spine [4 fingers apart] mid shoulder blade level).
H. 7 (on palm/little finger side of wrist crease [in hollow]).

SHOCK

K. 1 (on sole of foot centerline one-third from front).
GV. 6, 20 & 26 (GV. 6 on spine as shown, GV. 20 on top center of head [in line with tops of ears], GV. 26 is just under nose [on lip]).

AGGRESSION

GB. 20 (just below bottom of skull, 4 finger widths apart [i.e. 2 either side of center]).

CONFUSION

CV. 17 (on chest bone between nipples).

HYSTERIA

H. 4, 5, 6 & 7 (on little finger/palm side of wrist, starting 2+ fingers from wrist crease, [H. 7 in hollow at crease]).
CV. 17 (between nipples).
GV. 16 (in hollow at base of skull [1 inch above hair line]).
P. 6 (center of inside wrist 2 fingers from wrist crease).

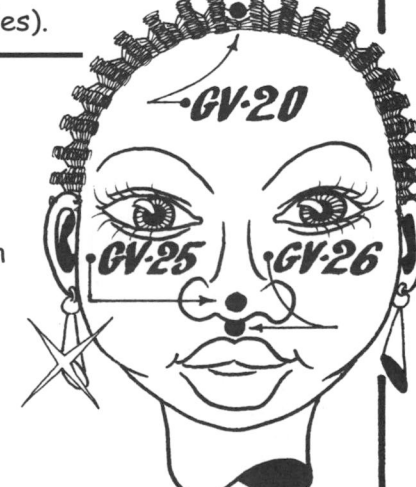

IMPORTANT NOTE
CULTURED ASIAN SMUGGLERS USUALLY HOLD TEACUPS LIKE THIS....

7 SECONDS PER TSUBO. REPEAT IF REQUIRED AFTER 10 SECONDS (3 IN ALL).

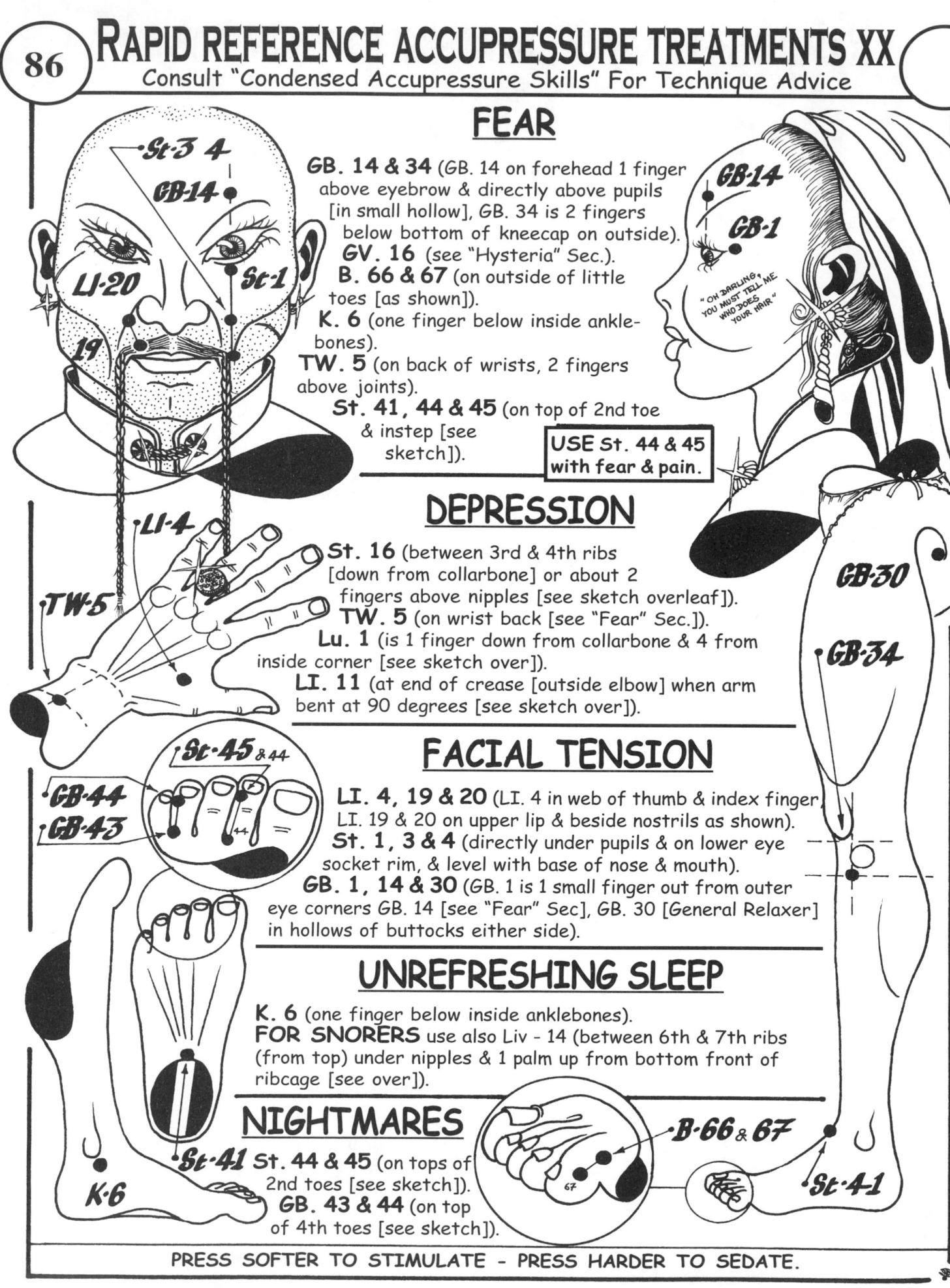

FEAR

GB. 14 & 34 (GB. 14 on forehead 1 finger above eyebrow & directly above pupils [in small hollow], GB. 34 is 2 fingers below bottom of kneecap on outside).
GV. 16 (see "Hysteria" Sec.).
B. 66 & 67 (on outside of little toes [as shown]).
K. 6 (one finger below inside ankle-bones).
TW. 5 (on back of wrists, 2 fingers above joints).
St. 41, 44 & 45 (on top of 2nd toe & instep [see sketch]).

USE St. 44 & 45 with fear & pain.

DEPRESSION

St. 16 (between 3rd & 4th ribs [down from collarbone] or about 2 fingers above nipples [see sketch overleaf]).
TW. 5 (on wrist back [see "Fear" Sec.]).
Lu. 1 (is 1 finger down from collarbone & 4 from inside corner [see sketch over]).
LI. 11 (at end of crease [outside elbow] when arm bent at 90 degrees [see sketch over]).

FACIAL TENSION

LI. 4, 19 & 20 (LI. 4 in web of thumb & index finger, LI. 19 & 20 on upper lip & beside nostrils as shown).
St. 1, 3 & 4 (directly under pupils & on lower eye socket rim, & level with base of nose & mouth).
GB. 1, 14 & 30 (GB. 1 is 1 small finger out from outer eye corners GB. 14 [see "Fear" Sec], GB. 30 [General Relaxer] in hollows of buttocks either side).

UNREFRESHING SLEEP

K. 6 (one finger below inside anklebones).
FOR SNORERS use also Liv - 14 (between 6th & 7th ribs (from top) under nipples & 1 palm up from bottom front of ribcage [see over]).

NIGHTMARES

St. 41 St. 44 & 45 (on tops of 2nd toes [see sketch]).
GB. 43 & 44 (on top of 4th toes [see sketch]).

PRESS SOFTER TO STIMULATE - PRESS HARDER TO SEDATE.

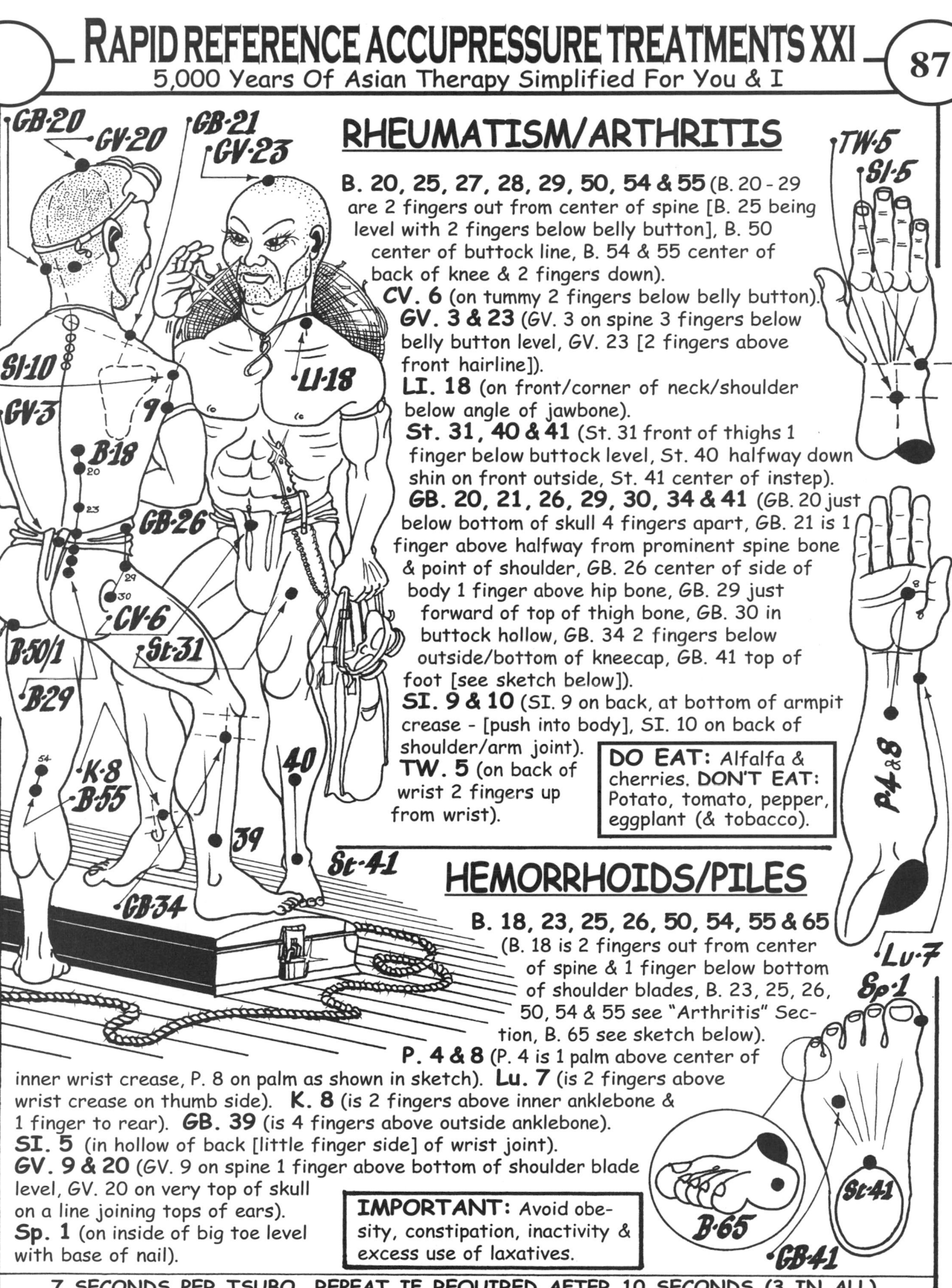

RHEUMATISM/ARTHRITIS

B. 20, 25, 27, 28, 29, 50, 54 & 55 (B. 20 - 29 are 2 fingers out from center of spine [B. 25 being level with 2 fingers below belly button], B. 50 center of buttock line, B. 54 & 55 center of back of knee & 2 fingers down).

CV. 6 (on tummy 2 fingers below belly button).

GV. 3 & 23 (GV. 3 on spine 3 fingers below belly button level, GV. 23 [2 fingers above front hairline]).

LI. 18 (on front/corner of neck/shoulder below angle of jawbone).

St. 31, 40 & 41 (St. 31 front of thighs 1 finger below buttock level, St. 40 halfway down shin on front outside, St. 41 center of instep).

GB. 20, 21, 26, 29, 30, 34 & 41 (GB. 20 just below bottom of skull 4 fingers apart, GB. 21 is 1 finger above halfway from prominent spine bone & point of shoulder, GB. 26 center of side of body 1 finger above hip bone, GB. 29 just forward of top of thigh bone, GB. 30 in buttock hollow, GB. 34 2 fingers below outside/bottom of kneecap, GB. 41 top of foot [see sketch below]).

SI. 9 & 10 (SI. 9 on back, at bottom of armpit crease - [push into body], SI. 10 on back of shoulder/arm joint).

TW. 5 (on back of wrist 2 fingers up from wrist).

DO EAT: Alfalfa & cherries. **DON'T EAT:** Potato, tomato, pepper, eggplant (& tobacco).

HEMORRHOIDS/PILES

B. 18, 23, 25, 26, 50, 54, 55 & 65 (B. 18 is 2 fingers out from center of spine & 1 finger below bottom of shoulder blades, B. 23, 25, 26, 50, 54 & 55 see "Arthritis" Section, B. 65 see sketch below).

P. 4 & 8 (P. 4 is 1 palm above center of inner wrist crease, P. 8 on palm as shown in sketch). **Lu. 7** (is 2 fingers above wrist crease on thumb side). **K. 8** (is 2 fingers above inner anklebone & 1 finger to rear). **GB. 39** (is 4 fingers above outside anklebone).

SI. 5 (in hollow of back [little finger side] of wrist joint).

GV. 9 & 20 (GV. 9 on spine 1 finger above bottom of shoulder blade level, GV. 20 on very top of skull on a line joining tops of ears).

Sp. 1 (on inside of big toe level with base of nail).

IMPORTANT: Avoid obesity, constipation, inactivity & excess use of laxatives.

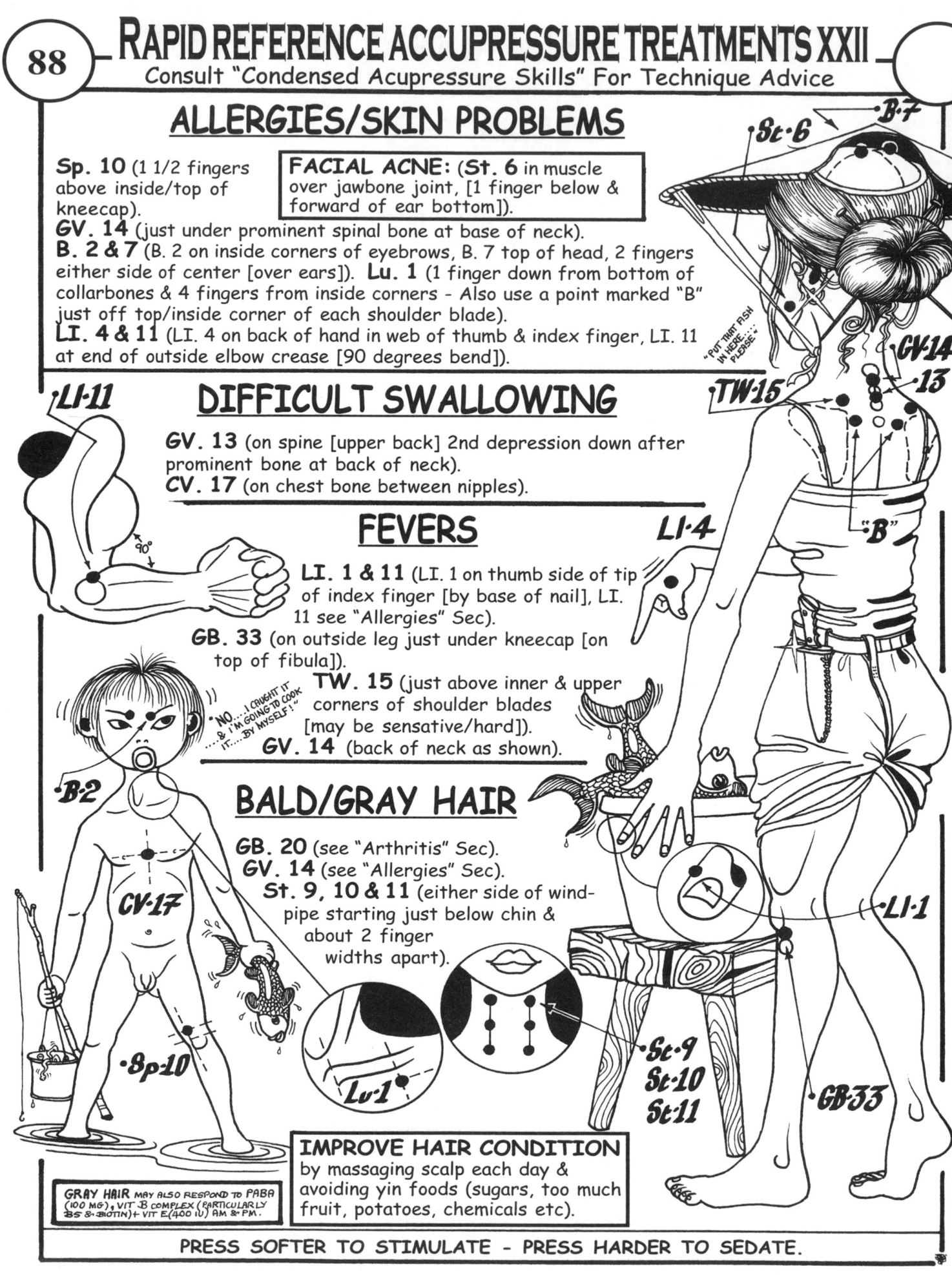

ALLERGIES/SKIN PROBLEMS

Sp. 10 (1 1/2 fingers above inside/top of kneecap).

FACIAL ACNE: (**St. 6** in muscle over jawbone joint, [1 finger below & forward of ear bottom]).

GV. 14 (just under prominent spinal bone at base of neck).
B. 2 & 7 (B. 2 on inside corners of eyebrows, B. 7 top of head, 2 fingers either side of center [over ears]). **Lu. 1** (1 finger down from bottom of collarbones & 4 fingers from inside corners - Also use a point marked "B" just off top/inside corner of each shoulder blade).
LI. 4 & 11 (LI. 4 on back of hand in web of thumb & index finger, LI. 11 at end of outside elbow crease [90 degrees bend]).

DIFFICULT SWALLOWING

GV. 13 (on spine [upper back] 2nd depression down after prominent bone at back of neck).
CV. 17 (on chest bone between nipples).

FEVERS

LI. 1 & 11 (LI. 1 on thumb side of tip of index finger [by base of nail], LI. 11 see "Allergies" Sec).
GB. 33 (on outside leg just under kneecap [on top of fibula]).
TW. 15 (just above inner & upper corners of shoulder blades [may be sensative/hard]).
GV. 14 (back of neck as shown).

BALD/GRAY HAIR

GB. 20 (see "Arthritis" Sec).
GV. 14 (see "Allergies" Sec).
St. 9, 10 & 11 (either side of windpipe starting just below chin & about 2 finger widths apart).

IMPROVE HAIR CONDITION by massaging scalp each day & avoiding yin foods (sugars, too much fruit, potatoes, chemicals etc).

GRAY HAIR MAY ALSO RESPOND TO PABA (100 MG), VIT B COMPLEX (PARTICULARLY B5 & BIOTIN) + VIT E (400 IU) AM & PM.

PRESS SOFTER TO STIMULATE - PRESS HARDER TO SEDATE.

• DIGESTION •

Sp. 4, 12 & 13 (Sp. 4 inside [side] of foot [just under bone] 2/5 from end of toe to heel, Sp. 12 & 13 in groin in front of thighbone to hip joint).
B. 66 & 67 (on outside of little toes).
St. 36 & 42 (St. 36 is 4 fingers down from bottom of kneecap & 1 finger out from shinbone, St. 42 is 2 fingers down from center of instep).

> **ALSO IMPROVE DIGESTION** by assuming "_Seiza_" (kneel with toes pointing back & buttocks on heels, hands on knees & back/head up straight. [**Also treats St. 42**]).

CV. 12 (one palm above belly button).

• DRAIN MUCUS •

LI. 3 & 4 (on back of hands as in sketch).

• OVERWEIGHT •

Sp. 6 (double height of inside anklebone on centerline).

• CLEAR TOXINS •

GB. 31 (on centerline of outside thigh where tip of mIddle finger rests when standing up straight).

• GENERAL PAIN •

P. 6 (on centerline of inside wrist 2'/2 fingers up from wrist crease).
B. 62 (two fingers below & forward of outside ankle-bones).

• SNEEZING •

GV. 25 & 26 (on tip of nose & upper lip under nose).
B. 2 & 7 (B. 2 on inner corners of eyebrows, B. 7 on top of head 2 fingers either side of center directly above ear tops).

• HEAT STROKE •

GV. 20 (on very top of head between tops of ears).

• SNOR-ING •

Liv. 14 (on ribs under nipples [see "No Milk" Sec.]).

• STITCH •
(FROM RUNNING)

Liv. 14 (see "No Milk" Sec).

• HEARTBURN •

St. 16 (between 3rd & 4th ribs, 2 fingers above nipples).

• BELCHING •

Liv. 14 (on ribs under nipples [see "No Milk" Section]).

• GENITAL BALANCE •

St. 29 (level with the top of hip to thighbone joint, but on the inside of hipbone [about 3 fingers from centerline of lower abdomen]).

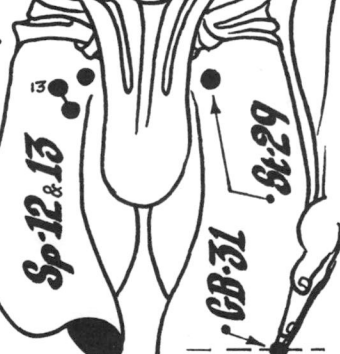

Labels on figure: B-2, GV-20, B-7, GV-25 & 26, St-16, CV-17, P-6, P-3, CV-12, Liv-14, GB-31, K-7, Sp-9, 6 & 4, St-36, St-42, 66, B-67, LI-3 & 4, P-3, B-62, Sp-12 & 13, GB-31, St-29

7 SECONDS PER TSUBO. REPEAT IF REQUIRED   AFTER 10 SECONDS (3 IN ALL).

RAPID REFERENCE ACCUPRESSURE TREATMENTS XXIV

Consult "Condensed Accupressure Skills" For Technique Advice

• (TOO LITTLE) ← SWEAT → (TOO MUCH) •

(Too little)

TW. 15 (just above inner/upper corners of shoulder blades).
Sp. 9 (center inside leg 3 fingers below kneecap - ([see sketch over]).
GB. 41 (top of foot as shown in sketch).

Bloating & water retention is also treated by the "too little sweat" points.

(Too much)

LI. 4 (on back of hand in web of thumb & index finger).
"B" (on inside of shoulder blades about halfway up).

• LOSS OF APPETITE •

B. 20 (two fingers either side of spine center, midway between bottoms of rib cage & shoulder blades).

• TOO THIRSTY •

P. 3 (inside of biceps tendon ([see sketch over])

• NO BREAST MILK •

GB. 21 (one finger width above the mid-point of line from shoulder tip to the prominent spine/neck bone).
CV. 17 (on chest bone between nipples [see over]).
Liv. 14 (between 6th & 7th ribs about 3 or 4 fingers below nipples).

Also massage breasts with warm hands clockwise.

• LABOR PAINS •
(BEFORE DELIVERY)

B. 22 (on lower back level with bottom of rib cage [2 fingers either side of spine]).
Sp. 6 (double height of inside anklebone on centerline [see over]).

• BLOATED STOMACH •

K. 7 (2 1/2 fingers up from inner ankle-bone [just inside tendon]).
Sp. 12 (in groin [see sketch over]. - Also good for pain).
Liv. 1 & 2 (on top of big toe as shown in sketch).
St. 44 & 45 (on top of 2nd toe as shown in sketch).

STOMACH CRAMPS: PRESS/MASSAGE MID/LOWER BACK & PRESS **Liv. 3** (SEE "FOOT AILMENTS") & **St. 34** (SEE "STOMACH ACHE") & DRINK CAMOMILE OR PEPPERMINT TEA.

• EMERGENCY •
(HEART ATTACK/ DROWNING ETC.)

CV. 1 (press with cap of pen or similar between anus and genitals).

• WILD EYES •

GV. 16 (on back of neck [central] in hollow at base of skull [just above hairline]).

• BODILY ENERGY •

LI. 4 & 11 (LI. 4 in web of thumb as shown, LI. 11 at end of outside elbow crease when arm is bent at 90 degrees).

GV. 4 (on spine opposite belly button).

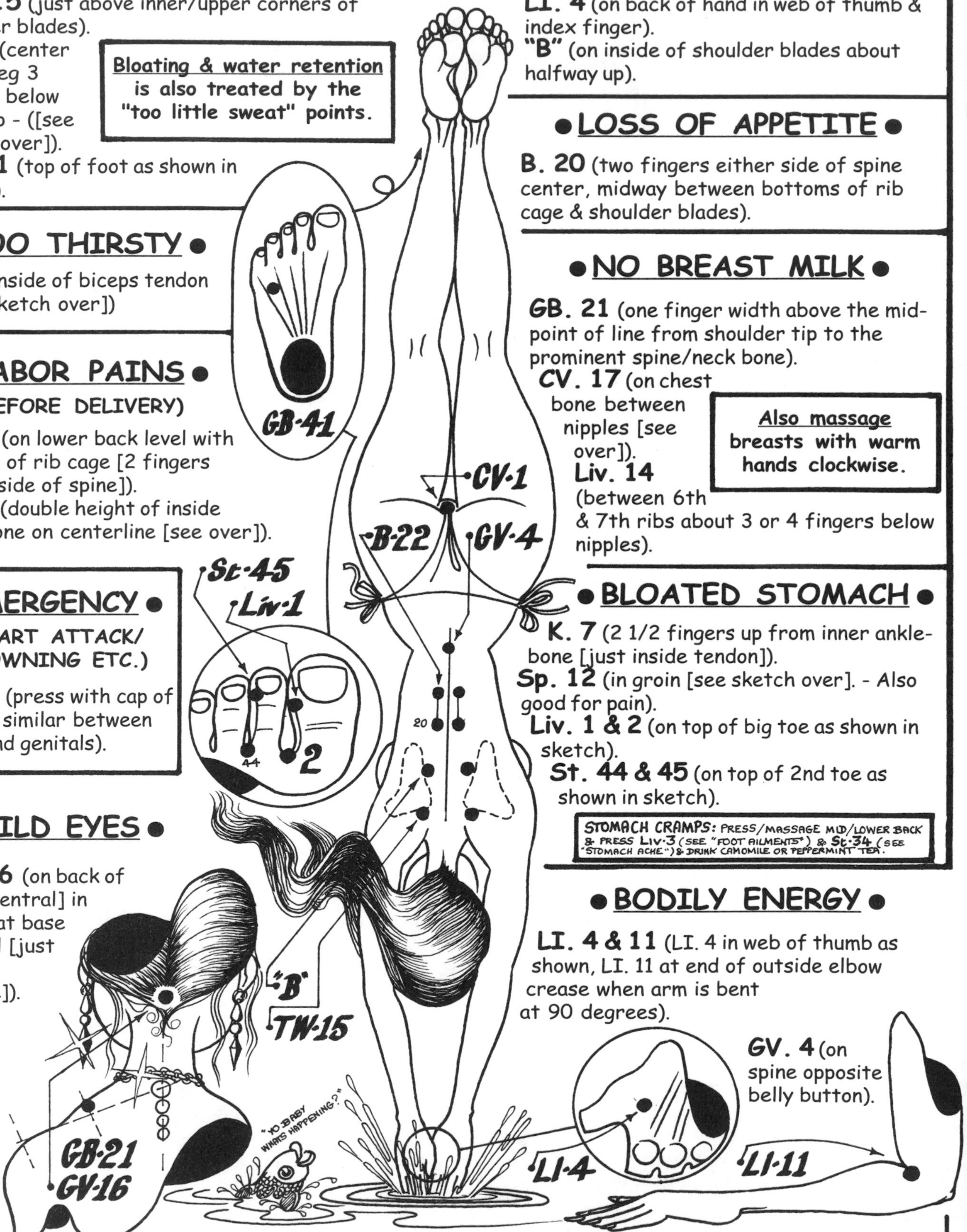

GB·41
CV·1
B·22
GV·4
St·45
Liv·1
44
2
20
"B"
TW·15
GB·21
GV·16
"YO BABY WHATS HAPPENING?"
LI·4
LI·11

PRESS SOFTER TO STIMULATE - PRESS HARDER TO SEDATE.

How To Read Symptoms As Possible Indicators Of Vitamin Shortages

NAME/SYMBOL & RDA	SYMPTOMS OF DEFICIENCY	BEST NATURAL SOURCES	ADDITIONAL NOTES
A RDA 1,500 mcg/ 5,000 IU 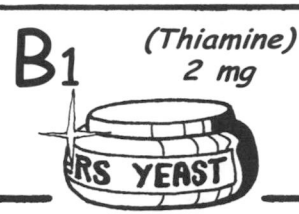	● Burning, itching, dry painful eyes. Scaly skin & scalp. Spine & lung infections. Frequent skin ulcers & viral diarrhea. Poor hair quality.	● Cod-liver oil. Liver. Carrots (one large fresh can supply 10,000 IU). Leafy greens. Egg yolk. Apricots. Beets. Margarine. Kidneys.	● Too little also causes kidney stones & night blindness. Too much (200,000 IU/day) is toxic (nausea, hair loss). Beta carotene (veg. Vit A) is nontoxic.
B1 (Thiamine) 2 mg 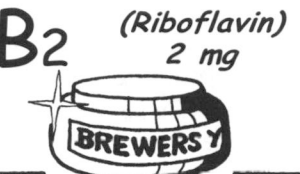	● Fatigue. Nausea. Depression. Beri Beri. Poor appetite & memory. Slow heartbeat. Muscle weakness. Gastric disorders. Breathless.	● Dried brewers yeast. Wholegrain rice. Wheatgerm. Fish. Legumes. Soya flour. Nuts. Poultry. Liver. All whole grains.	● Nontoxic orally. Alcohol, pregnancy, antacid drugs, fever & stress use it up fast. Used to treat heart, mental, back & gastric ailments.
B2 (Riboflavin) 2 mg	● Bloodshot & gritty eyes. Cracked lips. Slow growth. Hair loss. Trembling. Dizzy. Insomnia. Slow brain. Sore tongue. Indigestion.	● Brewers yeast. Eggs. Capsicum. Liver. Legumes. Yogurt. Wheatgerm. Soya flour. Meats. Milk. Leafy vegetables. Wholegrain cereals.	● Nontoxic. Destroyed by light. Deficiency causes birth defects. It is vital to make digestive enzymes. Vital for metabolic food to energy use.
B3 Niacin 20 mg (Nicotinic Acid. Nicot/Niacinamide). 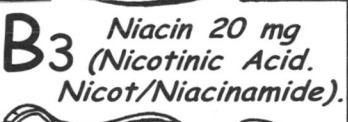	● Gastric ailments (inc. ulcers). Fatigue. Insomnia. Dermatitis. Headache & nausea. Used to treat acne, schizophrenia, leg cramps & arthritis.	● Peanuts. Kidney. Fish. Eggs. Figs. Yeast. Wheatgerm. Wholegrain cereals. Avocados. Dates. Prunes. Liver. White poultry meat.	● Basically nontoxic (but see note). Also used to treat high blood pressure, vertigo, bad breath (halitosis), tooth decay, stress, & migraine.
B5 (Pantothenic Acid) 10 mg 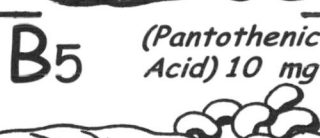	● Fatigue. Insomnia. Premature gray hair. Excess sleep needs. Irritability. Poor appetite. Reduced immunity. Depressed. Constipation. Asthma.	● Beans. Poultry. Wholegrains. Fish. Brewers yeast. Wheatgerm. Egg yolks. Legumes. Liver. Oranges. Peanuts. Cods roe.	● High dose (over 10g/day) may cause diarrhoea or water retention. Destroyed by stress & many drugs inc. alcohol. Used to treat allergies.
B6 (Pyridoxine) 2 mg	● Split lips. Dry scaly skin (face). Swollen belly/fingers &/or ankles. Sensitive to sun. Allergies. Anemia. Depression. Fits. Kidney stones.	● Wheat bran/germ. Brewers yeast. Milk. Fatty fish. Nuts. Soya flour. Eggs. Bananas. Liver. Kidney. Cabbage. Wholegrains. Potato.	● Although considered nontoxic don't exceed 25 mg in pregnancy or 200 mg at other times. This is a vital vitamin often low in modern diets.
B12 (Cyanocobalamin) 5 mcg	● Breathlessness. Heart palpitations. Sore smooth tongue. Feeling weak. Apathy. Degeneration of memory, nerves, brain, spine & premature aging.	● Eggs. Oyster. Clam. Liver. Milk. Cheese. Kidneys. Spirulina. Fermented soya beans. Pollen. Sea vegetables. Most animal products.	● Considered nontoxic. Strict vegetarians may be deficient. Used to treat shingles, alcoholism, asthma, allergies, insomnia, fits, hepatitis.
B15 (Pangamic Acid) 50 mg	● Fatigue. Premature aging (particularly nerve, glandular & heart ailments). Reduced oxygenation of cells leading to general deterioration.	● Wholegrains (in particular rice). Brewers yeast. Sesame seeds. Pumpkin. May be available as calcium pangamate in shops.	● Works as an antioxidant to detoxify the body. Extends cell life. Improves immunity. Protects liver & arteries. Improves vitality.
B17 (Laetrile) 250 mg	....**IS FOUND IN** raw (heat destroys it) apricot kernels (10 mg each), apple pips, cherry stones, millet seeds, buckwheat, plum stones, bitter almonds & some berries. It is a source of inorganic cyanide which destroys **CANCER CELLS** specifically, **BUT** too much is dangerous (not more than 1 gram of supplement [or a few apricot kernels] at one time) (5 - 25 apricot kernels spread over a day are considered sufficient) - **OVERDOSE SYMPTOMS:** cold sweats, blue lips, breathless, nausea, headache & low blood pressure.		

How To Read Symptoms As Possible Indicators Of Vitamin Shortages

NAME/SYMBOL & RDA	SYMPTOMS OF DEFICIENCY	BEST NATURAL SOURCES	ADDITIONAL NOTES
C (Ascorbic Acid) 100+ mg	● Reduced Immunity. Colds. Appetite Loss. Bleeding Gums. Allergies. Fatigue. Wrinkles. Anemia. Depression. Nerves. Frequent Infections.	● Cherry. Camu. Black Currants. Parsley. Citrus Fruit (eg. Orange & Grapefruit). Guavas. Kale. Broccoli. Green Peppers. Other Fruit & Veg.	● 1 - 4g/day required to protect immunity (supplement with magnesium to prevent kidney stones). Take more during illness, stress &/or pollution.
D (Sunshine Vit.) 400 iu.	● CHILDREN: Rickets. Bow Legs. Knock Knees. Head Sweats. ADULTS: Weakness. Porous, easy-to-break Bones & Teeth. Weak Muscles & Arthritis.	● Cod-liver Oil. Tuna. Kippers. Salmon. Mackerel. Eggs. Herring. - One hour of summer sun on your face reduces about 4 mcg.	● Toxic if too much eaten, symptoms: Loss of appetite, vomiting, thirst, head pain. Note that after you get a suntan the sun/skin stops producing Vit. D.
E (Tocopherol) 20 iu.	● Premature Aging including: Fatigue. Sterility. Infertility. Heart. Circulation. Kidney. Joint & Skin Diseases. Poor Healing of all Types.	● Wheatgerm Oil. Soyabean Oil. Maize Oil. Safflower Oil. Cod Liver, Peanut & Sunflower Oils. Green Vegetables. Eggs. Shrimp.	● Basically nontoxic but increase & decrease doses gradually. Enemies: Heat, freezing, oxygen, chlorine, iron & processing.

EXTRA B COMPLEX VITAMINS

NAME/SYMBOL & RDA	SYMPTOMS OF DEFICIENCY	BEST NATURAL SOURCES	ADDITIONAL NOTES
P.A.B.A. (Para Amino Benzoic Acid)	● Eczema. Senility. Wrinkles. Fatigue. Pigmentation Loss. Arthritis. Gastric.	● Brewers Yeast. Whole Grains. Liver. Kidney. Rice Bran. Wheatgerm.	● Take 20 - 100 mg/day. Treats Vitiligo. Gray Hair. Age Spots. Sunburn, Lungs.
FOLIC ACID (Vit. M) 400 mcg	● Anemia. Epileptic Fits. Depression. Poor Appetite. Sore Tongue. Gastric.	● Brewers Yeast. Soya Flour. Wheatgerm/bran. Nuts. Liver. Leafy Veg.	● Pregnancy, old age & drugs deplete this vitamin but over 15 mg/day can be toxic.
CHOLINE 500 - 1,000 mg	● Degeneration of Liver, Kidneys, Gall Bladder, Arteries & Nerves. Rapid Aging.	● Lecithin. Egg. Liver. Brain. Wheatgerm. Beans. Brewers Yeast. Green Veg.	● Used for stroke, angina, Alzheimers, senile dementia, high blood pressure.
INOSTOL 500 - 1,000 mg	● Dermatitis. Hair Loss. Hypertension. Constipation. High Blood Cholesterol.	● Lecithin. Liver. Nuts. Wheatgerm. Brains. Brewers yeast. Whole Grains. Beans.	● With choline vital for brain function. Nontoxic. Combats eczema & stress.
BIOTIN (Vit. H) 50 - 100 mcg	● IN BABIES: Dry skin & Diarrhea. ADULTS: Fatigue. Hair Loss. Eczema. Aches & Pains.	● Brewers Yeast. Whole grains. Fish. Liver. Kidney. Egg. Wheatgerm. Nuts.	● Stress, antibiotics, uncooked egg white & powdered baby milk can cause deficiencies.

OTHER VITAMINS

NAME/SYMBOL & RDA	SYMPTOMS OF DEFICIENCY	BEST NATURAL SOURCES	ADDITIONAL NOTES
F (Linoleic & Arachidonic) 50 - 100 mg	● Dermatitis. Acne. Eczema. Gray hair. Dandruff. Diarrhea. Heart diasese.	● Eve. Prim. Oil . Soya Oil. Safflower. Almond. Sunflower. Linseed. Wheatgerm. Peanuts.	● Protects skin, hair & arteries. Combats X - ray damage. No vit. F in Brazil/Cashew nuts.
K (There are 3: K1, K2 & K3) 300 mcg	● Usually shows as slow blood clotting (e.g.: Nose Bleeds & Poor Wound Closure).	● Cauliflower (best). Broccoli. Brussel Sprouts. Alfalfa. Yogurt. Kelp.	● Also helps stem excess menstruation. K1 & K2 are natural, K3 is synthetic.
P (Bioflavanoid Complex) 20% + of Vit. C intake	● Capillary Fragility inc.: Nose Bleeds, Easy Bruising, Gums Bleed & Red Lines on Skin.	● Citrus Fruit Pith & Segment Partitions. Apricots. Cherries. Buckwheat. Rose Hips.	● Vital for effectiveness of Vit. C. Nontoxic. Also use for Varicose Veins & Arthritis.

ADDITIONAL NOTES

● **RDA** (Recommended Daily Allowances) shown are for adults. - **g** = gram. - **mg** = milligram. - mcg (or) - **ug** = microgram. - **iu** = international unit.

● **B1** (Thaimin) also used as insect repellant 75 - 100 mg/day (orally). **Folic Acid** deficiency can also cause birth defects, premature births & abortions.

● **B6** (Pyridoxine) more deficiency signs: Swollen Tongue, Numb Hands/Feet, Linear Nail Ridges & Inability to recall dreams.

● **B3** one form of which (Niacin/Nicontinic Acid) may cause a temporary flush in doses over 100 mg (but this improves circulation & detoxifies capillaries).

NAME/SYMBOL & RDA	SYMPTOMS OF DEFICIENCY	BEST NATURAL SOURCES	ADDITIONAL NOTES
Calcium (Ca.) 800 mg	● Porous, brittle & painful bones. Rickets. Tooth decay. Fractures. Skin pigment loss. Cramps. Nervous. Sores. Slow growth.	● Hard cheese. Soft cheese. Yogurt. Milk. Proteins with bones in (i.e. tinned salmon & meat stew). Nuts. Dried beans. Green vegetables.	● Don't exceed 2,000 mg/day long-term. Vit. D required for efficient absorption. Enemies: Fat, Oxalic & Phytic acids. Stress & hard exercise require more.
Chromium (Cr.) 200 mcg	● High cholesterol/fat in blood. Tired. Hypertension. Slow growth. Nervous. Impaired glucose metabolism. Itchy. Depressed. Weak.	● Egg yolk. Molasses. Brewers yeast. Whole grains. Bran. Wheatgerm. Liver. Shellfish. Honey. Fruit juices. Meat. Fruit. Vegetables.	● Inhibits development of diabetes & artery hardening. Stimulates protein synthesis. Increases infection resistance. Older people retain less.
Copper (Cu.) 2 mg	● Fatigue. Anemia. Depigmentation of hair & skin. Bones brittle. Breathless. Loss of sense of taste. IN BABIES pale skin & diarrhea.	● Shellfish. Liver. Brewers yeast. Nuts. Soybeans. Whole grains. Prunes. Molasses. Pulses (beans). Legumes. Fish. Seaweed.	● Required for efficient use of Vit. C & iron, but excesses (from smoke, water pipes etc.) can cause: Arthritis, hypertension, heart attack & schizophrenia.
Iodine (I.) 150 mcg	● Hypothyroidism with swollen thyroid gland. Palpitations of heart. Reduced immunity. Irritable. Weakness. Rapid pulse & a cold body.	● Kelp. Shellfish. Haddock. Onions. Vegetables grown in iodine-rich soil. Iodised salt. Eggs. Milk. (In some countries - Check label).	● Certain foods inhibit iodine absorption these include: Raw cabbage, broccoli, brussel sprouts, kale, ground nuts, soya beans, turnips.
Iron (Fe.) men 10 mg women 20 mg	● Anemia. Fatigue. Headache. Insomnia. Dizzy. Breathless. Palpitations. Pale. Brittle nails. Slow growth in kids. Itching in old.	● Cockles. Winkles. Brewers yeast. Clams. Oysters. Liver. Egg yolk. Dried peaches, Beans, Raisins, Prunes. Green veg.	● Vital for oxygen supply to all cells. Often deficient in pregnancy, periods, babies, children & tea & coffee drinkers. Toxic in overdoses.
Germanium (Ge.)	● Premature aging in any of many forms e.g.: Senile dementia. Hair/memory loss. Age spots. Parkinson's disease. Cancer. Glaucoma etc.	● Ginseng. Garlic. Aloe Vera. Onion. Comfrey. Eggs. Fresh fruit. Green leafy vegetables. Sea foods/fish/shellfish/kelp.	● Reduces body's need for oxygen, making better use of what is available, enhancing immunity & recovery in multiple situations. No toxicity known.
Molybdenum (Mo) 500 mcg	● Irregular heartbeat. Irritability. Sexual impotence in men. Anemia. Cancer of gullet. Teeth decay easily. Can also cause coma.	● Buckwheat & all whole grains. Egg. Liver. Kidney. Soybeans. Most vegetables (dark green leafy best). Most fruits. Cocoa. Wheatgerm.	● Excess intake (over 10 mg/day) causes gout & copper depletion (loss of hair color). Metabolism of fats, carbohydrates & iron require Molybdenum.
Magnesium (Mg) 400 mg	● Fatigue. Vertigo. Convulsions. Heart attacks. Palpitations. Bed wetting. Kidney stones. Tremors. Nerves. Seizures. Hyperactivity. Weak.	● Soya beans. Nuts. Whole grains. Brewers yeast. Lobster/shrimp. Seafood. Dried fruit. Green leaf vegetables.	● Improves retention of urine, tooth enamel, nerves, heartbeat rhythm, energy & Vits E & C utilization. Used to treat kids hyperactivity.
Manganese (Mn) 4 mg	● Disproportionate skeleton (i.e. limbs too short/long for body). Schizophrenia. Convulsions. Poor muscle tone. Anemia. Impotence. Diabetes.	● Whole grains. Nuts. Beans (pulses). Vegetables (leafy green). Ginger. Tea. Most fruits. Cloves. Liver. Beets. Eggs. Peas.	● Important for sex hormones, bone formation, thyroid action, memory, nervous system & carbohydrates, Vits B & C function.

UNIT CODES: g = gram.   mg = milligram.   mcg (or ug) = microgram.   iu = international unit

NAME/SYMBOL & RDA	SYMPTOMS OF DEFICIENCY	BEST NATURAL SOURCES	ADDITIONAL NOTES
Phosphorous (P) 800 mg	● Rickets in children. Bone & joint pain/weakness. Tremor. Irritable. Numb. Pins & needles. Gum disease. Loss of appetite. Confused.	● Brewers yeast. Skimmed milk. Soya beans. Whole grains. Cheese. Wheatgerm. Nuts. Canned fish. Egg. High protein foods.	● Excess from diet can be a problem after 40 years as it inhibits absorption of Iron, Zinc, Magnesium & particularly calcium so supplement accordingly.
Potassium (K) 1 g	● Irregular heartbeat. Insomnia. Vomiting. Paralysis. Low blood pressure. Very weak/tired. Hypertension. Coma. Bloating. Thirsty.	● Soya flour. Banana. Dried fruit. Nuts. Wheatbran. Raw vegetables. Whole grains (particularly muesli). Molasses. Seeds. Potatoes.	● Dieting, vomiting, mental & physical stress, sugar, salt & fat all deplete it. It helps reduce blood pressure & increase oxygen to brain.
Selenium (Se) 50 mcg	● Immunity & infection resistance declining. Fatigue. Sex drive low (men). Cancer vunerablity. Early aging. Wrinkled/dry skin/dandruff.	● Crab. Lobster. Clam. Shrimp. Whole grains. Liver. Kidney. Onions. Broccoli. Brewers yeast. Raw wheatgerm. Fruit. Veg. Nut/seed.	● May be toxic over 200 mcg/day from supplements. Very broadly beneficial from skin condition to cancer enhancing protective ability.
Zinc (Zn) 15 mg	● White spots on nails. Dwarfism. Birth defects. Allergies. Slow mentality. Acne. Joint pain. Fatigue. Sexual immaturity. Sterility.	● Oysters. Brewers yeast. Liver. Hard cheese. Shell fish. Meat. Fish. Raw wheatgerm. Egg yolk. Pumpkin seeds. Wholegrains.	● Vital mineral but don't exceed 150 mg/day in supplements. Enemies: Smoking, alcohol, excess sex or sweat (up to 3 mg/day loss) & processing.
Fluorine (Fl) 1.5-4 mg	● Tooth decay. Stunted growth. Possible anemia. Weak bones & osteoporosis.	● Fluoridated water. China tea. Whole grain cereals. Kelp. Seafood. Milk.	● Excess (e.g. from water) is toxic causing mottled teeth & brittle bones.
Sodium (Na) 1-3 g	● Fatigue. Muscle wasting. Sunken eyes. Dehydration. Internal gas.	● Sea/table salt. Kelp. Shellfish. Cheese. Processed meat/fish/biscuits etc.	● Too much can cause high blood pressure, low potassium levels & swollen heart/kidneys.
Vanadium (V) RDA not established.	● Possible anemia. Slow growth of teeth/bones. High blood fat levels.	● Parsley. Lobster. Shrimp. Crab. Dill. Radish. Gelatine. Lettuce. Fish bones.	● Excess intake may be related to manic depression. Vit C helps balance levels.
Chloride (Cl)	● Stomach acid. Hair & dental loses.	● Sea/table salts. Processed foods.	● Too much (in water) destroys Vitamin E.
Cobalt (Co)	● Only known related symptom is anemia.	● Oysters. Scallops. Fish (e.g.. Cod). Liver.	● Is contained within Vitamin B12.

TOXIC BAD GUYS

ELEMENT & SYMBOL HIGHLY TOXIC OVER..	HOW IT GETS IN YOU	WHAT IT DOES TO U	HOW & WHAT TO FIGHT IT WITH
Cadmium (Cd) .5 part/million.	● Galvanized water pipes. Tobacco smoke. Dental amalgams. Air/food pollution.	● Stroke. Heart attack. Lung disease. Kidney & reproductive damage. Anemia.	● Adequate intakes of zinc, copper & selenium + Vit C (1 - 4 grams/day).
Lead (Pb) 500 mcg/day	● Car exhaust. Tobacco smoke. Water pipes. Contaminated food. Paint. Glazed pottery.	● Attacks brain, nerves, reproduction, liver, kidneys & immunity. Paralysis. Death.	● Vit C (2 - 4g), E & A, calcium, lecithin, penicillamine, kelp & selenium.
Mercury (Hg) 100 mcg/day	● Industrial waste in rivers etc. (thus into fish). Fungicides. Dental fillings.	● Progressive decline of brain, kidneys, nerves, intestines, liver & paralysis.	● Vits A, B Comp, C, E + selenium, penicillamine, lecithin granules, calcium.

Aluminium (from cooking pots) causes premature senility (e.g. Alzheimer's disease).

How To Use Nutritional Supplements & Herbs To Treat Common Ailments

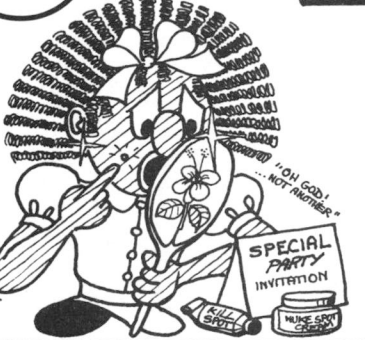

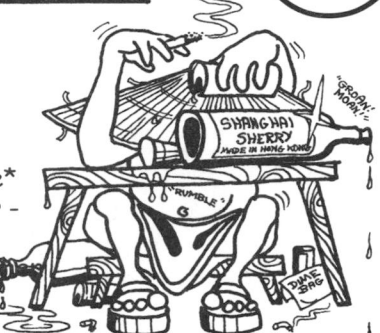

ACNE (Spots from overactive glands).
- Vits. A* - B Complex - C - E* - Zinc* - Oil of Evening Primrose* - Selenium - Potassium - Sulphur - Lecithin*. ● Burdock* - Chaparral - Dandelion - Ginseng. ● Adopt a Macrobiotic diet & avoid sugar, dairy & processed food.

ADDICTION (Unable to stop using a drug).
- Vits. A* - C* - D - E* - B Complex - Magnesium.
- Ginseng* - Saw Palmetto - Cayenne - Valerian - Licorice* - Camomile* - Passion Flower - Golden seal.
- FIRST FIND THE WILL, then use the above.

AGE SPOTS (Brown flat skin blotches).
- Vits. A* - B Complex* - C* - E* - RNA/DNA* - Selenium* - Calcium*.
- Ginseng* - Gotu Kola - Dandelion - Sarsaparilla.
- Asian medicine holds age spots caused by excess dietary sugar & fat. Change to a Macrobiotic diet.

AIDS (Acquired immune deficiency).
- Vits. A* - B5* - B6* - B12* - Folic Acid* - B Comp.* - C* - E* - Iron - Selenium* - Magnesium - Copper - Acidophilus - Zinc* - L' Arginine*.
- Garlic* - Ginseng* - Gotu Kola* - Ginger.
- Macrobiotic diet* - Acupuncture* - Yoga*.

ALLERGY (Excess immune responses).
- Vits. A - B5* - B6* - B Comp. - C* - E - Calcium - Magnesium - Manganese.
- Bee Pollen* - Alfalfa - Burdock - Comfrey - Eyebright - Papaya - Parsley. ● Bee Pollen doses should be built up gradually (over 1 month).

ANEMIA (Red blood cell malfunction).
- Vits. B6 - B12 - B Comp.* - C* - E - Folic Acid - Paba - Copper - Iron*.
- Dandelion* - Yellow Dock - Kelp - Comfrey - Chlorophyll - Hops.
- Different anemia's may require other programs but all require good diet.

ANXIETY (Worry, stress, depression).
- Vits. B6 - B Comp.* - C* - Magnesium* - Calcium* - L' Glutamin - L' Tryptophan.
- Chamomile* - Burdock - Passion Flower - Red Clover - Hops - Valerian.*
- Also try lecithin, massage, yoga, deep breathing & acupressure.

APPETITE LOSS (Do not make ill people eat as energy used up in digestion is needed for recovery). ● Vits. B12* - B Comp.* - C - Phosphorous* - Zinc*. ● Peppermint* - Garlic - Camomile - Alfalfa - Ginseng*.
- Start with exercise & multiple small meals.

ARTERIAL DISEASE (Artery deterioration).
- Vits. B3 - B5 - B6 - B Comp* - C* - E - F - Lecithin* - Silicon - Bioflavonoids* - Kelp - Magnesium - Dolomite - Selenium - Chromium. ● Garlic* - Hawthorn* - Rose Hips - Juniper. ● Macrobiotic diet & distilled water.

ARTHRITIS (Joint pain, wear, swelling).
- Vits. B2 - B3 - B5* - B6 - B12 - B Comp.* - C* - D - E* - F - P - Folic Acid - Magnesium* - Zinc* - Calcium - Phosphorous - Potassium - Oil of Evening Prim. ● Alfalfa - Burdock* - Yucca* - Licorice.
- Lots of light exercise.

ASTHMA (Allergy related breath spasm).
- Vits. A - B5 - B6* - B12 - B15 - B Comp.* - C* - E - F - P - Paba.
- Bee Pollen* - Thyme - Lobella - Licorice - Garlic - Camomile.
- Avoid allergens e.g.: fur, smoke, dust, aluminium pots, dairy products etc.

BACK ACHE (Non injury i.e.: Lumbago).
- Vits. B1 - B Comp.* - C - D - E - Calcium* - Phosphorous - Magnesium - Manganese.
- Comfrey* - Blue Cohosh* - Alfalfa - Slippery Elm.
- Lie on tummy & raise upper body & legs. Do sit-ups with bent knees.

BAD BREATH (From mouth, throat, tummy).
- Vits. A - B6* - C* - Zinc*. Parsley* - Myrrh - Mint - Chlorophyll* - Thyme - Alfalfa.
- Avoid processed carbohydrates, sugar & minimise dairy foods. Macrobiotic diet is best. Don't drink with meals.

BALDNESS (From genes or lifestyle).
- Vits. B3 - B5 - B12 - B Comp.* - C - E* - F - H - M - Lecithin* - Calcium - Copper - Zinc* - Oil Eve. Prim. ● Sage* - Burdock - Aloe Vera - Nettle - Water Cress. ● Massage scalp. Avoid all sugars. Macrobiotic Diet.

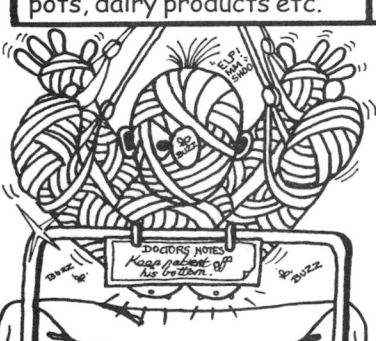

BED SORES (Skin ulcer from pressure).
- Vits. A* - B2 - B3 - B Comp.* - C* - D - E* - Magnesium - Potassium - Calcium - Lecithin - Copper.
- Cayenne* - Garlic - Bayberry* - Hyssop.
- Move subject often. Massage with alcohol. Macrobiotic diet.

BED WETTING (Boys under 5 are worst).
- Vits. A* - C - E - Magnesium*. ● Uva Ursi* - Corn silk* - Bee Pollen* - Buchu - Horsetail.
- May be allergy (eg. milk) related. Never scold the kid. Try 1 x tsp. honey, fennel seeds & parsley tea, 1 hr before bedtime.

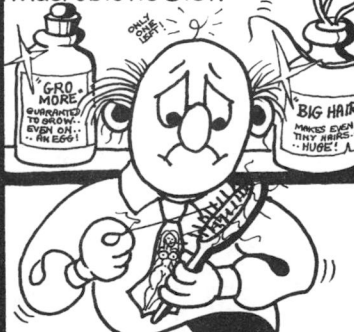

---

*Means considered an important supplement for that particular ailment.
● With all specific supplements also take a time-release multivit./min. tablet daily.
● Most sections have 4 parts: Heading, Vitamins/Minerals etc., Herbs etc., Extra notes.

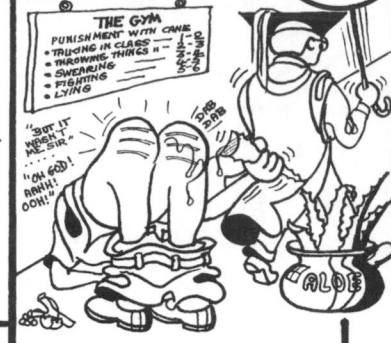

BLEEDING (Wound, nose, internal etc.)
- Vits. K* - C with bioflavonoids*.
- (Internal & external) Cayenne* - White Oak Bark* - Golden Seal* - Willow - Plantain.
- Avoid alcohol & aspirin. Eat cauliflower &/or chlorophyll (Vit. K).

BLOOD PRESSURE (Hypertension)
- Vits. B Comp. - C - E - P - Rutin* - Lecithin* - Magnesium - Tyrosine - Potassium.
- Garlic* - Cayenne* - Gotu Kola - Ginseng - Passion Flower.
- Exercise. Don't get fat/ smoke/drink/take drugs (inc. coffee). Avoid salt.

BODY ODOR (Smell from perspiration)
- Vits. B6* - B Comp - Paba* - Magnesium* - Zinc*.
- Chlorophyll* - Horsetail (feet) - Wood Betony (makes you sweat less).
- Caution: Smelly sweat means expelled toxins. Adopt a macrobiotic diet.

BOILS (Carbuncle, stye, very bad spot)
- Vits. A* - C* - Zinc*.
- Burdock* - Yellow Dock* - Chaparral* - Dandelion* - Red Clover - Comfrey.
- Bring to head by applying hot kaolin poultice. Then apply magnesium sulphate when it bursts. Avoid sugar. Exercise more.

BRONCHITIS (Lung/ airway infection)
- Vits. A - B12 - C* - E.
- Eucalyptus* - Comfrey* - Lobella* - (Try hot garlic soup &/or ginger with cayenne).
- Often follows a cold. Avoid fog/smoke/cold air/ exertion/dairy & refined foods. (Adopt a yang diet)

BRUISES (Sub-skin capillary ruptures)
- Vits. C* - P* - K* - Calcium.
- White Oak Bark* - St. Johns Wort* - Comfrey - Yarrow - Mullein - Aloe Vera.
- Eat cauliflower, pine-apple, yogurt. Apply aloe vera to bruise externally.

BURNS/SCALDS (Big ones serious - Get help)
- Vits. C* - E* - Paba* - Zinc*.
- Aloe Vera* - Burdock* - Comfrey* - Plantain.
- Bathe with iced water for 10 + mins & give cool drinks. Apply pure or fresh aloe vera gel. When partly healed apply Vitamin E oil.

BURSITIS (Joint sac/pad inflammation)
- Vits. A - B Comp. - C* - E - P* - Calcium - Magnesium - Chlorine.
- Chaparral* - Kelp - Comfrey* - Yucca - Alfalfa* - Burdock.
- Massage eucalyptus/ lavender oils in or apply a poultice with mullein.

CANCER (Out of control cell growth)
- Vits. A - B Comp.* - B6 - B17* - C* - E* - Zinc - Magnesium* - Germanium - Selenium*.
- Ginseng* - Garlic* - Chaparral* - Comfrey - Red Clover* - Taheebo.
- Adopt an organic veg diet & a fighting spirit. Beetroot juice.

CATARRH (Excess mucus in nose/throat)
- Vits. A - B5* - B6* - B Comp. - C* - E.
- Fenugreek* - Garlic* - Comfrey* - Hyssop - Slippery Elm - Thyme.
- Have an allergy test. Sniff golden seal or bayberry tea up nose. Avoid dairy/refined food. Eat more veg.

CHILBLAINS (Itchy inflamed finger/toes)
- Vits. B3 - B Comp.* - C* - E* - P* - K - Calcium* - Lecithin - Magnesium - Potassium.
- Cayenne* - Yarrow - Prickly Ash Bark.
- Keep warm & dry. Cut out caffeine & nicotine. Exercise & friction rub.

CHILDHOOD DISEASES (Chicken pox, mumps etc.)
- Vits. A - B Comp.* - C* - E.
- Catnip* - Burdock - Garlic* - Lobella* - Ginger - Yarrow.
- Avoid dairy/ refined foods & don't force feed (but give plenty of fluids). Use yellow dock for itching.

CIRCULATION (Blood stagnant/cold feet etc.)
- Vits. A - C* - B3* - B Comp.* - P* - Lecithin* - Calcium - Potassium - Magnesium - Iodine - Molybdenum.
- Bayberry* - Garlic* - Cayenne* - Hyssop.
- Macrobiotic diet. Exercise, exercise & exercise. No drugs.

COLDS (Respiratory viral/bact. infect.)
- Vits. A - B Comp. - C* - E - F - P - Calcium - Zinc* (Suck it)
- Garlic* - Cayenne* - Ginger * - Comprey * - Golden seal*.
- Sugar/refined foods = too yin = low resistance = catch colds = mucus (very yin) buildup
FIGHT IT WITH....

CHILBLAINS illustration
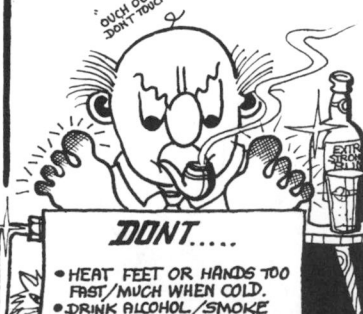

DON'T.....
- HEAT FEET OR HANDS TOO FAST/MUCH WHEN COLD.
- DRINK ALCOHOL/SMOKE
- BE LAZY (DO EXERCISE)

COLD SORES (Herpes virus mouth spots)
- Vits. A - B3* - B5 - B Comp. - C* - P - Zinc* (Suck it) - L - Lysine - Acidophilus.
- Golden Seal* - Sage & Ginger Tea* - Garlic* (int.).
- Contagious: Avoid sugar/refined food. Apply 50% lemon juice or zinc cream. Don't kiss (except enemies).

COLON (Improve sore bowel after illness)
- Vits. B5* - B6 - B Comp.* - C* - K - Pectin* - Acidophilus.
- Slippery Elm* - Myrrh* - Cascara Sagrada - Ginger.
- Avoid stress. Eat cooked veg & grain (cauliflower, brussel sprouts & brown rice). Avoid allergens.

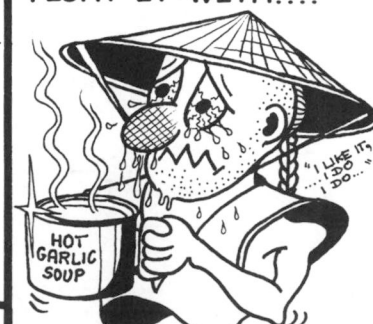

VEGETABLE BROTH + 1 TEASPOON GARLIC & GINGER EACH....WOW!

- See "Therapy Notes" (page 102) for dose/guidance etc.
- See "Herb or Vitamin" pages for function guidance.
- Always take a B complex supplement with single B vitamins.

How To Use Nutritional Supplements & Herbs To Treat Common Ailments

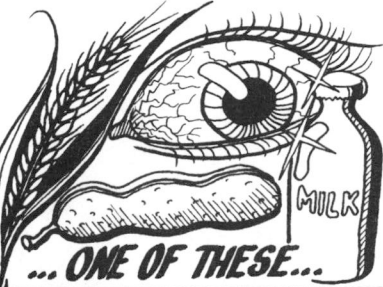

...IT MAY BE...
...ONE OF THESE...

CONJUNCTIVITIS
(Red, inflamed eyes)
● Vits. A* - B2 - B3 - B6 - B Comp.* - C* - Bioflavinoids (P)*. ● Eyebright* - Golden Seal* - Plantain*. ● May be infection or allergy or irritant, bathe with chickweed, camomile or red raspberry tea.

CONSTIPATION
(Stools difficult/infrequent). ● Vits. B1* - B Comp.* - C - Magnesium - Calcium - Potassium*. ● Dandelion* - Aloe Vera* Barberry - Cascara Sagrada*. ● Raise fiber & fluid intakes. Eat more veg, fruit & whole grains. Exercise & do yoga.

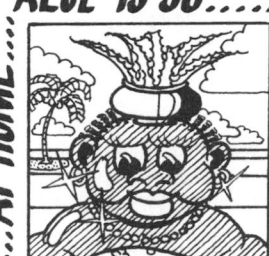

ALOE IS SO.....
VERY USEFUL...
AT HOME......
BETTER GROW IT

CONVULSIONS
(Fits, epilepsy etc.)
● Vits. A - B6* - B Comp.* - C - D - E* - Zinc - Folic Acid* - Calcium - Choline - Magnesium - Silicon - Selenium* - Manganese. ● Valerian* - Black Cohosh* - Lobella - Passion Flower*. ● Check for/eliminate allergies (food etc.).

COUGHS (Spasm of irritated airway).
● Vits. A* - B6 - B Comp.* - C* - Zinc - Garlic. ● Comfrey* - Licorice* - Marshmallow* - Cayenne - Lobella. ● Hot honey & lemon drinks. Hot water & cider vinegar mix (4 to l) as chest compress/inhaled. Avoid dairy, processed starch & sugar.

CRAMPS (Muscles involuntary spasm)
● Vits. B12 - B Comp.* - C - D* - E - F - Iron - Magnesium* - Calcium* - Potassium. ● Cayenne* - Alfalfa* - Peppermint* - Comfrey - Thyme. ● Can be caused by excess sweating & too little salt.

CUTS & SORES
(Wounds, grazes etc.)
● Vits. A* - B1 - B Comp.* - C* - E* - K* - Calcium - Zinc*. ● Aloe Vera* - White Oak Bark* - Yucca - Comfrey - Plantain. ● Grow aloe & slice off/ apply to all skin problems. Vit. E oil heals beautifully. Saliva also works.

DANDRUFF (Excess scalp skin flaking)
● Vits. A* - B6 - B Comp.* - Eve. Prim. Oil (F)*. ● Sage* - Camomile - Chaparral - Nettle. ● Massage sage tea into scalp daily. Eat polyunsaturated fatty acids (Vit. F) safflower, soya, wheatgerm oil. Avoid excess protein/dairy.

DERMATITIS (Skin allergy incl. eczema).
● Vits. A - B2* - B5* - B6* - B Comp.* - C - D - E - F - Zinc* - Biotin - Lecithin* - Sulphur - Magnesium - Calcium - Manganese. ● Bee Pollen* - Aloe Vera* - Alfalfa* Dandelion* - Camomile. ● Locate & eliminate allergen(s). Massage with Vit. E oil & aloe vera.

DIABETES (Insulin low from PANCREAS)
● Vits. A - B6* - B Comp. - C* - E* - Chromium* - Zinc* - Magnesium* - Lecithin - Potassium - Manganese. ● Golden Seal* - Uva Ursi* - Horseradish* - Chickweed* - Juniper*. ● Regular Macrobiotic diet & exercise.

DIARRHEA (Loose frequent stools).
● Vits. A - B3* - C - B Comp.* - Potassium - Magnesium - Garlic. ● Slippery Elm* - Peppermint - Red Rasberry* - Nutmeg*. ● Sip boiled water with honey, lemon, nutmeg & sea salt in. Avoid all foods for 24 hours.

DIGESTION (& mild stomach ailments)
● Vits. A - B1 - B3* - B5 - B Comp.* - C - E - Biotin - Folic Acid - Potassium - Iodine - Phosphorus - Zinc - Copper - Acidophilus. ● Peppermint* - Aloe Vera* - Camomile* - Ginger* - Papaya*. ● Observe combination rules. Go Macrobiotic.

DIRTY BLOOD (From toxins in circulation).
● Vits. A - B2 - B12 - B Comp.* - C - Folic acid* - Iron. ● Burdock* - Red Clover* - Yarrow - Sarsaparilla* - Myrrh* - Yellow Dock* - Dandelion - Chaparral. ● Drink 4 cups nettle tea/day to purify & start new blood cells.

DIZZINESS (& Fear of & falling/vertigo).
● Vits. B2 - B3 - B6 - B Comp.* - C - E - Potassium. ● Peppermint - Sage - Camomile - Cayenne* - Catnip - Bayberry. ● Limit/avoid refined & dairy foods. Dizzy spells often caused by poor circulation (so correct it & exercise).

DRY SKIN (Closed pores/wrinkled etc.).
● Vits. A* - B6* - B Comp.* - C* - Paba* - Biotin* - Lecithin*. ● Ginger* - Dandelion - Yellow Dock - Catnip* - Safflower* - Peppermint - Hyssop. ● Adopt Macrobiotic diet & eat P. U. F. A. (eg Evening Primrose oil).

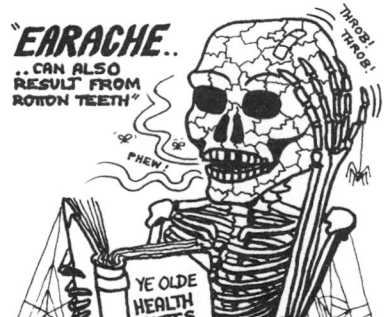

"EARACHE..
..CAN ALSO RESULT FROM ROTTON TEETH"
YE OLDE HEALTH NOTES

EAR AILMENTS
(Ache, ringing, block etc.)
● Vits. A - B2 - B Comp.* - C* - Zinc. ● Mistletoe (ringing)* - Yarrow (runny) or Yellow Dock* - Mullein. ● Causes: Allergies, wax, too much dairy/sugar, mucus, high blood p. For a boil use warm garlic oil & honey or almond oil drops.

ENERGY (Endurance vitality, anti-fatigue).
● Vits. B1 - B2 - B6 - B12 - B Comp.* - C* - D - E - F* - Biotin - Folic Acid - Magnesium* - Iodine - Potassium - Iron - Zinc. ● Ginseng * - Alfalfa* - Burdock* - Ginger - Licorice* - Dandelion*. ● Avoid refined foods adopt Macrobiotic diet & exercise.

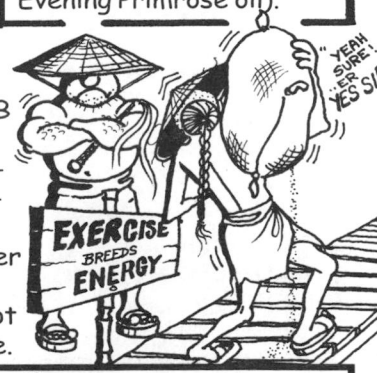

EXERCISE BREEDS ENERGY
"YEAH SURE! ..ER YES SIR"

* Means considered an important supplement for that particular ailment.
● With all specific supplements also take a time-release multivitamin/mineral pill daily.
● Most sections have 4 parts: Heading, Vitamins/Minerals etc., Herbs etc., Extra notes.

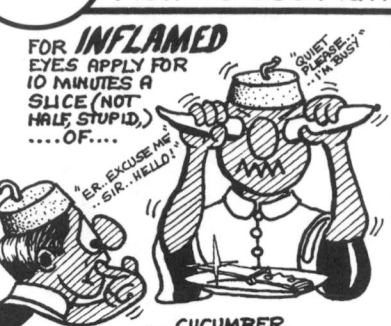

FOR *INFLAMED* EYES APPLY FOR 10 MINUTES A SLICE (NOT HALF, STUPID.) ....OF....

....CUCUMBER.

EYES (Cataracts, tired, glaucoma, weak)
● Vits A* - B1 - B2* - B6 - B12 - B Comp.* - C* - D - E - P - Lecithin - Protein - Zinc* (vital for retina).
● Eyebright* - Rue* - Rosemary* - Golden Seal* - Bayberry.
● Drink yarrow tea to relieve watery eyes. Rub sterile gold on a stye.

FEMALE FERTILITY (Hormones/ conceive).
● Vits A - B12 - B Comp.* - E* - Potassium - Iodine.
● Blessed Thistle* - Red Raspberry* - Don Quai* - Damiana* - Black Cohosh*.
● Vit. E is very important. Build up slowly - Do not take with iron - Eat more wheatgerm & soya oil.

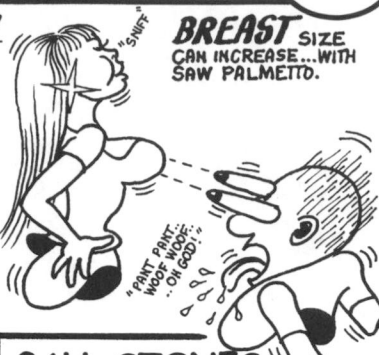

BREAST SIZE CAN INCREASE...WITH SAW PALMETTO.

FEVER (Raised body temp. from infection).
● Vits C* (no iron).
● Garlic* - Ginseng* - Catnip* - Sarsaparilla* - Yarrow - Lobella.
● Moderate fevers (up to 104 degrees) actually help the body fight infection - Over this cool down body with sponge etc. Do not let dehydration occur (frequent drinks).

FINGER/TOE NAILS (Ailments & condition).
● Vits A - B12 - B Comp.* - E* - F - Iron (brittle)* - Zinc (white spots)* - Silicon* - Sulphur* - Calcium - Iodine*.
● Horsetail* - Oat straw*.
● Flat, ridged, brittle nails = circulation poor (try bayberry* & cayenne*).

FLATULENCE (Gas in stomach from digestion).
● Vits B1* - B Comp.* - Activated Charcoal - Acidopholus. ● Peppermint* - Catnip* - Ginger* - Ginseng* - Cayenne*.
● Gas often caused by incompatible food combinations or drinks with meals, ulcers, hiatus hernia etc.

GALL STONES (Stone formation in G. Bladder). ● Vits A* - B Comp.* - C* - D - E* - F* - K - Lecithin* - Sulphur - Magnesium. ● Barberry* - Garlic - Burdock - Dandelion* - Cascara Sagrada*.
● Avoid obesity, coffee, alcohol & cholesterol. Exercise regularly.

GOUT (Uric acid/ arthritis in joints).
● Vits B Comp.* - C* - E* - Calcium - Magnesium - Potassium - Orotic acid.
● Primrose* - Corn silk* - Safflower* - Meadowsweet. ● Eat a few cherries daily. Avoid obesity, excess protein, fat, salt. Don't smoke.

HAIR (Condition of, graying, thickness).
● Vits A - B5 (gray)* - B Comp.* - Biotin (gray)* - E (gray)* - Paba (gray)* - Zinc - Manganese - Copper - Essential Amino Acids - Iron - Silica* - Lecithin* - Gelatin (thin)* - P.U.F.A. ● Nettle* - Oat straw* - Horsetail* - Sage. ● Macrobiotic diet.

HAY FEVER (Allergy to grass/pollen etc.).
● Vits A - B5* - B6 - B Comp.* - C* - E* - P* - Calcum. ● Cayenne - Nettle - Bee Pollen* - Alfalfa - Burdock - Confrey- Juniper - Red Clover.
● Build up bee pollen dose slowly. Avoid dairy & constipation.

HEADACHE (From diet, stress, sinus, allergy, pollution, drugs, injury etc.). ● Vits A - B3* - B6* - B12* - B Comp.* - F - Paba - Potassium* - Calcium* - Magnesium. ● Fenugreek* - Wood Betony* - Camomile - Peppermint - Thyme*.
● Macrobiotic diet & yoga.

HEART (Ailments of & relating to). ● Vits A - B1* - B6* - B Comp.* - C* - D - E* - F* - Lecithin* - Biotin - Pectin - Magnesium* - Calcium* - Iodine - Potassium* - Iron - Selenium* - Chromium* - Manganese.
● Hawthorn* - Garlic* - Cayenne* - Lobella*.
● Macrobiotic diet & exercise.

HICCUPS (Spasm of diaphragm).
● Vits B Comp.* - Charcoal Tablets (chew) ● Chew Dill*, Fennel or Caraway seeds (or sip tea) - Catnip - Ginger* - Peppermint*.
● Often caused by gas or indigestion. Lie on back, hug knees. Try teaspoon of honey.

IMPOTENCE (Male unable to copulate).
● Vits A* - B6 - B12 - B Comp.* - C - E* - Zinc* - Lecithin - Folic acid - Iodine - Brewers yeast.
● Sarsaparilla* - Licorice* - Ginseng - Damiana* - Chickweed - Plantain* - Catuaba.
● Avoid stress, fatigue, nicotine, alcohol etc.

INFECTIONS (Cuts, wounds, sores etc.).
● Vits A - C* - E - P - Zinc*. ● Golden seal* - Garlic* - Camomile - Sage - Poke Weed.
● Use ladys mantle or comfrey as a poultice. Mega doses of Vit. C should reduce over about a week after. (see p. 148)

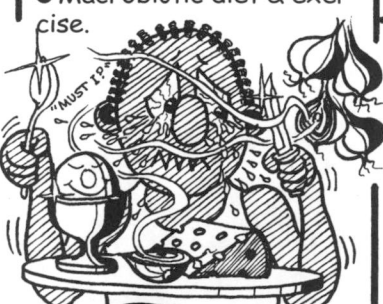

"MUST I...?"

INFLAMMATION (& swelling, red etc.).
● Vits A - C* -E - F - K* - P* - Calcium.
● Comfrey (sprains)* - Yucca (joints)* - Rose hips - Hyssop - Slippery Elm - Alfalfa. ● Apply poultice of :Valerian or onion or alum or comfrey or eucalyptus.

INSECT BITES (& stings & reactions).
● Vits B1 (take a week before to repel)* - C - Calcium - Magnesium.
● To repel rub with Pennyroyal* or Walnut Leaves or Eucalyptus* or Lavender. If stung apply vinegar or lemon juice or clay.
● Avoid blue & being wet.

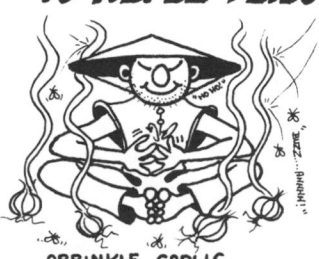

TO REPEL FLIES... .... SPRINKLE GARLIC, THYME OR PINE TEA.

● CUT CHOLESTEROL absorption by up to 40% (eat fresh/boiled onions w/ any saturated fat).

● See "Therapy Notes" (page 102) for dose/guidance etc.
● See "Herb or Vitamin" pages for function guidance.
● Always take a B Complex supplement with single B vitamins.

How To Use Nutritional Supplements & Herbs To Treat Common Ailments

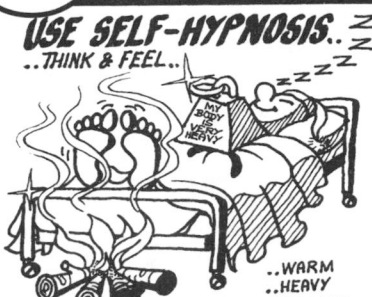

USE SELF-HYPNOSIS..
..THINK & FEEL..

..WARM
..HEAVY
..WARM ETC.

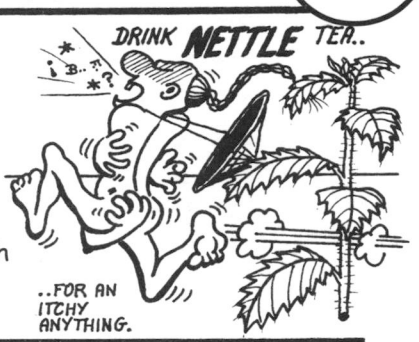

DRINK NETTLE TEA..

..FOR AN ITCHY ANYTHING.

INSOMNIA (Sleep difficulties long-term)
- Vits. B1 - B3 - B5 - B6* - B Comp.* - D - Calcium* - Magnesium* - Iron - Zinc - L - Tryptophan* - Manganese - Potassium.
- Valerian* - Hawthorn - Lobella* - Hops*.
- Avoid caffeine/stress. Try hot milk & nutmeg.

ITCHY (See also dry skin & allergies)
- Vits. B5 - B Comp.* - C* (Time rel.) - E* - F*.
- Yellow Dock* - Nettle* - Chickweed* - Ginger (dry skin)*.
- Try macrobiotic diet with oil of evening primrose & soya. Apply Vit. E oil/aloe.

KIDNEY AILMENTS (Inc. bladder & stones)
- Vits. A - B5 - B6* - B Comp. - C* - E - F - K* - Choline - Potassium - Magnesium* ● Lemon Juice & Thyme*- Nettle* - Uva Ursi* - Corn Silk - Dandelion. ● Avoid oxalic acid foods (inc. chocolate, tea, rhubarb etc.). Do use apple cider vinegar.

LACTATION (Breast milk production)
- Vits. A - B6* - B12 - B Comp.* - C - D - F - Choline - Manganese - Magnesium - Calcium - Zinc - Iodine.
- Alfalfa* - Fennel - Marshmallow* - Red Raspberry. ● To dry up milk: Take parsley or sage or dandelion (laxative). Also reduce fluid intake.

LICE (Blood-sucking hair parasites/nits)
- Vits. Thiamine 50 - 100 mg daily repels thru smell of sweat. ● Garlic (crush, let stand & strain in castor oil) massage in & leave an hour. Walnut leaf wash & massage daily.
- Apply cider vinegar 3 times/day (leave 1/2 hr.). Use nit comb.

LIVER (Including hepatitis/jaundice)
- Vits. A - B5 - B Comp.* - C* - E* - K - Folic acid - Lecithin - Sulphur - Copper.
- Barberry* - Aloe Vera* - Camomile* - Dandelion - Cascara Sagrada - Peppermint. ● Avoid excess fat & alcohol.

LONGEVITY (Incl. - senile dementia).
- Vits. A - B5 - B12* - B15* - B Comp.* - C - E* - Lecithin - Seleniom* - Calcium - Germanium* - RNA/DNA.
- Ginseng & Gotu Kola (take together)* - Don Quai & Damiana (ladies) - Licorice & Sarsaparilla (gents). ● Macrobiotics/exercise.

LUNGS (Ailments of incl. emphysema etc.).
- Vits. A* - C* - E*.
- Garlic* - Comfrey* - Fenugreek* - Licorice - Horsetail* - Mullein - Knotgrass - Ginger.
- Asian medicine holds that dairy & yin foods (e.g. sugar, drugs etc.) produce mucus. So avoid them & benefit.

LYMPH NODES (Swollen & ailments of)
- Vits. A - B5 - B Comp.* - C - E - Lecithin.
- Bedstraw (regulate)* - Golden Seal* - Burdock - Nettle. ● If swollen rub in St. johns wort oil. Weak lymph flow can lead to cancer. Exercise & deep breathing vital.

MEMORY (Loss of & in senility)
- Vits. A - B1* - B12* - B15* - B Comp.* - C - E* - F - Lecithin* - Germanium* - Paba - Zinc* - Calcium - Iron - Selenium.
- Speedwell* - Don Quai (F) - Ginseng* - Licorice (M) - Alfalfa - Gotu Kola*.
- Exercise & macrobiotics. Avoid aluminium.

MENOPAUSE (Female change of life)
- Vits. A - B6* - B Comp.* - C* - D - E* - Iron - Calcium* - Magnesium.
- Ginseng* - Ladys Mantle* - Yarrow - Black Cohosh* - Don Quai* - Misletoe - Valerian (calming)* - Passion flower - Kelp.

MISCARRIAGE (Premature birth)
- Vits. E (50 iu 3 times/day from 3 months before & during pregnancy)* - P* - B Comp. - C. ● Take together either Ladys Mantle & Yarrow or Lobella & False Unicorn - Catnip. ● Don't eat or drink anything you would not give a new baby.

MOTION SICKNESS (Also general nausea)
- Vits. B6 (20mg)* & Ginger (100 mg)* (kids half dose - Both every 2 hrs prior to & during journey as needed) - Also B Comp. & Calcium
- Ginger* - Alfalfa - Yarrow - Peppermint - Camomile - Kelp - Sage.
- Breathe deeply, suck a lemon & shut eyes.

MOUTH AILMENTS (Sores, gums etc.)
- Vits. A* - B2* - B3* - B12* - B Comp.* - C* - E - Folic acid - Calcium* - Zinc (suck)* - Iron - Phosphorus - Magnesium.
- Aloe Vera* - Sage* - Myrrh* - Garlic* - Golden Seal - Mallow - Red Raspberry - Horsetail.
- Upgrade diet. Avoid stress & sugar.

FOR HOT FLUSHES
USE DAMIANA + MODERATE DOSES OF VITS C & E + CALCIUM 3 TIMES DAILY.
(ABOUT 500 mg, 100 iu & 500 mg.)

USUALLY BETWEEN
45 & 55 YEARS OLD

MUSCLES (Swollen, shrunk, tics etc.).
- Vits. C - E (all)* - Calcium (all)* - B Comp. (tense)* - Potassium (tics & night cramps)* - Magnesium (tics). ● Shepards Purse & Ladys Mantle Tea (all)* - Comfrey (all)* - Thyme Oil Massage + take Amino Acids (shrunken).
- Stretching vital (see also "Cramps").

NIGHTMARES (& nerves/sweats etc.).
- Vits. B6* - B Comp.* - D - Dolomite* (all with hot milk & nutmeg before bed) - L' Tryptophane.
- Valerian* - Thyme* -Hops (good but is also a sex depressant)*.
- Stuff pillow with hops. Rub feet with garlic. Sniff lavender.

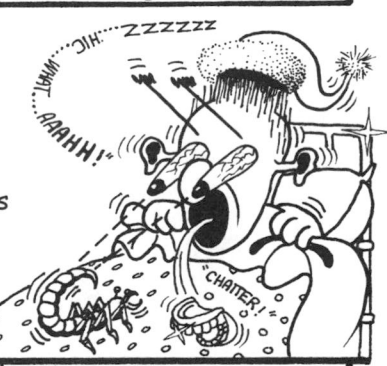

*Means considered an important supplement for that particular ailment.
● With all specific supplements also take a time-release multivitamin/mineral pill daily.
● Most sections have 4 parts: Heading - Vitamins/Minerals etc. - Herbs etc. - Extra notes

How To Use Nutritional Supplements & Herbs To Treat Common Ailments

CHICKWEED (STELLARIA MEDIA)... DECREASES APPETITE, HELPS DISSOLVE FAT & MUCUS.

& PUT SIMPLY.. EAT LESS & EXERCISE MORE!

OBESITY (Excess of body fat).
- Vits. B Comp.* - C - E - Lecithin* - Chromium - Iodine - Magnesium - Calcium - Potassium.
- Hawthorn* - Fennel* - Licorice - Burdock - Golden Seal* - Kelp. ● Macrobiotic diet. No sugar. Count calories. Lots of water.

PAIN (See also "Periods" & "Headache")
- Vits. B Comp.* - C - D - E - F - Tryptophan* - Magnesium* - Calcium*.
- Cattail Pollen (Pollen Typhae)* - Camomile* - Peppermint* - Wild Yam - Valerian* - Lobella - Taheebo. ● Exercise decreases pain sensitivity.

THIS SITUATION CALLS FOR.. **SELF-**

"ER.. LET ME.. SEE NOW.. WHOOPS WRONG ONE !"

RETIRING VERY SOON

-HYPNOSIS.

PERIODS (Monthly).
- **TOO MUCH:** A - B Comp.* - Iron* - Zinc - Cayenne* - Comfrey - Mistletoe.
- **TOO LITTLE:** B12 - Folic Acid - E - P - Camomile* - Ginger - St Johns Wort.
- **PAIN:** E* - F* - P - Calcium* - Peppermint* - Yarrow - Catnip.
- **GENERAL:** B6 - B12 - B Comp. - C - F - Folic Acid.

PROSTATE GLAND (& associated ailments).
- Vits. A - B6 - B Comp.* - C - D - E - F* - Zinc* - Dolomite - Lecithin.
- Bee Pollen* - Corn silk - Willow Herb* - Saw Palmetto* - Uva Ursi* - Buchu - Kelp.
- Adopt macrobiotics. Stimulate acu. point CV. 1. Exercise more.

PSORIASIS (Red, scaly, itchy patches).
- Vits. A (10,000 iu. [adults] 3 times/day, 6 days/wk.)* - B Comp* - C* - F* - Lecithin*.
- Dandelion* - Yellow Dock - Aloe Vera*.
- Avoid allergens & stress. Apply aloe & Vit. A to patches. Adopt macrobiotic diet.

RHEUMATISM (Muscle/Joint pain).
- Vits. B1* - B5* - B Comp.* - Magnesium - Calcium.
- Alfalfa* - Willow* - Horsetail - Cowslip - Chaparral - Yucca*.
- Avoid cold/damp. Massage with thyme or chamomile oil. Use hot water bottle.

RINGWORM (&/or ATHLETES FOOT).
- Vits. A* - C*.
- Walnut Leaf Wash (massage in well)* - Poke Weed - Golden Seal - Garlic - Taheebo.
- Keep dry & warm. Air & sun help. Apply lemon juice or cider vinegar or powdered Vit. C then honey or Vit. E oil.

SCHIZOPHRENIA (Illogical Paranoia).
- Vits. Nicotinamide (B3) & C together* - or Pyridoxine (B6)*. Also useful B12 - B Comp* - & Zinc.
- St Johns Wort* - Valerian* - Thyme - Passion Flower.
- Food allergies can precipitate wild mood swings.

SCIATICA (Spinal muscle/nerve spasm).
- Vits. B1* - B5* - B Comp.* - Calcium.
- Yucca* - Cayenne - Black Cohosh* - Valerian - Buckthorn.
- For arm/leg pains stroke 4 times with fresh nettles. For back, massage with warm St. johns wort oil.

SEX (Male interest in/ sperm count etc).
- **TO DEPRESS:** Hops* - Willow - Skullcap* - Sage - Marijuana* - Alcohol* - Nicotine* - Caffeine - Poor Diet*. ●**TO STIMULATE:** Vits. A* - B6*- C*- E* - Zinc* - Calcium - Magnesium - Manganese - Ginseng* - Licorice* - Chickweed* - Sarsaparilla*.

SEX (Female desire & hormones etc)
- **TO DEPRESS:** Hops - Willow - Skull Cap* - Sage - Nicotine* - Being Underweight* - Poor Diet* - Marijuana* - Caffeine* - Alcohol. ●**TO STIMULATE:** Vits. B6* - B12* - E* - Don Quai* - Blessed Thistle - Safflower - Plantain* - Damiana*.......

"NO MORE PLEASE"

"COME HERE DARLING"

"KISS KISS"

SHINGLES (Viral skin/nerve blisters)
- Vits. A - B3 - B5 - B6 - B12* - B Comp.* - C* - E* - L Lysine* - P - Acidophulis - B15*.
- Yellow Dock* - Red Clover* - Golden Seal - Yarrow - Sage.
- Detoxify body (fast or macrobiotics). Appy E & take C hourly.

SPLEEN (Ailments of & relating to).
- Vits. C* - Lecithin*.
- Dandelion* - Uva Ursi - Yellow Dock* - Nettle* - Arigmony - Barberry - Parsley.
- Every day pick, wash, deflower, chew well & eat raw four fresh dandelion stems.

SKIN (General skin conditions of).
- Vits. A* - B2 - B3 - B5 - B6* - B Comp.* - C* - E* - F - P* - Biotin* - Lecithin* - Silicon - Sulphur - Selenium* - Paba* - Germanium - Iron. ● Aloe Vera (inside & out)* - Yellow Dock* - Chickweed* - Horsetail.
- Macrobiotic diet.

SMOKING (To stop/ counter effects etc.)
- **TO COUNTER:** Vits. A* - B1 - C* - E* - Selenium* - Magnesium - Garlic* - Ginseng*.
- **TO STOP:** Vits. B Comp* - Tryptophan* - chew (& spit out) Calamus Root* - Valerian, Slippery Elm, Hops & Scullcap together.

SORE THROAT (Is it virus/bacteria/other?)
- Vits. A - C* - E - B Comp.
- Garlic* - Golden Seal* - Fenugreek - Marshmallow - Cayenne - Sage*.
- Gargle with apple cider vinegar in warm water hourly, & sip hot lemon & honey drinks to soothe.

- **BREATHING** big city air = 20 cigs./day
- **EACH** cig. destroys 25 mg of Vitamin C.
- **EACH cig. subtracts 10 minutes of life.**

THE GRIM REAPER

...& BLACK COHOSH*

- See "Therapy Notes" (page 102) for dose/guidance etc.
- See "Herbs or Vitamin" pages for function guidance.
- Always take a B Complex supplement with single B vitamins.

How To Use Nutritional Supplements & Herbs To Treat Common Ailments

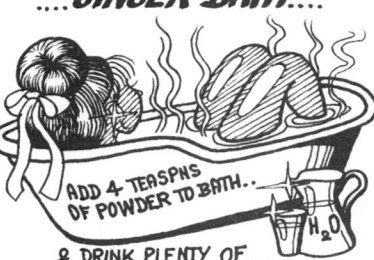

DETOXIFY WITH A....
....GINGER BATH....
ADD 4 TEASPNS OF POWDER TO BATH..
..& DRINK PLENTY OF.....
(jug of H₂O)

STROKE (Blood clot stops supply to brain).
● Vits. A* - B Comp. - C* - E* - F* - Lecithin* - Bioflavonoids* - Magnesium - Potassium. ● Mistletoe (tea)* - Garlic* - Cayenne*. ● Avoid stress, fat, salt & excess alcohol. Study Macrobiotics & exercise more.

SUNBURN (Excess ultra violet rays).
● PRE SUN TRAINING: Vits. B6* - B Comp.* - Paba* - C* - E* - Zinc* - Manganese*. ● IF BURNT: Bathe with cold water or Sage Tea. Apply Aloe* - E* - Paba. Take extra Vits. A, B Comp., Paba, C, D, E, Calcium & Zinc.

CONDITION SKIN....
..WELL BEFORE SUN....
..W/ MASSAGE (MIX APPLE CIDER VINEGAR & OLIVE OIL (IN A 2 TO 1 MIX)

SWEAT (Too little + smelly body/breath).
● B.O. = Toxins trying to get out, don't block them with roll on/deodorants etc. ● TOO LITTLE: Catnip* - Peppermint - Yarrow - Ginger* - Safflower. ● TOO SMELLY: Vits. B6* - B Comp. - C - Zinc* - Paba* - Magnesium* - Chlorophyll*.

TEETH (Enamel, roots, toothache).
● Vits. A - C (infection)* - B1 (sensitivity)* - D* - P (gums)* - Calcium - Magnesium* - Fluorine* - Vanadium - Phophorous* - Silicon - Molybdenum*. ● TOOTHACHE: Apply Aloe (or cloves or onion or garlic) &.... ● ....Drink camomile tea.

TONGUE (Ailments & deficiencies of).
● Vits. A - B1 (appears scared) - B2 (purple & sore) - B3 (bright red & sore mouth/throat) - B5 (swollen) - B6 (hot in mouth) - B12 (smooth & sore+mouth/lips) - B Comp* - C* - Zinc*. ● Bedstraw Tea* - Sage tea* - Marshmallow. ● Adopt Macrobiotics.

TRAVEL (Jet lag, culture shock etc.).
● Vits. A (eyes/smoke) - B2 & B3 (dizzy) - B6 (sick)* - B Comp. (stress/fatigue)* - C (bugs/immunity)* - E & Selenium (pollution)* - Calcium - Potassium - Iron (nerves/sleep)*. ● Ginger* - Ginseng* - Valerian (calm)*. ● Acidophilus (diarrhea).

ULCERS (Peptic [internal] & external).
● Vits. A* - B2 - B Comp* - C* - E* - P - Aloe Vera* - Folic Acid - Zinc* - Calcium. ● Horsetail (poultice or drink)*. - Slippery Elm* - Cayenne*. ● Avoid fat, aspirin, spice, sugar, stress, acidity, drugs, coffee. ● Use cabbage/carrot juice.

URINE (Problems & infections from/in).
● Vits. A - C (1 - 2g ev. 4 hrs reducing after)* - E - Zinc - Selenium. ● GRAVEL IN: Horsetail* or Nettle Tea* - PUS/INFECTION: Cranberry Juice twice daily* - RETENTION OF: Nettle* or Thyme - (Also try: Uva Ursi - Juniper). ● Excess C is urinated.

VAGINAL (Thrush/yeast/herpes etc.).
● Vits. E - B6 - Iron - Zinc + (A* & C* & Calcium & B5 [herpes]), + (B2* & Acidophilous* [itching]). ● YEAST INFEC: Garlic (eat & douche)* - HERPES: Drink Nettle or Calendula Tea* - ITCH: Marshmallow* ● Macrobiotic diet.

VARICOSE VEINS (Lumpy leg veins).
● Vits. B5* - C* - E* - P* - Iodine - Dolomite - Rutin* - Lecithin*. ● DRINK: White Oak Bark* - Cayenne* - Rosemary - Bayberry. ● APPLY: Calendula* - Agrimony* - Witch Hazel. ● Swim. Macrobiotics.

VENEREAL (Sexual contact) DISEASES.
● Vits. A* - B5* - B Comp.* - C* - E - Zinc* - Calcium. ● Taheebo* - Black Walnut* - Buchu with Uva Ursi* - Yellow Dock* - Burdock. ● If on antibiotics take extra Vits. K (cauliflower) & C & acidophilus.

VIRUS (The smallest of parasites).
● Vits. A* - B Comp. - C* - P* - Calcium - Zinc* - Lysine*. ● Goldenseal* - Red Clover - Garlic* - Calendula* - Nettle* - Burdock - Yellow Dock. ● Avoid aspirin, stress, yin diet, fatigue. Lots (p.148) of C can kill virus.

VITILIGO (Patchy skin depigmentation).
● Vits. Paba (100 mg AM & PM for up to 12 mths)* - B5* - B6* - B Comp.* - Zinc* - Manganese. ● Aloe Vera* - Yellow Dock* - Sarsaparilla*. ● Paba & folic acid also used to combat gray hair & wrinkles.

WARTS (Inc. genital & verrucae [all viral]).
● Vits. A* - C* - E*. ● INTERNAL: Cleavers - Garlic* - Poke Root. ● EXTERNAL: Rub AM & PM with Garlic or oil of Cinnamon or Vit E oil or Dandelion stalk juice or potato slice or Castor oil.. Also use self hypnosis.

IT MAY NOT BE FOOD.... MAKING YOU FAT BUT.... SALT..
"MORE MORE"
IT CAN.. BLOAT YOUR BODY.

WATER RETENTION (Body/fluid bloating).
● Vits. B6* - B Comp.* - C - Paba* - Calcium - Potassium*. ● Dandelion* - Kelp* - Parsely* - Yarrow* - Safflower - Uva Ursi - Fenugreek. ● Lecithin emulsifies fat. Allergies can also cause bloating.

WORMS (Inside body [tape/round etc.]).
● Vits. Folic acid - Garlic*. ● Pumpkin Seeds (20 four times/day & 1 teaspn. Castor oil 1 hour after each (kids half dose)*. - Raw garlic on rising* - Tansy (inside & out)* - Sarsaparilla - Cayenne - Thyme - Sage* - Black Walnut. ● They hate garlic.

WARTS MAY ALSO RESPOND TO APPLICATIONS 4 TIMES/DAY OF....
"GET LOST KID"
"EH WHAT....?"
"MUMMY MUMMY MAKS GOT A YELLOW NOSE!"
LEMON JUICE (EVEN ON YOUR NOSE)

---

*Means considered an important supplement for that particular ailment.
● With all specific supplements also take a time-release multivitamin/mineral pill daily. -
● Most sections have 4 parts: Heading, Vitamins/Minerals etc., Herbs etc., Extra notes.

HOW TO GATHER HERBS

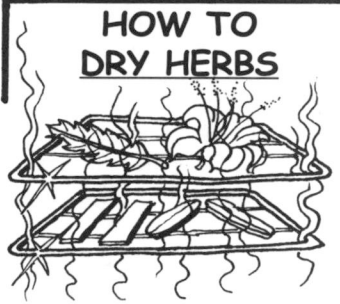

● Herbs are usually most potent at end of most active growth period (just before flowers open) so gather them on a sunny dry morning.

HOW TO DRY HERBS

● LEAVES & FLOWERS: Strip off & lay on racks in warm dry ventilated place till brittle enough to crumble easily.

● ROOTS: Wash/scrub well & trim off too thin shoots. Slice main root about 1/4 inch thick & lay on racks in warm dry place until all moisture is gone (usually 10 - 30 days [above stove is good]).

FOUR IMPORTANT FACTS

1. NO ONE KNOWS everything, & opinions differ widely (even "experts" get it wrong). So, do some basic research & compare doctrines/works before acting.

2. REACTIONS (to a dose or supplement) & interactions (between several different supplements) are complex & may vary widely between people & their circumstances.

3. ALL SUPPLEMENTS do more than the probably one thing you are taking it/them for (most do many things) & not all of these are necessarily what you want. So try to find out if any unwelcome secondary actions are likely before taking it/them - Listen to your body.

4. FINALLY all these are basically natural (& in most cases very old) therapies - So take your chosen one(s) with a positive outlook & "feel" the unique character of each working its magic on your life (self-hypnosis is a potent force - use it.)

VITAMIN/MINERAL DOSE EXAMPLES

NAME OF SUPPLEMENT..	THERAPEUTIC LIMITS	NAME OF SUPPLEMENT	THERAPEUTIC LIMITS
B1 (Thiamine)	10 -1,000 mg	BIOTIN	50 - 500 mcg
B2 (Riboflavin.)	10 - 1,000 mg	LECITHIN	1 - 15 g
B3 (Niacin)	50 - 5,000 mg	D	500 - 2,000 iu
B5 (Pant. Acid)	20 - 1,500 mg	ZINC	20 - 200 mg
B6 (Pyridoxine)	10 - 1,000 mg	MAGNESIUM	400 - 1,000 mg
B12 (Cyanocob.)	20 - 2,000 mcg	POTASSIUM	1 - 2 g
PABA	40 - 4,000 mg	IRON	20 - 200 mg
FOLIC ACID	400 - 2,000 mcg	Therapy doses usually 5 - 20 x RDA	
E	200 - 4,000 iu	BUT must be built up & declined slowly.	
C COMPLEX	2 - 40 g	BUT decrease slowly & use time release.	
A	10 - 75,000 iu	BUT split into 3 daily doses & taken only 5 days/week to prevent build-up.	

READ THIS PLEASE

● Nutritional therapies can include high doses of relevant supplements (not herbs) which may induce side effects (or even become toxic), therefore consult a qualified nutritionist &/or research a variety of opinions before acting.

● HIGH DOSES of C can cause diarrhea.

BUT CAROTENE IS OK.

HOW TO TAKE HERBS

AN INFUSION

● USE WITH fresh flowers &/or soft leaves or small particle dry herbs.
● MAKE IT: Put one heaped tsp. of herb in a glass or china cup and pour on boiling water. Let steep for 5 - 20 mins. Strain and drink within 12 hrs.

A DECOCTION

● USE WITH fresh roots and/or tough or woody stems and leaves or large particle dried herbs.
● MAKE IT: Put herb (25 g) in glass/china pot and simmer in one pint water for 10 - 20 mins. Strain and use (or can keep in fridge for max 24 hrs).

A TINCTURE

● USE WITH ground or finely chopped dried or fresh herbs.
● MAKE IT: Put 4 ozs of dried (or 8 ozs fresh) herb in a sealable glass jar & pour in 1 pint 30% (60 proof) Vodka. Seal & store in a warm place shaking twice daily for 2 weeks. Strain & squeeze out residue & store liquid (tincture) in dark airtight glass bottles. Adult dose about 2.5 (2 1/2) ml in a little water or in herb tea.

A POWDER

● MAKE FROM any suitable dry herb. Grind in a blender (or buy commercially) to mix & make your own personal mixture(s). Fill gelatine caps. or add to drinks/food (about 1/4 tsp.), or mix with a natural skin cream to make therapeutic ointment.

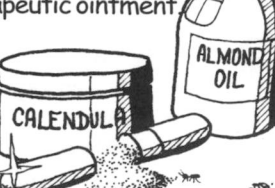

LOTION OR HAND/FOOTBATH

● Both infusion and decoction fluids can be used (where appropriate) as skin lotions or to soak hands or feet in. Can also be inhaled.

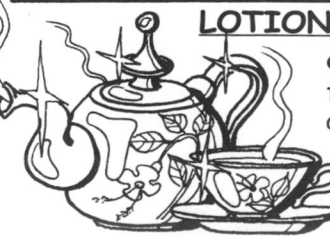

AGRIMONY
(Agrimonia Eupatoria)

- **USE:** Aerial parts.
- **FOR:** Tonic - Piles - Cystitis - Sores (ext)* - Mucus - Colitis* - Wounds (ext)* - Blood purifier - Appendici-tis* - Gallstones - Bruises (ext.)* - Inconti-nence (urine) - Diarrhea (kids)* - Sore throat (gargle).
- **NOTES:** Fragrant yellow flowers. Mild antibiotic. **May cause constipation.** Contains silica. Astringent action on digestive system.

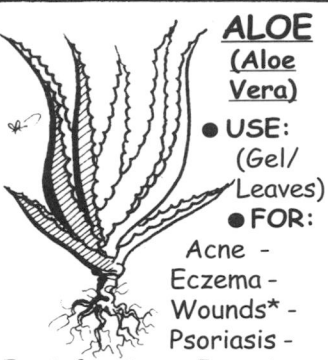

ALFALFA
(Medicago Salvia)

- **USE:** Herb & leaves.
- **FOR:** Flu - Gout - Bad breath - Hay fever - Blood vessel walls* - Energy - Diabetes - Allergies* - Intestinal cleaner - Rheumatism - Mothers milk - Stomach ulsers* - Old age - Cleans blood* - Pituitary gland* - Broken bones - Anti-cholesterol - Nausea (inc morning sick.) - Kidneys - Digestion - Cramps - Hypoglycaemia - Anemia - Arthritis* - General tonic - Teeth - Improve appetite - Thins blood - Bursitis - Uterus - Kidneys.
- **NOTES:** Blue/violet flowers. Also known as lucerne. **Prized for endurance & nutrition**

(Vits A, B, C, D, E , K, U, biotin, folic acid + amino acids, trace minerals & enzymes).

ALOE
(Aloe Vera)

- **USE:** (Gel/Leaves)
- **FOR:** Acne - Eczema - Wounds* - Psoriasis - Ear infections - Insect bites - Burns* - Ringworm - Sores - Cuts - Uterus - Mouth inflammation - Anus - Cankers - Fractures - Thrush - Fungi. **(ALL ABOVE EXTERNAL)** Constipation* - Liver - Tonsillitis - Colon - Digestion - Improve appetite.
- **NOTES:** Small doses increase menstrual flow.
- **CAUTION:** **Avoid use in first 4 months of pregnancy (stimulates contractions).** Use during breast feeding may give baby diarrhea. Do not use commercial aloe vera creams with lanolin on scalds/burns/sunburn etc.

ANGELICA
(Angelica Archangelica)

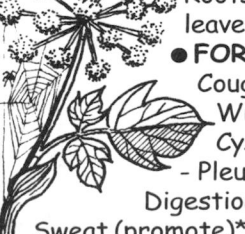

- **USE:** Roots & leaves.
- **FOR:** Cough* - Wind - Cystitis - Pleurisy - Digestion* - Sweat (promote)* - Bronchitis -Lung/chest congestion - Improves appetite - Rheumatism - Anemia - General tonic.
- **NOTES:** Lime/cream flower heads. Do not use if diabetic.

BARBERRY
(Berberis Vulgaris)

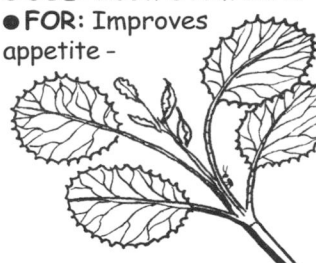

- **USE:** Root/Stem bark.
- **FOR:** Improves appetite - Douche - Bladder - Gall Bladder* (& stones) - Jaundice - Rheumatism - Boils - Gas (use with Wild Yam) - Liver* (& tumours) - Spleen (swollen) - Kidneys* - Mouthwash - Heartburn - Mild laxative - Arthritis - Anemia - Dysentery - Colon - Digestion - Fever - Malaria - Mouth sores - Purify blood* - Promote bile* - Sore throat - Skin ailments - Hepatitis - Antibacterial.
- **CAUTIONS:** Can be used to treat high blood pressure but **may dilate blood vessels.** Low dose stimulates heart, high dose slows it (& respira-tion). **Do not use if pregnant.**

BAYBERRY
(Myrica Cerifera)

- **USE:** Root, bark.
- **FOR:** Cuts - Eyes - Lungs - Douche - Circulation* - Miscarriage - Sore throat (garg.) - Sinus/mucus - Colitis* - Varicose veins - Diarrhea* - Fever - Children's diseases - Lumbago - Wounds* - Colon - Hay fever* - Dysentry* - Colds - Canker - Too heavy menstruation - Uterus

prolapse - Hemorrhage* - Ulcers - Catarrh* - Thyroid (low) - Voice loss - General tonic - Sores/boils (ext).
- **NOTES:** Combine with comfrey/agrimony for digestive ailments. Snuff powder or tea for sinus/mucus. **Large doses cause nausea/vomiting.**

BEE POLLEN
(Polen Grandular)

- **IS:** Male flower spores.
- **FOR:** Hay fever* - Age spots - Burns (ext) - Memory - Gangrene (ext) - Endurance* - Impotence* - Frid-gity - Hot flushes - Energy* - Allergies* - Prostate - Immunity* - Period cramps - Im-prove appetite -Asthma* - Eczema* - Hypoglycemia - Menopause - Skin (int. & ext.)* - Mental ability - Fertility* - Headache-Longevity*.
- **NOTES:** **Exceedingly nutritious** (Vits. A, B, C, D, E, P, enzymes, amino acids, minerals). For allergies build up dose over 1 month.

ROYAL JELLY (Bee)

- **PRODUCED** by worker bees for queen who eats it only (while laying 2,000 eggs/day).
- **FOR:** Immunity & longevity* - Stress - Anti-radiation - Tissue & cell regeneration*.

PROPOLIS (Bee)

- **FROM:** Leaf/bud/bark.
- **FOR:** **Strengthening** your body's defenses.

---

*Indicates that herb considered particularly effective for that ailment.
- See also "Rapid Reference Natural Therapy Notes" for extra details.

BISTORT
(Polygonum Bistortia)

- USE: Root.
- FOR: Acne - Wounds - Sores* - Insect Bites - Vagina - Anus (cracked) - Gums - Mouth (garg.)* - Toothache - Nosebleed (ALL ABOVE ext. in ointment or powder or tea form) - Diarrhea* - Worms - Bleeding* - Bed wetting - Ulcers - Hemorrage* - Small Pox - Jaundice - Period too heavy - Cholera - Measles - Dysentry* - Mucus - Miscarriage - Colon - Laryngitis (garg.) - Hemorrhoids (Oint.) - Gonorrhea.
- NOTES: Rose Pink flower & green/blue leaf with purple/ash grey underside.

BLACK COHOSH
(Cimicifuga Racemosa)

- USE: Dried Root.
- FOR: Skin ailments - Insect stings - Reptile bites - Period pain* - Female hormones* - Nerves - Delayed or light periods* - Cough - Lungs/Smoking - Rhuematism* - High blood p. - Menopause* - Whooping cough - Lumbago - Epilepsy - Bronchitis - Liver - Diarrhea - Diabetes - Arthritis - Thyroid - Fits* - Cramps (inc. period) - Circulation* - Asthma - Tinnitus - Cleans Blood/ Kidneys - Uterus - Hot Flashes*.
- NOTES: If pregnant don't use. If headache or nausea occur stop use. Lowers blood sugar. Contains estrogen.

BREWERS YEAST

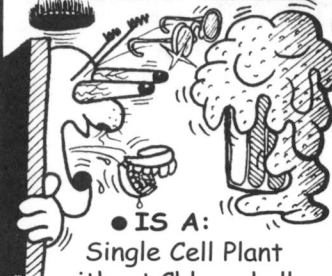

- IS A: Single Cell Plant without Chlorophyll (one cell can make 50 tons in 2 weeks).
- FOR: (as examples) Fatigue* - Stress* - Depression* - Bad temper* - Slow growth* - Anemia - Diabetes - Acne - Palpitations* - Beriberi - Gastric ailments - Memory - Muscles (weak) - Hair loss - Mouth sores - Breathless - Schizophrenia* - Gray hair - Kidney stones - Longevity* - Pigmentation - Fits - Sun sensitive - Nails (brittle) - Taste loss - Dizzy - Birth defects - Mental Agility - Hepatitis - Constipation - Liver - Hyperactivity - Bed wetting - Allergies - Metabolism - Asthma - Improve appetite - Insomnia* - Eyes (irritated) - Itching - Cholesterol - Skin Ailments - Headache.
- NOTES: Nutritional giant incl.: Vits B1, B2, B3, B5, B6, B15, paba, folic acid, biotin, choline, inositol, iron, selenium, phosphorous, zinc, potassium, copper, magnesium, calcium, chromium + 17 amino acids. It is a total protein. CAUTIONS: a) Excess yeast can cause uric acid, b) High doses require extra calcium, c) For high doses & allergies raise levels slowly.

BUCHU (Agathosma Betulina)

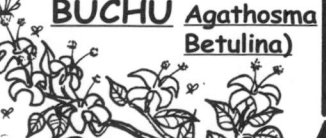

- USE: Leaves.
- FOR: Rheumatism - Venereal disease - Bladder (weak &/or sore)* - Bed wetting - Pancreas - Urine (burning or stones in, or mucus in, or retention of, or infection etc.)* - Diabetes - Kidneys - Urethritis - Prostatis.
- NOTES: Combine with yarrow (cystitis), corn silk (burning), or uva ursi (most/all).

BURDOCK
(Arctium Lappa)

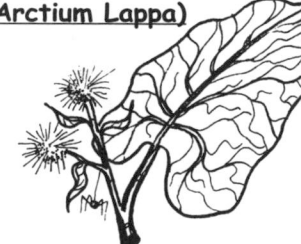

- USE: Seeds, Burrs, Roots*, Leaves.
- FOR: Dandruff - Clean blood* - Acne - Energy - Kidneys - Bladder - Cystitis - Hemorrhoids - Gout - Tonsilitis - Bursitis - Overweight - Itchy - Digestion - Lungs - Energy* - Gonorrhea - Colon cleaner - Lymph - Intestine cleaner - Arthritis* - Hair loss - Water retention (use burrs) - Nerves - Childhood diseases - Eczema (dry)* - Cankers - Burns & wounds (use leaves) - Sore throat (garg.) - Hay fever - Allergies - Psoriasis* - Ulcers/Old sores/Boils (use poultice) - Poison ivy - Constipation - Liver - Rheumatism* - Skin (dry/ scaly)* - Colds with fever (use seeds).
- NOTES: For skin problems use inside & out (can combine with red clover or yellow dock) - Aids protein metabolism. Reduces internal toxins. Reduces joint swelling.

CABBAGE
(Brassica Oleracea)

- USE: Leaves.
- FOR: Stomach ulcers - Cancer prevention - Rheumatism* - Gout - Arthritis* - Boils* - Premature ageing.
- NOTES: For joint inflammation &/or swelling (& boils) use a crushed or chopped warm to hot leaf poultice.

CHAMOMILE
(Matricaria Chamomilla/ Recutita)

- USE: Mainly the Flowers.
- FOR: Colic - Period pain - Toothache - Headache - Jaundice - Flatulence - Insomnia* - Dandruff - Bronchitis - Eyes (bath) - Styes (ext.)* - Swelling (ext.) - Parasites (kids)* - Hemorrhage - Drugs withdrawal - Catarrh (int. or ext.) - Digestion - Piles - Improve appetite* - Clean blood - Gas - Calluses (ext.) - Dizzy - Mouth sores - Worms (kids)* - Sore nipples - Gums (swollen) - Nerves & anxiety* - Pain - Spleen - Kidneys - Diaper rash (ext.) - Eczema (ext.) - Corns (ext.) - Nausea - Colds - Asthma - Earache - Bladder & colon - Food poisoning - Throat (garg.) - Children's diseases - Colitis - Bleeding - Cramps.
- NOTES: Suitable for kids. A hair rinse adds shine. Reduce swelling with poultice.

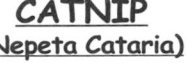

CATNIP
(Nepeta Cataria)
- **USE:** Leaves & flower tops.
- **FOR:** Flu* - Nerves* - Coughs - Insomnia* - Bronchitis* - Convulsions - Diarrhea (kids) - Flatulence - Water retention - Sweat (promotes) - Stress* - Miscarriage - Gas - Muscle tension* - Dizzy - Piles (oint.) - Hypoglycaemia - Pain - Upset stomach - Colds* - Parasites - Morning sickness* - Colic* - Smoking - Lymph - Nightmares - Kidney stones - Depression* - Croup - Toothache (chew leaves) - Digestion - Fever (enema if poss.) - Light periods - Cramps - Headache - Uterus - Kids diseases.
- **NOTES:** Suitable for kids (but cats & bees love it). Flowers are white with crimson dots or blue (leaves gray). For colds use with cayenne or yarrow.
- **CAUTION:** <u>Folklore holds that the root makes even a quiet man fierce!!</u>

CAYENNE
(Capsicum Annuum/ Fruteseems)
- **USE:** The fruits.
- **FOR:** Cuts/ Abrasions* - Muscle cramps - Chilblains - Shingles - Arthritis - Lumbago - Rheumatism - Neuralgia - Piles - (ALL ABOVE can also be treated externally with ointment) Varicose

veins* - Circulation* - Colds - Heart (stimulate & regulate)* - Lungs - Fits - Miscarriage - Paralysis - Spleen - Diabetes - Energy* - Period too heavy - Bleeding* - Kidneys - Capilliaries* - Gas - Plaque (remove)* - Glands (balance) - Hay fever - Arteries* - General tonic - Acne - Digestion - Nerves - Bronchitis (combine with ginger) - Ulcers* - Jaundice - Fatigue - Cough - Fractures - Shock - Pleurisy - Headache (int. & ext.)* - Throat/tonsils* - Douche/Vagina - Improve appetite - Sinus & asthma - Hemorrhage* - Kids diseases* - Tonic & antiseptic - Pancreas - Colitis - Eyes - Regulate blood pressure - Shock.
- **NOTES:** <u>Amplifies actions of other herbs</u> e.g. use with garlic to lower high blood pressure. Put in socks to help cold feet. Harvest fruit when ripe & dry in shade - Often sold as a powder.

CHLORELLA
- **IS:** <u>Green fresh water alga.</u>
- **FOR:** Acne - Cancer* - Liver* - Sore throat/Mouth - Constipation - Gas - High blood pressure - Clean blood* - Hemorrhoids - Body/Foot odor* - Bad breath* - Diabetes - Thyroid - Anemia - Fractures - Asthma - Period cramps - Immunity* - Warts - Arthritis - Colon - Digestion - Ulcers (ext.) - Blood cell growth - Heart - Allergies -

Tissue growth - Mothers milk (increase) - General detoxify* - Hemorrhage* - Energy* - Tonsils - Cholesterol - Cuts - Hypoglycaemia .
- **NOTES:** <u>Survived over 2 billion years.</u> Has richest known natural source of chlorophyll & is one of richest in DNA. Also has RNA, beta carotene, iron, iodine, cobalt, zinc & 19 amino acids. Use Chlorella during a fast for efficient detoxification (it <u>has 4 times more chlorophyll than spirulina</u>).

CIDER VINEGAR
(Fermented fresh apple juice)
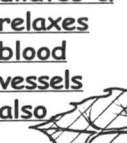
- **FOR:** Hair loss - Colon - Kidney stones - Dental decay (inhibits) - Enhances blood clotting ability - Ear infections - Period (too heavy) - Blood (oxygenates)* - Energy* - Obesity - Digestion* - Foul stools* - Stimulates metabolism* - Hay fever - Parasites (discourages) - Diarrhea - Varicose veins - Arthritis - Circulation - Kids diseases - Bad breath* - Mouth hygiene - Kidneys* - Stomach - Liver*
- **NOTES:** <u>As general tonic to stimulate metabolic rate & counter disease & fatigue</u> take 1 tablespoon breakfast & lunch. As antiseptic gargle use 1 tablespoon in glass water.

COMFREY
(Symphytum Officinale)
is omitted because of carcinogenic links.

CORN SILK
(Zea Mays)
- **USE:** Silk strands from maize cobs.
- **FOR:** Gout - Urethritis - Bleeding - Prostate - Bladder - Kidneys - Water retention - Urine ailments* - Urine odour - Bed wetting (irritant causes)* - Pain - Cystitis (combine with Yarrow)*
- **NOTES:** <u>Contains allantoin to speed healing.</u> Favored for childbirth (it encourages contractions of uterus).

CRAMP BARK
(Viburnam Opulus)
- **USE:** Dried bark.
- **FOR:** Constipation - Muscle relaxer* - Nerve relaxer* - Stimulate kidneys - Miscarriage (in prevention of) - Tics & spasms* - Colic* - Period pain - Urinary ailments.
- **NOTES:** Often is combined with wild yam particularly when used on cramps which it is effective on internally & externally (as ointment).
- **CAUTION:** <u>dilates & relaxes blood vessels also</u>

---

*Indicates that herb considered particularly effective for that ailment. See also "Rapid Reference Natural Therapy Notes" for extra details.

DAMIANA
(Turnera Aphrodisiaca)

- **USE:** Leaves.
- **FOR:** Fatigue* - Nerves* - Prostate - Senility - Aphrodisiac* - Period problems - Antidepressant* - Hot flashes* - Life extension (old age) - Increase appetite - Menopause* - Girl/Woman problems*.
- **NOTES:** Also called **Mexican Damiana.** Opinions differ on which sex this herb stimulates most but it is generally used by females to balance hormones but others say both frigidity & impotence benefit.

DANDELION
(Taraxacum Officinale)

- **USE:** Mainly dried roots (but fresh leaf used in salads).
- **FOR:** Acne - Anemia - Energy - Cancer - Spleen - Skeleton - Insomnia - Digestion - Heartburn - Kidneys* - Cramps - Jaundice* - Gall stones & bladder* - Builds blood - Tonsils/Flu - Diabetes - Age spots - Cleans blood* - Fever - Rheumatism - Gout - Skin ailments (incl spots, boils, eczema etc.)* - Constipation - Pancreas - Improve appetite - Bronchitis - Fractures (bones) - Hypoglycemia - Old age - Hemorrhage - Water retention* - Liver*

- Wounds.
- **NOTES:** **Efficient remover of acid/toxins from blood** but does also raise blood pressure. For liver/gall bladder combine with yarrow. Suitable for kids & as general tonic.

DANG GUI (Don Quai)
(Angelica Sinensis)

- **USE:** Root.
- **FOR:** Skin ailments - Insomnia - Cramps - Energy - Anemia - Bruises - Periods irregular & pain* - Lumbago - Blood clots - Menopause - Hypoglycemia - Mild laxative - Cleans blood* - Circulates blood* - Vitality - High blood pressure - Fits - Hot flashes* - Female problems - Longevity - Brain - Nerves/Anxiety.
- **NOTES:** **Also known as "Tong Kwai," "Don Quai," "Chinese Angelica" & "Womans Ginseng" (contains female hormones)** - It can be used by men, but may (long term) cause breast enlargement or facial hair loss. **Caution do not use just before or during pregnancy.** Good for elderly. Good after childbirth.

ECHINACEA
(Echinacea Angustifolia)

- **USE:** Root.
- **FOR:** Catarrh* - Acne - Carbuncles - Venereal diseases - Tonsils* - Sinus* - Snake & insect bites - Laryngitis* - Colds - Prostate - Wounds - Clean blood - Boils* - Septicemia* -

Hemorrhage - Gums - Bad breath - Infection* - Fever* - Kidneys - Smoking - Boils* - Sores* - Urine & bladder - Lymph glands (combine with Myrrh)* - Cystitis (combine with Yarrow)* - Cuts - Immunity* - Blood poisoning - Gingivitis.
- **NOTES:** **Also known as "Cone Flower"** & has purple petals. Can be used inside or out. This herb is **very versatile as it is antibacterial*, antifungal* & antiviral*** (& a fine lymph cleanser).

EUCALYPTUS
(Eucalyptus Globulus)

- **USE:** Oil & leaves.
- **FOR:** Sore throat/Cough* - Improve appetite - Fever - Nausea (dab on tongue)* - Catarrh* - Muscle spasm - Bronchitis/Lungs* - Dysentry - Ulcers/Sores - Circulation - Colds - Inhalations &/or Antiseptic bath - Wounds (dilute to clean/protect) - Paralysis - Cancer - Sleep (breathing put in/on pillow) - Uterus - Bowels - Sinus - Croup - Nerves.
- **NOTES:** **Caution: Take small doses (excess may cause headache &/or delirium &/or capillary dilation).** As insect repellent apply diluted oil to skin or simmer leaves in area to be protected.

EVENING PRIMROSE
(Oenetheris Biennis)

- **USE:** Oil from seeds.
- **FOR:** Pain - Arthritis* - Obesity* - Migraines - Glaucoma - Hangovers - Infertility - Circulation - Cholesterol* - Hyperactivity* - High blood p.* - Sedative - Nails* - Period pain - Acne (use with Zinc)* - Wounds - Eczema* - Stroke/Heart attack prevention* - Colds/Cough - Immunity* - Inflammation - Hair - Stress - Arteries* - Multiple sclerosis - Cancer* - Psoriaris - Depression (with B6 & E) - X-Ray damage - Skin.
- **NOTES:** Can be used inside or out. White/yellow flowers bloom for 1 night only. **It & blackcurrant seeds are richest natural sources of gamma linolenic acid.**

EYEBRIGHT
(Euphrasia Officinalis)

- **USE:** Herb.
- **FOR:** Sinus - Iritis* - Catarrh* - Cough - Glandular swelling - Blepharitis - Light sensitive/Weeping eyes* - Prostate - Inflamed eyes* - Allergies* - Ear/Headache (from cold) - Eye injuries* - Conjunctivitis* - Digestion - Cataracts* - Hay fever - Diabetes - Glaucoma - Colic.
- **NOTES:** Use internally or in eye bath/compress. Combines well with golden seal. Flowers white with purple.

FENNEL
(Foeniculum Vulgare)

● USE: Seeds.
● FOR: Bed wetting - Diabetes - Jaundice - Gout - Gas* - Liver - Fever - Colic* - Eyewash - Emphysema - Conjunctivitis (ext.) - Muscle ache (ext.) - Water retention - Increase mothers milk* - Energy - Increase period flow - Digestion* - Balance appetite* - Eyesight - Fits - Snake/Bug bites - Rheumatism (ext.) - Gall bladder - Gum disease/ Throat/Mouth (garg.) - Nerves - Morning sickness* - Obesity - Cramps - Coughs - Catarrh/Sinus - Bronchitis - Migraines - Swellings (ext.).
● NOTES: Can be used inside & out. Chew a few seeds after a meal for digestive & other benefits.

FENUGREEK
(Trigonella Foenum Graecum)

● USE: Seeds.
● FOR: Eyes - Catarrh* - Mucus* - Flu - Lungs - Colds - Stress - Bronchitis - Impotence - Frigidity - Heartburn - Diabetes - Vagina - Pneumonia - Fever - Pancreas* - Colon - Digestion* - Colitis -

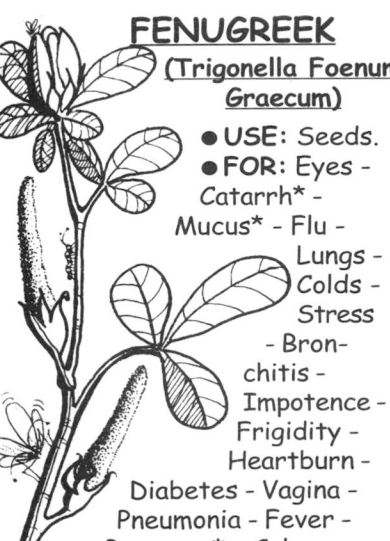

Emphysema - Period pain - Sore throat (garg.)* - Hay fever - Mothers milk (more)* - Bruises (ext.) - Headache* - Douche - Inflammed stomach/Intestines* - Cellulitis (ext.) - Boils/Abscesses/Sores/ Carbuncles (ext.)* - Water retention - Allergies - Sinus* - Migraines* - Nerves - Stomach/Kidney chills - Stomach ulcers* - Cholesterol (lower)* - Anemia - Stimulates appetite - Stomach cramps - Increase breast size - Glands - Reproduction - Skin ailments - Tumors - Metabolism - Enzyme production.
● NOTES: As poultice crush seeds & apply with fennel or aloe vera. Balances & lowers blood sugar. <u>Safe for nursing Mothers.</u> One of oldest recorded herbs.

GARLIC
(Allium Sativum)

● USE: Bulb.
● FOR: Gas* - Colds* - Liver - Croup - Warts - Fever - Sore throat - Ulcers - Thyroid - Ringworm - Increase appetite - Migraine - Cholera - Hemorrhoids - Food poisoning - Dissolves arterial plaque* - Cleans blood - Acne (int.) - Emphysema - High blood pressure* - Catarrh* - Diarrhea - Colitis - Constipation - Kids diseases* - Cramps - Depression - Heart* - Venereal disease - Rheumatism - Cough - Longevity - Vagina - Prostate - Digestion - Gall bladder - Flu -

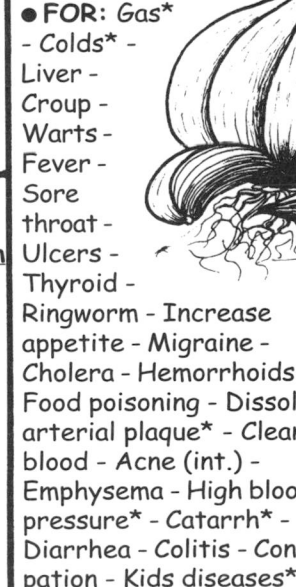

Cholestorol* - Aphrodisiac (men)* - Ring/Thread worms* - Arteries* - Sinus - Insect stings/ Bites - Dysentery - Cancer - Blood sugar control - Intestine tonic - Circulation* - Yeast infections.
● NOTES: <u>To lower blood pressure use with Cayenne.</u> To discourage external parasites wear in bag round neck. Some swallow cloves whole (peel & cut off sharp ends) for colon & worms. Encourages friendly intestinal bacteria. Eat with parsley to reduce smell. <u>Antiviral, antibacteria, antifungal.</u> Harvest when leaves start to whither. For infections use with echinacea. Doses from 1 clove to 2 lbs/day. 5,000 + year use history.

GINGER
(Zingiber Officinale)

● USE: Root.
● FOR: Energy - Improve appetite - Travel sick* - Morning sick* - Diarrhea - Lungs - Circulation* - Chilblains - Chills - Delayed periods - Toothache - Shock - Flatulence* - Sore throat (garg.) - Sinus - Sweat (increase)* - Hangover - Cough - Muscle ache/Sprain (ext.) - Paralysis - Kids diseases* - Cramps - Headache - Bronchitis - Colic* - Bad breath - Gout - Nausea* - Backache (ext.) - Hemorrhage - Digestion* - Colds & flu* - Douche - Sex (stimulate & balance) - Croup - Antacid* - Spasms of stomach &/or bowel - Pneumonia.
● NOTES: <u>A useful travellers herb (for stomach)</u> as is garlic (for

infection). <u>Detoxify your body in a ginger bath</u> (drink tea also). Excess use may cause dry eyes. Harvest root when leaves have dried. Wash well & dry in sun.

GINGKO BILOBA
(Gingko Biloba)

● USE: Leaves.
● FOR: Senility* - Varicose veins - Allergies - Cold feet/ Hands* - Mood swings - Headache - Circulation to brain* - Failing sight - Insomnia - Leg ulcers - Mental ability (particularly in old age)* - Post stroke recovery* - Tinnitus - Cancer - Alzheimers - Dizzy - Memory loss* - Metabolism*.
● NOTES: <u>Also known as "Maidenhair Tree."</u> <u>Probably world's oldest tree species</u> with exceptional resistance to fungi, parasites, insects, pollution & disease. A genuine fossil survivor, 250 million years old <u>(has significant anti-aging/longevity potential).</u>

THE LEAVES TURN AMBER IN AUTUMN

---

*Indicates that herb considered particularly effective for that ailment.
● See also "Rapid Reference Natural Therapy Notes" for futher details

GINSENG
(Panax Ginseng) (Korean/Chinese)

● USE: Root.

● FOR: Stress* - Fever - Inflammation - Increase red blood cells - Back pain - Hormones (balance)* - Acne - Impotence - Age spots - Prolapse - Headache - Gas - Insomnia - Lungs - Energy* - Sex stimulant* - General tonic* - Spleen* - Fits - Constipation - Rheumatism - Depression - Improve appetite - Morning sick - Cancer - Brain - Regulate periods - Hemorrhage - Chest ailments* - Drug withdrawal - Coughs - Digestion - Lower blood sugar - Lower blood fat - Asthma - Hiccups - Anemia - Antiaging* - Frigidity - Colds - Prostate - Pituatary - Metabolism (inc. Vit/Min use)* - Immunity.

NOTES: There are several varieties, most potent thought to be Manchurian, then Korean, Siberian, N. American. **Don't take within 3 hours of ingesting caffeine, or citrus, or vitamin C. Limit intake during pregnancy** & in any case avoid excess &/or long-term use.

GOLDENSEAL
(Hydrastis Canadensis)

● USE: Root.

● FOR: Liver - Burns - Flu* -
Hemorrhage* - Catarrh* - Sores (ext.)* - Spleen - Earache (ext. use with mullein) - Burns (ext.) - Uterus - Sore throat (garg.)* - Eczema (ext.) - Flu/Colds* - Colon/Bowels - Tonsils (garg.) - Prostate - Digestion (use with camomile)* - Itch/Rash (comb. w/ distilled witch hazel [ext.]) - Circulation* - Bad breath - Nosebleed (sniff)* - Improve appetite - Bronchitis - Constipation - Sinus* - Inflammation (ext.) - Eczema (ext.) - Gall bladder - Antiseptic* - Kids diseases - Conjunctivitis - Water retention - Morning sick - Hay fever - Venereal disease - Mouth/Gum sores (Gar.) - Ulcers - Anorexia - Cancer - Ringworm (ext.) - Helps mucus membranes* - Thyroid (low) - Lymph - Hemorrhoids - Insect repel (ext.) - Kidneys - Allergies - Nausea - Nerves - Vagina - Cuts/Wounds (ext.)* - Pancreas* - Asthma - Diabetes* - Puritis (ext.) - Psoriasis - Bladder - Obesity - Period flow (dec.) - Eye wash (use with eyebright)*.

● NOTES: Works well with other herbs. **Don't take if pregnant or have hypoglycemia. A powerful healer (natural antibiotic)** but use in moderation and not long-term.

GOTU KOLA
(Hydrocotlye Centella/Asiatica)

● USE: Herb/leaf.

● FOR: Memory* - Menopause - Skin ailments/Incl. scars (combine with Vit. E) (ext.)* - Energy* - Depression - Antiaging* - Colon - Water retention - Pituitary - Malaria - Mental agility* -
Leprosy - Nervous ailments - High blood pressure - Fever - Endocrine glands - Venereal diseases (ext.) - Age spots - Low endurance* - Rheumatism - Short attention span*.

● NOTES: Origin is India/China. Virtues similar to "**Fo Ti**" (in latin :**Polygonum Multiflorum**). Also known as "**Indian Pennywort.**" Works particulary well with ginseng.

HAWTHORN
(Crataegus Oxycantha - Monogyna - Laevigata)

● USE: Berries (& Flowers)

● FOR: Sore throat - Regulate pulse* - Swollen genitalia - Insomnia - Lumbago - Energy* - Kidneys - Angina - Cardiac tonic* - Diarrhea - Rheumatism - Arthritis - Palpitations* - Arteriosclerosis* - Hypoglycemia - Stress - Water retention - Miscarriage - Nerves - Digestion - Adrenal glands - Circulation* Regulate blood p* - Menopause.

● CAUTION : **Self-help with this herb may be tricky for heart ailments, as excess can cause dizziness.** For circulation ailments
combine with yarrow. Can be used as poultice to draw externally.

HE'S BLACK HAIR
(Polygonum Multiflorum)

● USE: Root (tuber).

● FOR: Liver* - Clean blood* - Vagina - Energy* - Jaundice - Hair loss - Hepatitis - Circulation* - Longevity - Boils - Impotence* - Gray hair* - Arteries - Kidneys* - Sex/Age.

● NOTES: Also known as "**Multiflower Knotweed**," "**Foti**," "**He Shou Wo.**"

HOPS
(Humulus Lupulus)

● USE: Female Flower.

● FOR: Headache - Nightmares - Liver - Antiseptic - Fever - Sex depressant* - Nerves* - Ulcers - Swollen joints &/or deep bruises (ext. poultice)* - Pain* - Earache - Cough - Bloating - Digestion* - Parasites - Aches - Toothache - Anemia - Stress/Anxiety* - Improve appetite - Bed wetting - Obesity - Jaundice - Period pain - Insomnia (use with valerian)*.

● NOTES: Poultice for inflammations, boils & skin irritations. **Don't use if depressed or impotent.** Hangovers respond to tea on rising. **For good sleep put in pillow.**

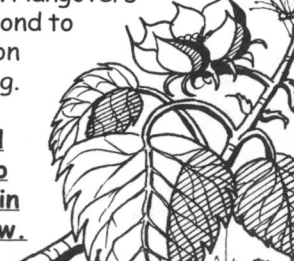

HORSETAIL
(Equisetum Arvense)

- **USE:** Herb.
- **FOR:** Eyes & swollen eye lids (ext.) - Jaundice - Fractures - Bladder - Toothache - Prostate* - Hair loss - Nosebleed* - Hemorrhage* - Rheumatism (ext) - Finger/Toe nails* - Water retention - Bleeding wounds (ext)* - Nerves* - Hair condition* - Liver - Chillblains (ext.) - Bed wetting* - Mucus - Earache - Vagina - Body odor - Lungs - Stomach ulcers* - Cystitis - Douche - Heart - Feet - Fits - Bronchitis - Tooth enamel - Obesity.
- **NOTES:** High silica content (aids hair & nails) assists calcium absorption. Be wary of adverse reactions in excess usage.

HYSSOP
(Hyssopus Officinale)

- **USE:** Herb.
- **FOR:** Gall stones/ Bladder - Anemia - Inflammation - Gas - Sore throat (use with sage[gargle]) - Burns (ext) - Circulation - Parasites - Clean blood - Liver - Lice - Colds (use with peppermint)* - Digestion - Catarrh* - Kids diseases - Diarrhea - Anxiety* - Lungs - Ears - Eyes - Coughs* - Colon

- Feverish chills* - Kidneys - Insect bites/ Stings (ext.) - Bruises (leaves ext.) - Blood pressure (reg) - Asthma - Hysteria - Cuts/Wounds (ext.) - Congestion* - Fits - Rheumatism - Ulcers.
- **NOTES:** Also known as "Holy Herb." Is safe for kids. Boil herb in cider vinegar & use as mouthwash for toothache.

KELP
(Incl. Various seaweeds eg.: Fucus Vesiculosus or Ascophyllum Nodosum)

- **USE:** Plant.
- **FOR:** Colds - Fractures - Psoriasis - Goiter* - Kidneys - Diabetes - General tonic* - Obesity - Heart - Eczema - Glands* - Builds blood vessels - Menopause - Hypoglycemia - Constipation - Dry skin - Prostate/Adrenal/ Pituitary/Thyroid* - Colitis - Cold hands/Feet - Slow Nail growth - Nerves* - Arteries - Nausea - Morning sickness - Brittle hair - Skin ailments - Anemia - Fat hips - Arthritis/Rheumatism/Joints (int. & ext.) - Fatigue - Cancer - Pregnancy - Bursititis - Hot flashes.
- **NOTES:** Caution: Many of the above ailments relate to iodine deficiency (kelp very rich in) (if you get too much it may cause headaches). Kelp has extremely wide nutritional spectrum. It

can reduce radioactive absorption by up to 80%. Also known as "Bladderwrack." Avoid taking during thyroid ailments or at bedtime.

LAVENDER
(Lavandula Augustifolia)

- **USE:** Oil & flowers.
- **FOR:** Colic - Antiseptic - Anxiety* - Repels insects - Muscle ache (ext.) - Digestion - Stress* - Migraine - Depression* - Rheumatism.
- **NOTES:** Rub or massage dilute oil for aches or insect repellent (for headache, massage temples with oil & take the tea with valerian). Put a few drops of oil on pillow for restful sleep.

LICORICE
(Glycyrrhiza Glabra)

- **USE:** Root.
- **FOR:** Leukemia - Adrenal glands - Age spots - Pneumonia - Spleen* - Detoxify - Constipation - Sex stimulant - Clean blood - Lower blood fat - Menopause - Hypogycemia* - Boils (Ext.) - Bronchitis - Pancreas - Asthma - Toothache (chew root) - Drug withdrawal* - Arthritis - Vagina - Carbuncles - Flu - Sore throat* - Stomach pain - Burns (ext.) - Pain - Laryngitis - Digestion -

Sores (ext.) - Stomach ulcers* - Emphysema - Cough* - Colic - Protect liver - Catarrh* - Anti aging - Fever - Mothers milk (incr.) - Colds - Energy* - Lungs - Kidneys - Tonic.
- **NOTES:** Use with marshmallow or comfrey for gastric ailments. Asian kids chew the root to promote muscle growth. Opinions differ to which hormones (Male or Female) predominate.
- **CAUTION:** Excess or long-term use may cause heart pains &/or higher blood pressure &/or fluid retention.

LOVAGE
(Levisticum Officinale)

- **USE:** Aerial parts.
- **FOR:** Bad breath (chew seeds)* - Gas - Kidneys* - Body odor (Drink tea &/ or apply to body)* - Tonsils (garg.) - Eye wash - Oily skin cleaner - Digestion - Jaundice - Detoxify* - Spots - Freckles - Colic.
- **NOTES:** Chew as tobacco subsitute. Ginseng family. Tastes like celery. Use as antiseptic wash. Wear in bag round neck as deodorant.

*Indicates that herb considered particularly effective for that ailment.
- See also "Rapid Reference Natural Therapy Notes" for further details.

MARIGOLD
(Calendula Officinalis)

- **USE:** Yellow Flower Heads.
- **FOR:** Acne - Eyewash - Dry skin (oint.)* - Eczema - Chilblains* - Bleeding - Sebaceous cysts* - Skin lesions - Gall bladder - Period pain - Indigestion - Gastric ulcers* - Wounds* - Conjunctivitis - Thrush - Cuts* - Delayed periods - Bruises* - Burns/Scalds* - Insect bites/Stings - Corns - Sprains/Strains.
- **NOTES:** <u>Quick healing antibacteria, antifungal, anti-inflammatory</u>, use inside or out (poultice/compress). <u>Cleans lymphatic system</u>. For gastric ailments combine with marshmallow.

MARSHMALLOW
(Althea Officinalis)

- **USE:** Root (& leaves).
- **FOR:** Sore throat/ Mouth/Gums (garg.)* - Allergies/Hay fever - Diarrhea - Hemorrhage - Boils (ext.) - Pneumonia - Varicose veins (ext.) - Kidneys/Stones* - Enteritis - Vagina - Hypoglycemia - Bed wetting - Mothers milk (incr.)* - Period flow (dec.) - Bladder* - Emphysema - Cystitis - Pain - Eye wash - Flu - Lungs -

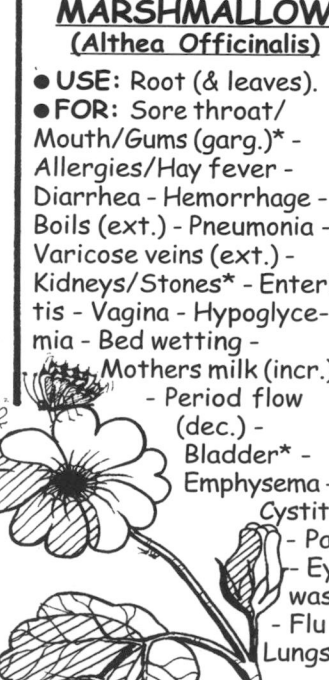

Burns - Inflammation* - Mucus membranes* - Sore colon - Urinary tract (incl. bleeding)* - Gastritis - Coughs - Ulcers (int. & ext.) - Diabetes - Abscesses.
- **NOTES:** <u>Rub leaves on insect stings/bites.</u> For bronchitis, use with licorice. Soothes & heals as a poultice.

MEADOWSWEET
(Filipendula Ulmaria)

- **USE:** Herb.
- **FOR:** Arthritis - Nausea - Stress - Kidneys - Headaches* - Toxicity - Joint pain - Hyperacidity* - Gastric/Peptic ulcers - Fever* - Muscle pain - Morning sickness - Bladder - Indigestion - Gastritis - Inflammation - Heartburn - Rheumatism - Digestion*.
- **NOTES:** Also known as <u>"Queen of the Meadow." Acts in a similar way to aspirin</u>. Often combined with marshmallow. <u>Suitable for kids.</u>
- **A VARIATION....** **(Eupatorium Purpureum)** is also recommended ....**FOR:** Bladder & Kidney stones* - (& associated low backache)* - Diabetes - Nerves - Uterus/Vagina (sore) - Gout - Water retention*.

MISTLETOE
(Viscum Album)

- **USE:** Leafy Twigs (not berries).

FOR: Asthma - High blood pressure* - Fits - Heart - Nerves* - Gall bladder - Palpitations - Capillaries* - Circulation* - Energy (female) - Hemorrhage* - Hypoglycemia - Hysteria - Epilepsy - Cancer/Tumors - Immunity* - Increase urine - Menstruation* - Arteries* - Kidneys.
- **NOTES:** <u>Considered by some to be a narcotic</u> but used to stop bleeding after childbirth (or miscarriage) &/or to expel placenta.
- **CAUTION:** <u>Don't eat berries—may cause abortion in high doses.</u>

MYRRH
(Commiphora Myrrha)

- **USE:** Gum resin.
- **FOR:** Bad breath* - Thrush - Douche - Colds - Lungs - Colon - Sinus - Mouthwash - Cuts - Acne - Gums - Shock - Ulcers* - Asthma - Laryngitis - Leucorrhea - Hypoglycemia - Bronchitis - Tonsils - Catarrh - Sores/ Wounds (ext.)* - Indigestion - Low thyroid - Nerves/Stress - Improve appetite - Antisep-

tic* - Clean blood - Boils (ext.)* - Colitis - Douche - Period pain - Chilblains.
- **NOTES:** Combine with enchinacea for infections. Take internally for bad breath. Stimulates production of white blood cells.

NETTLE
(Urtica Dioica)

- **USE:** Herb.
- **FOR:** Flu - Diarrhea - Hair loss* - Obesity - Anemia - Kidneys* - Heavy periods - Bladder/Urine* - Insect bite/Stings - Backache - Asthma - Dandruff (ext.) - Cuts/ Wounds - Eczema (use with burdock) - Rheumatism* - Colds - Pain (ext.) - Fever - Bleeding* - Lymph Glands - Rashes - Gout - Hemorrhage/hoids - Nosebleed - Ulcers.
- **NOTES:** <u>Strengthens & supports whole body</u> particularly if used with cayenne (Hair/Eyes protein metabolism). Expels stones from organs.

NUTMEG/MACE
(Myristica Fragrans)

- **USE:** Seed/Oil.
- **FOR:** Anxiety* - Nausea - Vomiting - Insomnia* - Colic - Gas - Flatulence* - Diarrhea - Muscle/Birth pain (oil ext.).
- **NOTES:** <u>Mildly narcotic. Excess causes dreams, dizzy, headache.</u>

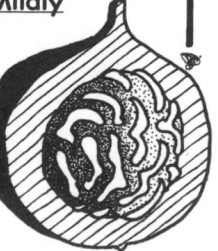

PAPAYA
(Carica Papaya)

- **USE:** Fruit.
- **FOR:** Freckles (ext)* - Worms - Wounds (leaves ext.) - Digestion - Liver - Gas - Allergies - Dyspepsia - Fainting - Mucus membranes - Angina pectoris (use with Vit. E 1,000 iu & Lecithin 15 g/day) Colitis - Burns/

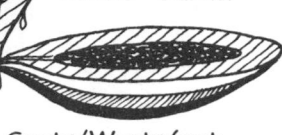

Spots/Warts (ext. poultice).
- **NOTES:** <u>Very high enzyme (papain) aids protein digestion</u> & its metabolic use in the body.

PARSLEY
(Petroselinum Crispum/ Sativum)

- **USE:** Leaves, oil, root.
- **FOR:** Bed wetting - Lumbago - Colic - Urine ailments* - Gall/Kidney stones* - Blood pressure (low) - Improve appetite - Cancer prevention - Allergies - Asthma - Venereal disease - Delayed periods - Glands (prostate/thyroid/pituitary) - Period pain - Bladder* - Bruises - Cough - Gout - Gas - Eyewash - Bile flow - Fever - Arthritis - Spleen* - Liver* - Rheumatism - Flatulence - Water retention* - Kidneys - Bad breath

(chew raw)* - Insect bites/Stings - Stomach* - Jaundice - Hay fever - Fractures - Earache (oil/ juice in) - Gall bladder - Freckles (apply crushed seeds).
- **NOTES:** <u>For puffy eyes or enlarged pores apply cool tea</u>. Rich in Vits. A, B, C, iron & potassium. Dries up mothers milk after birth. <u>Cancels garlic breath smell.</u>
- **CAUTION:** <u>Don't use much if pregnant (can cause abortion) or with kidney disease.</u>

PEPPERMINT
(Mentha X Piperita)

- **USE:** Aerial parts (& oil)
- **FOR:** Collc* - Diarrhea - Insomnia - Bronchitis - Bile flow - Improve appetite* - Nose/Throat - Colds/Flu - Vomiting - Antiseptic - Nightmares - Congestion - Stress/Worry* - Palpitations - Circulation/Heart - Rheumatism (ext. oil) - Anaesthetic (mild) - Morning sickness* - Nausea - Smoking - Migraine/ Headache* - Fever - Dizzy - Gas/Flatulence* - Period pain - Heartburn* - Muscle/Gut cramps - Digestion* - Skin ailments (ext.) - Pain - Liver - Tonic - Cough - Kids' diseases - Gall bladder - Itchy (ext.).
- **NOTES:** <u>Very good for nervous stomach (i.e. swallow air)</u>. Combine with elder to sweat.

PLANTAIN
(Plantago Major)

- **USE:** Leaves (& root, seeds)
- **FOR:** Boils/Carbuncles/Sores/ Ulcers/Insect bites/Stings/ Cuts/Wounds etc. (crushed leaf poultice)* - Diarrhea - Jaundice - Fractures - Thrush - Lungs - Eyewash - Bed wetting (weak tea) - Lumbago - Weak stomach* - Hemorrhage* - Kidneys - Dropsy - Antibacterial - Toothache (chew root) - Cystitis - Rheumatism - Constipation (seeds) - Burns (ext.)* - Snake bite - Coughs - Period flow (dec.) - Mucus membranes - Wasting diseases - Bleeding* - Bronchitis* - Blood poisoning - Stones in organs - Itchy - Hemorrhoids - Sore throat (garg) - Vagina - Impotence/ Frigidity - Semen* - Fertility - Leucorrhea - Plant stings - Backache - Asthma - Eczema - Bladder - Rashes*.
- **NOTES:** <u>Also known as the soldiers' herb (so useful in battle).</u>

PUMPKIN
(Cucurbita Pepo)

- **USE:** Seeds (also oil, juice, flesh)
- **FOR:** Enteritis - Gastritis - Worms* - Burns (ext. - oil) - Prostate* - Urine ailments - Tumors - Immunity* - Gonorrhea -

Virility (male)* - Internal cleanse.
- **NOTES:** <u>To expel worms</u> crush seeds & eat with milk/ honey before breakfast for 3 days & then purge with castor oil. <u>For red skin blotches</u> apply juice/flesh. <u>For freckles</u> mix crushed seed & olive oil. <u>Safe for kids. Rich in zinc.</u>

RED CLOVER
(Trifolium Pratense)

- **USE:** Flowers.
- **FOR:** Rheumatism - Clean blood* - Skin cancer* - Ulcers - Improve appetite - Bronchitis - Gout - Insomnia - Anemia - Arthritis - Breast cancer* - Athletes foot - Detoxifying - Childrens' diseases (whooping cough, mumps, measles) - Psoriasis (ext.)* - Eczema (ext.)* - Tumors* -Fertility - Dry cough - Pancreas - Nerves -Boils - Acne - Burns - Flu.
- **NOTES:** Can be taken inside and applied externally at same time. Combine with chaparral for anti-cancer use.
- **CAUTION:** <u>Do not use this herb internally in high doses or long-term.</u>

---

*Indicates that herb considered particularly effective for that ailment.
- See also "Rapid Reference Natural Therapy Notes" for extra details.

RASPBERRY
(Rubus Idaeus)

- **USE:** Leaves.
- **FOR:** Flu - Period pain* - Colds - Ulcers - Fever - Canker - Nausea* - Dysentry - Diabetes - Fractures - Eyewash - Constipation - Sore throat - Vomiting* - Childbirth* - Painful labor* - Irregular periods - Mucus membranes - Leucorrhea (Douche) - Morning sickness* - Miscarriage (prevent) - Rheumatism - Birth defects (prevent)* - Diarrhea (kids)* - Bronchitis - Thrush - Vaginal discharge* - Kidneys - Bladder - Afterpain* - Nerves - Burns/Wounds/ Cuts/Bleeding (wash) - Pregnancy* - Gums - Uterus (strengthen)* - Sore nipples (bathe) - Mothers milk (increase) - Period flow (decrease) - Kids diseases - Tongue - Digestion problems.
- **NOTES:** <u>Can use this herb thru pregnancy</u>. Not a painkiller but <u>strengthens entire female reproductive system.</u> To prevent hemorrhage use with bayberry. <u>O.K. for kids</u>. Nutritionally rich.

ROSEMARY
(Rosmarinus Officinalis)

- **USE:** Leaves (also flowers, twigs & oil).
- **FOR:** Sore throat - Bad breath - Gray hair (ext./to darken) - Mouthwash - Allergy* - Memory* - Colds - Depression - General tonic - Hair loss (ext. oil) - Sores - Female reproduction - Neuralgia - Nerves - Circulation - Heart - Headache* - Anemia - Deodorant (ext.) - Antiaging - Antiseptic - Hair conditioner* - Flatulence/Gas - Digestion - Eczema (ext.) - Rheumatism - Muscle ache (ext./oil) - Arthritis (ext./oil) - Disinfectant - Fatigue - Dandruff - Eyesight - Bruises - Energy (use in bath) - Wounds (ext.) - Bile (increase) - Cough.
- **NOTES:** <u>Also called "Dew of the sea."</u> Mix 2 parts golden seal & 3 parts each rosemary, rue & eyebright for a **POTENT EYE TONIC** (take several times daily for 3 months). Rosemary <u>reputed to keep bad dreams away if under pillow.</u>
- **CAUTION:** <u>Don't take essential oil internally or overdose on herb.</u>

RUE
(Ruta Graveolens)

- **USE:** Leaves.
- **FOR:** Malaria - Digestion - Delayed periods* - Headache (chew leaf) - High blood pressure - Nightmares* - Menopause* - Palpitations - Circulation* - Eye (nerves)* - Eye lens/ Pupil* - Blood vessels - Cough - Rheumatism (ext.) - Sciatica (ext.) - Bruises - Capillaries (broken)* - Flatulence - Poison antidote - Eye wash (weak tea) - Dizziness.
- **NOTES:** Powerful herb. Rich in rutin. <u>Holy herb reputed to ward off evil.</u> Crush leaves & spread round any other insect affected plant & watch them evacute.
- **CAUTION:** <u>Avoid if pregnant. May cause rashes if handled by sensitive skin.</u>

SAFFLOWER
(Carthamus Tinctorius)

- **USE:** Flowers (Also seeds/oil)
- **FOR:** Gas* - Heartburn - Hysteria - Gout* - Colds* - Cramps - Dropsy - Sweat (promote) - Frigidity - Period flow (inc.) - Gall bladder - Constipation - Improve appetite - Hemorrhoids - Water retention* - Kids' diseases (e.g. measles) - Skin ailments - Post exercise fatigue* - Periods (reg.) - Heart - Hypogycemia - Fever - Gray hair (oil) - Liver* - Dandruff (oil)* - Digestion* - Joints (arthritis)*.
- **NOTES:** <u>Combats uric/lactic acid buildup</u> (gout). Oil is very high in vit. F which <u>repairs X-ray damage.</u> Also known as <u>"Wild Saffron."</u> Leaves are spiny.

SAGE
(Salvia Officinalis)

- **USE:** Leaves.
- **FOR:** Wounds (ext.) - Schitzophrenia - Flu - Memory* - Brain* - Sore throat/Gums/Tonsils etc. (garg.)* - Antiseptic - Cough - Epilepsy - Dizzy - Gas/Flatulence - Diarrhea - Rheumatism - Sex depressant - Lungs - Digestive ailments* - Depression* - Morning sickness - Headache (sinus)* - Insect bites - Mucus membranes - Sunburn (bathe) - Clean blood - Longevity* - Bleeding - Liver - Kidney - Nausea - Gall bladder - Cold with fever* - Stitch/Cramp - Dandruff (rinse) - Hair loss* - Night sweats (take cold)* - Quinsy - Ulcers - Worms (kids)* - Tonsils - Stomach ailments - Senses* - Nerves - Palsy - Fertility (female) - Saliva (dry up).
- **NOTES:** To dry up mothers milk (drink cold). To restore gray hair (rinse). Various varieties. <u>Believed by ancients to ward off evil</u>. High in estrogen (hormone).
- **CAUTION:** <u>Do not boil this herb. Avoid while pregnant.</u>

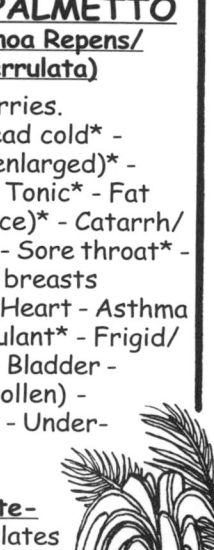

SAW PALMETTO
(Serenoa Repens/ Serrulata)

- **USE:** Berries.
- **FOR:** Head cold* - Prostate (enlarged)* - Diabetes - Tonic* - Fat cells (reduce)* - Catarrh/ Bronchitis - Sore throat* - Flu - Small breasts (enlarge) - Heart - Asthma - Sex stimulant* - Frigid/ Impotent - Bladder - Glands (swollen) - Alcoholism - Underweight.
- **NOTES:** <u>Contains steroids</u>. Regulates hormones. Sedative. <u>Use with kola & damiana for reproduction enhancement.</u> Also called <u>"Dwarf Palmetto/ Palm."</u>

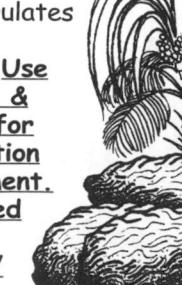

SARSAPARILLA
(Similax Officinalis)

- **USE:** Root.
- **FOR:** Acne* - Psoriasis* - Ringworm - Glands - Stress - Mucus - Flu - Antiseptic - Digestion - Eyes - Liver - Longevity - Frigidity - Impotence - Fertility - Anti-aging - Dysentery - Heartburn - Rheumatism* - Menopause - Blood (clean)* - Water retention - Gas - Flatulence - Age spots - Tonic - Venereal disease - Joints (swollen) - Circulation - Gout - Testosterone (activate) - Child birth (painful) - Hot flashes* - Colds - Hormones (balance)* - Eyewash - Fever - Boils - Inflammation - Cough.
- **NOTES:** Use with ginseng for male acne. Use with burdock or yellow dock for scaling skin. **Contains both male & female hormones.**

SKULL CAP
(Scutellaria Lateriflora/Galericulata)

- **USE:** Herb.
- **FOR:** Bed wetting - Pain - Smoking - Rheumatism - Hyperactive* - Miscarriage - Alcoholism - Headache - Hydrophobia - Hysteria* - Insomnia* - High blood pres.* - St. Vitus dance - Hypoglycemia - Cholesterol* - Hemorrhage - Depression* - Blood tonic - Hiccups - Stress - Bladder - Fits* - Anxiety* -

Diarrhea - Fever* - Kids' diseases - Sex depressant* - Cough - Arthritis - Stings/Bites - Insanity - Rabies - Paralysis - Epilepsy - Kidneys - Digestive ailments - Jaundice - Periods delayed/Tension.
- **NOTES:** Calms yet revitalizes central nervous system (use with valerian). **– Also called "Mad Dog Weed" & "Blue Pimpernel".**
- **CAUTION:** **Considered dangerous in excess. Lowers sex appetite.**

SLIPPERY ELM
(Ulmus Fulva)

- **USE:** Inner Bark.
- **FOR:** Hemorrhoids* - Diarrhea* - Cold sores - Bladder - Stomach - Pleurisy - Lumbago - Growths* - Eczema - Tonsils - Lungs* - Douche - Ovaries - Cramps - Bowels - Kidneys - Gastritis - Smoking - Poultice* - Splinters* - Fractures* - Constipation - Inflammation - Sore throat (garg.)* - Hemorrhage - Sex stimulant - Tumors* - Colds - Boils/Ulcers (ext.)* - Sores/Wounds (ext.)* - Burns/Scalds (ext.)* - Water retention - Flu - Heartburn - Coughs - Mucus membranes* - Cancer - Digestion - Catarrh* - Colitis* - Tape worms - Eyes - Breasts (caked) - Asthma.
- **NOTES:** For poultice (can mix with golden seal) make paste with hot water. Use inside or out. Hairy long tooth leaves (also called "American Elm"). Can use with marshmallow for digestive disorders.

SOYA LECITHIN
(Soja Hispida [Bean])

- **IS:** a fat solvent found in all human cells.
- **FOR:** Acne - Hair loss - Liver - Brain* - Nerves* - Obesity* - Psoriasis - Alzheimer's - Clean blood* - Cholesterol* - Hypertension - Arteries* - Antiaging - Kidneys - Constipation - Parkinson's disease - Memory* - Eczema - Gall bladder/Stones* - Concentration - Bile (to make) - Dermatitis - Longevity* - Wrinkles.
- **NOTES:** **Transports fat. Very valuable nutritionally** (partic. choline & inositol). 30% of dry weight of brain is Lecithin.

SPIRULINA

- **IS:** Spiral blue/green single cell warm freshwater algae. FOR: Anemia - Liver - Wounds (heal)* - Body odor* - Growth* - Stomach ulcers* - Antiaging* - Longevity - Energy* - Hepatitis - Circulation - Blood builder* - Breathing - Cholesterol - Ulcers (ext.) - Metabolism* - Intestines - Diabetes - Bad breath - Cell growth* - Detoxify*.
- **NOTES:** **Very high in nutrients & protein (70%)** with all essential 8 amino acids + all cell salts

& enzymes + many vits & mins. Antibacterial. High in chlorophyll & low in sodium. Take small doses before meals to lower appetite (is 5 times easier to digest than meat/soy).
- **CAUTION:** **Excess use may cause gout &/ or urine stones.**

ST. JOHN'S WORT
(Hypericum Perforatum)

- **USE:** Herb (internal) & oil (ext.).
- **FOR:** Anxiety - Diarrhea - Uterus - Tumors - Jaundice - Burns (oil) - Venereal disease* - Varicose veins (oil)* - Gout - Wounds (oil) - Bed wetting - Heart - Nervous - Sleepwalking - Backache (oil)* - Water retention - Detoxify blood* - Breasts (caked - oil) - Depression - Bad temper - Anemia - Sunburn (oil)* - Pain - Skin rashes/Boils/ Styes/Ulcers (int.) - Menopause - Urine (pus in) - Immunity - Sciatica (oil)* - Lungs - Hemorrhage - Worms - Rheumatism (oil)* - Glands (swollen - oil) - Whitlow (oil) - Cough - Mucus - Catarrh - Periods (irreg.)
- **NOTES:** Antiseptic/ anti-inflammatory (insect stings, snake bites, bruises). Use oil outside & herb tea inside. **Believed to protect from devil.**
- **CAUTION:** **Oil may remove hair. Long term herb intake may cause photosensitivity of skin.**

---

*Indicates that herb considered particularly effective for that ailment.
- See also "Rapid Reference Natural Therapy Notes" for extra notes.

113

...s)
...(int.) & oil (ext.)
● **FOR:** Lungs* - Sweat (induce) - Nightmares - Metabolism - Leucorrhea - Mouthwash - Bad breath - Wounds (oil) - Bed wetting - Gout (oil)* - Warts (oint) - Strains (oil) - Nerves - Colic - Antiseptic (oil)* - Energy (in bath) - Childhood diseases - Appetite (improve) - Bronchitis - Fever - Hair loss (rinse) - Flu - Sore throat (garg.) - Hookworms - Asthma - Kidney stones - Head lice (tincture) - Cramps - Swelling (oint.) - Eyes - Catarrh - Periods (reg./pain) - Bowels - Cough* - Muscle tics - Digestion - Eczema - Rheumatism (oil) - Gas - Headache - Athletes foot (tincture) - Liver - Diarrhea (kids).
● **NOTES:** For migraine &/or sinus take herb with fenugreek. Bees & butterflies love it.
● **CAUTION:** <u>Avoid high doses</u> (may be toxic or overstimulate thyroid).

VALERIAN
(Valeriana Officinalis)

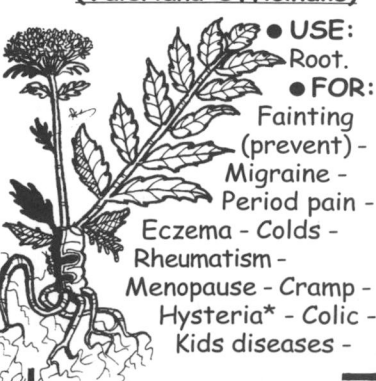

● **USE:** Root.
● **FOR:** Fainting (prevent) - Migraine - Period pain - Eczema - Colds - Rheumatism - Menopause - Cramp - Hysteria* - Colic - Kids diseases -

---

Gas - High blood p.* - St. Vitus' dance - Ulcers (stomach) - Smoking/Alcohol/(Reduce need) - Memory loss* - Eyes (stimulate) - Sores/Spots/Wounds (ext.) - Paralysis - Typhoid - Palpitations - Shock - Gallstones - Muscle spasm - Neuralgia - Swollen joints (ext.) - Digestion/Heartburn - Insomnia* - Stress* - Tumors - Anxiety* - Hypoglycemia - Fever - Fits (kids) - Afterpain - Lumbago (ext.) - Pain.
● **NOTES:** <u>Tranquilizer similar to valium but non addictive. Lore holds that a lady who wears it will never be short of suitors.</u>
● **CAUTION:** <u>Prepare & take it cold to keep effectiveness. Avoid long-term/high doses (may cause depression). It also slows heart.</u>

WHEATGERM/OIL
● **IS:** Part of seed that grows.
● **FOR:** Antiaging* - Pins & needles - Stress* - Fatigue* - Strength* - Cholesterol - Fertility* - Miscarriage* - Endurance* - Arthritis (pain) - Joints* - Heart attack (prevent) - Toxemia - Dizzy - Muscle spasms - Healing* - Nails (brittle) - Itching (old age) - Dizzy - Slow growth (kids) - Improve appetite - Circulation - Kidneys - Bad temper - Insomnia -

---

Headache - Tremor - Rickets - Skin.
● **NOTES:** <u>The best natural source of Vit. E</u> (also high in protein, B Comp. & minerals).
● **CAUTION:** <u>Very high in estrogen (female hormone) men don't take more than 2 teaspoons oil/day (or may shrink balls).</u>

YARROW
(Anchillea Millefolium)
● **USE:** Flowers (also oil & leaf).
● **FOR:** Bruises - Ulcers - Fever* - Bowels - Kidneys - Allergies - Pleurisy - Insomnia - Catarrh* - Blood (clean) - Hay fever - Bladder* - Antiseptic - Colic - Flu* - Arthritis - Cystitis - Sore throat* - Cuts/Wounds/Sores (ext.) - Hair loss (ext.) - Kids diseases - Jaundice - Lungs (& blood in)* - Improve appetite - Digestion - Liver - Dandruff - Spleen - Earache (ext.) - Burns (rinse) - Headache - Periods (dec./reg.) - Skin ailments (ext.)* - Fractures - Sweat (inc.)* - High blood p.* - Varicose veins* - Incontinence (urine) - Hemorrhoids* - Toothache (chew leaves) - Diarrhea - Urine (inc.) - Worms (leaves with garlic) - Nerves - Heart -

---

Menopause - Diabetes - Pores (open) - Gas.
● **NOTES:** For fever use with ginger/cayenne.
● **CAUTION:** <u>Fresh herb contact may cause rash. Avoid if pregnant</u> (uterus stim.). <u>Long-term use may cause photosensitivity. Contains steroids.</u>

YELLOW DOCK
(Rumex Crispus)
● **USE:** Root.
● **FOR:** Liver* - Itchy (int. & bath)* - Rheumatism - Clean blood* - Acne/Psoriasis/Eczema/Wounds/Hemorrhoids/Ringworm etc (all ext.)* - Arthritis - Colon mucus* - Styes - Energy* - Swelling/Tumor (ext.). - Tonic* - Constipation* - Ears - Flu - Fever - Digestion - Gout - Cancer* - Spleen - Glands (swollen)* - Anemia* - Gall bladder - Kids' diseases - V.D. - Pancreas - Urine.
● **NOTES:** Use inside or out. Rich in iron. Use with burdock or dandelion.

YUCCA
(Yucca Baccata)
● **USE:** Root.
● **FOR:** Joints* - Scalp/Hair* - Clean blood - Arthritis/Rheumatism* - Bursitis - Wounds - Gout - Swelling*.
● **NOTES:** <u>Contains steroids.</u> Keep in bathroom (plant eats urine smell).

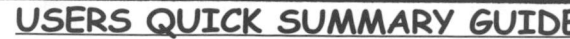

USERS QUICK SUMMARY GUIDE

1. <u>**Identify the herb(s)**</u> applicable to your situation (consult other works as even "Experts" opinions differ).
2. <u>**Check there are no known conflicting effects**</u> from it <u>**(E.G. RELATING TO PREGNANCY).**</u>
3. <u>**Pay particular attention to your body's response(s)**</u> during the first days & weeks of use.
4. <u>**As a rough guide**</u> only use a particular herb for 1 - 4 months and then rest for one month (to maintain effectiveness).

GOOD HEALTH &/OR HAPPINESS

A Traveler's Guide to Beating Sex Problems
Who Amongst Us Is Not Capable Of Improvement?

It is natural to be sexy - & unnatural to be unsexy - So don't be ashamed of it.

NOTICE FOR NOSY CHILDREN

....YOU <u>are not supposed to be reading this, so beat it!</u> - What, are you still here? - O.K, if I tell you **WHERE BABIES COME FROM** will you go .... because I'm busy? - Good, it's a deal then .... <u>Well first of all</u> a man & woman have to fall in love & usually get married, then they can sleep in one bed together & cuddle - <u>So, every month the wife</u> makes an **EGG** inside her tummy, BUT the egg won't become a baby unless it is fertilized (which means it has to meet up with a **SPERM** - & what is a sperm? - Well it's like another very tiny egg with a tail which is made inside the husband's tummy. <u>Now the problem</u> is how to get the sperm from inside the husband, to the egg inside the wife - <u>Well because they like cuddling,</u> the husband puts his penis (my son calls it his "**WILLY**") inside his wife's vagina (which my daughter calls her "**FUNNY**") & the sperm comes rushing out of the husband's willy (which gets hard, otherwise it won't go in) & tries to wiggle quickly to the egg, where it joins together to make a baby - But the **BABY** <u>takes 9 months to grow inside the wife's tummy</u> & then pops out of her funny very hungry & wants some milk immediately or it will cry very loudly (like you did) - <u>But don't forget</u> that you must be grown up & in love & really married before you make a baby or some very bad things can happen - Got it? - **OH! ONE LAST THING** ..... if anyone tries to touch your "Willy" or "Funny" tell your mom or dad immediately - Got it? - Right that's it - <u>Stop reading my book</u> - OUT! OUT! *GO & PLAY!!!*

ADULT SECTION

● **WET DREAMS** most common in adolescence being an involuntary ejaculation during a sexual dream - often due to a buildup of semen producing tension (which is then markedly relieved - <u>It is quite common & natural</u>, a kind of safety valve).

● **TO INCREASE SPERM QUANTITY** <u>abstain from ejaculating for several (3 or 4) days</u> BUT either stimulate erections &/or cultivate thoughts of sexual subjects periodically through this abstinence period.

● **AFTEREFFECTS** (on the man) of ejaculation are despite folklore limited to temporarily <u>low sperm count & a relaxed outlook</u> - There is no medical evidence of any ill effects from reasonable activity.

● **A SPERM** looks like a microscopic tadpole - Each carrying the complete gene blueprint of the father (& of his parents etc.) - The tail wiggles & propels the sperm in search of the egg - <u>Sperms are very susceptible to high temperatures</u> around the scrotum & lose mobility if for example a hot bath is taken.

● **SEMEN AS A COSMETIC** is prized by knowledgeable women as it contains prostaglandins with <u>reputed dramatic effects of rejuvenation on skin texture</u> (use fresh &/or from fridge/freezer).

● **SEMEN AS AN APHRODISIAC** is <u>provenly effective on females</u> when worn by a man dabbed on neck or behind ears & allowed to dry (on man) & then for example dancing cheek to cheek.

● **SPERM NUMBERS** vary with age & virility but can be as high as 300 million in one ejaculation with an average volume of 3 ml of semen of which about 10% is actually sperm.

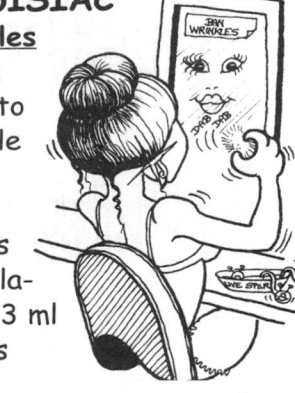

CHOOSING THE SEX OF YOUR BABY

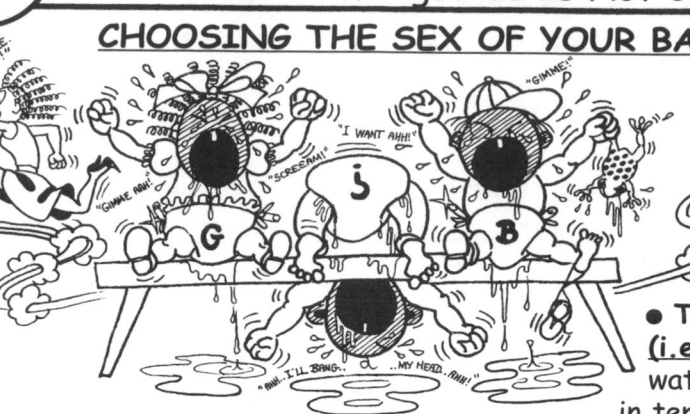

BEFORE CONCEPTION

● **TO HAVE A GIRL:** <u>Have sex 2-3 days before egg comes (or day after)</u> - Have sex every day except egg day. **- DON'T DRINK COFFEE.** - Wife orgasm after husband. - Have sex facing & don't come too deep inside wife.

● **TO HAVE A BOY:** <u>Have sex when egg comes (i.e.: about 14 days after period starts)</u> (clear watery sticky mucus discharge & a 1 degree rise in temperature). - **NO SEX 4-5 DAYS BEFORE.** - Strong coffee 15 mins before. - Orgasm after wife. - Sex from behind & deep penetration. - Husband wear loose underwear.

● **SPERM PROFILES:** <u>Female sperm</u> are larger but slower swimmers, but have better endurance & resistance to heat, stress & toxins - they also tolerate acidity better. - <u>Male sperm</u> are smaller, faster & more numerous, but more susceptible to bad conditions. - **THE MATURE EGG ONLY LIVES FOR ABOUT 24 HOURS SO TIMING IS CRITICAL.**

PERFORMANCE HINTS

● **IMPOTENCE (MENTAL** origin about 60% of cases): <u>Caused by worry, inhibitions, preoccupation (with work &/or money etc.)</u> - Often curable by use of hypnosis, self-hypnosis, more time/leisure pursuits (go fishing & stop thinking about the office) also try yoga & meditation <u>(ladies be VERY careful not to damage your lover's self confidence).</u>

● **IMPOTENCE (PHYSICAL** origin about 40% of cases): Often <u>a result of medication (e.g.: blood pressure, drugs) &/or too much smoking/alcohol etc. - Asian writings also blame excess sugars</u> (confectionery, fruit, cakes etc.) - & both blame poor general fitness (work out, go jogging etc.).

● **DIET** (general): **AVOID** <u>processed, chemically preserved, canned, saturated fat & salted foods.</u> Cut down on hydrogenated vegetable oils, red meats & yin vegetables (potato, eggplant, tomato). - (& for sex): **AVOID** sugar, sweets, radish & too much fruit (most except apples, cherries & strawberries are very yin). - (General): **DO EAT** <u>natural unprocessed whole foods without additives/ chemicals</u> (grains, fresh vegetables [& some fresh fruits], low-fat proteins [white fish, turkey etc.]). - (& for sex): **DO EAT** asparagus, burdock, black beans, oysters & garlic.

● **APHRODISIACS (SUPPLEMENTS):** Ginseng (not continually), royal jelly, sarsaparilla tea (contains testosterone & progesterone). -

● **(VITAMINS & MINERALS):** <u>Daily Mega multivitamin/Mineral (timed-release),</u> + extra: B Complex, Vit C (2,000 mg/day time release), **zinc (men)*** (20 - 40 mg/day), E (400 - 800 iu/day).

● **NOTE:** Do not start/stop supplements/ vitamins erratically & suddenly as this is something of a **SHOCK TO THE BODY.** - Do it over a week or so.

● <u>**LONG TERM** sexual relationships rely heavily on the woman to keep her man interested.</u> - Use imagination & variety to stay sexy (look in a mens magazine <u>for ideas on what his tiny mind lusts after).</u> Keep your dress sense & stay in shape. - Old age doesn't preclude your sex appeal.

● **IF HE WANTS YOU TO WEAR THIS** - <u>do it, you will both be happier</u>.

MANY NUTRIENTS ARE LOST IN SPERM BUT.......PARTICULARLY SELENIUM & ZINC

BREWERS YEAST

Understand, Analyze & Redirect Your Body's Excess Reactions

AN ALLERGY IS an abnormal reaction by the body's immune system. Enhance Immunity via a) Mother to baby. b) Lifestyle. c) Natural exposure. d) Vaccination.

UNDERSTANDING IT

BALANCE OF IMMUNITY

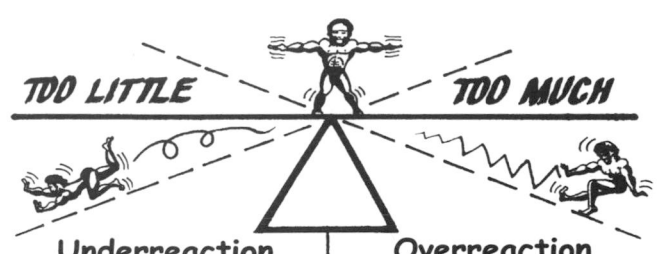

TOO LITTLE   *TOO MUCH*

Underreaction   Overreaction

- **Immune deficient,** prone to: Aids, cancer, pneumonia/infections.
- **Allergic to** eating, touching or breathing common items.

COMMON ALLERGEN TYPES

- **MITES** (House dust, grain etc).
- **FOOD** (See separate list).
- **POLLEN** (Flower, grain, grass etc).
- **MOLDS** (Fungus, spores etc).
- **ANIMAL** (Hair, waste products, fur, parasites from pets/livestock etc).
- **MEDICINES** (Drugs, antibiotics etc).
- **CHEMICALS** (Food additives, [preservatives/ colorings] gases, smoke, insecticides etc).
- **INSECTS** (Stings, bites, waste products, parasites etc).

COMMON FOOD ALLERGENS

- **Cows milk, wheat,** eggs (chicken), corn, coffee, tea, pork, soya, **preservatives,** yeast, **colorings,** additives, **nuts (pea),** chocolate, fish, **shellfish,** peas, goats' milk, beef, chicken, tomatoes, oats.

OVERPROTECTIVE IMMUNITY

- If you suffer from allergies to everyday foods & substances **then your immune systen is trying too hard on your behalf** - Rushing to fight off infections & intrusions - It usually does a great job & correctly identifies what is & is not wanted - **Unfortunately it occasionally becomes over- zealous in its duties** & rejects not only undesir- able substances but also harmless & even desir- able ones too.

- **This is why** a blood transfusion must be your exact blood type.
- **This is why** a skin graft must come from your own body.

A=YOUR IMMUNE SYSTEM.
B=BAD GUY.
C= GRANNY.

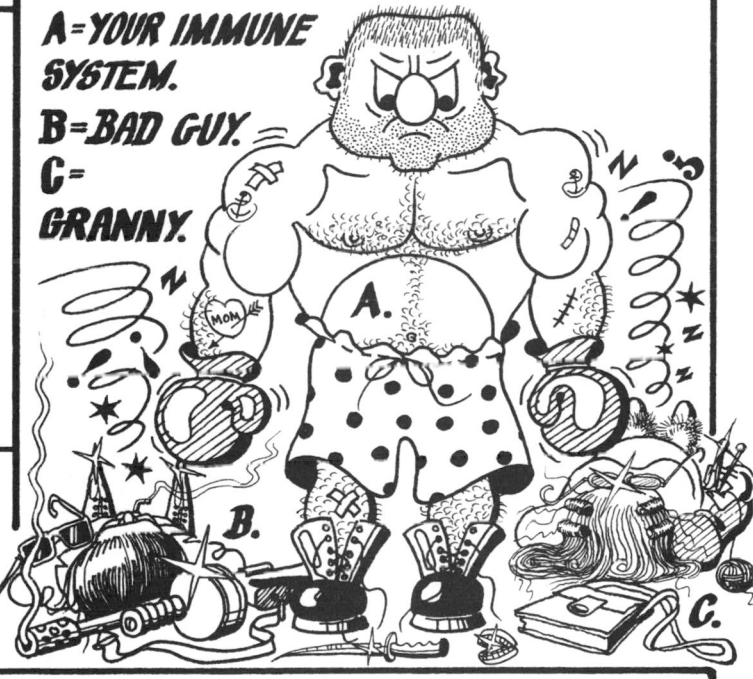

TRIGGER INFLUENCES....

....are apparently unrelated substances or situations or activities which precipitate an allergic attack from another allergen WHICH MIGHT OTH- ERWISE HAVE REMAINED DORMANT.

- **COMMON EXAMPLES** are ● VIGOROUS EXERCISE immediately after eating ● STRESS & emotional upsets ● TEMPERATURE &/or humidity changes ● DRUGS &/or medicinals ●PERFUMES &/or air-fresheners (particularly aerosols) ● AIR POLLUTION (from traffic, industry etc).

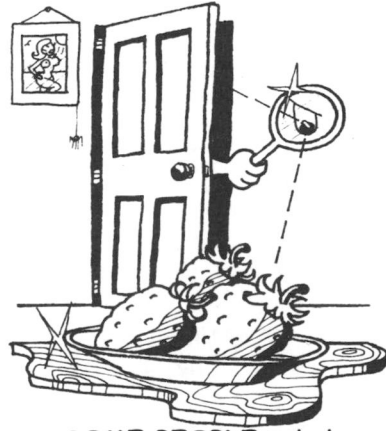

- **SOME PEOPLE** only have to go into a room with their allergen to start sneezing & wheezing.

FREQUENCY

- An allergy to a sub- stance or food only devel- ops AFTER MULTIPLE EXPOSURES TO IT.

AMOUNT

- Large amounts of a suspect food (or other substance) can precipitate an aller- gic reaction WHEN A SMALL AMOUNT MIGHT NOT.

MICROSCOPIC HOUSE DUST MITES

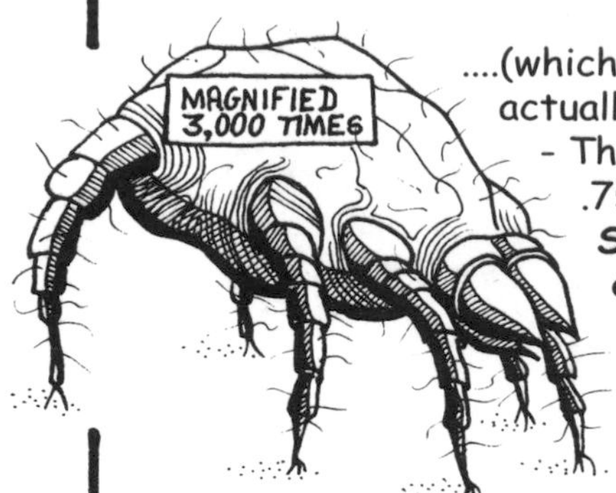

MAGNIFIED 3,000 TIMES

....(which are flecks of dust [0.3mm] size) **are a major cause of allergies** - It is actually the droppings (which are small enough to be inhaled) which are the allergen - The mite lives in dust & consumes discarded skin flakes - A human sheds about .75g/day, mainly in bed **(WHICH IS ENOUGH TO FEED SEVERAL THOUSAND MITES FOR SEVERAL MONTHS).**

- **BEDDING USUALLY HAS THE MOST MITES** as ideal climatic conditions are about 25 degrees C & 75% humidity (which they require to extract water) - **TURN BEDS BACK & OPEN A WINDOW IN DAYTIME.**

HOW TO REDUCE HOUSE DUST MITE INFESTATIONS

- **CARPETS** harbor mites **(change to woodblock, tiles or linoleum).**
- **CURTAINS** to a lesser degree also harbor mites (roller or slat blinds are best).
- **MATTRESS:** Preferably a new one **(immediately cover with waterproof slip-on cover).**
- **PILLOWS - DUVETS - BLANKETS:** Preferably synthetic (should be hot-washed [130 + degrees F] **a minimum of once a month).**
- **SHEETS - PILLOWCASES:** Should be changed **a minimum of once a week** (& hot washed).
- **VACUUM:** (for dust) Several times a week **with a disposable bag** (or outside exhaust).
- **HUMIDITY:** Should be kept low.
- **PETS:** Should not be allowed inside (particularly in bedrooms).
- **LOWER BUNKS:** **Are bad places to sleep** (mites "shower" down from the upper mattress).
- **SOFT FURNISHINGS - TOYS:** Etc. (hot wash regularly).

VIEW OF INNER FOREARM
CONTROL
TEA
COWS MILK
HOUSE DUST MITE
BEE POLLEN COMBATS ALLERGIES
ESSENCE OF TEA

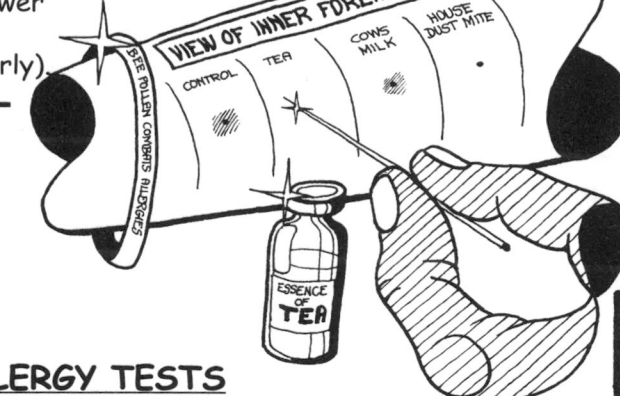

ALLERGY REACTION TIMES

- **IMMEDIATE** **reactions to eating a problem food include** a) tingling mouth/swollen lips, b) nausea/stomach ache, c) burning sensations, d) illogical fatigue, e) joint pain (toxin buildup), f) blurred vision, g) swollen inner ears.
- **DELAYED** **reactions might occur in different forms** & in different parts of the body when the food has been digested & "reaches" the part which reacts to it, or when a certain level of ingestion of that food occurs.

ALLERGY TESTS

- **Include:** Blood tests, patch tests, food elimination programs, hair analysis & nasal smears but probably the quickest & clearest results are from **SKIN TESTS** **which are a needle prick thru a drop of allergen.** An allergic reaction will usually result in strong itching after a few minutes & a weal + redness after about 10 - 20 minutes. This test is usually done on the inside of the forearm except on babies & young children.

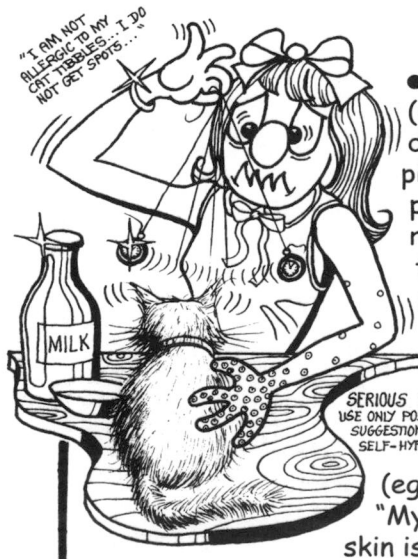

MIND POWER

"I AM NOT ALLERGIC TO MY CAT TIBBLES... I DO NOT GET SPOTS..."
MILK
SERIOUS NOTE: USE ONLY POSITIVE SUGGESTIONS IN SELF-HYPNOSIS.

- **ALLERGIC ATTACK** (e.g.. sneezing & breathing difficulties) can be precipitated in many of those prone by them entering a room with, say, plastic, flowers (no pollen) - **Conversely this "control" of mind over body** can be used (via self-hypnosis) to **REDUCE** unwanted reactions to allergens (eg. THINK & BELIEVE "My body likes cat fur.... my skin is smooth & calm etc.").

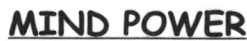

ELIMINATION DIETS

- Are simple in principal in that all foods suspected of causing a problem are eliminated from the diet for a minimum of four days (preferably a week), & then reintroduced **one at a time** (at intervals of four days) & reactions (if any), carefully monitored.
- **NOTES:** Be sure to study ingredients **minutely** to check they do not include "eliminated" foods.
- **WATCH NUTRITION DURING DIETS.**

Understand, Diagnose & Look After Your Skin Better Today

SKIN, OUR FIRST DEFENSE AGAINST THE WORLD....
self-healing, self-repairing & self-regenerating, virtually unchanged since the Stone Age.

STRUCTURE

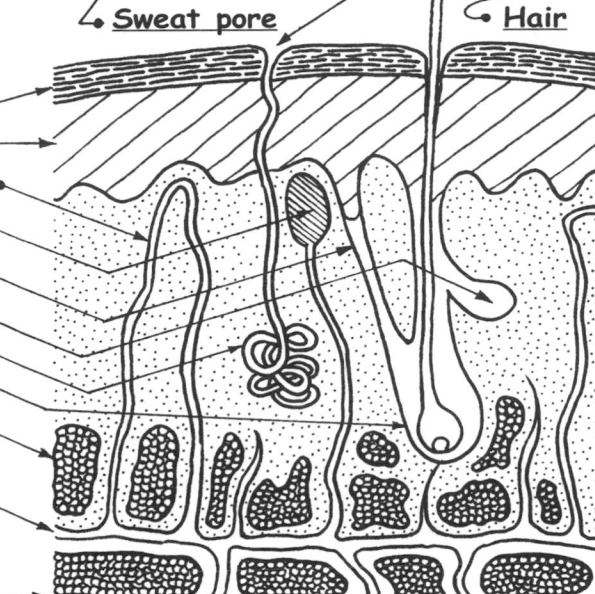

→ Sweat pore → Hair

A. Living skin cells growing outward (A & B together) are known as the epidermis.

B. Dead skin cells being shed.

● **Blood vessels** (capillaries) & nerves.
● Relay organ for **sense of touch.**
● Muscle for activating **goose pimple.**
● Oil producing **sebaceous gland.**
● **Sweat gland.**
● **Hair follicle.**
● **Fat cells.**
● **Blood supply** eventually goes back to heart (& nerves to brain).
● **Elastic fibers** & area immediately on top of limb muscles.

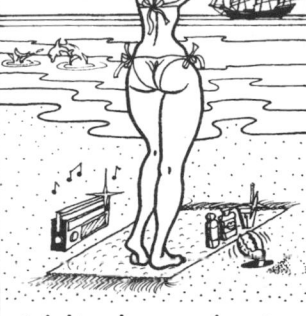

Adults have about 20 sq. ft. of it. - Look after it while you are young & it will last a lifetime!

UNDERSTANDING IT

● **NERVES:** The skin has a greater variety of nerves than any other organ.
● **SWEAT GLANDS:** More than 2 million over the body (the largest under the armpits) (the most numerous, on the palms of the hands) disposing of excess water (according to temperature & activity), organic matter & toxins - DON'T USE ANTIPERSPIRANTS (they prevent your sweat glands working).
● **SEBACEOUS GLANDS** are tiny sacks of oil (to lubricate skin & hair) attached to each hair follicle & controlled by a tiny muscle and activated by temperature (goose bumps), hormones (oily skin/acne), fright (hair standing on end). **LYMPH GLANDS & BLOOD VESSELS:** Responsible for supplying nutrition to skin & hair - & delivery of waste products to the sweat glands.

LOOKING AFTER IT

● **ABSORPTION** thru your skin is limited (but possible) **so don't put chemicals etc. on it - They may end up in your bloodstream.**
● **CLOTHING** not only restricts the flow of toxins excreted by the sweat glands (& then causes reabsorption of these poisons if it is not changed often) - but also prevents your skin "breathing." **So wear as little as possible.**
● **BATHING:** The skin itself is self-cleansing in that it continually renews itself from the inside out, but regular (daily) bathing will ensure the prompt removal of excreted toxins & dead skin cells - **TRY THIS** a) Warm (100 degree F.) shower b) Rubover with a loofah & P.H balanced (5.5) soap, c) Rinse with warm, d) Brief (10 - 60 seconds) cold shower, e) Brisk friction rub with rough clean towel....WOW!....FEELIN' GOOOOD!
● **FOOD: By far the best way to care for your skin** is the same way it grows - **FROM THE INSIDE....**

3 SUGGESTED MEAL CATEGORIES DAILY

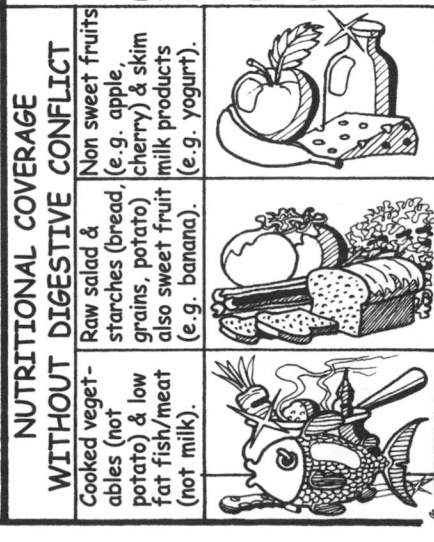

NUTRITIONAL COVERAGE WITHOUT DIGESTIVE CONFLICT

Non sweet fruits (e.g. apple, cherry) & skim milk products (e.g. yogurt).

Raw salad & starches (bread, grains, potato) also sweet fruit (e.g. banana).

Cooked vegetables (not potato) & low fat fish/meat (not milk).

SKIN CONDITION OFTEN MIRRORS GENERAL HEALTH -
Therefore healing internally is invariably evidenced externally.

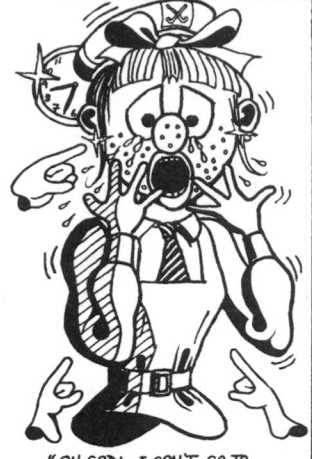

"OH GOD! I CAN'T GO TO SCHOOL LIKE THIS!"

ACNE (CP,CS,S)

● (APPEARANCE) - Familiar spots & blackheads of adolescence on face & upper trunk.
● (CAUSES) - Male hormonal influences on sebaceous glands, aggravated by poor hygiene, diet & stress (even contact with oils &/or chemicals etc.).
● (TREATMENTS) - Some exposure to natural sunlight - Diet "A"* minus high iodine foods (shellfish, iodized salt etc) plus extra yellow veg. (eg. carrots) - **MULTIVITAMIN/MINERAL** supplement + extra A, B6 (+ B Comp.), C, E, potassium, zinc, sulphur, evening primrose oil, & acidophilus - Drink plenty of pure water between (not at) meals - Don't pick/squeeze spots - Deep cleanse with clay mask - Use Aloe Vera inside & out - Take plenty of exercise - **CUT STRESS** with yoga & deep breathing - **HERBS:** Burdock, chaparral, chickweed, dandelion, ginseng, red clover, sarsaparilla, yellow dock.

AGE SPOTS (S)

● (APPEARANCE) - Brown blotches.
● (CAUSE) - Deteriorating structure of cells - Also chemicals/radiation.
● (TREATMENTS) - Diet "A"* - **MULTIVITAMIN/MINERAL** + Extra A, B Comp, C, E, selenium, zinc, calcium, evening primrose oil - Use aloe vera + almond oil externally - **HERBS:** Aloe Vera, dandelion, garlic, gotu kola, ginseng, sarsaparilla, licorice.

BALDNESS (KS, NM, S)

● (APPEARANCE) - Falling hair from head.
● (CAUSES) - Poor diet/circulation, heredity, chemicals/radiation.
● (TREATMENTS) - Diet "A"* minus yin foods (e.g. potato, sweet fruits etc - Study yin/yang) - Massage with aloe vera & almond oil - **MULTIVIT/MIN** + extra B Comp, E, copper, inositol - **HERBS:** Sage, burdock, chaparral, watercress, nettle, evening primrose oil.

BOILS (CS, S)

● (APPEARANCE) - Large swollen red spot often without head.
● (CAUSE) - Low general health &/or blocked/infected pore.
● (TREATMENTS) - Diet "A"* + extra bran - **MULTIVIT/MIN** + extra A, C, B6, B Comp, E, iron, selenium, zinc, calcium, acidophilus - Bring to head with compress of molasses & honey - **HERBS:** Burdock, dandelion, chaparral, sarsaparilla, red clover.

CELLULITE (CF, CP, KP)

● (APPEARANCE) - Puckered, pitted, bloated flesh on trunk & limbs.
● (CAUSES) - Excess bodily estrogen - Poor circulation - Toxin buildup under skin.
● (TREATMENTS) - Diet "A"* - **MULTIVIT/MIN** + extra A, C, E, B Comp, niacin, lecithin, calcium, potassium, magnesium - Use cypress, lemon, juniper or rosemary essential oils (rotate biweekly) in warm bath then hard massage (use carrier oil) - Use deep breathing - **HERBS:** Bayberry, cayenne, garlic, rose hips.

ECZEMA (KS, NM)

● (APPEARANCE) - Red scaly, blotchy, itchy (sometimes weeping).
● (CAUSES) - Heredity, allergies, diet, irritants (e.g. soap, rubber, even light etc).
● (TREATMENTS) - Diet "A"* - Locate & remove irritants - **MULITVIT/MIN** + extra A, B Comp, C, E, zinc, bioflavenoids, selenium, evening primrose oil, lecithin, acidophilus - **CUT STRESS** with yoga & deep breathing, self-hypnosis & exercise - Bee pollen (allergies) - Aloe vera inside & out - **HERBS:** Chickweed, dandelion, red clover.

DIET "A" *

● **DON'T EAT:** Fatty animal foods (including non skimmed dairy foods), sugars (including sweets & soft drinks), foods with chemicals, preservatives, drugs in.
● **DO EAT:** Whole unprocessed organic foods, grains, cereals, seeds, fresh green vegetables, apple, garlic, white fish, turkey, evening primrose oil, Vits. A, C, E & zinc. Study & use food-combining rules.

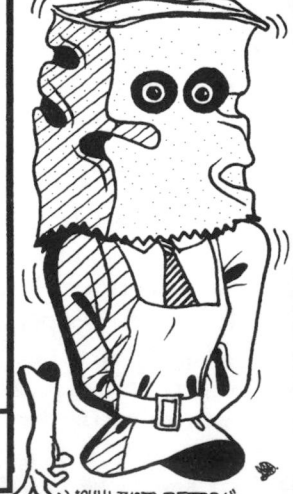

"AHH! THATS BETTER!"

HOMEOPATHIC CURES: Calc Flour (CF), Kali Phos (KP), Kali Sulph (KS), Calc Phos (CP), Calc Sulph (CS), Nat Mur (NM), Silicea (S). - See "TISSUE SALTS" (P.123/4)

A TRAVELER'S GUIDE TO FOOD COMBINING

A Simple Solution For Some Complex Ailments

If we are what we eat, then how we eat now is what we will become soon (try this program for a week & feel the change).

AM I EATING WRONG ?.. & WHAT COULD IT BE DOING TO ME?

● **TO SIMPLIFY** a complex process: <u>Different food groups are digested by different enzymes for different periods in different parts of the digestive tract</u> - **THEREFORE** when incompatible foods are eaten together (or within a couple of hours of each other) then the wrong enzymes (& acids) end up trying to digest the wrong foods for the wrong amount of time - **FIRST RESULT** is incomplete digestion & metabolic usage by the body of the nutrients in the food. <u>Followed by fermentation & putrification of the undigested remains,</u> which then generate toxic poisons that are by association absorbed into the blood stream, tissues & skeleton. - **END RESULTS** over a long period can be disastrous. Directly causing or contributing to <u>a multitude of diverse ailments including:</u> All gastric, all skin, all allergic, bad breath, obesity, malnutrition, fatigue, high blood pressure, arthritis, cancer etc. etc. & **GENERAL ILL HEALTH.**

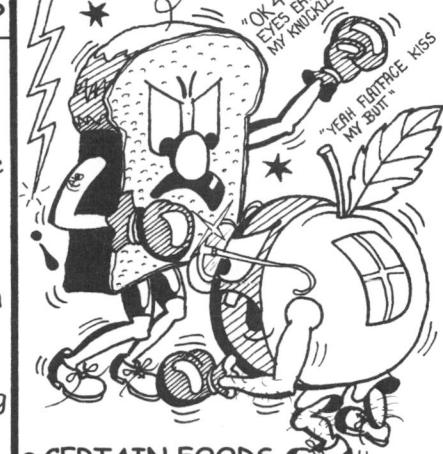

● **CERTAIN FOODS FIGHT VIOLENTLY IN THE DIGESTIVE SYSTEM**

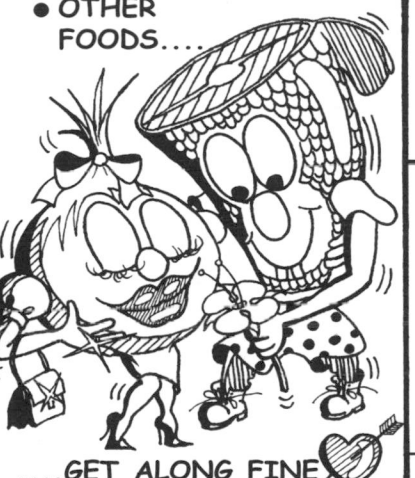

● **OTHER FOODS....**

....GET ALONG FINE

FOUR-STEP QUICK TEST

● **DO YOU** (despite chewing your food well) get cramps, heartburn, acidity, indigestion etc. after eating?
● **DO YOU** (despite eating nutritious foods) suffer from mystery maladies such as allergies & fatigue?
● **DO YOU** (despite a low calorie diet) gain/retain weight inexplicably or conversely fail to thrive on high quality foods?
● **DO YOU** suffer from bad breath, body odor, flatulence etc.?

● **IF YOU** ANSWERED YES TO ANY OF THE ABOVE THEN READ ON....

SAMPLE IDEAL COMBINATION MEAL PLANS

BREAKFAST CHOICES	LUNCH CHOICES	DINNER CHOICES
● ACID FRUIT (8 AM). A bowl of fresh diced sour apples & strawberries. ② ● SWEET FRUIT (10 AM). A ripe banana & a bowl of dried figs. ②	● STARCH & GREEN VEGETABLES (12 NOON). Boiled brown rice, carrots & broccoli with garlic & ginger sauce. ⑤	● PROTEIN (animal) & GREEN VEGETABLES (5 PM). Grilled cod steak with spinach & asparagus in fish stock & fresh herb sauce. ⑫
● ACID FRUIT (8 AM). A bowl of fresh orange & grapefruit segments. ② ● SWEET FRUIT (10 AM). Half a papaya & a saucer of dried raisins. ②	● STARCH & GREEN VEGETABLES (12 NOON). Baked jacket potato, boiled cabbage & fresh spring onions with mushroom and parsley sauce. ⑤	● PROTEIN (fat) & GREEN VEGETABLES (5 PM). Avocado & cheese salad (with assorted fresh greens, celery, radish, sprouts etc.) with stuffed olives. ⑫
● STARCH & GREEN VEGETABLES (8 AM). Organic oat porridge followed by hot garlic soup & wholemeal noodles & fresh chopped herbs. ⑤	● STARCH & GREEN VEGETABLES (12 NOON). Toasted wholemeal garlic bread & mixed vegetable stew followed by a bowl of savory almonds .... mmmm! ⑤	● SWEET FRUIT (5 PM). 2 ripe bananas & a bowl of mixed dried fruit. ② ● MILK (7 PM) 2 or 3 glasses of skim milk. ⑩

● **DONT DRINK** during or close to meal times (it impairs digestion).
● **RINGED NUMBERS** above indicate digestion times for that food group.

COMBINE ONLY GROUPS WITH A COMMON BORDER

PROTEIN (animal) ⑫

- Offal
- Turkey • Eel
- Chicken • Egg
- Lobster
- Fish (all)
- Rabbit • Hare
- Goose • Pork
- Mutton
- Lamb • Duck
- Pheasant
- Venison
- Caviar
- Crab • Squid
- Snake • Goat
- Cod Roe
- Beef • Veal
- Frog • Snail

GREEN VEGETABLES (nonstarch) ⑤

- Asparagus
- Artichoke
- Broccoli
- Cauliflower
- Chicory • Okra
- Chive • Garlic
- Escarole
- Bell Pepper
- Lettuce • Kale
- Spinach
- Bok Choy
- Turnip Top
- Green Bean
- Eggplant
- Parsley • Mint
- Mushroom
- Cabbage
- Cucumber
- Carrot Top
- Spring Onion
- Radish • Peas (raw)
- Bamboo Shoots
- Leek • Celery
- Brussel Sprouts
- Onion • Cress
- Collard • Chard
- Kale • Endive
- Sprouts (all)
- Zucchini
- Dandelion

PROTEIN (vegetable) ⑩

- Beans (dry)
- Peas (dry)
- Soya • Tofu

PROTEIN (fat) ⑫

- Cheese
- Avocado
- Nuts (raw) *
- Olives • Seeds
- Cream (sour)
- Yogurt (full fat)

FAT ⑫

- Coconut
- Margarine
- Butter • Oil
- Cream • Palm

STARCHES   (& sub starches) ⑤

- Potato • Yam
- Pumpkin • Oat
- Maize • Corn
- Flour • Noodle
- Bread • Rice
- Barley • Pasta
- Peanut (raw)
- Chestnut (raw)
- Wheat • Rye
- Squash
- Grain • Cereal
- Spaghetti
- Parsnip
- Turnip
- Beet
- Carrot

MILK ⑩
- All

• EAT ALONE <u>any food group not connected to another with a shared border</u> (i.e. eat green vegetables with any single adjoining group but do not for example eat proteins with starches).

• ALLOW IN HOURS <u>the ringed number before eating another incompatible group</u> (i.e. allow 2 hours after eating melon before eating any other group). * Except peanuts & chestnuts.

FRUIT (sweet) ②

- Banana
- Mango • Date
- Papaya • Fig
- Most dried e.g. raisins.

MELONS ②

- Casaba
- Muskmelon
- Watermelon
- Cantaloupe
- Honeydew

FRUIT (neutral) ②

- Apple (sweet)
- Cherry(sweet)
- Peach (sweet)
- Pear • Plum
- Guava • Kiwi
- Blackberry
- Fig (fresh)

SUGAR ②

- Malt
- Molasses
- Carob • Honey
- Maple Syrup

FRUIT (acid) ②

- Apple (sour)
- Cherry (sour)
- Peach (sour)
- Strawberry
- Pineapple
- Tomato
- Tangerine
- Lemon • Lime
- Cranberry
- Grapefruit
- Pomegranate
- Raspberry

Self-Diagnosis & Therapy Of Common Problems Using Tissue Salts

*Although the principles of therapeutic use of mineral salts are ancient
The specific remedies here are only about a century old.*

WHAT ARE THEY?

CODE	MINERAL NAME	FULL LATIN NAME	SHORT LATIN NAME	CHEMICAL FORMULA	ASSOCIATED STAR SIGN
1	Calcium Flouride	Calcarea Fluorica	Calc. Fluor.	CaF_2	Cancer
2	Calcium Phosphate	Calcarea Phosphorica	Calc. Phos.	$Ca_3(PO_4)_2$	Capricorn
3	Calcium Sulphate	Calcarea Sulphurica	Calc. Sulph.	$CaSO_4$	Scorpio
4	Iron Phosphate	Ferrum Phosphoricum	Ferr. Phos.	$Fe_3(PO_4)_2$	Pisces
5	Potassium Chloride	Kali Muriaticum	Kali. Mur.	KCI	Gemini
6	Potassium Phosphate	Kali Phosphoricum	Kali. Phos.	K_2HPO_4	Aries
7	Potassium Sulphate	Kali Sulphuricum	Kali. Sulph.	K_2SO_4	Virgo
8	Magnesium Phosphate	Magnesia Phosphorica	Mag. Phos.	$Mg\,HPO_4.7H_2O$	Leo
9	Sodium Chloride	Natrum Muriaticum	Nat. Mur.	$NaCI$	Aquarius
10	Sodium Phosphate	Natrum Phosphuricum	Nat. Phos.	$Na_2HPO_4.12H_2O$	Libra
11	Sodium Sulphate	Natrum Sulphuricum	Nat. Sulph.	$Na_2SO_4.10H_2O$	Taurus
12	Silicon Dioxide	Silicea	Silica.	SiO_2	Sagitarius

CODE	ESTABLISHED COMBINATIONS CONTENTS
A	4-6-8
B	2-4-6
C	8-10-11-12
D	3-5-7-12
E	2-8-10-11
F	6-8-9-12
G	1-2-6-9
H	8-9-12
I	4-7-8
J	4-7-9
K	7-9-12
L	1-4-9
M	2-5-10-11
N	2-5-6-8
P	1-2-6-8
Q	4-5-7-9
R	1-2-4-8-12
S	5-10-11

THE THEORY OF TISSUE SALT THERAPY

● **GOOD HEALTH** requires normal cell metabolism. ● Normal cell metabolism requires adequate nutrition. ● Adequate nutrition requires mineral tissue salts.

● **SHORTAGES** of mineral tissue salts result in impaired assimilation/utilization of nutritional intakes (& excretion of toxins/waste) <u>adversly effecting cell metabolism/& encouraging the onset of disease.</u>

● **SELF-DIAGNOSIS** of tissue salt shortages is best achieved by cross-reference of symptoms (see over) - If numerous symptoms are present concentrate on & treat the most severe.

● **DOSAGE** exactitude is not as critical as most other medicinals as excess consumption will within reason be excreted. - **CHRONIC PROBLEMS** such as rheumatism are usually treated with a lower but longer term dose while **A SERIOUS COLD** may call for hourly dosage decreasing as the symptoms subside.

● **FORM** is usually tablet in a lactose base which is very rapidly absorbed into the bloodstream.

A TRAVELER'S GUIDE TO TISSUE SALT THERAPY
Self-Diagnosis & Therapy Of Common Problems Using Tissue Salts

SYMPTOMS & THERAPIES

SKIN
- Acne - 3 - D.
- Blisters - 9.
- Burns - 5 - D - M.
- Dry/Hard - 1 - 7.
- Sweat (lack of) - 7.
- Warts - 5 - D - K.
- Grow new - 7.
- Festering - 3.
- Wrinkled - 6 - 9 - 1.
- Eczema - D.
- Greasy - 10 - C.
- Scaling - 2 - 7 - D.
- Shingles - 5 - 9.

CIRCULATION
- Varicose veins - 1.
- Anemia - 4 - 2 - B.
- Chilblains - 2 - 6 - 5 - P.
- Weak - 2 - 6 - 1.

RESPIRATION
- Asthma - 6 - J.
- Catarrh - 7 - Q.
- Wheezing - 5 - 4 - Q.
- Coughs - 4 - J.
- Coughs (convulsing) - 8 - H.
- Chest cold - 4 - 9.
- Phlegm (thin) - 9 - J.
- Phlegm (thick) - 12 - 7.
- Hawking - 2.
- Hay fever - 9 - 8 - 12 - H.

STOMACH
- Bloated - 2 - 8 - E.
- Travel sickness - 6 - 10.
- Indigestion - 8 - E.
- Heartburn - 2 - 11 - 12.
- Belching - 4 - 10.
- Vomiting - 10 - C.
- Upset - 10 - 11 - S.

NOSE
- Bleeding - 4.
- Sneezing - 9 - 12.
- Mucus blocked - 1 - 7 - Q.
- Dry - 9 - 12.

EARS
- Noises - 5.
- Swollen inside - 5 - 7.
- Throbbing ache - 1 - 4.
- White discharge - 5.

HEAD
- Ache (tummy) - 11 - S.
- Ache (body) - 8 - F - I.
- Ache (nerves) - 6 - F.
- Hair loss - 7 - 9 - 12.
- Dandruff - 7 - 9 - D

NERVES
- Mental fatigue - 6.
- Dejected/Crying - 9.
- Shy/Moody - 6.
- Bad memory - 2 - 6 - 8.
- Twitching (sleep) - 11.
- Jerks/Trembling - 8.
- Neuralgia - 2 - 5 - 6 - 8 - 10.
- Emotional - 6.

EYES
- Lid twitching - 8.
- Weak sight - 6.
- Stye on lid - 12.
- Bloodshot - 4 - H.
- Yellow discharge - 10 - 3.
- Too dry/Too wet - 9 - Q.
- White discharge - 5.
- Drooping lids - 6 - 8.

WHAT THEY DO

1:	Builds elastic tissues.
2:	Forms new blood cells.
3:	Blood purifier.
4:	Oxygen carrier.
5:	Blood conditioner.
6:	Nerve nutrient.
7:	Cell oxygenator.
8:	Antispasmodic.
9:	Body water balancer.
10:	Acid neutralizer.
11:	Water eliminator.
12:	Waste eliminator.

CHILDREN
- Bad tempered - 6.
- Bed wetting - 6 - 4 - B.
- Nightmares - 6 - 2.
- Teething - 2 - 9 - R.
- Hyperactive - 6.
- Poor appetite - B - 2 - 5.
- Itching - P.
- Hiccups - 8 - E.
- Thrush - 5.
- Colic - 8 - E.

THROAT
- Glands swollen - 5 - 2.
- Laryngitis - 2 - J.
- Tonsils - 4 - Q.
- Sore & dry - 9 - J.
- Tickling - 1.
- Lost voice - 4.
- Chronically hoarse - 2.

MOUTH
- Gums bleed - 6.
- Gums pale - 2.
- Bad taste in morn. - 2.
- Bad breath - 6 - 10 - C.
- Cracked lips - 1 - 3 - P.
- Ulcer (mouth) - 10 - C.
- Ulcer (lip) - 12 - D.
- Swollen gums - 4.

TONGUE
- Coated - 10 - C.
- Blister on tip - 9 - 2.
- Inflamed - 5 - 4 - Q.
- Swollen - 1.

TEETH
- Root ulcer - 3.
- Toothache - 8.
- Rapid decay - 2.
- Enamel thin - 1.
- Sensitive - 8 - 1.

WASTE
- Itchy anus - 1 - 10.
- Constipation - 9 - S.
- Diarrhea - 5 - S.
- Flatulence - E.
- Hemorrhoids - 1.

FEMALE
- Frigidity - 6 - 8.
- Period (heavy) - 4.
- Period (sparse) - 9 - L.
- Period pain - 6 - 8 - N.
- Morning sickness - 10 - S.

VARIOUS
- Won't get up in AM - 2 - 9.
- Insomnia - 6.
- Sleepy in day (old) - 12 - 2.
- Yellow face - 11.
- Colds/Flu - 4 - 10 - J.
- Freckles - 2.
- Lethargy - L - 11.
- Insect stings - 9.
- Symptoms bad in cold/ wet - 2 - 11.
- Sedentary - L.
- Convalescence - 2 - B.
- Joint cracking - 10.
- Cries easily - 6.
- Muscles stiff - 4.
- Bow legs - 2.
- Fever - 4 - 8 - I.
- Sprains - 4.
- Gout - 10 - 11 - 4.

Diagnose & Treat Bodily Ailments With Specific Zone Foot Massage

WHY DOES IT WORK?

NERVE ENDINGS	CIRCULATION	TOXIC DEPOSITS
There are estimated to be about 70,000 nerve endings in each foot which relate to & effect (directly or indirectly) every body part & function, making possible diagnosis &/or treatment of (for example) internal organs from specific foot zones.	Without adequate blood circulation any body part will die, & any blockages (very often in feet because of cold, age, constriction etc.) will in some way effect all other parts. Specific zone massage will improve blood supply to the site & its related remote area(s).	Areas of concentrated nerve endings (& poor circulation) frequently accumulate toxin buildup (uric acid, excess calcium [in crystal form] etc.) which are seriously detrimental to health/ mobility, but which respond well (break up) to specific zone massage.

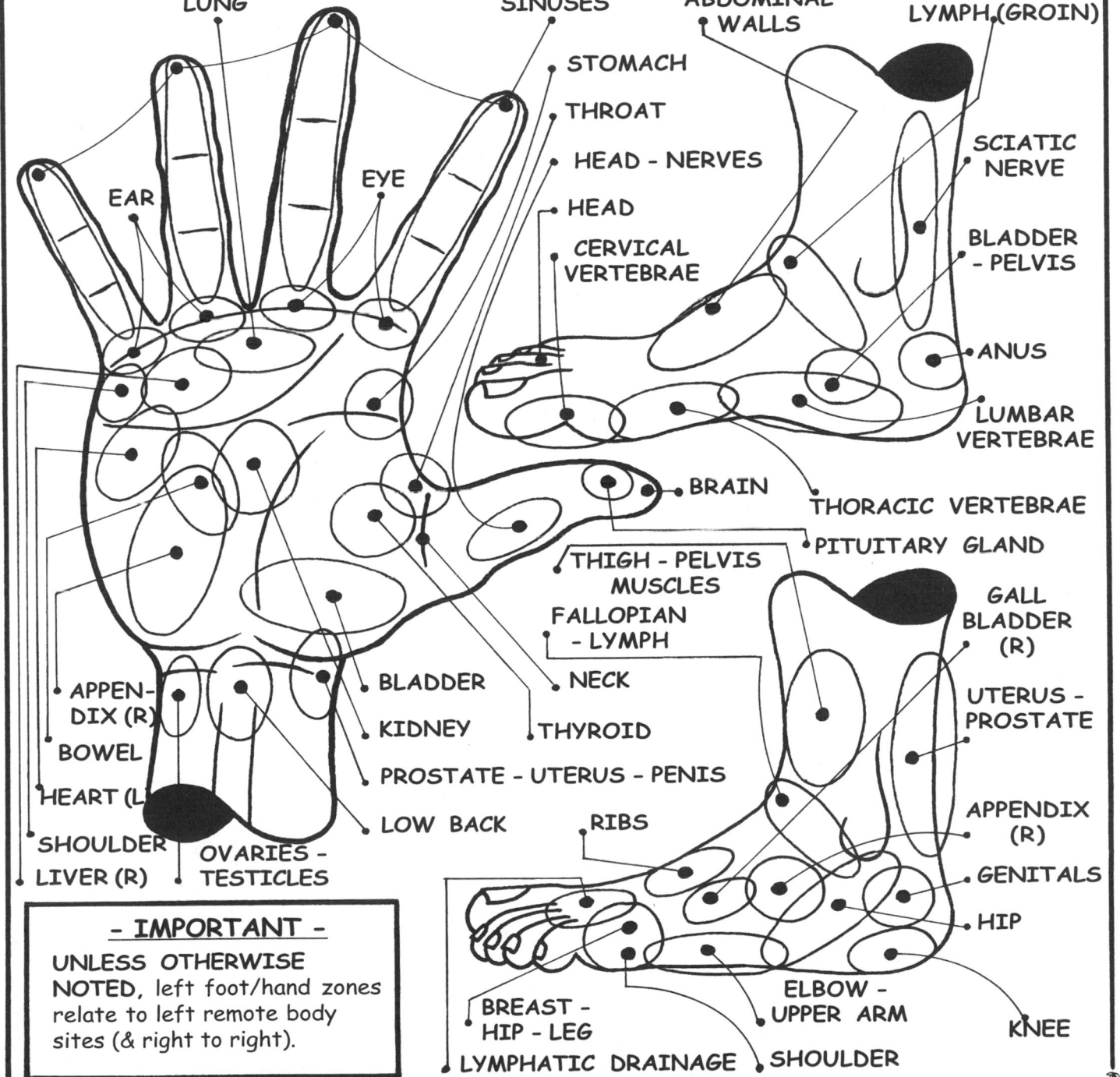

LUNG SINUSES ABDOMINAL WALLS FALLOPIAN - LYMPH (GROIN)

STOMACH

THROAT

EAR EYE HEAD - NERVES SCIATIC NERVE

HEAD BLADDER - PELVIS

CERVICAL VERTEBRAE

ANUS

LUMBAR VERTEBRAE

BRAIN THORACIC VERTEBRAE

PITUITARY GLAND

THIGH - PELVIS MUSCLES GALL BLADDER (R)

FALLOPIAN - LYMPH

APPEN-DIX (R) BLADDER NECK UTERUS - PROSTATE

BOWEL KIDNEY THYROID

HEART (L) PROSTATE - UTERUS - PENIS APPENDIX (R)

SHOULDER LOW BACK RIBS GENITALS

LIVER (R) OVARIES - TESTICLES HIP

- IMPORTANT -
UNLESS OTHERWISE NOTED, left foot/hand zones relate to left remote body sites (& right to right).

BREAST - HIP - LEG ELBOW - UPPER ARM KNEE

LYMPHATIC DRAINAGE SHOULDER

Technique Of Therapeutic Massage (probable origin: China)

HOW TO DIAGNOSE

<u>Consider any non-injury-related tenderness in a particular foot/hand zone</u> as a possible indication of trouble in its related remote site - But also treat any other sensitive foot/hand zones (all being interconnected) as an entire body therapy. **(see also p 205 & 206)**

HOW TO TREAT

<u>Administer massage with thumb, knuckle or other blunt pointed object</u> (e.g. round pen cap) using (if required) baby powder or oil (e.g. peanut, olive, safflower, coconut or aromatherapy) treat each zone for several minutes or until less tender. **(see also p 65 & 66)**

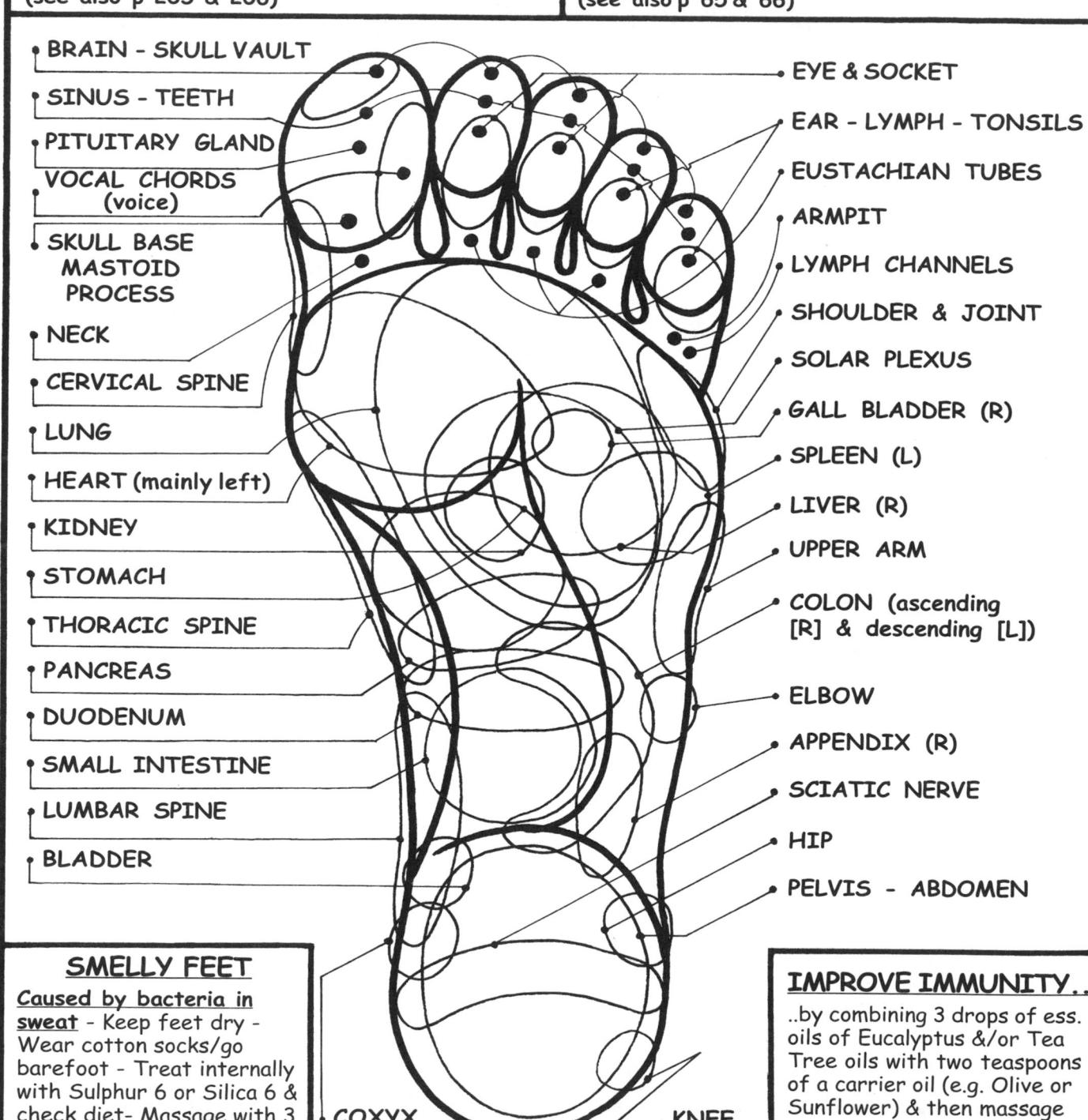

- BRAIN - SKULL VAULT
- SINUS - TEETH
- PITUITARY GLAND
- VOCAL CHORDS (voice)
- SKULL BASE MASTOID PROCESS
- NECK
- CERVICAL SPINE
- LUNG
- HEART (mainly left)
- KIDNEY
- STOMACH
- THORACIC SPINE
- PANCREAS
- DUODENUM
- SMALL INTESTINE
- LUMBAR SPINE
- BLADDER

- EYE & SOCKET
- EAR - LYMPH - TONSILS
- EUSTACHIAN TUBES
- ARMPIT
- LYMPH CHANNELS
- SHOULDER & JOINT
- SOLAR PLEXUS
- GALL BLADDER (R)
- SPLEEN (L)
- LIVER (R)
- UPPER ARM
- COLON (ascending [R] & descending [L])
- ELBOW
- APPENDIX (R)
- SCIATIC NERVE
- HIP
- PELVIS - ABDOMEN

COXYX

KNEE

SMELLY FEET

<u>Caused by bacteria in sweat</u> - Keep feet dry - Wear cotton socks/go barefoot - Treat internally with Sulphur 6 or Silica 6 & check diet- Massage with 3 drops ess. oil of Cypress in 2 tsp. of a carrier.

IMPROVE IMMUNITY..

..by combining 3 drops of ess. oils of Eucalyptus &/or Tea Tree oils with two teaspoons of a carrier oil (e.g. Olive or Sunflower) & then massage (feel those tsubos!) feet & hands—MARVELOUS!

VALUABLE TRAVELERS HINT

Sit on a chair - Take your shoes off (a carpeted floor is best) - Put one large marble (wooden balls slightly smaller than golf balls are best) under each foot & roll around, pausing on sensitive spots. - MMM HIGHLY THERAPEUTIC ! — (on a plane/coach tie them (balls) on a string — because they ROLL AWAY!)

Almost any human mind can achieve beneficial results with almost any problem
ON THE FIRST ATTEMPT OF SELF-HYPNOSIS.

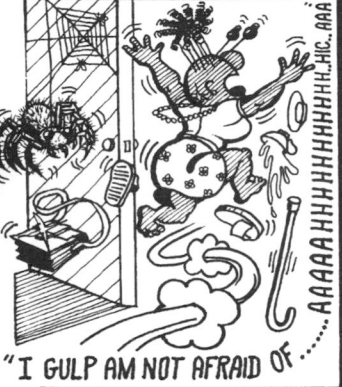

"I GULP AM NOT AFRAID OF ...."

● **WHAT CAN SELF-HYPNOSIS DO FOR ME?** - The answer is almost anything. The potential of our minds is barely touched. Many proven examples exist of e.g. a) **TELEPATHIC CONTACT** across long distances. b) **"REMOTE VIEWING"** (ability to "see" never before visited distant locations). c) **"BLOCK OUT"** intense pain (i.e. during operations or walking on hot coals) d) So-called **PHOTOGRAPHIC MEMORY** (recalling pages of names & addresses etc. after one quick reading). e) Dramatically improve (or conversely deteriorate) **PHYSICAL AILMENTS**/diseases etc. - There are many more: Stop smoking - Lose weight - Gain confidence - Improve work/sport - **THE LIST IS ENDLESS!**

● **PRINCIPLES OF HYPNOSIS:** To bypass the conscious mind by a) Concentrating its attentions on a single subject (light, pendulum, repetitive chant, counting etc.) or b) Putting it to sleep - (**then contact is made with the subconscious mind which accepts orders given to it** [by thought, voice or recording] **WITHOUT QUESTION**).

HOW TO (you can vary) ACQUIRE A TRANCE

● **POSITION:** <u>You should be warm</u> - Wear loose clothes - Have an empty bladder - Be in a quiet, dimly lit place - Lie on back (or sit with back & neck straight & feet/legs on floor).

TAPE RECORDER

● <u>Assume a comfortable position</u> (as above) & select a spot on the ceiling a bit above your front line of vision. Switch on your prerecorded tape (make your own) with a more lengthy version of this example (worded according to your particular needs).

● *"Take a few slow deep breaths & gaze at your chosen spot on the ceiling. Now progressively relax your body from toes to scalp - Completely relax each part in turn - Keep looking at your chosen spot - Focus only on my voice, nothing else matters - However if a crisis arose or this machine malfunctions your mind will return to full consciousness immediately, refreshed & alert - Therefore because you are safe in every way you can relax even more than before - Feel the tension drain away - Your body is very heavy - Your mind is very calm - Your heart & bodily functions continue normally. Even if you fall asleep it does not matter, you will awake refreshed - & now I will count down from 10 to 0 & at each number you will double your relaxation - & now you are in a self-induced trance & when you awake you will be more confident, healthier & much happier - & the next time you enter a trance it will be easier & deeper than this one - & now I will count from 1 - 5.... & when I reach 5 you will be wide awake.... & FEELING FABULOUS".*

BY THOUGHT

● <u>Close your eyes & look up about 20 Degrees</u> (encourages trance) then count backward from 100 at 2 second intervals (completely relaxing all tension from each body part in turn as you count) - If your mind wanders, push intruding thoughts away & return to your count - At zero (or before) **YOU WILL BE IN A TRANCE.**

TRANCES THEREAFTER

● <u>Can usually be achieved</u> from progressively lower numbers (e.g.: 7 nights from 80, 7 from 40, 7 from 20, 7 from 10 & finally try to achieve trances from 5).

COMING OUT

● Is usually acheived by counting from 0 - 5 with the prior statement to yourself that on 5 you will be awake & refreshed etc. - But it can be presuggested that on snapping your fingers & saying *"wake up"* you will come out.

● **HYPNOTISTS' HELP** to achieve effective self-induced trances is useful. <u>First be professionally hypnotized (& given key words to use later)</u> as required to induce a self-administered trance state .. SUCH AS ....

..." I AM AS LIGHT AS A RED BALLOON"....

Basic Techniques For Controlling The Subconscious Mind

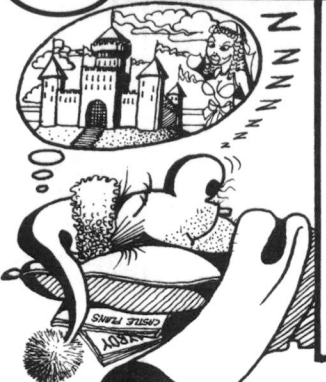

INSTANT ANTI-STRESS TECHNIQUE

• **PRIOR TO STRESSFUL SITUATIONS** preinstruct your subconscious mind (while in a trance) that at any future time **(PERHAPS AT A BUSINESS MEETING OR DURING A FAMILY ARGUMENT)** you will instantly acquire the same calm & focused state of mind that you have now (i.e. in the trance) by placing your hands (or fingers) in a certain position (do it). - **This usually requires 5 - 10 meditation sessions to condition the subconscious mind** but will be established thereafter & only require an occasional reconditioning (say weekly).

DREAM CONTROL

• **CAN USUALLY BE BEST ACHIEVED** by meditating prior to sleeping & while in a trance, state firmly to yourself (for example: _"Tonight I will dream about building my new house, I will think of a clever design & when I wake up tomorrow I will remember the details clearly"_) - This technique may require a week or so of nightly practice to perfect.

STUCK IN A TRANCE!

• **YOU WON'T**, so don't worry. **WHY?** - **Because a hypnotic trance is a delicate balance between being awake & being asleep** - & as such is difficult to maintain without slipping into one or the other (either of which will automatically bring you back to normality).

SUPERFAST TRANCE ACQUISITION

• **CAN BE ATTAINED** by posthypnotic suggestion (&/or try this): a) Close eyes, b) Progressively relax eyelids until they "won't" open, c) Test eyelids to be sure they "won't" open, d) Spread relaxation thru entire body, e) Proceed with suggestions.

• **SELF-HEALING** of any ailment/injury **IS POSSIBLE** while the mind is still capable of controlling the body.
• **THE PHONE TRICK** in any stressful situation: visualize yourself ignoring a ringing phone. **YOU WILL FEEL CALM & IN CONTROL.**

IMPORTANT HINTS

• **POSITIVE SUGGESTIONS** during a trance are more effective than negative ones (i.e. don't say _"I will not smoke"_ - say _"My willpower is strong & I can easily beat my nicotine habit"_).
• **DEEPER/FASTER TRANCES** are achieved by practice, & telling yourself **(prior to terminating each trance)** that on each successive occasion your trance will be easier & quicker to acquire, also deeper & more effective.
• **MILD TRANCES** such as beginners usually acquire will facilitate self-hypnosis & achieve results.
• **PLAN** your suggestions **before going into a trance (not during it)** as the thought processes required to do this reactivate the conscious mind (& weaken the trance).
• **AM I IN A TRANCE?** - You will know by the feeling of numbness (&/or detachment) which comes over the body (usually feet/legs first) - **Now is the time** to give yourself the self-help suggestions.
• **YOUR OBJECTIVES**, remember, are to: a) Achieve a trance, b) Give yourself the suggestions c) Terminate the trance.
• **POST TRANCE ACTION:** For rapid results after self-hypnosis always act out the subject of your suggestions (e.g. **if you would be brave then act brave**). **WITH PRACTICE THE ACT CHANGES TO REALITY.**

REPETITIVE CHANTING

• Either out loud or to yourself - **Pick any one syllable word (um, hu, om etc.)** & repeat it over & over, casting out all other thoughts - By this method are trances induced &/or **ANY HUMAN STRESS SITUATION CONQUERED.**

CLEANSING THE MIND

• **IMAGINE IN A QUIET PLACE** that you remove all negative thoughts & feelings from inside you (hate, jealousy, stress, worry etc.). Feel them flow out into a small metal box with an open lid. - Close the lid & cast the box into the sea. It sinks deeper & deeper, never to be seen again **- As it sinks a great feeling of relief comes over you. A burden is gone, you feel light, happy**, A NEW PERSON.

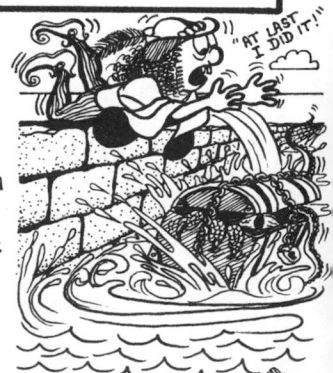

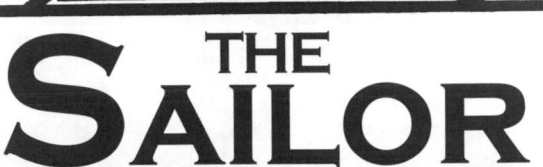

THE SAILOR

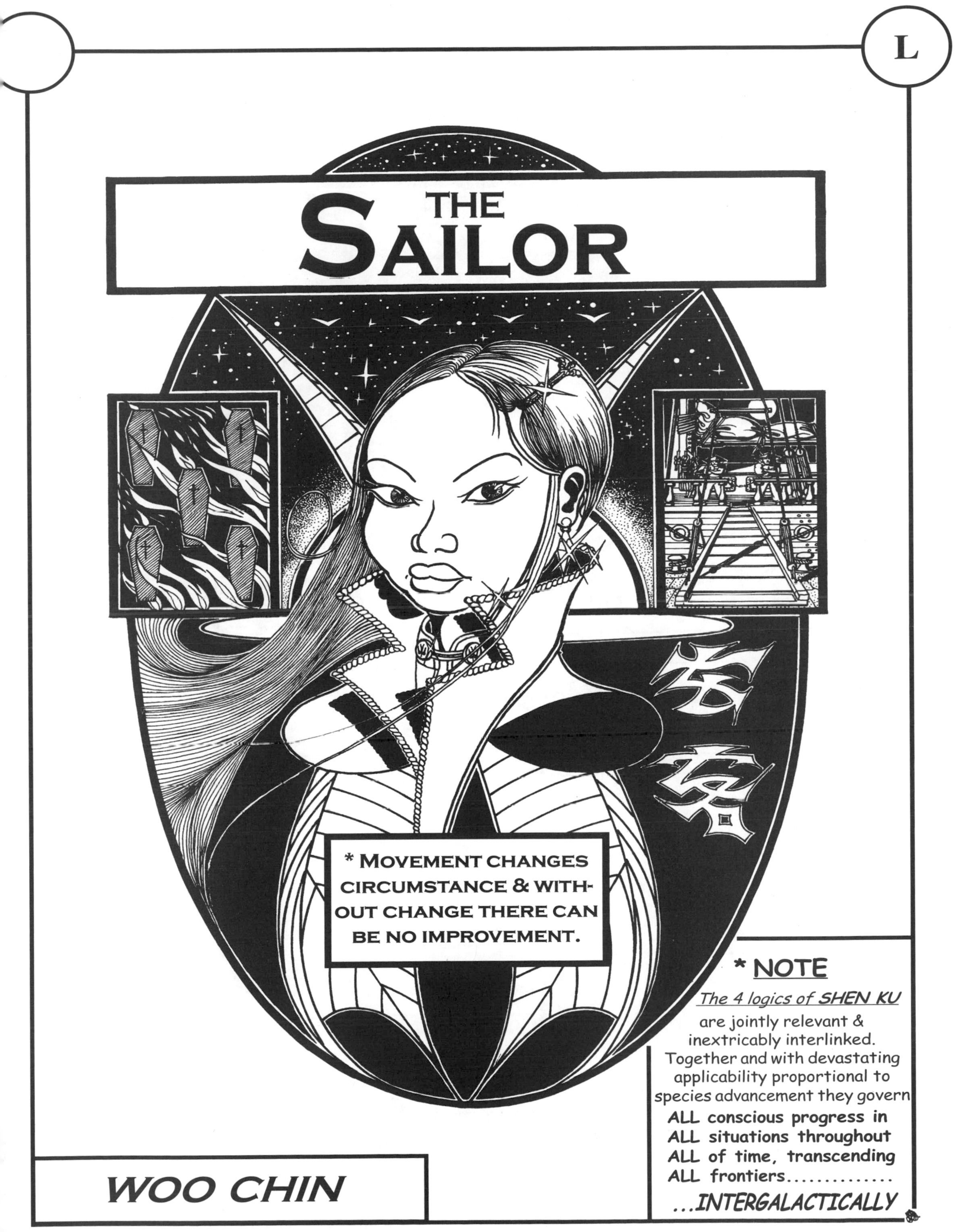
* MOVEMENT CHANGES CIRCUMSTANCE & WITH-OUT CHANGE THERE CAN BE NO IMPROVEMENT.

*** NOTE**

The 4 logics of SHEN KU are jointly relevant & inextricably interlinked. Together and with devastating applicability proportional to species advancement they govern **ALL conscious progress in ALL situations throughout ALL of time, transcending ALL frontiers.............. *...INTERGALACTICALLY***

WOO CHIN

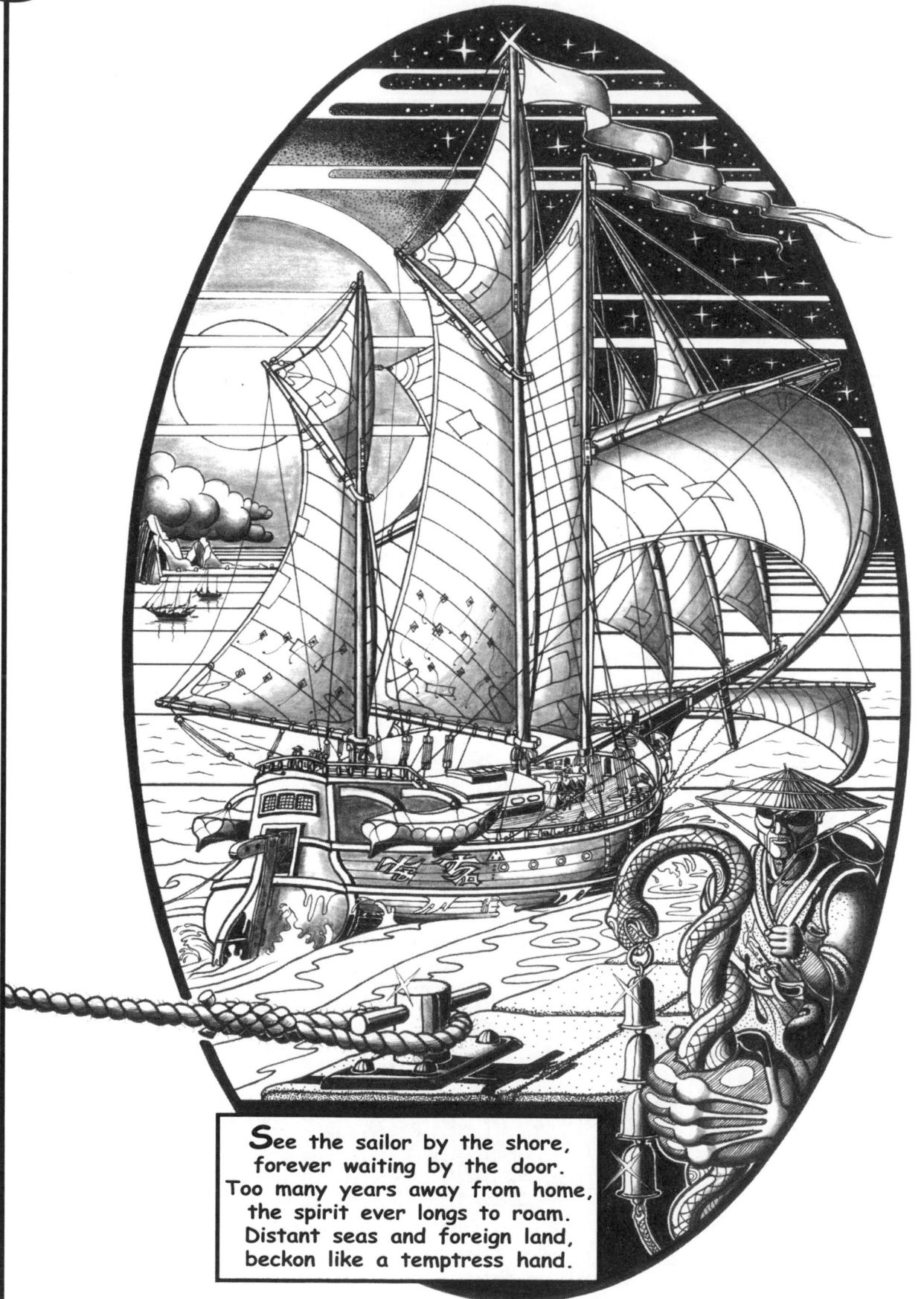

See the sailor by the shore,
forever waiting by the door.
Too many years away from home,
the spirit ever longs to roam.
Distant seas and foreign land,
beckon like a temptress hand.

- **AMPUTATION** (accidentally severed digit or limb) - Control bleeding as for "open wound" using elevation & pressure. - **Put severed item in sealed plastic bag & pack with ice**. - *GET SURGICAL HELP SOON.*
- **BRUISES** - Slow blood flow to injured area by elevation & cold compresses.
- **BURNS & SCALDS** (pain, red/gray skin, swelling, blisters, peeling). - **Immediately cool injured area for about 10 minutes in cold running water** (don't use ice). - Remove rings, shoes etc. as area may swell. - Cover with clean non-fluffy dressing (e.g.. torn sheet). - Do not touch burn. - *CHECK FOR SHOCK.*
- **CHILDBIRTH** - **Do not interfere unless problems develop**. - Mother on back or left side. - Observe scrupulous cleanliness. - Allow head to self deliver. - *CHECK FOR TANGLED UMBILICAL CORD.* - Clean baby's face & nose. - Support head & gently assist after shoulder delivers. - Hold baby up by ankles & *IF NOT BREATHING SLAP BACK TO STIMULATE.* - Wrap baby warmly. - Tie umbilical cord with sterile thread at 6, 8 & 10 inches from baby. - Cut cord between 8 & 10 inches from baby & dress end. - Afterbirth should deliver soon. - **Keep placenta for doctor to see.** - Give mother a warm drink & have her breastfeed baby.
- **CHOKING** (victim silent or gags, red face & grasps throat, blue lips & mouth) - Remove false teeth &/or mouth debris. - **Encourage victim to cough.** - Bend victim over with head lower than lungs & *STRIKE BETWEEN SHOULDER BLADES WITH FLAT OF HAND.*
- **CRAMP** (tight pain in muscle) - As a cramp is an involuntary contraction, **gently stretch** & massage muscle (e.g. calf, stretch by moving foot toward shin).
- **CUTS** - Clean with antiseptic. - Hold edges together with tape. - Keep dry.
- **FAINTING** - Lie victim with feet elevated or sit with head down.
- **FITS** (victim often cries out & falls down, muscles stiffen, back arches, violent vomiting) - **Don't panic (observer).** - Ensure safe location by moving objects. - Put rubber pad or book corner between teeth. - Let victim sleep after fit passes.
- **FOOD POISONING** (nausea, stomach pain [2 - 6 hours after eating], vomiting & diarrhea). - *VERY CONTAGIOUS.* - Rest. - **No food but a lot to drink.**
- **FRACTURES** - Align & immobilise limb with splints & elevate.
- **FROSTBITE** (extremities white, blue & black). - *WARM GRADUALLY.*
- **HEAT STROKE** (sweating, dizzy, nausea, cramps, collapse, unconscious) - Strip naked & cool slowly (e.g. in a cool [not cold] bath). - Give sips cold water with salt.

continued over ⟶

ABBREVIATED	C.P.R	TECHNIQUES
ADULT		**CHILD (extra notes)**
MOUTH TO MOUTH • UNCONSCIOUS OR NOT? (slap face). • SHOUT &/or send for help. • ROLL VICTIM on back. • OPEN/CLEAR AIRWAY & lift chin. • BREATHING OR NOT? (check). • GIVE 4 QUICK breaths. • PULSE OR NOT? (side of neck).		• OPEN AIRWAY by your hand under small of young child's back. • COVER MOUTH & NOSE of child with your mouth. • SHALLOW FAST BREATHS.
HEART MASSAGE • KNEEL CLOSE to side of victim. • LOCATE COMPRESSION POINT (just above where ribs meet) on breastbone. • WITH YOUR ARMS STRAIGHT & hands one on top of the other, compress victims chest 1 1/2 inches 75 times/minute BUT STOP EVERY 15 COMPRESSIONS TO GIVE 2 BREATHS.		• COMPRESS CHEST (between nipples) with FINGERS ONLY. • 5 COMPRESSIONS then 1 breath etc. • RATE OF 100/MINUTE.

(continued)

● **HEART ATTACK** (**sudden crushing pain in center of chest radiating into throat & arms [particularly left side]**) - Pain not reduced by antacid or belching. Ashen face. Weak pulse - Get professional help fast - If not Available : <u>**Minimise work of heart**</u> - Sit victim - Loosen clothes - Keep warm - Reassure - Check pulse & breathing & *BE READY TO GIVE C.P.R. - WATCH FOR SHOCK.*

● **HICCUPS** - Sit quietly - Take long drink - Hold breath - Put open paper bag (not plastic) over nose & mouth & breath in & out.

● **HYPOTHERMIA** (shivering to unconscious) - Warm victim - <u>**Starting with heart area first.**</u>

● **INSECT STINGS** - If sting still in skin, pull out with tweezers - Apply cold compress &/or surgical spirit - For jellyfish stings calamine lotion is helpful (vinegar, or alcohol also work).

"Doctor, Doctor,
I can't feel my foot........."

● **NOSEBLEED** - Sit up - Lean forward a little - Breath thru mouth - Keep still - Pinch nostrils together for 5 minutes - Apply cold compress to bridge of nose - *PLUG NOSE IF REQUIRED.*

● **OPEN WOUND** (serious blood loss) - *ACT FAST* - If wound is wide open, gently close - Elevate body part - <u>**Hold edges of "gash" type wounds together with butterfly bandaid plasters**</u> - Cover with clean pad & apply pressure (5 - 15 mins.) - If necessary apply additional dressings on top (but do not disturb original) - <u>**In serious cases apply intermittent pressure on supplying arteries**</u> - Removal of penetrating foreign bodies not usually recommended - *VICTIM MAY ALSO BE SUFFERING FROM SHOCK.*

● **SHOCK** (cold pale &/or gray skin, rapid but faint pulse, nausea, irregular breathing, possible collapse) - *DANGEROUS CONDITION*, treat seriously - Comfort physically - Keep warm - Don't move - Lie on side if sick - Loosen clothing - Reassure - No smoking.

● **STRAIN** (sudden sharp muscle pain usually during awkward or heavy exertion) - If strain serious : Immediately apply ice/cold compress for half hour - Elevate limb - Wrap site with layers of cotton wool & bandage firmly - Rest limb.

● **STROKE** (blockage in blood supply to brain, symptoms vary but are sudden) - Lie victim down with head to side - *GET TO HOSPITAL.*

● **TOOTHACHE** - Apply oil of cloves to tooth (not gum) & get help.

● **TRAVEL SICKNESS** - <u>**Prevention better than cure**</u> - Avoid acidic foods & alcohol on empty stomach - En route avoid confined spaces, getting cold, engine/cooking fumes & reading - Do look at horizon, get fresh air, eat crackers/soup - Get plenty of sleep. Take Vit B6 &/or ginger.

SAMPLE FIRST AID KIT	DRESSINGS	EQUIPMENTS	MEDICINALS	DRUGS
	● Assorted plasters. ● Cotton wool. ● Assorted bandages. ● Adhesive bandage. ● Eye dressing. ● Finger dressing. ● Burn dressing. ● Gauze swabs. ● Butterfly shape adhesive strips for closing open wounds. ● Larger size sterile pads in individual packs.	● Stainless scissors. ● Stainless tweezers. ● Thermometer. ● Eye bath. ● Safety pins. ● Disp. syringes. ● Inflatable splint. ● Sterile needle & thread in pack. ● Finger stalls.	● Antiseptic cream. ● Antacid tablets. ● Dilutable liquid antiseptic wash. ● High factor U.V. cream. ● Calamine lotion. ● U.V lip salve. ● Aspirin or similar. ● Travel sickness pills. ● Iodine.	● Several courses broad spectrum antibiotics (oral). ● Antibiotic powder (open sore/wound). ● Antibiotic eye drops or ointment. ● Antifungal ear drops. ● Strong nonaddictive pain relief (pref. oral).

English	Please	Where	Chemist	Doctor	Hospital
Spanish	Por Favor	Donde	La Farmacia	El Medico	El Hospital
French	S'il vous plait	Ou	La Pharmacie	Le Medecin	L' Hopital

Recognize & Understand Your Problems Earlier Not Later

NAME	SYMPTOMS	DIAGRAMS
ALLERGY	<u>Nasal congestion - Sneezing</u> - Diarrhea - Depression - Headache - Stomach ache - Rashes - Irritated eyes - Skin rashes.	CROSS EYES (both in) 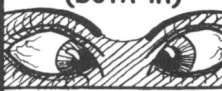
ANEMIA	<u>Fatigue - Pale skin, nails & hair</u> - Shiny tongue - Cracked mouth corners - Dizzy - Breathless - Fast pulse - Swollen ankles.	BOTH OUT 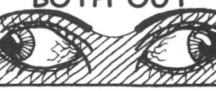
ARTHRITIS	<u>Joint swelling - Joint pain</u> - Stiffness of joints - Can be one, or several or all joints - Can come & even go erratically.	ONE O.K 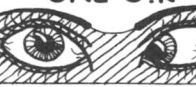
ASTHMA	<u>Short of breath - Wheezing</u> - Coughing - Tight chest feeling - Hard to breathe out - Can be caused by allergy in or out of body.	
BLOOD (press. high)	<u>Dizzy - Tired - Broken capillaries</u> in places (e.g. end of nose) - Tendency to cross eyes - Occasional blurred vision.	& ONE IN.
BLOOD (circ. bad)	<u>Face & nose red in the cold</u> - Dark bags under eyes - Tendency to skin ulcers - Dark lips & tongue - Red hands - Tummy ache.	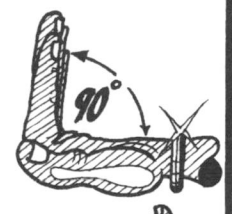
BLADDER (problem)	<u>Cloudy urine - Yellow tongue</u> - Dry throat - Frequent painful urination - Red heel on palm - Tired - Bitter taste - Backache.	
BOWELS (color)	<u>Yellow</u> = Faulty fat metabolism - <u>Red</u> = Blood from intestines - <u>Dirty white</u> = Liver or gall bladder - <u>Black</u> = Various (bleeding).	
CANCER	<u>Jaundice - Anemia - Nausea</u> - Green face - Eyes turn out - Chest & head pains - Black tongue root - Thin eyebrows - Fat tummy.	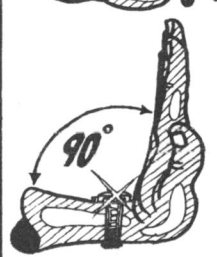
CANCER (children)	<u>Large pupils (eyes)</u> - Continuous nausea - Bumps - Lumps on body - Mole changes - Long-term pain in arms or legs - Anemia.	
CANCER (breast)	<u>When wet (bath/shower)</u> systematically examine all parts of breast for any lump or irregularity - Check nipple for discharge.	
CANCER (skin)	<u>Hands, face, neck, shoulders</u> - Check for unusual & changing marks (thickening, scaliness & moles [pearl, brown, black]).	MILK ALLERGY
CHOLESTEROL (too much)	<u>Bend fingers back</u> (should reach 90 degrees.) - Then bend hand back at wrist (should reach 90 degrees without undue pain).	● Cramps. ● Bloating. ● Fatigue.
CIRCULATION (check)	<u>Compare the temperature</u> of one foot with the other - Also the strength of pulse in each — a difference may be from narrow arteries.	● Depression. ● Rash etc.
CONSTIPATION	<u>Depression - Swollen tummy</u> (& lower lip) - Face red - Coated tongue - Anal spasms & hard stools - Acid & toxin irritation of intestines.	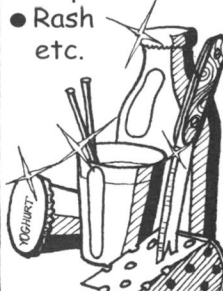
DIABETES	<u>Tired - Blurred sight</u> - One eye turned in - Dry skin with spots & boils - Thirsty & hungry - Feet & fingers hurt - Cramps - Itching.	
DYSENTRY	<u>Pain in tummy - Bloody stools</u> - Fever - Headache - Vomiting - Red eyes - Frequent small quantities of dirty brown urine.	
EPILEPSY	<u>Loud cry - Dizzy - Pale blank face</u> - Fat lips (with foam) - Big pupils - Blackout - Spasms with convulsive jerking (of entire body).	TO TEST
EYES (cataracts)	<u>Progressive blurring of sight</u> with bright objects (lights) appearing double - Sections of a viewed object appear to be missing.	● <u>On empty stomach</u> drink two glasses of cold milk.
EYES (detatched retina)	<u>Sight blurs from one side</u> like curtain - Flashes of light & small shadows which "float" around are common after.	
EYES (glaucoma)	<u>Poor side vision - Halos around lights</u> - Dull aches around eyes - Intermittant blurring of sight - Deteriorating night sight - Watering.	● <u>Check if your symptoms</u> (such as sinuses/joint
FEMALE SEX (organ trouble)	<u>Irregular periods - Dark shadows under eyes</u> - Split ends (head hair) - Darker lips (& gums) - Horizontal line on lip under nose.	pain) return.

A VOYAGER'S GUIDE TO AILMENTS BY PHYSICAL SYMPTOMS
Recognize & Understand Your Problems Earlier Not Later

NAME	SYMPTOMS	DIAGRAMS
GALLSTONES	**Fatty food intolerance** resulting in nausea & yellow tint to white of eye - Bloated upper eyelid - Upper tummy pain - Yellow coated tongue.	Name this problem
GASTRITIS	**Tummy pains** (more when empty [reduces with antacid or food]) - Very yellow urine - Smelly, watery, gassy stools - Feel cold & get fever.	"NOW IS YOUR INDEX WHY IS YOUR BIGMOUTH LIKE THAT?".
HEART (warning signs)	**Red face & bulbous nose** - Shiny red tongue with crack down middle - Bloated - Short of breath - Tired - Cleft nose - Swollen fingers & toes.	
HEPATITIS	**Dirty red/yellow foamy urine** - Yellow tongue - Nausea - Thirsty - Not hungry - Bitter taste in mouth - Headache - Feel cold with fever.	
HIATUS HERNIA	**Backwash of stomach acid** - Sharp pain in mid chest - Heartburn - Eased by alkaline foods, raising head in bed, loosening tight belts.	
HYPOGLYCEMIA (low blood sugar)	**Intermittent fatigue & anxiety** with fast pulse & cold hands - When hungry have dizzy spells, headaches - Eating lots of sugar snacks.	Shiny & red with split.
INTESTINES (problems)	**Nausea - Spots - Tummy cramps** - Swollen bottom lip - Side of thumb turns blue - Coated tongue - Thirsty - Chills & fever.	**MUSCLE BALANCE**
JAUNDICE	**Yellow palms, gums & whites of eye** - Dizzy after eating - Cold extremities - Coated tongue - Swollen tummy - Not hungry.	● Examine your footprints (wet or in sand).
KIDNEY (problems)	**Painful, difficult, frequent urination** (bloody or cloudy) - Dark bags under eyes - Back & headache - Tired - Red ears & Dark face.	
LEUKEMIA	**Anemia - Diarrhea - Dizziness** - Prone to bleeding (incl. urine & stools) - Swollen tummy - Aches in head & body - Pale - Fever.	
LIVER (problems)	**Yellow palms, nails & face - Dandruff** - Sides of tongue red - Swollen legs & upper lip - Red in eye white - Emotional - Not hungry.	
LUNG (problems)	**Spittle which is contaminated with pus** (green or yellow) - Coated tongue - Small nostrils - Pale skin - Intermittent chest pain & fever.	BALANCED
MENSTRUATION (problems)	**Backache - Low energy - Dizzy** - Dark red lips & gums - Blue shadows under eyes - Tongue tip red - Dark clots in menstruation - Cold hands.	
NERVES (problems)	**Tired - Ill-tempered - Insomnia** - Tongue will not stretch straight & trembles - Cuticles irritated - Dizzy - Headache - Fingers tremble.	
PARKINSON'S (disease)	**Pronounced trembling of hands & feet** - Rigidity of muscles (particularly noted in face) - Shuffling short steps - Arms in front.	LEFT SIDE OUT
PROSTATE (problems)	**Desire to urinate frequently** - Burning even painful (sometimes with blood) urination - Lower back & crotch pain - Bladder not empty.	
SCHIZOPHRENIA	**Hallucination - Paranoia** - Nonuniform horizontal lines on forehead - Increased suicidal tendencies - Illogical perspective.	
SINUSITIS	**Blocked nasal passages** - Feeling of weight in head - Sticky yellow nasal discharge - Dizzy - Headache - Memory poor - Fever.	
STOMACH (problems)	**Base & middle of tongue red** - Cyst(s) at side of chapped lips - Yellow tinge to face - Side of thumb blue tinge - Bad breath - Nausea.	RIGHT SIDE OUT
STOMACH (ulcers)	**In addition to above - Acidic burning** & pain + swelling - Dry throat - Frequent hiccups - Stools sticky/bloody - Relieved with alkaline foods.	
THYROID (underactive)	**Tired (low energy) - Heavy mens.** - Slow speech in constricted voice - Thick hair - Bloated face with dry skin - Feels cold easily.	
THYROID (overactive)	**Feels hot - Perspires easily** - Hair loss - Fast heartbeat - Highly strung - Losing weight - Light mens. - Heart palpitations - Trembling.	BOTH SIDES OUT

Ancient Origins From Across The Cultural & Geographic Spectrum

THE HEALING PLANT with a vast diversity of internal & external uses which is both pleasant to apply & easy to grow - MARVELOUS.

"WHAT, WHAT, WHAT IS IT ?"

● **CLINICAL COMPOSITION** is complex & not fully understood but works much better as a healer when all its many parts are used together - Some of its known contents are : ● Saponing ● Biogenic stimulators ● Zinc ● Mannose ● Calcium ● Galactose ● Tannin ● Potassium ● Organic acids ● Arabinose ● Glucose ● Copper ● Oxidase ● Iron ● Antibiotics ● Catalase ● Amylase ● Xylose ● Glucuronic acid ● Sodium ● Choline ● Steroids ● Manganese ● 18 amino acids ● Various vitamins, enzymes, hormones, pentoses, uronic acids etc.

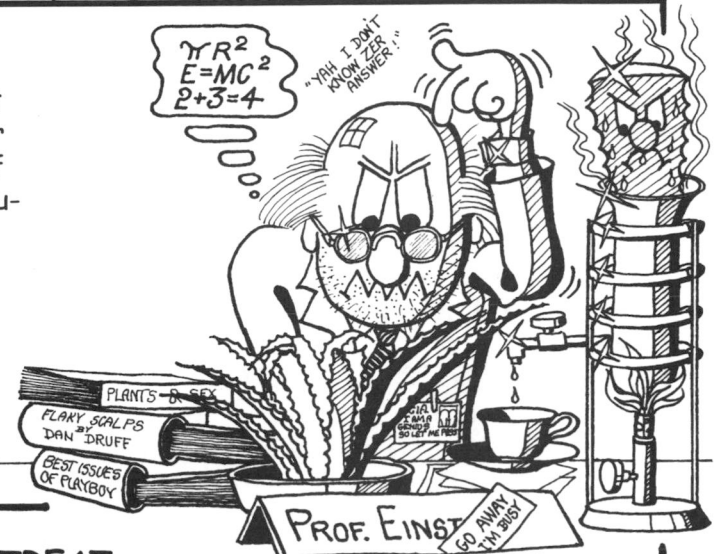

$$\Upsilon R^2$$
$$E = MC^2$$
$$2 + 3 = 4$$

"YAH I DON'T KNOW ZER ANSWER!"

PLANTS & SEX

FLAKY SCALPS BY DAN DRUFF

BEST ISSUES OF PLAYBOY

PROF. EINST...   GO AWAY I'M BUSY

WHAT HAS IT BEEN USED TO TREAT

● Acne ● Age/Liver spots ● Allergies ● Anemia ● Arthritis ● Asthma ● Bed wetting ● Bed sores ● Burns (heat, flame, electrical, chemical [wash first] & radiation) ● Bronchitis ● Boils ● Bleeding (reduction) ● Bile (cleanse liver of) ● Blood pressure (high) ● Colic ● Constipation ● Congestion (nasal) ● Chicken pox (blisters) ● Cataracts ● Dandruff ● Dermatitis ● Ezcema ● Eyesight (weak) ● Fatigue ● Festering sores ● Fever ● Gangrene ● Gum/Mouth problems ● Hair loss ● Headache ● Hemorrhoids ● Hair conditioner ● Impetigo ● Insect stings & bites ● Insomnia ● Itching ● Influenza ● Indigestion & gas ● Kidney stones ● Meningitis ● Menstruation (delayed) ● Muscle aches ● Nutritional supplement ● Parasitic worms ● Pain (burns, bites, rashes etc) ● Psoriasis ● Ringworm ● Sunburn ● Snake bite ● Strains/Sprains ● Shingles ● Toothache ● Tuberculosis ● Ulcers (all types including stomach) ● Upset stomach ● Varicose veins ● Venereal diseases ● Warts/Corns ● Wind/Sun protection - **CAUTION RECOMMENDED IF USING ALOE VERA WITH DIABETES &/OR PREGNANCY.**

ALOE VERA GEL — MADE IN THE JUNGLE

BOTANICAL DESCRIPTION

● **NAME:** Aloe Barbadenisis.
● **ALSO KNOWN AS:** "Lu - Hui" (China), "Ja - Dam" (Malaysia), "Sa - Vila" (Spain), "Crocodile Tail" (Thailand)
● **FAMILY:** One of about 200 worldwide "Xerolds" with the ability to self-seal cut ends & direct growth elsewhere (very hardy). ● **COLORS:** From bright green to gray (a few have stripes).

ALLERGIES

● In more than 99% of humans Aloe Vera acts as an anti-allergenic - However a small number (less than 1%) react adversely (test on inner forearm or underarm for rash or stinging usually in minutes.

Use **ALOE VERA** to: Reduce the pain, heal & combat the toxicity of RADIATION, BURNS.

TREATMENT EXAMPLES

● **ASTHMA**/Sinus : Boil a pint of water with peeled aloe vera leaves added. Inhale the vapors (or put juice in an atomizer & insert in nostril).
● **ARTHRITIS:** 2 - 4 tablespoons (according to body weight) several times daily of juice/gel (plus local external applications as required).
● **BURNS:** The ultimate natural treatment for burns of all types (sun, radiation, dry heat, scalds, acid (wash well first) - Even serious burns can be treated for pain, healing & anti-scarring by keeping the area wet with gel for 24 - 72 hours. AMAZING!

HOW TO GROW ALOE VERA

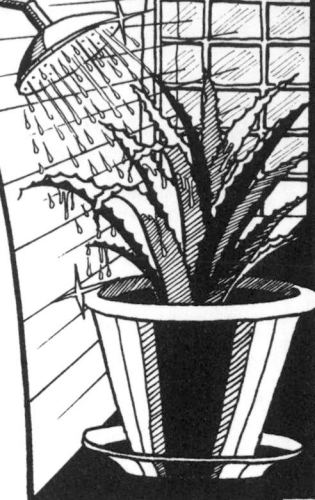

- **LIGHT:** Bright indirect sun produces best results (too much strong sun will turn the leaves brown - Too little light may cause leaves to lay flat).
- **POT GROWING:** Aloe Vera can stand most soil types (Excess alkalinity causes slow growth) & limited pot size (but must be well drained).
- **REPOT** only when mother plant gets top-heavy, turns bright green, sends out leaves horizontally &/or produces many baby shoots.
- **BABY SHOOTS:** Remove from mother plant when 3 1/2 inches long. Plant separately & water well (then withhold water [for 10 - 20 days] to force root growth) - May grow brown or grayish before recovering a stronger plant.
- **OUTDOOR** plants are usually stronger & grow faster.

- **WATERING:** Very little in winter (modestly once a week) - Too much causes slow growth (roots will rot & plant will fall over) - If leaves shrink & curl .... give water - In summer water freely (but ensure good drainage).
- **TEMPERATURE:** Semi - arid, tropical or temperate preferred (protect from freezing).
- **SIZE:** Larger plants are considered more potent (always use lower leaves first). - Young plants are still usable medicinally.

HOW TO USE ALOE VERA

- **INTERNAL USE:** Peel leaf & rinse gel very well to remove all the bitter yellow sap (which can be used as a **LAXATIVE**) the gel itself is almost tasteless (with a vague medicinal flavor).
- **GENERAL HEALTH SUPPLEMENT:** Take one tablespoon of juice/gel daily.
- **TO DRINK:** Either cube the gel & soak in a glass of water in the fridge, or mix liquidized gel (or juice) with a fruit (or other palatable drink). • **TO EAT:** Chop or mash chilled gel & use imagination to serve in a salad or dessert etc. • **REFRIGERATED** juice/gel/cut leaves will keep for several days (particularly if kept in an airtight container [or plastic wrap]).

- **EXTERNAL USE:** Slice off edges & skin from flat side .... apply directly to skin (when surface of gel dries, scrape with knife until wet again). • **ASTRINGENT** (drying) qualities in Aloe Vera mean that in some applications it is best applied with a moisturizing oil (such as olive or almond [either in or after the Aloe Vera]). • **VITAMINS A & E** are also sometimes added to futher enhance external healing qualities.

MORE TREATMENT EXAMPLES

- **CONGESTED/IRRITATED NASAL SKIN** surfaces (in & out) are soothed, healed & decongested (also cold sores) by applying Aloe Vera gel.
- **CONSTIPATION:** Soak leaf skin peelings in a glass of chilled water & use as required.
- **CUTS/WOUNDS/GRAZES:** Wash then dress with gel or juice to inhibit infection, aid healing & minimize scarring. • **DANDRUFF/FALLING HAIR** & other scalp problems: Apply gel or juice & leave on overnight (also conditions hair). • **DIGESTION, KIDNEY FUNCTION & STOMACH ULCERS** are all aided by ingesting a tablespoon of gel/juice several times daily.
- **EAR/EYE DROPS** of pure juice (or diluted 50/50 with sterile water [for eyes]) soothe & heal most irritations/ infections. • **HEMORRHOIDS & other ANAL PROBLEMS** respond well to the anal insertion of pealed leaf. • **SKIN PROBLEMS** of all types (even **CANCER**) have responded well to multiple (2 - 6) applications/ day of juice/gel (over a 2 - 6 month period [don't forget the moisturizer]).
- **SORE THROAT:** Mix juice/gel with warm water & gargle often.
- **VARICOSE VEINS & RUPTURED CAPILLARIES** can improve dramatically with a combination of both internal & external applications several times/day for 4 months. *ABSOLUTELY UNBELIEVABLE - BUT TRUE!*

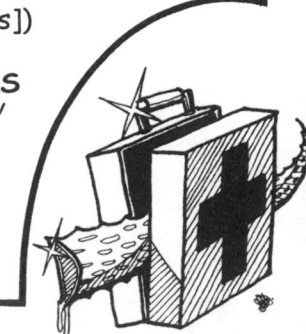

Exercise Your Eyes & See Better Without Glasses

As the girdle is to the flabby stomach, so glasses are to weak eye muscles - BOTH MAKE THE CONDITION WORSE, not better.

Some contributing (BEFORE STARTING) causes of bad vision.

- **WEAK EYE MUSCLES:** Caused mainly by letting glasses do the work of the eye muscles <u>(which progressively become weaker as the glasses become progressively stronger).</u>

- **PHYSICAL CONDITION:** If the body is run down (or out of condition) the operation of the eyes will be adversely affected - Therefore, maintaining the circulation, muscle tone (& general health) <u>of the entire body is of vital importance.</u>

- **MENTAL STRESS** is caused by/results in tense muscles & fatigue (which in turn causes inflexible eye muscles [unable to focus properly]) - Therefore, relaxation is of primary importance in improving vision (& <u>relaxing the eyes, relaxes the whole body</u> [& mind]).

- **FOOD** <u>is perhaps the most important factor</u>, because without adequate nutrition neither the mental nor physical (including eyes) status is likely to improve — Therefore, sufficient vitamins, minerals & natural healthy food are prerequisites to substantial progress.

- **ALLERGIES** can indirectly make a pronounced difference to the clarity of your vision by seriously effecting your metabolism (muscle & nerve responses can deteriorate markedly) - <u>Find out & eliminate yours as a matter of priority</u> (almost all of us have at least a few allergies).

- **THEREFORE** more exercise (& less visual aids) + better nutrition (& relaxation) = MEASURABLE SIGHT IMPROVEMENT IN 7 DAYS.

RELAXATION & CIRCULATORY STIMULATION TECHNIQUES

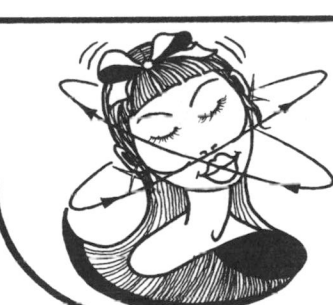

- **"ROLL THE HEAD":** Sight can be aided by relaxing the neck (which in turn relaxes the eyes), with eyes closed gently flop your head to the side & roll it slowly round (as if it were a heavy weight) a couple of times in each direction.

- **SWAYING** the whole body slowly & rythmatically from side to side is similar in principle to "Roll the Head," (but relaxes both body & mind [& thus benefits the eyes]) - Best position is in front of a window *(YOU MAY NOTICE A DREAMLIKE QUALITY DEVELOP WITH THIS EXERCISE).*

- **SHRUGGING** the shoulders as high as possible (hold for a few seconds & release) - Repeat several times & *FEEL THE TENSION DRAIN AWAY.*

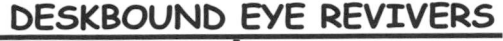

DESKBOUND EYE REVIVERS

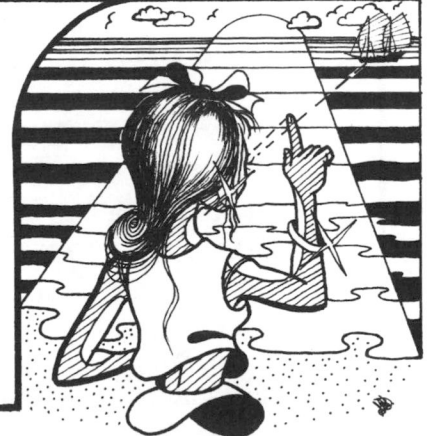

- **BLINKING** rapidly while rolling the eye <u>massages the eye balls,</u> exercises the lid muscles & improves blood circulation in the eye region (15 - 20 seconds is enough).

- **FOCAL LENGTH STRETCH** requires you to <u>use the muscles which adjust your distance focus</u> - Put your finger up & focus on it, then without moving anything focus beyond your finger on a more distant object (feel your eyes change shape) - Do it a few times looking to the front, to each side, up & down.

ON WAKING, EYE RELAXATION & EXERCISE PROGRAM

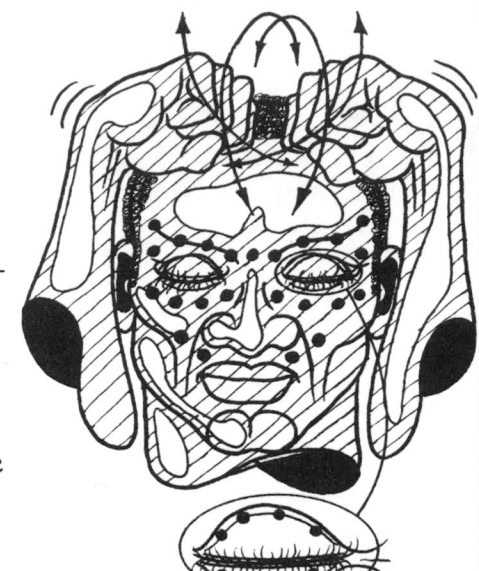

- **"KNUCKLE YOUR BROW"** using the first joints of your fists - *"Roll"* the knuckles slowly over your scalp & forehead - Pressing quite hard & pausing in sensitive places **(you will often feel a notable reduction in pressure [& increase in circulation] immediately).**

- **STIMULATE YOUR FACE** by pressing with rigid fingers (one each hand) around the face (see sketch) & temples - Press quite hard & hold for a few seconds in each position.

- **STIMULATE YOUR EYEBALLS** (with eyelids closed) by looking down & then gently press (one finger each eye) 4 points across the top of the covered eyeball (under the brow bone) - Then look up & press 4 points across the bottom of the covered eyeball.

- **PALMING (A)** __is a physically theraputic & mystically remedial practice__ which calms the mind & relaxes the body while encouraging the flow of energy forces thru & into the eyes - First cover your closed eyes with the palms of your (or someone else's) slightly cupped hands & tell yourself *"My eyes are very relaxed - My body is very realxed"* (& as you tell yourself this, consciously relax each part of your body, starting & finishing with your eyes - Then tell yourself *"When I remove my palms my eyes will be rested & strong."*

- **PALMING (B)** may also be continued while actually exercising the eye muscles. Cover the closed eyes as in (A) .... then (pausing a second or two at each station) commence *"looking"* as far as possible toward 12 o'clock, 1 o'clock, 2 etc. - When you reach 12 again return counterclockwise (do this several times).

- **FINISH** by turning both eyes toward the center (at the same time) & holding for a few seconds.

IMPORTANT HINTS

- **BLINK** on average about 10 times a minute (or once every 5 seconds) particularly when reading (or operating a computer) - **Your eye endurance will improve immediately.**

- **COLD BATHING** of your closed eyes (am & pm [splash cold water with cupped palms]) **will shrink bloodshot capillaries & immediately after, improve circulation** (feel the glow).

- **SUNBATHE** your closed eyelids for a few minutes, a few times a day & feel the penetrating warmth relax **(& encourage blood flow right thru)** your eyeballs.

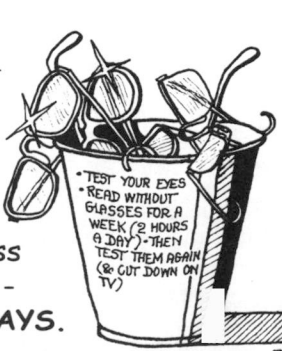

- **GLASSES** are a substitute for eye muscle usage - & like any muscle, the less you use it, the weaker it gets - Start today & try reading without them - YOU CAN DO IT.... & YOUR EYES WILL BE STRONGER IN JUST 7 DAYS.

*Your body is 65% water - Make sure it is pure water -
Or you may NOT LIVE NEARLY AS LONG as you otherwise might.*

THE PROBLEMS

● **WHAT** do indigestible, inorganic minerals in almost all available water supplies (including tap, reservoir, spring/mineral [including bottled] well, river etc.) do to our bodies starting from infancy until death?

● **BLOOD:** Cause the build up of <u>Atherosclerosis</u> (gummy deposits) on the walls of arteries, veins, blood vessels & capillaries resulting in <u>decreased blood supply to the whole body</u> (particularly extremities) with symptoms ranging from: <u>Cold hands/feet & broken capillaries to premature senility & heart attacks.</u>

● **JOINTS:** Contribute directly & indirectly to <u>arthritis, rheumatism & bone spurs etc.</u> (thru calcification) - <u>Thus to pain, reduced activity & more rapid aging.</u>

● **ORGANS:** Contribute to <u>the formation of calcified "stones" in the kidneys, gall bladder &/or pancreas, with possibly terminal complications</u> ● **A** = Water pipe when new ● **A1** = Artery at birth ● **B** = After 40 years of mineralized water, flow is decreased dramatically ● **B1** = After 40 years of poor diet & inorganic mineral saturated water the bodies blood supply system is close to critical ● **C** = After 80 years, high mains pressure is required to force any water thru! ● **C1** = <u>If, IF this person is still alive, blood distribution is extremely difficult!....</u>

A WATERPIPE   AN ARTERY

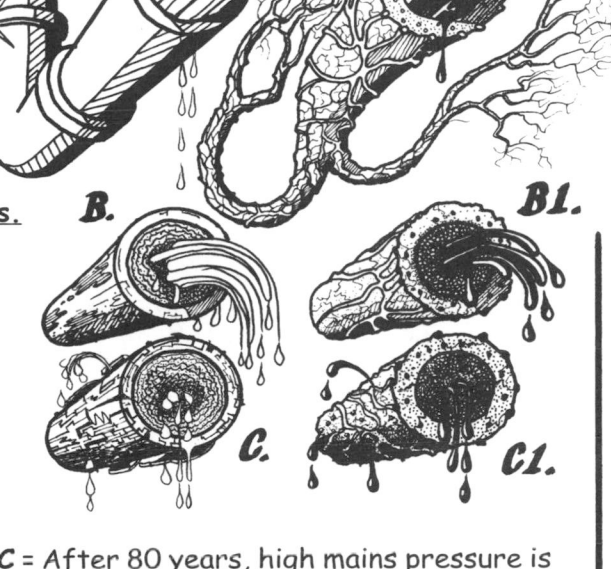

.....DON'T DO THIS TO YOURSELF - IT IS ENTIRELY PREVENTABLE.

HOW IT GETS INTO YOUR BLOOD

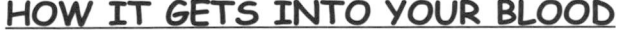

* **LIME** (calcium) along with many other minerals is in suspension in most water supplies (see it in kettles, sinks etc.) - <u>The particles are too minute to be effectively filtered out! - They pass thru the walls of the small intestine & into the liver</u> (which attempts to filter out impurities [& unwanted excesses]) & to supply the body with only that which is needed - **BUT IF THE BURDEN IS TOO GREAT ....** <u>the impurities are passed thru the liver & distributed around the body</u>, where they accumulate progressively (as detailed at top) clogging up living tissues until sooner or later (according to levels of toxicity) **THEY DIE.**

OTHER DEMONS IN WATER

● **FLUORIDE** in water has been blamed by respected researchers for <u>raising your risk by about 10% of developing cancer.</u>
● **CHLORINE** in water has been blamed in various sad examples as a major cause of <u>premature senility, birth defects, miscarriage, heart disease & cancer.</u>
* **LIME** is a broad name for: 1) Carbonate (chalk), 2) Sulphate (plaster of Paris), 3) Phosphate (bonemeal), which together with: Sodium, magnesium & nitrates are the most common inorganic mineral contaminants of "natural" drinking water.

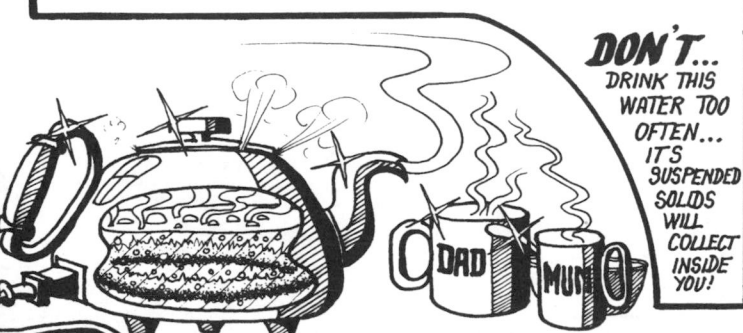

DON'T... DRINK THIS WATER TOO OFTEN... IT'S SUSPENDED SOLIDS WILL COLLECT INSIDE YOU!

DAD   MUM

SEA WATER....

.... (unpolluted) contains all known minerals required by the body, **BUT** not necessarily in the right proportions + vastly too much salt (sodium chloride).
SEA KELP tablets are a useful multimineral supplement.

WHAT OTHER DRINK CONTENTS ARE DOING TO YOU

● **SUGAR**, the most common ingredient of "leisure" drinks, but it: - Contributes dramatically to <u>dental decay</u>, - <u>Depletes the body's stock of minerals</u> - Attacks <u>mucus membranes</u> throughout the body - Contributes to susceptibility of diseases (such as <u>appendicitis, polio, diabetes & cancer</u>).

● **ALCOHOL**, apart from causing organ & metabolic stress, <u>literally dissolves various body substances</u> (such as cerebrose [a brain sugar] - which leads to <u>cerebral diabetes</u>).

● **ARTIFICIAL COLORS & PRESERVATIVES** etc. (in drinks such as carbonated colas etc.) are widely consumed by our children, & have been directly linked to disturbed brain activity (<u>such as aggression & hyperactivity) which can appear within minutes of consumption yet take weeks to be eliminated</u> (with possible residual cell damage).

SO WHAT **CAN** I DRINK?

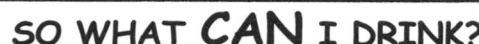

● <u>**DISTILLED** water is the ultimate in purity,</u> with maximum impurities left behind during evaporation - Drinking distilled water only, will in time flush away accumulated excess mineralized deposits in joints, organs & blood vessels (but will not remove minerals required for well-being already integrated into the body by metabolism).

● <u>**RAIN WATER** may be pure & distilled at cloud level,</u> but once it condenses & starts to fall to earth (or sea) it collects pollutants from the atmosphere (thru which it passes) - Chemical toxins can be concentrated in industrialized areas (& downwind of them for large distances [particles are wind-borne]).

● <u>**VEGETABLE & FRUIT** juices (raw & fresh) are naturally distilled fluids</u> full of enzymes, vitamins, organic (as opposed to inorganic) minerals & nutrients in natural balances, & are easily metabolized. - Buy (or make [my simple design at right]) an electric (or mechanical) juicer & **TRANSFORM YOUR BODY'S NUTRITION OVERNIGHT.**

● Sliding stainless cup with fruit in.

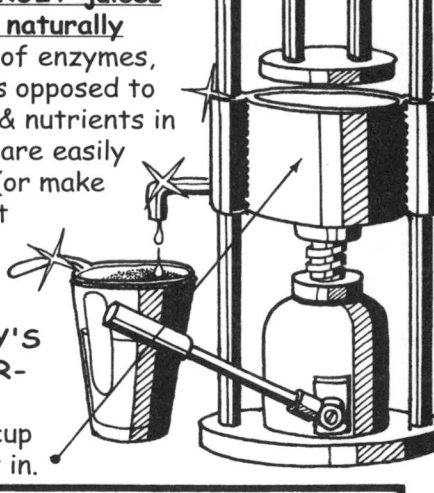

TEST NOW FOR CALCIFICATION

● **CAN YOU** put palms on floor (knees straight)?
● **CAN YOU** kick higher than your head?
● **CAN YOU** do a "crab" (upside down on floor)?
● **ALL TOO HARD** - Stand in a corner - O.K.? Do your fingers (together) bend back at 90 degrees? (see sketch p.131)

WATERMELON....

.... <u>is recognised as an efficient eliminator of crystallized inorganic mineral deposits in the body</u> - The most efficient form of elimination being a fast (up to a week) on watermelon juice & fruit only - Take a urine sample, seal it in a glass bottle & let it sit for a few months (6 better) - Observe (or have analyzed) the calcium & magnesium carbonates (& other toxins) which settle on the bottom - **FLUSHED FROM YOUR BODY!**

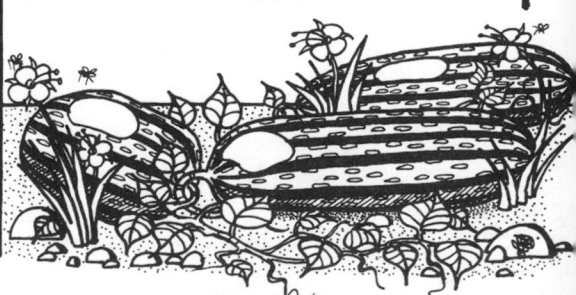

DISTILLER DESIGN

(Material = Stainless Steel)

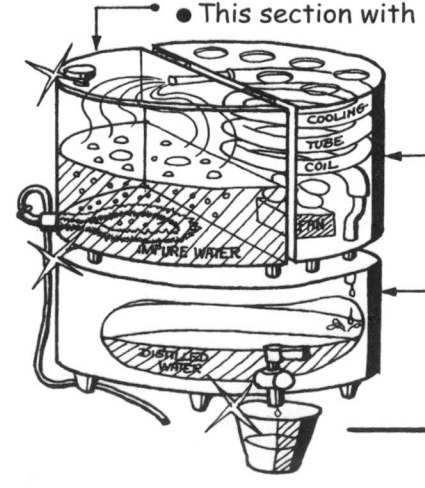

● This section with hinged sealing lid contains heating element (& impure water) with connecting pipe thru, insulated wall to this ....

● .... section (with vents on top & cloth-covered pipe kept damp with pinhole at start) cooled by fan at bottom (which condenses steam) going into this ....

● .... section which collects the pure distilled water. Build or buy this (or similar) simple unit & LIVE LONGER & HEALTHIER.

PARENTS/TEACHERS, our children are far more prone to initial infestation from poor hygiene. PROTECT THEM (& you) BY INSTRUCTION.

FLUKE WORM

● **DESCRIPTION:** Various different species & forms.

● **CONTRACTED:** <u>Usually by contact with, or ingestion of water which is contaminated by human feces - This could be in a river or on uncooked vegetables</u> (particularly those fertilized with human waste) - Usually requires an intermediate host (such as fresh water snails) - VERY COMMON IN AFRICA, ASIA & MIDDLE EAST.

● **SYMPTOMS:** Various, as this worm may lodge in organs, such as: Lungs, liver, spleen, bladder, rectum, intestines (& even veins) - Obstruction, pain & malfunction of the affected organ.

● **TREATMENT:** First requires identification - Then is difficult (as effective drugs can be toxic to humans). Prevention is much better - CLEAN WATER CRITICAL.

FLEAS

● **DESCRIPTION:** Tiny wingless (jump/crawl) insects which live on mammals - Animal fleas may jump on & bite humans - But only human fleas will stay on long.

● **CONTRACTED:** <u>By close contact with infected persons (or clothing or bedding, upholstered chairs, carpets etc).</u>

● **SYMPTOMS:** Flea bites are small punctures thru which blood is sucked - These then itch & (according to the hosts' skin reaction) show up as a red pimple or small lump - CERTAIN SPECIES OF FLEA TRANSMIT SERIOUS DISEASES (SUCH AS PLAGUE & MUSRINE TYPHUS).

● **TREATMENT:** Various forms & types of insecticide (shampoo for hair, dust for carpets & upholstery etc.) - Keep all away from infants & pregnant ladies - Calamine lotion for itching.

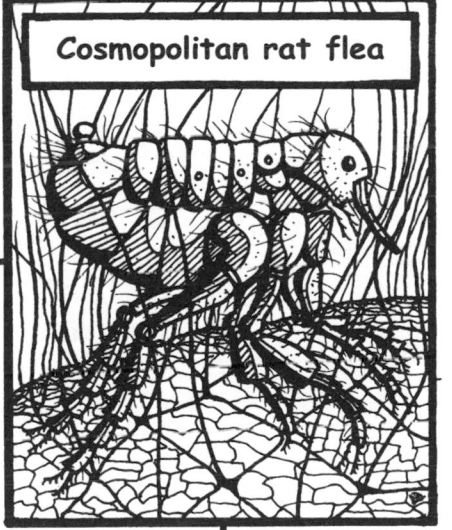

Cosmopolitan rat flea

SPECIFIC DISEASES

● **TOXOCARIASIS:** Infestation with round worm larvae - <u>Often contracted by children (playing in areas fouled by infected e.g. domestic pets)</u> - The eggs are swallowed & hatch in the intestine (migrating all over the body [liver, lungs, brain]) - Diagnosis by blood test - Treatment difficult - Prevention much better.

● **TOXOPLASMOSIS:** <u>Acquired by eating undercooked contaminated meat (or handling infected animals [or their products]</u> & not washing hands before eating) - Specifically applicable to pregnant mothers (who may not have symptoms, but pass the micro-organism to baby in womb) - Symptoms in baby: Rash, fever, jaundice & retina inflammation - DEATH A POSSIBILITY.

● **ANCYLOSTOMIASIS** (Hookworm Disease) : <u>Infection by not wearing shoes (in areas with fecal pollution)</u> - Larva enters the skin (thru usually the soles of the feet) - Symptoms include: Itchy points of entry, stomachache, diarrhea & anemia (iron deficiency).

● **ASCARIASIS** (Roundworm Disease) : <u>Eggs are passed in human feces (contaminating soil/water) & then by poor hygiene to the mouths of others</u> - After hatching in the intestine they traval thru the intestine wall to the lungs. (Symptoms: coughing, wheezing & fever) - ADULT WORMS PASSING INTO THE LIVER ETC. OF CHILDREN MAY CAUSE DEATH - Diagnosis by examination of feces - Treatments include Pyrantel Pamoate, Mebendazole & Piperzine Citrate.

● **RINGWORM** (Tinea): Not a worm but a group of fungal infections (including Athletes Foot) - Treatment by topical fungicides such as Miconazole or Griseofulvin.

IT IS VERY IMPORTANT (particularly in the tropics) TO BE AWARE of the nature & sources of contamination by parasites in humans.

HEAD LICE

- **DESCRIPTION:** Eggs are tiny (& cigar shaped) - Color: cream to darker - Adults look like miniature mosquitoes.

- **CONTRACTED:** Particularly (but not exclusively) by children - **Head to head contact + combs, towels, clothes even seat head rests** (recently used by a contaminated person).

- **SYMPTOMS:** As nits (eggs) are laid on & attach (very firmly) to hair - Inspect close to scalp for telltale white dots - Adult lice (louse) feed by biting the skin for blood & thus small red pimples (bites) may also be visible (these may also be itchy & irritated) - Bad cases may cause lymph glands to swell.

- **TREATMENT:** Insecticide shampoo for all the household - Wash all clothes & bed linens (repeat in 2 weeks) - Comb nits out of hair with very fine comb.

SCABIES

- **DESCRIPTION:** Microscopic burrowing mite.

- **CONTRACTED:** **By physical contact with a contaminated person (or animal) or clothes/bedding etc.**

- **SYMPTOMS:** The female mite burrows under the skin - Usual sites are between fingers, on wrists & flex zones of elbows, knees etc. (also genitals & waist) - Very bad itching with rash of small blisters (& zig - zag red lines) - Infection may result from scratching - These reactions may occur several months (2 - 4) after first contamination.

- **TREATMENT:** Microscopic identification of burrow scrapings - Locally apply Sulphur Ointment (or other scabicide [eg. Benzyl Benzoate]) after hot bath - Wash all clothes & linens.

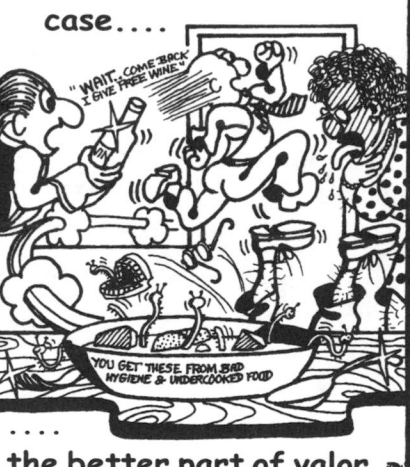

Discretion IS in this case....

.... the better part of valor.

YOU GET THESE FROM BAD HYGIENE & UNDERCOOKED FOOD

TAPEWORM

- **DESCRIPTION:** Ribbon shaped worms made up of segments in a chain, which in species such as Taenia Saginata (Beef tapeworm [the most often found in humans]) can reach 12 - 25 feet (yes you did read right: 12 - 25 ft).

- **CONTRACTED:** **Usually by eating the undercooked meat (beef, pork, fish etc.) of intermediate hosts** contaminated by the larval form of the worm.

- **SYMPTOMS:** Of infestation by adult worms in human infestenes are usually slight but diarrhea, gastric pain & weight loss are possible - Eggs or portions of worm may be passed in stool.

- **TREATMENT:** Drugs such as Quinacrine & Niclosamide are taken by mouth to loosen the worms attachment to the intestine wall (& partially dissolve them) prior to excretion.

THREADWORMS

- **DESCRIPTION:** (also known as pinworms) 1/4-1/2 inch long (like pieces of white thread).

- **CONTRACTED:** **By touching surfaces (almost any) which have been in contact with an infected person** (for example GIRLS ARE FAR MORE LIKELY TO BE INFECTED because of toilet seats).

- **SYMPTOMS:** Are often not obvious unless the anus is examined at night (when the worms may emerge to lay eggs [will retreat quickly if light shined on them]) - Anus area itchy - Insomnia - Worms sometimes seen in stools - Tape by side of anus in AM may reveal eggs microscopically.

- **TREATMENT:** Personal hygiene is the best preventive measure - Drugs include Piperazine & Thiabendazole - Treat whole house (& wash all fabrics/surfaces) twice, 14 days apart.

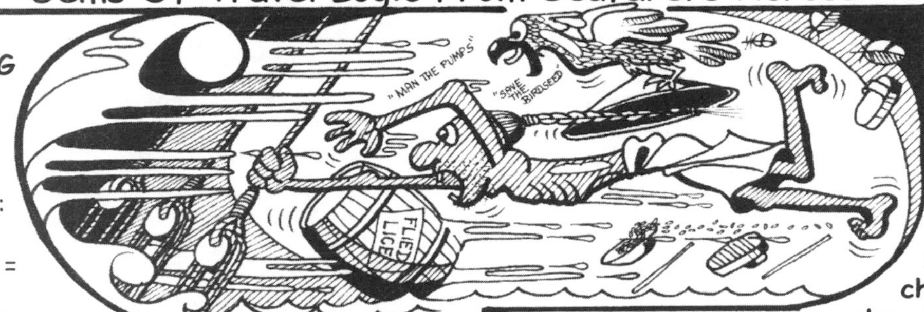

FORECASTING
Weather
CLOUDS

● **CIRRUS (𝟸):** High, wispy ("Mares' Tails") = Fine (but if not moving means gales moving in the direction of tails).

● **CIRROSTRATUS (𝟸):** Streaky, white & thin (ice crystals) - Makes sun halo (which gets bigger) = Fine - (Smaller = Rain).

● **STRATUS (—):** Low, misty, uniform cover = Some drizzle (may be fine later).

● **STRATOCUMULUS (⊌):** Low, rolling, lumpy, high % cover = Showers (clearing later).

● **CUMULUS (⌂):** Small, separate, puffy, white = Fine - Bigger & grouping = Showers - (In a clear sky they can mark land [heat]).

● **CUMULONIMBUS (𝟾):** "The King of clouds," towering, dark, low & very high, icy anvil top = Violent, erratic wind, rain - Thunder & lightning squalls.

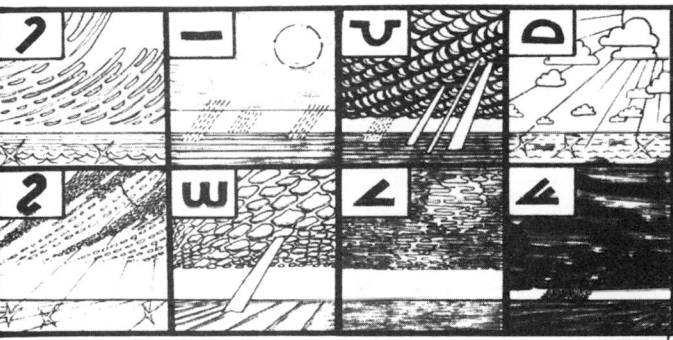

● **CIRROCUMULUS (𝟸):** White, small, high, shiny (no shadow) ("Mackerel Sky") = Post storm symptom (& fine coming).

● **ALTOCUMULUS (�w):** Similar to CIRROCUMULUS but thicker, medium height, with shadows = Post storm (becoming fine).

● **ALTOSTRATUS (⦜):** Mottled gray film thru which moon/sun faintly seen (if moon/sun goes = Rain).

● **NIMBOSTRATUS (⦜)"** Very dark, thick, gloomy, 100% cover = Persistent rain soon.

● **HIGHER CLOUD** = Better/Fine.
● **DIFFERENT LAYERS** = Change.
● **PM CLOUD ON HILLS** = Rain.

TEMPERATURE

	Winter	Summer
	Fast temp. rise = Bad	Fast temp. rise = Fine
	Fast temp. fall = Fine.	Fast temp. fall = Bad

SURVIVING
Storms
HURRICANES/ CYCLONES ETC....

....are what we sailors fear like chickens do a mad dog. We hide in deep landlocked coves or far into mangrove swamps or if we must we scamper across the ocean according to a magic formula **& only if cornered will we stand & fight. KNOW YOUR ENEMY....**

Where	Name	#/Yr.	Worst Months
N. Ind. Oc.	Cyclone	6	Sept. - Nov.
N. Atl. Oc.	Hurricane	10	Jun. - Nov.
S. Ind. Oc.	Cyclone	11	Dec. - Mar.
NE. Pac. Oc.	Hurricane	15	Jun. - Oct.
SW. Pac. Oc.	Willy Willy	15	Dec. - Apr.
NW. Pac. Oc.	Typhoon	25	Apr. - Dec.

TYPICAL N. ATLANTIC HURRICANE

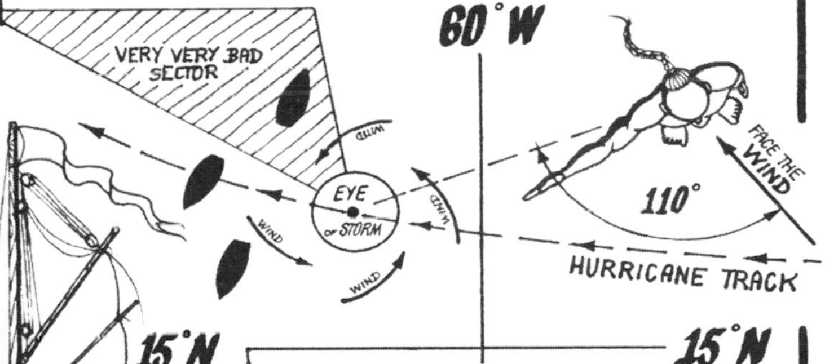

60°W

VERY VERY BAD SECTOR

EYE of STORM

FACE THE WIND

110°

HURRICANE TRACK

15°N   15°N

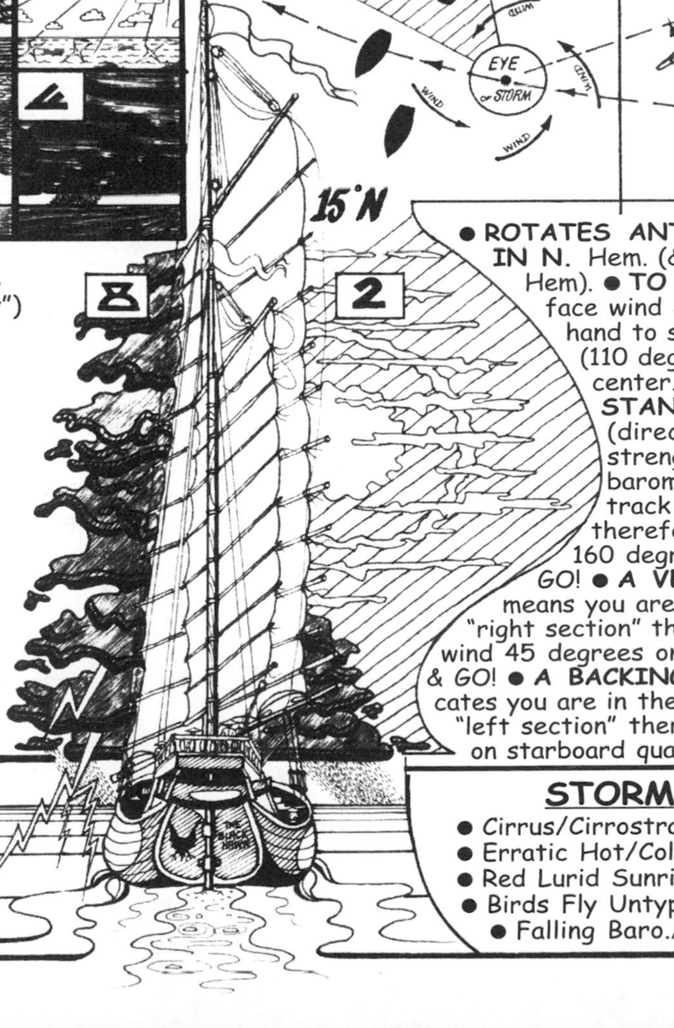

● **ROTATES ANTICLOCKWISE IN N.** Hem. (& opposite in S. Hem). ● **TO FIND CENTER** face wind & hold out right hand to side just behind (110 degree) it points to center. ● **A CONSTANT WIND** (direction), rising strength & falling barometer = Right in track of center therefore bring wind to 160 degrees relative & GO! ● **A VEERING WIND** means you are in the dangerous "right section" therefore bring wind 45 degrees on starboard bow & GO! ● **A BACKING WIND** indicates you are in the less dangerous "left section" therefore bring wind on starboard quarter & GO!

STORM COMING
● Cirrus/Cirrostratus Cloud.
● Erratic Hot/Cold Wind Puffs.
● Red Lurid Sunrise/Set.
● Birds Fly Untypically To Land.
● Falling Baro./Long Swell.

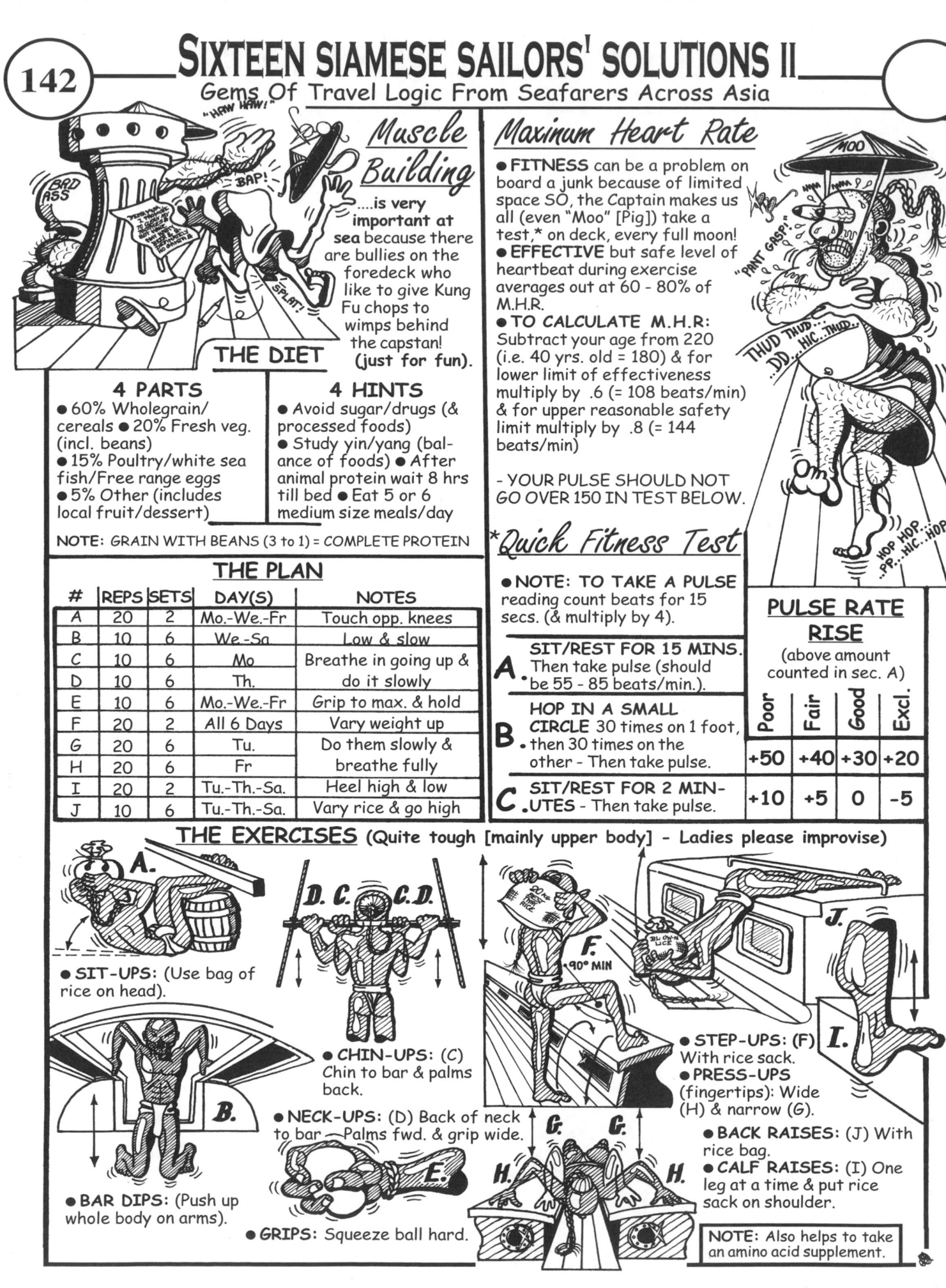

Muscle Building

....is **very important at sea** because there are bullies on the foredeck who like to give Kung Fu chops to wimps behind the capstan! **(just for fun).**

THE DIET

4 PARTS
● 60% Wholegrain/cereals ● 20% Fresh veg. (incl. beans) ● 15% Poultry/white sea fish/Free range eggs ● 5% Other (includes local fruit/dessert)

4 HINTS
● Avoid sugar/drugs (& processed foods) ● Study yin/yang (balance of foods) ● After animal protein wait 8 hrs till bed ● Eat 5 or 6 medium size meals/day

NOTE: GRAIN WITH BEANS (3 to 1) = COMPLETE PROTEIN

THE PLAN

#	REPS	SETS	DAY(S)	NOTES
A	20	2	Mo.-We.-Fr	Touch opp. knees
B	10	6	We.-Sa.	Low & slow
C	10	6	Mo	Breathe in going up & do it slowly
D	10	6	Th.	
E	10	6	Mo.-We.-Fr	Grip to max. & hold
F	20	2	All 6 Days	Vary weight up
G	20	6	Tu.	Do them slowly & breathe fully
H	20	6	Fr	
I	20	2	Tu.-Th.-Sa.	Heel high & low
J	10	6	Tu.-Th.-Sa.	Vary rice & go high

Maximum Heart Rate

● **FITNESS** can be a problem on board a junk because of limited space SO, the Captain makes us all (even "Moo" [Pig]) take a test,* on deck, every full moon!
● **EFFECTIVE** but safe level of heartbeat during exercise averages out at 60 - 80% of M.H.R.
● **TO CALCULATE M.H.R:** Subtract your age from 220 (i.e. 40 yrs. old = 180) & for lower limit of effectiveness multiply by .6 (= 108 beats/min) & for upper reasonable safety limit multiply by .8 (= 144 beats/min)

- YOUR PULSE SHOULD NOT GO OVER 150 IN TEST BELOW.

*Quick Fitness Test

● **NOTE: TO TAKE A PULSE** reading count beats for 15 secs. (& multiply by 4).

A. SIT/REST FOR 15 MINS. Then take pulse (should be 55 - 85 beats/min.).

B. HOP IN A SMALL CIRCLE 30 times on 1 foot, then 30 times on the other - Then take pulse.

C. SIT/REST FOR 2 MINUTES - Then take pulse.

PULSE RATE RISE
(above amount counted in sec. A)

	Poor	Fair	Good	Excl.
B	+50	+40	+30	+20
C	+10	+5	0	-5

THE EXERCISES (Quite tough [mainly upper body] - Ladies please improvise)

● **SIT-UPS:** (Use bag of rice on head).

● **CHIN-UPS:** (C) Chin to bar & palms back.

● **NECK-UPS:** (D) Back of neck to bar — Palms fwd. & grip wide.

● **BAR DIPS:** (Push up whole body on arms).

● **GRIPS:** Squeeze ball hard.

● **STEP-UPS:** (F) With rice sack.
● **PRESS-UPS** (fingertips): Wide (H) & narrow (G).

● **BACK RAISES:** (J) With rice bag.
● **CALF RAISES:** (I) One leg at a time & put rice sack on shoulder.

NOTE: Also helps to take an amino acid supplement.

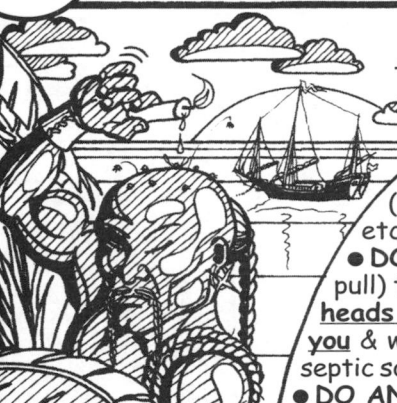

Tick Trouble
(Removing them)

● **AVOID THEM** (if possible) by covering up on shore trips (thru long grass/brush etc. [even grassy dunes]).

● **DON'T TRY TO** knock (or pull) them off (<u>as their heads & jaws are buried in you</u> & will break off [causing septic sores]).

● **DO ANY OF THESE:** a) Put drop of paraffin, alcohol, petrol or vaseline on (<u>& wait 10 - 60 mins. for it to let go</u>) - b) Put drop of candle wax (or clear nail varnish) on (suffocates it) - c) Put hot match on while gently & slowly easing out with tweezers - Disinfect bites after.

Licking

● **DON'T LET ANIMALS** (even the ship's cat [but particularly stray dogs etc.]) lick your hand, because bacteria & viruses (e.g. rabies) are carried in saliva (& <u>can pass into your body via any cut, scratch even pin prick on your hand</u> [rabies can be fatal]).

Swimmers Ear

● **DIVING** to free the propeller in dirty waters can result in this common inner ear infection.

● **BEFORE** entering (particularly tropical waters) <u>put a few drops of baby oil in ears.</u>

● **AFTER** swimming, evaporate residual water with <u>a teaspoon of Isopropyl Alcohol in ears</u> (&/or white vinegar [kills virus/bacteria]).

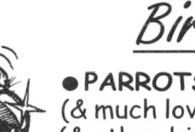

Bird Bugs

● **PARROTS** are a great laugh (& much loved at sea) but they (& other birds) can carry dangerous (& infectious) viral & bacterial diseases : <u>Exercise strict hygiene</u> while enjoying them.

● **EXAMPLES:** Salmonellosis is a very unpleasant food poisoning bacteria - & Ornithosis (Psittacosis in parrots) is a serious virus caught from birds!

Ear Bugs

● **AN INSECT** which crawls inside your ear can ruin your evening ashore.

● **DON'T POKE IT** with a pointed chopstick. Float it out with warm water.

Seasickness
(or Road/Air Sickness)

● **BEFORE DEPARTING** avoid alcohol, heavy &/or greasy foods - But do eat one egg white with lemon juice (& 20 mg Vit. B6 [6 hourly] .... kids 10 mg) & drink Ginger Root Tea.

● **UNDERWAY, DON'T** have greasy, sugary, salty (or alcoholic) foods/drinks <u>- Don't read books in stuffy cabins or work in engine rooms reeking of diesel oil.</u> *"Oh God! I feel terrible!"*

● **UNDERWAY, DO** travel at night if possible (alternate between sleep & fresh air if feeling sick) - <u>Look at the horizon when on deck</u> - Keep head still - Suck a piece of ginger root (very good [or slice of lemon]) - If sick take 20 mg Vit. B6 (kids 10 mg) 2 hourly (brewers yeast or B Complex also works) - <u>Always breathe deeply & slowly when nauseous</u> - Also try any of these herb teas (warm to hot): Alfalfa - Marjoram - Red raspberry - Ginger - Japanese green - Catnip - Savory - Peppermint - Eucalyptus - Camomile - Golden seal - Pennyroyal - Fennel - Sage - Cloves - Spearmint - Kelp - Basil - Anise - Peach - Asparagus - Clover.

PRESSURE POINTS ALSO WORK

● **KNEECAPS:** Massage around edges with "clawed" fingers for several minutes.

● **TUMMY:** Gently (but firmly) deep knead entire solar plexus for several minutes.

● **SHIN:** Press with thumb(s) (3 x 10 secs. each): a) One palm width down from kneecap (just behind shinbone on outside) & b) One palm width up from inside anklebone (just behind shinbone [both points may be sore]).

● **WRIST:** On inside centerline press 2 & 4 finger widths up from wrist crease (for 3 x 10 secs. each).

● **HEAD:** Massage (or specifically press [3 x 10 secs.]) particularly tender spots: a) In hollow at base of skull (back of neck) - b) On jawbone corner (below earlobe) - c) Scalp, forehead & behind ears (massage by rolling finger knuckles).

FINAL HINTS

● **REMEMBER:** Breathe deeply (& slowly) - Stay warm - Stay calm - Look at horizon (if up) - <u>Close eyes & lie down (if not)</u> - Suck ginger (crystallised is good for kids) - & STAY POSITIVE!

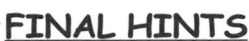
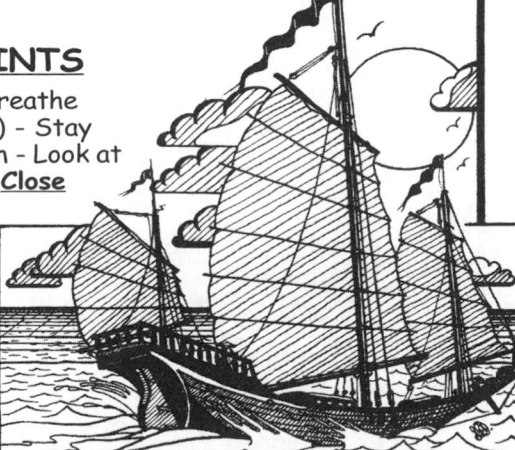

Hiccups....

....CAN INTERFERE with your steering & get you 3 lashes tied to the mizzen so try:

● **UPSIDE DOWN** drinking of water &/or followed by one minute massage of roof of mouth (where hard changes to soft at back center).

● **12 MORE HINTS** - **Pull** tongue - **Chew** charcoal tablets - **Eat** a teaspoon of honey - **Chew** fresh mint leaves - **Put** cold pack on back of neck - **Chew** dill seeds - **Sneeze** (use pepper) - **Let** a deep breath out slowly (thru pursed lips) - **Sip** a teaspoon of vinegar - **Drink** water with ears tightly covered - **Breathe** into paper bag for few minutes - **Assume** fetal position (on back) on floor (knees to chest).

Nosebleed

● **CAN BE A NUISANCE** particularly when serving dinner at the captain's table as you may drip in his soup

● COURSE OF ACTION ●

● **BLOW NOSE** once hard to remove clot (may be holding damaged vessels open).

● **"SCREW" A WAD** of cotton wool (can be soaked in white vinegar if available) into bleeding nostril & sit at table.

● **SQUEEZE** either side of nose just above nostril (in soft part) for 5 - 10 minutes.

● **COLD PACK** bridge of nose during above.

● **IF IT STOPS** leave cotton wool in for 20 minutes - If it doesn't stop, change wad & do it all again.

● **DON'T** lie down, take aspirin (stops clotting) or pick scab for a week after.

● **DO** take extra Iron, Vits. C & K & sip Yarrow Tea.

● **EXTERNALLY:** Gently sniff up nose (or use in cold compress) Golden Seal, White Oak Bark, Bistort or Mistletoe Tea (cool).

Birth Control

● **LADIES,** at sea you can easily lose count of days - SO, REMEMBER that vaginal mucus during ovulation becomes thin, clear & slimy (& can be stretched several inches) - After ovulation it is thicker (non-stretchy) & yellowish.

EGG PRESENT
(STRETCHES)

NO EGG
(BREAKS)

Black Eye(s)....

....CAN GET YOU in serious trouble with the Captain so:

● **APPLY** ice pack (frozen peas or drink can will do) 5 mins every 20 mins.

● **AVOID** aspirin (impairs clotting) - Don't blow nose (can cause air embolism) - Don't put head below heart (delays healing).

● **ALOE VERA** gel on skin speeds healing.

● **INTERNALLY** Take 1g Vit.C, 10mg Zinc, 300mg Bioflavonoids (all 4 times/day) - Eat pineapple &/or papaya (contains bruise healing enzyme) also green veg.

● **DURATION** usually 5 - 10 days, (passing thru black, green, yellow then gone).

Bad Breath

● **IN SMALL CABINS** can ruin a good friendship, so here are some well-tried remedies:

● **AVOID** spices, cheese, caffeine, meat, alcohol & rotten teeth.

● **AFTER MEALS** chew Cloves or Anise or Parsley or Fennel Seeds then floss & brush teeth (also tongue).

Warts

● **ELEGANCE** is difficult with a warty hand at the "Junk Owners Ball" therefore start early in the season to get rid of them.

● **WARNING:** Oriental logic associates warts with a tendency to cysts & tumors (so first eliminate excess fat/protein [which warts indicate]) - Also cut out sugar (& don't overeat) - Study Macrobiotics.

● **DANDELION STEM,** milky juice or crushed Marigold Leaves or Fig Tree milky sap (apply twice daily to warts until gone [few weeks]) - Also used are Garlic, Lemon Juice, Aloe Vera &/or pure Vit. E Oil.

● **CASTOR OIL:** Apply a drop twice daily in center of a "bandaid" twice daily (for 21+days).

● **SELF-HYPNOSIS** works on warts, see, feel them shrink "forcefully" for 5 minutes/day - AMAZING!

● **WARNING:** warts & verrucas (feet) are highly infectious & can spread thru any minute scratch to you or someone else.

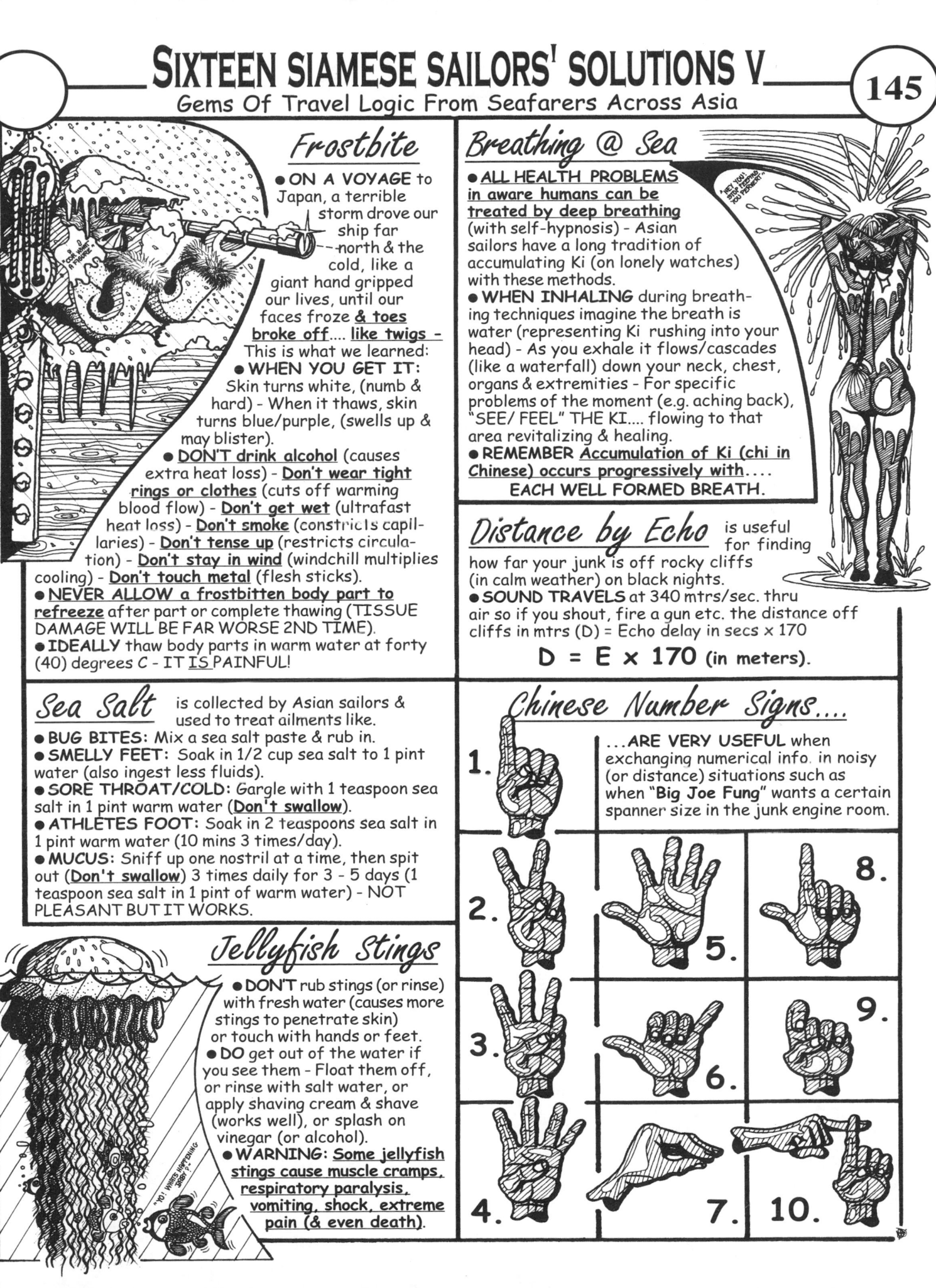

Frostbite

- **ON A VOYAGE** to Japan, a terrible storm drove our ship far north & the cold, like a giant hand gripped our lives, until our faces froze **& toes broke off**.... **like twigs** - This is what we learned:
- **WHEN YOU GET IT:** Skin turns white, (numb & hard) - When it thaws, skin turns blue/purple, (swells up & may blister).
- **DON'T drink alcohol** (causes extra heat loss) - **Don't wear tight rings or clothes** (cuts off warming blood flow) - **Don't get wet** (ultrafast heat loss) - **Don't smoke** (constricts capillaries) - **Don't tense up** (restricts circulation) - **Don't stay in wind** (windchill multiplies cooling) - **Don't touch metal** (flesh sticks).
- **NEVER ALLOW a frostbitten body part to refreeze** after part or complete thawing (TISSUE DAMAGE WILL BE FAR WORSE 2ND TIME).
- **IDEALLY** thaw body parts in warm water at forty (40) degrees C - IT _IS_ PAINFUL!

Breathing @ Sea

- **ALL HEALTH PROBLEMS in aware humans can be treated by deep breathing** (with self-hypnosis) - Asian sailors have a long tradition of accumulating Ki (on lonely watches) with these methods.
- **WHEN INHALING** during breathing techniques imagine the breath is water (representing Ki rushing into your head) - As you exhale it flows/cascades (like a waterfall) down your neck, chest, organs & extremities - For specific problems of the moment (e.g. aching back), "SEE/ FEEL" THE KI.... flowing to that area revitalizing & healing.
- **REMEMBER** <u>Accumulation of Ki (chi in Chinese) occurs progressively with</u>.... EACH WELL FORMED BREATH.

Distance by Echo

is useful for finding how far your junk is off rocky cliffs (in calm weather) on black nights.
- **SOUND TRAVELS** at 340 mtrs/sec. thru air so if you shout, fire a gun etc. the distance off cliffs in mtrs (D) = Echo delay in secs x 170

$$D = E \times 170 \text{ (in meters)}.$$

Sea Salt

is collected by Asian sailors & used to treat ailments like.
- **BUG BITES:** Mix a sea salt paste & rub in.
- **SMELLY FEET:** Soak in 1/2 cup sea salt to 1 pint water (also ingest less fluids).
- **SORE THROAT/COLD:** Gargle with 1 teaspoon sea salt in 1 pint warm water (**Don't swallow**).
- **ATHLETES FOOT:** Soak in 2 teaspoons sea salt in 1 pint warm water (10 mins 3 times/day).
- **MUCUS:** Sniff up one nostril at a time, then spit out (**Don't swallow**) 3 times daily for 3 - 5 days (1 teaspoon sea salt in 1 pint of warm water) - NOT PLEASANT BUT IT WORKS.

Jellyfish Stings

- **DON'T** rub stings (or rinse) with fresh water (causes more stings to penetrate skin) or touch with hands or feet.
- **DO** get out of the water if you see them - Float them off, or rinse with salt water, or apply shaving cream & shave (works well), or splash on vinegar (or alcohol).
- **WARNING:** <u>Some jellyfish stings cause muscle cramps, respiratory paralysis, vomiting, shock, extreme pain (& even death).</u>

Chinese Number Signs....

...ARE VERY USEFUL when exchanging numerical info. in noisy (or distance) situations such as when "**Big Joe Fung**" wants a certain spanner size in the junk engine room.

1. 2. 3. 4. 5. 6. 7. 8. 9. 10.

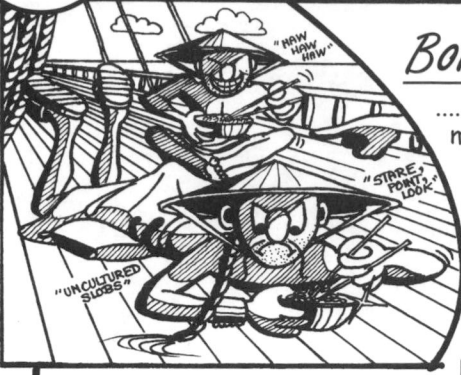

Boil on Bum....

.... is embarrassing at mealtimes (because rude & ignorant ruffians laugh when you lie on deck to eat rice).

● **WARNING: Boils indicate excess toxicity in body** - Change to a mainly bland diet of whole grains & cooked veg. (with no sugars, animal fats or refined carbohydrates).

● **SUPPLEMENT** with Vit. A (10,000 iu), C (2 g) & Zinc (20 mg) all 3 times/day.

● **BRING TO HEAD** using a warm compress (for 20 mins. 4 times/day) until boil(s) break (**up to 7 days**) - **Then for 3 days after** (to drain all remaining pus from surrounding tissue).

● **WARM POULTICES** (**to draw pus**) can also be made with mashed garlic, outer cabbage leaves, India tea bags, hot half tomato (or onion), mullein/lobella (3 to 1 mix) or burdock leaves.

● **DRINK** (**to clean blood**): Dandelion, burdock, comfrey, chaparral, red clover, sarsaparilla or yellow dock teas.

& DO REGULAR AEROBIC TYPE EXERCISE

Belching

.... is considered bad manners (even on the lower deck) & can lead to arguments & fighting so ....

● **NERVOUS** people swallow air (causes belching) - So **calm down** (deep breathe) - **Keep mouth open** (difficult to swallow air) - **Avoid gassy drinks** - **Also combine foods correctly** (e.g. eat fruits alone).

Bait Worms....

.... WORK VERY WELL catching the fat catfish that the Captain loves for lunch - But first you have to catch the worms.

● **SPRINKLE** water on vegetated soil (while poking with a fork) - Worms think it is raining (& come up to play).

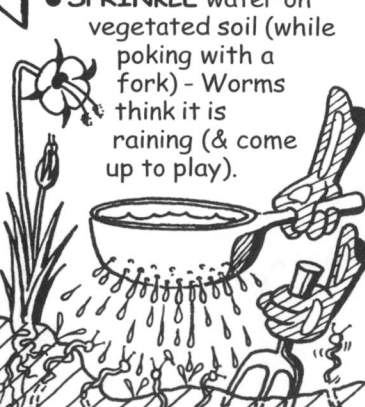

Flat Feet

● **LONG HOURS** standing at the helm (bare foot or in zero support shoes) can seriously flatten your arches.

● **TEST YOURS** with wet footprint(s) on a dry deck (or newspaper).

● **IF FALLEN** exercise (pick up pen with toes & roll instep on bottle) - Also wear support shoes.

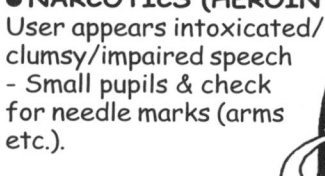

GOOD & BAD FOOTPRINTS

Stitches

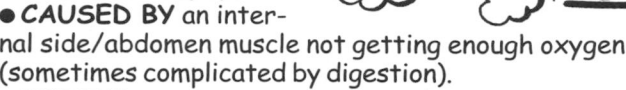

● **AS CABIN BOY** the Captain may sometimes require you to run quickly to the fish market (for a bottle of his favourite "Extra Strong Rice Wine") - **& too slow means no pay!**

● **CAUSED BY** an internal side/abdomen muscle not getting enough oxygen (sometimes complicated by digestion).

● **BEFORE** starting out, visit the toilet.

● **DURING** strenuous exercise breathe deeply (abdomen & chest) to ensure sufficient oxygen reaches muscles.

● **IF YOU GET ONE**, stop what you are doing (if possible) - If not possible (as when getting the Captain's wine) exhale totally & forcefully several times (massages internal organs/muscles) - Press &/or massage (with 3 fingers) center of pain - **DON'T, DON'T FORGET THE CAPTAIN'S CHANGE!**

CAPTAIN'S CORNER

Detecting drug use

● **BANANA REPUBLIC** governments may seize ANY excuse to impound your fine junk - **So, no "illegal drugs" allowed on board** - Check your crew for symptoms.

● **AMPHETAMINES (SPEED ETC.):** User becomes hyperactive, very talkative (possible dry lips/nose & throat), bad breath & hallucinations.

● **BARBITURATES (DOWNERS ETC.):** User first is relaxed/jovial then may appear drunk (clumsy/drowsy/slurred speech) but no alcohol smell.

● **MARIJUANA (GRASS/POT):** User first hungry/talkative/likes music/films - Often has idiotic smile - Red eyes/sleeps well - Residual "roaches" & sweet burnt rope smell.

● **NARCOTICS (HEROIN ETC.):** User appears intoxicated/clumsy/impaired speech - Small pupils & check for needle marks (arms etc.).

● **NOTE** ● Let us not misuse drugs (incl. nicotine & alcohol) IN FRONT OF CHILDREN.

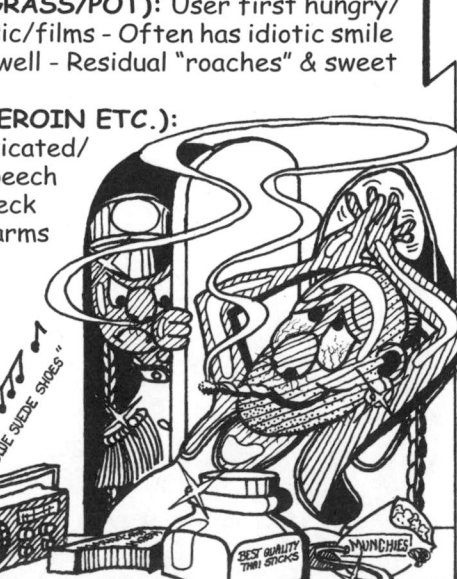

Gems Of Travel Logic From Seafarers Across Asia

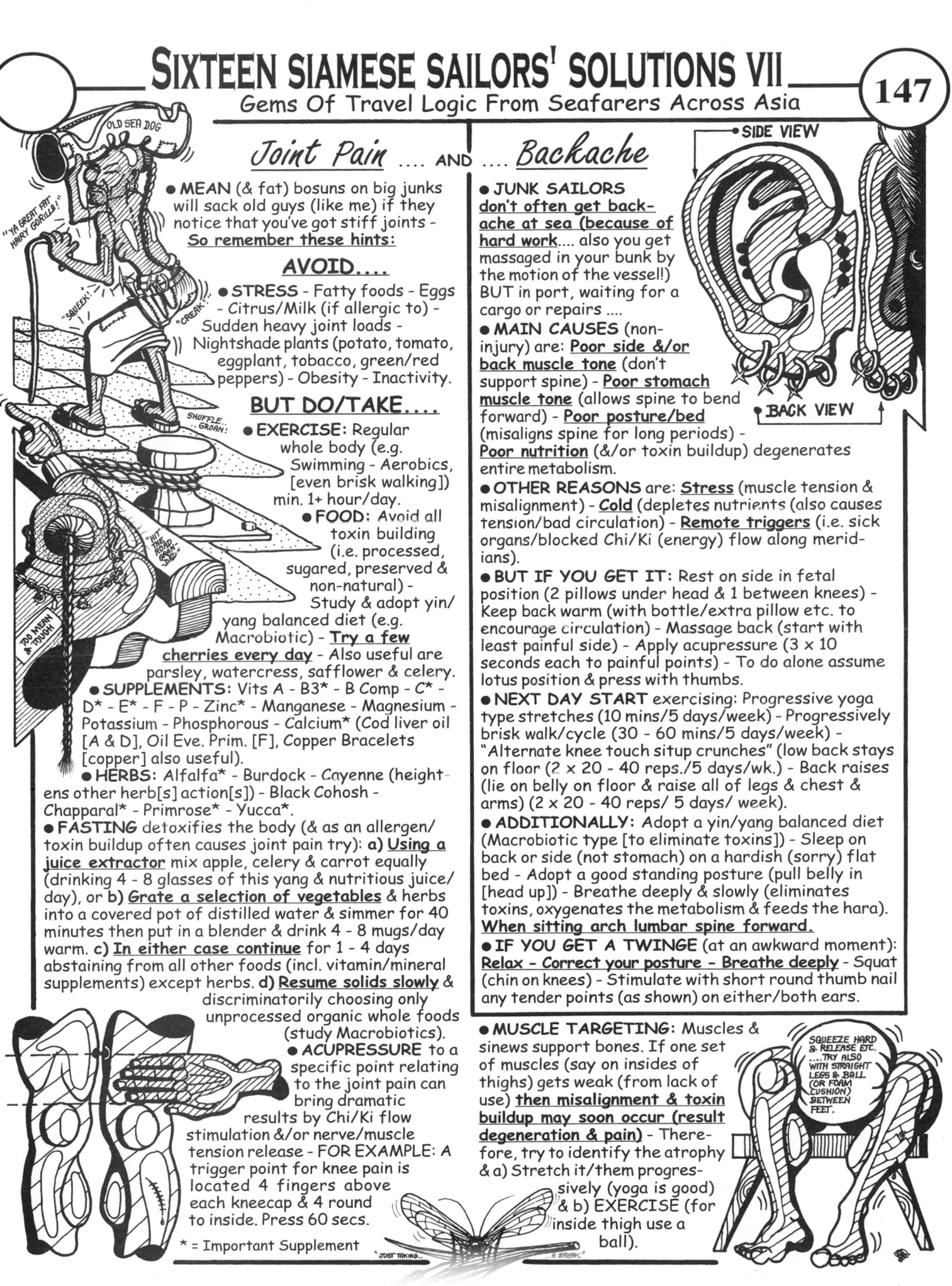

Joint Pain .... AND .... Backache

Joint Pain

- MEAN (& fat) bosuns on big junks will sack old guys (like me) if they notice that you've got stiff joints - **So remember these hints:**

AVOID....

- STRESS - Fatty foods - Eggs - Citrus/Milk (if allergic to) - Sudden heavy joint loads - Nightshade plants (potato, tomato, eggplant, tobacco, green/red peppers) - Obesity - Inactivity.

BUT DO/TAKE....

- EXERCISE: Regular whole body (e.g. Swimming - Aerobics, [even brisk walking]) min. 1+ hour/day.
- FOOD: Avoid all toxin building (i.e. processed, sugared, preserved & non-natural) - Study & adopt yin/yang balanced diet (e.g. Macrobiotic) - **Try a few cherries every day** - Also useful are parsley, watercress, safflower & celery.
- SUPPLEMENTS: Vits A - B3* - B Comp - C* - D* - E* - F - P - Zinc* - Manganese - Magnesium - Potassium - Phosphorous - Calcium* (Cod liver oil [A & D], Oil Eve. Prim. [F], Copper Bracelets [copper] also useful).
- HERBS: Alfalfa* - Burdock - Cayenne (heightens other herb[s] action[s]) - Black Cohosh - Chapparal* - Primrose* - Yucca*.
- FASTING detoxifies the body (& as an allergen/toxin buildup often causes joint pain try): a) **Using a juice extractor** mix apple, celery & carrot equally (drinking 4 - 8 glasses of this yang & nutritious juice/day), or b) **Grate a selection of vegetables** & herbs into a covered pot of distilled water & simmer for 40 minutes then put in a blender & drink 4 - 8 mugs/day warm. c) **In either case continue** for 1 - 4 days abstaining from all other foods (incl. vitamin/mineral supplements) except herbs. d) **Resume solids slowly** & discriminatorily choosing only unprocessed organic whole foods (study Macrobiotics).
- ACUPRESSURE to a specific point relating to the joint pain can bring dramatic results by Chi/Ki flow stimulation &/or nerve/muscle tension release - FOR EXAMPLE: A trigger point for knee pain is located 4 fingers above each kneecap & 4 round to inside. Press 60 secs.

* = Important Supplement

Backache

- JUNK SAILORS **don't often get backache at sea (because of hard work**.... also you get massaged in your bunk by the motion of the vessel!) BUT in port, waiting for a cargo or repairs ....
- MAIN CAUSES (non-injury) are: **Poor side &/or back muscle tone** (don't support spine) - **Poor stomach muscle tone** (allows spine to bend forward) - **Poor posture/bed** (misaligns spine for long periods) - **Poor nutrition** (&/or toxin buildup) degenerates entire metabolism.
- OTHER REASONS are: **Stress** (muscle tension & misalignment) - **Cold** (depletes nutrients (also causes tension/bad circulation) - **Remote triggers** (i.e. sick organs/blocked Chi/Ki (energy) flow along meridians).
- BUT IF YOU GET IT: Rest on side in fetal position (2 pillows under head & 1 between knees) - Keep back warm (with bottle/extra pillow etc. to encourage circulation) - Massage back (start with least painful side) - Apply acupressure (3 x 10 seconds each to painful points) - To do alone assume lotus position & press with thumbs.
- NEXT DAY START exercising: Progressive yoga type stretches (10 mins/5 days/week) - Progressively brisk walk/cycle (30 - 60 mins/5 days/week) - "Alternate knee touch situp crunches" (low back stays on floor (2 x 20 - 40 reps./5 days/wk.) - Back raises (lie on belly on floor & raise all of legs & chest & arms) (2 x 20 - 40 reps/ 5 days/ week).
- ADDITIONALLY: Adopt a yin/yang balanced diet (Macrobiotic type [to eliminate toxins]) - Sleep on back or side (not stomach) on a hardish (sorry) flat bed - Adopt a good standing posture (pull belly in [head up]) - Breathe deeply & slowly (eliminates toxins, oxygenates the metabolism & feeds the hara). **When sitting arch lumbar spine forward.**
- IF YOU GET A TWINGE (at an awkward moment): **Relax - Correct your posture - Breathe deeply** - Squat (chin on knees) - Stimulate with short round thumb nail any tender points (as shown) on either/both ears.
- MUSCLE TARGETING: Muscles & sinews support bones. If one set of muscles (say on insides of thighs) gets weak (from lack of use) **then misalignment & toxin buildup may soon occur (result degeneration & pain)** - Therefore, try to identify the atrophy & a) Stretch it/them progressively (yoga is good) & b) EXERCISE (for inside thigh use a ball).

SIDE VIEW

BACK VIEW

SQUEEZE HARD & RELEASE ETC. ....TRY ALSO WITH STRAIGHT LEGS & BALL (OR FOAM CUSHION) BETWEEN FEET.

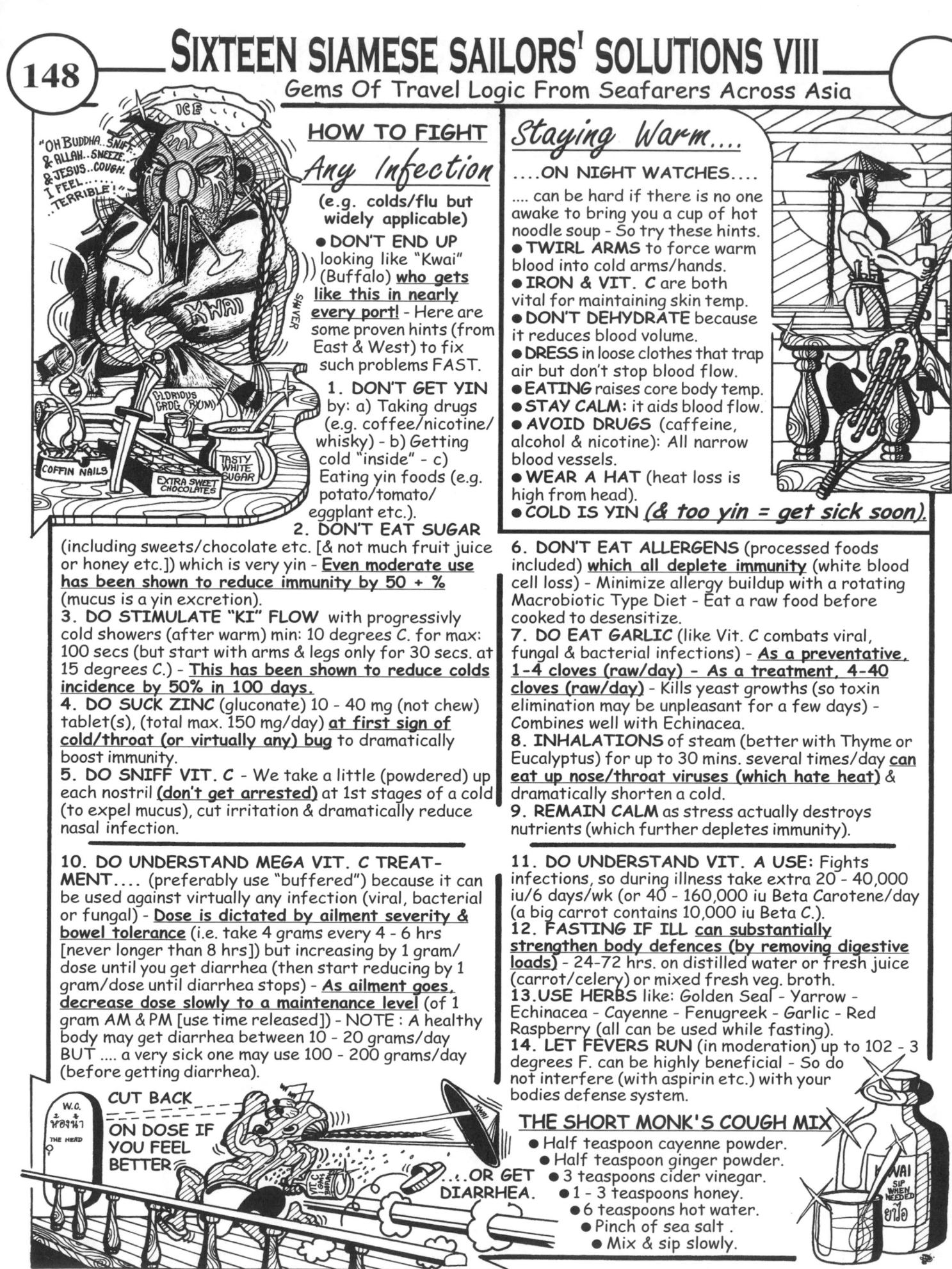

HOW TO FIGHT
Any Infection
(e.g. colds/flu but widely applicable)

- **DON'T END UP** looking like "Kwai" (Buffalo) <u>who gets like this in nearly every port!</u> - Here are some proven hints (from East & West) to fix such problems FAST.

1. DON'T GET YIN by: a) Taking drugs (e.g. coffee/nicotine/whisky) - b) Getting cold "inside" - c) Eating yin foods (e.g. potato/tomato/eggplant etc.).

2. DON'T EAT SUGAR (including sweets/chocolate etc. [& not much fruit juice or honey etc.]) which is very yin - <u>Even moderate use has been shown to reduce immunity by 50 + %</u> (mucus is a yin excretion).

3. DO STIMULATE "KI" FLOW with progressivly cold showers (after warm) min: 10 degrees C. for max: 100 secs (but start with arms & legs only for 30 secs. at 15 degrees C.) - <u>This has been shown to reduce colds incidence by 50% in 100 days.</u>

4. DO SUCK ZINC (gluconate) 10 - 40 mg (not chew) tablet(s), (total max. 150 mg/day) <u>at first sign of cold/throat (or virtually any) bug</u> to dramatically boost immunity.

5. DO SNIFF VIT. C - We take a little (powdered) up each nostril <u>(don't get arrested)</u> at 1st stages of a cold (to expel mucus), cut irritation & dramatically reduce nasal infection.

10. DO UNDERSTAND MEGA VIT. C TREATMENT.... (preferably use "buffered") because it can be used against virtually any infection (viral, bacterial or fungal) - <u>Dose is dictated by ailment severity & bowel tolerance</u> (i.e. take 4 grams every 4 - 6 hrs [never longer than 8 hrs]) but increasing by 1 gram/dose until you get diarrhea (then start reducing by 1 gram/dose until diarrhea stops) - <u>As ailment goes, decrease dose slowly to a maintenance level</u> (of 1 gram AM & PM [use time released]) - NOTE : A healthy body may get diarrhea between 10 - 20 grams/day BUT .... a very sick one may use 100 - 200 grams/day (before getting diarrhea).

CUT BACK ON DOSE IF YOU FEEL BETTER

....OR GET DIARRHEA.

Staying Warm....
....ON NIGHT WATCHES....

.... can be hard if there is no one awake to bring you a cup of hot noodle soup - So try these hints.

- **TWIRL ARMS** to force warm blood into cold arms/hands.
- **IRON & VIT. C** are both vital for maintaining skin temp.
- **DON'T DEHYDRATE** because it reduces blood volume.
- **DRESS** in loose clothes that trap air but don't stop blood flow.
- **EATING** raises core body temp.
- **STAY CALM:** it aids blood flow.
- **AVOID DRUGS** (caffeine, alcohol & nicotine): All narrow blood vessels.
- **WEAR A HAT** (heat loss is high from head).
- **COLD IS YIN** *(& too yin = get sick soon).*

6. DON'T EAT ALLERGENS (processed foods included) <u>which all deplete immunity</u> (white blood cell loss) - Minimize allergy buildup with a rotating Macrobiotic Type Diet - Eat a raw food before cooked to desensitize.

7. DO EAT GARLIC (like Vit. C combats viral, fungal & bacterial infections) - <u>As a preventative, 1-4 cloves (raw/day) - As a treatment, 4-40 cloves (raw/day)</u> - Kills yeast growths (so toxin elimination may be unpleasant for a few days) - Combines well with Echinacea.

8. INHALATIONS of steam (better with Thyme or Eucalyptus) for up to 30 mins. several times/day <u>can eat up nose/throat viruses (which hate heat)</u> & dramatically shorten a cold.

9. REMAIN CALM as stress actually destroys nutrients (which further depletes immunity).

11. DO UNDERSTAND VIT. A USE: Fights infections, so during illness take extra 20 - 40,000 iu/6 days/wk (or 40 - 160,000 iu Beta Carotene/day (a big carrot contains 10,000 iu Beta C.).

12. FASTING IF ILL <u>can substantially strengthen body defences (by removing digestive loads)</u> - 24-72 hrs. on distilled water or fresh juice (carrot/celery) or mixed fresh veg. broth.

13. USE HERBS like: Golden Seal - Yarrow - Echinacea - Cayenne - Fenugreek - Garlic - Red Raspberry (all can be used while fasting).

14. LET FEVERS RUN (in moderation) up to 102 - 3 degrees F. can be highly beneficial - So do not interfere (with aspirin etc.) with your bodies defense system.

THE SHORT MONK'S COUGH MIX
- Half teaspoon cayenne powder.
- Half teaspoon ginger powder.
- 3 teaspoons cider vinegar.
- 1 - 3 teaspoons honey.
- 6 teaspoons hot water.
- Pinch of sea salt .
- Mix & sip slowly.

Gems Of Travel Logic From Seafarers Across Asia

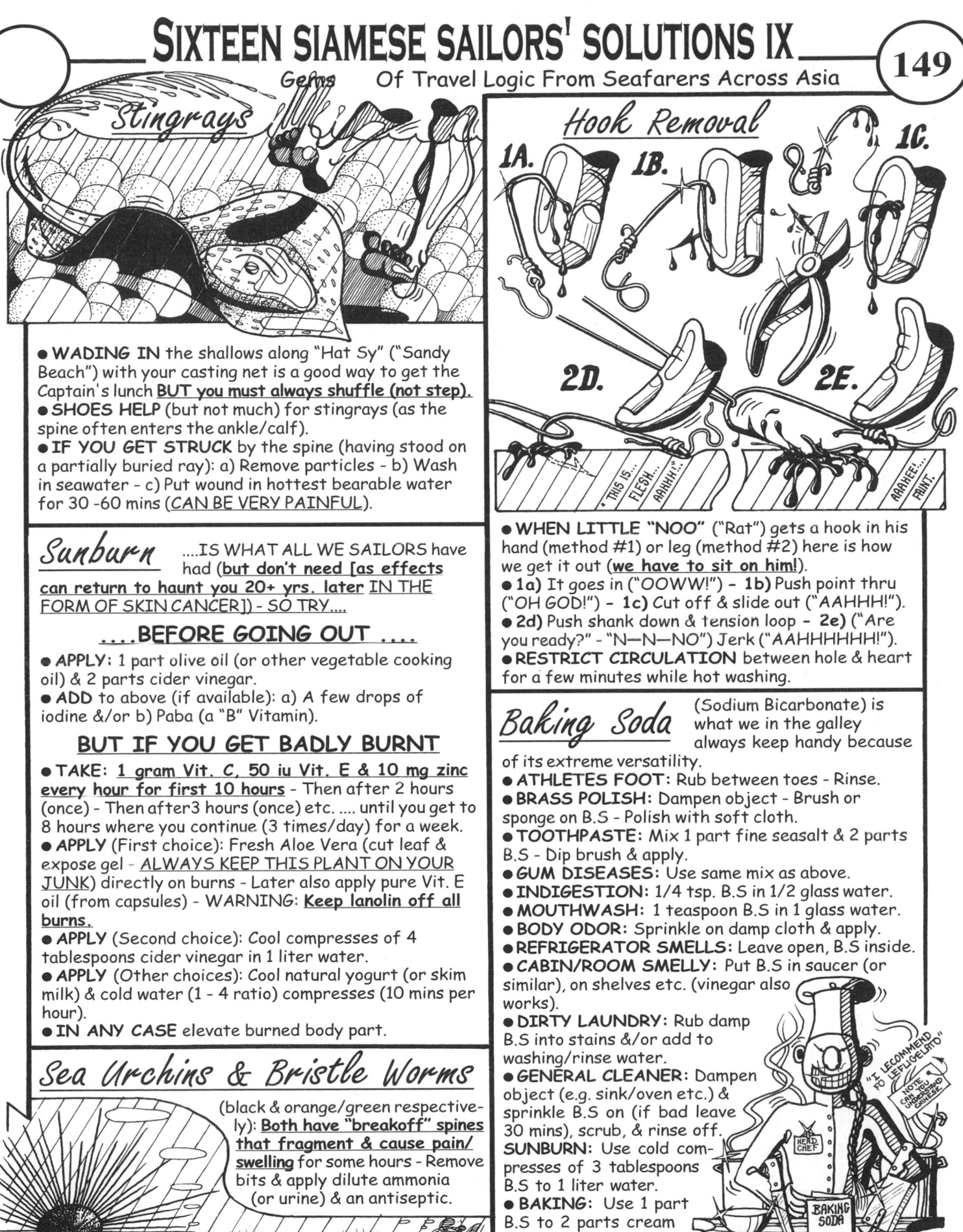

Stingrays

- **WADING IN** the shallows along "Hat Sy" ("Sandy Beach") with your casting net is a good way to get the Captain's lunch **BUT you must always shuffle (not step).**
- **SHOES HELP** (but not much) for stingrays (as the spine often enters the ankle/calf).
- **IF YOU GET STRUCK** by the spine (having stood on a partially buried ray): a) Remove particles - b) Wash in seawater - c) Put wound in hottest bearable water for 30 -60 mins (<u>CAN BE VERY PAINFUL</u>).

Sunburn

....IS WHAT ALL WE SAILORS have had (**but don't need [as effects can return to haunt you 20+ yrs. later <u>IN THE FORM OF SKIN CANCER]</u>) - SO TRY....**

....BEFORE GOING OUT ....

- **APPLY:** 1 part olive oil (or other vegetable cooking oil) & 2 parts cider vinegar.
- **ADD** to above (if available): a) A few drops of iodine &/or b) Paba (a "B" Vitamin).

BUT IF YOU GET BADLY BURNT

- **TAKE:** <u>1 gram Vit. C, 50 iu Vit. E & 10 mg zinc every hour for first 10 hours</u> - Then after 2 hours (once) - Then after3 hours (once) etc. .... until you get to 8 hours where you continue (3 times/day) for a week.
- **APPLY** (First choice): Fresh Aloe Vera (cut leaf & expose gel - <u>ALWAYS KEEP THIS PLANT ON YOUR JUNK</u>) directly on burns - Later also apply pure Vit. E oil (from capsules) - WARNING: **<u>Keep lanolin off all burns.</u>**
- **APPLY** (Second choice): Cool compresses of 4 tablespoons cider vinegar in 1 liter water.
- **APPLY** (Other choices): Cool natural yogurt (or skim milk) & cold water (1 - 4 ratio) compresses (10 mins per hour).
- **IN ANY CASE** elevate burned body part.

Sea Urchins & Bristle Worms

(black & orange/green respectively): **<u>Both have "breakoff" spines that fragment & cause pain/ swelling</u>** for some hours - Remove bits & apply dilute ammonia (or urine) & an antiseptic.

Hook Removal

1A. **1B.** **1C.** **2D.** **2E.**

"THIS IS... FLESH... AAHHH." "AARHHH... PRINT." "AAHHH!.. PRINT."

- **WHEN LITTLE "NOO"** ("Rat") gets a hook in his hand (method #1) or leg (method #2) here is how we get it out (**we have to sit on him!**).
- **1a)** It goes in ("OOWW!") - **1b)** Push point thru ("OH GOD!") - **1c)** Cut off & slide out ("AAHHH!").
- **2d)** Push shank down & tension loop - **2e)** ("Are you ready?" - "N—N—NO") Jerk ("AAHHHHHH!").
- **RESTRICT CIRCULATION** between hole & heart for a few minutes while hot washing.

Baking Soda

(Sodium Bicarbonate) is what we in the galley always keep handy because of its extreme versatility.

- **ATHLETES FOOT:** Rub between toes - Rinse.
- **BRASS POLISH:** Dampen object - Brush or sponge on B.S - Polish with soft cloth.
- **TOOTHPASTE:** Mix 1 part fine seasalt & 2 parts B.S - Dip brush & apply.
- **GUM DISEASES:** Use same mix as above.
- **INDIGESTION:** 1/4 tsp. B.S in 1/2 glass water.
- **MOUTHWASH:** 1 teaspoon B.S in 1 glass water.
- **BODY ODOR:** Sprinkle on damp cloth & apply.
- **REFRIGERATOR SMELLS:** Leave open, B.S inside.
- **CABIN/ROOM SMELLY:** Put B.S in saucer (or similar), on shelves etc. (vinegar also works).
- **DIRTY LAUNDRY:** Rub damp B.S into stains &/or add to washing/rinse water.
- **GENERAL CLEANER:** Dampen object (e.g. sink/oven etc.) & sprinkle B.S on (if bad leave 30 mins), scrub, & rinse off.
- **SUNBURN:** Use cold compresses of 3 tablespoons B.S to 1 liter water.
- **BAKING:** Use 1 part B.S to 2 parts cream of tartar.

"I LECOMMEND FO LEFLIGELATO"

NOTE: CAN YOU UNDELSTAND CHINESE?

HEAD CHEF

BAKING SODA

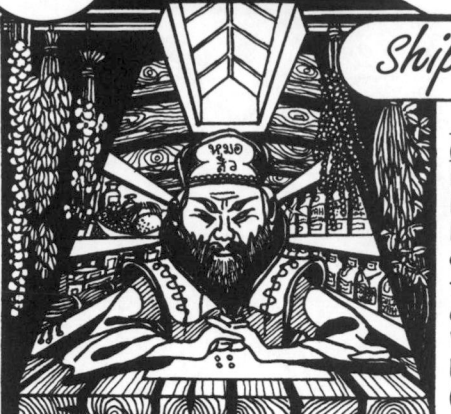

Ship's Doctor....

....is old "Koon Siw" (Mr. Pimple) - He lives in the forepeak & knows many tricks to keep us healthy ....

● **STYES:** Dab it 3 times a day with warm Camomile Tea - Take Vit E 200 iu & Oil of Eve. Prim. 1,000 mg (both 3 times a day for 3 months).

● **WATER QUALITY is vital to health** (Koon Siw always tells us) **because long-term use of impure water can cause many bad problems** (always he will taste before buying the ship's water in a port).

WATER	AILMENT
LIGHT	Hair loss & goiters.
HEAVY	Dropsy & Paralysis.
BITTER	Deformities & hunchbacks.
PUNGENT	Boils - Ulcers - Tumors.

● **HERPES (incl. cold sores/shingles/genital/chickenpox etc.)** - **EXTERNALLY:** Apply pure Vit. E Oil &/or fresh Aloe Vera gel - **INTERNALLY:** Mega B Comp. (time-release) - Acidopholus - Vit B12 (10-100 mcg) - L-Lysine (500 mg-1g) all AM & PM + Vit. C (1-4 g) every 4 hours DECREASING SLOWLY - Vitiman E is also useful internally.

VITAMIN & MINERAL LOSSES ....

.... At sea come mainly from storage & age of foods, but here are other causes that **CAN DRAMATICALLY DEPLETE BODY RESERVES.**

VITAMIN	LOSS CAUSED BY
B1	Alcohol - Stress - Fever - Antacids - Pregnancy - Heat.
B2	Alcohol - Tobacco - The pill.
B6	Alcohol - Drugs - Tobacco - Excess choline/Estrogen.
B12	Old age - Alcohol - Worms - Veganism - Pregnancy - Excess Vit. C/Estrogen.
Biotin	Antibiotics - Stress - Raw egg white - Estrogen.
C	Tobacco - Alcohol - Stress - Infection/Disease - Drugs - Old age - Diabetes.
D	Lack of animal protein/Sun.
E	Alcohol - Excess mineral oil/Iron/Chlorine/Heat/Oxygen - Liver disease.
F	Saturated fats - Oxygen - Heat.
Folic Acid	Drugs - Pregnancy - Heat - Old age - Excess Vit. C.
K	X Rays - Antibiotics - Aspirin.
Niacin	Alcohol - Drugs - Excess water.
B5	Antibiotics - Stress - Caffeine.
Paba	Sulpha drugs - Alcohol - Water.

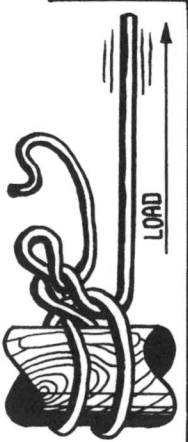

FAST HITCH (for quick releases)

Weather Wizard...

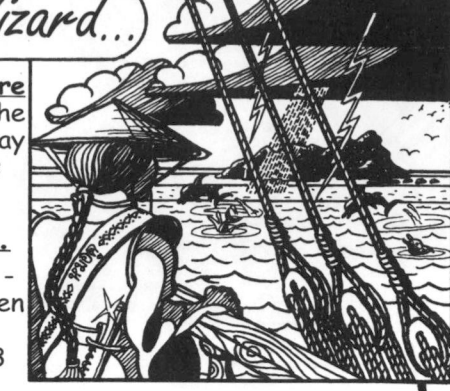

...on every junk there **must be one** to read the signs & to show the way - Here are some hints from our own....

HOW FAR OFF....

....IS THAT STORM? - Count seconds between flash & thunder, div. by 5 = miles, div. by 3 = kilometers.

BAROMETER	INDICATES
STEADY	No change.
SLOW RISE	Fine soon.
SLOW FALL	Wind soon.
FAST FALL OVER 1MB/HR	Strong wind/Rain/Storm.

BAROMETER....

.... readings vary with area, direction of wind & actual MB of reading (e.g. center of hurricane has no wind [= steady barometer] BUT a very low MB reading), however normally read as at left.

INDICATIONS ....

● **OF WIND:** Bright yellow sunset - Rapid rise or fall in barometer. *"Standby to shorten sail."*

● **OF RAIN:** Pale yellow or green sunset - Shrinking halo round sun/moon. *"Standby to scrub the decks."*

● **OF FINE WEATHER:** Silver moon - Growing halo round sun/moon - Red sunset - Dry strong wind - Birds feeding/flying offshore - Lots of jellyfish - Rising wind in AM & falling in PM - Sea with phosphorescense - (Fog/mist = no rain) - Rising barometer (slow/steady = best). *"Breakout the lotion."*

● **OF BAD WEATHER:** Red sunrise - Birds fly inland - Dolphins swim inshore - Decreasing cumulus by PM - A constant wind which suddenly changes direction - Rising wind in PM - Falling barometer. *"OH GOD!"*

MINERAL	LOSS CAUSED BY
Calcium	Low Vit. D - Excess phosphorus - Pregnancy - Oxalic/Phytic acids - Drugs - Excess fat.
Chromium	Alcohol - Processed foods.
Copper	Excess zinc/Molybdenum/Fluoride/Cadmium/Phytic acid (bran)/Processed food.
Iodine	Peanuts - Soya - Turnip - Rape.
Magnesium	Excess Vit. D/Calcium/Drugs/Alcohol - Cancer - Kidney disease.
Manganese	Processed foods - Excess copper.
Phosphorus	Excess dietary magnesium/Iron/Aluminium.
Potassium	Excess salt/Coffee/Sugar - Burns - Drugs - Injury - Flu.
Zinc	Alcohol - Liver &/or Kidney disease - Diuretics - Drugs - Processed foods - Excess bran.

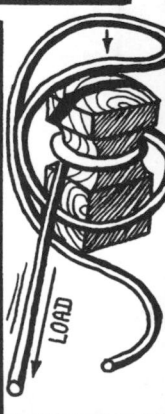

TOWING HITCH

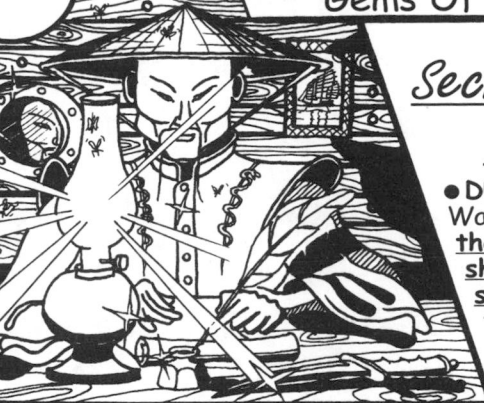

Secret Messages

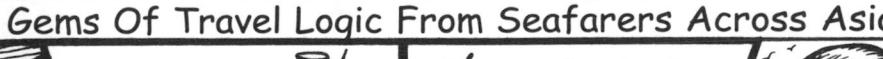

- **DURING** the "Great War" in Mongolia <u>there came on my ship four foreign spies</u> .... and from them I learned some modest skills which I .... AHHHHHHHHH!

WRITE DARK WORDS IN CLEAR INK

USE WHAT	MIX W/ WATER	TO DEVELOP	NOTES
Citrus Juice	Neat	Heat	Brown
Onion Juice	Neat	Heat	Brown
Candle Wax	-	Wash with weak ink	Or dust with powder
Sugar or Salt	1 to 40	Heat	Brownish
Lead Nitrate	1 to 80	Sodium sulphide 1 to 80	Black
Potato Juice	Neat	Heat	Brown
Vinegar or Milk	Neat	Heat	Brownish
Sodium Bisulphate	1 to 20	Heat	Gray (seal bottle)
Ammonium Chloride	1 to 160	Heat	Brown
Iron Sulphate	1 to 40	Sodium sulphide 1 to 80	Brown
Phenolphthalein	1 to 10	Ammonia 1 to 4	Red
Cobalt Chloride	1 to 80	Heat	Blue (reusable)

NOTES

- APPLY HEAT with iron/light bulb/stove top.
- APPLY DEVELOPER carefully (dab on/spray).
- WARM WATER is better for making ink.
- DON'T USE SHARP pens or press hard.

Credit Card Breakins....

....ARE A BIG PROBLEM IN OUR PORT - So we fit a row of tacks (head up a bit) here to stop these "worms" (who <u>will sometimes drug your water jug</u> then come back later TO CUT OUT YOUR GOLD TEETH).

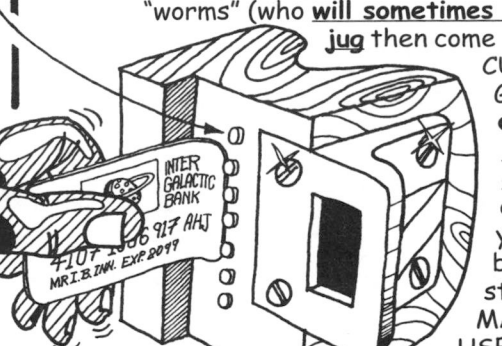

- **KEYS:** <u>Should never have your address/name on</u> or be attached to your wallet because if lost or stolen it (the key) MAY SOON BE USED TO ROB YOU.

ThrowingKnives

(or spikes [Shuriken])

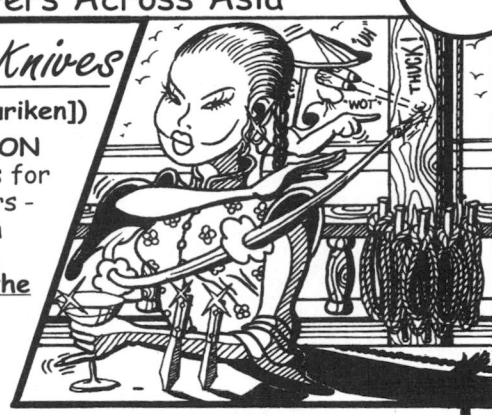

...A TRADITION of Asian sailors for a thousand years - Here, Woo Chin <u>(who can pin a cockroach to the mast at ten paces)</u> demonstrates the basic techniques.

GENERAL PRINCIPLES

- **BREATHING** is normally halted halfway thru the exhale cycle (mouth) <u>TO AVOID DEFLECTING THE THROWING ARM.</u>
- **PHYSICALLY** use the whole body (including hip twist) passing thru shoulder & wrist to deliver.... <u>MAXIMUM POWER.</u>
- **ANGLE OF IMPACT** must be at 90 degrees for.... <u>MAXIMUM PENETRATION.</u>
- **PREPARATION** (prior to a throw) should be minimal & subtle in bearing & position <u>TO AVOID GIVING AWAY YOUR INTENTIONS.</u>

STANCE, GRIP & TURNS

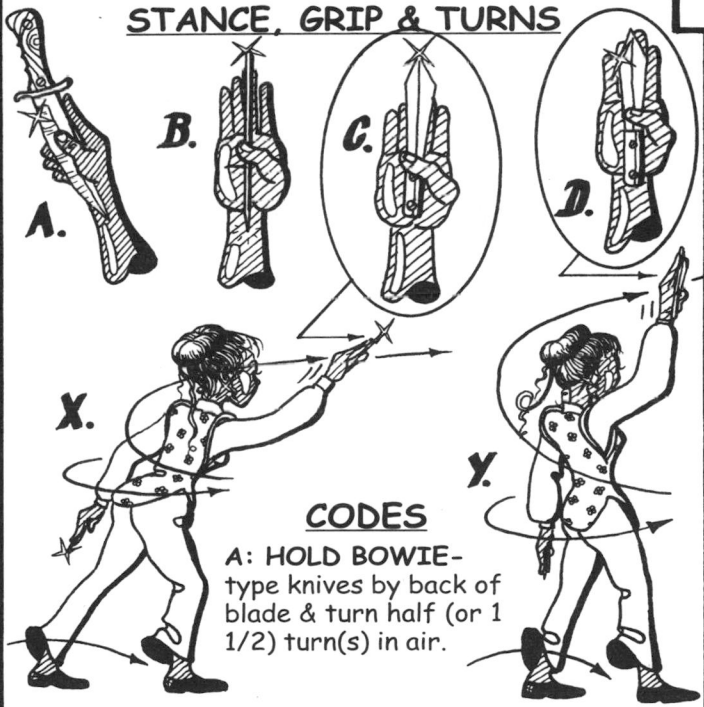

CODES

A: HOLD BOWIE- type knives by back of blade & turn half (or 1 1/2) turn(s) in air.

B: HOLD SPIKES (Shuriken [1/4 inch sq. steel]) either point in or out (according to style of throw & range of target)

C: THROWING KNIFE held for short range target (stance X.) (No turns).

D: THROWING KNIFE held for long range target (stance Y.) (No turns [or 1]).

- **AMBIDEXTERITY** is vital for advanced skills (in X & Y left hand holds next throw!).
- **SPIRITUALITY:** <u>Feel the weapon leave your hand like an attacking hawk</u> straight for the target - Empty the mind of all other thoughts **(THEY WILL DEFLECT YOUR AIM).**

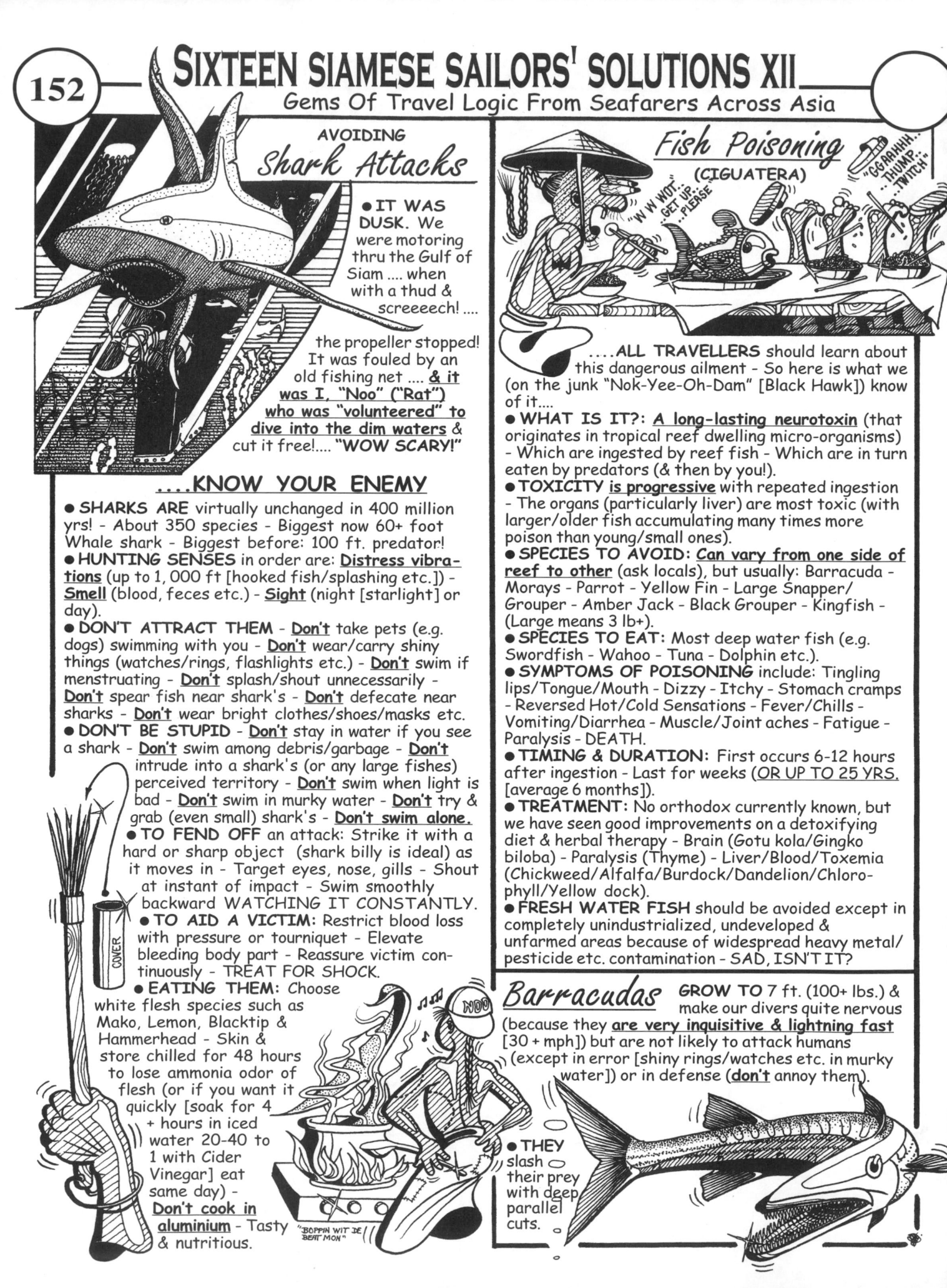

AVOIDING Shark Attacks

● IT WAS DUSK. We were motoring thru the Gulf of Siam .... when with a thud & screeeech! ....

the propeller stopped! It was fouled by an old fishing net .... **& it was I, "Noo" ("Rat") who was "volunteered" to dive into the dim waters** & cut it free!.... "WOW SCARY!"

....KNOW YOUR ENEMY

● SHARKS ARE virtually unchanged in 400 million yrs! - About 350 species - Biggest now 60+ foot Whale shark - Biggest before: 100 ft. predator!

● HUNTING SENSES in order are: **Distress vibrations** (up to 1,000 ft [hooked fish/splashing etc.]) - **Smell** (blood, feces etc.) - **Sight** (night [starlight] or day).

● DON'T ATTRACT THEM - **Don't** take pets (e.g. dogs) swimming with you - **Don't** wear/carry shiny things (watches/rings, flashlights etc.) - **Don't** swim if menstruating - **Don't** splash/shout unnecessarily - **Don't** spear fish near shark's - **Don't** defecate near sharks - **Don't** wear bright clothes/shoes/masks etc.

● DON'T BE STUPID - **Don't** stay in water if you see a shark - **Don't** swim among debris/garbage - **Don't** intrude into a shark's (or any large fishes) perceived territory - **Don't** swim when light is bad - **Don't** swim in murky water - **Don't** try & grab (even small) shark's - **Don't swim alone.**

● TO FEND OFF an attack: Strike it with a hard or sharp object (shark billy is ideal) as it moves in - Target eyes, nose, gills - Shout at instant of impact - Swim smoothly backward WATCHING IT CONSTANTLY.

● TO AID A VICTIM: Restrict blood loss with pressure or tourniquet - Elevate bleeding body part - Reassure victim continuously - TREAT FOR SHOCK.

● EATING THEM: Choose white flesh species such as Mako, Lemon, Blacktip & Hammerhead - Skin & store chilled for 48 hours to lose ammonia odor of flesh (or if you want it quickly [soak for 4 + hours in iced water 20-40 to 1 with Cider Vinegar] eat same day) - **Don't cook in aluminium** - Tasty & nutritious.

"BOPPIN WIT DE BEAT MON"

Fish Poisoning (CIGUATERA)

"W W WOT... GET UP... PLEASE"

"GGRHHH... THUMP... TWITCH"

....ALL TRAVELLERS should learn about this dangerous ailment - So here is what we (on the junk "Nok-Yee-Oh-Dam" [Black Hawk]) know of it....

● WHAT IS IT?: <u>A long-lasting neurotoxin</u> (that originates in tropical reef dwelling micro-organisms) - Which are ingested by reef fish - Which are in turn eaten by predators (& then by you!).

● TOXICITY <u>is progressive</u> with repeated ingestion - The organs (particularly liver) are most toxic (with larger/older fish accumulating many times more poison than young/small ones).

● SPECIES TO AVOID: <u>Can vary from one side of reef to other</u> (ask locals), but usually: Barracuda - Morays - Parrot - Yellow Fin - Large Snapper/Grouper - Amber Jack - Black Grouper - Kingfish - (Large means 3 lb+).

● SPECIES TO EAT: Most deep water fish (e.g. Swordfish - Wahoo - Tuna - Dolphin etc.).

● SYMPTOMS OF POISONING include: Tingling lips/Tongue/Mouth - Dizzy - Itchy - Stomach cramps - Reversed Hot/Cold Sensations - Fever/Chills - Vomiting/Diarrhea - Muscle/Joint aches - Fatigue - Paralysis - DEATH.

● TIMING & DURATION: First occurs 6-12 hours after ingestion - Last for weeks (<u>OR UP TO 25 YRS.</u> [average 6 months]).

● TREATMENT: No orthodox currently known, but we have seen good improvements on a detoxifying diet & herbal therapy - Brain (Gotu kola/Gingko biloba) - Paralysis (Thyme) - Liver/Blood/Toxemia (Chickweed/Alfalfa/Burdock/Dandelion/Chlorophyll/Yellow dock).

● FRESH WATER FISH should be avoided except in completely unindustrialized, undeveloped & unfarmed areas because of widespread heavy metal/pesticide etc. contamination - SAD, ISN'T IT?

Barracudas

GROW TO 7 ft. (100+ lbs.) & make our divers quite nervous (because they **are very inquisitive & lightning fast** [30 + mph]) but are not likely to attack humans (except in error [shiny rings/watches etc. in murky water]) or in defense (**don't** annoy them).

● THEY slash their prey with deep parallel cuts.

Gems Of... ...Travel Logic From Seafarers Across Asia

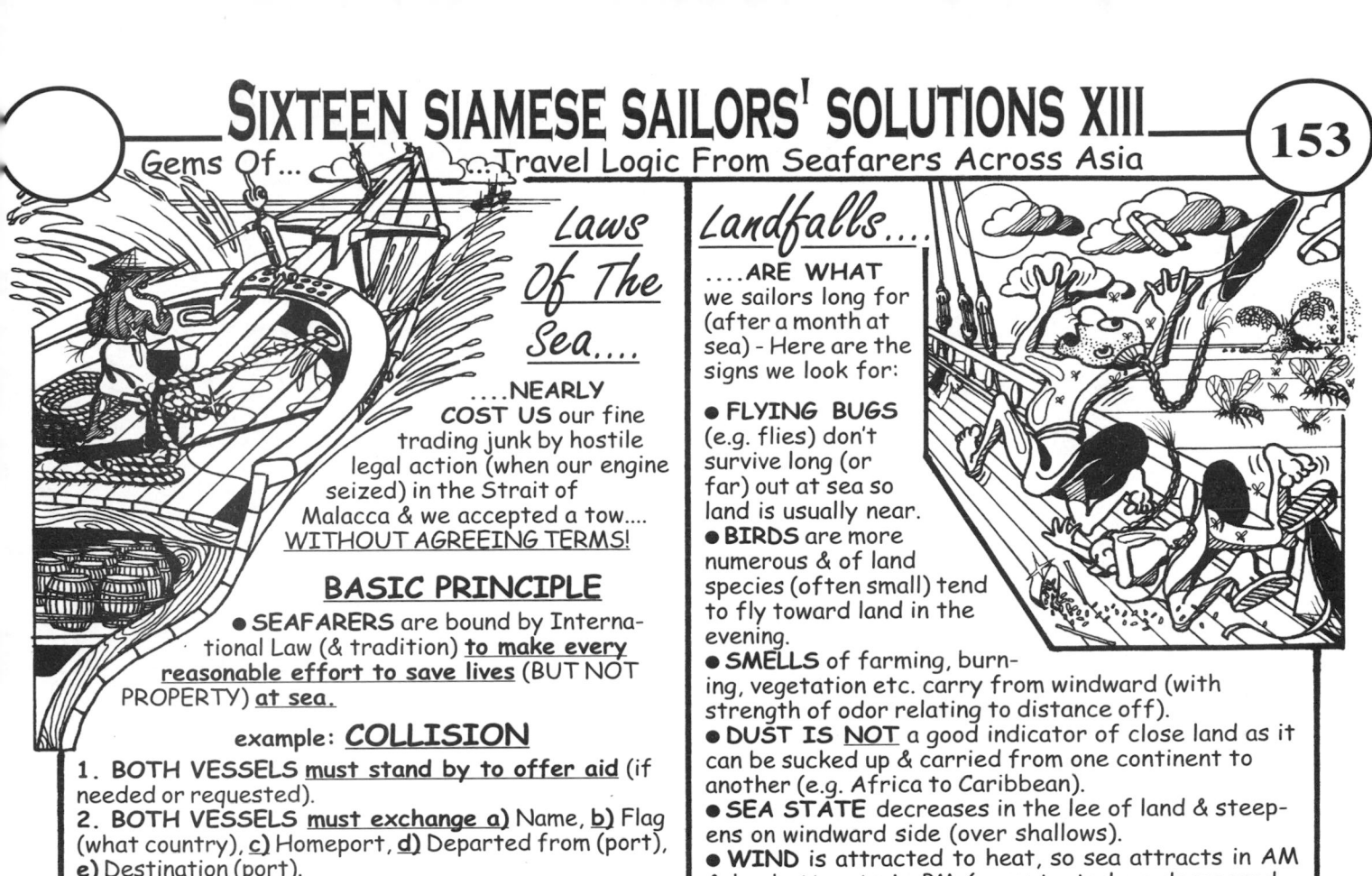

Laws Of The Sea....

....NEARLY COST US our fine trading junk by hostile legal action (when our engine seized) in the Strait of Malacca & we accepted a tow.... <u>WITHOUT AGREEING TERMS!</u>

BASIC PRINCIPLE

● SEAFARERS are bound by International Law (& tradition) <u>to make every reasonable effort to save lives</u> (BUT NOT PROPERTY) <u>at sea.</u>

example: COLLISION

1. BOTH VESSELS <u>must stand by to offer aid</u> (if needed or requested).
2. BOTH VESSELS <u>must exchange a)</u> Name, <u>b)</u> Flag (what country), <u>c)</u> Homeport, <u>d)</u> Departed from (port), <u>e)</u> Destination (port).

● NOTE: VIOLATION of the "Rules Of The Road" <u>does not necessarily indicate guilt</u> (as all available circumstances are considered).

YOU <u>must</u> know about SALVAGE

● <u>DISTRESSED PARTY MUST</u> (in order to avoid possibly unjust claims): 1. AVOID DISTRESS SIGNALS or flares (unless vital to life) - (White flares OK). 2. AVOID ACCEPTING AID (&/or warps) etc. from other vessels (if they throw you a tow line, attach yours to it & let them pull it in). 3. AGREE BEFORE WITNESSES (verbal will do) a towing fee in advance for safe passage to/from etc. ("no cure no pay" is best). 4. MAKE DETAILED LOG ENTRY of incident (& HAVE THE CREW SIGN IT).

● SALVOR MUST (in order to legitimize a claim) show beyond reasonable doubt that: 1. THE DISTRESSED VESSEL was in extreme danger of being lost. 2. HIS OR HER EFFORTS to save the distressed vessel were voluntary. 3. HIS OR HER VESSEL & CREW were put to expense (or endangered by the salvage). 4. HIS OR HER EFFORTS were successful.

REMEMBER

● PROVIDING A TOW LINE (or other aid) does not bestow salvage rights automatically.
● PASSENGERS/ CREW are unlikely to be granted salvage rights.
● A SALVOR <u>does not automatically own a salvaged vessel.</u>

Landfalls....

....ARE WHAT we sailors long for (after a month at sea) - Here are the signs we look for:

● FLYING BUGS (e.g. flies) don't survive long (or far) out at sea so land is usually near.
● BIRDS are more numerous & of land species (often small) tend to fly toward land in the evening.
● SMELLS of farming, burning, vegetation etc. carry from windward (with strength of odor relating to distance off).
● DUST IS <u>NOT</u> a good indicator of close land as it can be sucked up & carried from one continent to another (e.g. Africa to Caribbean).
● SEA STATE decreases in the lee of land & steepens on windward side (over shallows).
● WIND is attracted to heat, so sea attracts in AM & land attracts in PM (accentuated or decreased by prevailing area winds).
● SOUND (e.g. SURF) is particularly useful in bad visibility/at night (in quiet conditions) - IT CAN APPEAR EERILY CLOSE.
● SEA COLOR (Usually lighter = shallower).

CLOUD INDICATIONS

● LIGHT LOOM (from cities) can be seen on the underside of clouds 20-200 miles offshore.
● GREEN TINGE (from jungles/lagoons etc.) on underside of clouds 10-50 miles offshore.
● CUMULUS LINE often gathers along coastlines.
● CUMULUS STACK often hangs on mountains/hills & does <u>not</u> move with wind (like other clouds).

☐ Junk Sailors.... MUST BE TOUGH"

....says the seafaring martial artist Woo Chin....
"Because the sea takes no prisoners - So on your way to the fish market practice THE 4 TRADITIONAL ASPECTS OF WELL-BEING."

THINK POSITIVE	GOOD POSTURE
"<u>Avoid negative thought</u> & dwell on the good of all situations."	"<u>Is a therapy in itself</u> - Top of head up & bottom in."
BE VERY ACTIVE	BREATHE DEEPLY
"<u>Maximise time</u> during routine activity."	"<u>It is the staff of life</u> - In & out fully & slowly."

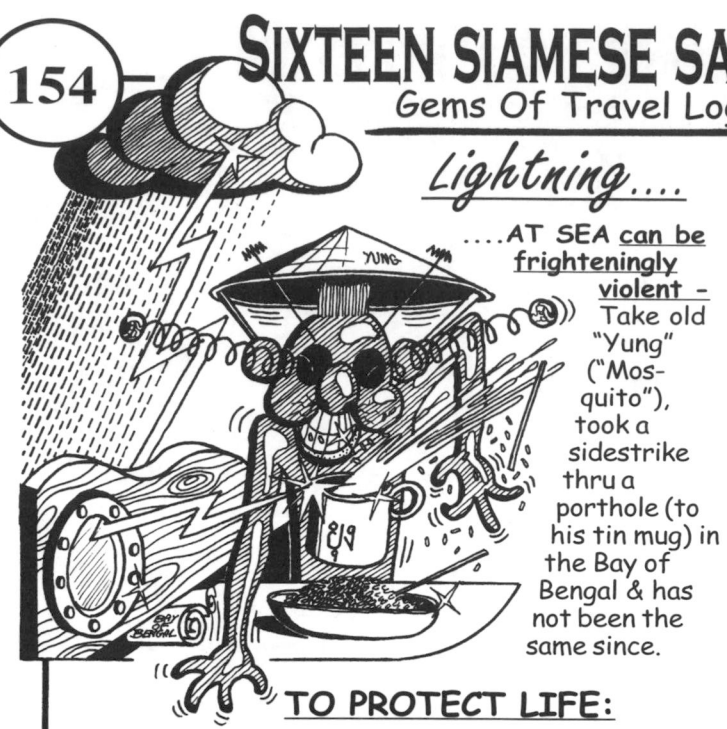

Lightning....

....AT SEA <u>can be frighteningly violent</u> - Take old "Yung" ("Mosquito"), took a sidestrike thru a porthole (to his tin mug) in the Bay of Bengal & has not been the same since.

TO PROTECT LIFE:

1. GO BELOW & stay dry.
2. KEEP AWAY FROM all metal & electric contact.
3. PARTICULARLY AVOID proximity (6 ft) to metal masts & chain plates - But also stove pipes, radio & engine rooms (even metal ships wheel - <u>GROUND IT</u>).

TO PROTECT THE VESSEL:

1. FIT A METAL ROD (6 - 12 inches) on top of tallest mast & bond it to both cap shrouds (shortest distance to water) also ground all other masthead fittings (instruments etc.) to it.
2. GROUND BOTH cap shroud chainplates to keel &/ or an external underwater plate <u>(or temporarily attach a chain/heavy wire to chainplate & throw it overboard)</u>.

NOTES

1. CONES OF PROTECTION extend about 60 degrees (on all sides of vertical) from lighting rod.
2. SIDE FLASHES (due to breaks in the conductor) CAN REACH UP TO 2 METERS OUT.
3. BURN THRU can occur if a struck conductor does not go to ground (or has too high a resistance [i.e. wood — CHECK THAT SHIP'S WHEEL]).
4. BE SURE all electric's are <u>well</u> grounded.

Bunk Wetting....

....CERTAIN SHORT CREW members suffer from this problem (& as laundry is difficult at sea) here are our remedies.

BASIC RULES

● DON'T CHASTISE the child for "accidents" (stress) - Give merit stars for dry days (in a row).
● NO EXCITEMENT before bed (movies/arguments etc.).
● DRINK ONLY IN AM & hold urine as long as possible (to stretch bladder & exercise muscles).
● AVOID ALLERGENS which irritate bladder, reduce flexibility & induce "drugged" sleep.
● KEEP WARM IN BED & sleep on side (not stomach).
● TRADITIONALLY JAPANESE parents tickle bedwetters 1 - 4 mins/ day.... "NO! STOP! HA HA HA HA!".
● AVOID DIETARY spice, salt, sugar.
● WAKE UP about 2 hrs after bed to go to toilet, thereafter as required.

SUPPLEMENTS

● BEE POLLEN (for allergies): Increase dose slowly over 1 month & take for 3 months.
● MAGNESIUM 200 mg/day for 1 month (don't take this with a meal [neutralises acid]).
● VIT A & B COMPLEX (are also both useful).
● CINNAMON (stick of): Chew at bedtime.
● HONEY (teaspoon of): Eat at bedtime.
● PARSLEY (sprig of): Eat 1 hour before bed.
● HERBS (take one for 2 months then stop or change): Corn silk - Buchu leaf - Fennel - Uva ursi - St. Johns wort - Hops - Parsley.

MASSAGE/ACU. SITES

● BELLY BUTTON (& 4 child finger widths below).
● IN WEB of big & next toes (on top side).
● BESIDE SPINE (level with tops of buttocks).
● ANKLE BONE (below & behind on outsides).
● BACK OF NECK (level with bottoms of ears).
● SHINS (1 hand width below outsides of kneecaps).

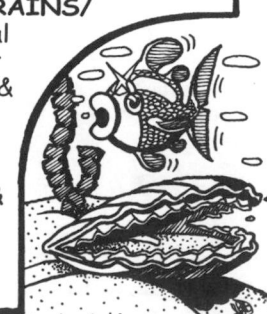

ALKALI FORMING

● MOST VEGETABLES (except onions/lentils).
● MOST FRUITS (figs & apricots particularly [not plums/ cranberries]).
● AVOID dried legumes.
● MOST NUTS (particularly almonds [except peanuts, walnuts]).
● MOST BEAN sprouts.

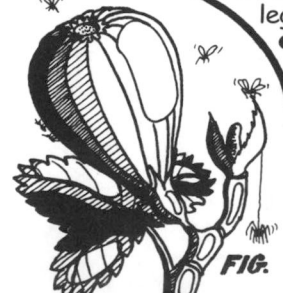

FIG.

Alkaline & Acid Forming Foods

● NORMAL BODY pH is ideally 7.4 for optimum health & immunity (skin 5.5).
● DIETARY EXCESS (particularly on the acid [protein] side) upsets a delicate balance & encourages ailments (e.g: Indigestion - Arthritis - Fatigue - Prostate - Ulcers - Kidneys - Low immunity).
● IDEAL RATIO of dietary alkaline forming foods to acid forming is: 4 to 1 (or 80% alkaline & 20% acid - But [in any case] never less than 50% & 50%).

NEUTRAL

● MOST MILKS, vegetable oils, yogurt.

ACID FORMING

● MOST FISH/seafood (particularly oysters).
● MOST MEAT (except horse) incl. poultry.
● MOST GRAINS/ flour/cereal etc. (except buckwheat & millet).
● CHEESE.
● EGGS.
● COCOA & SUGAR.
● SOME NUTS.

Toxic Oils....

....ARE WHAT all sailors (**particularly cooks** who get distracted [& then burn our fried squid in chilli sauce]) **need to know about.**

BASIC FACTS

1. SATURATED FATS (all animal origin + coconut/palm oils) are bad for you (**clogging arteries/heart [& metabolism] disastrously fast**).

2. UNSATURATED FATS (all other natural vegetable [non solid when cold] oils) in moderation (not more than 20% of diet) **are vital nutritionally** - (Aid Vits. A, D, E & K + calcium absorption + hormones [incl. sex] formation & use in the body).

3. BUT EITHER CAN BECOME VERY TOXIC in certain **apparently innocent conditions:**

HOW FATS/OILS BECOME DANGEROUS.

● UNSATURATED can be turned saturated by:

1. HYDROGENATION is commercial processing (in biscuits/cake etc.) - **Read packets carefully.**
2. OVERHEATING (e.g. in frying/B.B.Q/oven) e.g.: Olive oil max. 347 degrees F. (but corn oil max. is 450 degrees F.).

● ANY OIL CAN TURN rancid by:

1. OXIDIZATION (is exposure to oxygen for too long [left top off bottle etc.]).
2. LONG STORAGE, even in unused grains/nuts/seeds/legumes (but also in oils in bottles [check age]).

RANCID OILS ARE LETHAL....

....FROM TOO MUCH HEAT, AGE, OXYGEN (even light) form free radicals which can & do cause: Vit. E depletion, arthritis, ulcers, early aging, heart attack, metabolic breakdown & CANCER.

ACTION SUMMARY

● AVOID SATURATED FATS.
● AVOID FRIED FOODS.
● AVOID EXCESS (over 20% of total diet) of un-saturates.
● DON'T EAT old grains/nuts/oils
● DON'T OVERHEAT any dietary oil/fat.
● NEVER EVER reuse cooking oil.
● TAKE ANTIOXIDANT supplements daily (Vits. A, B6, B Comp, C, E + selenium & zinc).

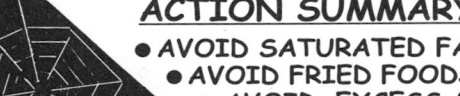

● EVEN OLD RICE (bran oil in) can turn rancid & become potentially CARCINOGENIC...

Toxic Food Combinations

....OF INDIVIDUAL-LY good foods can cause sailors like "Cha" ("Slow") many health problems (such as serious indigestion & fatigue [for hours after eating]) - *"Because the Bosun thought he was lazy & used to throw him overboard daily."*

● OTHER SYMPTOMS include: Obesity - Nerves - Headache - Dyspepsia - Irregular heartbeat - Heartburn - Metabolic slowdown - Allergies - Toxic buildup - Arthritis - Multiple skin ailments.

BASIC FACTS

● DIFFERENT FOOD GROUPS are digested in different organs, for different times, & with different "enzymes."
● EXAMPLE: "Cha" has a meal of fish & rice.
 - *THE FISH* (being a protein) requires about 12 hours in an acid medium (stomach) & the enzyme pepsin to be digested.
 - *THE RICE* (being a starch) requires about 5 hours in an alkaline medium (mouth & intestines [& different enzymes] to digest).
● RESULT: The rice (alkaline) not only stops complete digestion of the fish (acid) **but actually rots in the stomach** being unable to pass the fish to be digested in the intestines - *"Cha's" whole metabolism goes into mild shock as toxicity rises* (& fatigue/indigestion/allergies etc. set in).

BASIC RULES

1. DON'T combine protein (or acid fruit) with starch.
2. DON'T eat sweet desserts after protein.
3. DO combine starches, green veg., fats, sugars (all require alkaline [or neutral] medium).
4. DO combine proteins, fats, acid fruits, green veg. (all require acid [or neutral] medium).

ADDITIONAL HINTS

● DON'T DRINK with (or up to 2 hours after) meals.
● PAPAYA/pineapple aid lean protein digestion (enzymes).
● WATERMELON conflicts badly with cantaloupe.
● EAT NON-ACID fruits alone (very alkaline).
● BLENDED PROTEIN (& starch mixes [e.g. pancakes]) digest reasonably well.
● AVOID COFFEE/TEA (particularly after meals).
● HEARTBURN responds to 12 raw almonds or a glass of skimmed milk.

DO NOT COMBINE A & C

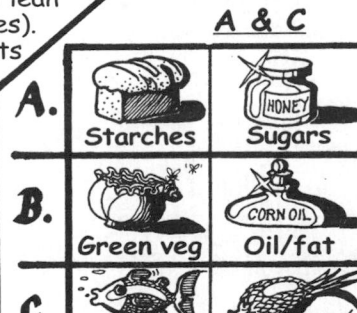

A.	Starches	Sugars
B.	Green veg	Oil/fat
C.	Proteins	Acid fruit

Gems Of Travel Logic From Seafarers Across Asia

Yang Food For Sailors

(ALMOST ALL ILLNESS RESULTS FROM EXCESS YIN - STAY YANG & WELL)

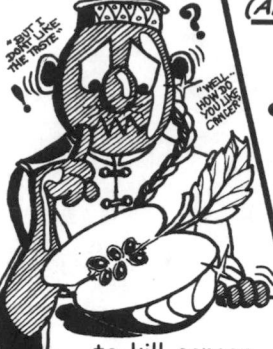

APPLE PIPS are believed....

....to kill cancer cells (with organic cyanide) also contains B17

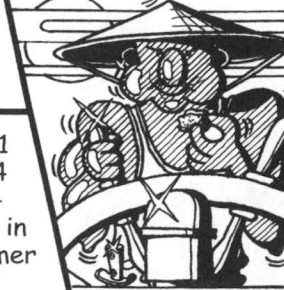

EATING RAW food....

....before cooked reduces allergies & aids digestion (also take Vit B Complex & 1 - 2 tsp. cider vinegar after).

STARTERS

● **YANG SIDE SALAD:** 4 carrots (grated) - 2 apples (cubed) - 2 cloves garlic (chopped) - 1 tbsp. cider vinegar - 1 tbsp. olive oil - Pinch of sea salt - Toss/Chill/ Serve. *"YES! FEELIN' GOOOD!"*

● **"SOOP GRA-TIUM" (GARLIC SOUP):** 1-4 cloves garlic (chopped) - 1/2 cup rice noodles - 1 stock cube - 1/4-1/2 tsp. cayenne pepper powder - 1/2 spring onion (chopped) - Pinch of sea salt - Pour on hot water/stir **(lowers high blood pressure & clears mucus)**. *"I FEEL BETTER ALREADY!"*.

● **"SALAT TOO-UH" (BEAN SALAD):** 8 oz mung bean sprouts - 1 red pepper (seed & slice) - 2 spring onions (chopped) - **DRESSING:** 2 tbsp. olive/groundnut oil - 2 tbsp. rice wine/cider vinegar - 1 tsp. honey - 1 tsp. tamari sauce - Pinch sea salt - Mix & shake dressing - Pour over mixed salad & toss - Let stand for 30 mins.

● **"BPO GLOM" (CRAB RINGS):** 1 cored cucumber filled with a blended mix of: 2 hard boiled eggs - 1 cup crab meat - 1/2 cup pickled onion + lemon juice & sea salt (pack/slice & top with ginger). —VELY VELY TASTY.

DESSERTS

● **NIGHT WATCH BISCUITS:** 3 oz dried dates - 4 oz unsweetened apple juice - 4 oz wholemeal flour - 4 oz tahini - 2 oz oats (rolled) - 1 tsp. cinnamon - Mash & blend dates with 1/2 of apple juice - Mix other ingredients in well - Add other 1/2 apple juice - Spread & cook in oven (preheated) 20 mins. @ 330 degrees F. *"AH LUUV THESE!"*.

● **"BAWL APUNN" (APPLE BALLS):** (Kids love 'em) - Boil 6 oz dried apricots in 6 oz water until all gone - Then blend into puree & add: 2 grated apples - 4 oz ground almonds - 2 egg whites (beaten) - 2 oz wheatgerm - 1/2 tsp. ground cloves - 1/2 tsp. cinnamon (ground) - Bake in blobs 15 mins @ 320 degrees F. *"I'LL SCREAM IF U DON'T GIMME MORE."*

● **"KOW WAN" (RICE PUDDING):** (This dessert a bit yin because of honey) 4 1/2 cups of skim milk - 1/2 cup skim milk powder - 2 cups whole grain rice - 1/4 cup honey - 1 tsp. cinnamon - Mix milk & powder well - Add & mix honey, cinnamon & rice - Bake in preheated oven @ 220 degrees F for 3 hours (stir ev. 30 minutes) - Serve hot or cold topped with nuts. *"MMMM."*

MAIN COURSES

● **"BPLA PAT" (FRIED FISH):** Dip fish fillet in lemon juice - Coat with ground nuts/seeds &/or wholemeal flour - Fry until crisp.

● **"SALAT GAI" (CHICKEN SALAD):** 1 small chicken (boil/skin/chop) - 4 apples (core/cube) - 2 cups roast nuts (partly crushed) - 1/2 cup unsweet-ened apple juice - 1 tsp. ginger (chopped root) - Pinch of sea salt - Toss/chill/serve. —OH YES, VELY SEXY.

● **HOT LENTIL SOUP:** 2 onions (chopped) - 4 cloves garlic (crushed) - 2 tbsp. veg. oil - 4 cups water - 1 cup red lentils - 1 bay leaf - 1/2 tsp. ginger (ground) - 2 tsp. cayenne pepper (ground) - 1/4 tsp. sea salt - 1/2 lemon juice - Parsley - Fry onions & garlic lightly in oil - Add other ingre-dients & simmer for 45 minutes - Add parsley & lemon at table.

● **"KOW HOONG" (STEAM/BOIL RICE):** 1 cup whole grain (brown) rice - 2 1/4 cups water - 1/4 tsp. sea salt - Rinse rice until water is clear - Boil on high heat until water starts to go & craters appear (5 - 10 mins.) - Cover pan tightly & steam on low heat for 40 mins. more - Remove pan & let stand for 10 mins. - Remove lid & fluff. —VELY EASY.

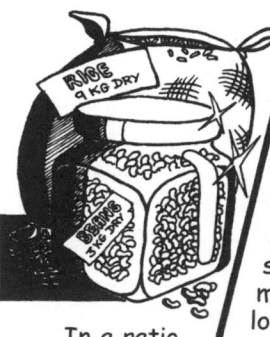

BEANS (or peas) & RICE (or grain)....

....In a ratio of 1 to 3 make a complete protein.

SPECIAL TREATS

● **"BPAWN TOO-UH" (NUT LOAF):** (1: 2 eggs - 3/4 cup veg. oil - 1/2 cup honey) - (2: 1 1/2 cups wholemeal flour - 2 tsp. nutmeg - 1 tsp. cinnamon - 1 tsp. baking powder - 1/2 tsp. sea salt) - (3: 1 1/2 cups grated carrots - 1 cup crushed nuts) - Preheat oven to 350 degrees F - Mix section 1 together well - Add section 2 & mix - Add section 3 & mix - Bake for 60 minutes. *"GREAT WITH HERB TEA."*

● **APPLE SHAKE:** 2 cups skim milk - 4 tsp. skim milk powder - 1 cup unsweetened apple juice - 1 tsp. vanilla - 4 ice cubes - Blend until frothy.

● **STRAWBERRY SHAKE:** 1 cup skim milk - 1/2 cup ripe straw-berries - 1 ice cube - 1 tsp. vanilla - Blend until it froths.

● **TOO YIN PANCAKES:** 2 eggs - 2 ripe bananas - 1 tsp. honey - pinch sea salt - Blend all together - Fry & turn when brown.

....OR TO SEPARATE GRAINS: 1 cup wholegrain (brown) rice - 2 1/4 cups water - 1/4 cup vegetable oil - 1/4 tsp. sea salt - Heat oil then stir in rice until brown - Add water & simmer for 40 - 50 minutes.

● **"KOW PAT" (FRIED RICE):** Use cold steamed rice in a little hot oil & stirfry with other ingredients.

ACID STOMACH!....

....On nightwatch we love to snack on....

....RAW ALMONDS & APRICOTS (DRY [very alkaline])

Useful Time-Saving "How To Do It" Tricks Around Your House

GENTLEMEN, HELP YOURSELF & IMPRESS YOUR LADY
(There is no more valued asset around the house than a useful man.)

SMELLS & HOW TO CONTROL THEM

- **DISH CLOTHS:** Boil (or soak) in bleach solution - DRY OUT OFTEN (in sun best).
- **ONION & GARLIC** smell on hands: RINSE IN ONLY COLD WATER & wipe with white vinegar (or lemon juice [on cutting boards rub with salt & rinse])
- **SINK DRAINS:** Pour half a cup of washing soda crystals down the plughole (& follow it with boiling water — <u>Watch out it doesn't "spit" back</u>).
- **CIGARETTE SMOKE** will be absorbed by: **a)** Hot weak solution of ammonia & lavender oil in open bowl - **b)** Open bowl of vinegar left overnight - **c)** For fast results wave a towel dampened with a weak ammonia solution (then wipe surfaces with it). *"WHAT A PARTY!"*
- **GARBAGE CANS:** Drop a few mothballs in the bottom of yours to keep odors down (& vermin away)... *"WOW STINKY."*
- **REFRIGERATORS** respond best to an open packet of baking soda (or charcoal) left in - Crumpled newspaper will also work. *"QUICK BEFORE MOTHER COMES."*
- **NEW PAINT & CHEMICALS:** Use either a peeled onion in a bucket of water (or a bowl of salt left overnight)... *"NICE JOB DAD."*
- **FISH** cooked in oil (with chopped celery will reduce odor) - To clean pan after: Boil saltwater in it - Add a dash of vinegar to washing up water (for plates etc.) *"HEY DAD CAN WE GO FISHING, PLEASE."*
- **CABBAGE** smells (when boiling) can be reduced by adding a squirt of lemon juice to cooking water. *"OH MUM NOT CABBAGE AGAIN."*
- **CUPBOARDS** (& the clothes in them) will stay fresh (& sweet) if you leave a saucer of bath salt crystals in a corner... *"MMM."*

MORE VINEGAR USES

- **WINDOW CLEAN - 1)** Add a couple of tablespoons of vinegar to a bucket of warm water - **2)** Use cloth or chamois leather to wipe windows with solution - **3)** Polish with crumpled newspaper... *"HEY DAD! WINDOW CLEAN FOR CASH?"*
- **MILDEW** can be discouraged (from developing) by wiping susceptible surfaces with vinegar... *"WHAT ABOUT THE SHOWER CEILING?"*
- **SLIMY SPONGES:** Will respond well to a soak in vinegar (1 tablespoon to 1 pint water) solution before washing... *"WOW SMELLY SPONGE."*
- **LIMESCALE** in kettles can be removed by covering element with vinegar - Boil & leave to cool - Empty & rinse well - A marble or small piece of loofah will discourage a reoccurrence... *"HEY DAD! I CAN FIX THAT KETTLE."*
- **LIMESCALE** in toilets: Plunge (or scoop) water out - Then brush with hot vinegar <u>& leave to stand</u> - Thereafter, when cleaning use vinegar in hot water (to disinfect & control reoccurring scale). ... *"OK MUM, I WILL CLEAN THAT DIRTY TOILET FOR...SAY $5...OK OK FOR YOU $3!"*

OVEN TEMPERATURE TABLE

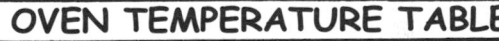

	ELECTRIC		GAS
	C	F	MARK
BRRR!	110	225	1/4
VERY COOL	120	250	1/2
	140	275	1
MEDIUM COOL	150	300	2
	160	325	3
MEDIUM	180	350	4
	190	375	5
MEDIUM HOT	200	400	6
	220	425	7
VERY HOT	230	450	8
	240	475	9
OUCH!	260	500	10

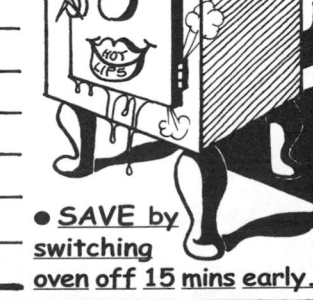

- <u>SAVE by switching oven off 15 mins early.</u>

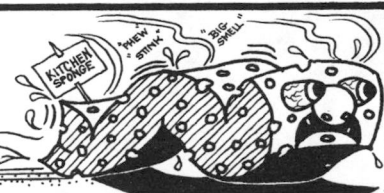

SEWING

● **SHORTEN DRESSES** by first getting the hemline straight - A chalked string between two chairs will mark your skirt evenly (wherever touched) - Or a second person can mark it with a pencil. *"HEY, MUM, CAN I DO IT, PLEASE?"*

● **FRAYED BUTTON HOLES:** Don't just cut bits off - Dab the edges with clear nail varnish. *"MUM, MUM, I CAN DO THAT TOO!"*

● **DRAWSTRINGS** in swimwear, pajamas, tracksuit bottoms etc. should be sewn "center back" (to avoid losing the ends).

● **BUTTONS:** Pick "four hole" types & sew each pair of holes separately (this way you rarely lose a button).

● **ANTI TWIST:** When hand sewing with double thread, knot each separately.

● **PLASTIC MATERIAL:** When machine sewed, tends to stick - Dust it with talcum powder (& slide)... *"WHOOPS SORRY, MUM."*

● **MACHINE THREAD BREAKING (TOP):** <u>Usually caused by</u> either too large a thread for the needle eye (or excess tension) - **(BOTTOM):** <u>Usually caused by</u> an overfull bobbin (or excess bobbin tension).

● **COMPLICATED** sewing jobs (e.g. erratically shaped covers) are best assembled using narrow (1/4 inch) two sided tape (which is left in the seams during [& after] sewing)... *"MUM, I LOVE PUTTING TAPE ON!"*

● **EXTRA THICK** (or hard) seams will sew (machine or hand) easier (& lie flatter) if a bar of soap is run along the inside of the material before the needle enters it. *"Sailors, these tips work on boats too!"*

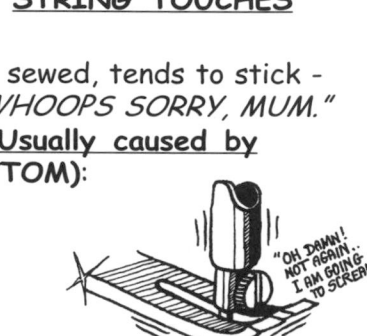

MARK WHERE STRING TOUCHES

Turn slowly

MISCELLANEOUS GEMS

● **STUCK GLASSES:** Be a hero & know this trick - Fill the inner one with cold water & hold the outer one in a sink of hot water - Pull apart... *"OH DARLING, YOU'RE SO...CLEVER!"*

● **AIRED BED** or not?: Check by leaving a small mirror between the sheets for a few minutes - If the bed is damp the mirror will mist up.

● **LIME SCALE** formation can futher be reduced by: Emptying the kettle completely each time it is boiled.

● **STEAMED UP** windows can be prevented by: Wiping them with a dab of dishwashing liquid on a dry cloth.

● **CONDENSATION** in bathrooms can be reduced by: Running the cold water into your bath before the hot.

● **TIGHT RUNNERS** (drawers): Will slide easier if rubbed with a bar of soap (or candle).

● **GLUE:** For paper (& kids) can be made with flour & water.

● **OLD FURNITURE POLISH** can be removed by rubbing with a rag dipped in (8 to 1) solution of warm water & vinegar.

● **DIFFICULT LIDS** to remove from jars & bottles are gripped easier if a rubber band is wrapped around - Or hold lid under hot water for 10 seconds... *"OH DARLING, YOU'RE SO STRONG TOO."*

● **WASHING LINGERIE** by machine can damage it - Put in a pillow case (& keep twice as long)... *"GULP! LET ME PUT THOSE IN, DEAR."*

● **TIDY KITCHENS** are difficult with kids leaving a stream of clothes, toys etc., behind them - <u>Solve this problem</u> by dumping all such items in a "Lost Property" box - & the person with the most things in it at the end of the month has to pay a fine (& put it all away!)... *"OH NO! NOT ME AGAIN!"*

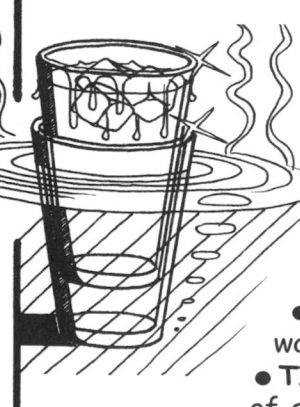

How To Diagnose, Treat & Look After Your Green Friends

CARE OF HOUSEPLANTS IS AN ART WITH MANY PITFALLS -
Watch carefully (even talk to) your charges & your thumb will turn green.

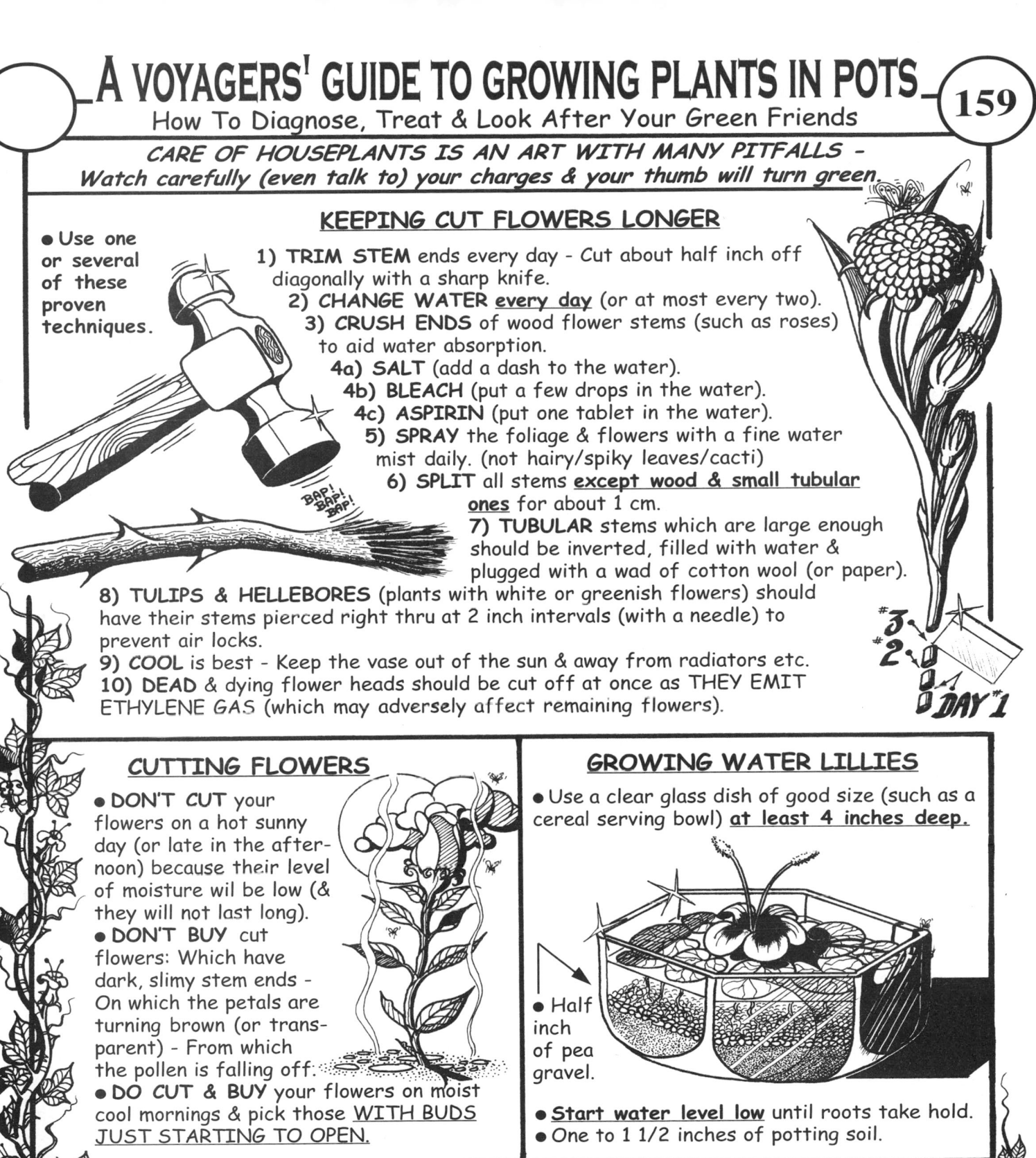

KEEPING CUT FLOWERS LONGER

● Use one or several of these proven techniques.

1) **TRIM STEM** ends every day - Cut about half inch off diagonally with a sharp knife.

2) **CHANGE WATER** <u>every day</u> (or at most every two).

3) **CRUSH ENDS** of wood flower stems (such as roses) to aid water absorption.

4a) **SALT** (add a dash to the water).

4b) **BLEACH** (put a few drops in the water).

4c) **ASPIRIN** (put one tablet in the water).

5) **SPRAY** the foliage & flowers with a fine water mist daily. (not hairy/spiky leaves/cacti)

6) **SPLIT** all stems <u>except wood & small tubular ones</u> for about 1 cm.

7) **TUBULAR** stems which are large enough should be inverted, filled with water & plugged with a wad of cotton wool (or paper).

8) **TULIPS & HELLEBORES** (plants with white or greenish flowers) should have their stems pierced right thru at 2 inch intervals (with a needle) to prevent air locks.

9) **COOL** is best - Keep the vase out of the sun & away from radiators etc.

10) **DEAD** & dying flower heads should be cut off at once as THEY EMIT ETHYLENE GAS (which may adversely affect remaining flowers).

BAP! BAP! BAP!

#3 #2 DAY #1

CUTTING FLOWERS

● **DON'T CUT** your flowers on a hot sunny day (or late in the afternoon) because their level of moisture wil be low (& they will not last long).

● **DON'T BUY** cut flowers: Which have dark, slimy stem ends - On which the petals are turning brown (or transparent) - From which the pollen is falling off.

● **DO CUT & BUY** your flowers on moist cool mornings & pick those <u>WITH BUDS JUST STARTING TO OPEN.</u>

GROWING WATER LILLIES

● Use a clear glass dish of good size (such as a cereal serving bowl) <u>at least 4 inches deep.</u>

● Half inch of pea gravel.

● <u>**Start water level low**</u> until roots take hold.

● One to 1 1/2 inches of potting soil.

TAKING CUTTINGS FOR TRANSPLANT

● **CHOOSE** an offshoot a couple of inches long (with several leaf buds forming)

- **CUT** <u>with a razor blade</u> diagonally (just below one of the buds)

- **REMOVE** (gently) any forming leaves on the lower section of the offshoot

- **PLANT** in sheltered, warm position in moist fertile soil.

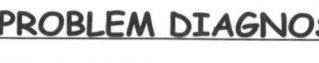

PROBLEM DIAGNOSIS

- **TALL & THIN:** Too little light relative to the amount of food & water available - Leaves may also be small & pale.
- **LEAVES GO YELLOW** (& drop off!) - Probable cause: Too much water.
- **LEAVES GO YELLOW** (& stay on) - Probable cause: Too much lime (or too little light).
- **BENT STEM:** Usually caused by a fixed position light source - Either turn or move plant regularly (a few times a week).
- **SLOW GROWTH** is usually caused by: a) Pot too small - b) Plant too cold - c) Too little food (&/or water).
- **BROWN EDGES** on leaves probably caused by: a) Cold winds - b) Too much bright light - c) Too much water.
- **ROTTEN ROOTS** are usually caused by: Too much water in the soil (which will often grow mold on top).
- **WHITE STREAKS** (or pale yellow/green patches) on leaves are usually viral (& contagious to other plants) - Throw it away & sterilize the pot.
- **CATERPILLARS:** Pick them all off by hand
- **GREEN FLY** (& other minature plant flies) which almost all suck sap (& encourage mold) - Wipe off those visible & spray with soap solution (keep contaminated plants away from healthy ones).

CLEANING HOUSEPLANTS

- **SHINE** thick leaved indoor plants with a drop of olive oil (on cotton wool) - Milk also works (but doesn't smell so good).
- **DAMP SPONGE** (or soft cotton cloth) any smooth surfaced leaves with clean (non-chlorinated) room temperature water.
- **BRUSH** (with a soft natural bristle paint brush) all hairy & spiky (cacti) leaved plants (which do not like moisture on their foliage [don't spray them]).

WATERING HINTS

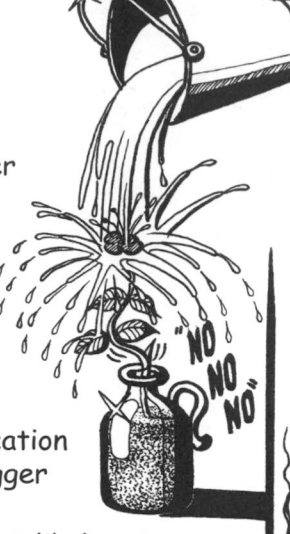

- **ONLY WATER** indoor (& potted) plants when they need it.
- **HOW TO KNOW:** Try pressing a piece of newspaper on the soil - If dry add water - If not, don't.
- **ROUGH GUIDE** for warmer months would be water 1 - 3 times a week - And for colder months 1 - 3 a month.
- **LEAF AREA** is a good indication of a plant's water needs (bigger area requires more).
- **CACTI** rarely need (& do not like) watering in winter - If their skin wrinkles give them a little.
- **TAP WATER** often contains chlorine (leave it to stand for a day & some will go) & other pollutants (it also may be the wrong temperature [room temp. best]) - Therefore use rain water if possible.
- **SPRAY** leaves (except hairy & cacti) occasionally (but not in direct sunlight as this can cause burning.

FEEDING HINTS

- **WHEN?:** In the growing season only (about every 2 weeks is good).
- **WHAT?:** Phosphates for the roots - Nitrogen for the leaves - Potash for flowers (& fruit).
- **HOW?:** Usually with liquid fertilizer (5 - 10 drops in a pint of water).
- **TOO MUCH** makes the plant lazy (& restricts root growth).
- **TOO LITILE** weakens resistance to bugs & disease.

OTHER

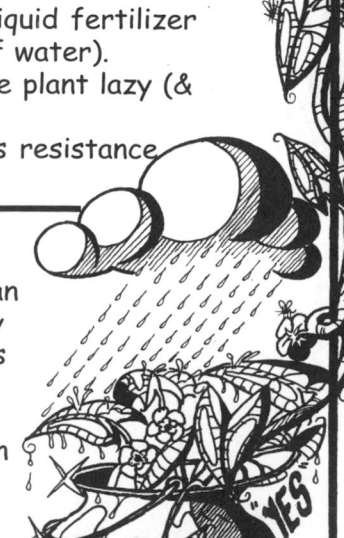

- **REPEAT BLOOMS:** Can be encouraged by gently pulling off dying flowers (before they seed).
- **BUSHY GROWTH:** Can be encouraged on tall plants by gently nipping off growing buds (on the top).

MOSQUITOES....

....**b**reed in still or stagnant water - Kill the larva with a few drops of paraffin (not on fish ponds) - Also use Pyrethrum spray (from Pyrethrum plant) or burn coils - **Put screens on doors & windows & sleep under a net** (which you first squashed into a ball) - **They do not like smoke or the smell of Basil** (herb) - SO GROW SOME ROUND YOUR HOUSE.

FLIES

Familiarity breeds contempt of this common but dangerous carrier of dozens of diseases - **From dung, sewer & dead/rotten meat direct to your kitchen (& food) where they regurgitate & lay eggs!** - Cover all food - Wipe all kitchen tops with disinfectant - Put screens on windows & doors - Keep moth balls in your rubbish bin - Keep the area around your house clean - **Plant some Lavender around the garden** (& rub surfaces with oil of Lavender) which they don't like - **Other herbs they do not like are Mint - Pennyroyal - Rue - Elder** - (Elecampane root is also good for a sticky fly trap [HANG A PIECE IN DOORWAYS]).

WOODWORM....

....**is** actually the grub of the furniture beetle **which can live for several years in almost any type of wood** (leaving pin head size holes & fine pale saw dust) - **Treatment is not easy** - Use a fine tipped can to squirt Paraffin or Kerosene in each hole (then follow with liquid Ammonia) - Leave for a day & wipe excess off - <u>CHECK FOR REINFESTATION.</u>

BEDBUGS

Very small, wingless brown night active bugs, with a sweet smell - Often leave dark stains on walls & bed linens - **Bites are itchy & some cause allergic reactions** - **Bugs live in wall/floor cracks, furniture & bed mattresses** - Treat affected areas with insecticide (e.g. Pyrethrum - Malthion or Lindane).

RATS & MICE....

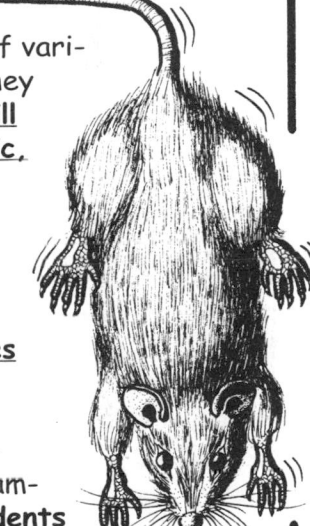

....**are** both carriers of various serious diseases - They are also destructive **& will gnaw thru wood, plastic, packages, even wire covers (sometimes causing fires)** - Discourage them by being very clean in (& around) your house - **Block all holes into (& in) your house - Rubbish in metal bins - Food in hard containers** - Watch for droppings (& damage) & listen at night - **Rodents do not like cat smells - Mint - Tansy - Peppermint** (grow some around the house) - Use oil of Peppermint to discourage entry - To kill, set traps at right angles to walls they run along - Bait with: Bacon/Peanut butter/Chocolate - Don't touch trap with your hands (smell) - <u>IF YOU MUST USE POISON BE CAREFUL.</u>

SILVERFISH

BOOK LICE

PLASTER BEETLE

THIS HAPPY TRIO OF BUGS (& their close relatives) **all love damp** & feed off its by-products (mold etc.) - <u>DRY EVERYTHING & THEY WILL GO.</u>

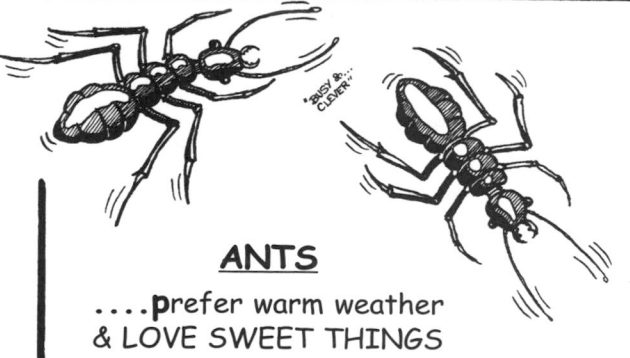

COCKROACHES....

....**d**ate back to prehistoric times & are a problem in most parts of the world (particularly tropical) - They come out at night & are light sensitive - THEY ARE A HEALTH HAZARD **(potentially contaminating any surface or food they touch)** - Difficult to eradicate completely due to their rapid movements/distant forays (& rugged constitution) - Some fly, some swim, some only run - TO GET RID OF THEM, BE SCRUPULOUSLY CLEAN WITH FOODSTUFFS, (sealing all soft packets in rigid tight fitting containers) - Clean up every crumb after a meal - **Don't bring boxes (cardboard worst) into your home** from elsewhere - Catch them with baited sticky traps - Kill them slowly with Boric Acid powder (or quickly with Insecticide) on their runs - Also try sprinkling with Pyrethrum powder (from Pyrethrum plant) **- KEEP POISONS AWAY FROM CHILDREN.**

WEEVILS....

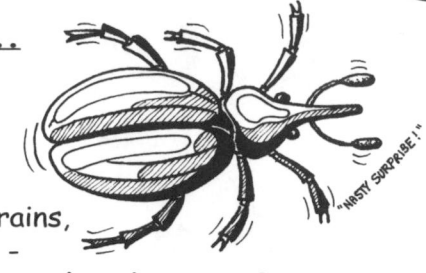

....**a**re small beetles which hatch from maggot eggs (laid mainly in grains, bread, biscuits) - **The egg stage can lay dormant for several months (& can actually hatch out in an apparently sealed e.g. biscuit tin)** - Throw away all contaminated foods & start again - A Bay leaf in each container of grain/flour will deter egg laying - Use **AIRTIGHT** jars.

MOTHS

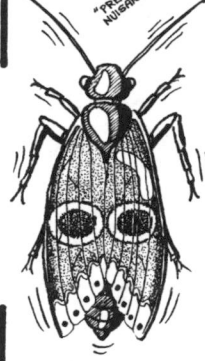

It is the larva (not the developed moth) that damages (by eating) any natural fibre (wool, cotton etc.) in clothes, curtains, carpets etc. - The moths lay their eggs in late summer - **IF CLOTHES** are contaminated, brush off larva (check in folds & pockets), wash well & dust with Epsom salts - Or use moth balls (& seal in plastic bags [for storage]) - **WITH CARPETS**, put damp rag on larva hole(s) and iron (steam will kill them).

ANTS

....**p**refer warm weather & LOVE SWEET THINGS

- Stand anything which attracts them on a table with its legs in water (which they won't cross unless given time & materials [they will bridge it]) - Dissuade them with either Penny Royal - Tansy - Rue in cupboards - Kill them by tracking their procession back to its source (hole) & pouring boiling water down, followed by a cotton wool plug soaked in Paraffin (which they hate) - Or mix equal parts Icing sugar & Borax (& put near nest entrance).

MITES

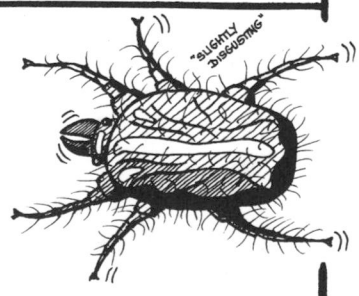

There are many types, most very small (& reasonably harmless) - Although many people do have allergic reactions to the droppings of house dust mites - **Certain species will seek warm-blooded hosts** (& bite soft creases of the skin on the body) causing itching & swelling (even fever) - Use powerful vacuum cleaner to remove all possible dust from (corners, cracks, fabrics etc.)- Treat with insecticide (REPEAT WEEKLY FOR A MONTH).

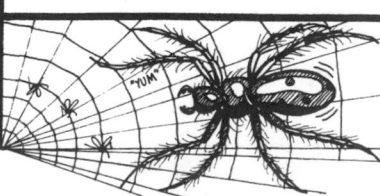

SPIDERS despite their reputations **are yours (& my) best friend - They don't eat or destroy anything (around the house)** & they DO eat all the bugs we hate - So if you don't like spiders put them outside.

Quick Reference Guide To Choosing & Storing Ten Food Groups

Buy foods in season, they are most likely to be free of chemicals, also cheaper

FOOD TYPE	CHOOSING IT	STORING IT
Bread-Cakes	● <u>Freshly baked from baker best</u> - No mold - Soft inside - DATE IF PACKAGED	● <u>For use soon: Cover but allow a little air</u> - REMOVE MOLD AT ONCE AS IT SPREADS - Freeze in bags for a month - Wrap stale loaf in foil & bake at 450 deg. F. (for 5-10 mins.).
Dairy	● <u>Dried milk (& hard cheeses) last longest</u> - IN LIQUID FORM USE HOMOGENIZED MILK (skim & whole)	● <u>Dried usually lasts over a year</u> (if unopened) - Refrigerated milk (4 days) & sealed hard cheese about 3 wks. - Cheeses in freezer about 3 mths. - Skimmed & homogenized milk freezes OK - DO NOT FREEZE WHOLE MILK, YOGURT ETC.
Dried-Packaged	● <u>Look for vacuum packages</u> & long "use by" dates - Ask shopkeeper how old if in doubt - AGE IS IMPORTANT.	● <u>Grains (even if well sealed) can be a problem</u> after 3 months with weevils - STORE ALL DRIED FOODS SEPARATELY (FROM EACH OTHER) IN AIRTIGHT CONTAINERS in a cool, dark (& dry) place - Most will freeze for 6 mths.
Eggs	● <u>Shell color is not important</u> (breed of hen) freshness is all - Test an egg in water (FLOATERS ARE STALE)	● <u>Don't wash even dirty eggs</u> (shortens store life) but you can coat with vaseline or plunge briefly in boiling water - Otherwise 2-3 wks. in fridge (1-2 out) - If you want to freeze eggs : Break shells & freeze whites & yolks separately (or beat a bit).
Fish	● <u>White fish (Cod - Sole - Plaice etc.) last twice as long as oily fish</u> (Mackerel - Salmon etc.) - Both to have fresh smell (& bright bulging eyes).	● Frozen <u>white fish 6 mths.</u> - Frozen <u>oily fish 3 mths</u>. - In fridge (cooked) 2-3 days - In fridge (uncooked) 1-2 days - WRAP FISH IN FOIL (to prevent odor spreading to other foods) - Fish can also be filleted, dried & salted.
Fruits	● <u>Avoid buying fruit in plastic wrappings</u> which can "leach" into the food - Buy green from markets & let fruits ripen.	● Frozen fruits are usually packed in dry/syrup sugar & will last 12 months or so - To prevent browning (e.g. apples) use Ascorbic Acid - In fridge hard fruit will last about 2 wks. - If no fridge keep cool & dark (ALSO WRAP IN FOIL).
Meat	● From a 4-legged animal, the finer meat usually comes from the rear - From a bird, the breast - <u>Big cuts keep better</u>.	● <u>Meats are a prime cause of food poisoning</u> so be very careful (particularly processed meats & pates) - In fridge a few days - In freezer from 1 mth. (small cuts pork) to 12 mths (large cuts beef/lamb) - POULTRY ABOUT 9 MONTHS ONLY.
Shellfish	● Look for freshness (ask when caught) - Should be firm, heavy & have a sea smell - <u>Carry home in a cool/ice box.</u>	● <u>Shellfish have a notoriously short shelflife</u> - Even when caught & frozen straight away a maximum of 6 wks. is recommended - If not to be frozen, catch (or buy fresh) & keep as cool as possible FOR HALF DAY ONLY.
Cans	● No dents/rust <u>(particularly no swollen cans)</u> - Cans with loose contents may be mushy if transported by sea or road.	● <u>Don't store cans with highly acidic contents</u> (e.g. rhubarb/prunes etc.) for more than 6 mths - Most other cans can theoretically be stored for years - BUT bear in mind that LEACHING OF SEAM MATERIAL INTO FOOD CAN (& does) OCCUR!
Vegetables	● <u>Avoid vegetables sold in plastic</u> (they deteriorate quicker) - All should be firm (& bright) with NO WRINKLES OR ROT.	● <u>Store all vegetables in a cool & well ventilated place</u> (not in plastic bags) - Keep all root vegetables (potatoes etc.) in the dark (& CUT OFF SHOOTS IF THEY APPEAR) - Most vegetables will freeze for up to 12 mths. (but "blanch" them first).

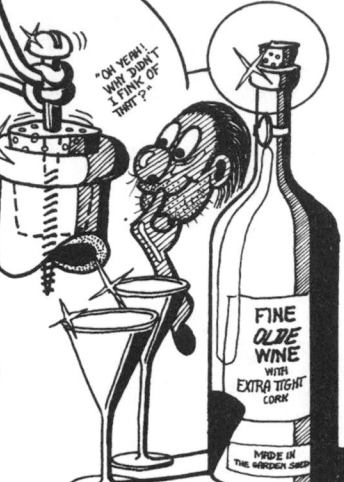

- **CRISP CRACKERS:** Can be kept that way by putting a couple of sugar cubes in the tin (with the biscuits) to absorb moisture — <u>Large containers have more air in (& THUS MOISTURE) than small ones.</u>
- **WINE SUBSTITUTION:** In recipes can usually be made with dry cider.
- **FEWER ADDITIVES** are found in unprocessed (also locally grown) & in-season foods — <u>Be cautious of long shelf life foods.</u>
- **NO CORKSCREW** don't panic - Screw a long screw into the cork - Attatch a piece of string - Pull hard. *"Darling you're so clever."*
- **CABBAGE SMELL** (& sprouts etc.) when cooking can be dramatically reduced by adding a teaspoon of sugar to the water.
- **CONDENSATION IN FRIDGES** is mainly caused by leaving the door open (or putting warm/hot foods in it).
- **GARLIC BREATH** can be reduced naturally by eating fresh parsley.
- **WEAK HERBS** (in flavor, color & effect) often result from storing in clear containers — <u>Particularly store medicinal herbs out of the light.</u>
- **HARD HONEY** can be restored by standing the jar in hot water.
- **GREEN TOMATOES** ripen best in a warm (& dark) place with one or two ripe ones (sharing the box) — *"But but, why the ripe ones?"*
- **BLANCHING** is a common preparation of vegetables prior to freezing - Plunge prepared vegetables into boiling water for 1-3 minutes - REMOVE & PLUNGE INTO COLD WATER - Dry & freeze.
- **CORK WON'T GO BACK IN** to that precious wine (or other) bottle - Plunge it briefly into boiling water (& it will) — *"Oh God! Darling you're so, so, KNOWLEDGEABLE. Let's do it NOW!"*
- **PLUCKING BIRDS** is much easier if it is briefly plunged into boiling water first.
- **BOILED EGG OR NOT:** They both look the same in their shells - But <u>only the boiled one will spin</u> (like a top) — or put a cross on the boiled ones.
- **HEATING MILK** in a pan is more easily cleaned off after if the pan was rinsed in water BEFORE PUTTING THE MILK IN.
- **DAMP SALT** can be prevented! - Keep a few grains of rice in the jar.
- **DON'T FREEZE** hard boiled eggs - They become rubbery - Or whole milk, cream & yogurt (which all separate [& will not remix when thawed]).
- **DON'T RE-FREEZE** anything - YOU RISK FOOD POISONING.
- **STORE WINE** bottles on their sides (to keep the cork moist [& thus sealed]) — Don't forget white goes best with fish & red with meat.
- **DISCOLORED APPLES**, bananas etc. can be prevented by adding lemon juice to fruit salads (or cooking water) — *"Yes, Yes, YES!"*

SPICE COMPATIBILITY

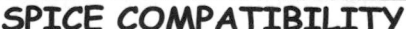

NAME	USE WITH
ANISEED	Bread - Cake - Shellfish.
CINNAMON	Pudding - Pies - Crumbles - Cakes.
CLOVES	Apples - Hams.
FENNEL	Fish - Buns - Bread.
GINGER	Cakes - Curries - Drinks - Jams - Confectionery.
MACE	Is the outer shell of nutmeg.
MUSTARD	Meats (particularly beef).
NUTMEG	Milk puddings & drinks (particularly at night) - Cakes - Cabbage - Potato.
PAPRIKA	Salad dressing & garnish.
SAFFRON	Rice - Cake & many southern European dishes.
SESAME	Gomasio - Bread - Salads.
TURMERIC	Rice - Curry - Pickles.

WINE TEMPERATURES

STORE all wines between 10-15 deg. C (50-59 deg. F).

SERVE WHITE wine at about 10 deg. C (50 deg. F) - Sweet, a little colder than dry.

SERVE RED wine at room temperature i.e. 18 deg. C (65 deg. F) - Open the bottle an hour or two before.

BURGUNDY & BEAUJOLAIS & some Italian light reds at 16 deg. C (61 deg. F).

SHERRY & PORT (the former before, & the latter after a meal) are served at 14 deg. C (57 deg. F).

SPARKLING wines (including champagne) at about 10 deg. C (50 deg. F).

BEER/LAGER complement vinegar (or curry base) dishes better than wine.

ONE OF THE FINEST REJUVENATING FOODS AVAILABLE -
Amazingly simple & cheap to grow at home (or on top of a mountain).

ADVANTAGES

- **VITAMIN** content of sprouts (as compared to the bean/grain or seed it came from) <u>can be as much as 7 times higher.</u>
- **FATS, PROTEINS & STARCHES** during sprouting become (respectively) FATTY ACIDS, AMINO ACIDS & SIMPLE SUGARS.
- **DIGESTION** of beans/grains/seeds is more difficult than their sprouts (which are NATURALLY EASIER TO METABOLIZE).
- **MUCUS** formation (stimulated by eating some beans/grains/seeds) IS MUCH REDUCED WHEN SPROUTED.
- **COOKING** causes nutritional losses but <u>sprouts lose less</u> because of short (if any) times required.

GROWTH SPEED

Ideal fast-growing temperature is 70-85 degrees F - If maturity has almost been reached (& you are not ready to use them) then <u>you can slow growth by continuing to rinse but in a cooler place.</u>

GET READY

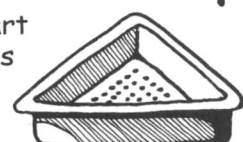

- **WHICH BEAN**/grain/seed to start with? - Mung - Alfalfa - Brown lentils - Fenugreek - Aduki - Chick peas.
- **WHAT IN?** - Wide mouth glass jars are ideal - But almost any container (even a plastic bag) will do - <u>A sieve on bottom &/or top</u> IS USEFUL.

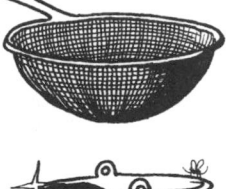

- **HOW MUCH?** - <u>On average allow for a 6-12 fold expansion</u> from bean/grain/seed to sprout - 2 full tablespoons of B/G/S produce about 1 cup of sprouts.
- **HOW LONG** to germinate? - Even the same bean/grain/seed type (in the same container) <u>may sprout many hours apart</u> - SO GIVE THEM A CHANCE.
- **LIGHT OR DARK** conditions? - Both will produce sprouting (but with different tastes & nutritional properties).

SIMPLE SIX-STEP SPROUT SYSTEM

1. Measure the amount of beans/grains/seeds you are going to use & pour onto a tray (or large sieve) - <u>Discard any damaged ones or debris</u> (husks, stones etc.).

4. The next morning pour off the "soak" water (use it in soups /drinks) - Cover the top with mesh/net (held with a rubber band) - <u>Lay the drained jar on its side away from light.</u>

2. Put the beans/grains/seeds in their jar & rinse (discard water) - Then cover with a couple of inches of pure water <u>(some chemicals such as chlorine MAY INHIBIT SPROUTING).</u>

5. Thereafter the B/G/S are germinating - <u>They need to be rinsed in clean warm water</u> 2-4 times/day (depends on temperature) <u>for the next 2-5 days</u> (depends on B/G/S type).

3. Leave the beans/grains/ seeds in a warm place to soak ([usually overnight] <u>but check overleaf as times vary).</u>

6. <u>As tiny yellow leaves appear expose sprouts to good light (indirect sunlight best)</u> to turn them green (4-24 hours) - Sprouts are now ready to eat - Rinse for last time & eat (or store in fridge [<u>most will keep for up to a week]).</u>

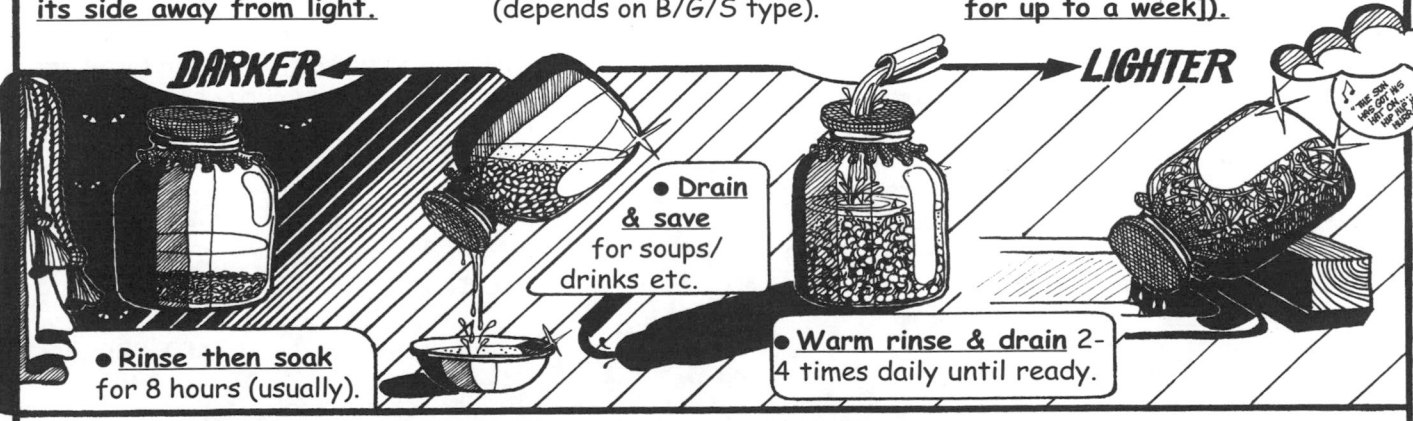

DARKER ← → **LIGHTER**

- **Drain & save** for soups/ drinks etc.

- <u>Rinse then soak</u> for 8 hours (usually).

- <u>Warm rinse & drain</u> 2-4 times daily until ready.

- **CAUTION:** Because of possible digestive complications associated with eating raw beans & peas & their sprouts <u>(BUT NOT GRAIN SPROUTS)</u> - THEY SHOULD BE COOKED FOR A FEW MINUTES BEFORE EATING.

EASY GUIDE TO 15 SPROUTS

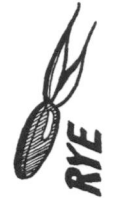

- **ADZUKI:** Grow for 3-5 days until 3 cms long - <u>Benefits kidneys</u> - Has nutty taste.
- **ALFALFA:** Grow for 5-6 days until 3.5 cms long - HIGH IN VITS. A & K, POTASSIUM, CALCIUM & CHLOROPHYLL - When little green leaves come eat <u>(or refridgerate immediately).</u>
- **BARLEY:** Grow for 2-3 days until sprout same length as grain - Initial soak 12-15 hrs. - CAN EAT RAW - HIGH ENERGY (produces a lot of sugar).
- **CHICK PEAS:** Grow for 3-4 days until 2.5-4 cms long - <u>Requires long initial soak</u> (10-20 hrs) & change water once - Cook for 6-8 mins.
- **FENUGREEK:** Grow for 3-4 days until 1.5-3 cms long - <u>USED FOR TOXIN ELIMINATION</u> - Curry taste.
- **LENTILS:** Grow for 3-5 days until 1-2.5 cms long (depending on type) - SPLIT LENTILS WILL NOT GERMINATE - Cook for 5 mins.
- **MILLET:** Grow for 3-4 days until sprout same length as grain - Initial soak not more than 8 hrs. - <u>THE ONLY ALKALINE GRAIN.</u>
- **MUNG:** Grow for 3-5 days until 2-6 cms long - Initial soak 15+ hours - Darker conditions produce sweeter sprouts - Cook for 3 mins <u>(entire sprout/bean edible).</u>
- **MUSTARD:** Grow for 4-5 days until 2.5 cms long - <u>No initial soaking required</u> - CAN BE GROWN ON DAMP PAPER TOWELS (cut off tops for salad).
- **OATS:** Grow for 3-4 days until sprout same length as grain - Initial soak not more than 8 hrs. - <u>Sprouting decreases mucus forming effect of oats</u> - Can eat raw.
- **RYE:** Grow for 2-3 days until sprout same length as grain - Initial soak 12-15 hrs. - DELICIOUS TASTE - GOOD FOR GLANDULAR SYSTEM - Can eat raw.
- **SESAME:** Grow for 1-2 days until sprout same length as seed - DO NOT GROW LONGER THAN 2 DAYS (as they develop a bitter taste).
- **SOYA:** Grow for 3-5 days until 3.5 cms long - Initial soak 18-24 hrs (change water 3 or 4 times) - Rinse often during growth - <u>Remove non-germinating beans after 24 hrs.</u> - HIGHEST PROTEIN OF ALL BEANS - Cook for 10-15 mins.
- **SUNFLOWER:** Grow for 1-2 days until sprout same length as seed - <u>DOES NOT KEEP WELL - SPROUT ONLY 1 DAY'S CONSUMPTION - HANDLE GENTLY</u> - Sometimes grown for greens.
- **WHEAT:** Grow for 2-3 days until sprout same length as grain - Initial soak 12-15 hrs. (use water for soup) - <u>DELICIOUS TASTE - HIGH IN B VITS.</u>

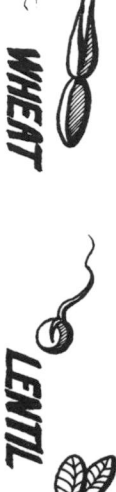

PROBLEMS

- **WON'T SPROUT:** Bean/grain/seed <u>is damaged</u> (i.e. is split [peas] or hulled [rice]) & THUS INCOMPLETE.
- **WON'T SPROUT:** B/G/S <u>is whole but dead</u> (either age or bad storage conditions - e.g. heat).
- **SPROUTS ROT:** <u>Too much water</u> - After initial soaking B/G/S must be well drained - After each rinsing LEAVE TILTED.
- **BROWN & WITHERED:** <u>Sprouts not rinsed frequently enough</u> (or in too hot/dry a position).
- **DON'T USE** B/G/S from growers' suppliers (as they <u>may have been treated with chemicals</u>).
- <u>**ENZYMES** ARE DESTROYED BY HEAT (TEMPERATURES OVER 130 DEG. F.).</u>

FINAL HINTS

- **MORE LIGHT** during growth reduces sweetness <u>BUT INCREASES VIT. C & CHOROPHYLL</u> (wound-healing) contents.
- **LESS LIGHT** during growth <u>increases sweetness & Vit. B2</u> (Riboflavin [vital for skin, eyes & food to energy conversion]).
- **COOKING:** <u>If adding salt &/or fat, do so at end</u> (as both inhibit water absorption by the sprouts [tenderness]) - Unless they are being stir-fried (which loses the least Vit. C).

    MAXIMUM PROTEIN (Amino Acids) utilization can be achieved by a mixture of 1 PART BROWN RICE TO 4 - 8 BEAN SPROUTS.

    (depends on type)

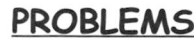
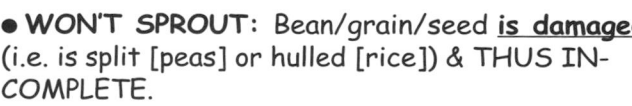
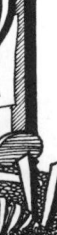
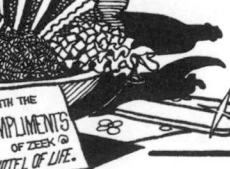

WITH THE COMPLIMENTS OF ZEEK @ THE HOTEL OF LIFE.

ADUKI

WHEAT

LENTIL

PINTO

RYE

ALFALFA

CORN

MUNG

An invaluable low technology technique with multiple product uses including:
HOUSEHOLD - TRIPS - SURVIVAL - TREATS ETC.

DRY IT & SAVE

- **NUTRITION:** <u>Almost all</u> of the Vitamins, Minerals, Enzymes & other Nutritional elements retained. <u>ABSOLUTELY MINIMUM LOSSES.</u>
- <u>COST is minimal as heating level is low</u> (95-110 deg. F.) & can often be derived from waste sources (e.g. fridge/water heater tops [OR EVEN A SINGLE LIGHT BULB]).
- **CHEMICALS** of any kind are NOT required in this process - <u>Making such foods ideal for sensitive constitutions (e.g. allergies etc.)</u>.
- **SIMPLE:** Dehydrators (dryers) are easy to build (basic tools & readily available materials).
- **VERSATILE** (& handy) foods can be eaten: at work or play - On the move or at the table - & in many forms — <u>Kids love dried fruits</u>, HEALTHY.
- **SPACE** required for storage is reduced by about 80% — <u>PERFECT NUTRITION FOR TRAVELLERS.</u>
- **QUICK:** Drying rarely takes more than 2 days (48 hrs) — <u>Dry in season foods when cheap to buy.</u>
- **SHELF LIFE** of well dried (& stored) foods should be a minimum of 12 months (& POTENTIALLY MUCH MORE).

STORAGE PRINCIPLES

- **EXCLUDE** air, water & light.
- **SMALL** containers are better.
- **TEMPERATURE** levels in long-term storage should not be high (or erratic).
- **RECOMMENDED** containers are: a) Food quality (waxed or plain) brown paper bag inside - b) Small sealed plastic bag (several of which inside) - c) Larger sealed plastic bag - <u>FOR EXTRA LONG TERM STORAGE</u>, use a third plastic bag (or other rigid air tight box).
- **NAME & DATE** <u>TAG ALL FOOD BAGS AS YOU FILL THEM</u> (easy to confuse).

FRUIT (& OTHER) LEATHERS

- **HOW TO MAKE THEM:** Take your choice of foods (say apples) - Core (but don't peel) - With a splash of water, liquidize - Spread about 1/4 inch thick <u>on alternate halves of consecutive drying racks</u> (see below) - Dry for about 2 days (depends on thickness).

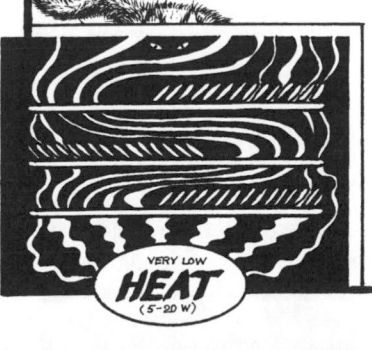

- **FINISHED PRODUCT** - Some leathers (e.g. bananas) dry quickly - Usual finished consistency can be cut (&/or just rolled) - Absolutely delicious (& very versatile [see next page for ideas]). **"MMMM"**

BUILDING A DEHYDRATOR

- **A** = <u>Rotating Air Vent</u> (hot damp air comes out here). • **B** = <u>Thermostat</u> (nice but not essential).

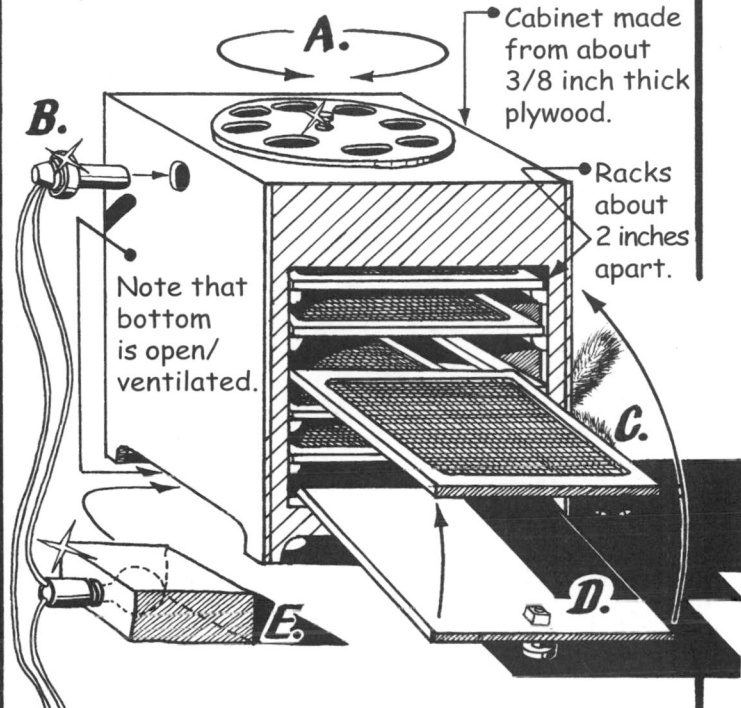

Cabinet made from about 3/8 inch thick plywood.

Racks about 2 inches apart.

Note that bottom is open/ventilated.

- **C** = <u>Wire Mesh Drying Trays</u> (slide in & out, & can be turned) on wooden runners.
- **D** = <u>Door on hinges</u> (to close off front).
- **E** = <u>Heater</u> (ideal is low watt fan heater .... but one shown is light bulb in metal box) - However certain positions (e.g. on top of refrigerator/hot water tank) may not require any heater.

OPERATING NOTES

- **TEMPERATURE** should be steady around 100 deg. F. (**not more than 110**) & is controlled by thermostat (or ventilation) on top of dryer.
- **AIR FLOW** from bottom to top **is critical** (for moisture removal) - THEREFORE, ENSURE THAT FOODS DO NOT TOUCH EACH OTHER (on the racks) permitting air flow up.
- **FOOD ON RACKS** <u>should be put so that the driest is the lowest</u> (thus permitting moisture from the "wettest" to go straight out of the top vent) - <u>Occasional 90 degrees &/or 180 degrees turns</u> of racks will ensure even drying of foods.
- **FOOD TYPES** (which can be dried) cover a very wide range & include: Fruit - Herbs - Vegetables - Fish - Meat - Breads - Berries etc.
- **SAVE MONEY** by drying excess stock (&/or leftover foods) almost as you would use a freezer.

VERY LOW **HEAT** (5-20 W)

A VOYAGER'S SIMPLE & HEALTHY DEHYDRATED RECIPES
The Traveler's Ideal Fare - Nutritious - Convenient - Light - Varied

Herbs

- **PICK** <u>in the season of that herb</u> - Away from polluted areas (e.g. roads) - WASH WELL (PARTICULARLY ROOTS).
- **DRY** by arranging loosely <u>(leave air space)</u> on racks - Turn racks at least once - DRY UNTIL CRISP (usually about 1 day).
- **STORE** in airtight bags/boxes <u>IN A DARK PLACE.</u>
- **TO USE** (when required) crush to powder for ointments etc - Add uncrushed leaves to hot water for teas - <u>FOR ROOTS ONLY</u>, boil on low heat until soft (10 mins.).

Fish & Meats

- **PICK** <u>only very lean meat</u> - Skin &/or clean off any fat from fish or poultry.
- **DRY:** Slice 1/4 inch thick & dust with sea salt &/or soy sauce - <u>DRY FAST</u> (up to 110 degrees F) <u>& VERY HARD</u> - Usually about 2 days.
- **STORE** in dry brown (food quality) paper, inside air tight bags/boxes, <u>in a cool dark place</u>.
- **TO USE:** Reconstitute & <u>COOK BY BOILING</u> (ideal protein in soup/stew).
- **NOTE:** <u>Wash dehydrator racks well</u> after drying fish & meat (to remove smell & bacteria).

Fruit & Vegetables

- **PICK** well ripened (<u>organic best</u>) produce of virtually any type (<u>better in season</u>).
- **DRY** by slicing <u>hard types</u> (e.g. apples) 1/4 inch thick - <u>Soft types</u> (e.g. apricots) in 8 or more segments (remove core/stones but not skin) - <u>Leafy types</u> (e.g. cabbage) dry same as herbs - **NOTE:** <u>DIP APPLE SLICES IN DILUTE LEMON JUICE</u> to stop browning - Dry all until hard (12 - 48 hours).
- **STORE** in <u>AIR TIGHT</u> plastic bags/boxes/bottles in <u>DARK PLACE.</u>
- **TO USE:** <u>Can be eaten in any stage of reconstitution from chewy hard to succulent soft</u> - Snack on & travel with dried fruits - Use vegetables in salads & soups (very healthy eating).

Sesame Snaps

- 2 cups sesame seeds.
- 1/2 cup sunflower seeds.
- 1/2 cup chopped dates.
- 2/3 cup of honey.
- 1/3 cup hot water.
- 1/2 cup crushed walnuts.

1. **MIX** honey & hot water in bowl.
2. **STIR** in everything else.
3. **SPREAD** & compact 1/4 inch thick on plastic sheet (on dry rack) - Put in dryer (100 degrees F) until firm.
4. **CUT** into squares - Remove plastic sheet - Turn over & dry (until crisp) - "MMMMMMM!"

Yang Fruit Leather

- 1 pint chopped apples.
- 1 cup pitted cherries.
- 2 tablespoons honey.
- 1 tablespoon lemon juice.
- 1 teaspoon nutmeg.

1. **LIQUIDIZE** everything.
2. **DRY** at about 100 degrees F until hard (see overleaf) - Macrobiotically balanced treat - "WOW! YEAH! YUMMY!"

Banana Crisps

- 2 cups very ripe bananas.
- 1 1/2 cups sesame seeds.
- 1/2 cup sunflower seeds.
- 1/4 cup chopped organic orange or lemon peel.

1. **LIQUIDIZE** bananas.
2. **MIX** in other ingredients.
3. **SPREAD** 1/4 inch thick on plastic film as per overleaf.
4. **DRY** until firm - Remove plastic - Cut into squares, turn over & dry (until crisp). "GOOD!"

Notes

- **WAXED PAPER** is fine outside but will melt inside the dryer. **STAINLESS STEEL** wire mesh is the best material for racks.
- **PLASTIC WRAP** should not be used to dry (or store) animal proteins. **PLASTIC WRAP** may need taping at corners (to hold flat on rack).
- **ENZYMES** are destroyed at temperatures over 120-130 degrees F. **BUTCHERS** (& bakers) paper can be used on racks (& to wrap dried foods for storage). "GO, GO, MOM!"

Easy To Prepare - Nutritionally Sound - Yin & Yang Balanced

Macrobiotics (translates as "BIG LIFE") is based on ancient practices of Buddhist monks balancing yin & yang (acidic & alkaline approximates).

STARTERS

Carrot Soup

- 1 medium/large onion.
- 1 lb (450g) carrots.
- 2 oz (55g) sunflower oil.
- 1/2 tablespoon wholemeal flour.
- 1/2 tablespoon thyme.
- 1 bay leaf.
- 1 pint (570ml) veg. stock.
- 1/2 pint (285ml) skim milk.
- Sea salt/peppers to taste.

1. **GENTLY** cook chopped onion & grated carrots (in oil) **in covered pan** for 10 minutes.
2. **ADD** veg. stock, flour, herbs & seasoning - Simmer for 10 mins.
3. **TAKE** out bayleaf (liquidize if wanted) - Add milk & bring to boil.
4. **SERVE** with toasted wholemeal bread croutons & shredded parsley. **"VERY YANG!"**

MILK VERY LOW FAT

Shrimp Cocktail

- 8 oz (225 g) prawns.
- 1 small celery.
- 2 slices ginger root.
- 1/2 teaspoon sea salt.
- 2 tablespoons rice wine.
- 1 tablespoon soy sauce.
- 2 teaspoons sesame oil.

1. **MARINATE** shrimp **(already cooked)** in the wine for 30 minutes.
2. **CLEAN** celery stalks (remove leaves etc.) - Slice diagonally & mix with salt (LEAVE STAND FOR 10 MINUTES.).
3. **TIP** prawns on top of celery - Add shredded ginger, soy sauce & sesame oil - **Toss well.**
4. **SERVE** immediately in small bowls (with a sprig of parsley). **"GOOOD!"**

MAIN COURSES

Turkey Rissoles

- 12 oz (340g) turkey meat.
- 1 wholemeal bread roll.
- 3 oz (85g) shelled walnuts.
- 1 bunch fresh parsley.
- 2 tablespoons sunflower oil.
- 1 teaspoon grated lemon rind.
- Sea salt/peppers to taste.
- 1 medium onion.
- 1 egg.

1. **SOAK** bread in water - Squeeze (THEN FLUFF OUT).
2. **CLEAN** turkey of skin/fat etc. - Finely chop it, the onion, the walnuts & parsley.
3. **MIX** everything **(except oil)** together well - With wet hands make rissoles.
4. **FRY** for about 5 minutes per side in oil.
5. **SERVE** with pumpkin side salad (& wholemeal rolls). **"YEAH!"**

White Fish In Wine

- 3 lbs (1.35kg) white fish.
- 1 med. chopped onion.
- 3 cloves garlic.
- 2 glasses white wine.
- 6 tablespoons olive oil.
- 1 tablespoon parsley.
- 1 tablespoon flour.
- 1 bay leaf.
- Sea salt.

1. **CUT** fish into 1 inch cubes & sprinkle with salt **(set aside for 10 minutes).**
2. **SAUTÉ** chopped onion & garlic in oil - Sprinkle flour on as you stir.
3. **ADD** 1 glass water, wine, & herbs - Simmer 15 mins.
4. **ADD** fish - **Cover pot** - Simmer 15 mins. more.
5. **SERVE** with organic rice. **"DEEELICIOUS!"**

Considerable & wide health benefits are attributed to Macrobiotics -
START BY AVOIDING INDUSTRIALIZED & EXCESSIVELY YIN FOOD/DRINK.

DESSERTS

Rice Pudding

- 1 cup organic whole rice.
- 2 cups soy milk.
- 2 tablespoons rice syrup.
- 1/4 teaspoon sea salt.
- Grated lemon rind.
- 1 cinnamon stick.

1. **WASH** rice under running water - Add all other ingredients to pot.
2. **BRING** to boil - Simmer gently for about 45 mins (in covered pot) till rice is soft - Pressure cooker requires about 25 mins.
3. **REMOVE** the cinnamon stick & serve in bowls (with a teaspoon of sugarless strawberry jam [or grated cinnamon on top]).
   4. **"VEERY TASTY!"**

Apple Crumble

- 8 medium/large apples.
- 1 cup apple juice.
- Cinnamon.
- 2 cups wholemeal flour.
- 1/2 cup sunflower oil.
- 1/2 teaspoon sea salt.

1. **THINLY** peel, core & slice apples - Lay neatly in baking dish - Pour on 1/2 cup apple juice (with cinnamon).
2. **IN** separate bowl mix flour, oil, salt & 1/2 cup apple juice (**until ingredients are "crumbly"**).
3. **SPRINKLE** crumble evenly over apples - Leave for 30 mins - Bake at 400 degrees **until top browns** (but apples juicy).
4. **SERVE** with sugar-free custard - **MMMM!**

OTHER TREATS

Baked Apple

- **The most yang of fruits** is very simply baked by: Carefully cutting out the core (but leave the bottom) -
  - **Fill the hole** with either:
    a) Tahini - b) Grated rind & cinnamon - c) Raisins.
  - **Bake** for 30 mins.
    "DDDELICIOUS!"

Unyeasted Bread

- **Mix 1 lb. (450g) wholemeal flour** & 1 teaspoon sea salt & water to make dough ● **Knead** for 5 mins then cover (& leave for 12-24 hrs. in warm room) ● **Knead** for 5 mins ● **Put** in oiled baking tin - Cover (& leave) for 2-4 hrs. ● **Bake** at 200 deg. C. (gas # 6) for 30 mins.

Strawberry Milk Shake

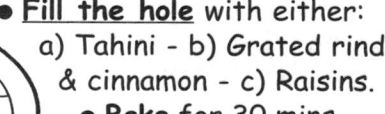

- **Blend 9 oz (250g) fresh strawberries,** 3 cups of soy milk & 3 tablespoons rice syrup thoroughly -
- **Pour** into glasses chilled (for smaller quantities divide by 3) - A delicious summer drink!

  "YEE HA! YEEEE HA!"

Apple Sauce

- **Thinly peel & core your choice of apples** (small red reputedly more yang)
- **Boil** with minimum water till soft - Then mash (or use blender) ● **Add** a touch of cinnamon, cloves or mint & serve cold with a wide variety of dishes (or as a dessert) - **"WOW!"**

A Traveler's Choice Of Easy To Prepare Nutritious Dishes

"Wholefood" broadly REFERS TO UNPROCESSED naturally grown foods such as are often eaten in rural/farming communities.

STARTERS

Pumpkin Soup

PENCIL NOTES

- 1 lb (450g) pumpkin.
- 1 large onion.
- 2 pints (1.15 lts) veg. stock.
- 2 teaspoons wholemeal flour.
- 4 oz (fl) (125ml) cream.
- 1/2 bunch fresh parsley.
- Sea salt/pepper/nutmeg.
- 1 tablespoon veg. oil.

1. **PEEL** & fine chop onion (sauté in oil) - Peel, clean & cube pumpkin (add to onion in pan) - MIX WELL.
2. **SPRINKLE** on flour (& add veg. stock) - Simmer (covered) for 10 minutes.
3. **STIR** soup well - Add spices & cream - Finally, sprinkle on chopped parsley.
4. **SERVE** with wholemeal croutons. "YO, DAD! COME & GET IT."

Baked Grapefruit

- **CUT** grapefruit(s) in half & remove pith core (**do not pierce bottom**) - Loosen segments & dribble several tea-spoons of thin honey in center & around segments - Sprinkle a little cinnamon on top.
- **BAKE** at 180 degrees C (gas number 4) for 15 - 20 minutes.
- **DELICIOUS** as starter or dessert. "MMM"

Roast Cashews

- **PUT** about 1 tablespoon of oil (sesame or sunflower good) into flat baking tin - Shuffle 1 lb (450g) nuts in until coated.
- **ROAST** at 180 degrees C (gas num-ber 4) for 15 minutes (turn occa-sionally) - Remove & sprinkle nuts with tamari (soy sauce) & shuffle till coated - **Then back in oven for 5 minutes.**
- **SERVE** as snack (or with other starters). "OH YES!"

MAIN COURSES

Quick Pizza

DOUGH
- 1/2 lb flour.
- 1/2 cup veg. oil.
- 2 teaspoons baking powder.
- 1 cup water.
- Sea salt/pepper

FILLING
- 2 tomatoes.
- 6 mushrooms.
- 1/2 onion.
- 2 cloves garlic.
- 4 oz (110g) cheese.
- Sea salt/pepper.
- Oregano.

1. **MIX** flour, baking powder & salt/pepper well.
2. **MIX** half the oil with water - Add flour mix - knead into dough (& ROLL FLAT).
3. **OIL** large flat pan - Brown **both** sides of dough.
4. **SLICE** vegetables (& arrange artistically on dough).
5. **GRATE** cheese - Put on top (followed by salt/pepper & Oregano).
6. **GRILL** pizza for about 5 minutes to cook veg. & melt cheese - "KIDS ABSOLUTELY LOVE IT!"

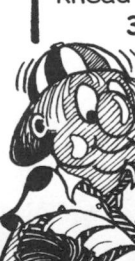

Steamed Trout

- 2 medium cleaned trout.
- 4 tablespoons dry sherry.
- 2 tablespoons soy sauce.
- 1 tablespoon sunflower oil.
- 1 teaspoon thin honey.
- 4 spring onions.
- 4 cloves garlic.
- 1/2 teaspoon sea salt.
- 2 in (5cm) ginger root.

PENCIL NOTES

1. **PREPARE** trout by cleaning (& drying).
2. **PREPARE** marinade by beating soy sauce, sherry, honey & oil - Then add the chopped/sliced garlic, ginger & two spring onions.
3. **SOAK** trout for about 30 mins. in marinade - Steam for about 20 mins.
4. **SERVE** with remaining marinade & spring onions, brown rice & side salad .... "DEELICIOUS."

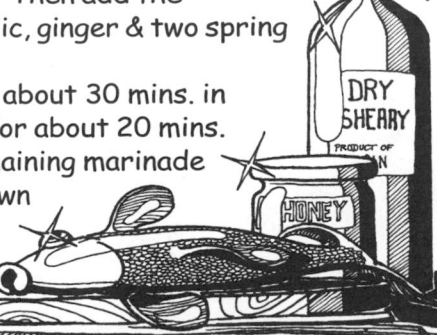

Keep body and soul HEALTHY & HAPPY by introducing more fresh unprocessed ingredients into your families daily diet.

DESSERTS

Cupcakes

PENCIL NOTES

- 1/2 lb. (225g) wholemeal flour (self rising).
- 5 oz (140g) thin honey.
- 5 oz vegetable margarine.
- 3 eggs.
- 1/3 tsp. sea salt.
- 1 tsp. baking powder.
- 1/2 cup apple puree.
  - A touch of cinnamon.

1. MIX well: Flour - Baking powder - Salt & cinnamon.
2. ADD: Beaten eggs - Puree - Margarine & honey - MIX VERY WELL.
3. 2/3 FILL nonstick (or greased) baking cups - Bake at 220 deg. C. (gas mark 7) for 25 mins - **Cakes should have risen** (& be brown on top). "MOM, MOM, I CAN EAT TEN!"

Fruit Trifle

PENCIL NOTES

- 1 pint (570ml) skimmed milk.
- 4 eggs (well beaten).
- 12 oz (340g) stale wholemeal cupcakes (or sponge cake).
- 2 tablespoons brown sugar.
- 1/2 tsp. vanilla essence.
- 2 large ripe oranges.
- 2 large ripe bananas.
- 1 tablespoon arrowroot.
- 1 oz (30g) roasted flaked almonds.
- 1/4 pint (140ml) whipped cream.

1. STIRRING <u>constantly</u>, heat milk & sugar - Add eggs, vanilla & arrowroot - <u>When custard thickens,</u> REMOVE FROM HEAT.
2. PLACE sliced cupcakes in bottom of trifle dish - Arrange peeled sliced fruit on top.
3. POUR custard over fruit (& refrigerate).
4. SERVE topped with almonds & cream - "VEERY TASTY!"

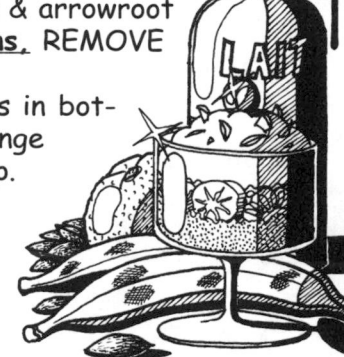

OTHER TREATS

Fruit Salad

- CUT into small cubes : 1 banana, 1 pear & 2 large red apples - Squeeze the juice of half a lemon over them.
- ADD 1 1/2 cups of strawberries (cut lengthways) & 1 cup of ripe cherries (stoned & cut)
- GARNISH with a sprig of mint - "DDDELICIOUS!" (& attractive to look at).

French Toast

- BEAT one egg, 1 tablespoon of milk, sea salt & pepper together - Dip 3 slices of lightly buttered wholemeal bread into mixture - Fry one minute per side in vegetable oil - Top with your choice of tomatoes, banana, cheese, mushrooms, honey (&/or chopped nuts) - "MMMM!"

Almond Milk Shake

- Put 1 oz (30g) blanched almonds in a dry pan & brown.
- Crush almonds to powder & mix (liquidizer best) with:
- 8 oz (250 ml) milk
- 1 tablespoon white rum
- 1 teaspoon thin honey
- <u>Serve chilled with a sprinkle of nutmeg on top</u> - On a warm evening - "YEE HO!"

Apricot Chaud

- TAKE 12 oz (340 g) of dried apricots & soak overnight - Simmer (for 15 mins) in 8 oz (225 g) water, 4 oz (110 g) white wine, 2 tablespoons thin honey, 1 tablespoon brandy, 1 teaspoon lemon juice & a dash of cinnamon.
- SERVE with flaked almonds & yogurt - "SSSCRUMPTIOUS!"

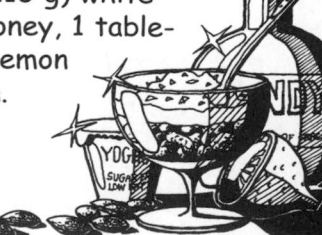

A Traveler's Choice Of Easy To Prepare Nonmeat Dishes

Vegetarians USUALLY RADIATE A CERTAIN "INNER STRENGTH" - Perhaps from the discipline of their regime - Perhaps from the diet itself.

STARTERS

Vegetable Broth

PENCIL NOTES

- 1/2 lb. (225g) of your choice of fresh vegetables.
- 1 pint of vegetable stock.
- 1 teaspoon yeast extract.
- 1 tablespoon vegetable oil.
- Sea salt/pepper to taste.
- Your choice of fresh chopped herbs (parsley, chives etc.).

1. **CHOP** the vegetables into small pieces - Sauté in oil for 2-3 mins.
2. **POUR** on the stock - Simmer until chopped veg. are just soft.
3. **FINALLY** stir in yeast - Add chopped herbs (on top).
4. **SERVE** with toasted wholemeal croutons.
"I FEEL GOOOD!"

Diced Salad

PENCIL NOTES

- 2 medium sweet red apples.
- 1/2 lb. (225g) firm tomatoes.
- 4 sticks crisp celery.
- 1 carrot.
- 1 onion.
- 1 red pepper.
- 1 green pepper
- 1 tablespoon olive oil.
- Small bundle mixed herbs.
- 1 lemon.

1. **DICE** apples into small (1 cm) cubes - Mix with 1 tablespoon lemon juice.
2. **DICE** other ingredients - Dress with 1 tablespoon lemon juice & olive oil.
3. **MIX** all together - Serve into bowls (& garnish with herbs)
"VVVERY HEALTHY!" (tasty too!)

MAIN COURSES

Vegeburgers

PENCIL NOTES

- 4 oz (110g) wholemeal bread crumbs.
- 1 large onion (diced).
- 8 oz (225g) ground nuts (hazel, walnut, almond combination).
- 1 egg.
- 1 teaspoon basil.
- 2 oz (55g) oat flour.
- 2 tablespoons sesame oil.
- 2 tablespoons oats.
- 2 tablespoons sesame seeds.
- Sea salt/pepper to taste.

1. **MIX** bread crumbs, onion, nuts, basil, flour & salt.
2. **MIX** beaten egg & oil - Add to dry mix above.
3. **FORM** into 4 burgers - Roll in oats & sesame seeds.
4. **GRILL** for 10 minutes (per side) & serve.

Hot Spinach Pie

PENCIL NOTES

- 2 lb. (900g) spinach.
- 2 medium onions.
- 4 ozs (110g) grated cheese.
- 4 large eggs.
- 4 tablespoons parsley.
- 1/3 pint (190ml) milk.
- 3 tablespoons oil.
- Salt/pepper to taste.

1. **PEEL**, chop & fry in oil the onions - Chop the spinach & mix with the onions - Arrange in an oiled pie dish.
2. **BEAT** eggs & milk well - Add seasoning & chopped parsley.
3. **POUR** egg mix over spinach & onions - Top with cheese.
4. **BAKE** at 190 deg. C (gas mark 5) **till set inside & brown on top** (30 mins.) - Serve with side vegetables.

THE ONLY WAY TO GET KIDS TO EAT SPINACH IS (DON'T TELL 'EM...) TO PUT MINTS IN IT!

Statistically vegetarians LIVE LONGER & in better general health than the rest of us - Is this because of more "good" food? - Or less "bad" ?

DESSERTS

Honey & Nut Ice Cream

PENCIL NOTE

- 4 oz (110g) honey.
- 8 oz (225g) thick cream.
- 4 oz (110g) roasted nuts.
- 1 egg (separate white & yolk).
  - Dash of vanilla flavoring.

1. **BEAT** egg yolk very well - Add honey & vanilla.
2. **BEAT** very well chilled cream (until quite stiff) - Mix well with "honey mixture."
3. **CRUSH** roasted nuts - Add to mix - Put in freezer until nearly firm.
4. **BEAT** egg white (did you forget?) - Fold into mix.
5. **RETURN** to freezer - Stir occasionally till hard - **"GGGOOD! YEE HA!"**
6. **SMALL** amounts of soft (or cooked) fruit can also be added. **"OH GOD!"**

Sugarless Buns

PENCIL NOTE

- 8 oz (225g) wholemeal flour.
- 3 oz (85g) veg. margarine.
- 2 teaspoons baking powder.
- 4 oz (110g) currants & raisins.
- 1 egg (beaten).
- 1/2 cup milk.
- 1 teaspoon cinnamon.
- 1 grated lemon rind.

1. **MIX** the flour, baking powder & cinnamon.
2. **ADD** currants & rind - Then margarine to achieve **crumbly** texture.
3. **MIX** milk & egg - Add to "dry mix."
4. **BAKE** at 200 degrees C. (gas mark 6) for about 15 mins. in paper baking cups. **"BUNTASTIC!"**

OTHER TREATS

Apricot Fool

- **SIMMER** 8oz (225g) of dried apricots **(which have been soaked overnight)** until tender - Blend into thick puree.
  - **MIX** puree with 1/2 pint plain yogurt & 2 tablespoons thin honey.
  - **FINALLY**, fold in 1/4 pint thick cream & chill well. **"NORTY BUT NICE!"**

Mint Chutney

- **CHOP** 8 oz (225g) peeled onions & 4 oz (110g) of fresh mint leaves very small - Then mix together with 1 tablespoon of vegetable oil & 1 tablespoon of Gomasio (mixed, roasted, finely crushed sesame seeds & sea salt [5 to 1 ratio]). **"LOVE IT!"**

Wholemeal Croutons

- **CUT** 2 slices of slightly stale wholemeal bread into small cubes - Shallow fry them in 1/2 tablespoon of vegetable oil & 1 tablespoon of vegetable margarine (turning often **until golden brown**) - Delicious in soups & salads - Store in **airtight** jar.

Salad Dressing/Cream

- **DRESSING:** 1 part vinegar (or lemon juice) 2 parts vegetable oil + seasoning/spice to taste (crushed garlic & parsley!).
- **CREAM:** 1 part vinegar (or lemon juice), 2 parts vegetable oil, 3 parts condensed milk + seasoning & spice to taste (**add crumbled blue cheese** for a change). **"YYYES!"**

A Traveler's Choice Of Easy To Prepare Asian Origin Dishes

A SOUGHT-AFTER SKILL is the balance of: Ingredients - Flavors - Colors - Shapes & textures TO SATISFY BODY & SPIRIT.

STARTERS

Bean Curd Soup

PENCIL NOTES

- 8 oz (225g) tofu.
- 4 green spring onions.
- 4 tablespoons celery tops.
- 2 tablespoons spinach.
- 2 cloves garlic.
- Soy sauce.
- 2 pints (1.15lts) chicken stock.

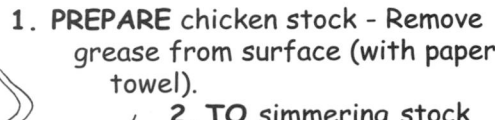

1. **PREPARE** chicken stock - Remove grease from surface (with paper towel).
2. **TO** simmering stock add: Chopped onions - Spinach & garlic - Cover for 5 minutes.
3. **CUT** tofu into 1 cm cubes - Add to simmering soup (for a few mins.).
4. **ADD** chopped celery leaves & onion tops - Serve in rice bowls (with soy sauce).

Canton Prawn Dip

- 1 lb. (450 g) unshelled fresh shrimp.
- 2 finely chopped hot chilies.
- 2 shredded spring onions.
- 2 slices shredded ginger.
- 2 tablespoons tamari (soy sauce).
- 2 tablespoons vegetable oil.
- 2 tablespoons sesame oil.
- 1 tablespoon vinegar.

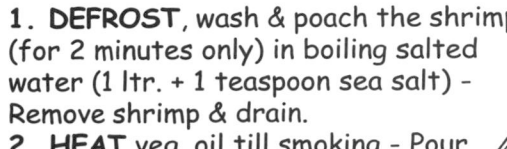
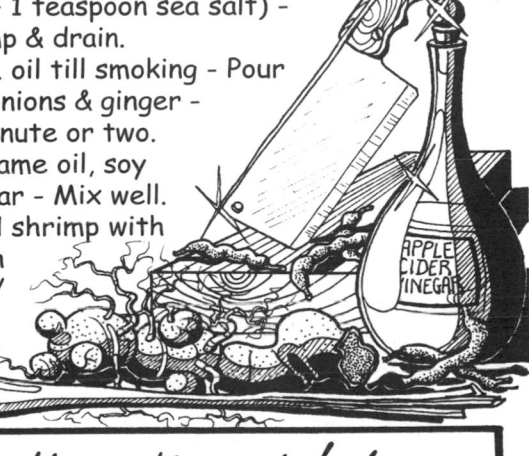

1. **DEFROST**, wash & poach the shrimp (for 2 minutes only) in boiling salted water (1 ltr. + 1 teaspoon sea salt) - Remove shrimp & drain.
2. **HEAT** veg. oil till smoking - Pour over chilies, onions & ginger - Wait for a minute or two.
3. **ADD:** Sesame oil, soy sauce & vinegar - Mix well.
4. **GARNISH** shrimp with parsley - Each diner to peel/ shell, hold tail & dip - **"MMM!"**

MAIN COURSES

Stir-Fried Chicken

- 4 chicken breasts.
- 2 tablespoons soy sauce.
- 2 tablespoons dry sherry.
- 6 oz (170g) mushrooms
- 1 tablespoon veg. oil.
- 3 tablespoons chopped walnuts.
- Gomasio (mixed, roasted, crushed sesame seeds & sea salt [5 to 1]).
- 1 bunch basil.
- 4 sticks celery.
- 2 cloves garlic.

1. **CLEAN**, bone & cut into strips the chicken - Soak in soy sauce & sherry for 30 mins.
2. **WASH,** clean & cut up the garlic, vegetables & basil.
3. **PUT** oil in wok - Stir-fry ingredients in this order: Garlic - Chicken - Mushrooms - Celery - Marinade - Nuts - Basil - Gomasio.
4. **SERVE** with brown rice - **"VELY VELY GOOD!"**

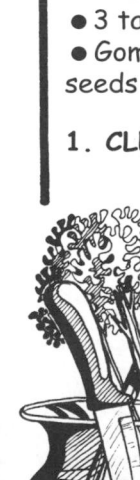
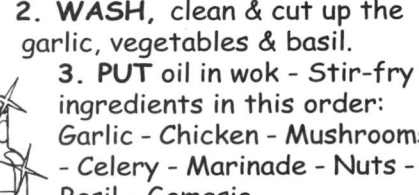

Hong Kong Lobster

PENCIL NOTES

- 1 lb. (450g) lobster meat.
- 4 onions (minced).
- 4 cloves garlic (minced).
- 3 tablespoons sesame oil.
- 3 tablespoons soy sauce.
- 1 teaspoon kazu (veg. gelatine).
- Parsley.
- 1 egg.

1. **CUT** lobster into 1 inch pieces - Sauté in oil with the garlic & onions **(keep stirring lobster).**
2. **ADD** soy sauce & 2 cups of boiling water - Mix well - Simmer (covered) for 10 mins.
3. **DISSOLVE** kuzu in 2 tablespoons of cold water - Add to lobster till sauce is thick (& smooth).
4. **BEAT** egg - Cut off heat - Pour over lobster - Stir - Garnish with parsley - Serve with brown rice - **"VELY VELY DELICIOUS!"**

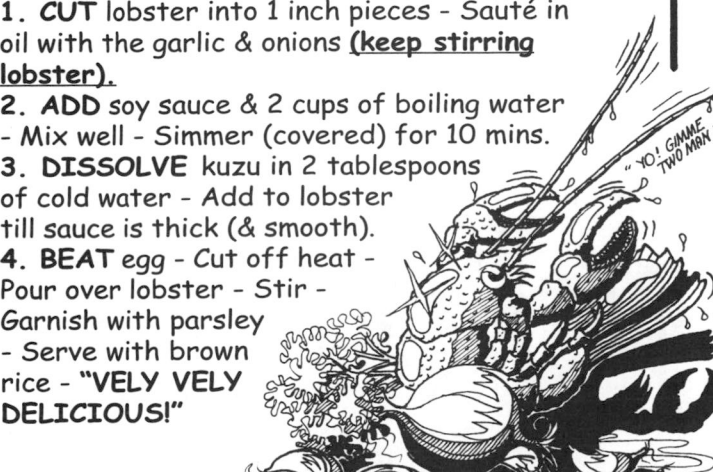

"YO! GIMME TWO MAN."

FROM ROTTERDAM TO ROAD TOWN cuisine can be found
in almost every habitated corner of our planet - *TRY THESE FAVORITES.*

DESSERTS

Nut Kanten

PENCIL NOTES

- 1 pint (570 ml) soy milk.
- 1 pint (570 ml) water.
- 1/2 cup rice syrup.
- Few drops vanilla extract.
- 1/4 teaspoon sea salt.
- 8 oz (225 g) nut butter (almond, hazelnut, cashew [even peanut]).
- Agar (seaweed jelly - also known as Kanten) or other unflavoured gelatine (for 2 1/2 pints of liquid).
  - 2 tablespoons crushed nuts.
  - 1/2 cup whipped cream.

1. **MIX** all ingredients **(except cream & nuts)** - Stirring constantly bring to boil - Simmer for several minutes.
2. **POUR** into contoured setting bowl(s) - Leave to firm (in refrigerator).
3. **UP** end & serve topped with nuts & cream. "VELY FANTASTIC!"

Peking Date Sandwich

PENCIL NOTES

- 1 lb. (450 g) wholemeal flour.
- 12 oz (335 g) seedless dates.
- 8 oz (225 g) walnuts.
- 2 cups rice syrup.
- 1/2 cup soy milk.
- 1/2 teaspoon sea salt.
- Ground cinnamon.

1. **CHOP** dates very small - Chop walnuts medium small - Mix.
2. **MIX** flour & salt - Add date/nut mix - Add rice syrup & soy milk **(should be dough like)**.
3. **ROLL** dough 1/2 inch thick - Fit into oiled pan - Bake at 220 degrees C (gas mark 7) for 30 minutes.
4. **CUT** into squares - Spread with rice syrup - Sprinkle with cinnamon - "GLEAT SNACK!"

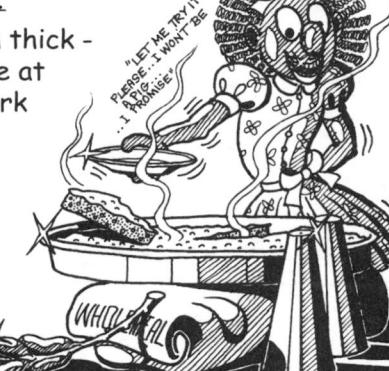

OTHER TREATS

Salad Dressing

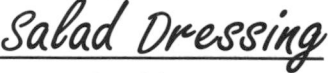

- 2 tablespoons soy sauce.
- 2 tablespoons olive oil.
- 2 tablespoons lemon juice.
- 2 teaspoons thin honey.
- 1 teaspoon grated ginger.
- 1 teaspoon grated lemon rind.
- Vinegar to taste.
  - **MIX** well & serve with side (or starter) salad.

Sweet & Sour Sauce

- **HEAT** wok with 2 tablespoons vegetable oil - Add 2 slices ginger, 2 cloves garlic & 2 spring onions **(all chopped small).**
- **THEN** add 2 tablespoons of rice wine (sherry OK) & 2 of tamari (soy sauce) + 1 tablespoon honey & 1 of vinegar.
- **FINALLY**, bring sauce to boil - Add half a cup of water mixed with 2 teaspoons Kuzu (corn starch OK) - Stir well (& serve with fish or chicken).

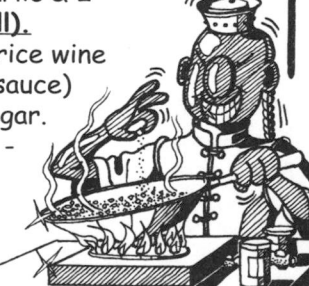

Apple Chutney

- **THINLY** peel, core & dice 1 lb. (450 g) of cooking apples - Mix with 1 tablespoon of each of the following:
  - **SESAME** oil (cold pressed).
  - **SPLIT** mustard seeds.
  - **GOMASIO** (mixed, roasted, finely crushed sesame seed & sea salt [5 to 1 ratio]). "EXTLA TASTY!"

Flowering Egg Soup

- **THE** ultimate natural convenience soup (for those unexpected guests).
- **BRING** 1 pint (570ml) of stock to a rapid boil - "Dribble" **(very slowly)** 2 beaten eggs into it.
- **SEASON** with sea salt & ground peppers - Garnish with 2 finely chopped spring onions - Warming, quick & nutritious. "VELY VELY FAST"

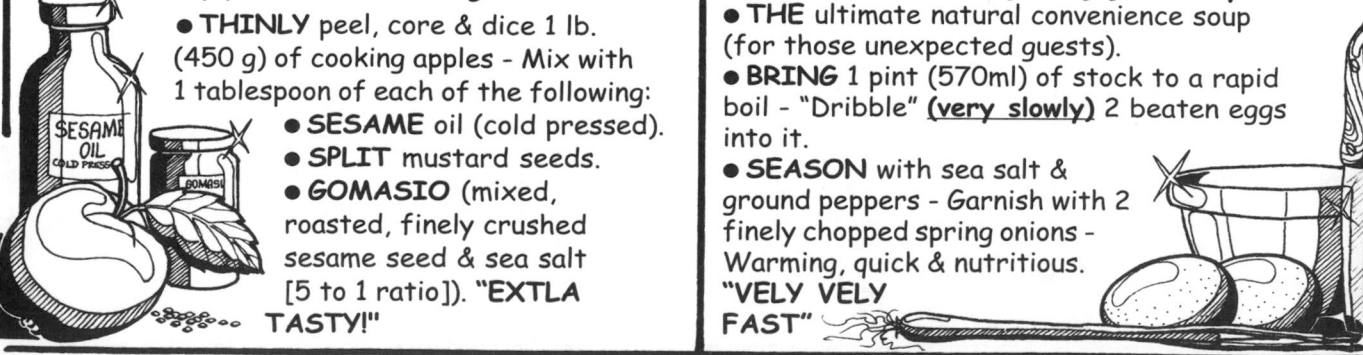

Illustrated Guidance To Getting Names Right Under Sail

"It would seem "SAID THE TOURIST ON THE DOCK" that almost nothing on a sailing vessel is called by a normal land name" ....

RIG NAMES

● REFERS TO: The configuration of sails & mast(s).

● **SLOOP** (1 mast & 1 headsail).

KETCH (mizzen forward of rudder).

● **YAWL** (mizzen aft of rudder).

CUTTER (1 mast & 2 + headsails).

● **GAFF RIGGED** (look for this spar).

SCHOONER (aft mast(s) higher than forward).

SAIL NAMES

● REFERS TO: Each sail according to its shape, size & position.

- SPINNAKER.   HEAD.
- MAINSAIL.   ROACH.
- STAYSAIL.   LEECH.
- JIB.   LUFF.

● CLEW.
● FOOT.

● TACK.

REEF POINTS.

● MIZZEN STAYSAIL.   ● MIZZEN.

RUNNING RIGGING

● REFERS TO: Sail or mast control lines which move (or run).

BOOM VANG/ KICKING STRAP.

OUTHAUL

DOWNHAUL. STARBOARD JIB SHEET. STARBOARD STAYSAIL SHEET.

MAIN-SHEET.

MIZZEN-SHEET.

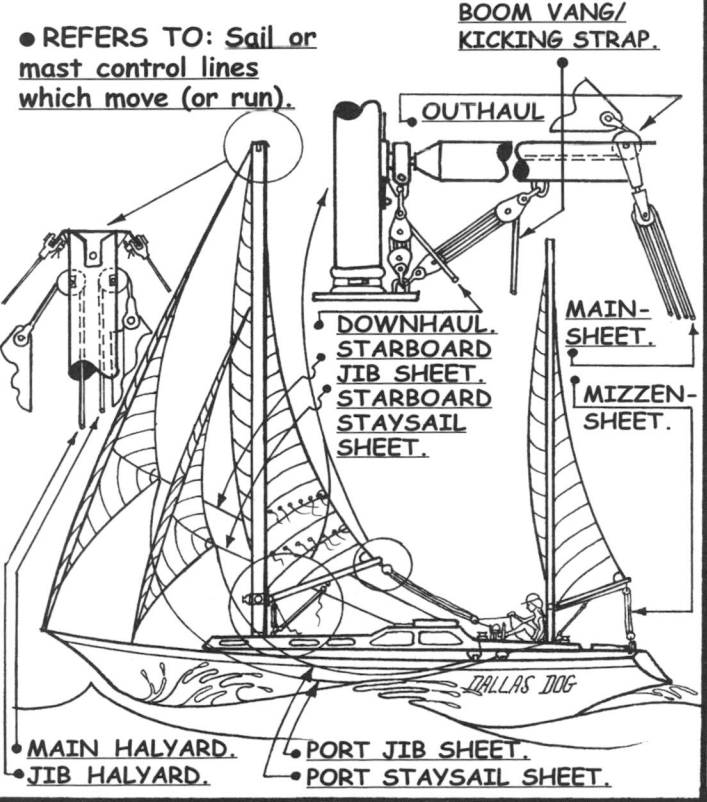

● MAIN HALYARD.
● JIB HALYARD.

● PORT JIB SHEET.
● PORT STAYSAIL SHEET.

STANDING RIGGING

● REFERS TO: Mast wires which are fixed in position.

- TRIATIC STAY.
- MAIN TOPPING LIFT.
- MAIN PORT CAP SHROUD.
- INNER FORESTAY.
- SPLIT BACKSTAY.
- MIZZEN TOPPING LIFT.
- PORT MIZZEN CAP SHROUD.

FORESTAY.

MAIN STARBOARD CAP SHROUD.

MAIN STARBOARD FORWARD LOWER SHROUD.

MIZZEN PORT AFTER LOWER SHROUD.

MAIN STARBOARD AFTER LOWER SHROUD.

Salty Instructional Sketches From A Seadog's Diary

.... *"That,"* replied the sailor, *"Is because, A SAILING VESSEL AT SEA IS to all intents IN A WORLD OF ITS OWN."*

POINTS OF SAILING

✿ **Use preventor** (stops spar swinging back).

☐ **Use boom vang** (keeps boom end down).

△ **Use spinnaker pole** (keeps sail out).

☐ **CLOSE REACH**

• **CLOSE HAULED**

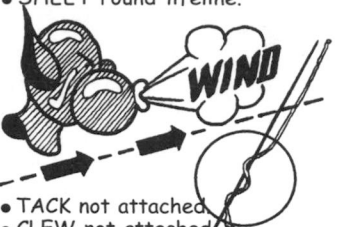

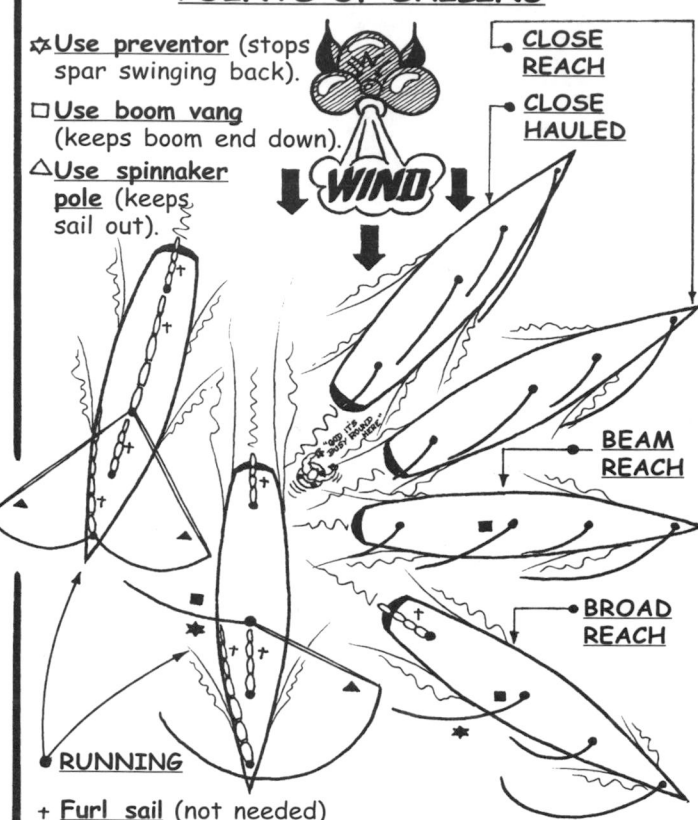

BEAM REACH

BROAD REACH

• **RUNNING**

+ **Furl sail** (not needed)

SAIL HANDLING (HOISTING)

- DON'T -	- DO -
(Identify in circles)	1.) **HEAD** 10 degrees-20 degrees off the wind whilst hoisting.

• HANK upside down (i.e. luff is twisted).
• SHEET round lifeline.

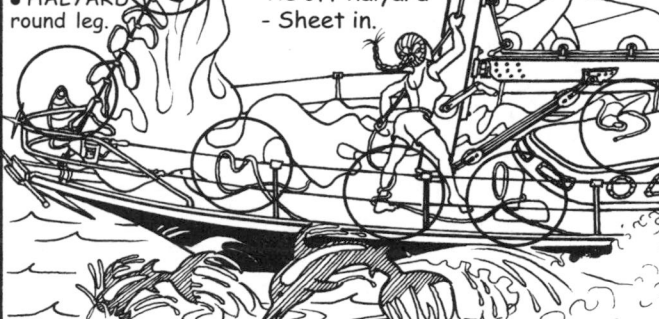

2.) **CHECK** all is ready: Hanks, halyard & sheets (all led correctly).

• TACK not attached.
• CLEW not attached.
• HALYARD round ventilator.
• HALYARD round forestay.
• HALYARD round leg.

3.) **HOIST** quickly by hand - Take up the last tension with the winch (2-6 wraps clock- wise depending on sail size) - Tie off halyard - Sheet in.

SAIL HANDLING (THE GYBE)

• **CONTROL** is the first word here.
• **DANGER** is the second word (the larger the yacht and the stronger the wind <u>THE MORE CHANCE OF ACCIDENTS</u>).

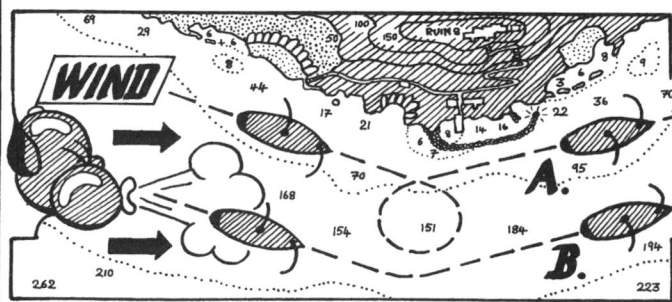

"A" ALTERNATIVE IN STRONG WINDS.
"B" CONVENTIONAL GYBE.

SAILS ON BOOMS ARE THE PROBLEM
(handle them like this):
1) **WAIT** for a lull (if any).
2) **BRING** the wind onto the quarter.
3) **SHEET** the boom in hard amidships.
4) **TAKE** the stern thru the eye of the wind (gybe) - Ease out the sheet - <u>Don't forget the preventor.</u>

INTERNATIONAL ROAD RULES FOR VESSELS UNDER SAIL

• **WIND ON DIFFERENT SIDES:** Vessel with wind on port side <u>STAYS CLEAR.</u>
• **WIND ON SAME SIDES:** Vessel to windward <u>STAYS CLEAR.</u>

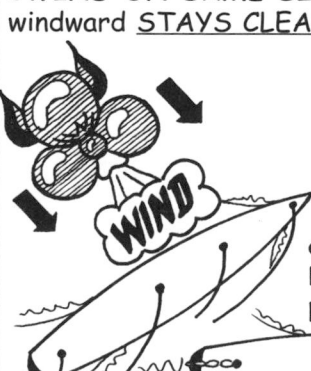

• **A VESSEL** also powered by machinery is classed as a power-driven vessel.

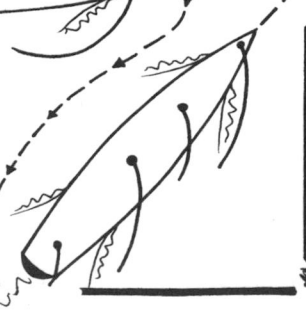

• **A VESSEL** with the wind on port side (unable to determine which side a vessel to windward has the wind) shall <u>STAY CLEAR.</u>

Sail: One of the oldest & probably still the "freest" form of
INTERNATIONAL TRAVEL AVAILABLE TO THE 21ST CENTURY.

BASICS OF ANCHORING

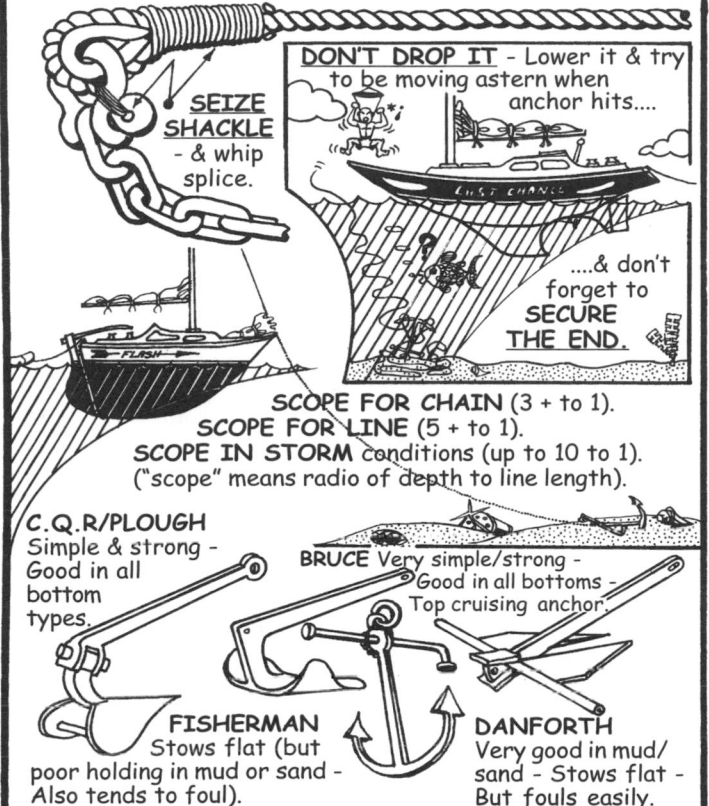

SEIZE SHACKLE - & whip splice.

DON'T DROP IT - Lower it & try to be moving astern when anchor hits....

....& don't forget to **SECURE THE END.**

SCOPE FOR CHAIN (3 + to 1).
SCOPE FOR LINE (5 + to 1).
SCOPE IN STORM conditions (up to 10 to 1).
("scope" means radio of depth to line length).

C.Q.R/PLOUGH
Simple & strong - Good in all bottom types.

BRUCE Very simple/strong - Good in all bottoms - Top cruising anchor.

FISHERMAN
Stows flat (but poor holding in mud or sand - Also tends to foul).

DANFORTH
Very good in mud/sand - Stows flat - But fouls easily.

DECK SIGNALS

● **WHEN APPROACHING MOORING** (or anchorage) it is often useful to have a "body" on the bow to direct the helmsperson.

GO in that direction (including reverse).

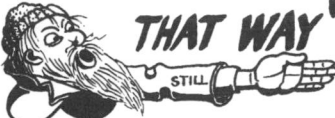

THAT WAY STILL

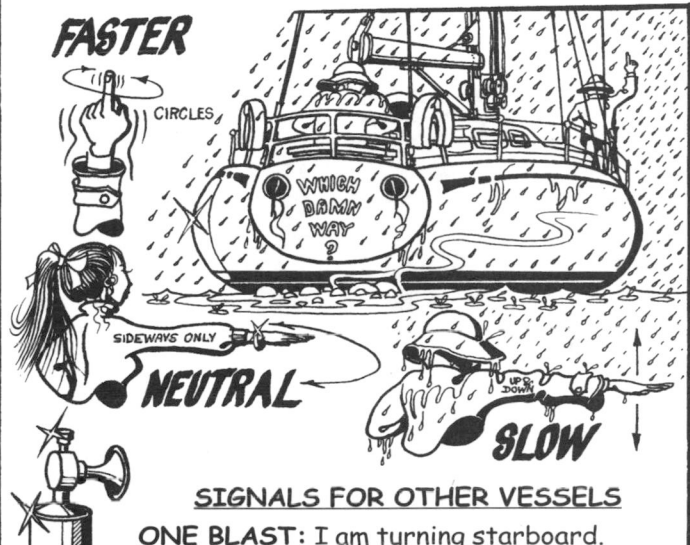

FASTER CIRCLES

WHICH DAMN WAY ?

NEUTRAL SIDEWAYS ONLY

SLOW UP & DOWN

SIGNALS FOR OTHER VESSELS

ONE BLAST: I am turning starboard.
TWO BLASTS: I am turning to port.
MULTIPLE BLASTS: I am going astern.

APPROACHING A MOORING

● **WIND & congestion** are often the problem factors.
● **PLAN your approach** carefully & approach from leeward (downwind).
● **IF** this is the mooring you want....

BE PREPARED WITH

● **DINGHY** painter short.
● **CREW** forward with boathook.
● **YACHTS carry their way, a long way** (maybe a boat length per knot in light airs & seas).
● **ABOUT** half a boat length away: You will probably lose sight of the bouy (under the bow) - **Line it up before you do** - Steer straight - Watch for signals from bow.

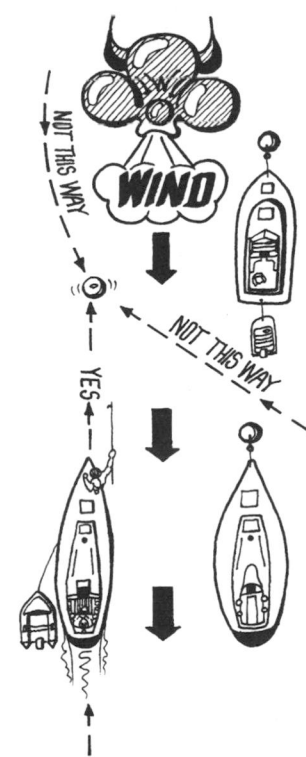

NOT THIS WAY
WIND
NOT THIS WAY
YES

CHOOSING A POSITION

● **RECONNOITER & PLAN** your choice of position - Here is an example.

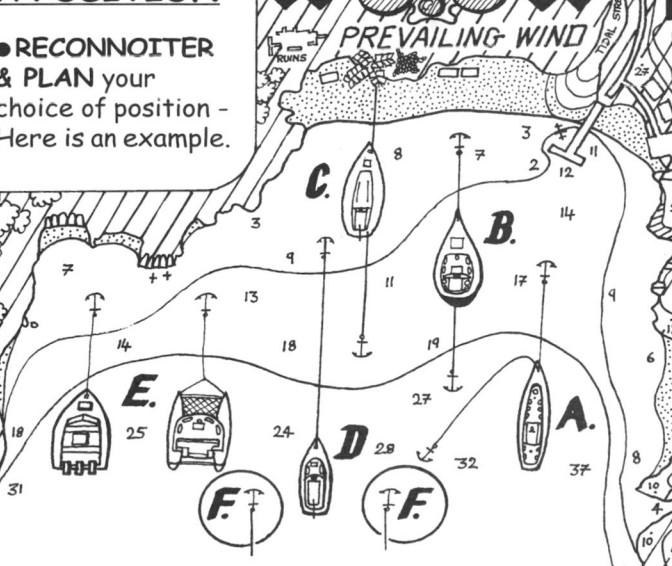

PREVAILING WIND

RUINS

TIDAL STREAM

A - **BAHAMIAN** moor (to stay off the rocks).
B - **FORE** & aft anchor (to stay off the beach).
C - **BOW** line around tree (& stern anchor).
D - **EXTRA** scope (may swing into others).
E - **MULTI** & power (swing differently).
F - **LOWER** your anchor HERE.

A SAILOR'S BASIC DOCKING REMINDERS

The Condition Of Your Vessel Almost Certainly Depends On These

THE WEATHER & LADY LUCK make going to sea a game of "RUSSIAN ROULETTE," but preparation will improve your odds dramatically.

TYING UP ALONGSIDE

- **LIKE THIS** on cleats & posts with crossbars.

- **FIRST ASHORE....** attach one end of bow line to bow cleat - Coil rest neatly (tail out)* - Be ready to throw (or jump) with it.

OR THIS....

on anything (but particularly rings).

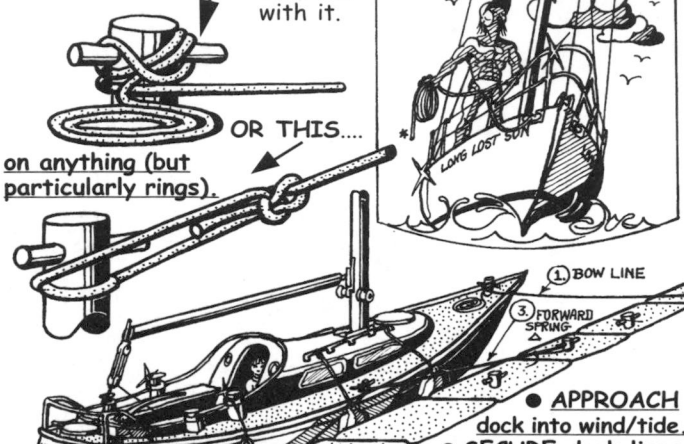

LONG LOST SON

1. BOW LINE
3. FORWARD SPRING
2. STERN LINE
4. AFTER SPRING

- **APPROACH** dock into wind/tide.
- **SECURE dock lines** in order of numbers.
- **DOUBLE lines** (& fit chafe guards) in strong winds/tides.

- **APPROACH** dock like this.

DOCKING A ROWING DINGHY

OAR BLADE ANGLE

A = **Blade enters** water at this angle.
B, C & D = **Blade stays** at same angle while under water (keeps it down & also handle in rowlock).
E = **Blade exits** water at end of pull (twist wrist now).
F & G = **Flatten blade** angle to avoid "crabs" (& to reduce air resistance during return stroke).

- **BODY POSITION:** Legs, back & arms all straight.

"ONLY ANOTHER 100 LESSONS DEAR...."
"BUT I ROW BETTER THAN YOU DEAR.."

T.T. LAZY DOG

- **USE THE WRISTS** to twist/flick blades just before exit from water (at "E") & **LEAN BACK** - Use body weight ("A" to "E").

WHEN APPROACHING DOCK: Maintain speed (1 & 2) - Dip & hold seaward oar (3) - Ship dockside oar & fend off (4) - Don't give up if you mess it up the first few times - **PATIENCE.**

INTERNATIONAL ROAD RULES FOR VESSELS UNDER POWER

- **TWO VESSELS MEETING HEAD ON:** Each shall alter course to starboard giving one blast on the horn.

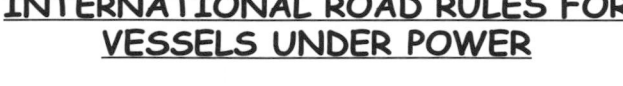

B. **B.**

- **IN A CROSSING SITUATION:** The vessel with the other on her own starboard side shall give way.

B.

- **OVERTAKING:** An overtaking vessel is one approaching another from 22 1/2 degrees or more aft of the beam & **shall stay clear.**

CAUTION
B = Burdened.
R = Right of way.
BUT don't force your rights on any other vessel - Use **COMMON SENSE.**

R.

22½° **R.** **22½°**

OVERTAKING STAY CLEAR

B. **B.**

BACKING UP UNDER POWER

- **SAILING VESSELS usually do not behave well under power in reverse.** - Particularly if fitted with racing/folding props.

USUAL TECHNIQUE

- **BUILD UP sternway** at medium R.P.M (helm central if unsure).
- **CUT BACK R.P.M.** to idle (& keeping a very tight grip) attempt steering.
- **IF CONTROL is lost:** Engage "ahead" with helm hard over (to correct position) - Then try again in "reverse."

- **EXAMPLE:** This is a "left hand" prop viewed from the stern with engine going ahead - It will:
- **PULL the stern to port in "ahead"**
- **PULL the stern to starboard in "reverse."**

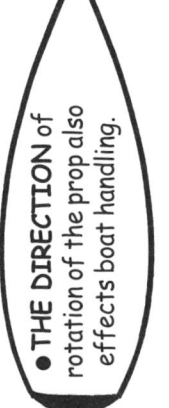

THE DIRECTION of rotation of the prop also effects boat handling.

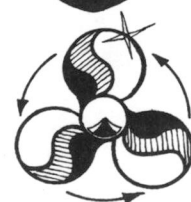

1 Nautical mile = 6,080 feet = 1.8532 Kilometres = 1 minute of latitude = (at the equator only) 1 minute of longitude.

RADIO POSITION FINDING
(use any directional radio)

● **TUNE IN** a strong station - Listen for its location.
● **ROTATE SET** carefully for <u>MINIMUM</u> signal - Record compass bearing.

NOTE: <u>Mountains (& long distance etc.) cause errors.</u>

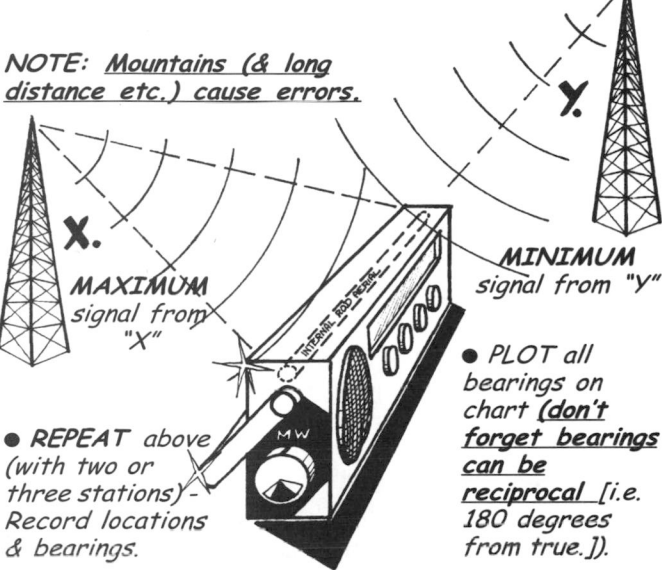

MAXIMUM signal from "X"

X.

Y.

MINIMUM signal from "Y"

● **PLOT** all bearings on chart *(<u>don't forget bearings can be reciprocal</u> [i.e. 180 degrees from true.])*.

● **REPEAT** above *(with two or three stations) - Record locations & bearings.*

CHOOSING SHELTER
(e.g. for a vessel of 6 ft draft)

A = Good anchorage.
B = Good anchorage (in prevailing winds).
C = Shallow.

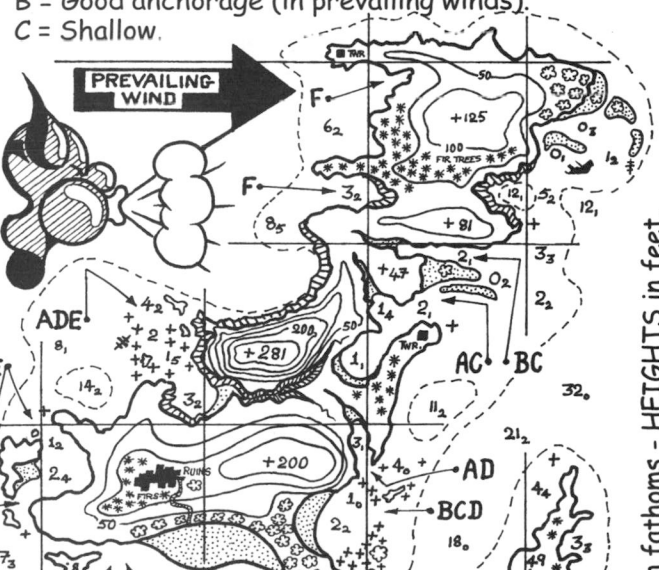

PREVAILING WIND

SOUNDINGS in fathoms - HEIGHTS in feet.

D = Tricky approach & exit.
E = Swells may enter.
F = No good (in prevailing winds).

LATITUDE FROM NOON SIGHT

● **YOU NEED:** A sextant - Almanac - Chart & watch.
● <u>HANDLE the sextant very carefully</u> - It is used to measure the angle between sun, horizon & the observer - <u>Don't forget to use the sextant shades.</u>

BEFORE THE SIGHT

● **CALCULATE G.M.T.** of Sun's Meridian Passage by converting approximate (D.R.) longitude to time (see over) e.g....
D.R. long : 64 degrees 30' W = 4 hrs 18 mins.
*Meridian Passage for date (6 Aug. '88) in Greenwich England 12 hours 06 mins therefore Meridian Passage locally = 16 hrs 24 mins

THE SIGHT

● **START** observing sun's altitude about 10 mins before expected passage.

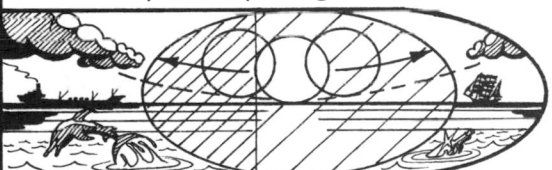

● **SWING** sextant in gentle arc (to skim horizon with bottom of sun).
● **RECORD** maximum altitude & time.

THE CALCULATION		+	−
* Ht. of eye above sea (8 ft)		−	2.7
* Other corrections		16.1	−
Sextant index error		−	−
Observed altitude		88°	15.5'
Subtract from 90 degrees written as		89°	60'
Corrected altitude		−88°	28.9'
Therefore Zenith distance N/S	=	1	31.1'N
* Sun's Declination N/S		16°	30.8 N
Therefore Latitude N/S	=	18°	1.9'N

NOTES

* These values from Nautical Almanac for year/day/hour.
● N. or S. (for Zenith D.) determined by observer (being either N. or S. of the sun).
● If Zenith D. & Dec. are both N. or S: Add together - If different: Take smaller from larger.
● <u>Longitude calculations are more complex</u> - But a rough check can be had by graphing exact time of Meridian Passage & comparing it with that of Greenwich (see Almanac [& over]).

.... Find Your Way Across Planet Earth

*WHY IS IT THAT, the more experienced the navigator,
the more suspicious of the apparently obvious they appear to become?*

COMPASS ERRORS

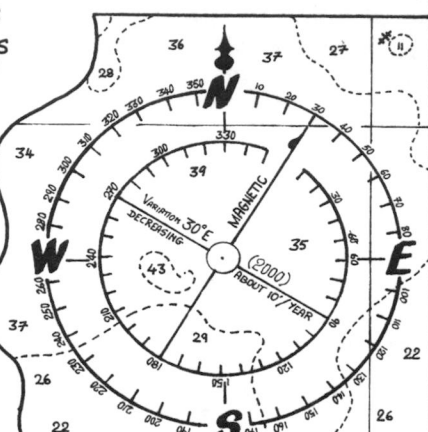

- **MAGNETIC** variations are caused by the earth's magnetic field.
- **DEVIATION** is caused by ferrous objects onboard/ near the vessel.
- **ONE OR BOTH** of the above can mean that the compass you look at is probably not showing a true reading.
- **IN THE EXAMPLE** at right, the magnetic var. is 30 degrees E - In other words if you want to go True North - Then you must steer 330 degrees on the compass.
- **CONVERSELY** if the variation was say 20 degrees W - Then the compass course for True North would be 020 degrees.
- **MEMORIZE** this rhyme: **"Error west compass best (more), Error east compass least (less)."**

LATITUDE & LONGITUDE

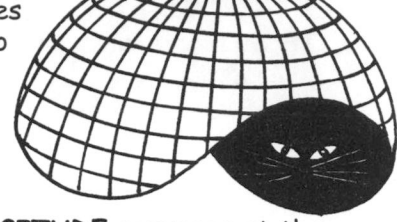

- **LATITUDE** goes around (E to W).
- **LONGITUDE** goes up & down (N to S).
- **LINES OF LATITUDE** run parallel to each other.
- **LINES OF LONGITUDE** converge at the poles.
- **ZERO DEGREES OF LONGITUDE** runs thru Greenwich, England.
- **ONE MINUTE (1') OF LATITUDE** = 1 nautical mile - One degree of latitude = 60 nautical miles (60' = 1 degree).
- **AT THE EQUATOR** (0 degrees of latitude), 1 degree of latitude = 1 degree of longitude - BUT north or south longitude decreases to nothing at poles.
- **1 DEGREE OF LONGITUDE** = 4 minutes of time (irrespective of the latitude) - And 15 degrees of longitude = 1 hour of time (irrespective of latitude).
- **CONFUSING?** - ONLY AT FIRST!

PLOT COURSE & DISTANCE

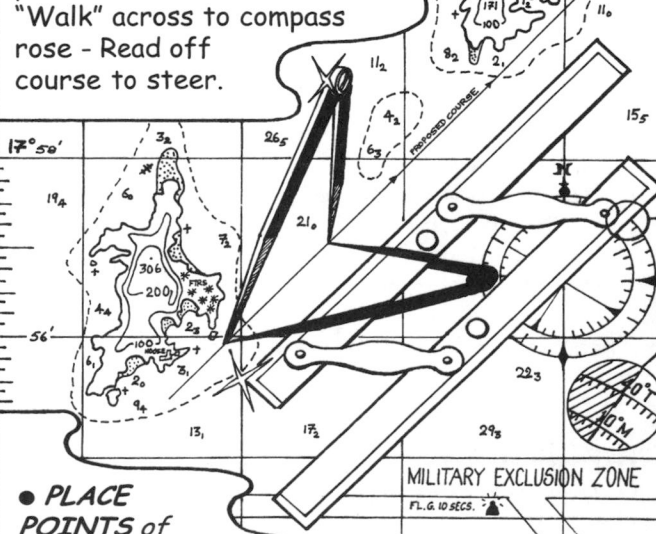

- **DRAW A LIGHT LINE** with a soft pencil on the chart (between the points to be transited).
- **PLACE ONE EDGE** of parallel rulers on line - "Walk" across to compass rose - Read off course to steer.

MILITARY EXCLUSION ZONE
FL.G. 10 SECS.

- *PLACE POINTS* of dividers on distance to be measured - Transfer to LATITUDE.

COASTAL POSITION FINDING
(Examples of common techniques)

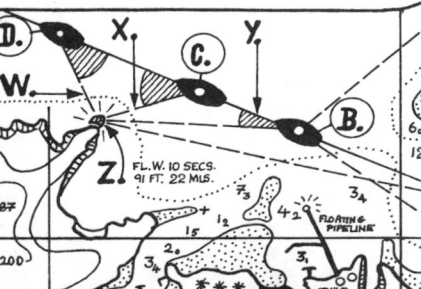
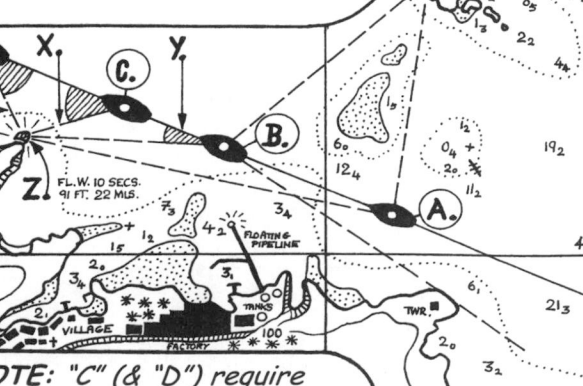

- **WESTERLY** points of two islands in line & compass bearing on lighthouse Z ("A").
- **WESTERLY** & Easterly points of two islands in line & compass bearing on prominent point ("B").
- **DOUBLING** the angle on the bow makes sides X & Y equal ("C").
- **ISOSCELES** triangle with two equal angles & sides (W & X) ("D").

FL.W. 10 SECS.
91 FT. 22 MLS.

- *NOTE:* "C" (& "D") require log readings (& allowance for current &/or tide).

NO ONE CAN ESCAPE MATH, from infancy ("I got more toys 1.2..3...errr?") to the rocking chair ("I got more teeth 3.2..1...errr?") BUT SAILORS NEED IT ALL THE TIME!

	$+$	$-$	$\times$	$\div$
WHOLE NUMBERS	69,498 + 307 + 1,679,784 =	187,016 - 4,931 =	4,207 × 315 =	447,984 div.by 102 =
	(1) 69,498 / 307 / 1,679,784 / **1,749,589** / 1 1 1 1 1 ← • Tens are carried forward to next column.	(2) 6 +9 +10 18⟋,016 - 4,931 **182,085** • Because you can not take 3 from 1 borrow from the next number (7).	(3) 4,207 ← × 315 1 262 100 / ₁ ₂ 42 070 21 035 / ₂₁ ₃ **1,325,205** / ₁ ₁ • Start with 3 →	(4) 4392 102)447984 408↓ 399 306↓ 938 918↓ 204 204 000 • 102 into 4 doesn't go - 102 into 44 doesn't go etc. etc.
DECIMALS	1.247 + 42.8 + 101.01 =	4920.31 - 1.0279 =	47.61 × .83 =	7.4612 div.by .23 =
	(5) 1.247 42.8 101.01 **145.057** 1 • Keep decimal points in a vertical line.	(6) 1 10 2 9 9 10 492⟋0.3⟋1 ⟋ 1.0279 **4919.2821** • Read notes of 2 & 5 which are relevant here.	(7) 47.61 × .83 38 08 80 / ₆ ₄ 1 42 83 / ₂ ₁ **39. 51 63** / ₁ ₁ • Digits after point in question = Same in answer.	(8) 32.44 .23)7.46 12 6 9↓ 56 46↓ 10 1 92↓ 92 92 00 • Proceed as per number 4 but move point as per divisor.
FRACTIONS	(9) $\frac{1}{3} + 2\frac{1}{2} =$	(10) $1\frac{1}{2} - \frac{3}{5} =$	(11) $4\frac{1}{4} \times \frac{2}{5} =$	(12) $1\frac{1}{9} \div \frac{5}{6} =$
	$\therefore$ as $\frac{1(\times 2)}{3(\times 2)} = \frac{2}{6}$ & $\frac{1(\times 3)}{2(\times 3)} = \frac{3}{6}$ then write sum as: $\frac{2}{6} + 2\frac{3}{6} = 2\frac{5}{6}$ • Bottoms of fractions either side of sign (+ or -) must be the same.	$\therefore$ as $\frac{1}{2}(\times 5) = \frac{5}{10}$ & $\frac{3}{5}(\times 2) = \frac{6}{10}$ & $1 = \frac{10}{10}$ then write sum as: $\frac{15}{10} - \frac{6}{10} = \frac{9}{10}$	First change all to fractions $\therefore 4\frac{1}{4} \frac{(4 \times 4 + 1)}{4}$ $= \frac{17}{4} \times \frac{2}{5}$ then multiply top by top & bott. by bott. $= \frac{34}{20} \times 1\frac{14}{20} = 1\frac{7}{10}$	$\therefore 1\frac{1}{9} \frac{(9 \times 1 + 1)}{9}$ $= \frac{10}{9} \div \frac{5}{6}$ then invert the right side—it becomes "×" (as in (11)) $= \frac{10}{9} \times \frac{6}{5} = \frac{60}{45}$ $= 1\frac{15}{45} = 1\frac{1}{3}$

	DECIMALS	**FRACTIONS**
	Take as an example 12.21% of $150. Work out both ways for practice.	
%	• Move decimal 2 places to left & drop % sign. = **.1221 × 150** = (Work this out as per example (7) above - The answer will be $ & figures to right of point in cents) → **$18.315** ←	• As a fraction lay out like this $\frac{12.21}{100*} \times \frac{150*}{1} = \frac{12.21}{2} \times \frac{3}{1} =$ (* Divide by 50 to reduce the numbers) $= \frac{36.63}{2}$ • Divide top by bottom (answer is in $ & cents).

A SAILOR'S BASIC FORMULA REMINDERS

....To Make The Blocks - To Build The Bridge - To Cross The Abyss

LAND	1 SQUARE MILE = 640 acres - 1 acre = 4,840 square yards,: 1 SQUARE KILOMETER = 1 million square meters = 100 hectares

CIRCLES

Π (THE GREEK ALPHABET LETTER PI) = **3.14159 or 22/7**

CIRCUMFERENCE OF A CIRCLE: Π x D (where D is diameter).	AREA OF A CIRCLE: Π x R x R (where R is radius).

TEMPERATURE

FAHRENHEIT TO CENTIGRADE	CENTIGRADE TO FAHRENHEIT
(....°F - 32) x 5/9 = °C.	(....°C x 9/5) + 32 = °F.

DISTANCE

MILES P.H. TO KILOMETERS P.H.	KILOMETERS P.H. TO MILES P.H.
....m.p.h. x 8/5 = k.p.h.	....k.p.h. x 5/8 = m.p.h.

WATER

1 LITER weighs 1 Kilogram	1 GALLON weighs 10 lbs.
1 CU. MTR. weighs 1,000 K.Grams	1 CUBIC FOOT weighs 62.4 lbs.
1 CUBIC METER = 1,000 Liters	1 TON = 224 Imperial galls.

PHYSICS

F = MA   (FORCE = MASS X ACCELERATION [Newton's laws 1 & 2]).
$E = MC^2$ (ENERGY = MASS X VELOCITY OF LIGHT SQUARED [Einstein]).

GAS LAWS   PRESSURE is inversely proportional to volume (Boyle's Law).
PRESSURE is directly proportional to temperature (Charles' Law).

CONVERSIONS

TO CONVERT column A to column B, multiply by column C.
TO CONVERT column B to column A, multiply by column D.

A	B	C	D	A	B	C	D
AREA				**WEIGHT**			
sq. ins.	sq. cms.	6.4516	.155	grams	ozs.	.035	28.35
sq. ft.	sq. mtrs.	.0929	10.764	lbs.	kgs.	.454	2.205
LENGTH				tons	tonnes	1.016	.984
1/16 inch	mm	1.587	.63	**VOLUME**			
inches	meters	.025	39.37	cu. ins.	cu. cms.	16.387	.061
feet	meters	.305	3.281	cu. ins.	litres	.016	62.5
miles	k.mtrs.	1.609	.621	cu. ft.	cu. mtrs.	.028	35.315
sea mls.	meters	1853.1	.00054	imp. gals	U.S. gals	1.205	.830
SPEED				U.S. gals	liters	3.785	.264
k. p. h.	m. p. sec.	.278	3.6	imp. gals	liters	4.546	.22
ft. p. sec.	m. p. sec.	.305	3.281	**STRESS & ENERGY**			
ft. p. sec.	m. p. h.	.682	1.467	kg/sq. m.	lbs./sq. ft.	.205	4.88
m. p. h.	m. p. sec.	.447	2.237	k. w.	h.p.(U.K.)	1.34	.746
m. p. h.	k. p. h.	1.609	.621	**ELECTRICITY**			
DENSITY				WATTS = Volts x Amperes.			
lbs./cu. ft.	kg./cu. m.	16.019	.0624	AMPERES = Watts div. by Volts.			

A Professional's Choice Of The World's Best (& Easiest)

*Don't waste your next plane, train, bus or boat trip -
Take a meter of line & PRACTICE YOUR KNOTS - You may need one soon.*

TYING OFF A CLEAT

- **START BY** going round the back of the cleat.

LOAD

NOTE the "figure 8."

DRESS TIE KNOT

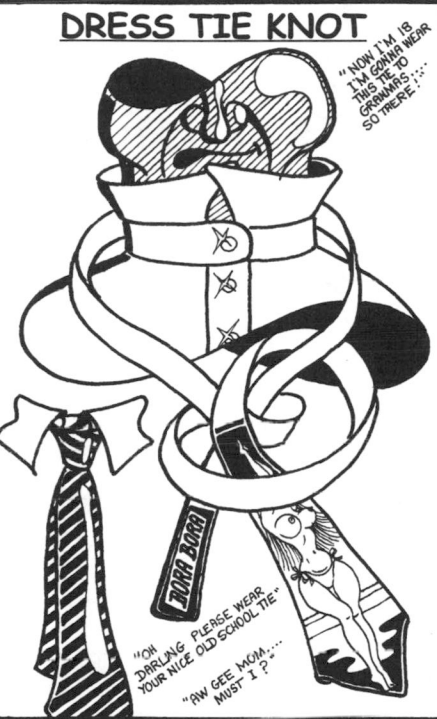

"NOW I'M 18 I'M GONNA WEAR THIS TIE TO GRANMA'S SO THERE!"

"OH DARLING PLEASE WEAR YOUR NICE OLD SCHOOL TIE"

"AW GEE MOM.... MUST I ?"

A COIL OF LINE

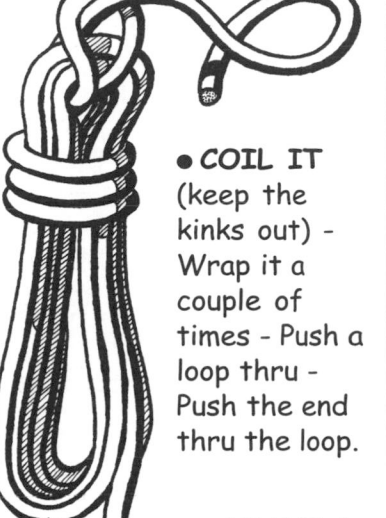

- **COIL IT** (keep the kinks out) - Wrap it a couple of times - Push a loop thru - Push the end thru the loop.

- **LEAVE** the "tail" out of the coil

MAKING UP A COIL ON A CLEAT

- **TIE OFF** the cleat (as top left) - Then coil the "fall" - Reach thru & twist a loop next to the cleat - Pull it thru the coil & hook it back on the cleat.

HUNTERS BEND

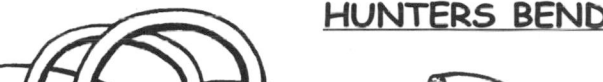

- **USE AS** a secure method of joining 2 (similar sized) lines.

- **ALSO HOLDS WELL** with modern synthetics.

HIGHWAYMAN'S HITCH

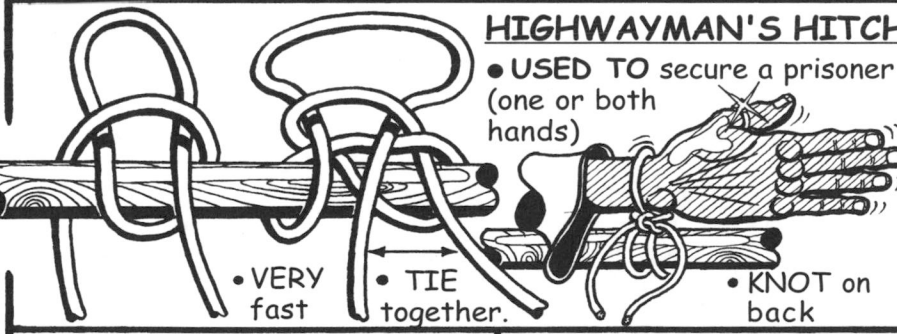

- **USED TO** secure a prisoner (one or both hands)

- **VERY fast**
- **TIE together.**
- **KNOT on back**

BRAID

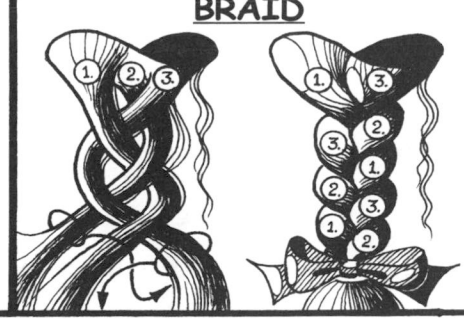

SURGEONS KNOT

- **USED TO** tie stitches in wounds (or other slippery lines).

FISHERMAN'S BEND

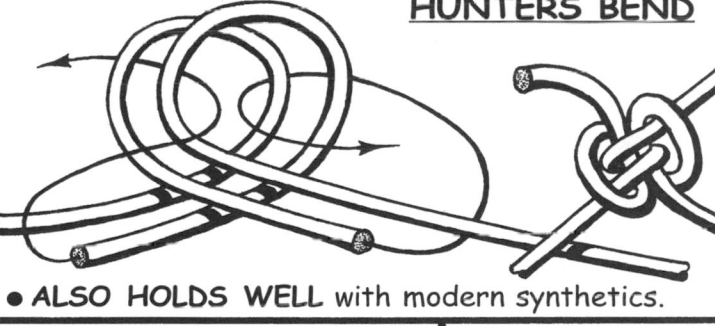

- **USED AS** a secure knot (to anchor or dock).

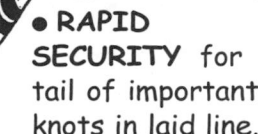

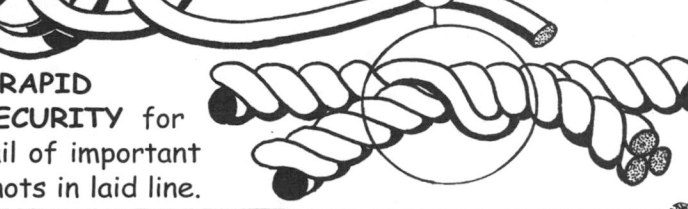

- **RAPID SECURITY** for tail of important knots in laid line.

A Professional's Choice Of The Worlds Easiest (& Best)

THE KNOWLEDGE of how to tie a simple knot fast could be THE factor which saves THAT "rapid response" situation - DON'T MESS IT UP.

FIGURE OF EIGHT   BABIES FIST   CLOVEHITCH

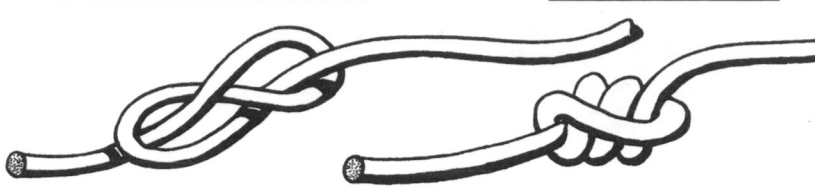

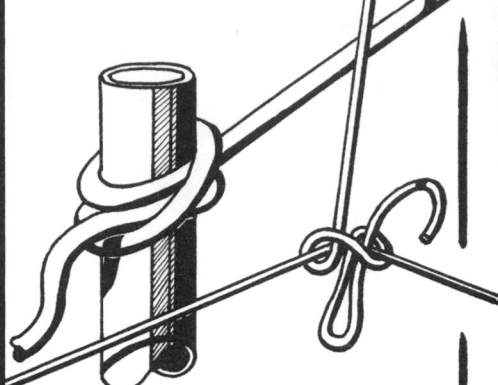

● BOTH THE ABOVE ARE "STOP" KNOTS used on the end of a line to <u>stop it going thru something</u>: Kit bag - Pulley block - Fair lead or YOUR PANTS - Also easy to undo.

● A VERY SIMPLE (& useful) knot - Use it to tie up your yacht - Or tie down your sun awning (with a slip end) - <u>It is self-tightening (yet easy to undo)</u> - ALMOST INDISPENSABLE AT SEA.

TRUCK DRIVER'S HITCH

LOAD

● AROUND THE HOUSE, the boat, at work, or on the road, this little known knot is simple to tie & very effective - <u>Use it whenever you need extra power to pull two objects together</u> - To tighten a parcel tie - A boat lashing - A truck load - <u>It can be repeated again & again on the same line</u> (to multiply power!).

→ PULL HERE

DOUBLE SHEET BEND

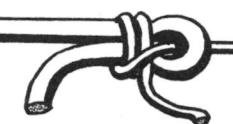

● USE THIS KNOT to join two lines of <u>unequal</u> diameter (also easy to undo).

BOWLINE

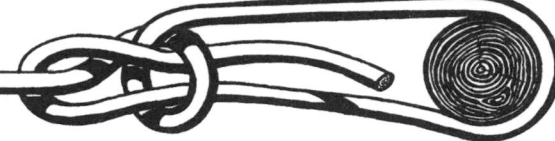

● A VERY IMPORTANT, (simple & effective) knot with a wide range of uses - Wherever a secure loop is required - <u>Will not slip under load</u> - YET CAN EASILY BE UNDONE.

REEF KNOT

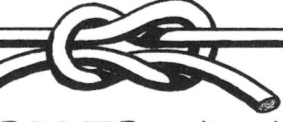

● USE TO TIE two lines (of equal size) - <u>Not completely trustworthy</u> - Use on bags/ parcels/sails (with or without a slip end).

ROLLING HITCH

● A KNOT WHICH could (more than most) <u>save your life (or your ship)</u> - Used to attach a line (perhaps your safety or escape line) TO ANOTHER LINE (OR WIRE) under load.

● RIGGERS USE <u>two of these knots in a row</u> to attach their safety line to a <u>VERTICAL</u> wire!!!!

FISHERMAN'S KNOT

● USED TO JOIN broken fishing line etc.

SHEEPSHANK

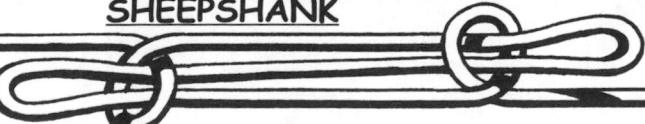

● USED TO SHORTEN (the middle of) a line.

FROM THAILAND TO TAHITI, Mauritius to Martinique (with some variations),
ALL sailors speak the internationally understood "language" of these pages.

3 STRAND EYE SPLICE

- **TAPE** &/or burn ends.
- **UNTWIST** about 10 times the diameter of line.
- **A TURN** of tape here.
- **START** with middle one.

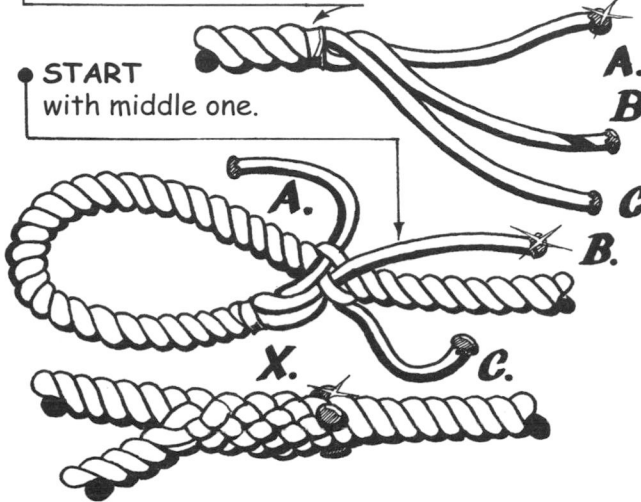

- **THEN** the other two (A & C) each side.
- **YOU** should have **three ends, coming out of three different holes** (BUT ALL LEVEL).
- **TAKE OFF** tape & pull each tight - Then take each end in turn & go over one strand, then under one strand etc. - After each round, **check that each end comes out of a different hole** (BUT IS LEVEL WITH THE OTHER TWO) - Pull tight.

END SPLICE

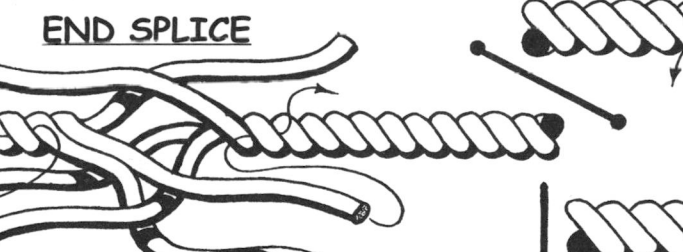

- **TO JOIN** two (3 strand) lines start as above (don't forget the tape) - Continue both sides in opposite directions (as in "X" at top).

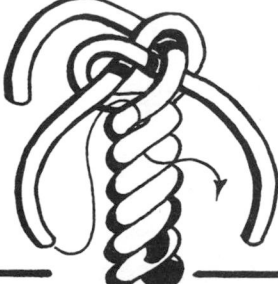

BACK SPLICE

- **TO TERMINATE** a (3 strand) line neatly - Start off the splice (as at left) - Then proceed as in "X" (at top).

WHIPPINGS

- **START** like this.

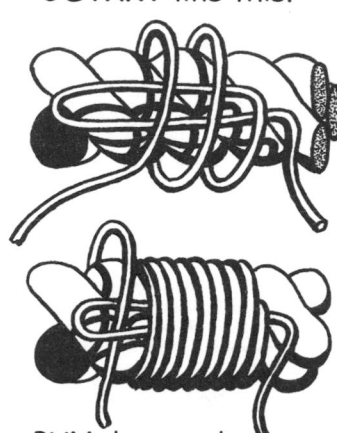

- **PULL** loop under.

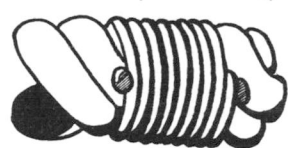

- **LOOP** is **under** whipping - Cut off ends (& BURN THEM IF SYNTHETIC).

- **START** like this.

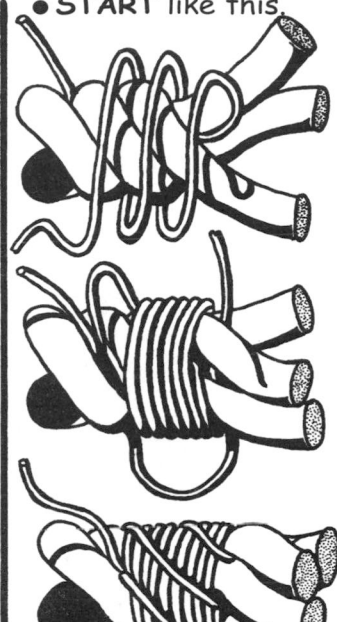

- **ENDS** should meet inside lay - Cut off (& **burn if synthetic**).

WIRE TO 3 STRAND LINE SPLICE

FINISHED SPLICE

- **IDENTICAL** in principle to the "End Splice" (opposite) except that on the line side, the ends of the strands are tapered (& usually waxed) - **On the wire side** THE STRANDS ARE TUCKED IN PAIRS.

NOTES

- **SEE OVER** for tools to assist with wire & braid splices.
- **WHIP** splice joints/ends.
- **TAPE** wire center strand & feed down center of line lay.
- **MEASUREMENTS** in braid splices are approximate & may vary.

THIS SECTION IS MORE ADVANCED, but without these simple facts, the end result is VERY difficult - Think of it as a key to a door.

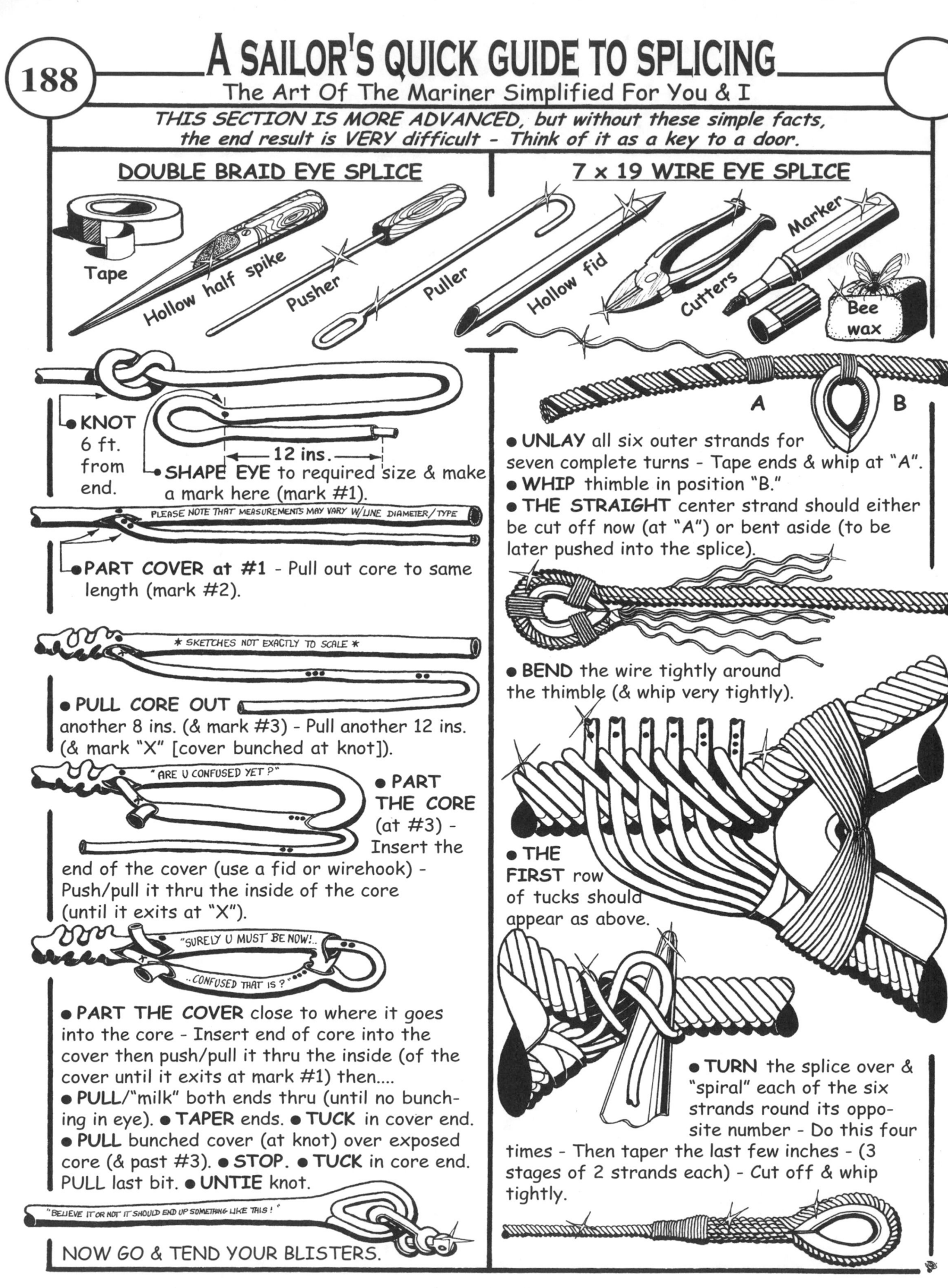

DOUBLE BRAID EYE SPLICE

Tape
Hollow half spike
Pusher
Puller

- **KNOT** 6 ft. from end.
- **SHAPE EYE** to required size & make a mark here (mark #1).

12 ins.

PLEASE NOTE THAT MEASUREMENTS MAY VARY W/LINE DIAMETER/TYPE

- **PART COVER** at #1 - Pull out core to same length (mark #2).

* SKETCHES NOT EXACTLY TO SCALE *

- **PULL CORE OUT** another 8 ins. (& mark #3) - Pull another 12 ins. (& mark "X" [cover bunched at knot]).

" ARE U CONFUSED YET ?"

- **PART THE CORE** (at #3) - Insert the end of the cover (use a fid or wirehook) - Push/pull it thru the inside of the core (until it exits at "X").

"SURELY U MUST BE NOW!.."

..CONFUSED THAT IS ?"

- **PART THE COVER** close to where it goes into the core - Insert end of core into the cover then push/pull it thru the inside (of the cover until it exits at mark #1) then....
- **PULL**/"milk" both ends thru (until no bunching in eye). • **TAPER** ends. • **TUCK** in cover end.
- **PULL** bunched cover (at knot) over exposed core (& past #3). • **STOP.** • **TUCK** in core end. PULL last bit. • **UNTIE** knot.

"BELIEVE IT OR NOT IT SHOULD END UP SOMETHING LIKE THIS !"

NOW GO & TEND YOUR BLISTERS.

7 x 19 WIRE EYE SPLICE

Hollow fid
Cutters
Marker
Bee wax

A   B

- **UNLAY** all six outer strands for seven complete turns - Tape ends & whip at "A".
- **WHIP** thimble in position "B."
- **THE STRAIGHT** center strand should either be cut off now (at "A") or bent aside (to be later pushed into the splice).

- **BEND** the wire tightly around the thimble (& whip very tightly).

- **THE FIRST** row of tucks should appear as above.

- **TURN** the splice over & "spiral" each of the six strands round its opposite number - Do this four times - Then taper the last few inches - (3 stages of 2 strands each) - Cut off & whip tightly.

Decorative Line & Rope Work From Phuket To Panama

GRATIFY A FRIEND OR LOVED ONE with a valuable gift -
A length of line & an hour of your time!

CROWN KNOT

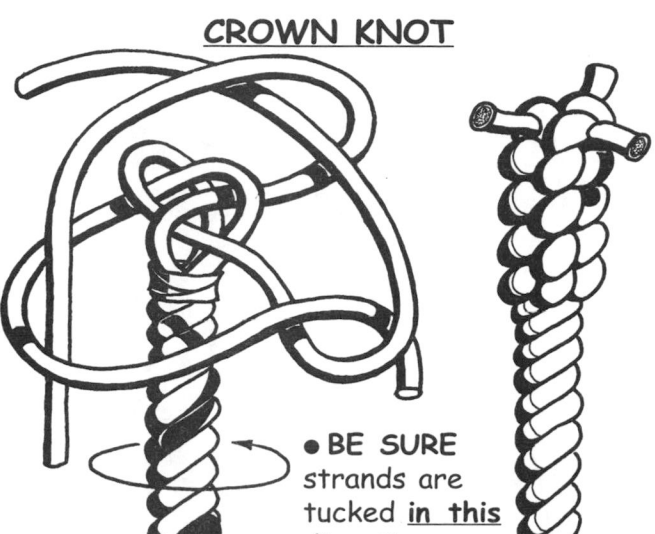

● **BE SURE** strands are tucked **in this direction.**

● **USED AS** an end decoration, finishing or handling aid - Start as at left, & keep going - Cut ends close - Burn or whip.

WALL KNOT

● **THIS RELATIVE** of the Crown Knot is "conjured up" by tucking the strands **under (instead of over)** the next strand.

MONKEYS FIST

● **IT LOOKS** difficullt **(but it's not)** - Start at "A" & keep going - Has many uses (from a heaving line [a metal ball in the middle] to a fob on your keyring).

● **START WITH** these 3 loops.

● **THEN THESE.**

A.

● **& LAST THESE.**

● **TUCK ONE** of the ends in when finished.

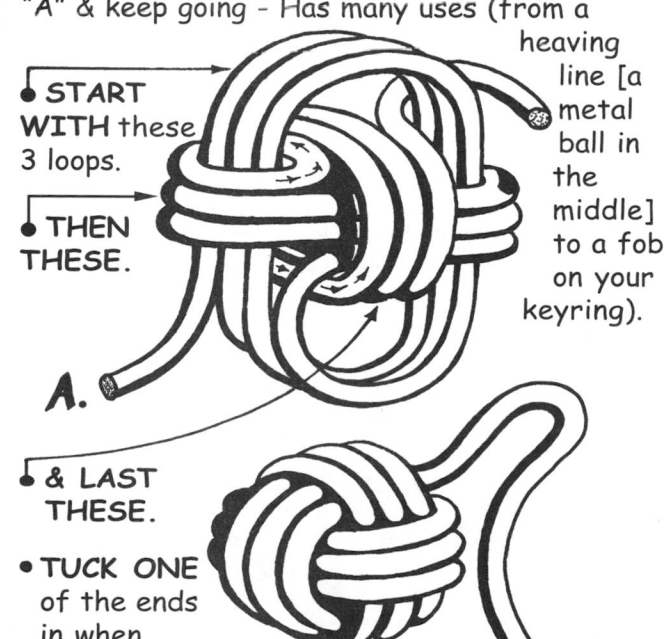

KIDS LOVE THESE.

FRENCH WHIP

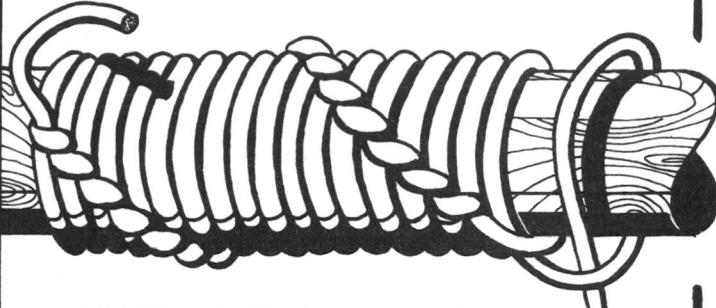

● **DECORATIVE** whipping with many uses - Usually to cover posts, tillers, wheel rims etc. - Often ends are covered with TURKS HEADS.

SQUARE SENNIT

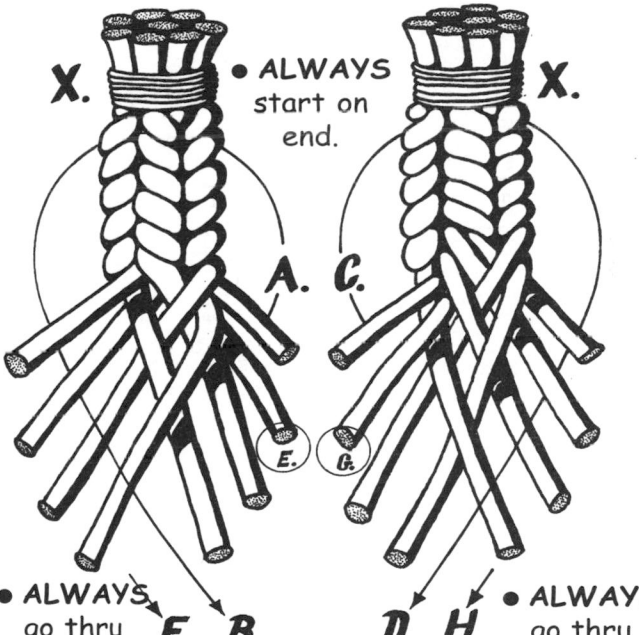

X.   ● **ALWAYS** start on end.   **X.**

A. C.

E. G.

● **ALWAYS** go thru middle. **F. B.**   **D. H.** ● **ALWAYS** go thru middle.

A HEAVY BRAID used for bell pulls, whip handles, leads etc.

● **START** with 8 equal lines (or 4 folded in half [if a loop is required at the top]).
● **WHIP** at "X".
● **PART** strands in half (4 on left & 4 on right).
● **LAY** strands out flat (with a gap in the middle).
● **TAKE** strand "A" to "B" ● **TAKE** strand "C" to "D" ● **TAKE** strand "E" to "F" ● **TAKE** strand "G" to "H" etc. - **HAVE FUN!**

RECOMMENDED LINE SIZES & types for works such as: Sennits - French Whip or Turks Head are usually braided dacron (2-5 mm)

TURKS HEAD

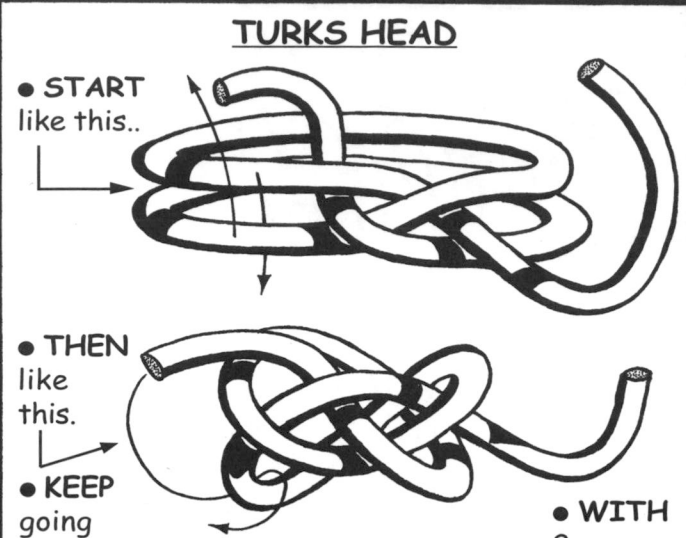

- **START** like this..
- **THEN** like this.
- **KEEP** going
- **WITH** 2 wraps it should look like this.
- **TUCK** ends in when finished.

- **A VERY USEFUL** & popular "artform" - Do one on your best friend's wrist **(or decorate almost anything cylindrical)** - ENJOY!

SAIL REPAIR STITCH

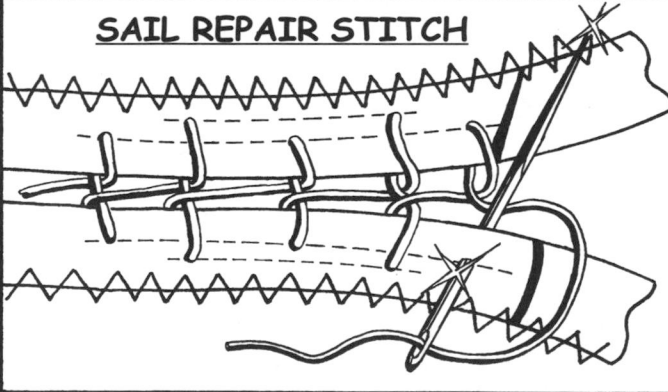

ROPE MAT

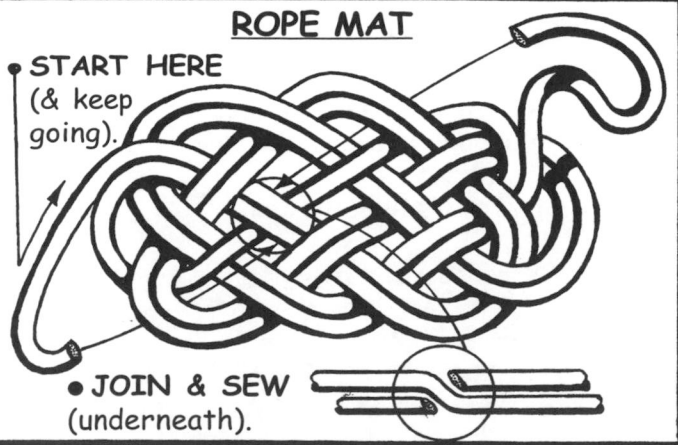

- **START HERE** (& keep going).
- **JOIN & SEW** (underneath).

ALTERNATE CROWN SENNIT

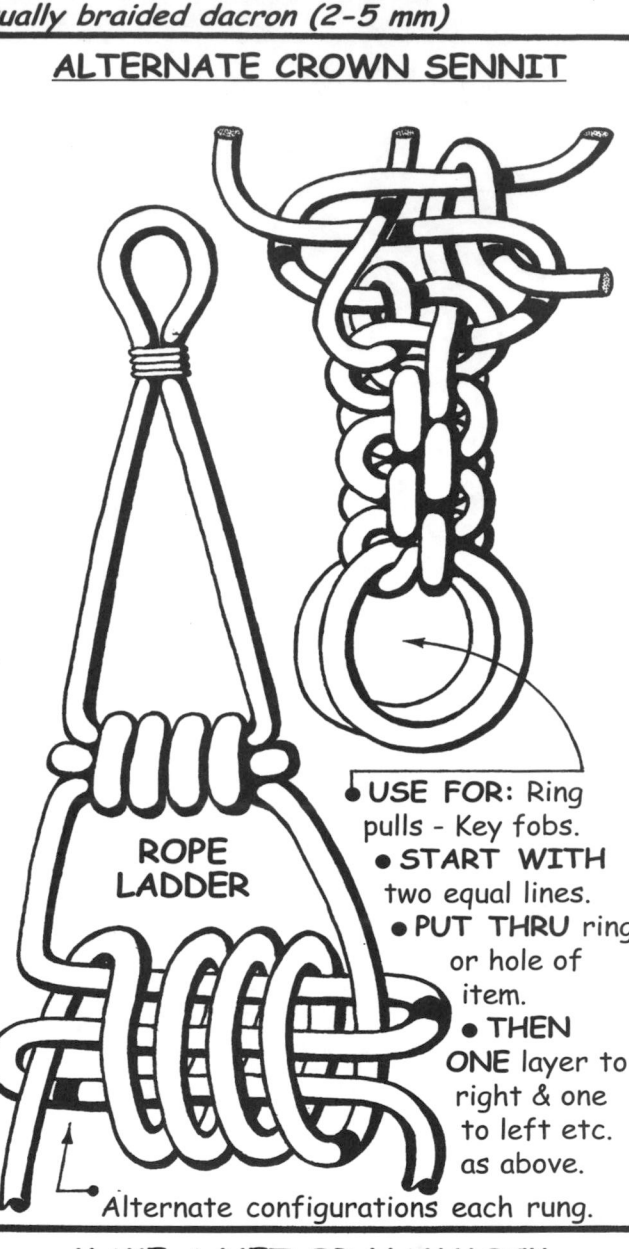

ROPE LADDER

- **USE FOR:** Ring pulls - Key fobs.
- **START WITH** two equal lines.
- **PUT THRU** ring or hole of item.
- **THEN ONE** layer to right & one to left etc. as above.

Alternate configurations each rung.

MAKE A NET OR HAMMOCK

- **MAKE "FRAME"** to size first then start tying.

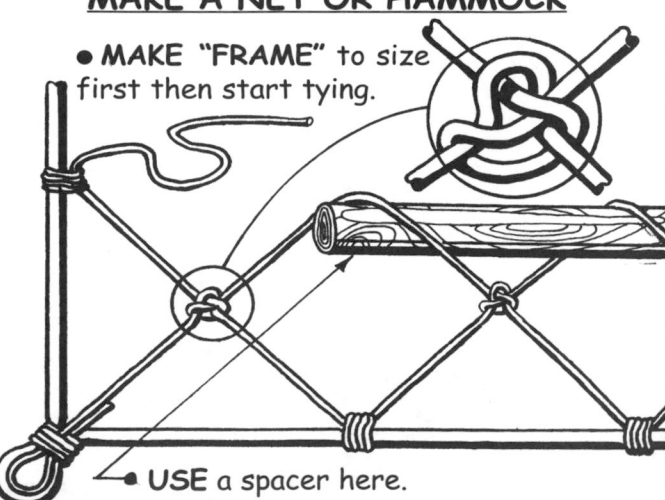

- **USE** a spacer here.

A Simplified Fast Results Course Of Elementary Board Sailing

(2+2) = 2 HOURS TO STUDY (& memorise theory) - & 2 HOURS TO GO OUT (calm water, steady gentle breeze) & do it - ENJOY!

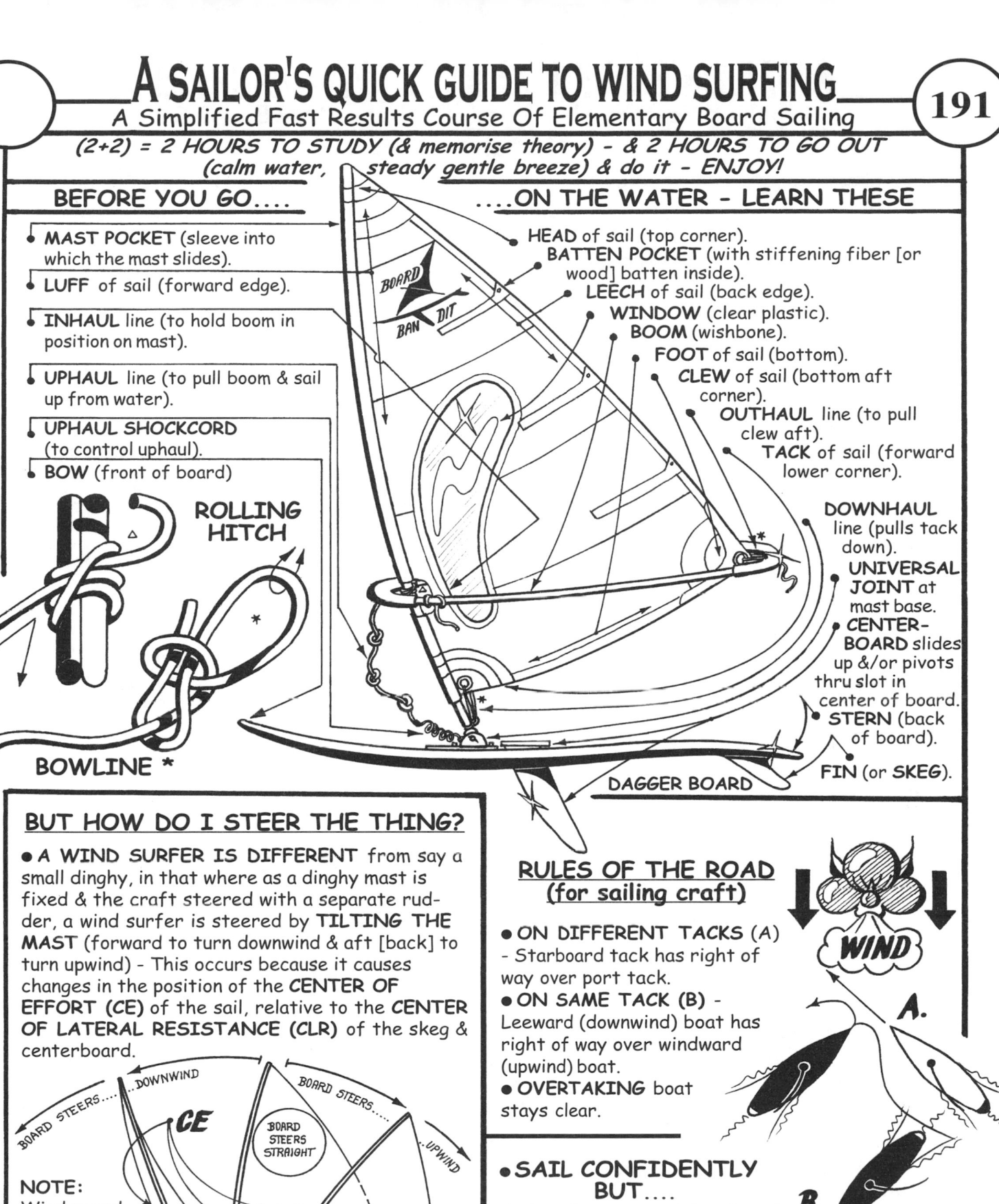

BEFORE YOU GO....

- **MAST POCKET** (sleeve into which the mast slides).
- **LUFF** of sail (forward edge).
- **INHAUL** line (to hold boom in position on mast).
- **UPHAUL** line (to pull boom & sail up from water).
- **UPHAUL SHOCKCORD** (to control uphaul).
- **BOW** (front of board)

ROLLING HITCH

BOWLINE *

....ON THE WATER - LEARN THESE

- **HEAD** of sail (top corner).
- **BATTEN POCKET** (with stiffening fiber [or wood] batten inside).
- **LEECH** of sail (back edge).
- **WINDOW** (clear plastic).
- **BOOM** (wishbone).
- **FOOT** of sail (bottom).
- **CLEW** of sail (bottom aft corner).
- **OUTHAUL** line (to pull clew aft).
- **TACK** of sail (forward lower corner).
- **DOWNHAUL** line (pulls tack down).
- **UNIVERSAL JOINT** at mast base.
- **CENTER-BOARD** slides up &/or pivots thru slot in center of board.
- **STERN** (back of board).
- **FIN** (or SKEG).

BOARD BANDIT

DAGGER BOARD

BUT HOW DO I STEER THE THING?

- **A WIND SURFER IS DIFFERENT** from say a small dinghy, in that where as a dinghy mast is fixed & the craft steered with a separate rudder, a wind surfer is steered by **TILTING THE MAST** (forward to turn downwind & aft [back] to turn upwind) - This occurs because it causes changes in the position of the **CENTER OF EFFORT (CE)** of the sail, relative to the **CENTER OF LATERAL RESISTANCE (CLR)** of the skeg & centerboard.

BOARD STEERS.....DOWNWIND
BOARD STEERS.....
BOARD STEERS STRAIGHT
...UPWIND
CE

NOTE: Wind speed (& lateral mast movement) also change the position of the CE.

CLR

RULES OF THE ROAD (for sailing craft)

- **ON DIFFERENT TACKS (A)** - Starboard tack has right of way over port tack.
- **ON SAME TACK (B)** - Leeward (downwind) boat has right of way over windward (upwind) boat.
- **OVERTAKING** boat stays clear.

WIND

A.

B.

- **SAIL CONFIDENTLY BUT....** don't enforce your right of way over other craft (even if you are technically correct) - **PARTICULARLY** stay well clear of large vessels (sail & power) which may maneuver with difficulty - Also avoid rowboats, canoes etc.

DOING IT

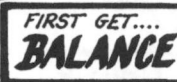

INITIAL TRAINING

FIRST GET.... BALANCE

- **BALANCE IS IMPORTANT,** so start by standing on the board in the water WITHOUT THE RIG.
- **THEN WITH MAST & SAIL RIGGED (but lying in the water)** stand with one foot just forward of the mast (& the other on the dagger board slot) - Turn the board beam (side) on to the wind (with sail to leeward [downwind]) - Then with knees bent (& back to wind)
  - **PULL ON THE UPHAUL** (straighten legs as sail comes up)
  - **YOU SHOULD BE IN THIS POSITION** (with sail flapping).
  - **IF LATER YOU GET CONFUSED** (or fall off) RETURN TO THIS POSITION for a new start.

WIND →

SECOND GET.... MOBILITY

- **PRACTICE TURNS** by holding uphaul (or front of boom) - Tilt mast towards stern - Put your weight on aft foot - Board will turn bow to wind (enabling you to carefully step forward of mast to other side) - Use your feet to continue turning (until you complete 360 degrees) - Then practice from the opposite direction (until confident either way).

WIND →

THIRD GET.... CONTROL

- **TO GET UNDER WAY** grasp the wishbone boom just aft of the mast with one hand (mast hand) - Then twisting body & board slightly to windward, grasp with the other hand (sail hand) the boom at shoulder width & gently "harden" (fill with wind) the sail as shown.
  - **AT THIS STARTING STAGE** the mast is usually inclined slightly to windward (& the wishbone about parallel with water).

WIND →

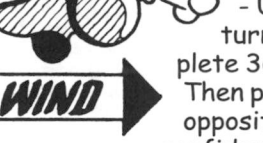

POSTURE (at start)

- **BACK** (straight). ● **BOTTOM** (in). ● **KNEES** (slightly bent). ● **MAST ARM** (bent).
- **SAIL ARM** (nearly straight). ● **TORSO** (twisted partially toward bow). ● **CALF** of forward leg (touches mast [not when running]).

- **NOW PRACTICE** the above until the stance & starting techniques become natural (from both sides).

ANY PROBLEMS?

- **WIND TOO STRONG?** - Ease sail hand (& "spill" wind). ● **EMERGENCY STOP?** - Drop sail (& rig) in water.
- **NO WIND?** - Take sail off, (roll it up & lay with mast [& boom] on board) then paddle with hands (or dagger board).
- **CAN'T GET TO WINDWARD?** - Try tacking the "zigzag" course of about 45 degrees (necessary to sail into the wind).
  - **FALLING OFF DOWNWIND?** - Running (sailing with wind astern) requires the board rider to stand (with feet either side of the daggerboard) aft of the boom which is arthwart-ships (crossways).
  - **HOW TO GYBE?** (To "tack" downwind) - The rider lets the boom go downwind (flapping sail) over the bow & grabs it (the boom) from the other side (still standing aft of the mast) **balance & visibility may be troublesome at this point of sailing.**

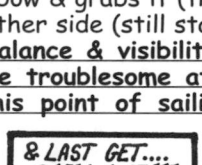

& LAST GET.... SKILLFUL

STRONG WINDS

- **DON'T GET BLOWN AWAY!** .... by strong offshore (blowing out to sea) winds - But if you do .... **DON'T ABANDON YOUR BOARD** .... because it will: **a)** Help rescuers to find you - **b)** Keep you afloat & **c)** Provide transport when the storm abates.
  - **OTHER OPTIONS: a)** "Derig" board & paddle at an angle to wind (to shore) - **b)** Reach (wind on beam) across wind with sail (& boom tip) in water to leeward & sail luffing (part flapping) to shore.
    - **CE:** Strong winds move the center of effort in the sail aft thus tilt mast futher forward.
- **STARTING: a)** Raise sail quickly - **b)** Tilt mast well forward - **c)** Bend knees & "harden" sail - **d)** Push board into position with feet - **e)** .... H H HANG ON!

- **SAIL SHAPE** should be fuller (ease luff & clew tension) in light winds **but flatter in strong winds.**

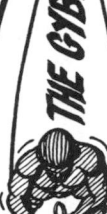
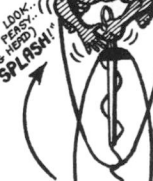
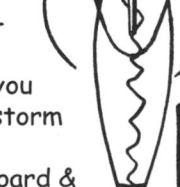
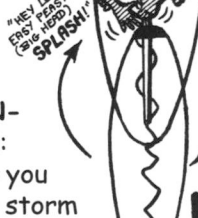
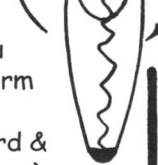
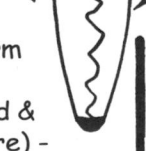
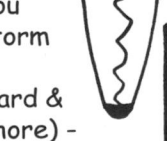
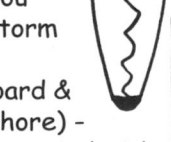
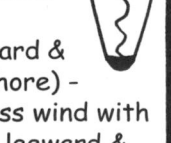
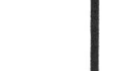

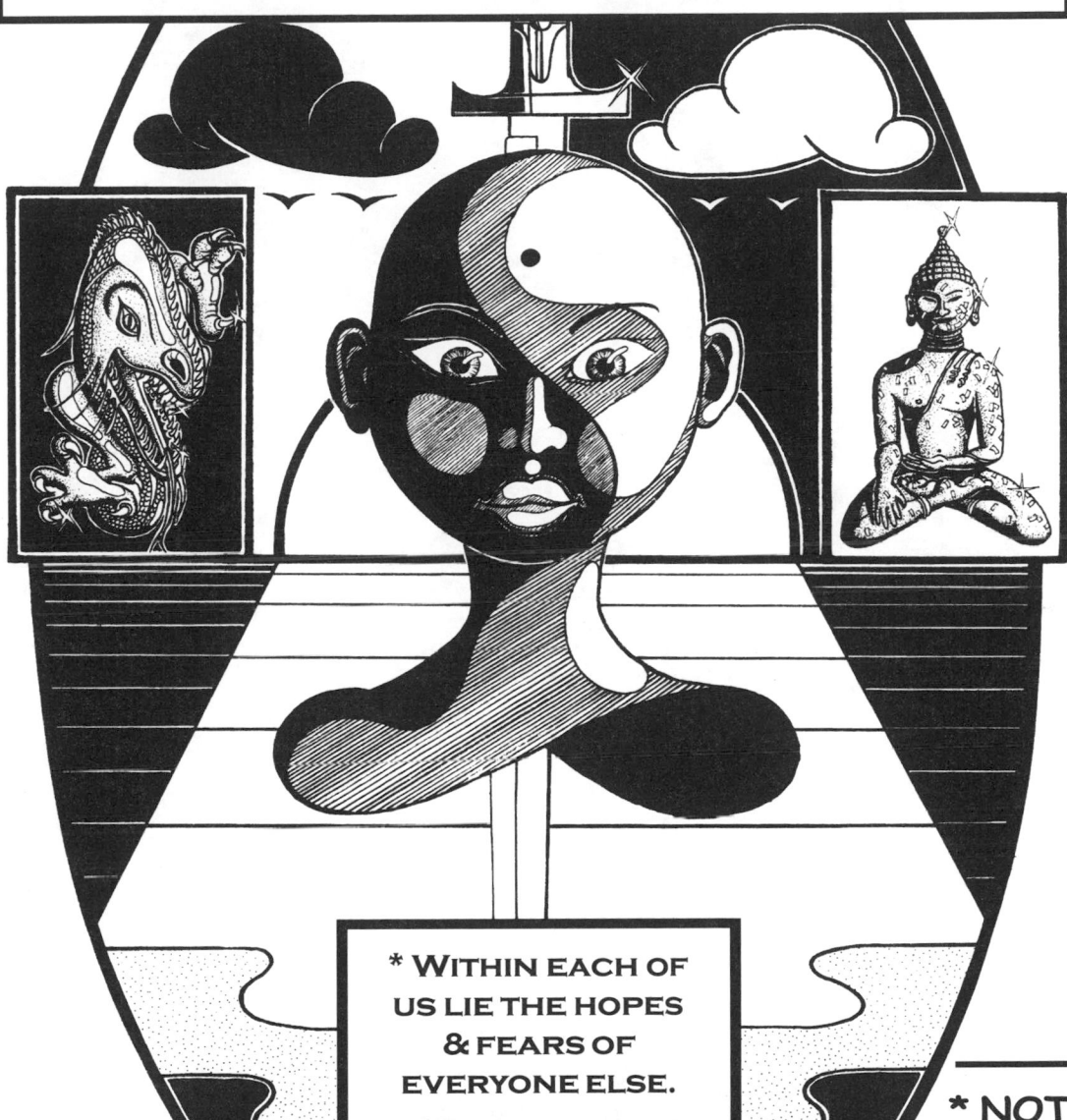

THE MARTIAL ARTIST

* WITHIN EACH OF
US LIE THE HOPES
& FEARS OF
EVERYONE ELSE.

* NOTE

The 4 logics of SHEN KU
are jointly relevant &
inextricablly interlinked.
Together and with devastating
applicability proportional to
species advancement they govern
ALL conscious progress in
ALL situations throughout
ALL of time, transcending
ALL frontiers..............
...INTERGALACTICALLY

LOM PING

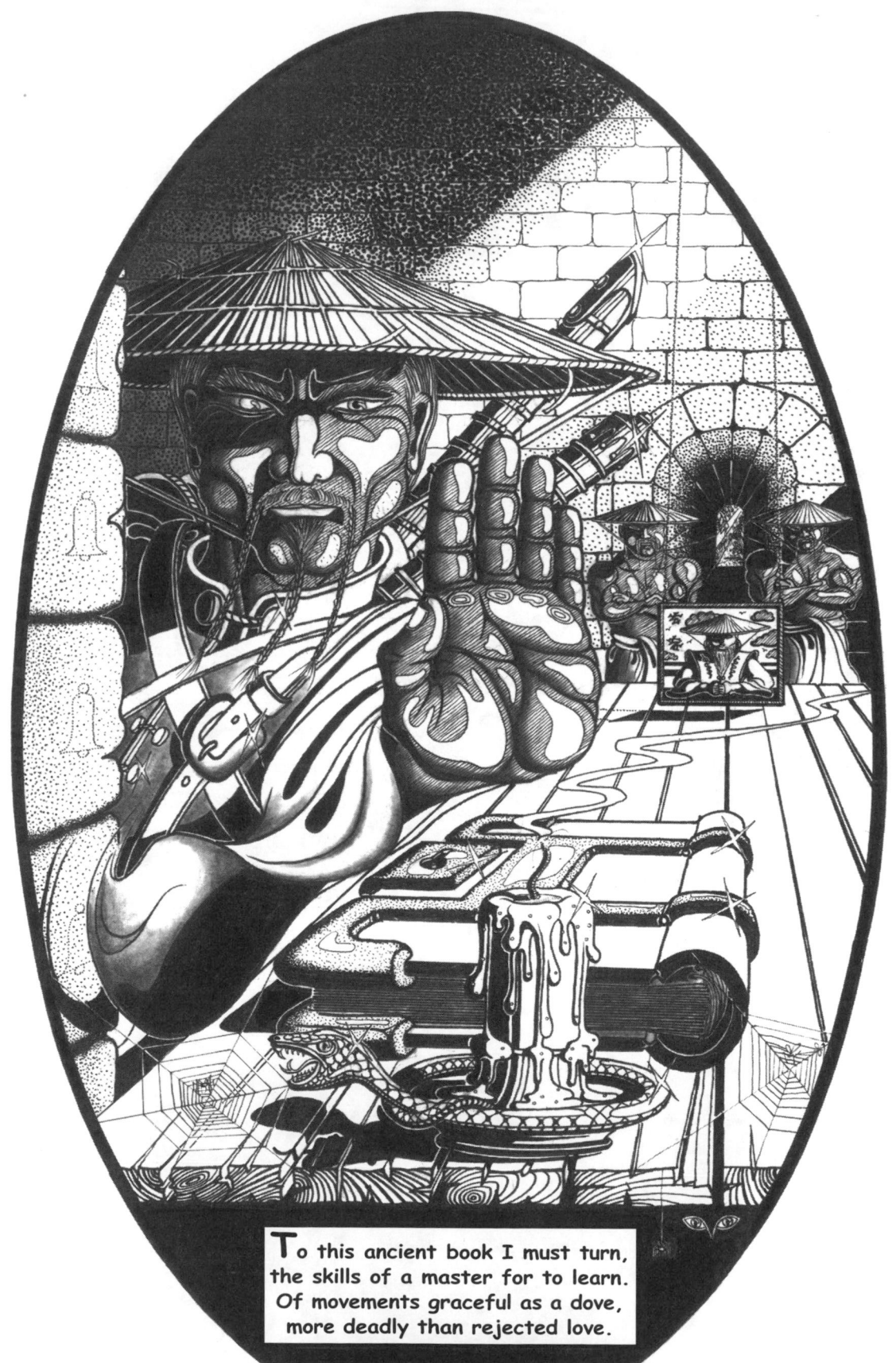

To this ancient book I must turn,
the skills of a master for to learn.
Of movements graceful as a dove,
more deadly than rejected love.

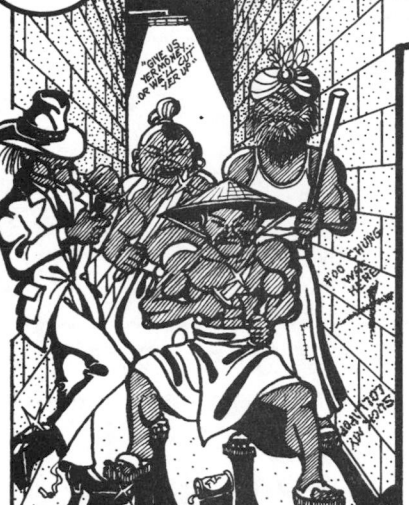

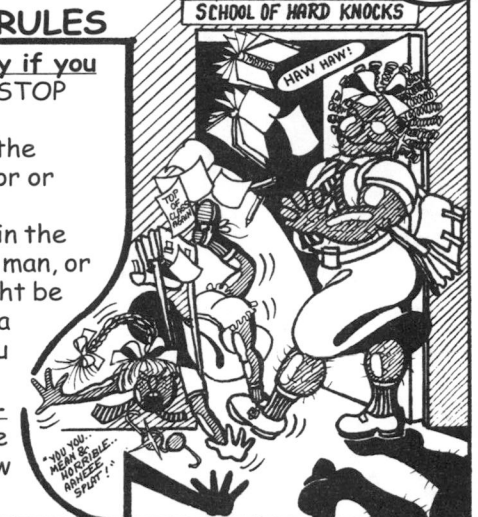

UNDERSTANDING THE 4 BASIC RULES

1. <u>REMEMBER</u> **when trouble comes, walk away if you can** - Don't fight unless you have to - Even then STOP WHEN YOUR SAFETY IS NOT THREATENED.

2. <u>DON'T ARGUE</u> **with guns & knives**, (unless the holder is clearly an amateur) - Even then wait for or MAKE A DIVERSION BEFORE ACTING.

3. <u>DON'T THREATEN</u> anyone (bumps into you in the street, dangerous driver etc.) - Because the old man, or the fat lady, or the skinny kid you threaten, might be Bruce Lee's relative or a homicidal maniac with a .44 magnum under their coat waiting to blow you away for YOUR bad judgement.

4. <u>BE PREPARED</u>, **mentally, physically & strategically** (have a plan) - Study & practice these two condensed pages with a friend (until you know by heart the response for each situation).

GETTING READY

....CROOKS LOOK FOR EASY TARGETS IN ISOLATED SITUATIONS - SO DON'T BE WHAT THEY LOOK FOR.

● **APPEARANCE:** If you might have to transit a dubious area <u>don't look like "a million dollars"</u> (jewelry, designer/provocative [ladies] clothes etc.) - <u>Dress like the natives</u> & immediately cut your crime risk by 10-50% - Try wearing a cheap long coat & old hat over your finery - <u>Dress poor/tough & probably get left alone</u>.

● **USE MONEY SENSE** <u>in bad areas by carrying a "decoy" wallet/purse</u> (with old credit cards, fake keys & a bit of money in) - While your real valuables are in a money belt or secret pocket etc.

● <u>AWARENESS is an infinite quality, which you should strive to improve continually</u> - Look, listen, "sense" & memorize more of your surroundings every time you venture out - This skill can save the day (or night) for you - Have you ever looked up at roofs/windows while hurrying to work? - Why is that man wearing a coat in summer? - Cross now & avoid 3 alleys on this side - Have I seen that same man twice in 5 min?

● **BODY LANGUAGE** tells its own story & <u>is read instinctively by criminals like this.</u>

WEAK & NERVOUS = easy pickings
STRONG & CONFIDENT = too much trouble

● **THEREFORE** walk briskly, purposefully, head up, shoulders back - <u>In conversation</u>: Look people in the eye, speak clearly, be alert but stay relaxed (DON'T FIDGET/SMILE TOO MUCH).

● **CAN YOU RUN?** - Ladies, you know we love to see you in those tight skirts & high heels, but <u>your life might depend on how fast you can run</u> (or climb a wall), so choose carefully.

● **DON'T TALK** too much (or in a loud voice) about travel/money plans, <u>because thieves may follow you home</u> (to see where you live) then visit later - & NEVER, NEVER OPEN A FAT WALLET IN PUBLIC.

● <u>AVOID ROUTINES which are predictable</u> (i.e. don't walk thru the same quiet park at 6 PM every weeknight) - You are just begging some idiot to plan a crime on you!

....HOW TO MAKE LIFE DIFFICULT FOR THEM....

● **IN RESTAURANTS** beware of "bag snatchers" (who target unwary diners sitting with backs to/or too close to, street/exit doors) - <u>Always choose a seat with your back to a wall (& with good visibility).</u>

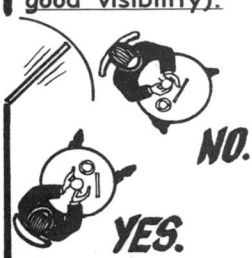

● **COMING HOME** (or into any supposedly empty building) - <u>Stay alert - Push doors right back before entering</u> - Check windows have not been forced - Check cupboards & store rooms etc. are empty

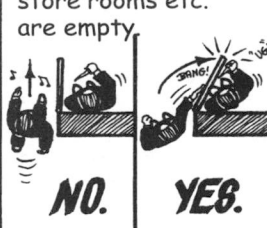

● **ON SIDEWALKS** <u>stay in the middle</u> (particularly when approaching alleys, corners & doorways [which are all favorite ambush site for muggers]).

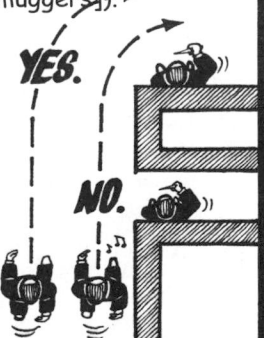

● **"HAVE YOU GOT A LIGHT**, the time, a quarter" <u>are all favorite muggers' tricks (to get close to you)</u> - Never take your eyes off (or let them within striking distance) & always side step.

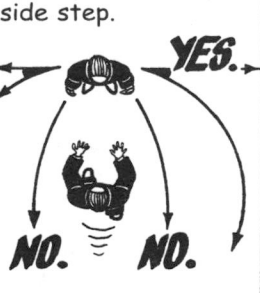

● **IN TRAINS** DON'T <u>sit with your back next to a door (as you are begging to be the victim of a "grab & run thief")</u> - Also avoid the muggers' favorite .....the "dead end" carriage.

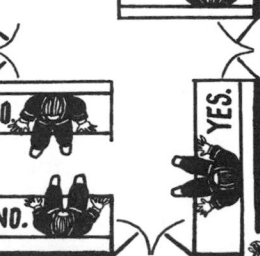

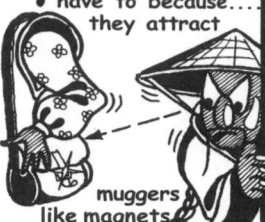

DON'T CARRY BAGS unless you have to because.... they attract

muggers like magnets

ON THE STREET

....<u>DO</u> USE YOUR EYES TO ....<u>BUT</u>.... <u>DON'T</u> USE YOUR EYES TO....

....<u>look for potential trouble spots</u> (corners, doorways, suspicious figures/actions) - <u>Plan ahead</u> to avoid dark (&/or isolated) areas - Sweep your eyes from side to side (starting low & moving higher then repeating) - & DON'T FORGET BEHIND YOU.

.... stare at people (confrontational), glance then move on - Don't look down (submissive) - <u>If you find an idiot staring at you</u> (e.g. in a train or line), make a small physical turn away (dismissive) - Pick something to gaze at (while maintaining surveillance on the nuisance peripherally).

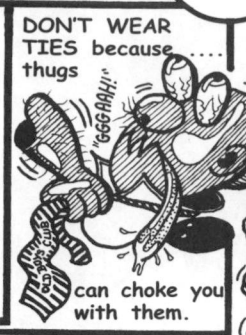

DON'T WEAR TIES because.... thugs

"GGGRAH!"

can choke you with them.

? LEGAL WEAPONS ?

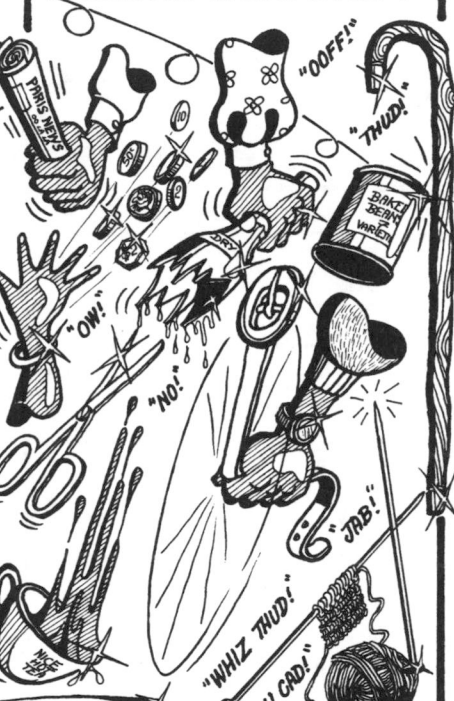

HOW TO SURVIVE HOSTILE CONFRONTATIONS

- **DON'T SHOUT "HELP" because** (depending on country) <u>about 50% of such cries are ignored</u> - But "RAPE" gets better results (65%) - However try the best "FIRE" GOT A 95% RESPONSE.

- **SEIZE INITIATIVE** if you know you are going to be attacked (i.e. a thug makes a grab for [or a hit at] you) - <u>It is usually better to reverse the tables</u> - With a shattering yell, charge forward - Deliver your best blows (with lightning speed) - Don't stop yelling (or attacking) for an instant (until you can escape safely).

- **LYING:** In semi-hopeless situations (i.e. thug wants to kill/rape you & is holding a gun/knife on you) then lie - <u>"I have $ 62,300 in cash</u> (drug or tax money) <u>buried in my grandmother's back garden</u> in .... (another town) - & I could give you half" - This is an almost irresistible "plum" for the attacker (& gives you many opportunities to turn the tables).

- **THUGS' EXPECTATIONS** are that you will quiver & shake & comply with their demands - So, (circumstances permitting) <u>you must make this "cozy" plan more trouble than it's worth</u> (by any means) - Run, scream, fight, blabber "in Greek," drop/throw your purse etc. (or all together).

- **DIVERSIONS** in confrontational situations (muggers, gangs, louts etc.) are a valuable tool to tip the scales in your favor at a critical time e.g....
<u>COUGHING FIT:</u> Clutch throat, cough convulsively & stagger.
<u>EPILEPTIC FIT:</u> slobber, jerk, stagger, eyes wide.
<u>HEART ATTACK:</u> clutch chest, jerk, stagger, gasp, stare.
<u>WHEN YOU</u> are in position to, make a miraculous recovery, & either strike or run.

LAST RESORT DEFENSES
(on the ground)

- **1st CHOICE - LIE ON BACK & PIVOT** (as required kicking fast [& hard] at shins & knees).

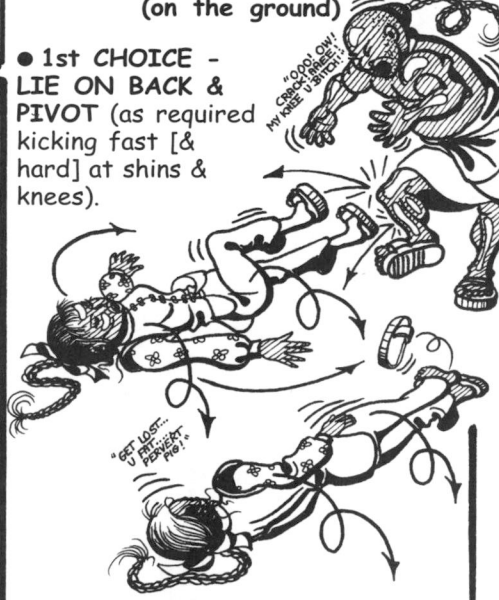

HOW TO DEAL WITH PARTICULAR IDIOTS

- **BULLIES** <u>are looking for a victim to have some "fun" at the expense of</u> - So, to stop this you must make the "fun" more trouble than it's worth - Fight back thru any reasonable means at every possible opportunity (provoked & otherwise) - Bullies are impressed (& deterred) by force (&/or power) .... not peaceful discussion.

- **CAR HIJACK** occurs in various ways (for example from a hidden assailant in the back seat of a parked car at night) - If a thug forces entry (or jumps) into your car & says "DRIVE" - Do so until you get to busy place, <u>then deliberately drive into another vehicle</u> (a police car would be nice!).

- **GANGS** are more trouble (because of numbers) & the usual best action (if threatened) is to <u>without warning charge the weakest member</u> (on the side of group) - With a wild yell, shove him/her into the others & (still yelling) run, BUT if they are catching you ....
<u>PICK UP ANY MAKESHIFT WEAPON</u> (pipe, bottle, stick etc.).
<u>AMBUSH THEM</u> (one at a time) by jumping out from doors/corners etc. (& striking).
<u>MAKE A STAND</u> as a last resort in a narrow entrance (where only one can get at you at a time).

- **MUGGERS are often armed (but basically want your money)** - So, if you transit bad areas get smart: Look poor - Look tough - <u>Carry a "MUGS" wallet (with fake everything)</u> which you tearfully (& reluctantly) hand over (or drop & run).

- **2nd CHOICE - RAPID ROLL** (to gain distance to stand in).

- **3rd CHOICE - FETAL BALL** (to minimize injury in a mob fight [or riot]).

THE LAW...

● IN MOST COUNTRIES OF THE WORLD <u>permits the use of "reasonable force," to be used in the prevention of actual bodily harm</u> perpetrated on yourself (or another person unable to defend themselves) by an attacker - <u>But YOU CANNOT LEGALLY STRIKE THE FIRST BLOW in an unarmed conflict</u> - Armed attackers (who threaten to use their weapon on you) can (for what it's worth) USUALLY BE STRUCK FIRST.

ACQUIRING THE 4 BASIC ABILITIES

MENTAL

● <u>KNOWLEDGE</u> is what you are hopefully acquiring now - <u>Without it you (& I) are like a baby in the jungle</u> - Study & memorize the legalities & psychology, defensive & offensive ploys, martial arts counters & strikes - The list is long (but start here).

● <u>STAYING CALM is critical to your performance in crisis situations</u> - Practice with: Yoga, meditation, self-hypnosis - <u>& at any time, deep breathing</u> - All the way in thru nose (fill belly then chest) to slow count of 4 - Hold for 4 - All the way out thru mouth (chest then belly) to a slow 4 - <u>Feel better in just 1 min.</u>

PHYSICAL

● <u>FITNESS though not vital is very valuable so start with</u> - a) Yoga, stretching for flexibility (then alternate days of) - b) Cardiovascular workout (aerobic/running/circuit training etc.) - c) Strength training (weights/press-ups etc.) - <u>Do this program 6 days/week</u> (EVEN 10 MINS/DAY IS A START).

● <u>PRACTICE is vital for any reasonable efficiency</u> - Try & find a training partner you can alternate "attacker" roles with - <u>Strive for technical excellence, speed, continuity & power (in that order)</u> - Get ....tall punch bag to get mean with.

....BUT ONLY....

JUST DO IT ... IF YOU HAVE TO.

● <u>PERSONAL SPACE: Keep all strangers out of it (particularly suspicious & "have you got a....." persons)</u> - Be on instant guard if they try to enter it (because within that circle [about 60 in. dia.] you can easily be surprised [or grabbed/struck] WITHOUT WARNING).

● <u>COMBINATIONS are strikes/moves rapidly sequenced (one after the other), used to try & end any fight very fast (less than 10 secs)</u> - Each move should be automatically chosen because of: a) Opponents position/vulnerability - b) Your position/ability - c) Degree of injury sought - EXAMPLE (for a right-handed person) against life-threatening attacker: 1) Left star hand to eyes - 2) Right sword hand/palm/fist to throat/chin/face - 3) Left snap/mule kick to groin/knee - 4) Withdraw (or continue [depending on attackers status]).

PERSONAL   SPACE

● <u>GUARD STANCE: Distribute weight evenly (with feet 18 inches apart)</u> - Keep moving (but maintain foot spacing) by - Moving front foot 1st (to go forward), & rear foot 1st (to go back) - Best kicking foot is usually back (stance diagonal to attacker) - Keep elbows in, & fingers spread (gives no clue to intentions & lulls attacker into false security) - Leading hand at throat level (chin down), rear (& best punching hand) below.

● <u>BLOCKS & DEFLECTIONS are usually taken on the forearm pivoting at the elbow (up & out for high blows, down & out for low)</u> - Your left arm blocks attacker's right, & your right blocks attacker's left arm - Front leg & rear arm (on lower pivot) protect groin - <u>Practice this very efficient system (called Chinese blocking) with a partner (slow then fast).</u>

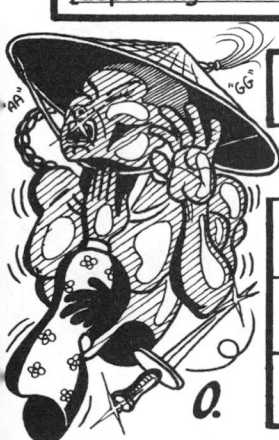

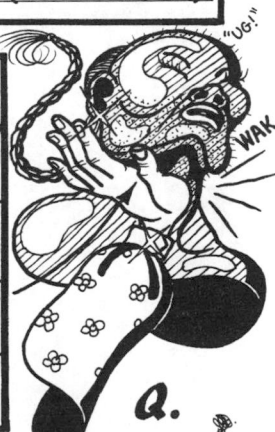

QUICK REFERENCE ACTION PLAN

TYPE OF SITUATION	Best Choice	2nd Choice	3rd Choice	Worst Choice
BULLY	Ignore for a set time then assess.	If worse then fight by all means.	Report to parents/ authorities.	Run away (very bad for spirit).
ARMED MUGGER	Reluctantly give "mugs" (fake) wallet.	Lie about will bring cash tomorrow.	Activate ploy then run & shout wildly.	Activate ploy then disarm/ fight/shout.
RAPIST	Activate ploy then run & shout wildly.	Activate ploy then fight hard & shout.	Shout "stop" then lie you have AIDS.	Shout "stop" & lie you have big $ hidden.
GANG	Activate ploy charge, barge run & shout.	Activate ploy run & ambush individually.	Lie about big $ cash in bank box.	Ploy & fight but in narrow space 1 by 1

State Of The Art Crisis Techniques From Phuket To Panama City

WARNING

....**ONLY STRIKE HARD at vulnerable body targets IF YOU CAN JUSTIFY SERIOUS INJURY TO YOUR ATTACKER** e.g.:-

- **ABDOMEN**: Kicks or hard strikes can cause serious (even fatal) organ damage (or internal bleeding).
- **EARS**: Simultaneous cupped hand clapping can permanently damage hearing.
- **SKULL**: Hard strikes to "soft" parts (e.g. temple) can cause brain damage/coma/death.

- **BACK**: Hard kicks/strikes with elbow to spine can result in paralysis &/or years of pain.
- **EYES**: Even moderate jabs can permanently blind.
- **NECK**: Even moderate blows to throat (asphyxiation) & neck (spinal damage) can cause permanent injury (e.g.: paralysis) or even death.

BONUS TIP
- Grab balls & squeeze/twist hard. OWWWEEEE!

NOTE: THIS IS ATTACKERS RIGHT HAND...WATCH OUT FOR... ...THE LEFT.

WARNING THIS MOVE IS DANGEROUS BUT POSSIBLE W/ TRAINING

ACTION PLAN

	ATTACKER DOES THIS TO YOU....	CHOICE OF RESPONSE CODES
FROM BEHIND	• GRABS you round waist pinning arms	A - B - I
	• GRABS you round waist (arms free)	A - B - C - D - I - W
	• GRABS you by hair with one hand	B - E - F - I - S
	• GRABS you with arm round your neck	B - C - H - I
	• GRABS you by shoulder with one hand	B - F - I - S - N
	• POINTS GUN/knife at you VERY CLOSE	J - D - R
FROM FRONT	• GRABS you in bearhug pinning arms	K - L - B - I
	• GRABS you round waist (arms free)	Z - L - K - M - B - D
	• GRABS you round neck in stranglehold	Z - N - P - O - Q - S
	• GRABS you by hair with one hand	Z - N - S - R - O - T
	• GRABS you by shoulder/arm with one hand	N - P - S - Q - R - I
	• POINTS GUN/knife at you VERY CLOSE	U - J - R

....SO YOU DO THIS TO ATTACKER ("X")

- **A** • STRIKE "X's" face with back of your head (aim at nose). "SPLAT!"
- **B** • STAMP on "X's" instep (or toes) with your heel. "CRUUUNCH!"
- **C** • STRIKE "X" in face with either fist (over shoulder) "VERY SNEAKY"
- **D** • JAB at "X's" eyes with spread fingers (look at target first) "BAAD!"
- **E** • GRAB "X's" hand (on hair) with both yours - Twist 180 deg. (hard).
- **F** • PIVOT 90 deg. - Use swinging backchop (edge hand) to "X's" head.
- **H** • MOVE hips (to either side) & elbow "X" in kidneys (hard). "UGGG!"
- **I** • RAKE "X's" shinbone with outside of your shoe edge (strike down).
- **J** • LIGHTING back/side chop to outside/back of "X's" gun hand "BANG"
- **K** • STRIKE "X's" nose with your front hairline/forehead "SPLUNCH!"
- **L** • KNEE strike to genitals (wear box in practise) "OH GOD!"
- **M** • HARD clap both cupped hands on "X's" ears ... "PARDON!"
- **N** • SNAP kick to genitals (wear box in practise) "NO...PLEASE!"
- **O** • KNIFE handstrike to throat or solar plexus "GGGKKK!"
- **P** • SNAP kick to kneecap (practise accuracy) "NO, THAT'S MY BAD ONE"
- **Q** • HEEL of palm strike (up & in) to "X's" nose "ALLAH, NOT AGAIN!"
- **R** • PUNCH to throat/face/solar plexus (depending on position) "OOFFF"
- **S** • MULE kick to instep/lower leg/ belly (depending on position)
- **T** • STRIKE hard with your knee at outside/ front of "X's" thigh "THUD!"
- **U** • CREATE a diversion, e.g.: Bad cough, fit, heart attack etc. "ZZZZ!"
- **W** • WHEN "X" looks down strike at face with either elbow "CHEAT!"
- **Z** • CLAW (& briefly hold) "X's" face (fingers in eyes). "AAAAA!"

BONUS TIP
- GRAB little finger & bend it back AHHHKRAK!

NOTES ON

- **E** • TWIST to side **which turns attacker's back to you**.
- **F** • OFTEN helps to grasp attacker's "hair" hand (with your free hand) while executing strikes.
- **J** • THIS IS RISKY & must - a) **Be followed up fast with disabling strike** - b) PRACTICED WELL WITH A FRIEND.
- **Z** • THIS MOVE IS **both attack & diversion** (IN THAT THE ATTACKER IS UNABLE TO SEE/AVOID OTHER STRIKES COMING).

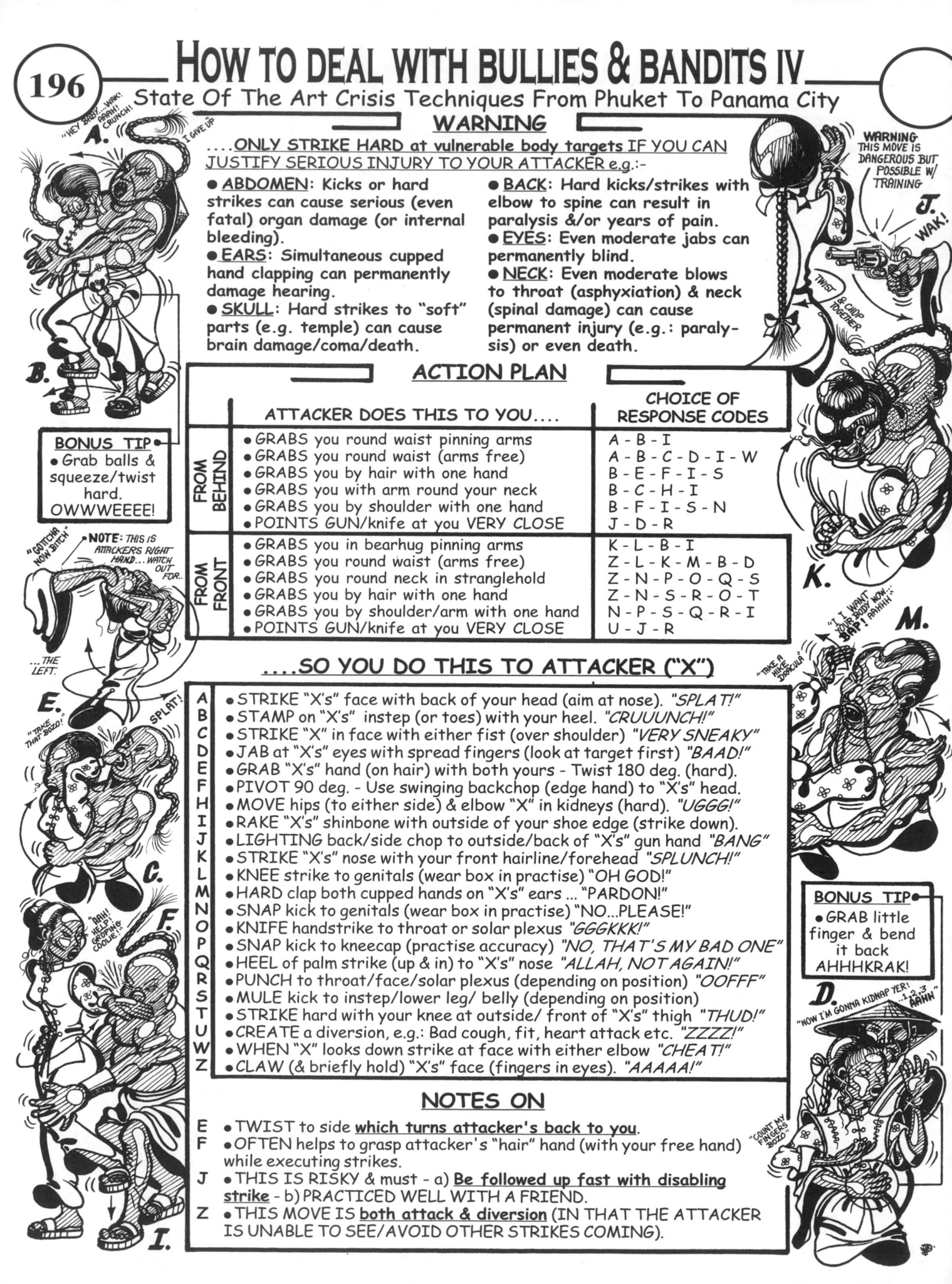

Asian Techniques On Reading Wrist Pulses For Vital Health Indications

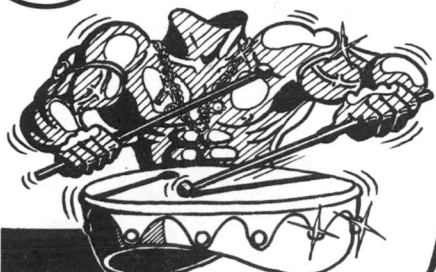

"a **HARD PULSE** is like a tight drum".

CHINESE PULSE DIAGNOSIS

- **CREDIBILITY: An ancient skill** - Almost entirely scoffed at by western medicine - As was its cousin "acupuncture" .... (not many years ago.... BUT NOT NOW!)
- **PRINCIPLES hold that there are not one, but twelve different pulses** (to be felt in each person) **which indicate yin/yang balance** (or lack thereof) in 12 related organs (&/or body functions) - Full diagnosis is complex, as up to 27 different qualities (or faults) are considered detectable in each of the 12 pulses (total up to 300).

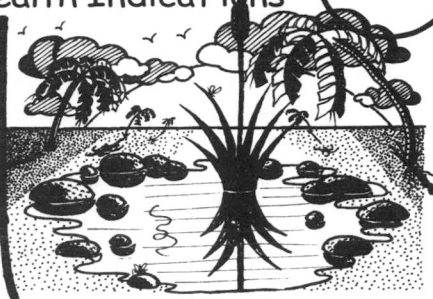

"a **SOFT PULSE** is like a floating thread".

HOW TO READ IT

- **PHYSICIAN: first takes own pulse** as irregularities in it (e.g. too fast or slow) may affect his/her reading of patient (who sits/lies quietly [for 5 - 10 minutes]).
- **A MAN'S left (yang) wrist is read first** - A woman's right (yin) is read first.
- **THE READING is taken with the tips of the first 3 fingers** (about half inch apart) of opposite hand, all at the same time (i.e. 3 pulses read at once).
- **PRESSURE first apply it lightly** (readings) - Then deeply (more readings) - Then proceed to the other hand.
- **PULSE SPEED is ideally 4 beats per "in & out" breath** (taken at same time as other readings).
- **FOUR MAIN pulse classifications** (including speed) to be checked for first, are shown at right.
- **EVERY PULSE should be:** Firm - Calm - Flowing - Elastic - Regular.
- **BUT IT MIGHT BE:** Tight - Slippery - Hollow - Floating - Leaping - Crouched - Overflowing - Wiry (& many more) - EACH RELATES TO BODY STATUS.

TOO MUCH (DO)

- **TOO MUCH LOOKING** (Reading/T.V etc.) weakens the "heart" meridian (also blood).
- **TOO MUCH SITTING** (Office/Factory/Old age etc.) weakens the "spleen" meridian (also flesh & spine condition).
- **TOO MUCH STANDING** (Stationary) weakens the "kidney" meridian (also bones & joints).
- **TOO MUCH LABOR** (Physical work/Walking etc.) weakens the "liver" meridian.
- **TOO MUCH LYING** in bed weakens the "lung" meridian (also respiration).

TOO MUCH (AIR)

- **TOO MUCH HEAT** damages the "heart."
- **TOO MUCH HUMIDITY** damages the "spleen."
- **TOO MUCH DRYNESS** damages the "kidneys."
- **TOO MUCH WIND** damages the "liver."
- **TOO MUCH COLD** damages the "lungs."
- **TOO MUCH COLD WIND**, if not countered fast (sweat & garlic soup) will quickly harm first: "Lungs" (a cold) - Then "liver" (vomit) - Then "spleen" (fatigue) - Then "kidneys" (discharges) - Then "heart" (SPASMS EVEN DEATH).

PULSE SITES

LEFT HAND		RIGHT HAND

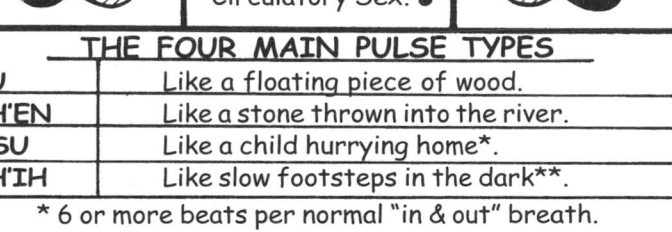

LIGHT PRESSURE
- Bladder.
- Gall Bladder.
- Small Intestine.
  - Triple Heater.
  - Stomach.
- Large Intestine.

HARD PRESSURE
- Heart.
- Liver.
- Kidney.
  - Lung.
  - Spleen.
  - Circulatory Sex.

THE FOUR MAIN PULSE TYPES

FU	Like a floating piece of wood.
CH'EN	Like a stone thrown into the river.
HSU	Like a child hurrying home*
CH'IH	Like slow footsteps in the dark**

* 6 or more beats per normal "in & out" breath.
** 3 or less beats per normal "in & out" breath.

HOW AILMENTS AFFECT PERSONALITY

MERIDIAN WEAK	USUAL TIME OF MOOD SWING TO:		
	Quiet & peaceful	Clarity of thinking	Lively & animated
LUNGS	Midnight	Pre dusk	Noon
LIVER	Midnight	Morning	Pre dusk
SPLEEN	Afternoon	Post dusk	Dawn
KIDNEYS	Pre dusk	Midnight	Late season
HEART	Morning	Noon	Midnight

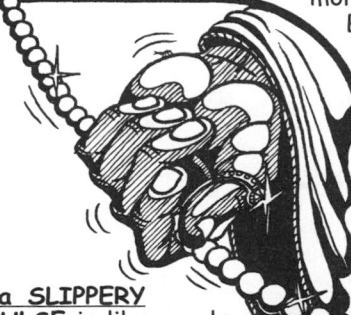

"a **SLIPPERY PULSE** is like pearls thru the fingers".

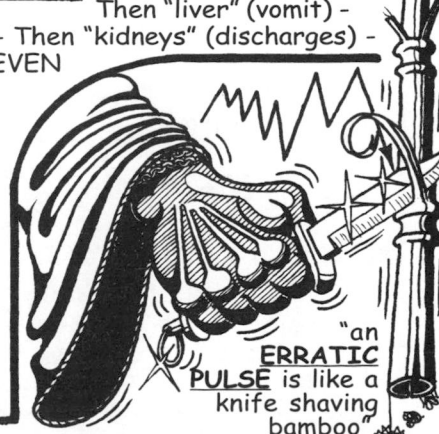

"an **ERRATIC PULSE** is like a knife shaving bamboo".

SYMPTOMS	CONCLUSIONS	DIAGRAMS

EYES

SYMPTOMS	CONCLUSIONS
Black spots on eye white.	Check for kidney malfunction.
Brown spots on eye white.	Suspect internal stones (&/or cysts).
Yellow spots on eye white.	Indicate stagnating blood supply.
Green spots on eye white.	Indicative of cancerous growth.
Red spots on eye white.	Indicate stagnating blood supply.
Whole eye white is red.	If no irritation, probably liver.
Whole eye white is yellow.	Probable jaundice (liver/bile).
Whole eye white is blue/gray.	Local regenerative failure (with sight loss).
Descending purple/blue inner eye corner skin stain.	"Stagnant" blood (circulation &/or purification poor) darker = worse.
Sudden descending curtain across vision of one eye.	Follows hard impact (e.g. boxing, fall etc.) causes detached retina.
Gritty itch in lower eyelid with tiny spot(s) (&/or blurring).	Chaio Tz'ang (infectious) excess yin diet (sugar, fruit, liquid &/or dairy).
Hyperactive nonstop eye movements.	Excess dietry yin = nervous tension (with probable irregular heartbeat).
Bits & shadows float in vision.	Indicates damaged (bits off) retina.
Double image (& near sight).	Excess yin in diet (see yin/yang sec.).
Lower eyelid edge is white.	Deficient in red blood cells (anemia).
Puffy under eye bags.	Excess fluid straining kidneys.
Hard bags with pale face.	Probable kidney stone formation.
Clear eye discharge.	Normal healthy body function.
Yellow eye discharge.	Excess dietary mucus (dairy foods).
White eye discharge.	Excess dietary toxins (animal fats).

NOSE

SYMPTOMS	CONCLUSIONS
Nostril holes very small.	Weak lungs (lack of exercise) & yin diet.
Bulbous red nose tip.	Probable high blood pressure.
Non-injury nose bleeding.	Excess yin diet (or protein) = Thin tissues.
Cleft (split) in nose tip.	Indicates mismatched heart chambers.

SPOTS

Read digestion on shoulders.
Read lungs on back.
Read liver here.

SYMPTOMS	CONCLUSIONS	
Pimples on/around nose.	Heart	**WARNING: Corresponding organ is being adversely affected** by mucus (&/or fat) accumulation from excess dietary, animal/dairy fats, sugars, liquids.
Pimples on cheeks.	Lungs	
Pimples around mouth.	Reproduction	
Pimples on forehead.	Intestines	
Pimples around jaws.	Kidneys	

LIPS

SYMPTOMS	CONCLUSIONS	
Dry &/or chapped lips.	Indicate dietary toxin build up.	
Cracked/splits on lip(s).	Serious digestive toxicity.	Upper Lip = Stomach
Cyst/pus-filled spot on lip.	Similar or worse in organ.	Corners = Duodenum
Dark red/purple lips.	Diet imbalance, illness prone.	Lower Lip = Intestines
Swollen/puffy lips.	Swollen stomach/intestines.	
Thin puckered lips.	Indication of extreme yin.	
Pasty colorless lips.	Anemia or scarlet fever.	
Red face with red lips.	Internal heat/fever (lungs?).	

● Also read lungs & heart on chest.

READ INTESTINES HERE

● **BASIC INTRODUCTION TO YIN/YANG FOOD BALANCE** - **Yin foods are: Acid** - Sweet - Sour - Spicy - Liquid (avoid extreme yin e.g: Potato - Tomato - Egg plant - Sugar - Sweets - Soft drinks - Drugs - Coffee - Chemicals etc.) - **Some yang foods are:** Carrots - Onions - Turkey - White fish - Strawberries - Apples - Cherries (AVOID WHEN PRACTICAL: SALT - DAIRY - RED MEAT - FATS/OILS - PROCESSED FOODS).

Detect & Analyse Health Problems By Hair Growth Study

Asian medicine holds that the condition of hair (or lack thereof) on various parts of the head CORRESPONDS TO PARTICULAR BODILY FUNCTIONS &/or ailments.

Symptom(s), Location(s) & Indication(s)

HAIR ZONES

ZONE 1. Relates to the LIVER & GALLBLADDER.

ZONE 2. Relates to the STOMACH & SPLEEN.

ZONE 3. Relates to the HEART, CIRCULATION & SMALL INTESTINE.

ZONE 4. Relates to the LUNGS & LARGE INTESTINE.

ZONE 5. Relates to the BLADDER, BOWELS & KIDNEYS

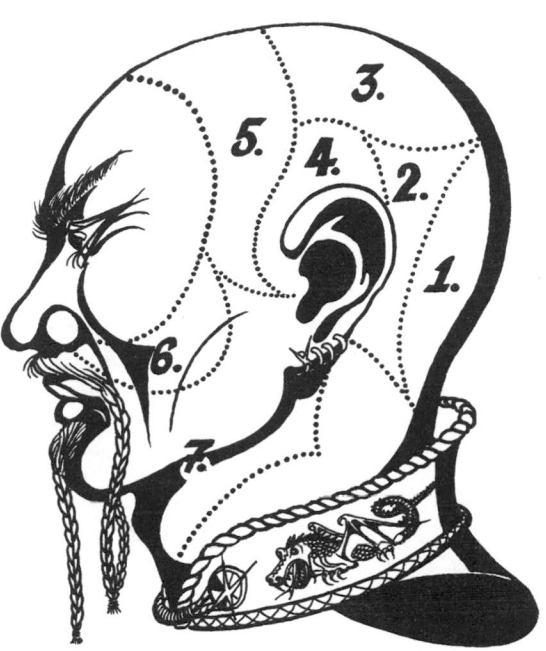

DANDRUFF results

from overeating & the elimination of excess food (particularly protein & fat of animal origin) in the form of flaking skin cells - **It can also indicate** kidney problems (& an irritable disposition).

BALDNESS ZONE 3.

Resulting from the consumption of saturated fats (which also cause an accumulation of cholesterol, digestive problems, hard arteries, heart disease, tumors & cancer) - An aggressive & often materialistic view may also be evident - **The offending foods** here (particularly) are animal proteins & fats (including dairy).

SHADE & THICKNESS

	DARK	LIGHT
THIN	Cooked, salted vegetables.	Animal protein &/or cooked salt. veg.
THICK	Carbohydrates & veg., protein & oil.	Animal protein & fat (including dairy).

● **HEREDITARY** genes are the primary hair structure influence - Food is the major secondary factor.

STRAIGHT OR CURLY

● **BALANCED YIN/YANG** diet of cooked grains, vegetables & some animal foods (not dairy).

● **HIGHER QUANTITIES** of animal/dairy foods with salt in cold places (or more carbohydrates in hot places).

● **BEARDS ZONE 7. Growth in men (& lack of in women) relates to the status of sexual hormones in their bodies** - It is adversely affected by either excess animal/dairy or yin foods/drinks -
● **ZONE 6.** Particurly relates to ANIMAL FAT INTAKE.

● **SPLIT ENDS are evidence of extreme yin** caused by imbalance in the diet (too much sugar, fat, animal protein, fruit/juice & yin vegetables) & a shortage of grains - THE REPRODUCTIVE SYSTEM IN PARTICULAR DEGENERATES.

● **GRAY HAIR** occurs naturally with age - **However it is also brought on (prematurely) by excess consumption of** salty foods (particularly animal &/or overcooked vegetables) - EAT MORE FRESH LEAFY VEGETABLES & NATURAL GRAINS.

BALDNESS ZONE 5.

Resulting from the consumption of yin drinks & fruits (such as alcohol, soft drinks, juices etc.) also sugar, sweets & drugs - Also very yin vegetables (such as potatoes & tomatoes) - **Symptoms include** decline in sexual interest, bowel, kidney, digestive & circulation problems - A more intellectual & passive personality.

ASIAN HEALTH SECRETS OF NAIL DIAGNOSIS

Detect & Analyze Health Problems By Fingernail Study

THE EXAMINATION OF PHYSICAL CHARACTERISTICS
is a proven Asian diagnostic tradition, established over thousands of years.

SYMPTOM(S) & INDICATION(S)	SKETCH(ES)
● **WHITE FLECKS caused by shortage of zinc** - &/or drug/chemical consumption - &/or stress - &/or elimination of excess dietary sugar (can be in form of soft drinks, sweets, alcohol, even fruit) - POSITION OF FLECK INDICATES TIME OF OCCURRENCE.	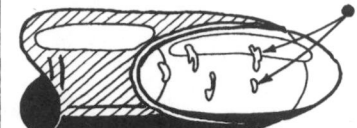
● **LONGITUDINAL RIDGES are indicative of an imbalance in the nutritional side of the diet** - This effect varies with individuals (but usually shows a shortage of digestible protein & fat [&/or an excess of salt & carbohydrate]). ALSO PRONE TO ARTHRITIS	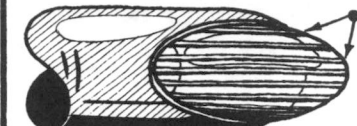
● **HALF MOONS**: With the exception of children (& those with a rapid metabolism) large half moons on nails (except thumb) **indicate a yin constitution** (the larger the half moons, the more toxins may have built up in the body). MAY ALSO MEAN OVERACTIVE THYROID	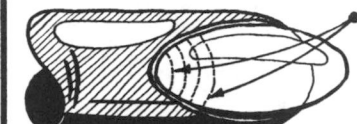
● **LATERAL RIDGES are an indication of a shock to the body's metabolism** (normally brought about by a pronounced dietary change [PERHAPS FROM SLIMMING OR MOVING TO ANOTHER LOCATION]) - Position(s) indicate time(s).	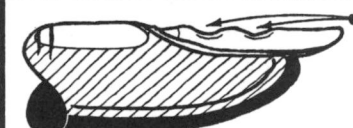
● **SPLIT & PEELING nails are signs of a strongly yin constitution** caused by the excess consumption of yin foods (fruit, sugar, chemicals etc.) - The position of the problem relates to the location of bodily troubles. SPLITS CAN ALSO MEAN WORMS	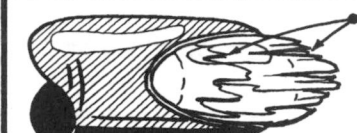
● **CONCAVE OR SPOON nails** (which are hollow when viewed from the side) **indicate an iron deficiency** - OR A LONG STANDING INTERNAL PARASITE INFESTATION (probable origin: Poor hygiene - Undercooked meat - Unwashed vegetables etc.).	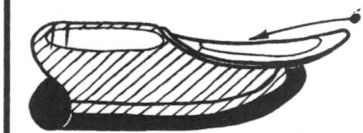
● **THICK CUTICLES**: Raised (& sometimes red) **is an indication of excess consumption of (usually) animal protein** (& OFTEN OCCURS IN CONJUNCTION WITH OVERPRODUCTION OF SKIN CELLS IN OTHER PARTS [i.e. dandruff &/or flaking facial skin etc.]).	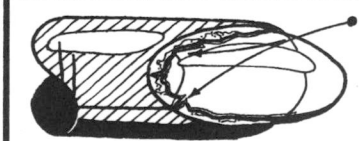
● **CONVEX OR ROUNDED nails** (when viewed from side [& end]) **are signs of a yang (& healthy) constitution** (as are: Short - Broad - No half moon - Longitudinal grain nails [grain refers to visible lines not raised ridges]). **But tip down could mean lung/heart/liver ailment(s).**	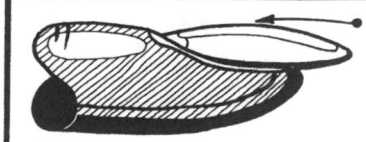

● **GROWTH TIME** of a complete nail depends on metabolism (young & active = Quicker) - It is usually between 6-9 months - Therefore a fault halfway occurred about 4 mths. ago.	● **THICK** = High dietary protein (or fat) intake (or as a result of yang diet [more favorable]). ● **THIN** = Vegetarian (&/or yin diet [too much fruit/sugar/coffee etc.]).
● **COLORS: Pink** = Healthy - **Dark red** = Too much animal protein (or Vit. B12 deficiency) - **Yellow** = Jaundice (or lymph system problem &/or Vit. E deficiency) - **White** = Anemia.	● **BRITTLE** nails can result from either: Protein &/or iron deficiency - &/or Bad circulation - &/or Exposure to external chemicals (cleaners, solvents etc.).

How To Analyze General Health from Foot Condition

Asian health & well-being (mental, spiritual & physical) traditionally rely heavily on principles of "balance" in all things (therefore first study "Yin/Yang Values" Sec.).

TRADITIONAL ASIAN FOOT-TO-BODY-RELATED ZONES (MAY DIFFER FROM REFLEXOLOGY)

SOLE

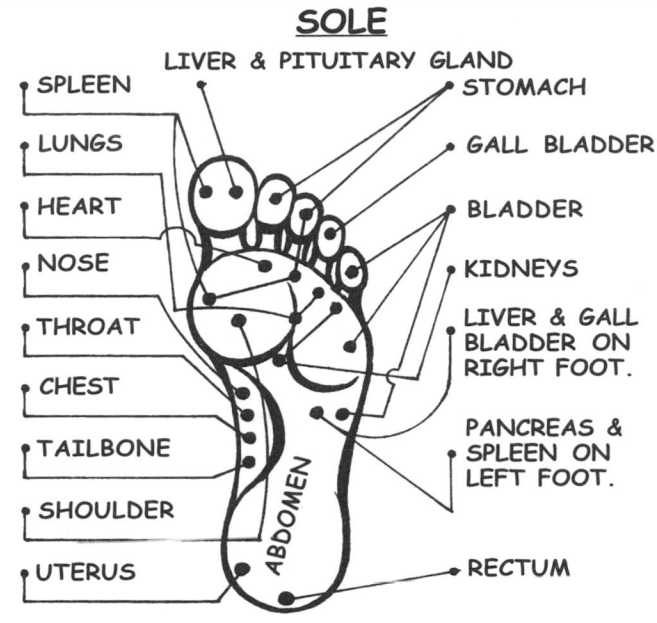

- SPLEEN
- LUNGS
- HEART
- NOSE
- THROAT
- CHEST
- TAILBONE
- SHOULDER
- UTERUS
- LIVER & PITUITARY GLAND
- STOMACH
- GALL BLADDER
- BLADDER
- KIDNEYS
- LIVER & GALL BLADDER ON RIGHT FOOT.
- PANCREAS & SPLEEN ON LEFT FOOT.
- RECTUM
- ABDOMEN

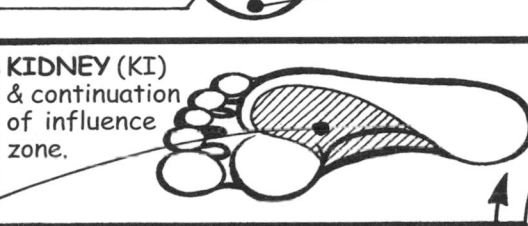

- KIDNEY (KI) & continuation of influence zone.

TOP/SIDES

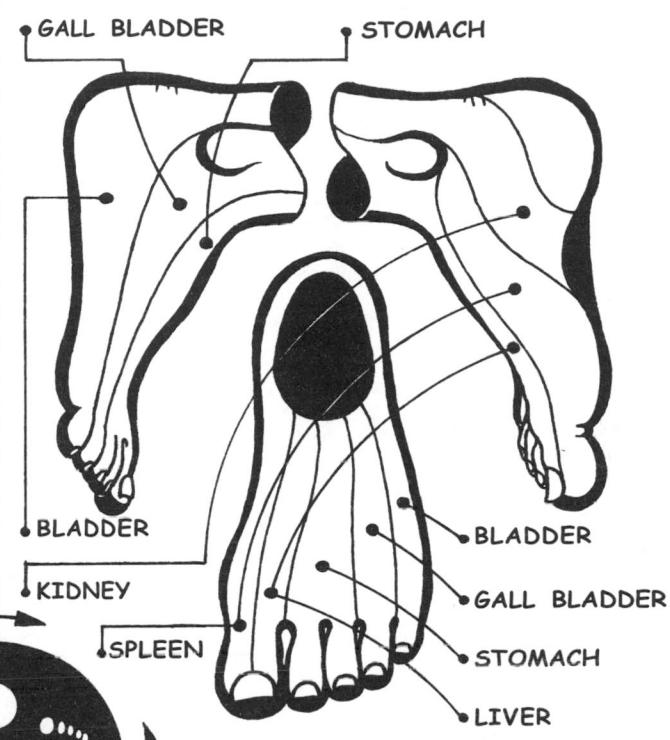

- GALL BLADDER
- STOMACH
- BLADDER
- KIDNEY
- SPLEEN
- BLADDER
- GALL BLADDER
- STOMACH
- LIVER

HOW TO INTERPRET

- **SIZE: Small feet indicate** inherited physical vitality (& non-central abdomen sited organ strength [e.g. lungs, heart, intestines]) - **Large feet indicate** central abdomen sited organ strength (e.g. liver, kidneys, stomach) & mental vitality.
- **WIDTH: Wide feet indicate** less physical vitality (& a past yin diet but usually an inquiring mind) - **Narrow feet (less than 1-3) indicate** past yang diet (with less liquid + usually mental & physical vitality).
- **INSTEP ARCH: High indicates** past yang diet (tight muscles & high physical potential) - **Low indicates** past yin diet (high liquids, sugar etc.) usually more inclined to be studious, arty etc.
- **TOE LENGTH:** 2nd & 3rd toes longer than big toe indicate prebirth diet imbalance (with later tendency to stomach problems [see "B"]).
- **FLEXIBILITY** decrease in foot joints (& sinews) reflect general bodily decline (OFTEN PREMATURE BECAUSE OF EXCESS DIETARY SALT, FAT, CALCIFIED WATER ETC.).

FOOT CHARACTERISTICS

- **BALL OF FOOT** (if protruding sideways [see "A"]) indicates long-term diet imbalance (e.g. with salt use) often causing personality inflexibility (& central organ [kidney, liver, stomach] ailments).
- **TOE TIPS** which harden for no good reason, indicate stagnation (or ailment) in the corresponding organ (usually because of overindulgence [or nutritional &/or yin yang] imbalance).
- **TWISTED TOES** (not from tight shoes [see "C"]) indicate imbalance between adjoining toes (organs) usually from excess yin food &/or animal fat, salt etc. overburdening one or both organs.
- **PIGEON-TOED** (see "D") indicates past yin diet (& usually passive personality).
- **SPLAYFOOTED** (see "E") indicates past excess animal protein intake, spinal base constriction & AGGRESSIVE MOODS.
- **NAILS** (MAIN DETAILS : 11, 55, 200 & 202) but non-pink color (&/or irregularities) indicate problems in the corresponding organ.

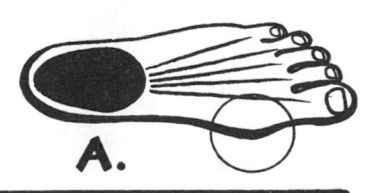 **A.**

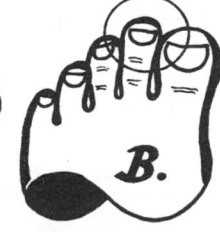 **B.**

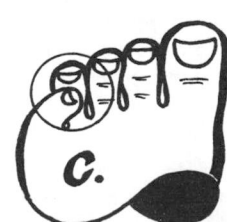 **C.**

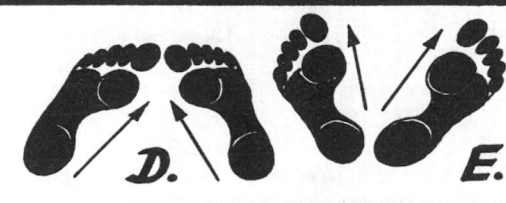 **D.** **E.**

CATEGORY			OBSERVATIONS	DIAGRAMS
COMMON PROBLEMS	*Remember foot abnormalities (moles, warts, toe nail & color changes) as well as indicating their own specific problems also relate to (& are diagnostic aids for ailments within) remote body organs (acupressure/reflexology).*	ATHLETES FOOT (RING WORM)	● **HIGHY CONTAGIOUS** fungal peeling between toes (caused by infection from showers/towels etc.) - But encouraged by excess dietary yin (& liquid [sugar, fruit &/or juices, drugs etc.]) - Correct diet - Keep feet dry/aired - Take extra Vits. A & C - Dab with lemon juice (or cider vinegar) then apply honey.	**BRITTLE NAILS**
		CALLUSES	● **FROM EXTERNAL PRESSURE** &/or overeating (usually animal/dairy [but also sugar/ starch]) with resulting mucus/fat elimination from related organ at contact point (see "Acup. Sec.") - Correct diet - Soak, then abrade (in hot water) with baking soda - Apply oil & vinegar (4 to 1 ratio).	● Low body iron. ● Circulation poor. ● Kidney problems. ● Solvent exposure
		CHILBLAINS	● **DIETARY EXCESS** of extreme yin (sugar/drugs etc. [&/or animal fats]) damage major organs = Poor circulation = Cell damage = Chilblains - Correct diet - Take extra Vits. B Comp & C + Calcium - Keep feet warm (not hot, not quickly) & dry - Wash feet in salt water (then turnip/beet water) - Massage with oil of onion.	**MASSAGE TOE** tip & nail with warm olive oil.
		CORNS	● **HARD SKIN** "turned in" from abrasion - Also caused by excess dietary fat/protein (mainly animal) - &/or high yin intake (sugar, drugs etc.) which both overload organs - Remove abrasion - Correct diet - Massage with Castor Oil (twice daily) - Or soak in warm water/vinegar (2 to 1) - &/or rub in lemon juice.	**BIG MOONS** (see page 200)
		INGROWING TOENAILS	● **NAILS CUT WRONG** + tight shoes (excess dietary animal protein/fat CAUSES THICK IRRITATED CUTICLES.) ● Correct diet - Soak in strong sea salt solution - Cut nails in gentle curve (not in at corners).	● **TOO MUCH** dairy/ animal protein (often occurs with dandruff).
		SMELLY FEET	● **BACTERIA/SWEAT** caused by excess dietary yin fluids (soft drinks, alcohol, fruit juices etc. [thirst caused by excess dietary animal protein/fat/salt etc.]) - Correct diet - Go barefoot (or wear sandals or cotton socks) - Massage with oil of Cypress/Pine.	**DEAD NAIL** (from knock)
		VERRUCAE	● **WART ON SOLE** of foot (with tiny black spot) - Highly contagious virus (wear shoes) - Encouraged to form by excess dietary protein & fat (elimination of which is impaired by excess dietary yin [sugars/chemicals etc.]) - Correct diet - Take dandelion root (&/or garlic) internally & apply dandelion sap (&/or garlic) externally.	
FOOT COLOURS		WHITE	● **INDICATES ANEMIA** - &/or underactive circulation (&/or digestion) - Caused by excess dietary animal products (e.g. meat, dairy, salt etc.).	● **TO SOFTEN:** Wash in vinegar (often). ● **TO REMOVE:** Apply (& leave on) paste of milk & ground apricot kernels.
		YELLOW	● **INDICATES JAUNDICE** - &/or liver/gall bladder ailments (from excess dietary meat, fat, eggs, alcohol, dairy etc. [also overeating]) - Excess bile in blood.	
		GREEN	● **INDICATES CIRCULATION** &/or lymph or spleen ailments - &/or cysts (or cancer) from excess dietary toxicity/fat (e.g. butter/bacon/cheese/pastry/sugar).	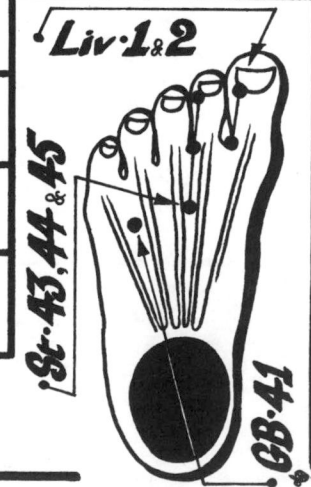
		RED	● **INDICATES OVERACTIVE** circulation, urinary & excretory functions (with heart, kidney & mental fatigue) - Caused by excess dietary yin (& liquid).	
		PURPLE	● **AS IN "RED"** but additional toxicity probable (e.g. additives, colorings, preservatives, insecticides etc.) - REPRODUCTION AILMENTS LIKELY.	
		BLACK	● **OFTEN WITH SWELLING** indicates stagnant kidney, blood & excretory functions (from excess dietary animal/ dairy/salt/chocolate/oxalic acid foods.	

<u>**SOME FOOT TOP DIAGNOSIS POINTS**</u> - (IF TENDER PRESS 3 X 10 SECONDS TO TREAT) - **GB. 41** (fatigue, menstruation, arthritis) - **Liv. 1 & 2** (lungs, fatigue, insomnia) - **St. 44 & 45** (stomach & fear) - **GB. 41** (fatigue).

Detect & Analyze Health Problems From Specific Skin Areas

EXTERNAL PROBLEMS ON YOUR FACE (such as dry skin, spots, tenderness etc.) can indicate more complex ailments elsewhere.

FACIAL ZONES RELATING TO BODY ORGANS

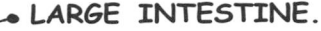

THIS ZONE NOT IDENTIFIED YET.

- BLADDER.
- SPLEEN.
- LIVER.
- KIDNEYS.
- HEART.
- LARGE INTESTINE.
- GALL BLADDER.
- STOMACH.

- LARGE INTESTINE.
- SMALL INTESTINE.
- PANCREAS.
- SEX ORGANS.
- INTESTINES.
- LUNGS.
- SPLEEN.
- BRONCHI.
- DUODENUM.

- **THE EYES** also represent SEX ORGANS & KIDNEYS.
- **THE EYEBROWS** relate to the NERVOUS & DIGESTIVE SYSTEMS.

- **NOTE**: If an organ (e.g. lungs) is shown on (e.g. the left cheek only) then the right cheek will relate to the right lung.

GENERAL ASIAN ORGAN INFLUENCES

A PROBLEM IN	MENTAL CAUSES	A PROBLEM IN	PHYSICAL AFFECTS
The heart.	Worry - Anxiety.	The heart.	Circulation - Arteries.
The lungs.	Melancholy - Sadness.	The lungs.	The skin & hair.
Liver. Spleen.	Impatience - Temper.	The liver.	Muscles & tissue.
Intestines.	Nervous disposition.	Kidneys.	The bones & nails.
Nervous sys.	Suspicion - Aloofness.	The spleen.	Condition of flesh.

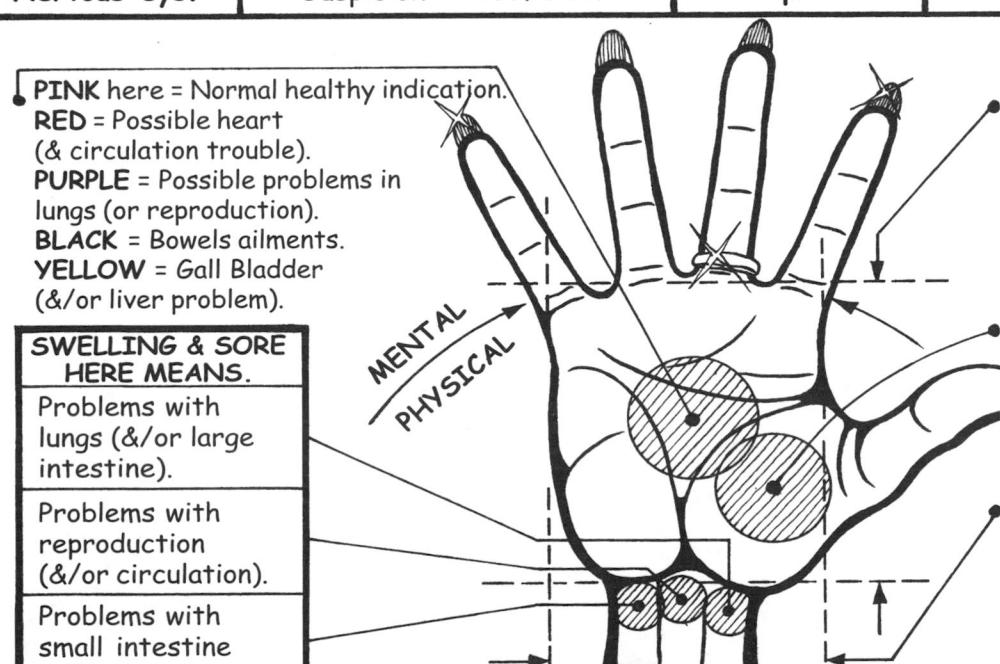

PINK here = Normal healthy indication.
RED = Possible heart (& circulation trouble).
PURPLE = Possible problems in lungs (or reproduction).
BLACK = Bowels ailments.
YELLOW = Gall Bladder (&/or liver problem).

SWELLING & SORE HERE MEANS.
Problems with lungs (&/or large intestine).
Problems with reproduction (&/or circulation).
Problems with small intestine (&/or heart).

MENTAL
PHYSICAL

PALM LENGTH longer than finger length indicates a more developed physical (than mental) constitution - If the fingers are as long (or longer) then the opposite applies.

RED/BLUE here = Diet caused trouble in intestines.
GREEN indicates developing cancer in bowels.

PALM WIDTH is an indication of yin (or yang) constitution with wide, indicating physical strength & a long life - Narrow the opposite.

SKIN IS		LIKELY CAUSE	CONCLUSIONS	DIAGRAMS
TOO OILY		● **FAULTY** fat metabolism or excess dietary fat &/or oil - &/or general overeating (e.g. of sugar, animal products, white flour, fruit juices etc.).	● **DANGER:** Overburdened organs (e.g. liver, gall bladder, lungs, kidneys, colon etc.) can develop mucus buildup, stones, cysts & tumors - CUT OUT ALL FATTY FOODS - EAT LESS.	**TONGUE ZONES** RELATING TO:
TOO DRY		● **DEHYDRATION** or excess dietary fat &/or oil (resulting in a layer of under skin fat) which blocks perspiration.	● **AS ABOVE** but toxins (&/or oils) not being sweated out - Thus saturating blood (& metabolism) endangering arteries (& heart particularly) - Eat less (not more) fats.	
TOO WET		● **EXCESS** dietary fluids & sugars (e.g. fruit juices, soft drinks, milk, yogurt, soup & fruit) - &/or excess protein salt (& carbohydrates)= Thirst.	● **INDICATES** possible fits, aches in teeth (& jaws), glaucoma, memory (& hair) loss, detached retina, physical (& mental) fatigue etc. - Balance diet - REDUCE URINATIONS TO 4 TIMES PER DAY.	● **Back** = Kidneys. ● **Middle** = Stomach. ● **Sides** = Liver. ● **Tip** = Heart.
NON RACIAL COLORS APPEARING ON ANY BODY PART	WHITE	● **SHOCK** (or fever) & cold (or excess dietary animal fat [incl. dairy]) & salt etc.	● **INDICATES** mental rigidity - &/or diverse ailments of liver, kidneys, spleen, lung cells, gall bladder & veins.	**BLOOD ACIDITY**
	YELLOW	● **IN COLD** wind (after sweat) or excess dietary yang (e.g. meat, fish, salt, eggs etc.).	● **INDICATES** liver, bile, pancreas, kidney, excretory & gall bladder ailments - &/or flatulence/ aggression.	
	BLUE	● **OPPOSITE** dietary excesses (yang [animal/salt etc.]) - & yin (sugar, pastry, fruit juices).	● **INDICATES** overload of any/all of spleen, liver, pancreas, kidneys - Also inflexibility & temper.	**TOO ACID** ● Oversize Pupils. ● Cross Eyes.
	GREEN	● **DAMP/cold** - Or excess yin (sugar, drugs, oils) - Or excess yang (animal, salt, fat).	● **INDICATES** danger of infection with boils, cysts, tumors & cancer - Also ailments of liver (& emotions).	
	PURPLE	● **EXTREME** dietary yin (i.e. sugar, potato, tomato, drugs, sweet fruit etc.).	● **INDICATES** ailments of stomach, intestines, kidneys & reproduction - May also be insecure (even suicidal).	**TOO ALKALINE** ● Eyes Turn Out. ● Tend To Worry.
	RED	● **STRESS** &/or excess dietary yin (eg. alcohol & sugar drinks, spices, drugs)	● **INDICATES** ailments of veins, heart, lungs & nervous system - Fast for few days then rice & yang veg. diet.	
	BROWN	● **EXCESS** dietary animal fat/ protein - &/or yin fruits, vegetables, drinks etc.	● **INDICATES** ailments of stomach, intestines (incl. colon) & kidneys - May have narrow mental outlook.	**TOO MUCH SALT**
	BLACK	● **COLD** (wet) in abdomen or excess dietary yin (e.g. sugar, drinks, juices etc.).	● **AILMENTS** as for "brown" (but also reproductive/hormonal & mental paranoia) - Rest & change diet.	
TOO PUFFY		● **EXCESS** dietary fat (& mucus) producing foods (& drinks) particularly dairy (e.g. milk, butter, yogurt, cheese etc.) but also meats, sugar, processed flours etc.	● **POTENTIALLY** dangerous indication - Usually most obvious on body front - Showing serious fat/mucus buildup, causing: Colds, fatigue, ear/sinus, lung, artery/heart, liver & thyroid ailments - POSSIBILITY OF TUMORS & CANCER.	
YIN	TOO ROUGH	● **EXCESS** dietary yin foods (such as sugar, pastry, cakes, chemicals, sweets, fruit juices, drugs, alcohol etc.).	● **OFTEN** flush (& sweat) heavily - Pulse beat varies - Kidney (& bladder) overload (with frequent urination & loose bowels) - Cry easily - Eat more grain & YANG vegetables.	● Constipation. ● High Blood P. ● Insomnia. ● Red Ears.
YANG	TOO ROUGH	● **EXCESS** dietary protein/fat (e.g. milk, butter, cheese, meat, sausage, eggs, yogurt, bacon, coconut etc.).	● **POTENTIALLY** dangerous buildup of body fat deposits - Threatens arteries/heart, liver, kidneys, flexibility/mobility - GENERAL METABOLIC DECLINE - Change diet.	● Bow Legs. ● Brown Urine. ● Dry Skin. ● Flushed Skin.

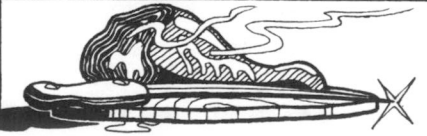

● **TOO MUCH MEAT** = THICK IRRITATED CUTICLES - Bulbous nose - Big half moons on nails - Hair loss on head - Dark lips - Red ears - Red face - Red nails.

Asian D.I.Y Maintenance & Repairs For Body & Spirit

PRACTICE THESE VALUABLE TECHNIQUES in spare moments - On a bus -
At the office - In the bathroom (you do have time) - Feel the difference in minutes.

REVITALIZE YOUR BODY - PART I

● **STIMULATE THE FLOW OF "CHI"** (life force) - Momentarily restrict (a few seconds) then release the flow (as shown) - This works on the same principal as a kinked hose which when released <u>FLUSHES OUT BLOCKAGES & THEREAFTER FLOWS BETTER THAN BEFORE.</u>

── FEET ──

A. TO INVIGORATE "CHI" flow to & from the <u>Kidney, Liver, Bladder, Spleen, Gallbladder & Stomach meridians</u> - Bend each toe (in turn) up & back (as far as it will go) - Hold for a few seconds - Then (in turn) bend each toe under (as far as it will go) - Hold for a few seconds.

A.

B. PINCH EITHER SIDE of each toe level with base of each nail (e.g. big toe stimulates <u>Liver & Spleen meridians</u>) - Also used for headaches, fits, fainting & bloated stomach - Hold 5-15 seconds, repeat 1-3 times).

Sp·1 **B.** *Liv·1*

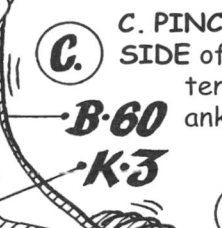

C. PINCH EITHER SIDE of Achilles tendon (hard) just behind anklebones stimulates <u>Bladder & Kidney meridians</u> - Used for ankle, foot, hand & low back ailments - Also dizziness/fits & to enhance sexuality - Hold 5-15 seconds, repeat 1-3 times.

C. *B·60* *K·3* **D.**

D. GET 2 BIG MARBLES <u>(or golf balls) & put one under each bare foot while sitting at your desk</u> - Pressing firmly roll feet back & forth (lingering on any tender places) - This procedure stimulates (& treats) all reflexology zones (which are scattered over the bottoms of feets & toes), & relate to all body parts & functions - <u>A very effective & valuable (to you) technique.</u>

── HANDS ──

E. TO ENCOURAGE "CHI" flow to/ from <u>Small Intestine, Triple Warmer & Large Intestine meridians</u> (also used for fever & diarrhea) - Bend each digit (including thumb) at first joint to form 3 sides of a square for several seconds.

E.

F. ONE AT A TIME bend each digit back at 90 degrees (for several seconds) - Stimulates <u>Lung, Pericardium & Heart meridians</u> - Used for hand/arm ailments - Also sore throat/coughs.

90° **F.**

G. "ACTIVATE" LI. 4 (one <u>thumb joint in on web of index finger & thumb)</u> - Grip top & bottom & squeeze 5-15 seconds (repeat 1-3 times) - This important & easy to reach point traditionally aids: Rashes - Insomnia - Too much sweat - Worry/stress - Toothache - Allergies - Facial tension - Constipation - Sinuses - Dizziness - Diarrhea - Periods - Obsession - Confusion & General Health.

LI·4 **G.**

H.

H. SQUEEZE THE TIP of each digit tightly (either side of the base of each nail) - The little finger positions stimulate the heart - <u>IN AN EMERGENCY SQUEEZE, TWIST, SHAKE BOTH OF VICTIMS DIGITS VIGOROUSLY.</u>

(YIN)	MERIDIAN CODES	(YANG)	
CV	- Conception Vessel	**B**	- Bladder
H	- Heart	**GB**	- Gall Bladder
K	- Kidney	**GV**	- Governing Vessel
Liv	- Liver	**LI**	- Large Intestine
Lu	- Lung	**P**	- Pericardium
Sp	- Spleen	**SI**	- Small Intestine
TW	- Triple Warmer	**St**	- Stomach

REVITALIZE YOUR BODY - PART II

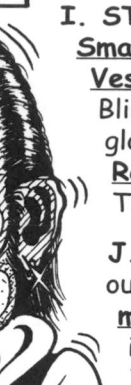

IMAGINE YOU HAVE A FLY ON YOUR NOSE & YOU ARE ALL TIED UP!

I. STIMULATE "CHI" FLOW to/from the <u>Gall Bladder, Stomach, Triple Warmer, Small Intestine, Governing Vessel, Large Intestine, Bladder & Conception Vessel meridians</u> by (do it in private) - Wiggling face, mouth, cheeks, ears - Blink eyes at speed - Do all simultaneously (& with vigor) until your face glows (& its muscles ache) - <u>Dramatically improves circulation - Rejuvenates the tissues</u> - BRINGS A RAPID HEALTHY GLOW TO PALLID FACES.

J. RAPIDLY SLAP cheeks & lips with loose fingers (in an outward & up direction) for 30 seconds - <u>Stimulates all meridians in "I" (except TW & B)</u> - Also brings an instant improvement in FACIAL CIRCULATION, TISSUE NUTRITION, SKIN COLOR & FIRMNESS.

"WHIP SLAP! OW OOO" "SLAPITY OUCH."

K. THREE IMPORTANT meridians <u>(Bladder, Stomach & Gall Bladder)</u> all start on the edges of each eye socket - They affect many other body functions (besides those in their names) - Particularly eye ailments, headaches & tension - <u>They are well worth stimulating</u> (PARTICULARLY BY THOSE WITH HEAVY VISUAL LOADS [like me!]).

<u>MEN ONLY - (A certain pop star has the right idea)</u> put your hand in your pocket & maintain your interest in sex well into old age by - **a)** Squeezing your balls once for every year of age (once a day [this is an ancient Japanese technique]) - **b)** Press CV. 1(between anus & genitals) to stimulate sex glands (<u>works for women too</u> [press 3 x 10 sec.]).

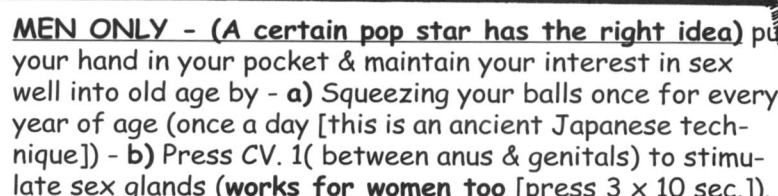

St·1
B·1
GB·1
"IN DO"
"....& WILL U PLEASE WIPE YOUR NOSE"

L. <u>USE THE 2nd FINGER knuckles of both clenched fists in a back & forth rolling action across forehead & skull</u> - Pause & repeat if a tender spot is found (this often indicates a tsubo [acupressure point] requiring treatment) - Stimulates <u>Triple Warmer, Bladder, Governing Vessel & Gall Bladder meridians</u> - Strongly encourages circulation & hair nutrition - Also treats a wide range of ailments including nausea, toothache, hemorrhoids, headache, swollen eyes, colds, dizziness & nosebleed - Plus heatstroke, stiff neck/face <u>& CALMS/ STOPS APPREHENSION/FEAR.</u>

N. PRESS W/ 1 THUMB: St. 9, 10 & 11 on either side of windpipe (10 secs. each/ 3 times) <u>to stimulate Thyroid gland & Stomach mer. - Used to keep skin supple (& to combat gray hair</u> [also treats high blood pressure]).

O. <u>A KEY AREA not to miss is where the neck meets the base of skull</u> (GV. 16 & GB. 20) & 1 finger down (GV. 15 & B. 10) - Press these points (3 x 10 secs.) even in public to treat many ailments - Such as headaches, fear/hysteria, insomnia, stress, colds/sinus & nosebleed - Also nausea, strokes, balding, dizzy, fatigue & aggression.

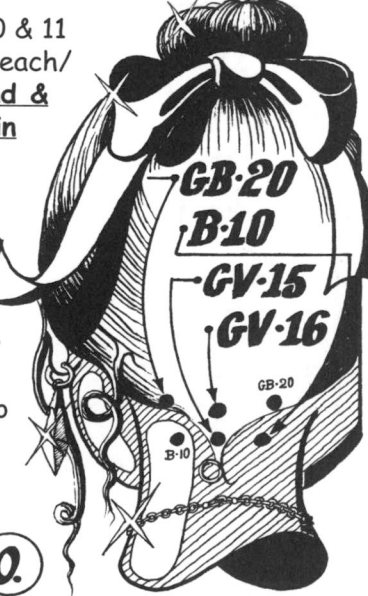

GB·20
B·10
GV·15
GV·16
GB·20
B·10

O.

P. IMPORTANT FINAL HINTS
a) <u>BREATHE DEEPLY (fill abdomen & chest completely) & slowly,</u> in thru nose & out thru mouth to oxygenate your entire body, rise out of depression & fight fatigue in minutes -
B) <u>STAND & SIT UP straight with stomach and shoulders back (& head high)</u> - Exercises a wide range of muscles - Dramatically improves circulation/digestion etc. - & LOOKS GREAT ON ANYONE!

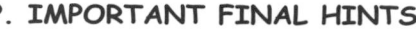

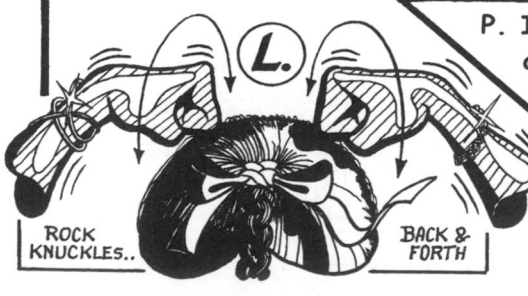

ROCK KNUCKLES..   BACK & FORTH

L.

The Ancient Asian Principles Of Health

MACROBIOTICS is a Buddhist monks tradition of balancing opposites (as applied to foods & life) - The word comes from the Greek for BIG LIFE.

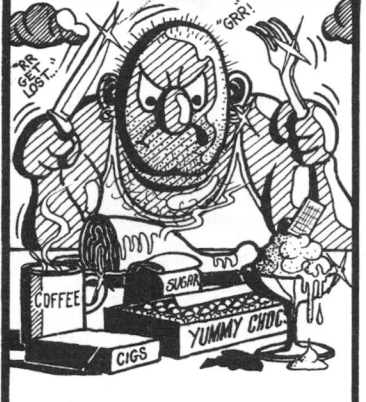

THE 7 PRINCIPLES OF MACROBIOTICS

1. <u>AVOID industrialised & processed, artificially fertilized & preserved foods & drinks</u> (such as canned foods & soft drinks) - Because of factors such as the DEPLETION OF NATURAL NUTRIENTS & THE ADDITION OF TOXINS.

2. <u>AVOID fruit, vegetables & livestock/fish not grown or reared in the area in which you currently live</u> & not harvested in the season in which time it now is - Because of factors such as the natural evolution & development of these living things to ACQUIRE NUTRIENTS & ANTITOXINS SUITED TO A PARTICULAR PLACE & TIME.

3. <u>AVOID drinking immediately before, during or (in quantity) immediately after eating</u> - In any case avoid very hot or very cold (or large quantities of) liquids because of factors such as OVERBURDENING OF THE BODIES FILTRATION SYSTEMS & DILUTION OF DIGESTIVE JUICES.

4. <u>AVOID drugs (such as coffee, nicotine, alcohol, strong spices etc.)</u> & other artificial stimulants because of factors such as disruption to the bodies natural resistance to infection - Also UNPREDICTABLE LEVELS OF INTERFERENCE WITH YIN/YANG BALANCE.

5. <u>AVOID excessively yin foods & drinks</u> (such as potatoes, eggplant, tomatoes, sweets, alcohol, sugared cordials juices etc.) - Maintain a balance (according to your personal circumstances) between yin & yang (& alkaline/acid forming foods) IN ORDER TO MAINTAIN THE BODIES NATURAL & ESSENTIAL EQUILIBRIUM.

6. <u>AVOID eating to excess (i.e. stop before full)</u> - & chew foods very well because of factors such as not overburdening the digestive system (leaving UNDIGESTED FOODS IN THE STOMACH TO PARTIALLY PUTREFY & DEVELOP INTO TOXINS).

7. <u>CULTIVATE a calm & tolerant spirit capable of versatility</u> - <u>ACQUIRE THE KNOWLEDGE TO RE-BALANCE YOUR BODY IN THE EVENT OF OCCASIONAL INDISCRETIONS.</u>

THE 7 FOOD PLAN GUIDELINES & HOW TO USE THEM

● <u>START WITH THE PLAN closest to your present meal structure</u> - Stay on it for 7 days before progressing to the next higher number (on which you stay for 7 days etc.) - When you reach plan #7, stay on it for 7 days (before decreasing to the plan on which you feel most suited) - Always maintain the balance between yin/yang foods - USE THE MOST NATURALLY BALANCED OF THE GRAINS AS THE BASIS OF YOUR PLANS **(ORGANIC BROWN RICE).**

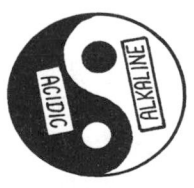

ACID OR ALKALINE FORMING FOODS ....

....<u>are related to but not exact parallels of yin & yang.</u>

<u>ALKALINE forming foods are not necessarily alkaline before digestion</u>, but end up being so after - Almost all fresh fruit & vegetables, some nuts (almonds & brazil) & whole grains (millet) WILL MAKE YOUR BODY & BLOOD MORE ALKALINE.

<u>ACID forming foods are multitude</u> - They include all meat, fish, eggs, poultry, processed carbohydrates, sugar, coffee, drugs, chemicals, soft drinks, most beans, some nuts, many breads etc. - EXCESS BODY ACIDITY CAUSES MANY ILLNESSES.

<u>TO FUTHER CONFUSE</u>: Combining starches &/or sugars with proteins &/or acid fruits at the same meal will build up toxic residues - STUDY "FOOD COMBINING" (PG. 121/2) FOR DETAILS.

#	Cooked whole grains	Fresh vegetables	Fresh fruit	Animal protein	Desserts
7	100%				
6	90%	10%			
5	80%	10%	10%		
4	70%	15%	10%	5%	
3	60%	15%	15%	5%	5%
2	50%	20%	15%	10%	5%
1	40%	20%	20%	10%	10%

Avoid drinking at mealtimes

YIN & YANG VALUES FOR SAMPLE FOODS

- **VERY YANG**: Pheasant - Ginseng - Burdock - Dandelion root (rotate herb use quarterly)

- **MEDIUM YANG**: Buckwheat - Carrot - Pumpkin - Watercress - Duck - Turkey - Egg - Shrimp - Sardine - Caviar - Herring - Snapper - Goat's cheese - Mu tea - Sage - Apple (sweet less yang).

- **YANG**: Rice - Wheat - Millet - Lettuce - Onion - Parsley - Pigeon - Sole - Salmon - Dutch cheese - Strawberry - Chestnut - Cherry (fried foods are less yang than boiled/steamed).

- **YIN**: Barley - Corn - Rye - Oats - Lentil - Beet - White Cabbage - Chicken - Octopus - Eel - Oyster - Lobster - Trout - Halibut - Camembert & Gruyere cheese - Olives - Sunflower oil - White sesame nuts - Corn oil - Well water - Soda water (read labels for fat/sugar/chemicals content).

- **MEDIUM YIN**: Garlic - Celery - Peas - Red cabbage - Beef - Pork - Hare - Frog - Snail - Milk - Peach - Peanut - Cashew - Hazel - Coconut - Olive oil - Safflower oil - Ale - Beer - Dry wine.

- **VERY YIN**: Potato - Tomato - Eggplant - Yam - Spinach - Cucumber - Mushroom - Most beans - Asparagus - Margarine - Butter - Cream - Yogurt - Ice cream - Chocolate - Soft drinks - Fig - Banana - Orange - Grapefruit - Lime - Lemon - Pineapple - Mango - Papaya - Pear - Melon - Molasses - Honey - Sugar - Most jams - Lard - Coffee - Sweet wines - Ginger - Sweets & junk foods.

* Values for the above list are for organic grown foods.

COOKING NOTES

- **ALUMINIUM pots can leach into the food** (& be absorbed by you) - Use clay, lead-free glass or stainless steel to cook in.

- **VEGETABLES should be brushed** under running water (not peeled) to keep nutrients.

- **CLIMATE IF cold is yin** (therefore eat more yang) - If hot is yang (therefore eat a little more yin in hot climate - Some local fruit?).

- **BALANCE all your meals** (according to each person's need) to contain both yin & yang.

- **EXTREMES of yin or yang in meals** (i.e. excess addition of salt) should not be resorted to - Extreme reaction is likely.

- **COOKING ORGANIC WHOLE RICE** is slower than processed rice - Wash 1 cup of brown rice under running water - Drain - Add 2 cups of pure water (1 1/2 in pressure cooker) - 1/4 teaspoon of sea salt - Bring quickly to boil **in covered pot** - Simmer over very low heat for 45 mins (25 mins. in pressure cooker) - **Do not stir the rice while cooking it.**

- **GOMASIO is used as a table seasoning** in Macrobiotics (it is also a heartburn remedy) - To prepare, toast 1 part sea salt till crystalline, then grind to powder - Then rinse (in good water) 5 parts of sesame seeds - Toast evenly (keep moving) until brown (should crumble when pinched) - Grind seeds & salt together - STORE IN AIRTIGHT CONTAINER IN COOL PLACE - REMAKE WEEKLY.

HEALTH NOTES

- **EXCESS YIN** (& acidity) is often indicated by: Heartburn - Cramps - Itching - Coughing - Pimples - Sneezing - Hiccups - Crying - Mucus.

- **OBESITY** is a problem not to be found at all among genuine longer-term practitioners of Macrobiotic principles. (Mental discipline)

- **SEXUAL DESIRE may be decreased** by eating sweets, dairy foods, yin fruits (& vegetables) - **May be increased** by eating ginseng, royal jelly, burdock, most fish (e.g. oysters, anchovies) & lean protein (e.g. turkey). **Avoid stress**

- **DANDRUFF** is often a result of consuming too much milk & other yin proteins.

- **TRAVEL SICKNESS?** ..... Try gomasio!

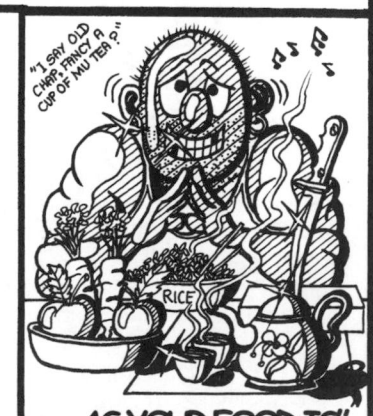

.....AS YOUR FOOD IS"

Invigorate & Rejuvenate Your Body With A Simple Juice Fast

JUICE FASTS ARE SAFER (& more versatile) than water only -
But both types have been used therapeutically since ancient times.

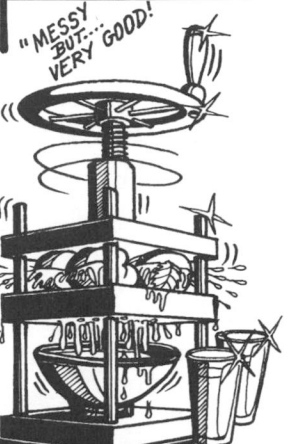

"MESSY BUT... VERY GOOD!"

INTRODUCTION

● **THE THERAPEUTIC** effects of fasting are well-known across many cultures - <u>Major benifits include:</u> Detoxification (& cleansing) of accumulated waste products - Strengthening of stamina & resistance to infections.

● **WHAT HAPPENS?** .... After a few days of fasting the body selects those of its own cells & tissues which are superfluous, diseased &/or damaged & burns these first - <u>**Then incredibly stimulates the building of new healthy cells.**</u>

● **ELIMINATION OF TOXINS** & metabolic waste matter is considerably quicker when fasting <u>**(as much as ten times normal urine-carried toxins are expelled)**</u> - The body is spared the burden of digestion & can concentrate on elimination of long-standing accumulations - The result is such **TYPICAL** FASTING SYMPTOMS as: DARK URINE - BAD BREATH - SPOTS - SMELLY & HEAVY SWEATING - NASAL MUCUS/DISCHARGE ETC.

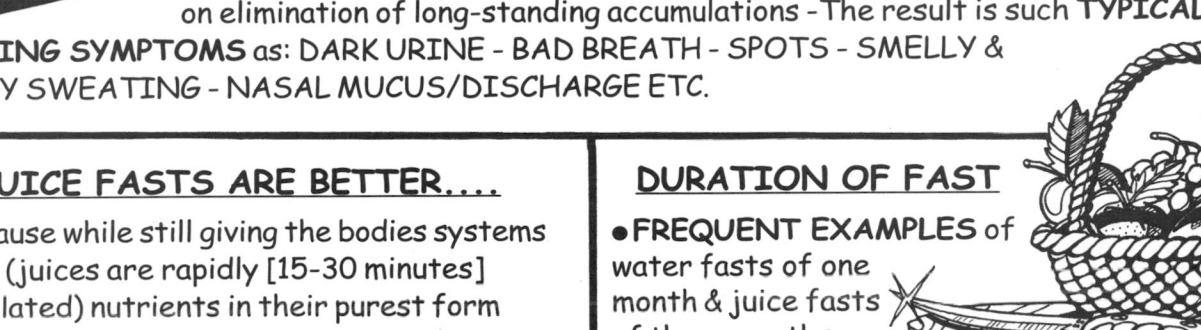

JUICE FASTS ARE BETTER....

....because while still giving the bodies systems a rest (juices are rapidly [15-30 minutes] assimilated) nutrients in their purest form (vitamins, minerals, enzymes & trace elements etc.) proceed virtually straight to the bloodstream & thence to the body's newly rejuvenated cells.

● <u>**MENTAL CLARITY (& perception)**</u> during fasting <u>**are markedly heightened**</u> by the stimulation (& balancing) of body functions.

● <u>**SEXUAL URGES are frequently revived**</u> during (& after) fasting due to stimulation & rejuvenation of hormones, glands & tissues.

DURATION OF FAST

● **FREQUENT EXAMPLES** of water fasts of one month & juice fasts of three months have been recorded with no ill effects - <u>**For normal cleansing a week is sufficient to achieve results.**</u>

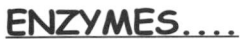

ENZYMES....

● **ARE DESTROYED** by heating to temperatures over 125 deg.F.
● **IN SEEDS & NUTS** are in a suspended state.
● **CAN SURVIVE** almost indefinitely in low temperatures.

CHOICE OF JUICES ....

....(VEGETABLE & FRUIT DON'T MIX) & herb teas should be structured to the fasting persons own state of health - <u>**However diversification is important to give as wide a coverage of nutritional factors as possible**</u> (as all have different remedial qualities) - Typical base juices are carrot (veg.) & apple (fruit) & peppermint herb tea - RESEARCH & ADD OTHERS TO SUIT NEEDS.

● **POSITIVE MENTAL OUTLOOK** is critical to successful fasting (think <u>**"I am happy"**</u> - <u>**"I am cleaner"**</u> etc.) - Don't think negatives.

● **CONTAMINANTS** such as insecticides & chemicals are usually retained in the fibers of fruit (& vegetables), leaving the juices clean.

A JUICE FAST PROGRAM

- **PRIOR TO STARTING** eat only uncooked (BUT WELL CHEWED) fruit & vegetables (BUT DO NOT MIX THE TWO AT ONE MEAL) for 2 days - **Then cleanse bowels with a purge** (such as Castor Oil). "NO, PLEASE, NOT CASTOR OIL!"

- **SUGGESTED DAILY PLAN:** • **7:00** breathing (&/or yoga) exercises. • **8:00** glass of warm herb tea. • **9:00** cleanse bowels with enema - Dry brush massage (& hot then cold shower). • **10:00** glass of warm herb tea. • **11:00** moderate physical exercise (e.g. swimming). • **12:00** glass of fresh fruit juice (diluted 50% with spring water). • **13:00** rest/read. • **14:00** glass of fresh vegetable juice. • **15:00** moderate physical exercise (e.g. walking). • **16:00** glass of fresh fruit juice (diluted 50% with spring water). • **17:00** breathing (&/or yoga) exercises. • **18:00** glass of fresh vegetable juice. • **19:00** manipulative massage & therapeutic bath. • **20:00** glass of warm vegetable broth. • **21:00** bed.

- **AFTER FINISHING** gradually (**one piece of fruit or a small bowl of salad etc. per meal**) re-introduce solid foods at meal times - BE SURE TO CHEW THEM ALL VERY WELL - This (in addition to juices) should continue for 2 days - Then return to a normal diet.

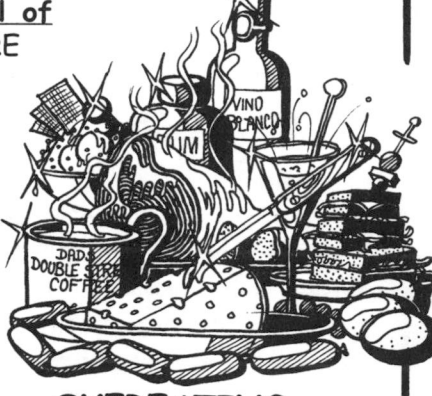

ENEMAS

- **ARTIFICIAL FLUSHING OF THE BOWEL** is considered important when fasting - This is because with no feces being passed **toxins accumulate & can putrefy, sometimes dangerously.**
- **HOW?**... A plastic or rubber bag is filled with warm (100 degrees F) water (1-2 pints) with a few drops of lemon juice (or some Camomile Tea) in & hung 2-3ft. above the kneeling body - The bag has a hose & nozzle which is inserted into the anus **& gravity fed into the bowels** - Retain liquid for a short while - Turn over & massage stomach - Then go to toilet & empty bowels.
- **CAUTION: Do not take enemas routinely for prolonged periods** as: a) They weaken the bowel emptying muscles - b) **ARE CONSIDERED HABIT FORMING.**

OVEREATING....

....**is detrimental to health & life expectancy** in normal circumstances - BUT **after a fast it is particularly vital to:** a) Eat moderate quantities - b) Eat a carefully selected natural diet (Macrobiotic or similar).

DRY SKIN BRUSHING

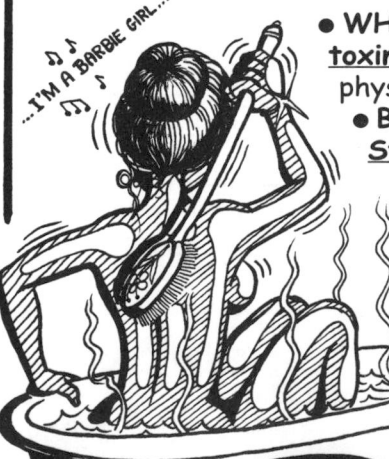

- **WHY?**... **The skin continuously eliminates toxins & waste products thru its surface**, but dead skin cells (unless physically removed) WILL CLOG & RESTRICT THIS PROCESS.
- **BENEFITS** - **Loosens** & removes dead skin cells - **Increases** blood flow - **Stimulates** oil & hormone glands - **Rejuvenates** the nervous system (thru the nerve endings) all over the skin.
- **WITH** any medium stiff natural fiber brush (preferably long handled [no synthetics]). • **HOW?**... With a vigorous circular movement - Brush whole body for about 10 minutes (skin should glow) - **Start from feet**, legs, hands, arms, buttocks, back, tummy, chest, neck, face. • **WHEN?**... Before going to bed (&/or on rising).
- **AFTER** - Take a hot (then cold) shower to remove any remaining loose/dead skin cells. "WOW! FEELIN' GOOOOD!"

- **CAUTION: Fasting is not considered advisable if pregnant** or suffering from cancer/major organ disease etc. (seek "expert" advice).

THE EXTRACTED AROMATIC OILS OF PLANTS & SPICES *have been used therapeutically since before the pyramids of Egypt were built!*

GENERAL PRINCIPLES

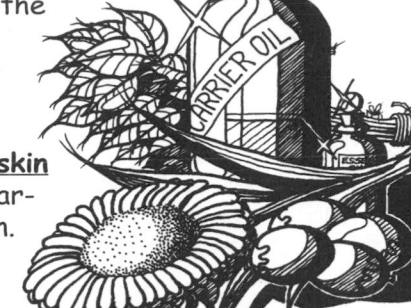

- **WHAT DO THEY DO?**... By penetrating the skin during massage (& the lungs during inhalation), they are absorbed into the body, effecting "the whole" & specific areas (e.g. circulation, respiratory, nervous, hormonal etc.) according to the oil used. ALSO VERY PSYCHOLOGICALLY RELAXING (& HEALING).
- **HOW IS IT MADE?**... With some difficulty by cold pressing, distillation or dissolving - Yielding usually less than 1 % of the plant part being treated - Thus being very concentrated (& sometimes expensive).
- **HOW IS IT USED?**... **In its pure form, essential oils may burn the skin** & are therefore usually diluted in sterile water (for bathing) - Or in a carrier oil (e.g. sunflower or olive) for massage &/or therapeutic application.
  - **STORE** in opaque (or dark) stoppered glass containers - **At not more than 20 degrees C (70 degrees F).**

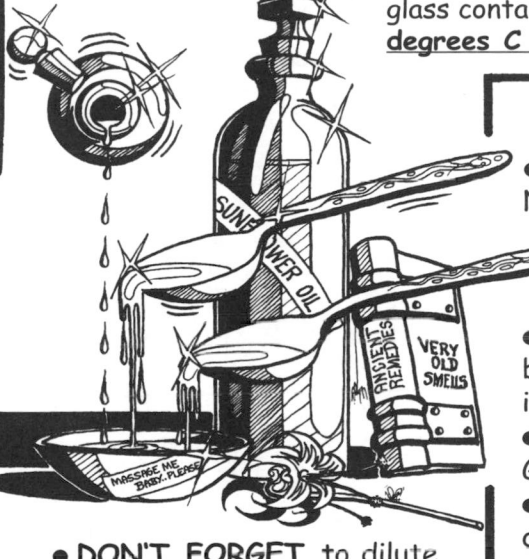

- **DON'T FORGET** to dilute essential oils for massage uses.

SELECTED EXTERNAL REMEDIES

- **ACNE** - Dab effected areas with 10% essential oil of JUNIPER in an olive oil carrier.
  - **BATH** (skin tonic) - Into a half full bath of warm water add 250g of sodium bicarbonate, & 15g essential oil of LEMON. "VEERY RELAXING!"
- **BOILS** (& wounds) - Boil a sliced ONION in a little water & bathe the boil with the water (hot) - Wounds (bathe warm if infection present, & cold if not).... Avoid dietry sugar with boils.
- **BREASTS** (congestion) - Bathe with 1g of essential oil of GERANIUM in 1 pint of warm water.
- **BURNS** - Bathe with 2% essential oil of either GERANIUM or ROSEMARY in sterile water & paint with either 10% essential oil of Geranium or LAVENDER (or 5% essential oil of Rosemary in olive oil carriers).

- **CATARRH** - Mix one drop each of EUCALYPTUS, CAMOMILE, LAVENDER & either TEA TREE or PEPPERMINT essential oils with 2 teaspoons of a carrier oil (e.g. sunflower) & massage into chest (or upper back) - This combination of oils can also be used as a steam inhalation with a pint of boiling water (put a towel over your head & breathe deeply).
- **CHILBLAINS** - Apply 10% of either ROSEMARY, LEMON or ROSEWOOD & CYPRESS essential oil(s) mixed in an olive or sunflower carrier - **If skin broken use lemon & keep warm not hot/cold.**
  - **COLD - FLU** - Combine 1 drop each of TEA TREE & EUCALYPTUS & 2 drops of LAVENDER essential oils in 1 1/2 teaspoons of a carrier oil - Massage on chest, upper back, soles of feet & palms of hands - Anticongestion, antibacteria & antifungal.
  - **COUGHS** - Add 2 or 3 drops each of SANDALWOOD & FRANKINCENSE essential oils to a pint of boiling water - Use as a steam inhalation (put a towel over your head & breathe deeply). "OH YES! FEEL MUUCH BETTER."
    - **DERMATITIS** - Bathe with 2% essential oil of SASSAFRAS in sterile (boiled) water....ALSO CHECK CAREFULLY FOR ALLERGIES.
    - **ECZEMA** (dry) - Bathe with 2% essential oil of SAGE in sterile water - Dress with 10% sage in an olive oil carrier. Also cut out dietary animal fats.

PUT A TOWEL OVER YOUR HEAD.

continued

continued ————→ ● <u>ECZEMA</u> (weeping) - Bathe with 10% essential oil of JUNIPER in sterile (boiled) water. <u>Also again cut out dietry animal fats (incl.dairy)</u>

● <u>HERPES</u> - Bathe with 2% essential oil of either LEMON or GERANIUM in sterile (boiled) water.

● <u>INSECT STINGS</u> - Apply to the bite (or sting) one drop neat of any of the following essential oils: BASIL, LAVENDER, LEMON, SASSAFRAS or SAGE.

● <u>INSECT REPELLANT</u> - Scatter a few drops of essential oil of PEPPERMINT on clothes (&/or bed sheets) - <u>Works well with mosquitoes.</u>

● <u>LOST VOICE</u> - Gargle with 2% essential oil of SAGE in sterile (boiled) water.

● <u>NAILS</u> (brittle) - Apply 10% essential oil of LEMON in a warm olive oil carrier (see also p. 202).

● <u>SPORTS INJURIES</u> (sprains, bruises, impact grazes etc.) - Apply compress with 2% essential oil of LAVENDER (antiseptic & anti-inflammatory) in cold water.

● <u>SKIN PROBLEMS</u> (General) - Dab on 5% of essential oil of CAJEPUT in a sweet almond oil carrier (see also ALOE VERA).

● <u>SORE THROAT</u> - Gargle with 2% essential oil of LEMON in sterile (boiled) water.

● <u>WARTS</u> - Dab on essential oil of LEMON neat. <u>(Also avoid overeating).</u>

● <u>WOUNDS</u> - Bathe with 2% essential oil of either CLOVES, SAGE, HYSSOP, ROSEMARY, GERANIUM, SAVORY or LAVENDER in sterile water - Dress with 10% geranium, lavender or savory in olive oil carrier.

● <u>WOUNDS</u> (bleeding) - To slow bleeding (& clean) - Bathe with 2% essential oil of LEMON in sterile (boiled) water.

● <u>PIMPLES</u> - Bathe with 2% essential oil of LAVENDER in sterile (boiled) water.

● <u>SLEEP WELL</u> with a relaxing & antiseptic drop each of CHAMOMILE & LAVENDER essential oils on your pillow. "ZZZZ."

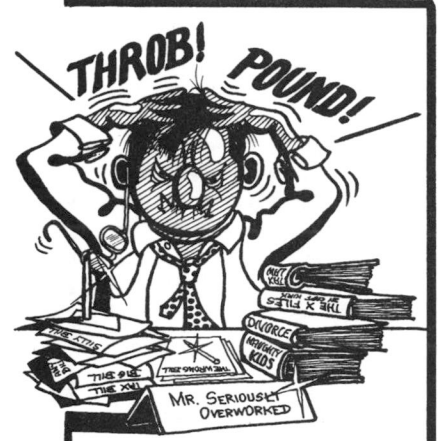

● <u>HEADACHE</u> - Add one drop of essential oil of LAVENDER or PEPPERMINT to 1/3 of a teaspoon of carrier oil - Massage into temples. "MMMM."

● <u>RHEUMATISM giving trouble?</u> - Any of the following essential oils LAUREL, NUTMEG, CARAWAY, GINGER, CAJEPUT or CORIANDER mixed (at 10%) with a warm olive oil carrier & massaged in will help. "AAAA."

● <u>SICK ROOMS</u> - A few drops of SANDALWOOD will freshen the air. "HEY I FEEL BETTER ALREADY!"

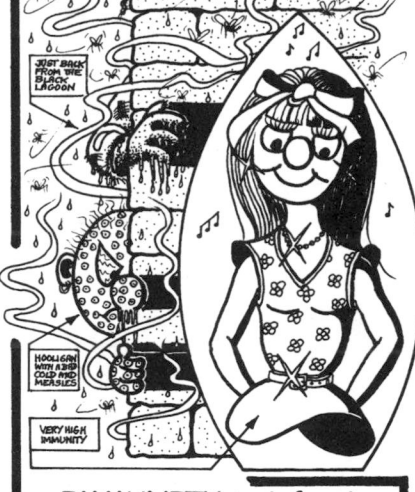

● <u>IMMUNITY</u> to infection can be improved (& general well-being enhanced) by combining 3 drops of essential oils of TEA TREE &/or EUCALYPTUS with 2 teaspoons of a carrier oil - Massage it into glands in groin & neck - Also into soles of feet & palms - Morning & night for a week or so. "YESSSS."

● <u>SNAKEBITE - Promote bleeding - Bathe with sterile (boiled) water</u> - Dab on neat essential oil of LAVENDER (mixed with either CINNAMON or ASPIC) or BASIL.

● NOTE: Many essential oils (being herbal extracts) are also used internally - <u>BUT do not attempt to self-prescribe without research (or consultation) AS SOME ARE TOXIC IF MISUSED.</u>

Multiple Benefits From This Simplified Study Of Techniques

A COMPLEX TRADITION OF CONTROL - Encompassing physical, mental & spiritual well being - Yoga reputedly originated in NE India well OVER 5,000 YEARS AGO.

BEFORE STARTING

● **WHEN TO DO IT?** - Although early morning is ideal, any time will do, **except 1-4 hours (depending on size & type) after a meal** at which time the body's energy if diverted from digestion to physical activity will impair the METABOLISM OF NUTRIENTS.

● **WHERE?** - **Indoors:** A quiet, warm place with good air (ideally a wooden floor) - **Outside:** an isolated, peaceful (& if possible beautiful) location with CLEAN AIR (NOT COLD OR WINDY).

● **HOW LONG/OFTEN?** - First select those postures which suit your needs best & assume those **from 10 seconds to several minutes** each (depending on circumstances) - Then allowing for a short warm-up of stretches (at the start) & a few minutes in the relaxation posture (at the end) **your yoga session should take from 10-60 minutes, at least once a day**.

● **WEAR as little as possible** (loose fitting) & bare feet - Use towel &/or cushion on hard floors - **DON'T GET COLD.**

● **HOW TO BREATHE DURING YOGA** - **As a general rule breathe in when** stretching up or out (with arms or body) - **& breathe out when** bending over (forward) or bringing arms or legs into (or across) chest or stomach - Breathe naturally (relaxed) - BUT fill & empty the rib cage & abdomen fully with each breath - **Breathing sequence** times range from **BEGINNER:** In = 3 secs., out = 3 secs. - **EXPERT:** In = 8 secs., hold = 32 secs., out = 16 secs., hold = 4 secs.

● **WHAT TO THINK DURING YOGA?** - To obtain maximum benefit, concentrate on breathing sequences & the following categories of thought - **INHALING** (energizes): imagine/visualize energy, health **flowing into your body** - **EXHALING** (calms): imagine/visualize all disease, toxicity & negative thoughts (incl. stress) **flowing out of your body**. DON'T NEGLECT THIS IMPORTANT ASPECT.

THE LOCUST

● **HINTS** - **If you have high blood pressure** BE CAREFUL WITH THIS.
● **BENEFITS** - Strengthens entire back (& makes spine supple) - Also buttocks & backs of thighs - Adrenal glands - Lungs - Bladder - Organs of abdomen - Circulation - Sexuality - Digestion.

STRAIGHT

● GREAT FOR LOWER BACK (DO EVERY AM & PM)

THE COBRA

● **HINTS** - Start by lying on floor (facedown) with hands under shoulders - **Use back muscles for lift & arms for support** - KEEP HIPS DOWN & HEAD UP.
● **BENEFITS** - Relaxes - Strengthens - Elongates & aligns back (spine) & neck - Also for Indigestion - Abdominal organs - Adrenal glands - Chest expansion - Flexibility & wind.

"CLICK!"

● BE VERY CAREFUL W/ THIS AT FIRST

THE PLOW

● **HINTS** - Arms/hands can be reversed to grasp toes to - a) Complete energy flows - b) Stimulate pressure points - c) For balance.
● **BENEFITS** - Thyroid gland - Neck - Spine - Back - Circulation - Sore throat - Shoulders - Headache - Bloating - Fever - Brain - Fear.
Varicose veins - Urination - Anxiety - Eyes.

U CAN PUT KNEES DOWN HERE ALSO

● STRETCHES <u>ALL</u> OF SPINE

SHOULDER STAND

● **HINTS** - Can be used in less vertical position according to ability.
● **BENEFITS** - Thyroid gland - Arm/Neck/Shoulder problems - The brain - Energy levels - Varicose veins - Sexuality - Dropped stomach organs - Circulation - Rejuvenation - Constipation - Dyspepsia - Resistance to colds - Nerves - Sore throats - Anger - Eyes - Heart. **(Feel your neck & upper spine STR....ETCH)**

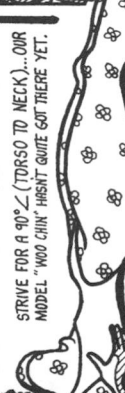

STRIVE FOR A 90° ∠ (TORSO TO NECK)...OUR MODEL "WOO CHIN" HASN'T QUITE GOT THERE YET.

THE BOW

- **HINTS** - More difficult - **Use back muscles for lift** (& arms only for assist & balance).
- **BENEFITS** - Sexuality - Digestive organs - Circulation - Opens rib cage - Central nervous system - Stretches all muscles along front of body - Supple spine - Back & neck muscles - Endocrine glands - Constipation - Brain.

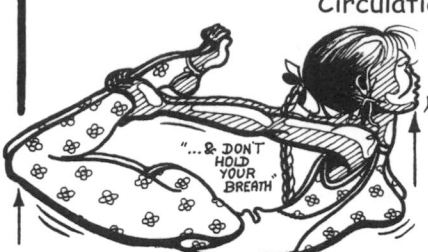

"...& DON'T HOLD YOUR BREATH"

FORWARD STRETCH

- **HINTS** - Bend with trunk **NOT by pulling with arms** - Twin this posture with "Cobra" after.
- **BENEFITS** - Flexibility - Bladder & abdominal organs - Sexuality - Knee problems - Fatigue - Hemorrhoids - Heart - Sciatica - Circulation to feet - Muscular cramps (calves & instep etc.) - Stiffness - Lumbago - Digestion.

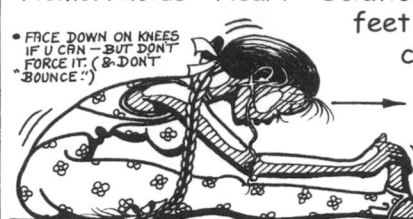

• FACE DOWN ON KNEES IF U CAN - BUT DON'T FORCE IT. (& DON'T "BOUNCE.")

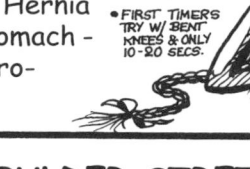

THREE VALUABLE SITTING POSTURES

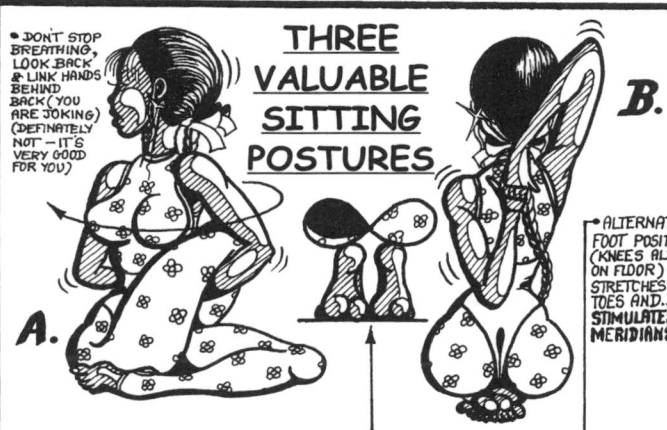

• DON'T STOP BREATHING, LOOK BACK & LINK HANDS BEHIND BACK (YOU ARE JOKING) (DEFINATELY NOT — IT'S VERY GOOD FOR YOU)

B.

→ ALTERNATE FOOT POSITION (KNEES ALSO ON FLOOR) — STRETCHES TOES AND.. STIMULATES MERIDIANS.

A.

C.

A. **SPINAL TWIST** - Comprehensive stretch & flexibility posture with many other benefits (including abdominal organs).

B. **COW STRETCH** - Stretch & flexibility (for arms & shoulders) & alternate crossed feet for: Fits - Cramps - Abdominal pains - Middle back pain - Circulation - Vertigo & madness.

C. **LOTUS** - Mainly a meditation posture but also benefits general health.

THIS REQUIRES LOTS OF PRACTICE (BUT IF YOUR KNEE JOINTS HURT DO EVERY 2ND DAY)

HEADSTAND

- **HINT** - Beginners do in a corner - Interlock fingers behind head - **Do NOT use if you have high blood pressure - Detached retina - Glaucoma - Period - Concussion etc.**
- **BENEFITS** - Pituitary gland - Circulation - Varicose veins - Organs of abdomen - Headache - Hernia - Asthma - Dropped stomach - Pineal gland - Mental processes.

• FIRST TIMERS TRY W/ BENT KNEES & ONLY 10-20 SECS.

SHOULDER STRETCH

•DON'T WORRY IF YOUR SPINE GOES **"CLICK."**

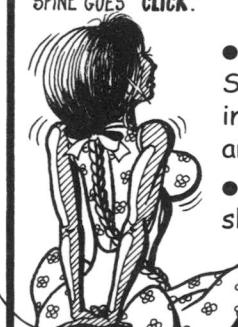

- **HINTS** - Link fingers palm up - Shoulders back & up - Head back inhale & move linked hands (with arms straight) away from body.
- **BENEFITS** - Strain/pain of shoulder/upper back - Resistance to illness - Breathing - Heart problems - Asthma - Colds/Bronchial problems - Posture - Flexibility.

SPINAL ROCKING

- **HINTS** - Select acupressure points on feet or knee (St. 36) to stimulate during rocking.
- **BENEFITS** - Wide ranging **as entire spine is massaged** including all pressure points thereon relating to many different bodily functions (also very good for fatigue & tension).

St.36

GOOD FOR: COUGHS, HIGH BLOOD PR., IMPOTENCE, STOMACH & HEADACHE.

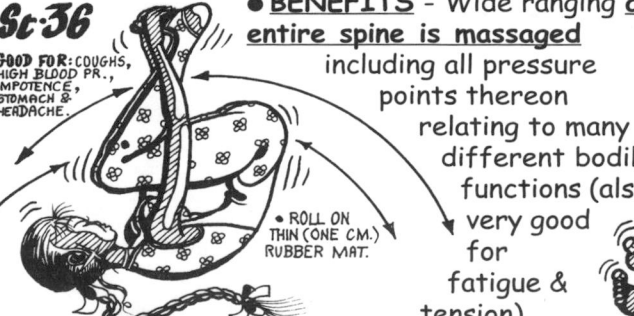

• ROLL ON THIN (ONE CM.) RUBBER MAT.

RELAXATION

- **HINTS** - Use after (& if required during) exercise - Feet out & palms up - **Keep warm** - Start with toes & consciously relax body parts ending with scalp/eyes - **Count backward at 2 second intervals, (mentally) doubling relaxation** at every count - When coming out of relaxed state breathe deeply & slowly for several minutes.
- **BENEFITS** - Maximizes other postures.

•LIE ON HARD BUT PADDED SURFACE..& WOD CHIN PRESS YOUR LOWER BACK DOWN & TURN YOUR PALMS OVER

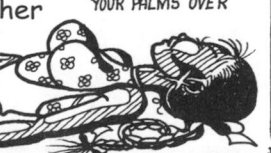

STUDY "NING" (the Ningpo Cat) - How can she be so apparently lazy (& inactive), yet remain so supple (& lightning fast)? - Her secret can (with practice) be yours

WHAT WILL IT DO FOR ME ?

- **STIMULATE** BLOOD (& NUTRIENT) CIRCULATION with **multiple** benefits.
- **PROMOTE** MENTAL (& spiritual) WELL-BEING by approximating various yoga positions.
- **STRENGTHENS** MUSCLES, LIGAMENTS & BONES - **Helps prevent injury.**
- **STIMULATE** ACUPRESSURE MERIDIANS - Thus **boosting metabolism (& immunity).**
- **PROGRESSIVELY** **improve flexibility well into old age.**
- **DRAMATICALLY** **reduce muscle tension** - Improves physical relaxation/MENTAL CALM.
- **IMPROVES** coordination - & THUS SPORT/PHYSICAL PERFORMANCE.

HOW DO I DO THEM ?

- **GENTLY** **& don't bounce** (to avoid tearing muscle fibers - **WHICH ACTUALLY REDUCES FLEXIBILITY.**)
- **PROGRESSIVELY** (as flexibility increases) - **But only until mild tension is felt each time.**
- **BREATHE** out when first bending trunk forward (or bringing limbs across trunk) - Breathe in when first straightening trunk (or moving limbs away from trunk) - **In either case continue breathing slowly & deeply thereafter.**
- **DURATION:** From 15 seconds (for loosening up) - To 60+ seconds (for increased range).

"FLOP THE RICE SACK"
(Neck - Shoulders)

....With back straight, very slowly roll/loll in a circle (4 times in each direction) - Pausing at any position with tension. "VEERY RELAXING."

"FLOAT IN RIVER"

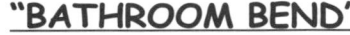

— STRETCH —

1 (All longitudinal muscles & ligaments) ....**On a hard floor** lie on back & stretch arms & feet in opposite directions - 4 stretches of 4 seconds each (pause between).

"YES SIR"
(Biceps - Forearms - Rib Cage - Pectorals - Shoulders)

....With fingers **(palm up)** interlinked behind back, twist arms to bring **palms down** - Then raise arms (keep chin down) - Very good for posture - Do whenever you find yourself slumping - **Extra effective for ladies bustlines & manly pectorals** (hold 15 secs.).

9.

"BATHROOM BEND"
(Knees - Lower Back - Shins - Groin - Ankles - Antilles Tendons)

....With knees above toes **(& outside shoulders)** - Squat with curved back (& loose arms) for 60+ secs -**Very good for low back tension.**

5.

TIP: USE THIS POSITION ON **ALL** SUSPECT TOILETS WHEN TRAVELLING.

"TREE IN WIND"
(Sides of Arm/ Shoulder/Waist/ Hip - Spine/Back)

....Link hands above head & lean sideways for 15 seconds each side (pull one hand with the other) - Feet straight ahead (& apart) - **Knees slightly bent** - Also good for waist.

7.

"DAWN STAR"
(Low Back - Hip Side - Bottom - Hamstrings - Neck)
....With shoulders flat on floor **bring one knee across body & grip foot on floor (difficult)** - Stretch opposite arm (palm down) & leg straight - Turn head to that **side** - Hold 20-40 secs. **(each side).**

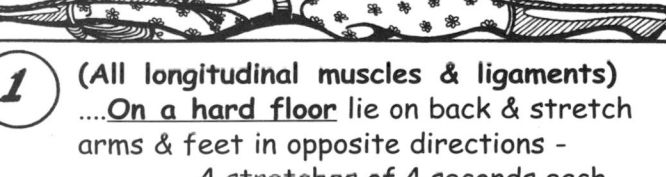

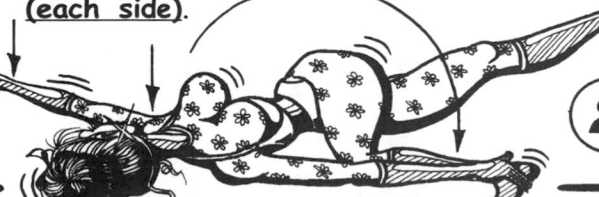

2.

A TRAVELER'S CONCISE GUIDE TO THERAPEUTIC STRETCHING
Simple Stretching Techniques To Revitalize Your Body

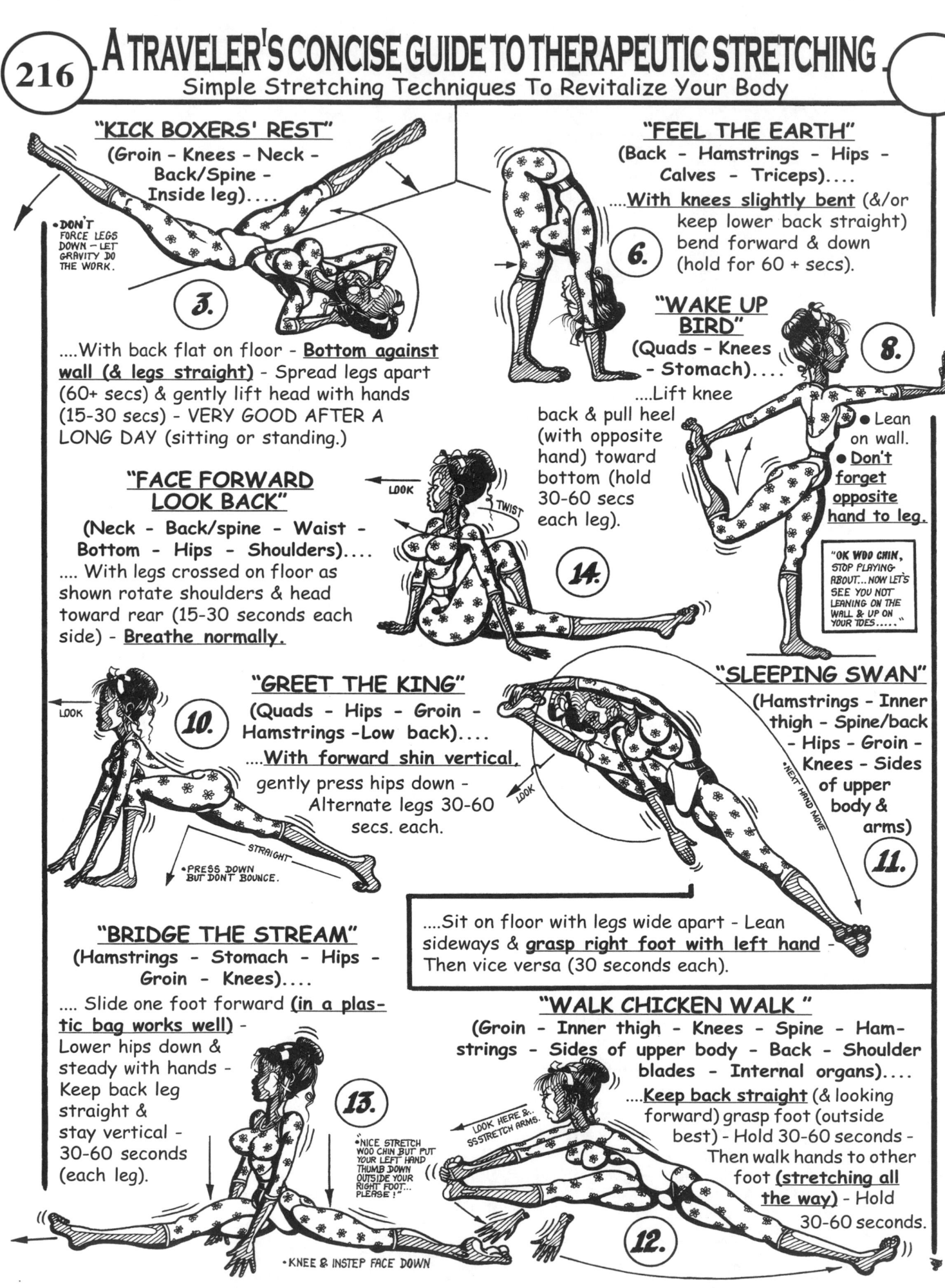

"KICK BOXERS' REST"
(Groin - Knees - Neck - Back/Spine - Inside leg)....

• DON'T FORCE LEGS DOWN — LET GRAVITY DO THE WORK.

3.

....With back flat on floor - **Bottom against wall (& legs straight)** - Spread legs apart (60+ secs) & gently lift head with hands (15-30 secs) - VERY GOOD AFTER A LONG DAY (sitting or standing.)

"FACE FORWARD LOOK BACK"
(Neck - Back/spine - Waist - Bottom - Hips - Shoulders)....
.... With legs crossed on floor as shown rotate shoulders & head toward rear (15-30 seconds each side) - **Breathe normally.**

LOOK
TWIST
14.

"GREET THE KING"
(Quads - Hips - Groin - Hamstrings -Low back)....
....With forward shin vertical, gently press hips down - Alternate legs 30-60 secs. each.

LOOK
10.

STRAIGHT
• PRESS DOWN BUT DON'T BOUNCE.

"BRIDGE THE STREAM"
(Hamstrings - Stomach - Hips - Groin - Knees)....

.... Slide one foot forward **(in a plastic bag works well)** - Lower hips down & steady with hands - Keep back leg straight & stay vertical - 30-60 seconds (each leg).

13.

•NICE STRETCH WOO CHIN BUT PUT YOUR LEFT HAND THUMB DOWN OUTSIDE YOUR RIGHT FOOT... PLEASE !"

•KNEE & INSTEP FACE DOWN

"FEEL THE EARTH"
(Back - Hamstrings - Hips - Calves - Triceps)....
....**With knees slightly bent** (&/or keep lower back straight) bend forward & down (hold for 60 + secs).

6.

"WAKE UP BIRD"
(Quads - Knees - Stomach)....
....Lift knee back & pull heel (with opposite hand) toward bottom (hold 30-60 secs each leg).

8.

• Lean on wall.
• **Don't forget opposite hand to leg.**

"OK WOO CHIN, STOP PLAYING ABOUT... NOW LET'S SEE YOU NOT LEANING ON THE WALL & UP ON YOUR TOES....."

"SLEEPING SWAN"
(Hamstrings - Inner thigh - Spine/back - Hips - Groin - Knees - Sides of upper body & arms)

•NEXT HAND MOVE

LOOK

11.

....Sit on floor with legs wide apart - Lean sideways & **grasp right foot with left hand** - Then vice versa (30 seconds each).

"WALK CHICKEN WALK "
(Groin - Inner thigh - Knees - Spine - Hamstrings - Sides of upper body - Back - Shoulder blades - Internal organs)....
....**Keep back straight** (& looking forward) grasp foot (outside best) - Hold 30-60 seconds - Then walk hands to other foot **(stretching all the way)** - Hold 30-60 seconds.

LOOK HERE &: SSSTRETCH ARMS.

12.

Balancing Yin & Yang For A Long & Healthy Life

THE TAO (WAY) ORIGINATED +/- 10,000 years ago & is based on principles which are as simple (or complex) as you make them.

A SIMPLIFIED CHANG MING HEALTH REGIME

Illness is caused by imbalance	Health is gained thru balance

DON'T EAT

- Coffee
- Alcohol
- Soft drinks
- Chocolate
- Sweets
- Fudge etc.
- Preservatives
- Colorings
- Processed (& Refined foods)
- Tomatoes
- Potatoes
- Eggplant
- Animal fat
- Lard
- Dripping
- Butter
- Dairy cheese (& yogurt)
- Ice cream
- Lollipops
- Pudding
- Sugar
- Molasses
- Sweeteners
- Animal Meat (pork, beef etc.)
- Birds (& fish) with high fat levels
- Meat extract (soups & gravies)
- Spices
- Peppers
- Curries
- All white flours (& grains)
- Salmon
- Mackerel
- Tuna
- Shark
- All deep-fried foods
- Cream
- Spinach
- Rhubarb
- Cucumber

DO EAT

- Any natural (unrefined) grain
- Brown rice
- Wheat (buckwheat etc.)
- Bread
- Cake etc. (made from above)
- Omelettes or scrambled eggs only
- Vegetables in season (except at left)
- Carrots
- Onions
- Burdock etc.
- Vegetable oils (& margarines)
- Sunflower
- Sesame
- Safflower
- Soya & mung bean shoots
- Some unsalted roasted nuts
- Undyed china & herb teas
- Vegetarian & low fat cottage cheese
- Natural low fat yogurt
- Soya sauce
- A little gomasio
- A little local fruit in season
- Herbs (thyme, parsley, ginger etc.)
- Seaweed
- A little dried fruit

USE SPARINGLY

ANIMAL	VEGETABLE	FRUIT	OTHER
• Low fat fish	• Celery • Radish	• Durian	• Skimmed milk
• Low fat birds	• Garlic	• Coconut	• Natural honey
• Lobster	• Green peas	• Apricot	• Almond • Hazel
• Turkey • Duck	• Most beans	• Peach	• Sea salt
• Partridge	• Red cabbage	• Lime • Melon	• Raw vegetables

USE RARELY

• Crab meat	• Bamboo shoots	• Banana • Fig	• Very hot liquids
• Pigeon • Hare	• Sweet potatoes	• Pineapple	• Cold food/drink
• Chicken	• Asparagus	• Grapefruit	• Peanut • Cashew
• Mussels • Clam	• Artichoke	• Orange • Pear	• Fruit juices
• Snail • Frog	• Mushrooms	• Mango • Papaya	• Other milk

FOUR GOLDEN RULES

- **DRINK SPARINGLY** - Not before an hour after eating (dramatically improves digestion).
- **NEVER OVEREAT** - and anyway stop before being full (dramatically reduces toxin buildup).
- **BREATHE COMPLETELY** (from abdomen) - At all times (invigorates entire metabolism).
- **CHEW ALL FOOD** very well - Until no lumps remain (dramatically reduces digestive loads).

SOME VERY YANG FOOD & DRINK

- Apple
- Strawberry
- Ginseng
- Goat cheese
- Mu tea
- Pheasant
- Burdock
- Watercress
- Carrot
- Dandelion root coffee
- Pumpkin
- Sardine
- Turkey
- Shrimp
- Snapper
- Eggs

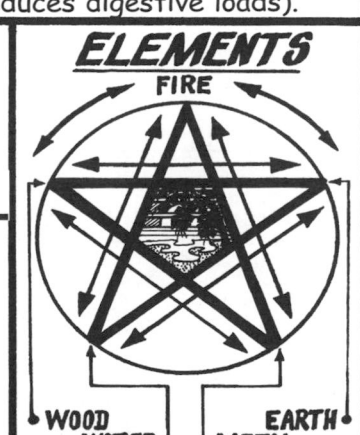

ELEMENTS

FIRE

WOOD
WATER

EARTH
METAL

POINTS TO REMEMBER

- **IT IS NEVER TOO LATE TO MAKE AN EFFORT IN LIFE** - But toxins (& damage) require time to be eliminated - For example, <u>it takes your body about 3 months to banish all traces of 1 aspirin!</u> - & about 3 years to banish 1 trip on cocaine! (or 1 cortisone injection) - YOUR HEALTH IS IN YOUR OWN HANDS!

A SIMPLIFIED ORDER 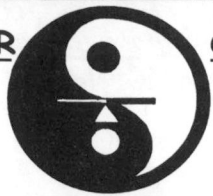 OF THE UNIVERSE

- NOTHING IS IDENTICAL.
- EVERYTHING CHANGES.
- Opposites are complementary.

- That with a front has a back.
- Bigger front - Bigger back.
- That with a start has an end.

● ALL THINGS ARE VARIATIONS OF ONE INFINITY ●

YIN ATTRACTS YANG - YANG ATTRACTS YIN - YIN REPELS YIN - YANG REPELS YANG.

- BIG YIN ATTRACTS SMALL YIN - BIG YANG ATTRACTS SMALL YANG.
- NOTHING IS TOTALLY YIN - NOTHING IS TOTALLY YANG.
- EXTREME YIN PRODUCES YANG - EXTREME YANG PRODUCES YIN.
- PHYSICALLY THE SURFACE IS YIN AND THE CENTER IS YANG.
- EITHER YIN OR YANG IS ALWAYS MORE OR LESS.
- EVERYTHING IS CHANGING FROM YIN TO YANG OR VICE VERSA.
- CHANGE IS PROPORTIONAL TO THE STATUS QUO OF YIN & YANG.

A SIMPLIFIED TABLE OF YIN - YANG VALUES

	VERY YANG	YANG	MIDDLE	YIN	VERY YIN
Element	Wood	Fire	Earth	Metal	Water
Day	Morning	Noon	Afternoon	Evening	Night
Planet	Jupiter	Mars	Saturn	Venus	Mercury
Season	Spring	Summer	Late summer	Autumn	Winter
Emotion	Shouting	Laughing	Singing	Weeping	Groaning
Color	Green	Red	Yellow	White	Black
Organ	Liver	Heart	Spleen	Lungs	Kidneys
Climate	Heat	Wind	Humid	Cold	Ice
Fluids	Tears	Sweat	Saliva	Mucus	Urine
Senses	Sight	Hearing	Taste	Smell	Touch
Direction	East	South	Equator	West	North
Tendency	Implosion	Contraction	Stability	Growth	Expansion
Drinks	Ginseng	Mu tea	Thyme	Beer	Coffee
Dairy	Goat's milk	Veg. cheese	Skim milk	Yogurt	Butter
Fruit	Apple	Strawberry	Olive	Peach	Orange
Vegetable	Leek	Carrot	Onion	Garlic	Potato
Meat	Pheasant	Turkey	Chicken	Rabbit	Pork-Beef

A SIMPLIFIED GUIDE TO THE NATURE OF YIN - YANG

	YANG	YIN		YANG	YIN
Speed	Fast	Slow	**Sex**	Male	Female
Length	Short	Long	**Attitude**	Aggressive	Defensive
Size	Small	Big	**Nature**	Alkaline	Acidic
Weight	Heavy	Light	**Outlook**	Material	Spiritual
Structure	Hard	Soft	**Dimension**	Time	Space
Light	Light	Dark	**Humidity**	Dry	Wet
Temperature	Hot	Cold	**Time**	Past	Future
Direction	Down-Side	Up	**Particle**	Proton	Electron
Frequency	Low	High	**Taste**	Salt	Sweet

OUT (BREATH)
& IN.... (SLOW)

P.D.   P.D.

1.

HORSE (STANCE)

(PALM POSITION)

OUT & IN...

P.U.   P.D.

2.

CAT

MIND POWER

● **IN ASIA** it is called Ki or Chi - In the West, will or spirit, even life force - <u>Whatever name you favor ITS EFFECT ON YOUR LIFE IS LITERALLY PROFOUND.</u>

NEGATIVE THOUGHTS SHORTEN LIFE

● **EACH OF US** has a unique genetic code (different from everyone else) which is our "program" for life (& death) - <u>BUT the mind is an incredibly powerful tool</u> - For example, a healthy person who genuinely believes themselves ill (or old, or without hope) will, in a surprisingly short time actually develop symptoms of that situation - & seeing such evidence of decline, <u>WILL SPIRAL EVER DEEPER DOWN.</u>

POSITIVE THOUGHTS EXTEND LIFE

● **THEREFORE,** fellow passenger, thru time - Make use of this amazing & proven adaptability of life - <u>EXTEND YOUR HEALTH & HAPPINESS BY:</u>

IMMUNITY DRAINS

- ○ **DON'T** be a sacrificial goat for others.
- ○ **DON'T** live in the past (plan for future).
- ○ **DON'T** be elitist (tolerate differences).
- ○ **DON'T** hold grudges/anger (let it go).
- ○ **DON'T** be bullied (action defeats fear).
- ○ **DON'T** be a 100% perfectionist.
- ○ **DON'T** keep sorrow (cry & let go).
- ○ **DON'T** worry (do something).
- ○ **DON'T** overwork (designate).
- ○ **DON'T** take criticisms to heart.
- ○ **DON'T** be obsessively neat.
- ○ **DON'T** ever get depressed.

IMMUNITY BOOSTS

- ○ **DO** always have an exciting future goal.
- ○ **DO** love & be loved (in family or group).
- ○ **DO** have mental/actual security (on any income).
- ○ **DO** be confident & pleasantly self-assertive.
- ○ **DO** be an individual (dare to be different).
- ○ **DO** practice prompt decision making.
- ○ **DO** stay calm inside during conflict.
- ○ **DO** relax/have fun without guilt.
- ○ **DO** practise healing visualization.
- ○ **DO** ask for help unashamedly.
- ○ **DO** develop quiet self-esteem.
- ○ **DO** be an outrageous optimist.

PLACE POWER

● <u>**ENVIRONMENT has a massive effect on our immunity levels**</u> - Which with widely snowballing permeation of our "modern" world from chemical, radiated & other pollutants devastate our health & shorten our lives by huge portions - Is it any wonder that toxin-related diseases such as cancer & birth defects are so feared today?

● <u>**HORRIFYINGLY simple examples of how we daily deplete immunity are:**</u> - Plastic covers/bags, furniture, foam etc. emit allergenic Formaldehyde Gas - Microwave exposure can cause cancer &/or birth defects - Professional painters have a 40% higher risk of lung cancer than average - <u>**Over 50% (& rising) of all food, water (including rain) & air in our world is now polluted by varying amounts of PESTICIDES/CHEMICALS/HEAVY METALS.**</u>

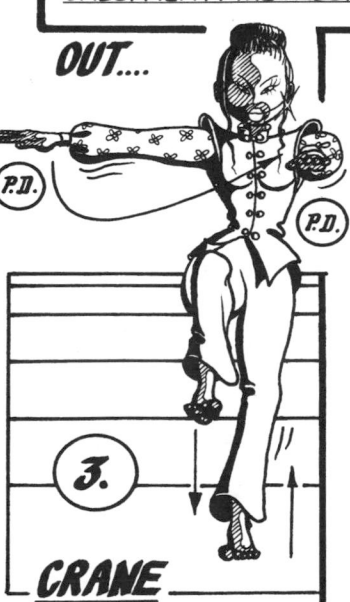

OUT....

P.D.   P.D.

3.

CRANE

DON'T

- ○ **DON'T** live near factories.
- ○ **DON'T** live in big cities.
- ○ **DON'T** work in heavy industry/construction.
- ○ **DON'T** live near a tip.
- ○ **DON'T** live anywhere near nuclear power stations.
- ○ **DON'T** live/work near pylons/transformers etc.
- ○ **DON'T** work/live near/with granite rock (Radon).
- ○ **DON'T** live/work near intensive farming (pesticide vapors).
- ○ **DON'T** have anything to do with asbestos (on roofs, round pipes).
- ○ **DON'T** use fly sprays (swat).
- ○ **DON'T** use cosmetics/soaps with chemicals.
- ○ **DON'T** live/work around Formaldehyde plastics (packing/cavity walls).

DO

- ○ **DO** heat with central (not in room) fuel burning.
- ○ **DO** avoid breathing in paint/thinner vapors.
- ○ **DO** avoid using garden chemicals/weed killers.
- ○ **DO** avoid exercise in polluted/dusty air.
- ○ **DO** place your bed away from sockets/appliances.
- ○ **DO** avoid wearing dry cleaned clothes (solvents).
- ○ **DO** avoid regular long city commuting journeys.
- ○ **DO** clean home etc. with vinegar/baking soda etc.
- ○ **DO** try to sleep with window open (oxygen).
- ○ **DO** avoid smoky rooms/bars & people.
- ○ **DO** use air-conditioned transport in cities.
- ○ **DO** avoid D.I.Y dusts/glues/solvents etc.

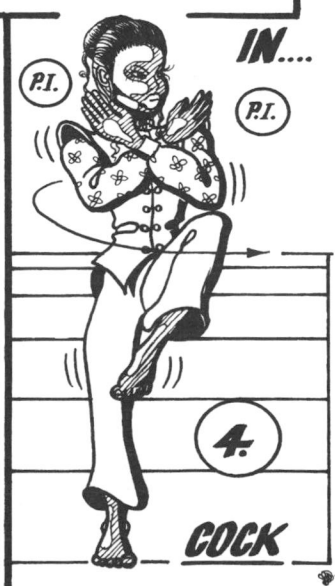

IN....

P.I.   P.I.

4.

COCK

A TRAVELER'S CONCISE GUIDE TO THE 4 SECRETS OF LONGEVITY
What, How & Where You Think, Eat, Act & Live Dramatically Affect Your Life Span

OUT...

P.U.

P.D.

5.

DOG

IN...

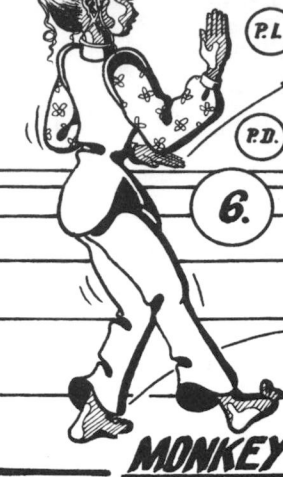

P.L.

P.D.

6.

MONKEY

FOOD POWER

- **WHAT YOU EAT strengthens or weakens immunity**.
- **30+% OF CANCERS** originate from diets/drinks

FOOD PLAN
- 50-70% cooked whole organic grains.
  - 20-30% raw/lightly cooked fresh veg.
  - 5-15% local fruit.
- 5-15% white sea fish, poultry, organic eggs.
- 5-10% veg. soup/juice.
- 0-5% low fat dairy

VIT. PLAN (adults & time-release)
- High pot. multivit. & chel. mins. **breakfast & dinner.**
- Vit. A: 20-30,000 iu total (incl. above) **6 days/week.**
- Super Vit. B Complex **at lunch & bed time.**
- Vit. C with bioflavs. 4-16g **spread over all daytime**.
- Vit. E: build up to 1,000 iu **spread over all daytime.**

• **EXTRAS:** RNA/DNA - Zinc - Selenium - Royal jelly - Dolomite - Lecithin - Eve. prim. oil - Chlorella.

DON'T
- ○ DON'T cook with heavy fat/oil (free radicals.)
- ○ DON'T eat any refined/processed foods.
- ○ DON'T eat red meat or fat content dairy foods.
- ○ DON'T eat sugar/canned/smoked foods.
- ○ DON'T cook in microwave/aluminium/teflon.
- ○ DON'T eat a lot or animal protein after lunch.
- ○ DON'T drink coffee/sugar/fruit drinks.
- ○ DON'T eat very cold or spicy food.
- ○ DON'T eat if stressed or fevered.
- ○ DON'T eat too much raw food.
- ○ DON'T drink at/or close to meals.
- ○ DON'T drink tap water.

DO
- ○ DO chew food well & digest without haste.
- ○ DO cook in glass or stainless steel.
- ○ DO drink/use herb teas selectively.
- ○ DO seek out organic/additive free foods.
- ○ DO cook food lightly & serve it warm.
- ○ DO identify & remove allergens from diet.
- ○ DO promote appetite with exercise.
- ○ DO study Yin/Yang (macrobiotics).
- ○ DO eat & drink in moderation.
- ○ DO study food combining*.
- ○ DO avoid protein/starch together*.
- ○ DO vary diet from day to day.

ACTION POWER

AN IMMUNITY BOOST
- **SOAK** a small towel in half a pint of warm castor oil - Fold & lay on tummy - Cover with plastic - Lay hot water bottle on top - Lie & relax for 1 hour/day for 1 month - Then alternate days for 1 month - Then as required.
- **REMEMBER all ailments are OPPORTUNISTS (take weak first).**

TO TEST i**mmunity/ longevity potential** - Pencil in every "O" (93 in all) you conform to - Count total & add one for every relative (up to 7) that ever got to 93 years old - Enter on graph next to date. **TRY TO IMPROVE.**

THE STANCES
1-8 (then repeat with other side) & all interconnecting moves are martial arts based - **But in this case are executed slowly - Pay attention to technique, breathing** (all in/all out slowly) **& positive suggestions** - Pick a quiet (& if possible beautiful) place - **& FEEL YOUR "KI" GROW!**

DO

OUT...

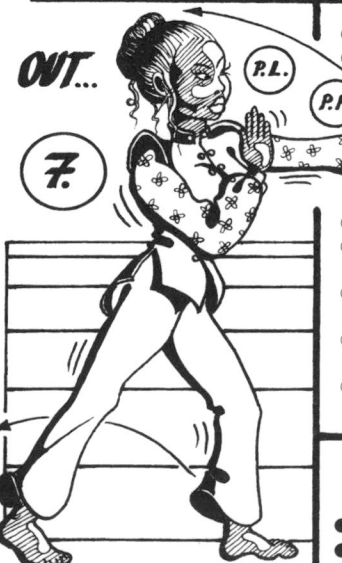

P.L.

P.F.

7.

DRAGON

- ○ DO chart progress to goals
- ○ DO take up yoga/tai chi
  - ○ DO work to a schedule
  - ○ DO laugh a lot
  - ○ DO enjoy music
  - ○ DO think young/well/ happy/expectant
  - ○ DO be very creative
- ○ DO listen to your body
- ○ DO find a friend to talk out problems with
- ○ DO make a change for the better now, not later
- ○ DO avoid crossing arms/legs (inhibits "Ki" flow)
- ○ DO avoid taking any drugs unnecessarily

- ○ DO sleep at set times
- ○ DO stretch/flexibility exercises 6 days/week
- ○ DO enjoy sex with one long-term partner
- ○ DO avoid TV/PC/Radar/ microwave radiation
- ○ DO strength/weight exercises 3-5 days/week
- ○ DO aerobic/heart exercise 3-5 days/week
- ○ DO be adventurous in experiencing life
- ○ DO avoid more than 1 glass of wine 3 days/week
- ○ DO deep breathing exercises 6 days/week

IN...

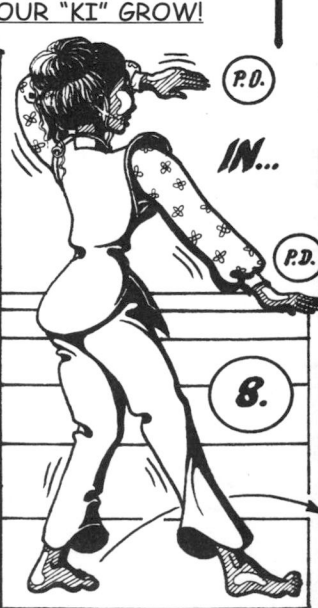

P.D.

P.D.

8.

DUCK

IMMUNITY/LONGEVITY HERBS
(study & alternate usage monthly)
● Bee pollen ● Ginseng ● Gingko biloba ● Gotu kola ● Garlic ● Licorice ● Alfalfa ● Don quai ● Burdock ● Fenugreek ● Golden seal ● Cats claw ● Damiana ● Sarsaparilla ● Echinacca ● Astragalus ● Guarana ● Shiitake ● False unicorn ● Reishi.

Graded - Easy To Follow - No Equipment - Well Demonstrated By Delicia Penn.

*LADIES, FOR YOUR LOVED ONES (& yourself) PLEASE STAY IN SHAPE
- We all enjoy looking at a trim figure (at any age).*

PRESS-UPS

A.

◄ # DO ON <u>finger tips</u> for strong hands.

KEEP body straight.

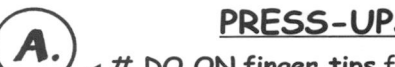
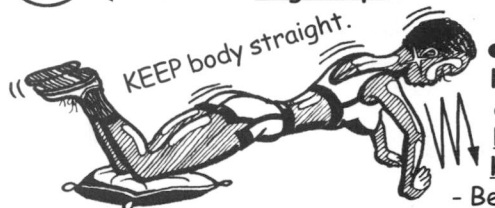

● **WITH KNEES ON** cushion (<u>keep body and head straight</u>) - Bend arms & <u>touch</u> <u>chest</u> <u>on</u> <u>floor</u> - Then up (vary hands apart width [& angle] for different muscle groups).

BACK PRESSES

B.

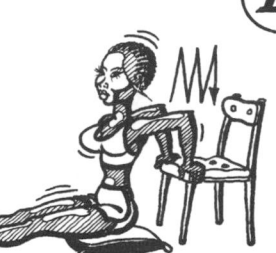

● **HEELS ON FLOOR** - Hands on chair/bath/box etc. - Cushion under bottom - Push up, down etc. - <u>Touch</u> bottom on cushion each time - <u>Harder version</u> = Put feet on another chair. "**NICE FIGURE !**".

STAR JUMPS

C.

● **STAND TO** attention in cushioned soled shoes - Jump with legs apart & <u>clap hands above head</u> - Back to attention etc. - Do it in front of mirror - Good for heart & BURNING CALORIES.

NECK TENSION

W. **X.** **Y.** **Z.**

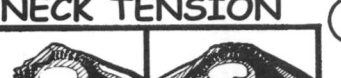
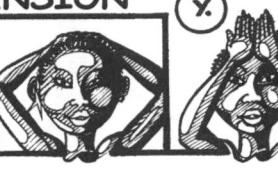

W = **LEFT** side of head - X = **RIGHT** side of head - Y = **BACK** of head - Z = **FRONT** of head
Pull/push each one <u>very hard</u> for 15 seconds (THAT IS <u>ONE</u> SET*).

D.

SIT-UPS

E.

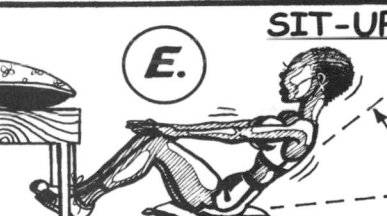

● **SIT ON CUSHION** - Hook feet under bed or similar - Lie back on floor <u>with knees bent</u> - Sit up & reach to right - Lie back (<u>BUT DON'T TOUCH FLOOR</u>) - Sit up & reach to left etc.

LYING OVERHEAD LEG RAISES

● **LAY ON TOWEL,** on back, on floor (with hands under bed) - Raise legs over body & touch bed - Down again, but <u>DON'T TOUCH FLOOR</u> with heels - Up again etc.

F.

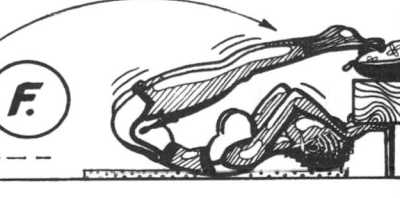

BACK RAISES

G.

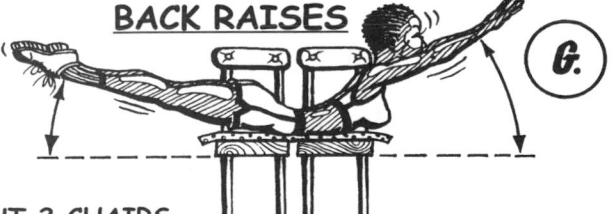

● **PUT 2 CHAIRS** together with cushions on (& lie on) - Keep arms & legs straight - Raise as high as you can - Hold a second & lower (<u>but don't touch floor</u>) - Then up etc.

JOGGING

● **OUTSIDE:** Pick pleasant route - If you are going for say 20 mins - Go in one direction for 10 mins - Then turn back - END WITH A SPRINT.
● **IN ROOM:** Get heartbeat up by lifting knees high & doing arm movements (e.g. overhead claps) - PUT ON SOME INSPIRING MUSIC.
● **BOTH:** <u>Wear cushioned heel shoes</u> (to protect joints) - Use self-hypnosis - "I feel strong" - "I feel fresh" etc. (<u>NOTE: Overleaf "M" = Minutes</u>).

STAND-UPS

I.

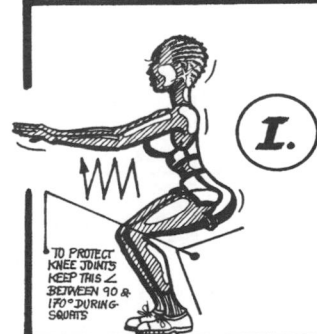

TO PROTECT KNEE JOINTS KEEP THIS ∠ BETWEEN 90 & 170° DURING SQUATS

IT IS BETTER to do these without holding on (it improves your balance) - But if you prefer you can hold on - Then squat down, stand up, squat etc. - <u>Watch out for aching thigh muscles</u> a day or two later - Have fun! "OH YEAH !"

CALF RAISES

J.

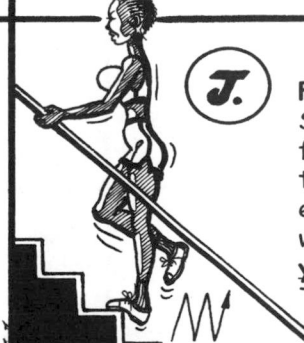

FIND A STEP (& a hand rail) - Stand on it with the ball of one foot (wear soft shoes) - Raise the other foot - Then raise entire body by pressing down with your toes - <u>Up as high as you can & then low</u> etc. - Then change feet - "**WOOO!.. FEELIN' GOOOODD!**"

WOMEN'S NO-EQUIPMENT EXERCISE PLAN
3 Women's Exercise Programs For Non-Gym Situations

HEALTH IS MORE PRECIOUS THAN DIAMONDS - GET RICH WITH EXERCISE.

REPS = Repetitions (Number of times an exercise is done without stopping).
SETS = Numbers of groups of repetitions. *"EEENJOY IT YEAH!"*

E·F·A A△
A·B   D

"...R. NO U MAY NOT HAVE A DATE..."

I·C·H I·HC
J·H·C·I

I·G·H·C G
A·B·F G·H

"...BUT I MIGHT GO TO THE MOVIES WITH U... DUTCH TREAT THAT IS "

J·H·C·I
H·J·C·I

EASY PROGRAM

Exercise	MON REPS	MON SETS	TUE REPS	TUE SETS	WED REPS	WED SETS	THU REPS	THU SETS	FRI REPS	FRI SETS	SAT REPS	SAT SETS	SUN REPS	SUN SETS
Press-Ups	5	1			5	1			5	1				
Back Presses			5	1			5	1			5	1		
Star Jumps	20	1			20	1			20	1				
Neck Tension			*	1			*	1			*	1		
Sit-Ups	10	1			10	1			10	1				
Lying O'hd L.R.			10	1			10	1			10	1		
Back Raises	15	1			15	1			15	1				
Jogging													15 M.	
Stand-Ups			20	1			20	1			20	1		
Calf Raises	20	1			20	1			20	1				

MEDIUM PROGRAM

Exercise	MON REPS	MON SETS	TUE REPS	TUE SETS	WED REPS	WED SETS	THU REPS	THU SETS	FRI REPS	FRI SETS	SAT REPS	SAT SETS	SUN REPS	SUN SETS
Press-Ups	10	2			15	1			10	2				
Back Presses			10	2			10	2			15	1		
Star Jumps	40	2			60	1			40	2				
Neck Tension			*	2			*	2			*	2		
Sit-Ups	20	2			30	1			20	2				
Lying O'hd L.R.			20	2			20	2			30	1		
Back Raises	15	2			25	1			15	2				
Jogging													30 M.	
Stand-Ups			40	2			40	2			60	1		
Calf Raises	40	2			60	1			40	2				

HARD PROGRAM

Exercise	MON REPS	MON SETS	TUE REPS	TUE SETS	WED REPS	WED SETS	THU REPS	THU SETS	FRI REPS	FRI SETS	SAT REPS	SAT SETS	SUN REPS	SUN SETS
Press-Ups	20	4			30	1			20	4				
Back Presses			20	4			20	4			30	1		
Star Jumps	80	4			120	1			80	4				
Neck Tension			*	4			*	4			*	4		
Sit-Ups	40	4			60	1			40	4				
Lying O'hd L.R.			40	4			40	4			60	1		
Back Raises	40	4			60	1			40	4				
Jogging													60 M.	
Stand-Ups			80	4			80	4			120	1		
Calf Raises	100	4			150	1			100	4				

Graded - Easy To Follow - No Equipment - Well Demonstrated By Small Joe Fung

GENTLEMEN DO YOURSELF A FAVOR - Stay strong - Besides it is useful (for taking lids off pickle jars).

A. PRESS-UPS

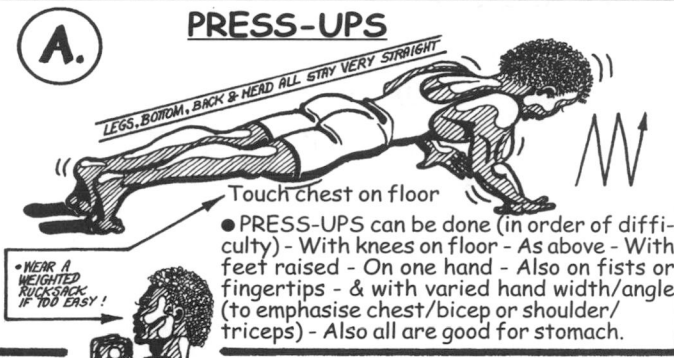

LEGS, BOTTOM, BACK & HEAD ALL STAY VERY STRAIGHT

Touch chest on floor

● PRESS-UPS can be done (in order of difficulty) - With knees on floor - As above - With feet raised - On one hand - Also on fists or fingertips - & with varied hand width/angle (to emphasise chest/bicep or shoulder/triceps) - Also all are good for stomach.

• WEAR A WEIGHTED RUCKSACK IF TOO EASY!

B. BACK PRESSES

● SUSPEND BODY between 2 chairs - Then either rest feet on one seat (& hands on the other) or one hand on each chair back (knees bent & off floor) - You can also use a weighted rucksack - Then bend & straighten arms slowly.

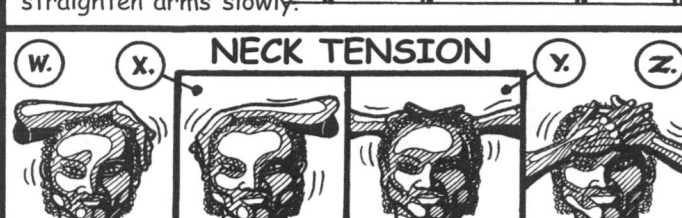

UP & DOWN

C. PULL-UPS

• DON'T REST &/OR STAND BETWEEN REPS.

Up & down

● FIND SUITABLE DOOR frame (or stairway or bar) & grip - a) Palms toward face or - b) Palms away from face, with - c) Narrow grip or - d) Wide grip, & pull up - e) In front of head or - f) Behind head - <u>All use different muscle groups.</u>

NECK TENSION

W. X. Y. Z.

W = LEFT side of head - X = RIGHT side of head - Y = BACK of head - Z = FRONT of head - <u>Pull/push each one very hard for 16 secs.</u> (THAT IS ONE SET*.)

D.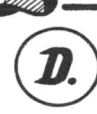

E. SIT-UPS

• TRY "CRUNCHES" (SIT UPS BETWEEN "A" & "B")...UDO AHH!

● SIT ON CUSHION - Hook feet under bed (or similar) - Lie back on floor <u>with knees bent</u> - Sit up & touch left elbow on right knee - Lie back (but don't touch floor) - Back up & right elbow to left knee etc. **Do "E" & "G" daily to prevent LOW BACKACHE.**

• CAN ALSO BE DONE W/ WEIGHTS (EG BOOKS) NO

LYING OVERHEAD LEG RAISES

● LAY TOWEL on floor next to bed - Lay on back with hands under bed - Raise legs over body & touch bed with toes - Go back <u>(but don't rest feet on floor)</u> - Then up again etc.

• WEAR YOUR HEAVY BOOTS IF TOO EASY.

F.

NO

G. BACK RAISES

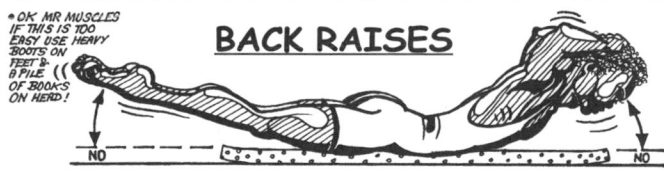

• OK MR MUSCLES IF THIS IS TOO EASY USE HEAVY BOOTS ON FEET & A PILE OF BOOKS ON HEAD!

NO   NO

● LIE ON FACE on towel on floor - Put hands behind head - Keeping legs straight, raise feet & head as high as possible - Hold for a second - Down (<u>but don't touch floor</u>) etc.

JOGGING

● OUTSIDE: Pick a pleasant route - If you are going for say 20 minutes - Go in 1 direction for 10 minutes, then turn back - **END WITH A SPRINT.**
● IN ROOM: Get heartbeat up by lifting knees high & doing arm movements (shadow boxing) - Put on some music. "PUT ON DE BOB MARLEY, MAN!"
● BOTH: Wear cushioned heel shoes to protect joints - Use self-hypnosis "<u>I feel strong</u>" - "<u>I feel fresh</u>" etc. (note overleaf "M" = minutes).

• "HEY MAN I DON'T NEED NO SHOES!"

I. STAND-UPS

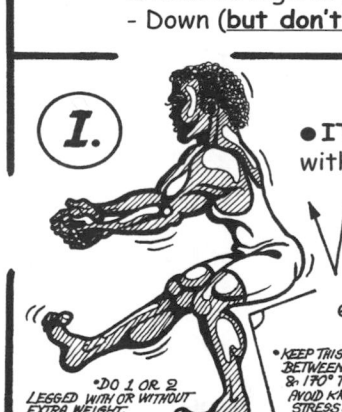

● IT IS BETTER to do these without holding on (as it improves your balance) - But if you prefer hold on - Squat down, stand up, squat down etc. - Watch out for aching thigh muscles a day or 2 later - <u>Can also do with weighted rucksack.</u>

• DO 1 OR 2 LEGGED WITH OR WITHOUT EXTRA WEIGHT.

• KEEP THIS ∠ BETWEEN 90° & 170° TO AVOID KNEE STRESS.

J. CALF RAISES

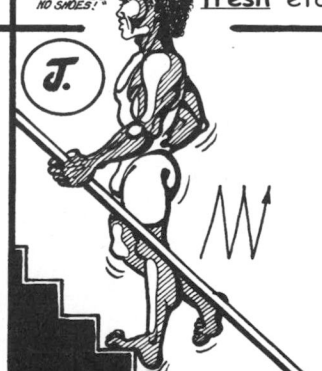

● FIND A STEP - Stand on it with the ball of one foot (wear soft shoes) - Raise the other foot - Hold on & start going up & down <u>as far as you can</u> - Then change feet - YEAH!... FEEEEL DE BURN!

MEN'S NO-EQUIPMENT EXERCISE PLAN
3 Men's Exercise Programs For Non-Gym Situations

EXERCISE IS LIKE A BANK ACCOUNT – YOU CAN GET OUT ONLY WHAT YOU PUT IN!

REPS = Repetitions (number of times an exercise done without stopping)
SETS = Number of groups of repetitions. (one minute between sets.)

C·D I·H·F
A·B·C D

"HEY! WHATS HAPPENIN MAN ?"

H·I
E·F·A
D·C·A H·J·I
A·C

"LONG TIME NO SEE.. HOW YER DOIN ?"

G·H·I
G·B J·H·G
A·B·C G·H

Program	Exercise	MON REPS	MON SETS	TUE REPS	TUE SETS	WED REPS	WED SETS	THU REPS	THU SETS	FRI REPS	FRI SETS	SAT REPS	SAT SETS	SUN REPS	SUN SETS
EASY PROGRAM	Press-Ups	10	1			10	1			10	1				
	Back Presses			10	1			10	1			10	1		
	Pull-Ups	2	1			2	1			2	1				
	Neck Tension			*	1			*	1			*	1		
	Sit-Ups	10	1			10	1			10	1				
	Lying O'hd L.R.			10	1			10	1			10	1		
	Back Raises	20	1			20	1			20	1				
	Jogging			10	M.			10	M.			10	M.		
	Stand-Ups	20	1			20	1			20	1				
	Calf Raises			20	1			20	1			20	1		
MEDIUM PROGRAM	Press-Ups	20	2			30	1			20	2				
	Back Presses			20	2			20	2			30	1		
	Pull-Ups			4	2			4	2			6	1		
	Neck Tension					*	2					*	2		
	Sit-Ups	20	2			30	1			20	2				
	Lying O'hd L.R.			20	2			20	2			30	1		
	Back Raises	20	2			30	1			20	2				
	Jogging													30	M.
	Stand-Ups	40	2			60	1			40	2				
	Calf Raises			50	2			50	2			75	1		
HARD PROGRAM	Press-Ups	40	4			60	1			40	4				
	Back Presses			40	4			40	4			60	1		
	Pull-Ups			16	4			16	4			16	4		
	Neck Tension					*	4					*	4		
	Sit-Ups	40	4			60	1			40	4				
	Lying O'hd L.R.			40	4			40	4			60	1		
	Back Raises	40	4			60	1			40	4				
	Jogging													60	M.
	Stand-Ups	80	4			120	1			80	4				
	Calf Raises			100	4			100	4			50	1		

How To Trim & Shape Specific Body Parts - Well Demonstrated By Aloe Vera

YOU NEED: 1 x sit up bench, 4 x dumbbell bars, 2 x long bars, selection of weights, grips & ankle weights (all quite easy & cheap to get).

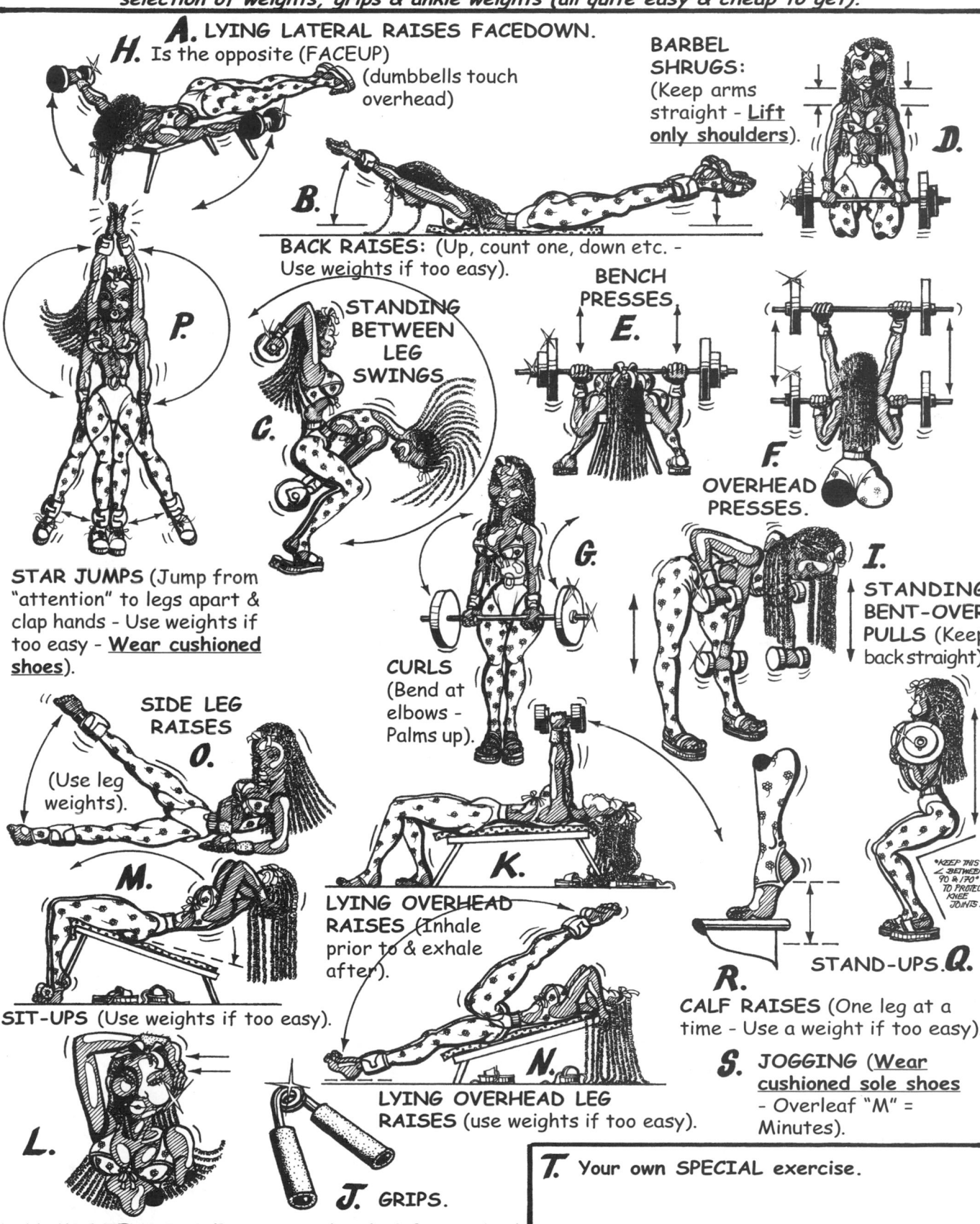

H. A. LYING LATERAL RAISES FACEDOWN. **H.** Is the opposite (FACEUP) (dumbbells touch overhead)

BARBEL SHRUGS: (Keep arms straight - <u>Lift only shoulders</u>). **D.**

B. BACK RAISES: (Up, count one, down etc. - Use <u>weights</u> if too easy).

P. STANDING BETWEEN LEG SWINGS **C.**

BENCH PRESSES E.

F. OVERHEAD PRESSES.

STAR JUMPS (Jump from "attention" to legs apart & clap hands - Use weights if too easy - <u>Wear cushioned shoes</u>).

G. CURLS (Bend at elbows - Palms up).

I. STANDING BENT-OVER PULLS (Keep back straight).

O. SIDE LEG RAISES (Use leg weights).

M. SIT-UPS (Use weights if too easy).

K. LYING OVERHEAD RAISES (Inhale prior to & exhale after).

N. LYING OVERHEAD LEG RAISES (use weights if too easy).

L. DYNAMIC TENSION (Press on each side & front & back of head very hard for 15 seconds each, this is one set).

J. GRIPS.

R. CALF RAISES (One leg at a time - Use a weight if too easy).

STAND-UPS. Q. *KEEP THIS ∠ BETWEEN 90 & 170° TO PROTECT KNEE JOINTS.*

S. JOGGING (<u>Wear cushioned sole shoes</u> - Overleaf "M" = Minutes).

T. Your own SPECIAL exercise.

BODY SCULPTURE PROGRAM FOR WOMEN
The Shaping Of Your Own Body By Selective Exercise

OBESITY = EATING MORE CALORIES THAN YOU USE IN EXERCISE

REPS = Repetitions (number of times exercise done without stopping).
SETS = Number of groups of repetitions. "ALOE U ONE"

M·N·S G·H·I L·D· B
E·H·K·I
Q·S·P R·S·P
Q·S·P·C KA·I
J·L·I D
A·I D
A·C·B·I
B·C·I C·B·I
O·P·S R·P·S·I
Q·C·B·S C·B·S

ADJUST YOUR WEIGHTS SO YOU CAN **JUST** DO THE REPS & SETS AT RIGHT

MUSCLE DEFINITION PROGRAM

NOTES

HIGH PROTEIN DIET definition = 1 gram of protein for each 1lb of nonfat body weight to be eaten daily.

DIET: Very low fat - Moderate protein & high carbohydrate (50-70 %) balanced wholefood - EXERCISE PRINCIPLE: High reps (15+) done quickly - & low sets (1-3) with 1 minute rest between sets.

	MON REPS	MON SETS	TUE REPS	TUE SETS	WED REPS	WED SETS	THU REPS	THU SETS	FRI REPS	FRI SETS	SAT REPS	SAT SETS	SUN REPS	SUN SETS
A	30	1					30	1						
B			30	3					30	3				
C					100	1					100	1		
D	20	2					20	2						
E			20	2					20	2				
F					30	1					30	1		
G	20	2					20	2						
H			20	2					20	2				
I					30	1					30	1		
J	100	1					100	1						
K			30	1					30	1				
L					*	3					*	3		
M	20	2					20	2						
N			25	2					25	2				
O					100	1					100	1		
P	100	1					100	1						
Q			100	1					100	1				
R					100	3					100	3		
S													50 M	
T														

MUSCLE BULK PROGRAM

NOTES

DIET: Low fat (10-20%) - High carbohydrate (& high protein) balanced wholefood - EXERCISE PRINCIPLE: Low reps (5-15) done slowly - High sets (3-9) with 1 minute rest between sets.

	MON REPS	MON SETS	TUE REPS	TUE SETS	WED REPS	WED SETS	THU REPS	THU SETS	FRI REPS	FRI SETS	SAT REPS	SAT SETS	SUN REPS	SUN SETS
A	10	3					10	3						
B			15	5					15	5				
C					30	3					30	3		
D	10	4					10	4						
E			10	5					10	5				
F					10	3					10	3		
G	10	5					10	5						
H			10	5					10	5				
I					10	3					10	3		
J	30	3					30	3						
K			10	3					10	3				
L					*	5					*	5		
M	15	3					15	3						
N			15	3					15	3				
O					30	3					30	3		
P	50	1					50	1						
Q			10	5					10	5				
R					30	5					30	5		
S													25 M	
T														

BODY SCULPTURE PROGRAM FOR MEN

How To Trim & Shape Specific Body Parts - Well Demonstrated By Carl .... Ski

YOU NEED: 1 x Sit-up bench, 4 x Dumbbell bars, 2 x Long bars, selection of weights, grips & ankle weights (all quite cheap & easy to get).

A. LYING LATERAL RAISES FACE-DOWN.

H. Is the opposite (FACEUP) - (dumbbells touch overhead)

BACK RAISES (Up, count one, down etc. - Use weights if too easy).

B.

D. BARBEL SHRUGS (Keep arms straight - Lift only shoulders).

C. STANDING LATERAL RAISES.

F.

G.

E. BENCH PRESSES.

CURLS (Palms up - Bend at elbows).

OVERHEAD PRESSES.

I. STANDING BENT-OVER PULLS (Keep back straight).

J. FRENCH CURLS (Inhale as you lower - Exhale as you raise).

K. LYING OVERHEAD RAISES (Inhale prior to & exhale after).

L. WRIST CURLS (Do as shown [or palm up] - Move wrist & hand only [can rest forearm on knee]).

O. GRIPS.

M. SIT-UPS (Touch alternate elbows on knees - Use weights if too easy).

CALF RAISES (One leg at a time - Use a weight if too easy). **R.**

(Use weights if too easy).

S. JOGGING (Wear cushioned soled shoes - Overleaf "M" = Minutes).

T. Your own SPECIAL exercise.

N. LYING OVERHEAD LEG RAISES

Q. STAND-UPS.

* KEEP THIS ∠ BETWEEN 90 & 170° TO PROTECT KNEE JOINTS.

P. DYNAMIC TENSION (Press on each side & front & back of head very hard for 16 seconds each, * this is one set).

BODY SCULPTURE PROGRAM FOR MEN

The Shaping Of Your Own Body By Selective Exercises

OBESITY = EATING MORE CALORIES THAN YOU USE IN EXERCISE

REPS = Repetitions (number of times exercise done without stopping).
SETS = Number of groups of repetitions.
"CARL WHERE U HIDE DE $?"

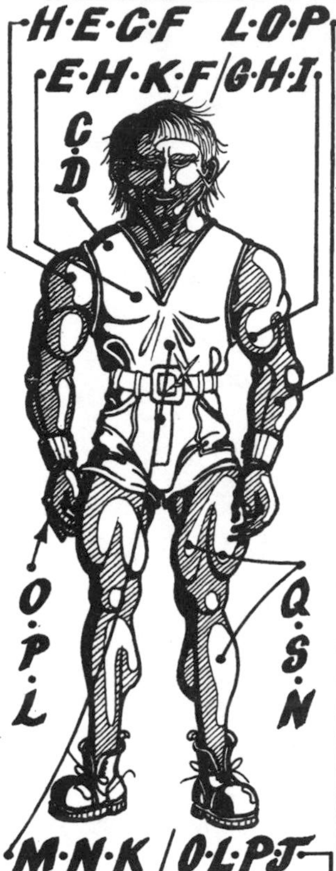

H·E·C·F
L·O·P
E·H·K·F
G·H·I
C
D
O·P·L
Q·S·N
M·N·K
O·L·P·T

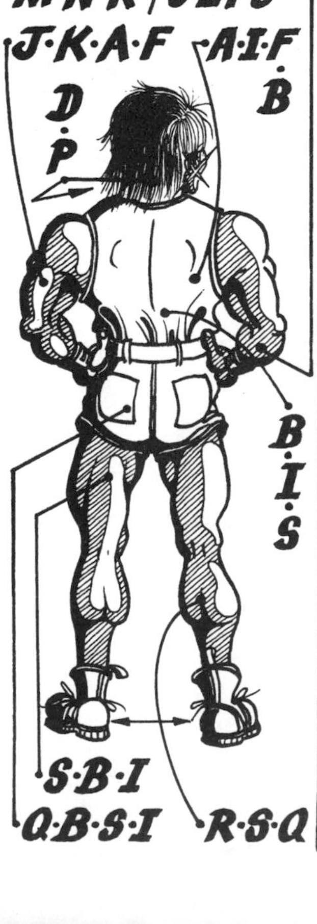

J·K·A·F
A·I·F
B
D
P
B·I·S
S·B·I
Q·B·S·I
R·S·Q

ADJUST YOUR WEIGHTS SO YOU CAN JUST DO THE REPS & SETS AT RIGHT

MUSCLE DEFINITION PROGRAM

NOTES

DIET: Very low fat - Moderate protein & high carbohydrate (50-70 %) balanced wholefood - **EXERCISE PRINCIPLE:** High reps (15+) done quickly - & low sets (1-4) with 1 minute rest between sets.

	MON REPS	MON SETS	TUE REPS	TUE SETS	WED REPS	WED SETS	THU REPS	THU SETS	FRI REPS	FRI SETS	SAT REPS	SAT SETS	SUN REPS	SUN SETS
A	20	2					20	2						
B			40	4					40	4				
C					20	2					20	2		
D	20	2					20	2						
E			20	2					20	2				
F					20	2					20	2		
G	20	2					20	2						
H			20	2					20	2				
I					20	2					20	2		
J	20	2					20	2						
K			20	2					20	2				
L					20	2					20	2		
M	20	2					20	2						
N			20	2					20	2				
O					60	4					60	4		
P	*	4					*	4						
Q			40	2					40	2				
R					80	4					80	4		
S													60	M
T														

MUSCLE BULK PROGRAM

HIGH PROTEIN DIET definition = 1 gram of protein for each 1lb of nonfat body weight to be eaten daily.

NOTES

DIET: Low fat (10-20 %) - High carbohydrate (& high protein) balanced wholefood - **EXERCISE PRINCIPLE:** Low reps (5-10) done slowly - High sets (4-10) with 1 minute rest between sets.

	MON REPS	MON SETS	TUE REPS	TUE SETS	WED REPS	WED SETS	THU REPS	THU SETS	FRI REPS	FRI SETS	SAT REPS	SAT SETS	SUN REPS	SUN SETS
A	10	4					10	4						
B			20	4					20	4				
C					10	4					10	4		
D	10	4					10	4						
E			10	4					10	4				
F					10	4					10	4		
G	10	4					10	4						
H			10	4					10	4				
I					10	4					10	4		
J	10	4					10	4						
K			10	4					10	4				
L					10	4					10	4		
M	10	4					10	4						
N			10	4					10	4				
O					30	6					30	6		
P	*	6					*	6						
Q			10	4					10	4				
R					40	6					40	6		
S													30	M
T														

An Expert's Choice Of Simple Yet Effective Holds & Locks

DO NOT ATTEMPT HOLDS (except in sport or practice) on persons of considerably greater strength than yourself.

WRISTLOCK

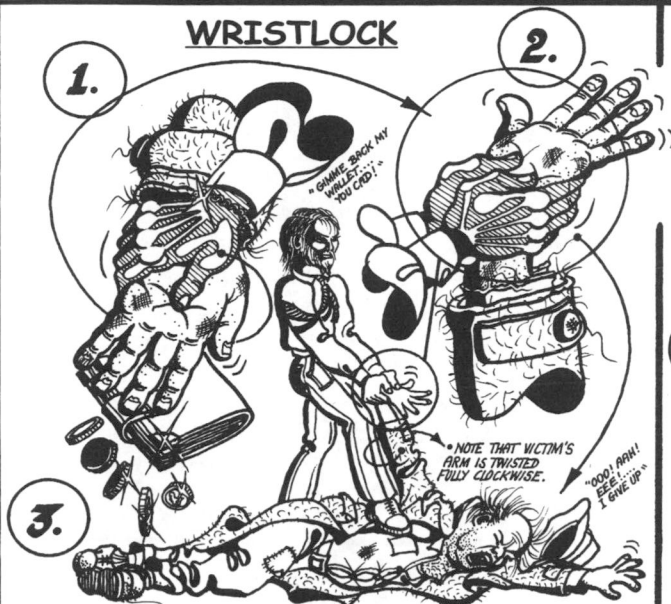

• NOTE THAT VICTIM'S ARM IS TWISTED FULLY CLOCKWISE.

ARMLOCK

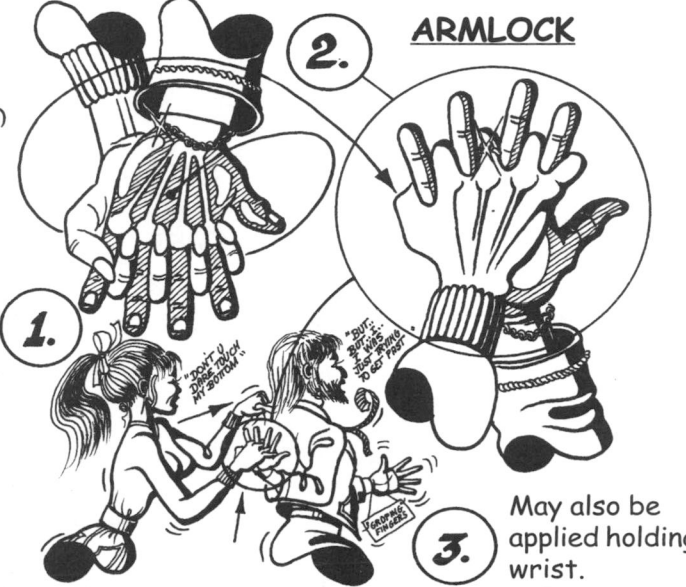

May also be applied holding wrist.

LEGLOCK

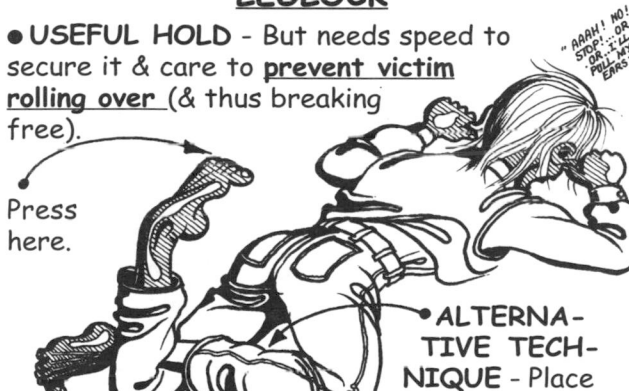

• USEFUL HOLD - But needs speed to secure it & care to **prevent victim rolling over** (& thus breaking free).

Press here.

• ALTERNATIVE TECHNIQUE - Place your foot in triangle between victim's legs - Use other foot to hold toes down (leaves both hands free).

NECKLOCKS*

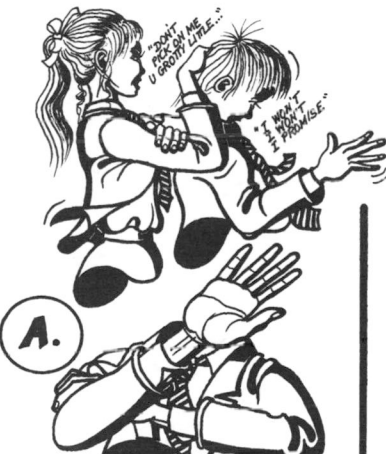

• FROM REAR ("A") & from side ("B") - These holds (if well applied) **difficult to escape from (without resorting to blows).**

• ALSO BRINGS pressure on windpipe & carotid artery (side of neck) **thus making submission (&/or unconsciousness) possible.**

HEADLOCK*

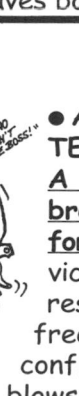
Link fingers here

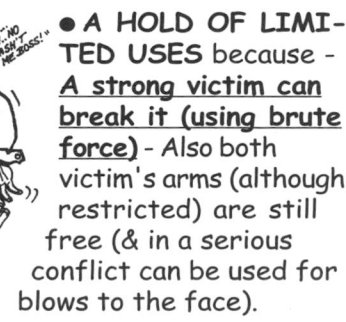

• A HOLD OF LIMITED USES because - **A strong victim can break it (using brute force)** - Also both victim's arms (although restricted) are still free (& in a serious conflict can be used for blows to the face).

• HOWEVER A USEFUL SPORTING HOLD (in, for example, the restraint of a non violent person) - *NOTE: **In a serious conflict** a victim of this hold can precede blows to the face by stamping on attacker's foot.

• THE MAJOR WEAKNESS of these holds **is that the victim's hands are free** & the hands of the attacker are occupied.

• IF YOU ARE THE VICTIM (& the contest is not a friendly one) with "A" strike elbow hard into attackers kidneys - With "B" grasp & twist genitals.

• FOLLOW BOTH of these with a violent fist to the attacker's face (nose is best).

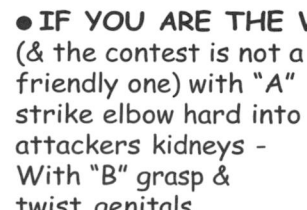

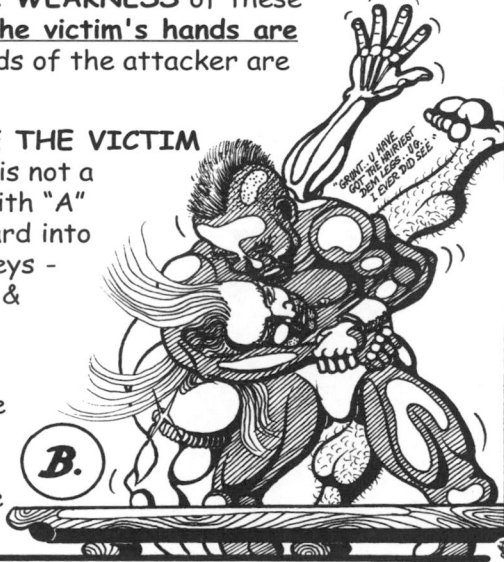

HOW TO EXECUTE BASIC JUDO THROWS

An Expert's Choice Of Simple, Yet Effective, Trips & Throws

"OVERCOMING A WEIGHT OF 1,000 CATTLE BY 4 OUNCES"
(or the art of turning an attacker's movements against them).

LEG TRIP

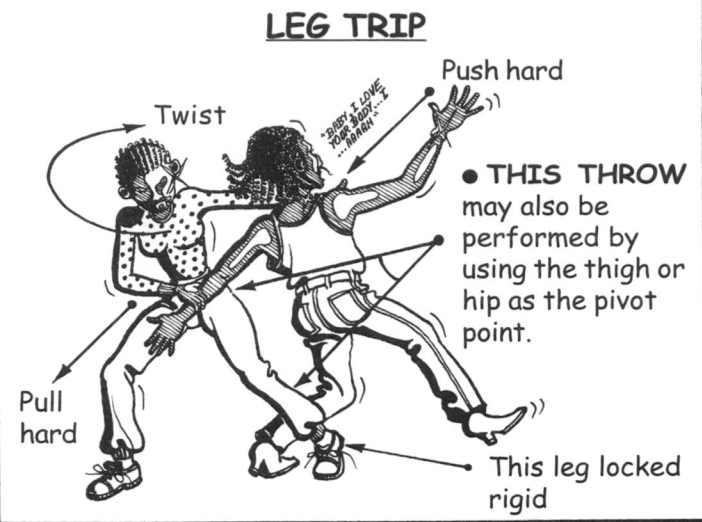

Twist

Push hard

● **THIS THROW** may also be performed by using the thigh or hip as the pivot point.

Pull hard

This leg locked rigid

LEG SWEEP

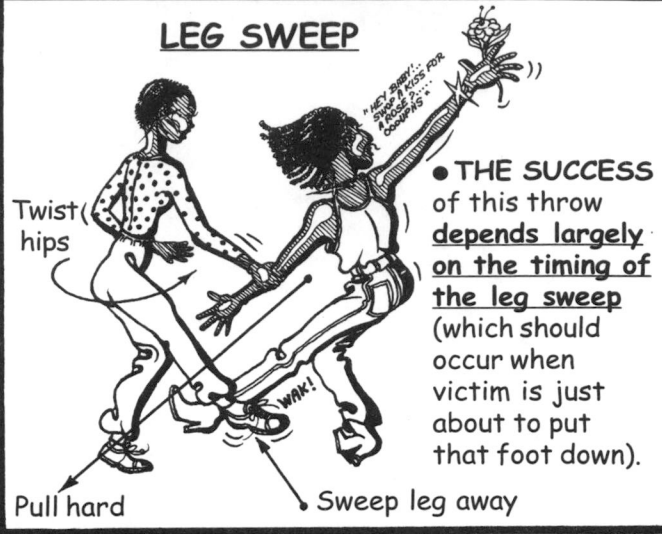

Twist hips

● **THE SUCCESS** of this throw <u>depends largely on the timing of the leg sweep</u> (which should occur when victim is just about to put that foot down).

Pull hard

Sweep leg away

HIP THROWS A, B & C

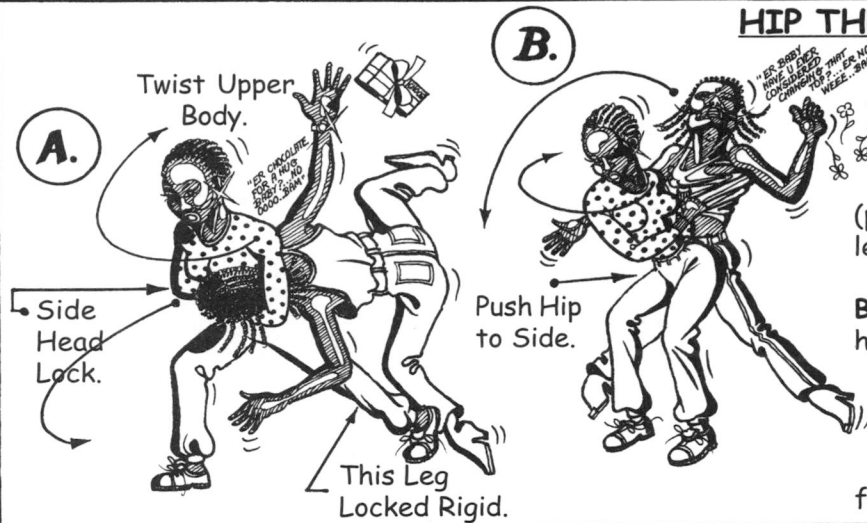

A. Twist Upper Body.

Side Head Lock.

This Leg Locked Rigid.

B. Push Hip to Side.

A. HIP THROW FROM SIDE headlock position: With a tight hold on victim's head (you don't want to lose it!) - Twist your upper body away (pulling victim over your hip & extended leg) - To fall on back (or side).

B. HIP THROW FROM DOUBLE handed coat (or lapel) grip - Start face-to-face - Twist away from victim & jut hip out at same time - Twist further & bend forward pulling victim clear of ground (& over hip) to fall (usually heavily) on back (or side).

C. HIP THROW FROM WRIST or cuff grip - Start face-to-face - From a blow (or push) grasp attacker's wrist (or cuff) "X" - Twist & (at same time) grasp attacker's lapel (or underarm) - Perform hip throw as in "B"

STOMACH THROW

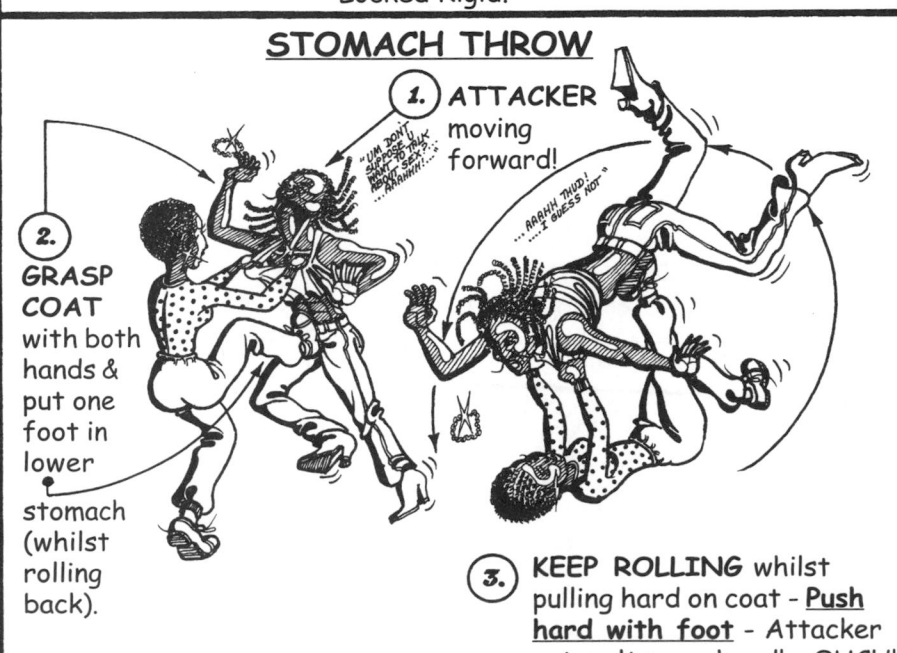

1. ATTACKER moving forward!

2. GRASP COAT with both hands & put one foot in lower stomach (whilst rolling back).

3. KEEP ROLLING whilst pulling hard on coat - <u>**Push hard with foot**</u> - Attacker catapults overhead!... OUCH!

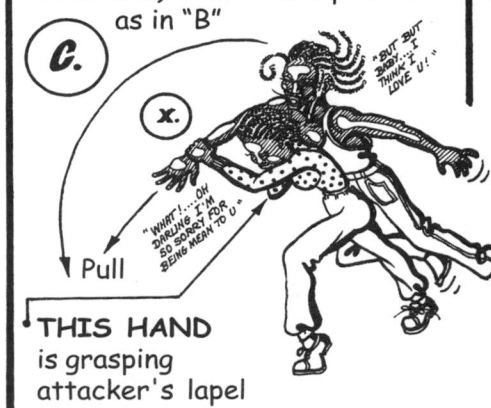

C.

X.

Pull

● **THIS HAND** is grasping attacker's lapel (or underarm).

AIKIDO IS A MARTIAL ART WITH A HIGH LEVEL OF SUBLETY & SOPHISTICATION with over 3,000 recorded strategies - Its "in depth" study requires a lifetime.

VITAL AIMS

- **WEAKER <u>can control stronger THRU TECHNIQUE.</u>**
- **<u>TECHNIQUE is using minimum force to achieve maximum effect</u>** in turning an opponent's force against his or herself.
- **<u>CULTIVATE an alert (& flexible) mind to "share" an opponent's feelings,</u>** in a smooth nonemotional reflex utilization of their aggression - Turning it against them.
- **<u>PERFORMED CORRECTLY aikido requires no undue effort or strength</u>** - & if it does, probably indicates the move was not done well - Is thus suitable for both sexes (young & old).
- **<u>AIKIDO MOVES are almost all spherical</u>** (using principles of physics) such as centrifugal, centripetal & deflective forces (in any plane) **<u>to redirect an attackers energy AGAINST THEMSELVES.</u>**

READY POSTURE ("KAMAE")

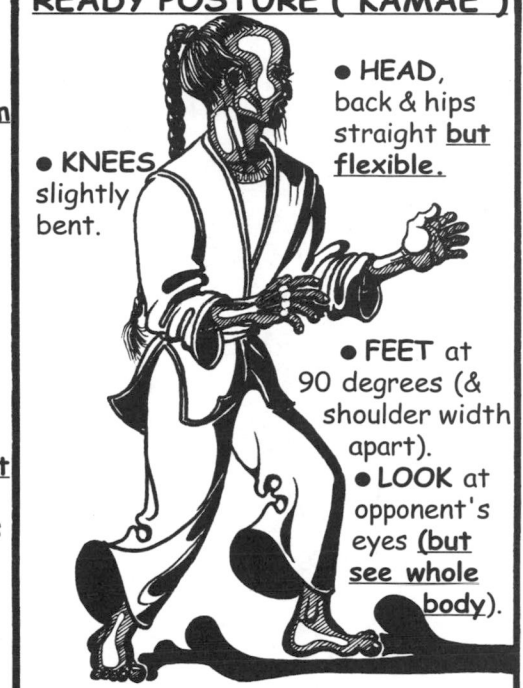

- **KNEES** slightly bent.
- **HEAD,** back & hips straight **but flexible.**
- **FEET** at 90 degrees (& shoulder width apart).
- **LOOK** at opponent's eyes **(but see whole body).**
- **WHEN** changing defensive position **<u>slide feet</u>** (to maintain stability).
- **<u>FEEL the power flow from soles of feet to spread fingertips.</u>**

VITAL SKILLS

- **<u>SPEED of reaction</u>** (& response) **<u>to be cultivated to the extreme</u>** - Many aikido moves require matching an opponent's direction (& speed) before acting.
- **<u>TIMING</u>** (as with a surfer catching a wave) **<u>is critical</u>** - Good timing = Less speed (&/or strength required) - Bad timing may mean failure of the move - Practice playing catch with a ball.
- **<u>CENTER OF GRAVITY</u>** (position) of your body (when you execute your move) **<u>is critical in order to use your weight against an opponent effectively</u>** - Thus requiring less speed (&/or strength).
- **<u>CONCENTRATING FORCE</u>** by mental effort into 1 action &/or muscle group (e.g. a finger hold or leg sweep) is an ability aquired by concentration (& practice) - **<u>It can MULTIPLY an exponent's power</u>**.

PROTECT YOURSELF BY LEARNING TO FALL (UKEMI)

FORWARD

- **<u>TURN FALL into a roll</u>**, going diagonally across back from one shoulder to opposite hip.
- **<u>STRIKE GROUND with straight arm & palm</u>** (hard) at instant of impact (to lessen shock of fall).

BAM!

- **CONTINUE ROLL** (back onto feet), twisting **<u>to retain view of opponent.</u>**

BACKWARD

- **<u>BEND KNEES</u>** going down (lowers center of gravity & increases rolling moment).
- **<u>CURVE SPINE</u>** & lift head (encourages roll & deflects impact).

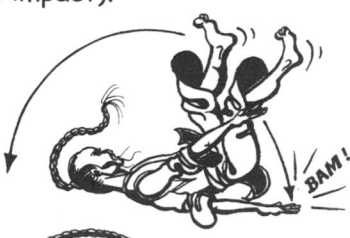
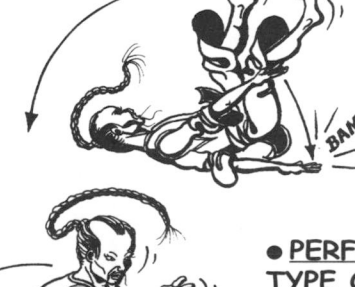

BAM!

- **<u>STRIKE FLOOR with straight arms & palms</u>** (reduces shock of hitting).
- **<u>PERFORM ANY TYPE OF ROLL to gain distance</u>** - But preferably a diagonal one (a buttock to opposite shoulder) - It is with practise **<u>SMOOTH & FAST.</u>**

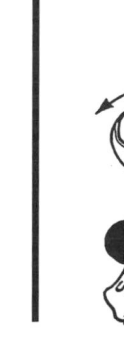

SIMPLE SUBMISSION HOLD FROM A FALSE CHOP

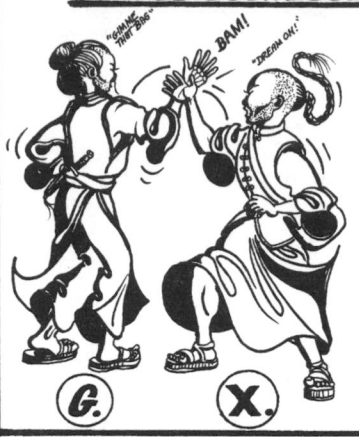

● **DURING AN ATTACK** by "G" - "X" <u>makes a false chop</u> toward "G's" head - Then grasps "G's" blocking wrist (or hand).

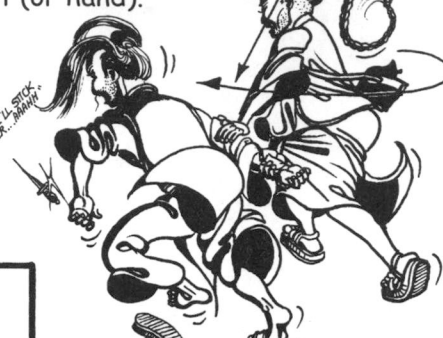

SIMPLE ARM PULL DEFENSE ("IRIMI")

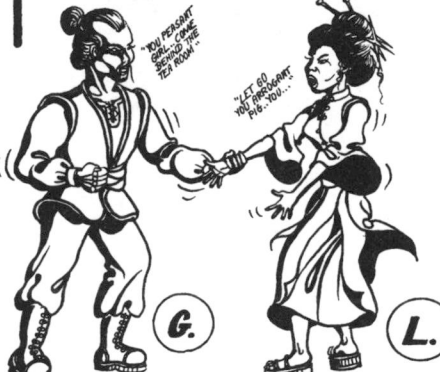

● **"X" PULLS "G's" WRIST**/ hand quickly down & to the right while stepping forward & bringing his left hand down sharply on "G's" elbow.

● **"G" IS FORCED** to the ground <u>in a spherical move</u> (with "X" following).

● <u>"G's" ARM IS HELD AT 90 degrees to his body</u> - With "X's" left knee in his armpit.

● <u>"X" SHOULD BE on his knees with straight arms, back & hips pressing down & out with left hand.</u>

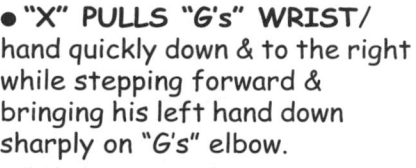

● **"G" GRABS "L's" WRIST** & pulls aggressively.

● **"L" SLIDES RIGHT FOOT** forward & drives right hand "sword like" over "G's" shoulder.

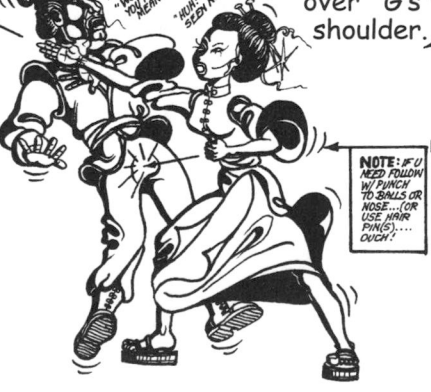

NOTE: IF U NEED FOLLOW W/ PUNCH TO BALLS OR NOSE...(OR USE HAIR PIN(S)... OUCH!

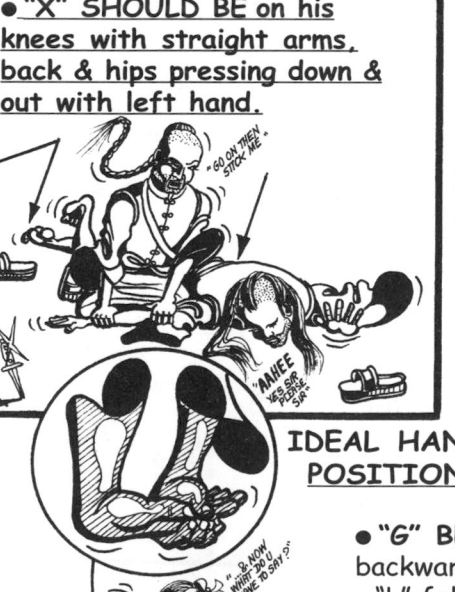

IDEAL HAND POSITION

● **CONCLUSION:** "G's" hostile move was redirected & broken <u>in the direction of easiest deflection (i.e.: Sideways & in direction of pull)</u> - Resulting in "G" being uncoordinated, off balance & without a grip on "L" - Thus being open to an aggressive counter by "L" if required.

ONE-HAND COMBAT THROW ("KATATA MOCHI")

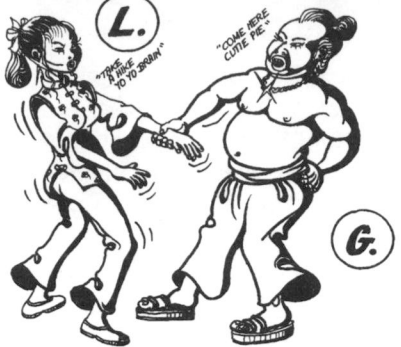

● **"G" GRABS "L's" WRIST** & pulls aggressively.

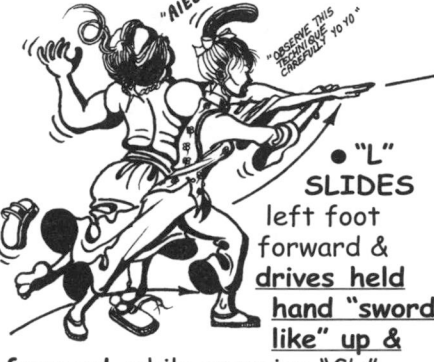

● **"L" SLIDES** left foot forward & <u>drives held hand "sword like" up & forward</u>, while grasping "G's" hand (with her other hand).

● **"L" PIVOTS THRU 180 DEGREES** & twists "G's" hand over his shoulder, while <u>driving forward & down "sword like"</u> (& stepping forward).

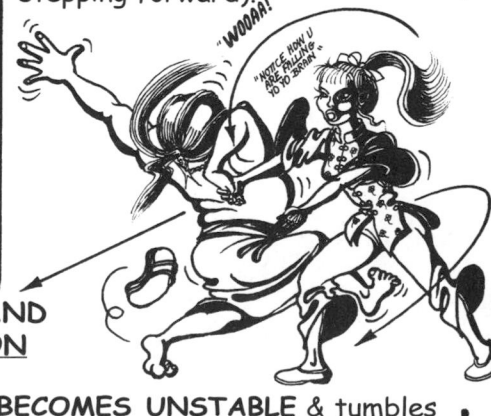

● **"G" BECOMES UNSTABLE** & tumbles backward <u>(use leg sweep if necessary)</u> - "L" follows "G" to ground (maintaining grip) - If required delivering blow(s) to "G's" face.

● **WITH SMALL VARIATIONS** the above move can be used <u>against an armed attacker</u> - Use both hands to twist & hold (as the fingers are forced open).

You Don't Have To Be Bruce Lee To Enjoy (& Benefit Vastly From) This Page

STRETCH INTO EACH POSITION GENTLY & HOLD FOR UP TO 60 SECONDS

PRE - STRETCH (FORWARD)

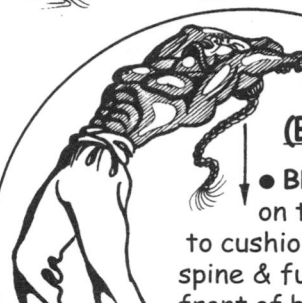

- **OFTEN STARTED** from upright with full lungs to further stretch spine.
- **ACCORDING TO** ability, grip toes & pull.
- **BEGINNERS CAN** slightly bend knees.

1.

PRE - STRETCH (BACKWARD)

- **BREATHE IN** on the way back to cushion curve of spine & further stretch front of body.

COMMON POSTURE FAULT: LOW BACK TOO STIFF (PRACTICE CRAB & BOW POSTURES MORE -ALSO THE COBRA HELPS).

2.

PRE - STRETCH (SIDES)

- Low hand behind back.
- Keep body & hips facing to front.
- Stomach in.
- Feet flat.

3.

PRE - STRETCH (TWISTS)

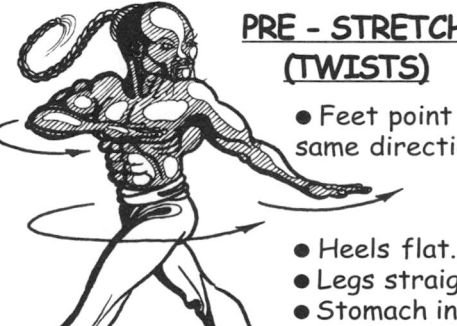

- Feet point in same direction.
- Heels flat.
- Legs straight.
- Stomach in.

4.

BREATHING

- **DURING MOVE-MENTS** (unless otherwise stated) **breathe out when bending trunk for-ward** (or when bring-ing limbs across the trunk) - **Breathe in when straightening trunk** (or moving limbs away from trunk).
- **WHEN STATION-ARY** during stretches **continue breathing deeply & slowly** (in thru nose & out thru mouth).

DON'T

- **DON'T bounce** (**"Ballistic Stretch"**) because this can (easily) tear muscles.
- **DON'T consecu-tively stretch the same muscle group** (if possible) except in P.N.F. technique (over).
- **DON'T force the stretch** - Use only moderate tension & no more.
- **DON'T (beginners) stretch each muscle group more often than alternate days** (at first) to give **RECOVERY TIME.**

BENEFITS (MIND)

- **STRESS release** is an actual fact with many stretches similar to yoga.
- **CONFIDENCE thru ability** generates a positive outlook.
- **STIMULATION of multiple sites** up-grades mentality.
- **SPIRITUALITY is revived thru creativ-ity** & the awareness/ pleasure of a close mind/body link.

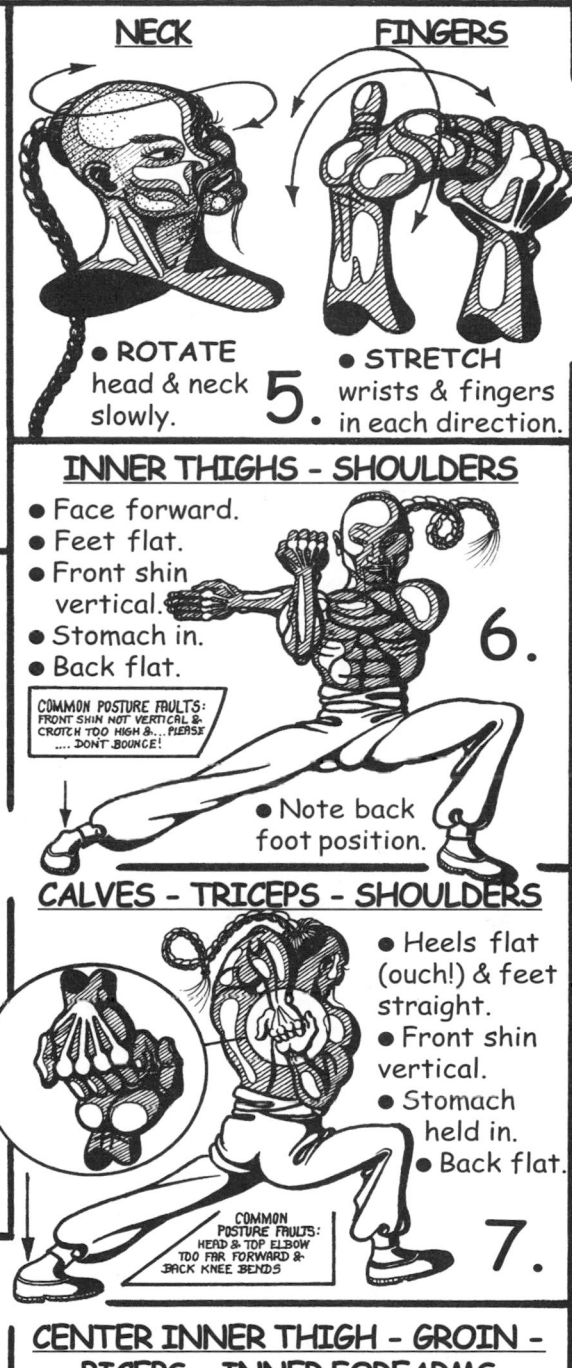

NECK   FINGERS

- **ROTATE** head & neck slowly.

5.

- **STRETCH** wrists & fingers in each direction.

INNER THIGHS - SHOULDERS

- Face forward.
- Feet flat.
- Front shin vertical.
- Stomach in.
- Back flat.

COMMON POSTURE FAULTS: FRONT SHIN NOT VERTICAL & CROTCH TOO HIGH &... PLEASE .... DON'T BOUNCE!

6.

- Note back foot position.

CALVES - TRICEPS - SHOULDERS

- Heels flat (ouch!) & feet straight.
- Front shin vertical.
- Stomach held in.
- Back flat.

COMMON POSTURE FAULTS: HEAD & TOP ELBOW TOO FAR FORWARD & BACK KNEE BENDS

7.

CENTER INNER THIGH - GROIN - BICEPS - INNER FOREARMS

- Feet flat & facing forward.
- Palms down & fingers back.
- Progressively slide feet sideways.

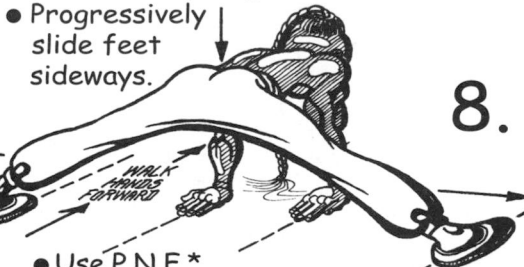

WALK HANDS FORWARD

- Use P.N.F.*

8.

FRONT INNER THIGHS - GROIN - STOMACH - CHEST - SHOULDERS

● **FROM POSITION #8** - Reverse hands - Drop hips to floor (feet on side) - Raise upper body slowly (keep hips on floor) AHHHH!

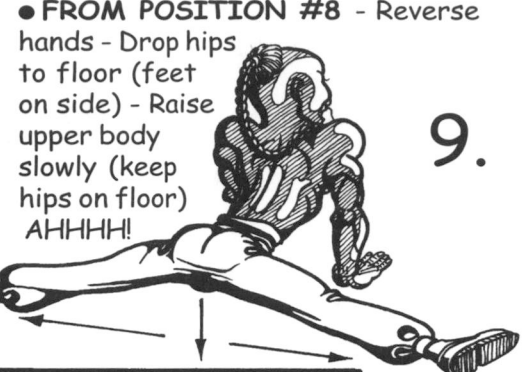

9.

CHEST - FRONT OF ARMS - TOES

● Back straight. ● Stomach in.

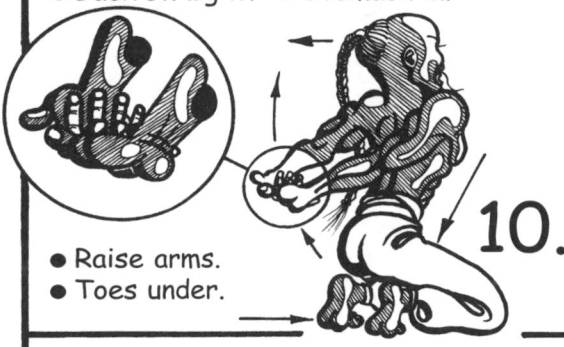

● Raise arms.
● Toes under.

10.

BACK - INNER & REAR THIGHS - BUTTOCKS - KNEES - GROIN - TRICEPS - DELTOIDS

● Back straight as possible.
● Stomach pulled in.
● Point toe & grip it.
● Can use 1 hand to....

11.

....push bent knee down.

BENEFITS (BODY)

● **IMPROVE** posture & joint/spine alignment.
● **ELONGATES** & tones muscles (& significantly reduces muscle tension).
● **HELPS** reduce sports injuries, aches, strains, sprains etc.
● **EFFECTIVELY** warms muscles/body prior to further sport/exercise etc.
● **KEEPS YOU** mobile & flexible into advanced old age.
● **PROVIDES** a very versatile exercise form which can be done virtually any-where/anytime.
● **CIRCULATION** & the elimination of toxic deposits are both improved.
● **AS A "WIND DOWN"** sequence at the end of strenuous (or prolonged) exercise - Signifi-cantly reduces resulting aches, stiffness, tensions.
● **ACU. POINTS (TSUBOS)** & their associated meridians relating to every body function are variously stimulated during stretching - Result is broad meta-bolic enhancement of the entire body.

GROIN - BUTTOCKS - DELTOIDS - BACK - INNER & REAR THIGHS - KNEES

● Heels into groin.
● Soles of feet together.
● Grasp toes & pull down.
● Knees down.

12.

QUADRICEPS - INSTEP & ANKLES - GROIN - STOMACH - KNEES

● Keep heels to sides of buttocks & pointing up.
● Keep knees on floor.

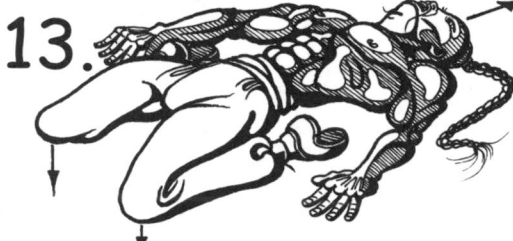

13.

FRONT & REAR THIGHS & GROIN

● **ADVANCED STRETCH-ERS** (not kids) use P.N.F.* for this stretch.

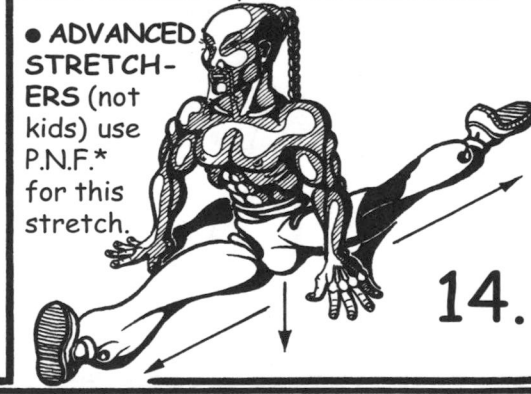

14.

P.N.F.

WHAT IS IT?

● **STANDS FOR:** PROPRIOCEPTIVE NEURO-MUSCULAR FACILITATION....
● **AND THAT IS....** an advanced stretching system - Which by the use of isometric tension blocks out the muscle in question's "early pain" ([Golgi Organ Signal] which inhibits further stretching) - **This permits additional muscle elongation without injury** (providing the technique is not abused) or used by the wrong people.
● **KIDS** (immature joints) & beginners (untoned muscles) - AVOID USING THIS SYSTEM.
● **WARM UP WELL before using P.N.F. TO DE-RIVE MAXIMUM RESULTS.**

HOW DO I DO IT ?

A. **ASSUME A STRETCH POSITION** (e.g. #8 or 14) - Until moderate tension is felt.
B. **TENSE HARD THE MUSCLE(S)** being stretched for 16 secs. - Then relax for 2 secs. (& push a little further into the stretch).
C. **REPEAT STEP "B" 4 TIMES** in all - Except on Set 4 tense for 1 - 4 mins. (& relax for 1 min.).
D. **THE ENTIRE PROCEDURE** (A, B, & C) can be repeated up to 4 times (at one session).

RECOVERY TIME NOTE

P.N.F. CAN ACHIEVE **much faster results (e.g. with splits)** BUT REQUIRES 48-96 HRS TISSUE ADAPTATION TIME **between full sessions.**

4 BASIC RULES

KNOWLEDGE OF MARTIAL ART TECHNIQUES CARRIES MORAL & LEGAL RESPONSIBILITIES.

1. NEVER STRIKE THE FIRST BLOW.
2. DON'T USE EXCESSIVE FORCE.
3. STOP WHEN OUT OF DANGER.
4. TEMPER & MARTIAL ARTS ARE INCOMPATIBLE.

THE FIST

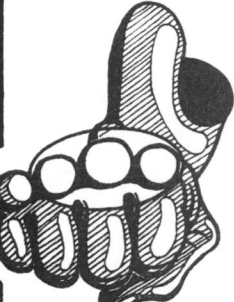

- IDEALLY strike with first two knuckles - **Ensure back of hand & forearm are in straight line** - Condition for 1-2 years.

THE PALM

- VERY POWERFUL & fast to train (3-6 months) - **Effectiveness depends on correct body co-ordination** - Favorite targets are under chin & chest.

THE FORK

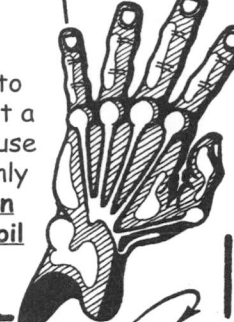

- TAKES VERY LONG (1-4 years) to condition well - But a useful strike because of long reach to only target (eyes) - **Even a miss causes recoil** (& loss of concentration).

THE HAMMER

- POWERFUL & quite easy to condition (6-18 mths) - Use on low targets (e.g. back of neck/skull) - Also sideways/back to face.

CONSIDER 1st THAT

FORCE = MASS × ACCELERATION

THE CLAW

- VERY USEFUL in grappling situations (to cover attacker's face [fingers in eye sockets]) - Conditioning improves power (but can be used without).

MAXIMUM IMPACT....

- **MOMENTUM:** Twist hips & body into strike - **MOVE ENTIRE BODY FORWARD ON IMPACT.**
- **A STRAIGHT LINE** thru max. body mass **achieves max. impact.**
- **RIGIDITY & SPEED:** Relaxed muscles contribute to more delivery speed (& thus impact) .... - **BUT tense muscles are required at the instant of impact** (to transmit body weight efficiently [particularly buttocks]).

"G..KUK"
'YAH!'

....& BREATHING

- **EXCEPT IN RAPID COMBINATIONS** use 1 breath for 1 technique - **So that at moment of impact all air is forced out of mouth** (in combat shout) - This violent exhalation also helps muscle rigidity & spine alignment by involuntary tensing of stomach muscles (also distracts opponent[s])

THE BLOCK

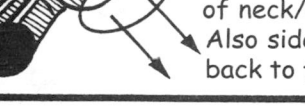

- USE TO STRIKE sideways & out (incoming blows & kicks) - Your left blocks attacker's right etc.

....& SECOND THAT....

EVERY ACTION HAS AN EQUAL & OPPOSITE REACTION

THE HOOK **A.**

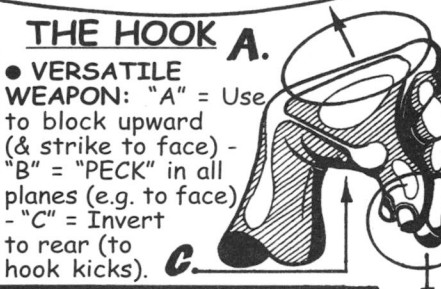

- **VERSATILE WEAPON:** "A" = Use to block upward (& strike to face) - "B" = "PECK" in all planes (e.g. to face) - "C" = Invert to rear (to hook kicks). **C.** **B.**

THE ELBOW

- POWERFUL close-in weapon - For use to head (sideways) - To back (down) - To kidneys/groin /belly (backward) - Conditioning much improves strike ability.

THE CHOP

- A VERY POWERFUL strike - Requires minimal (to use) conditioning (1-6 mths) - Targets include side/back of neck - Also hands/arms (holding weapons).

THE SPEAR

- A DEADLY WEAPON used to strike primarily at throat (or belly) - **But requires long (2-6 years) conditioning** - NOTE: Slightly curved fingers.

HOW TO CONDITION FOR MARTIAL ART STRIKES
Practice Theory, So That Theory Will Work In Practice

(INTERNAL) SOFT SCHOOL TRAINING
- **PROGRESSIVE CONDITIONING** of tissues, ligaments, nerves, circulation & joints WITH LITTLE EXTERNAL (SKIN) EVIDENCE.

(EXTERNAL) HARD SCHOOL TRAINING
- **AS PER "SOFT SCHOOL"** (but far more extreme) - Increased injury risk - HEAVY SKIN THICKENING - CALLUS FORMATION.

STRIKE PROGRESSIVELY EACH POSITION 4 - 100 TIMES.

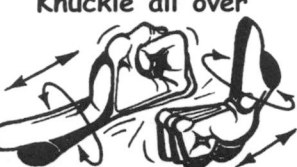 Push fingers sideways
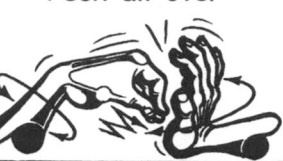 Force in & out
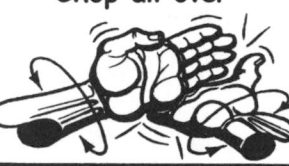 Knuckle all over / Peck all over
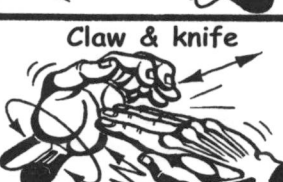 Chop all over / Hit palms all over
Hammer all over / Claw & knife

IN BOTH SCHOOLS START SLOWLY & BUILD UP POWER, TIME & TECHNIQUE OVER ABOUT 2 YRS.

STRIKE PROGRESSIVELY (TOTAL 4-60 MINS/DAY).

SAND BUCKET....
- **FILL INITIALLY** with rice - Drive strike (e.g. fist) in as far as possiblble - **Change quarterly** to dried peas, sand, small stones.

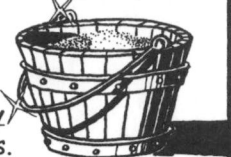

IMPACT BLOCK....
- **COVER** a 12 x 12 inch soft wood block (with 2 layers of leather) - Strike progressively.

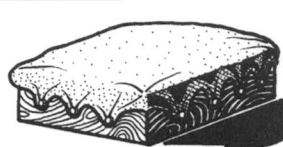

CONDITIONING BAG....
- **SECURE** a canvas bag on firm surface - Vary filling with progress (foam to gravel).

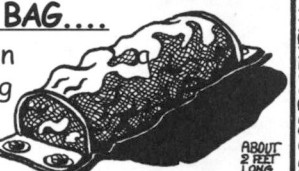 *ABOUT 2 FEET LONG*

TREE TRUNKS....
- **....PARTICULARLY** old ones (with thick crumbling bark) are ideal for progressive strike training.

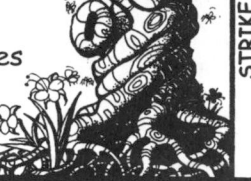

TECHNIQUES ADAPTABLE TO EITHER SCHOOL

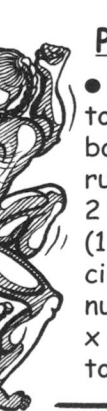

POWER TRAINING
- **SECURE BAGS** at top with chain (& bottom with rubber) - Draw 2 figures on tall (1 x 6 ft) bag - & circles with numbers on heavy (2 x 4 ft) bag (in order to target strikes).

REFLEX TRAINING
- **SECURE** 4 filled balls (1 ft dia.) at shoulder ht. (between floor/roof) - Double rubbers above balls & single below (in a 6 ft square) - Strike as many balls as fast as possible - BUT DON'T GET HIT. *"WAK!"*

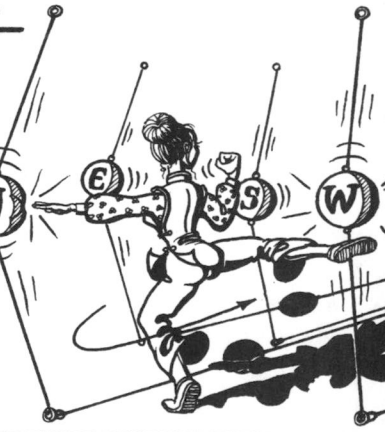

TRAINING PARTNER(S)
- **ALWAYS STRETCH/** warm up first - **Wear at least head & groin protection** - Blocks are very important (so swap defense & attack roles) - During sparring "pull" strikes to just touch the target - Martial arts are both useful & fun so - ENJOY IT! *"OUCH!"*

SPARRING POST
- **BUILT FROM** greased "slices" of hardwood tree trunk (1 ft dia. x 6 ins thick) - With a "pin" down the middle - & 2 inch x 3 ft arms (wrapped in 1 inch rope) stuck in each side.

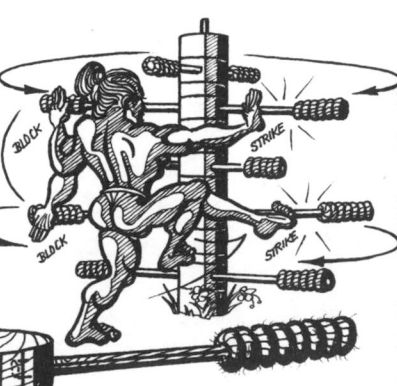

4 BASIC RULES

KNOWLEDGE OF MARTIAL ART TECHNIQUES CARRIES MORAL & LEGAL RESPONSIBILITIES.

1. NEVER STRIKE THE FIRST BLOW.	2. DON'T USE EXCESSIVE FORCE.	3. STOP WHEN OUT OF DANGER.	4. TEMPER & MARTIAL ARTS ARE INCOMPATIBLE.

4 BASIC PRINCIPLES

1. ON DELIVERY STRIVE FOR A STRAIGHT LINE through leg & body - THIS ENSURES BODY WEIGHT IS TRANSMITTED TO TARGET (& not deflected) - Also helps balance.

2. MAXIMUM POWER ONLY ON IMPACT - This requires all muscles tense for solidity - UNTIL THEN, RELAX IN ORDER TO ACHIEVE MAXIMUM SPEED.

3. RAISE KNEE/LEG PRIOR TO STRIKES - THIS MAKES THE KICK FASTER & MORE POWERFUL - Also more difficult to predict (& block).

4. DON'T GIVE AWAY YOUR INTENDED TARGET by glancing at it USE PERIPHERAL VISION - Also don't change stance too early - Unless either are deliberate false indications.

8 KICK STRIKE ZONES

KNEE (K) · SHIN (S) · ARCH (A) · HEEL (H) · BALL (B)

INSTEP (I) · BACK OF HEEL (BH) · OUTSIDE EDGE (O)

16 DEVASTATING KICKS

FRONT SNAP KICK

- EASY to learn.
- MINIMAL body movement.
- FAST & hard to counter.
- STRIKE & snap back from knee.

B/I.

- IDEAL targets are kneecap (B), groin (I) & abdomen (B).

BACK SNAP KICK

- LOOK over intended strike shoulder - Fold leg at knee - Strike with heel - Refold leg.

H.

- MOST usual target belly (or kneecap).

INSIDE CRESCENT KICK

A.

- START with left foot forward.
- TWIST upper body to left.
- BEND knee - Twist hip & kick (all in one move).
- TENSE all muscles on impact.
- SNAP leg back at knee & change stance (all in one move).

FRONT THRUST KICK

- MOVES similar to above (but used to stop advancing attacker).

THIS FOOT (LEFT) STAYS PUT, BUT PUSH BACK & STRAIGHTEN LEG JUST PRIOR TO IMPACT.

H or B.

- TWIST hips & hold strike longer (to belly/chest/chin [H] or to belly [B]) before snapping leg back at knee.

SPINNING BACK KICK

- DIFFICULT to time (& target) but devastating if done well.

H/O/B.

"WRONG YO YO! YOU NEED TEETH!"

OUTSIDE CRESCENT KICK

O/H.

- START with right foot forward.
- BEND knee - Strike - Twist hips (& upper body) all in one move.
- TENSE all muscles on impact.
- SNAP leg back at knee - Change stance (all in one move).
- CRESCENT kicks are quite effective (& simple) to learn - PRACTICE THE SPLITS.

GROUND SIDE KICK
- **USE** against an advancing attacker if you have fallen (target belly, knee, groin).
- **CAN** also strike back with heel (Ground Back Kick).

O/H.

GROUND SWEEP KICK
- **USED** to sweep an attackers supporting leg away (at a critical moment).

"PLEASE WOO CHIN SON ME HELP ME UP...AHH!"

"SHOW ME YOUR BEST KICK... FALL-TO-YO"

I.

GROUND ROUND HOUSE KICK
- **USE** to strike belly, head (crouched), kidneys or weapon hand of unwary attacker - Tense muscles on impact.

I. or B.

SIDE SNAP KICK
- **FOR** maximum impact start with kicking foot back.

O/H.

- **SNAP** leg back.
- **TWIST** upper body first - Bend knee & strike in a straight line (with muscles tensed).

STANDING SWEEP KICK
"WHY U LITTLE... I'LL SHOW U M' BEST KICK!... AAH-BAM!"

"NOW THAT WAS NO GOOD AGAIN!"

- **USE** forward.... ....or back

ROUND HOUSE SNAP KICK
- **VERSATILE** & fast - Can be used at various heights.

B. or I.

- **"RUBBER band"** snap out & back is critical.
- **RETURN** to original (or opposite) "Ready Stance."

SIDE THRUST KICK
- **AS ABOVE**, except used when requiring more power - Particularly effective against an advancing attacker - Be wary of leg/foot grabs.

O/H.

▲ SIDE KICKS OFTEN EXECUTED CONSECUTIVELY W/ ALTERNATE LEGS

- **BODY** is more in line - Leg is left in position slightly longer.

A KICK....
....**HAS SEVERAL TIMES** (<u>about 3.5 on average</u>) the "destructive" power of a punch.

....**CAN ATTACK BODY PARTS** which are very hard to defend ie. knees/shin/groin.

....**HAS A MUCH LONGER** reach than a punch - <u>Thus a short person can strike a tall one</u> (or a child an adult).

MOST KICKS....
....**CAN BE EXECECUTED** in variations of the basic strike - For example <u>sliding kicks</u> are when a given kick is combined with a slide toward the target increasing momentum & impact.

....**JUMPING KICKS** take the above one step futher - <u>The aim being</u> (in both cases) <u>to put as much rigid</u> (muscles tensed) <u>body weight</u> (traveling as fast as possible) <u>behind each kick at the moment of impact,</u> as possible.

....& TOUGHEN UP THOSE FEET

REVERSE ROUNDHOUSE KICK
- **"RUBBER BAND"** snap is important.

B/I/H.

- **A SLIGHTLY** <u>awkward kick to learn</u> - But covers a useful angle (therefore worthwhile).

AXE KICK
- **BE CAREFUL** <u>of grabs</u> with this kick.

H.

- **USED** to strike a horizontally exposed target from above (e.g. collar-bone, chest, back of neck, spine etc.).

USE OF THE KNEE
- **IF YOU** are too close to kick - Then use the knee - Simple, powerful & easy (multiple strikes).

| to BELLY or KIDNEYS |
| to THIGH or BELLY |
| to GROIN or FACE (use hands to hold). |

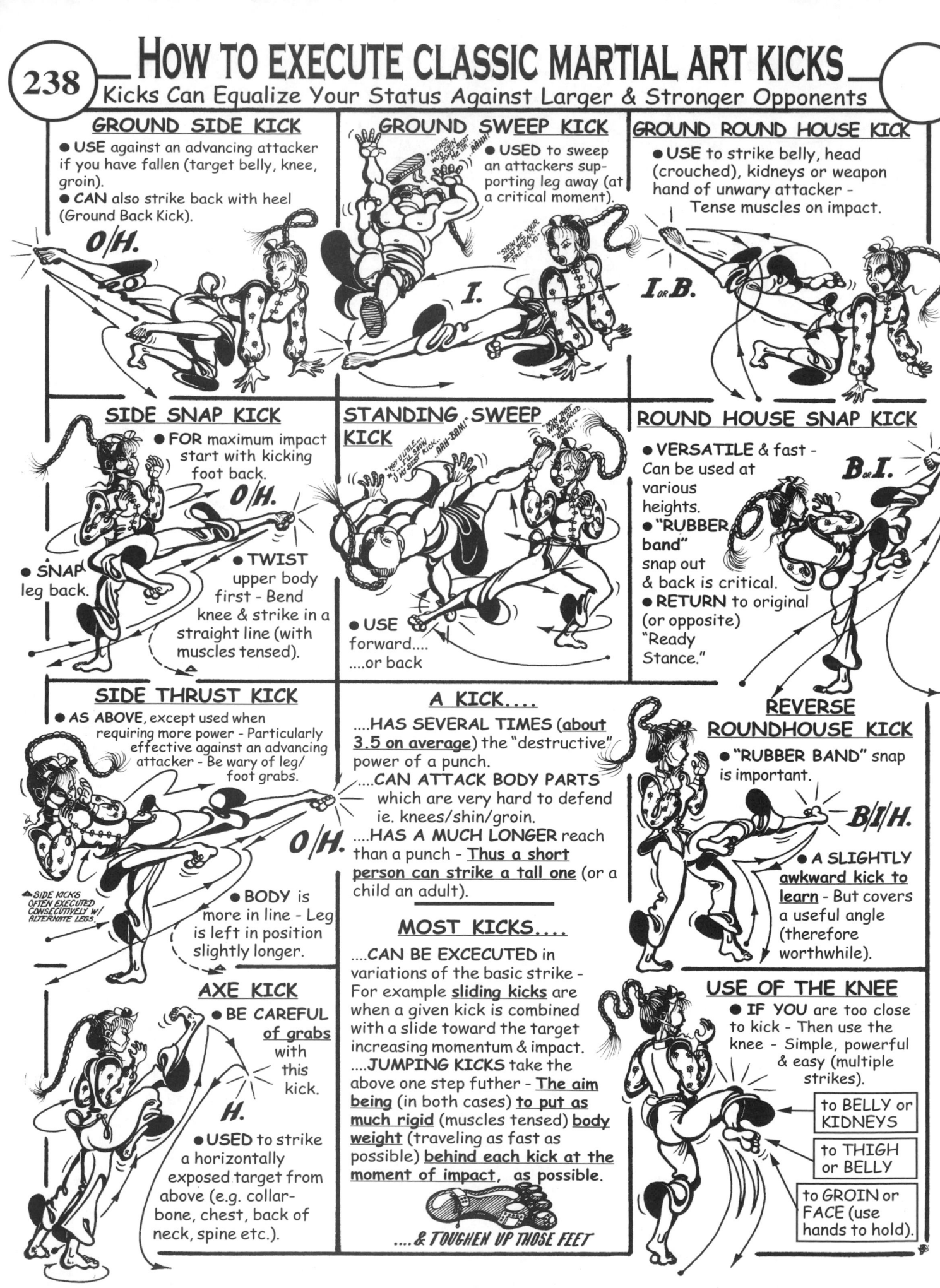

Formal Exercise Sequence ("Striking Snake" 1-36)

PRACTICE & STUDY THE PURPOSE OF EACH POSITION & MOVEMENT -
Until able to deliver any random combination - Automatically & at speed.

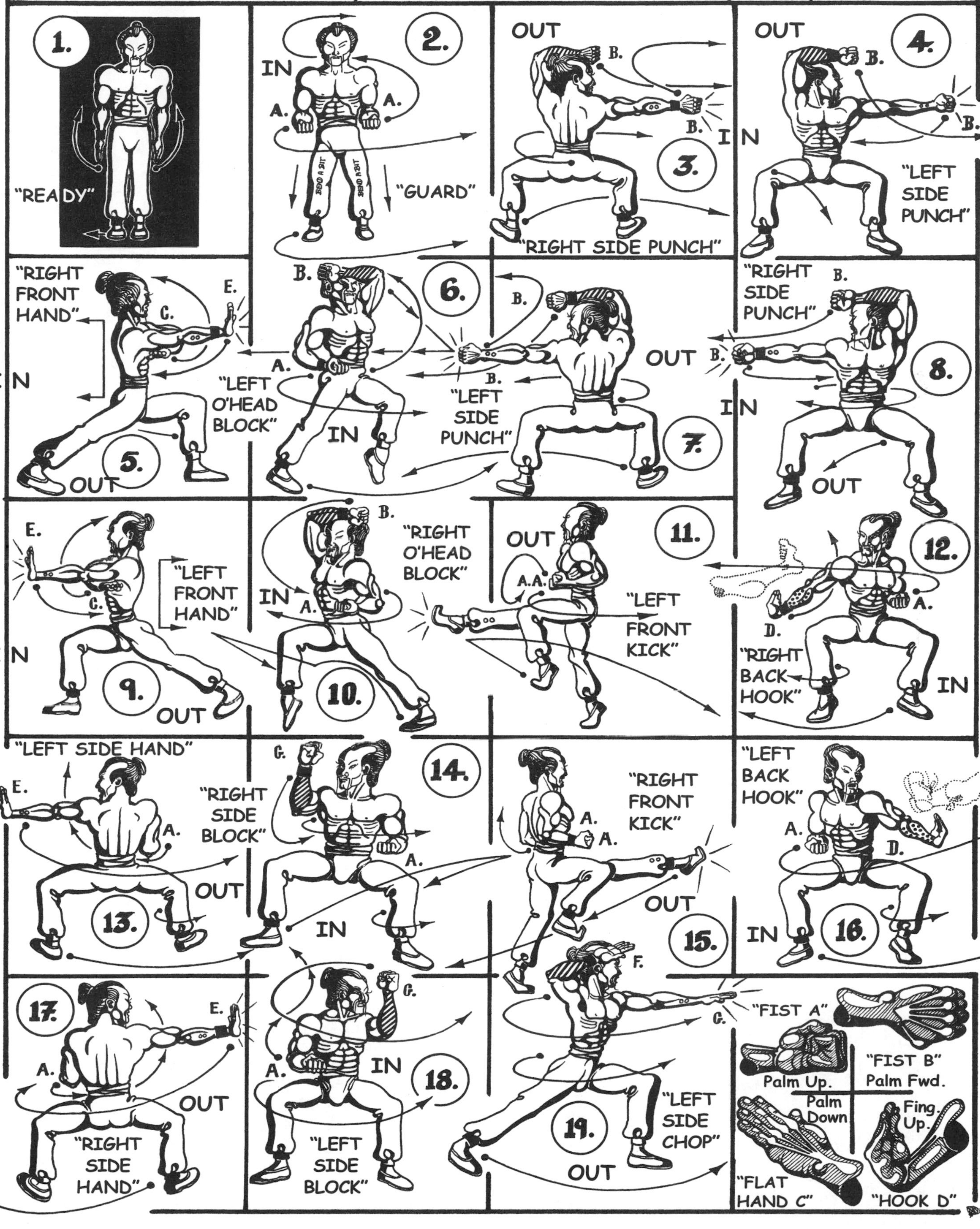
1.
"READY"
2.
IN
A.
A.
"GUARD"
OUT
B.
B.
IN
3.
"RIGHT SIDE PUNCH"
OUT
4.
B.
B.
"LEFT SIDE PUNCH"
"RIGHT FRONT HAND"
E.
C.
IN
5.
OUT
B.
6.
A.
"LEFT O'HEAD BLOCK"
IN
B.
B.
"LEFT SIDE PUNCH"
OUT
7.
"RIGHT SIDE PUNCH"
B.
B.
8.
IN
OUT
E.
"LEFT FRONT HAND"
C.
IN
9.
OUT
B.
"RIGHT O'HEAD BLOCK"
IN
A.
10.
OUT
11.
A.A.
"LEFT FRONT KICK"
12.
A.
D.
"RIGHT BACK HOOK"
IN
"LEFT SIDE HAND"
E.
A.
"RIGHT SIDE BLOCK"
OUT
13.
G.
14.
A.
IN
"RIGHT FRONT KICK"
A.
A.
OUT
15.
"LEFT BACK HOOK"
A.
D.
IN
16.
17.
E.
A.
OUT
"RIGHT SIDE HAND"
G.
A.
IN
18.
"LEFT SIDE BLOCK"
F.
G.
"LEFT SIDE CHOP"
19.
OUT
"FIST A"
"FIST B"
Palm Fwd.
Palm Up.
Palm Down
Fing. Up.
"FLAT HAND C"
"HOOK D"

HOW TO EXECUTE CLASSIC KUNG FU MOVES

Formal Exercise Sequence ("Striking Snake" 1 - 36)

INCREASE POWER OF A DELIVERED BLOW BY BODY ROTATION.
REDUCE IMPACT WHEN RECEIVING A BLOW BY DEFLECTION.

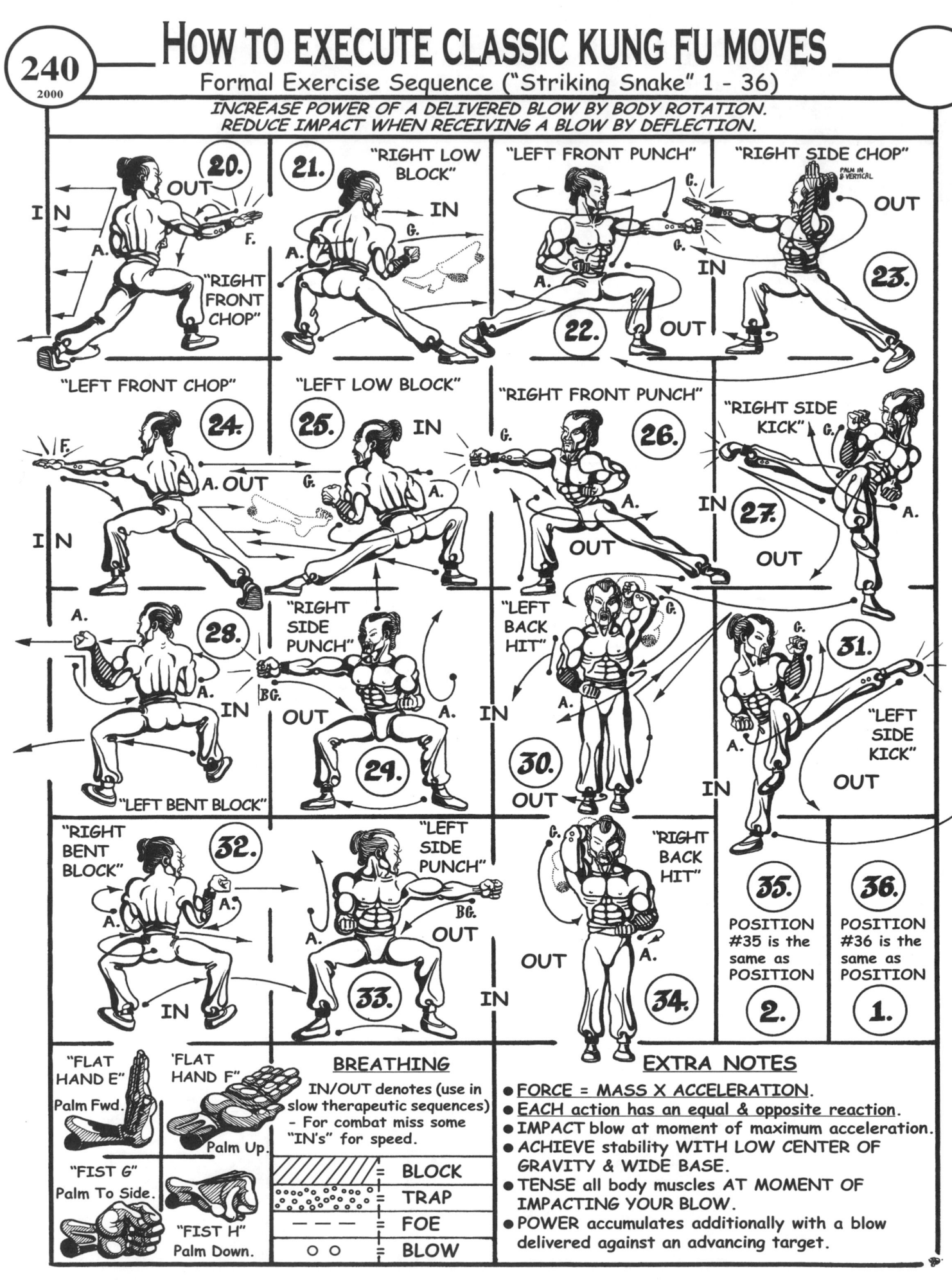

20. OUT — IN — A. — F. — "RIGHT FRONT CHOP"

21. "RIGHT LOW BLOCK" — IN — A. — G.

22. "LEFT FRONT PUNCH" — C. — G. — A. — OUT

23. "RIGHT SIDE CHOP" — PALM IN & VERTICAL — OUT — IN

"LEFT FRONT CHOP"

24. F. — A. OUT — IN

25. "LEFT LOW BLOCK" — IN — G. — A.

26. "RIGHT FRONT PUNCH" — G. — A. — OUT

27. "RIGHT SIDE KICK" — G. — IN — OUT — A.

28. A. — IN — BG. — OUT

29. "RIGHT SIDE PUNCH"

30. "LEFT BACK HIT" — G. — A. — IN — OUT

31. G. — A. — "LEFT SIDE KICK" — IN — OUT

"LEFT BENT BLOCK"

32. "RIGHT BENT BLOCK" — A. — A.

33. "LEFT SIDE PUNCH" — BG. — OUT — IN — A.

34. "RIGHT BACK HIT" — G. — OUT — A.

35. POSITION #35 is the same as POSITION **2.**

36. POSITION #36 is the same as POSITION **1.**

"FLAT HAND E" Palm Fwd.

'FLAT HAND F" Palm Up.

"FIST G" Palm To Side.

"FIST H" Palm Down.

BREATHING

IN/OUT denotes (use in slow therapeutic sequences) – For combat miss some "IN's" for speed.

⧄ =	BLOCK
⠿ =	TRAP
--- =	FOE
○○ =	BLOW

EXTRA NOTES

- FORCE = MASS X ACCELERATION.
- EACH action has an equal & opposite reaction.
- IMPACT blow at moment of maximum acceleration.
- ACHIEVE stability WITH LOW CENTER OF GRAVITY & WIDE BASE.
- TENSE all body muscles AT MOMENT OF IMPACTING YOUR BLOW.
- POWER accumulates additionally with a blow delivered against an advancing target.

Devastating Short Stick Techniques Demonstrated By Mistress Hoo Chin

SHORT STICK HISTORY

ANCIENT FORMS (BOTH SINGLE & DOUBLE) ABOUND IN ASIA, EXAMPLE "ESCRIMA" a Philippino art originating in India but imported into the Philippines via the Thai peninsula & Indoneasian islands....
....BY ROVING MERCHANT ADVENTURERS MORE THAN 1000 YEARS AGO.

SPIRITUAL PREPARATION

- **IN COMBAT** (due to emotional stress) <u>awareness of surroundings can shrink to a single spot (e.g. attacker's knife) ignoring other dangers.</u> • This condition must be trained against by: Meditation or self-hynosis (use a trigger word to invoke a calm but alert state).
- **SPAR PHYSICALLY** with training partners to detraumatize the experience. • <u>MAKE A CONSCIOUS</u> effort <u>NOT TO DEVELOP "TUNNEL VISION"</u> prior to & during confrontational situations.

THE STICK(S)

....**FOR THIS** form is/are arm length (i.e. Wrist to Armpit).

"LOOK! THIS LONG"

....**DEPENDING ON** material (Rattan Vine traditionally) about 1 inch thick - <u>Weight depends on user's strength</u> - Heavier stick strikes harder but is slower - Lighter stick is faster but has less impact - THEREFORE COMPROMISE.

PHYSICAL PREPARATION

- **PROFICIENCY** in Escrima (as in any art) requires practice & dedication.
- <u>No one is perfect therefore even the best can improve.</u>
- **STRIVE** before a mirror to perform each move exactly.
- Then swap hands & try again.
- Then progress to combinations of moves (<u>FROM BOTH SIDES & WITH BOTH HANDS</u>).
- Then speed the sequences up not forgetting accuracy & force. Seek out training partners to spar & swap ideas with.

BASIC STRIKE FORMS

"TRAINING STRIKE"

"I'M GONNA CUT YER UP!"
"STOP!"

- **DELIVERED** with force but stopped at strike site (to permit counters to be applied).

"BOUNCING STRIKE"

"OUCH! MAYBE NOT"
"DONK!"

- **STRIKE** & withdraw technique (as if hitting rubber) - Used in multiple strikes & fakes - Difficult strike to counter.

"POWER STRIKE"

"CRACK! ...DEM THAT HURTS... AAAH! ...OK OK I GIVE UP!"
AIM TO FINISH HERE

- **DELIVERED** "thru" the target - Clumsy but bone crushingly forceful (if it connects) - But open to counters if missed.

"TWIRLING STRIKE"

"OOOO! ...VERY FANCY!"
START HERE

- **TECHNIQUE** where (prior to a strike) stick is twirled from the wrist (maintain finger grip) - To confuse target.

"FAN STRIKE"

"WOW! ...DO THAT AGAIN!"

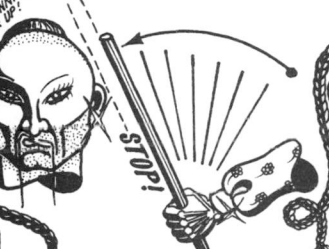

- **POWERFUL** whipping technique where stick, wrist, elbow & upper arm is fanned (any plane) - To confuse prior to a strike.

"SWORD STRIKE"

- **STICK IS** thrust end first (like sword) - Effective strike, but stick must be held very tight

"HAAH! ...INSULT! DON'T FRIGHTEN ME LIKE THAT!"

....**also <u>vulnerable to grabs & counters</u>** - Used in small spaces (or when blocked) & at long range - Good follow-up move.

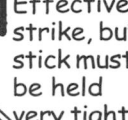

"LONG BACK STRIKE"

- **REQUIRES** a change from conventional grip (thumb up) to stick on little finger side - Used to strike backward from awkward (longer range) positions (e.g. holds).

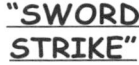

"SHORT BACK STRIKE"

"G. AAAH! NO MORE PLEASE. ...I'LL BEE YOUR SLAVE!"

- **USING THE 1 inch** of stick protruding from bottom of hand - Strike (usually head targets) from awkward positions (or holds).

- **THE "LIVE HAND"** (in single stick Escrima combat) is the hand not holding the stick - <u>It is traditionally held close to the central chest</u> (palm forward or "in") - <u>This position best avoids attacks on it</u> (until required for blocks, counters, grabs, strikes etc.).

ASIAN SECRETS OF SHORT STICK COMBAT
With Practice, Effective Against All Non-Projectile Weaponry

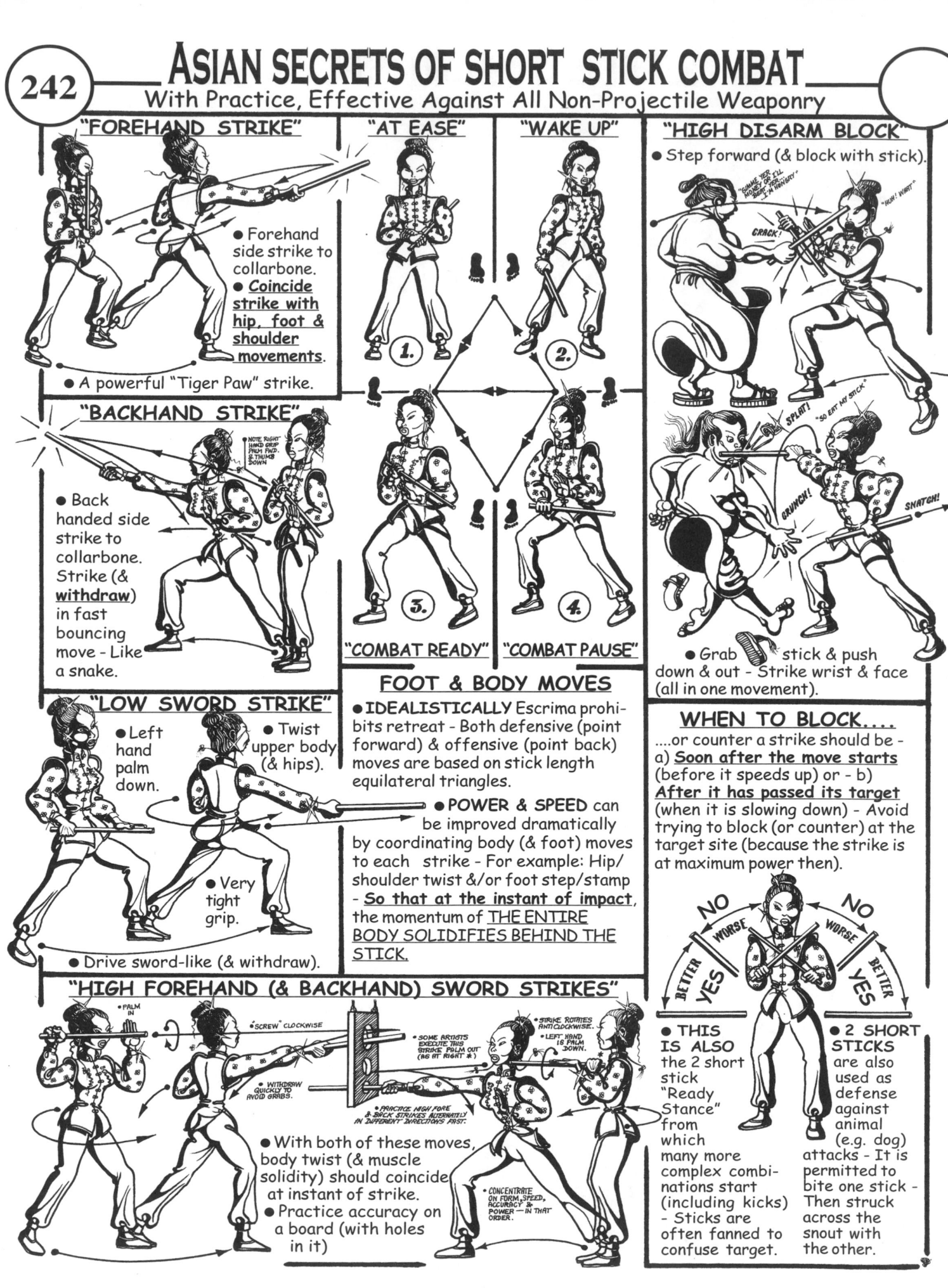

"FOREHAND STRIKE"

- Forehand side strike to collarbone.
- **Coincide strike with hip, foot & shoulder movements**.
- A powerful "Tiger Paw" strike.

"BACKHAND STRIKE"

- Back handed side strike to collarbone. Strike (& **withdraw**) in fast bouncing move - Like a snake.

"LOW SWORD STRIKE"

- Left hand palm down.
- Twist upper body (& hips).
- Very tight grip.
- Drive sword-like (& withdraw).

"AT EASE"
1.

"WAKE UP"
2.

3.

4.

"COMBAT READY"   "COMBAT PAUSE"

FOOT & BODY MOVES

- **IDEALISTICALLY** Escrima prohibits retreat - Both defensive (point forward) & offensive (point back) moves are based on stick length equilateral triangles.
- **POWER & SPEED** can be improved dramatically by coordinating body (& foot) moves to each strike - For example: Hip/shoulder twist &/or foot step/stamp - **So that at the instant of impact**, the momentum of THE ENTIRE BODY SOLIDIFIES BEHIND THE STICK.

"HIGH DISARM BLOCK"

- Step forward (& block with stick).

CRACK!

SPLAT!   "SO EAT MY STICK"

GRUNCH!   SNATCH!

- Grab stick & push down & out - Strike wrist & face (all in one movement).

WHEN TO BLOCK....

....or counter a strike should be - a) **Soon after the move starts** (before it speeds up) or - b) **After it has passed its target** (when it is slowing down) - Avoid trying to block (or counter) at the target site (because the strike is at maximum power then).

NO   NO
WORSE   WORSE
YES   YES
BETTER   BETTER

- **THIS IS ALSO** the 2 short stick "Ready Stance" from which many more complex combinations start (including kicks) - Sticks are often fanned to confuse target.

- **2 SHORT STICKS** are also used as defense against animal (e.g. dog) attacks - It is permitted to bite one stick - Then struck across the snout with the other.

"HIGH FOREHAND (& BACKHAND) SWORD STRIKES"

- With both of these moves, body twist (& muscle solidity) should coincide at instant of strike.
- Practice accuracy on a board (with holes in it)

Devastatingly Demonstrated In Actual Conflict By Mistress Hoo Chin (& Yo Yo Brain)

"READY STANCE"

BACKGROUND

● **OVER 400 RECORDED** stick fighting styles (& many moves & techniques within each style) - Applicable to various lengths from the **"Wing Chun Long Pole"** (7 ft, 2 ins) to **Japanese "Tessen Iron Edge Fan Style"** (+/- 1 foot) - Now sadly most of these ancient arts are almost forgotten.

ADVANTAGES

● **PRACTICE** can make this a highly effective defense form against most forms of personal attack (incl. knives etc.)
● **RESPONSE** easily variable from mild pain to serious injury.
● **STRENGTH** requirement is low.
● **CHEAP** & legally permissible.

HOW?

● **HANDS** (palm back) & feet apart (at shoulder width).
● **RELAX** spiritually & physically - BUT BE AT ALL TIMES VERY ALERT.
● **LOOK** at your attacker's eyes - BUT SEE HIS/HER WHOLE BODY.

WHY?

● **THIS STANCE** is deceptively nonaggressive in appearance.
● **IT PERMITS** a large choice of blocks & strikes (with minimum position change).

POWER

● **BELIEVE** the stick to be a part of (& strike with) your whole body.
● **STRIKE** with the end 6" of the stick.

"START POSITION"

PRACTICE UNTIL YOUR TRAINING PARTNER CAN ATTACK WITH EITHER HAND, WITH FULL POWER & SPEED.

the 8 BASIC DEFENSE & COUNTERMOVES

"OUTSIDE CHEST STRIKE (step back)"

A 1

● **LEFT** foot step back diagonally.
● **SLIDE** left hand to end of stick.
● **RIGHT** foot slide to left a bit.
● **WHILE** striking slide right hand & twist upper body.

"OUTSIDE CHEST STRIKE (step forward)"

A 2

● **LEFT** foot step diagonally forward.
● **SLIDE** left hand to end of stick.
● **RIGHT** foot slide after left a bit.
● **WHILE** striking slide right hand.
● **FOLLOW** with "F."

"INSIDE ONE HAND JAB"

B

● **LET** go right hand and swing.
● **WIDEN** & lower stance.
● **JAB** at solar plexus/face with whole body.
● **MANY** good follow-up moves.

"INSIDE CHEST STRIKE"

C

● **LEAN** & step to right (slide right hand to stick end).
● **STRIKE** at ribs (using body) while sliding left hand.
● **FOLLOW** with "D2" or "B."

"OUTSIDE WRIST STRIKE"

D 1

● **LEFT** foot short step left - Right foot in arc to rear.
● **CHANGE** grip as per "C" - & strike wrist.
● **FOLLOW** with "F" or "B."

"ROTATING OUTSIDE WRIST STRIKE"

D 2

● **LEFT** foot step left rear (& slide right foot).
● **LEFT** hand to end - Right slides & "whips" stick (in tight C.W circle).
● **STRIKE** & withdraw quickly.

"INSIDE WRIST STRIKE"

E 1

● **PIVOT** & swing right foot (to left rear).
● **SLIDE** right, then left hands - & strike wrist in short arc.
● **FOLLOW** with "F" or "B."

"ROTATING INSIDE WRIST STRIKE"

E 2

● **LEFT** foot to left rear.
● **STRIKE** & withdraw quickly.
● **HANDS** move as in "D2."

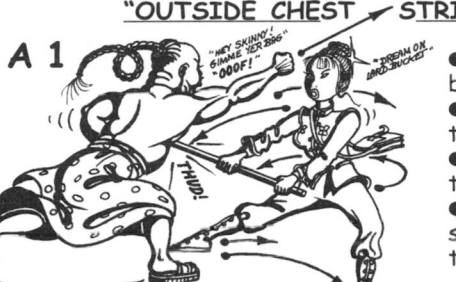
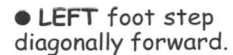
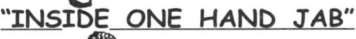
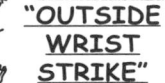
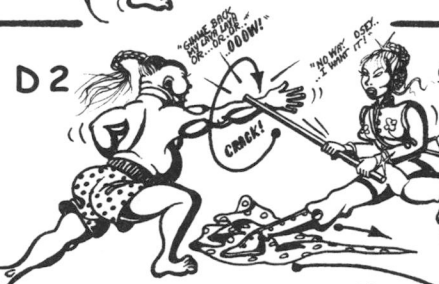
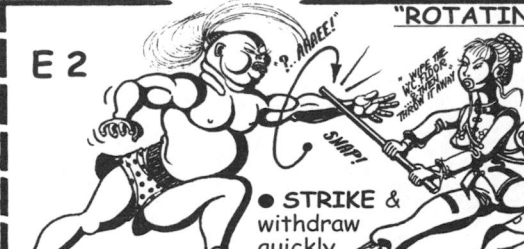

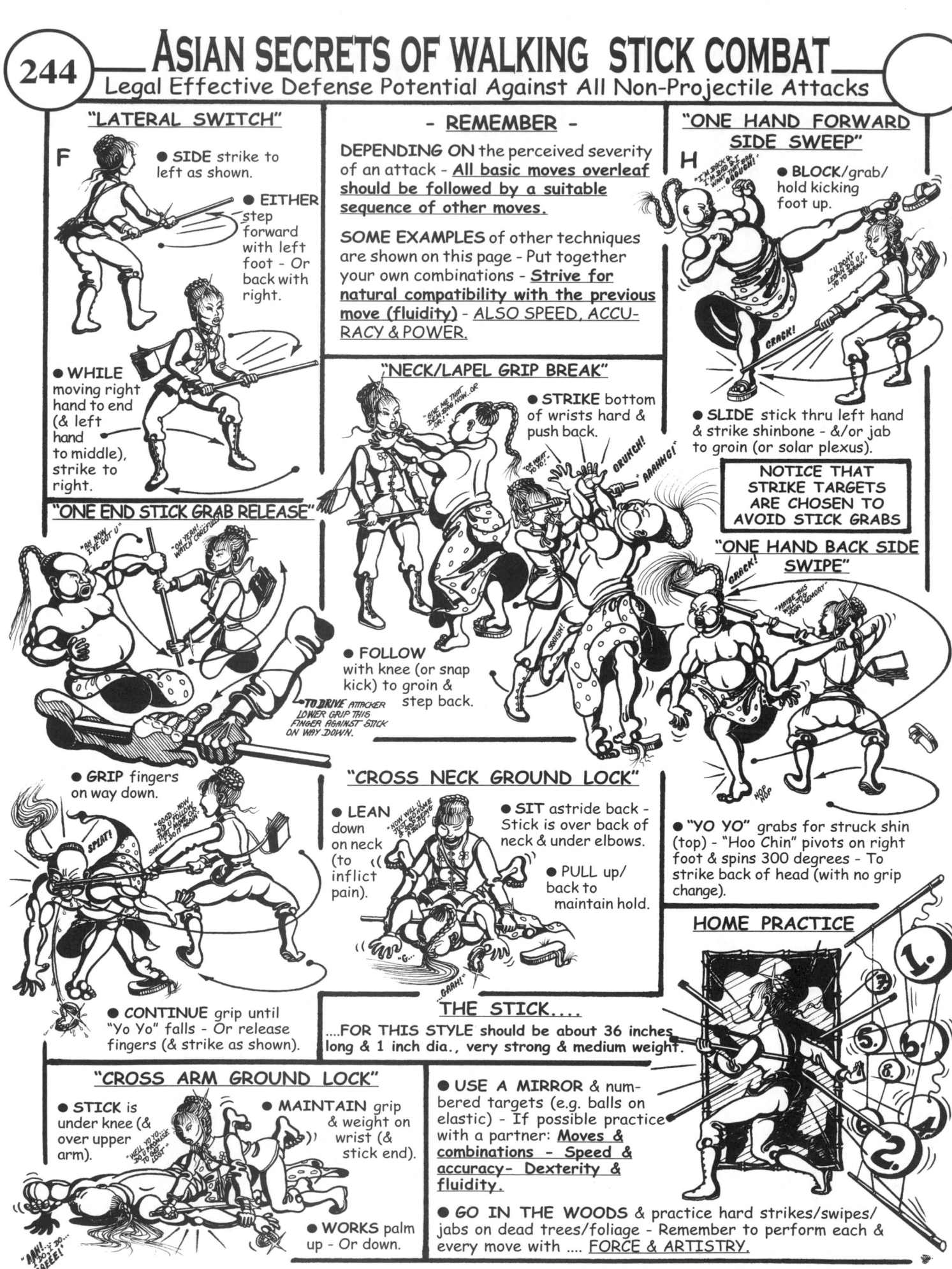

"LATERAL SWITCH"

- **SIDE** strike to left as shown.
- **EITHER** step forward with left foot - Or back with right.
- **WHILE** moving right hand to end (& left hand to middle), strike to right.

"ONE END STICK GRAB RELEASE"

- **GRIP** fingers on way down.
- **CONTINUE** grip until "Yo Yo" falls - Or release fingers (& strike as shown).

"CROSS ARM GROUND LOCK"

- **STICK** is under knee (& over upper arm).
- **MAINTAIN** grip & weight on wrist (& stick end).
- **WORKS** palm up - Or down.

- REMEMBER -

DEPENDING ON the perceived severity of an attack - All basic moves overleaf should be followed by a suitable sequence of other moves.

SOME EXAMPLES of other techniques are shown on this page - Put together your own combinations - Strive for natural compatibility with the previous move (fluidity) - ALSO SPEED, ACCURACY & POWER.

"NECK/LAPEL GRIP BREAK"

- **STRIKE** bottom of wrists hard & push back.
- **FOLLOW** with knee (or snap kick) to groin & step back.

TO DRIVE ATTACKER LOWER GRIP THIS FINGER AGAINST STICK ON WAY DOWN.

"CROSS NECK GROUND LOCK"

- **LEAN** down on neck (to inflict pain).
- **SIT** astride back - Stick is over back of neck & under elbows.
- **PULL** up/back to maintain hold.

THE STICK....

....FOR THIS STYLE should be about 36 inches long & 1 inch dia., very strong & medium weight.

- **USE A MIRROR** & numbered targets (e.g. balls on elastic) - If possible practice with a partner: Moves & combinations - Speed & accuracy - Dexterity & fluidity.

- **GO IN THE WOODS** & practice hard strikes/swipes/jabs on dead trees/foliage - Remember to perform each & every move with .... FORCE & ARTISTRY.

"ONE HAND FORWARD SIDE SWEEP"

- **BLOCK**/grab/hold kicking foot up.
- **SLIDE** stick thru left hand & strike shinbone - &/or jab to groin (or solar plexus).

NOTICE THAT STRIKE TARGETS ARE CHOSEN TO AVOID STICK GRABS

"ONE HAND BACK SIDE SWIPE"

- **"YO YO"** grabs for struck shin (top) - "Hoo Chin" pivots on right foot & spins 300 degrees - To strike back of head (with no grip change).

HOME PRACTICE

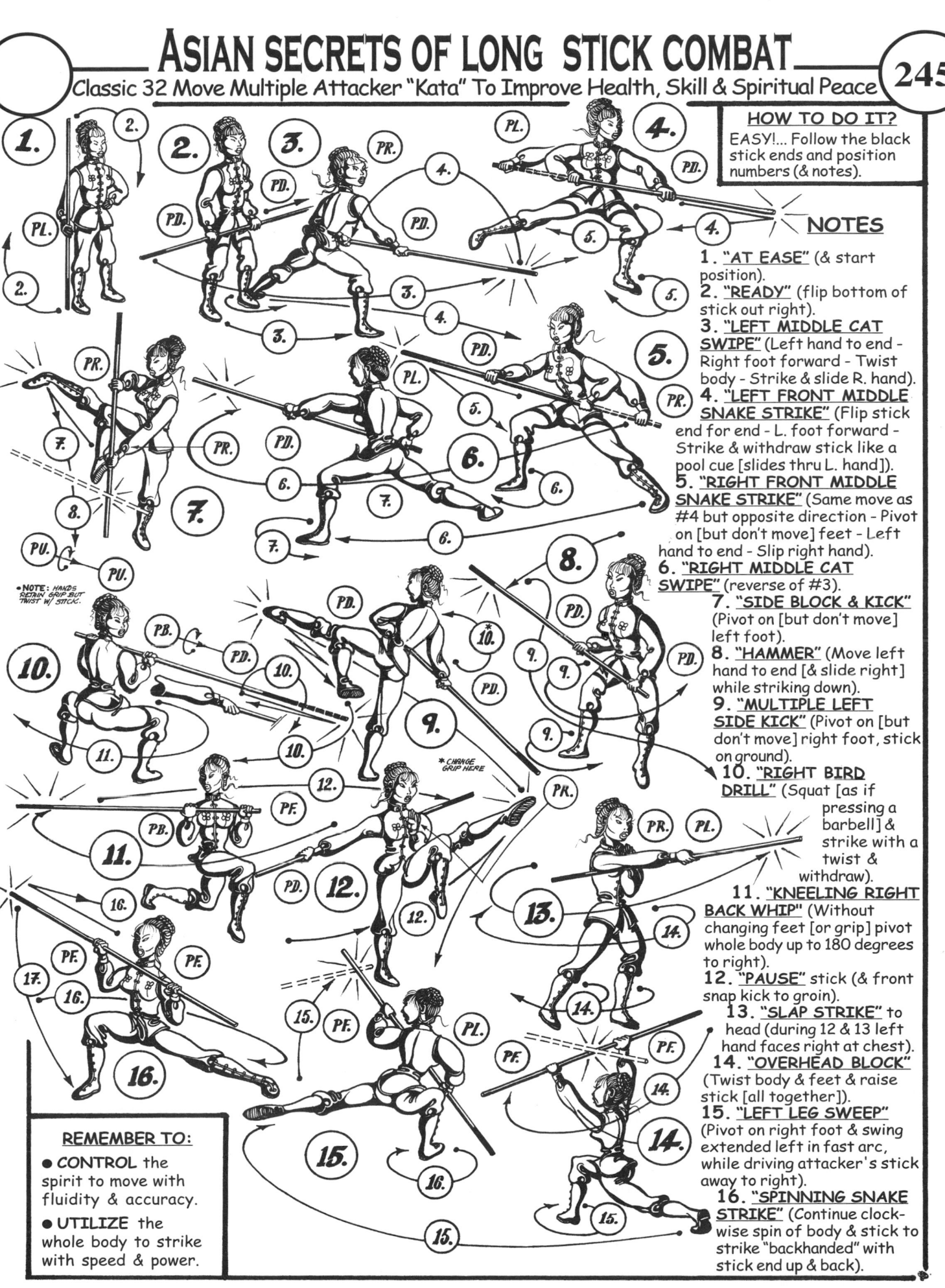

HOW TO DO IT?

EASY!... Follow the black stick ends and position numbers (& notes).

NOTES

1. "AT EASE" (& start position).

2. "READY" (flip bottom of stick out right).

3. "LEFT MIDDLE CAT SWIPE" (Left hand to end - Right foot forward - Twist body - Strike & slide R. hand).

4. "LEFT FRONT MIDDLE SNAKE STRIKE" (Flip stick end for end - L. foot forward - Strike & withdraw stick like a pool cue [slides thru L. hand]).

5. "RIGHT FRONT MIDDLE SNAKE STRIKE" (Same move as #4 but opposite direction - Pivot on [but don't move] feet - Left hand to end - Slip right hand).

6. "RIGHT MIDDLE CAT SWIPE" (reverse of #3).

7. "SIDE BLOCK & KICK" (Pivot on [but don't move] left foot).

8. "HAMMER" (Move left hand to end [& slide right] while striking down).

9. "MULTIPLE LEFT SIDE KICK" (Pivot on [but don't move] right foot, stick on ground).

10. "RIGHT BIRD DRILL" (Squat [as if pressing a barbell] & strike with a twist & withdraw).

11. "KNEELING RIGHT BACK WHIP" (Without changing feet [or grip] pivot whole body up to 180 degrees to right).

12. "PAUSE" stick (& front snap kick to groin).

13. "SLAP STRIKE" to head (during 12 & 13 left hand faces right at chest).

14. "OVERHEAD BLOCK" (Twist body & feet & raise stick [all together]).

15. "LEFT LEG SWEEP" (Pivot on right foot & swing extended left in fast arc, while driving attacker's stick away to right).

16. "SPINNING SNAKE STRIKE" (Continue clockwise spin of body & stick to strike "backhanded" with stick end up & back).

• NOTE: HANDS RETAIN GRIP BUT TWIST W/ STICK.

* CHANGE GRIP HERE

REMEMBER TO:

● **CONTROL** the spirit to move with fluidity & accuracy.

● **UTILIZE** the whole body to strike with speed & power.

ASIAN SECRETS OF LONG STICK COMBAT
Devastatingly & Artistically Demonstrated By Mistress Hoo Chin

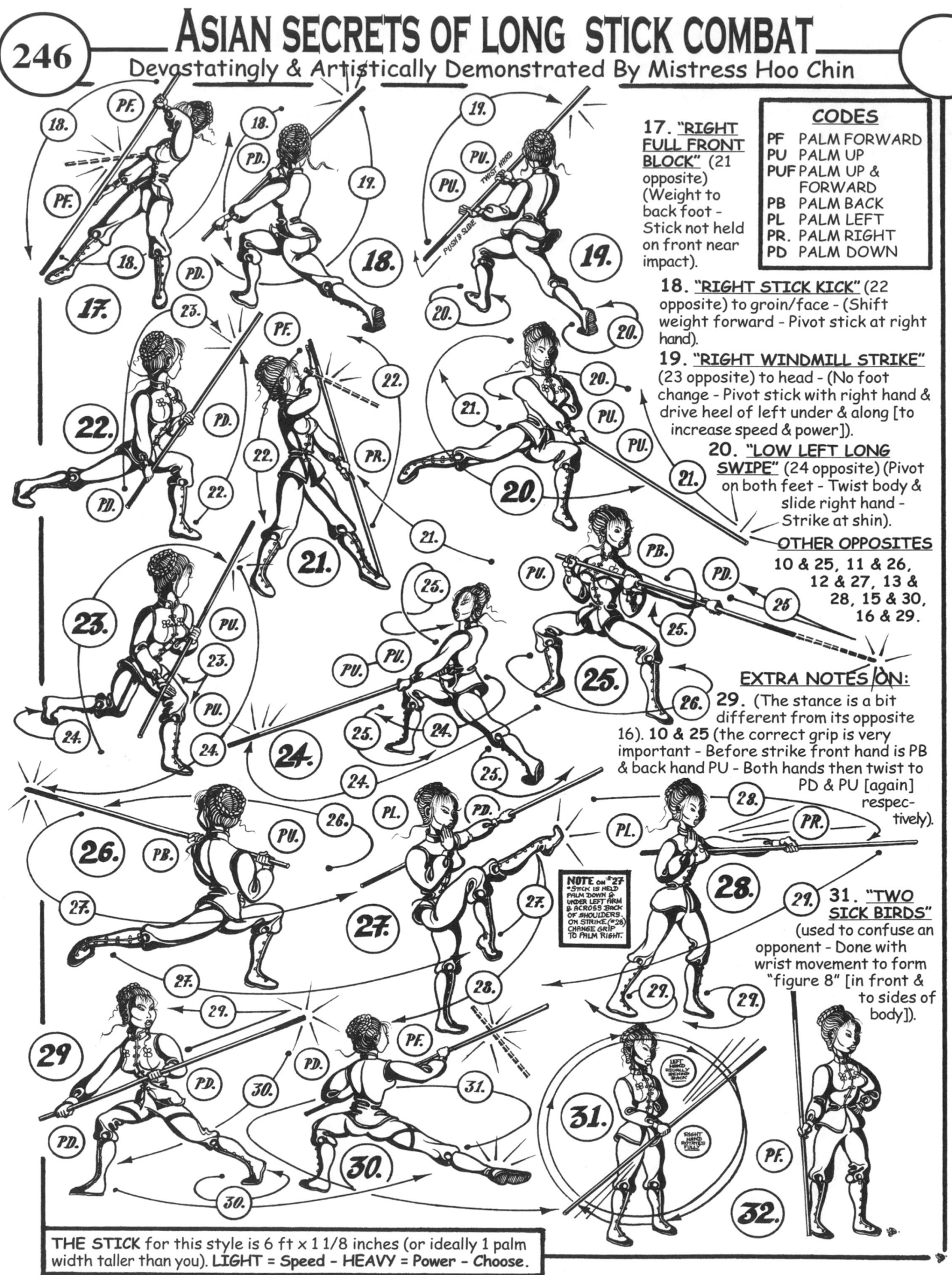

CODES

PF	PALM FORWARD
PU	PALM UP
PUF	PALM UP & FORWARD
PB	PALM BACK
PL	PALM LEFT
PR.	PALM RIGHT
PD	PALM DOWN

17. "RIGHT FULL FRONT BLOCK" (21 opposite) (Weight to back foot - Stick not held on front near impact).

18. "RIGHT STICK KICK" (22 opposite) to groin/face - (Shift weight forward - Pivot stick at right hand).

19. "RIGHT WINDMILL STRIKE" (23 opposite) to head - (No foot change - Pivot stick with right hand & drive heel of left under & along [to increase speed & power]).

20. "LOW LEFT LONG SWIPE" (24 opposite) (Pivot on both feet - Twist body & slide right hand - Strike at shin).

OTHER OPPOSITES
10 & 25, 11 & 26, 12 & 27, 13 & 28, 15 & 30, 16 & 29.

EXTRA NOTES ON:
29. (The stance is a bit different from its opposite 16). **10 & 25** (the correct grip is very important - Before strike front hand is PB & back hand PU - Both hands then twist to PD & PU [again] respectively).

NOTE on *27 *STICK IS HELD PALM DOWN & UNDER LEFT ARM & ACROSS BACK OF SHOULDERS, ON STRIKE (*28) CHANGE GRIP TO PALM RIGHT.

31. "TWO SICK BIRDS" (used to confuse an opponent - Done with wrist movement to form "figure 8" [in front & to sides of body]).

THE STICK for this style is 6 ft x 1 1/8 inches (or ideally 1 palm width taller than you). **LIGHT** = Speed - **HEAVY** = Power - Choose.

ASIAN SECRETS OF MANRIKIGUSARI (CHAIN) COMBAT

The Almost Lost Defensive Skills Of The Gusari (Chain) Martial Artist

BE ADVISED....

....that knowledge of martial arts carries moral & legal responsibilities -Seek spiritual peace before physical skill.

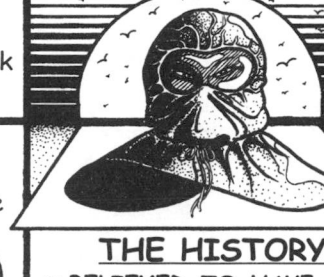

THE 4 RULES

- **NEVER** strike the first blow.
- **DON'T** use excess force.
- **STOP** when out of danger.
- **TEMPER** & martial arts don't mix.

HAND POSITIONS

B.

- **CATCH** & release one handed with....

....index finger & thumb in this position.

A.

- **HOLD**, hide & prepare to strike like this

THE HISTORY

- **BELIEVED TO HAVE ORIGINATED IN FEUDAL JAPAN** where it was known as "Manriki - gusari" (10,000 x chain) & was widely used as a defensive weapon.

THE WEAPON

- **USUALLY** carried in the waist sash - It is simply an 18-30 inch chain with a weight at both ends*

HIDDEN BUT READY

- In clasped hands at front.
- Over shoulder or behind trouser leg.
- Behind back.

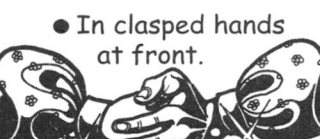
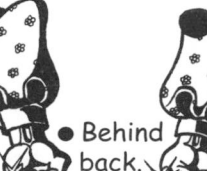
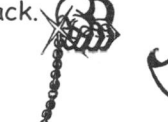

THE 4 PRINCIPLES

- **CULTIVATE** spiritual peace to achieve speed.
- **CULTIVATE** speed to achieve surprise.
- **CULTIVATE** secrecy to protect surprise.
- **CULTIVATE** variety to protect secrecy.

"AAAAAAAEEEEEEEEEEGTHUK!"

ADVANTAGES...

....are many e.g.
- **SIMPLE** to make (even for peasants).
- **COLLAPSES** to a very small size.
- **EASILY** concealed on body (or in bag).
- **EFFECTIVE** against most other weapons (e.g. knives/sticks, even guns [close up]).

STAND-OFF FORMS

- **PRACTICE** horizontal & vertical "figure 8's" (& circles) - Into & out of strikes - **Until you don't tangle (or hit yourself).**

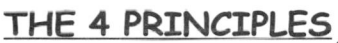
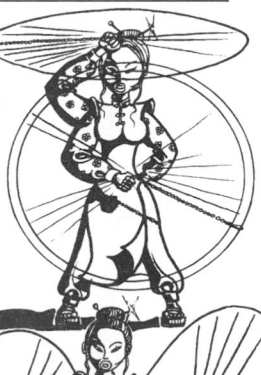
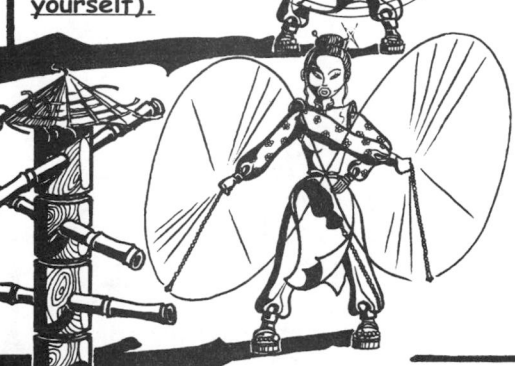

USE COMBINA-TIONS

of moves when possible - **This dramatically increases the success likelihood of each individual strike** (or counter) - It might be a kick to the shin to draw the attacker's attention followed by a chain strike to the face - **In our example above** "Woo Chin" strikes her attacker's sword hand, pulling it to the outside, while executing a spinning back kick to the groin with the opposite foot - Whatever your choice of combination, make sure each move FLOWS SMOOTH & FAST INTO THE NEXT.

READY TO STRIKE

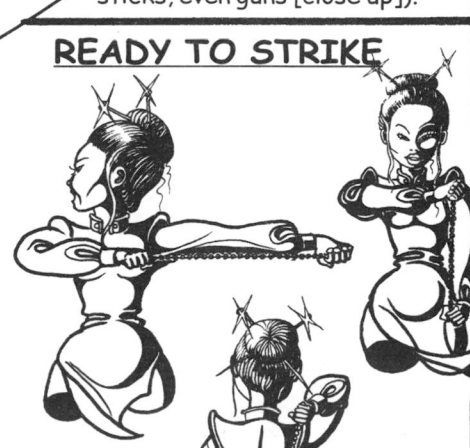

- **ALL SHOWN** for right hand strikes (but **train for equal ability with both hands**).
- **IN ALL CASES** release left hand & whip right hand.

GRAB COUNTERS

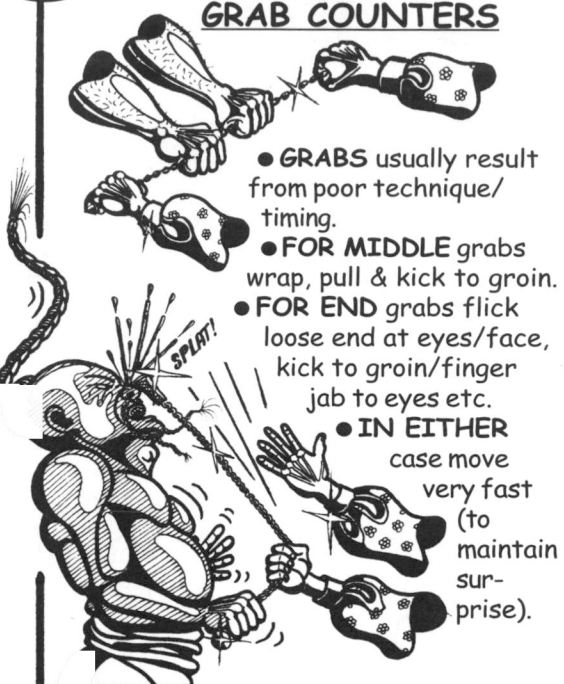

- **GRABS** usually result from poor technique/timing.
- **FOR MIDDLE** grabs wrap, pull & kick to groin.
- **FOR END** grabs flick loose end at eyes/face, kick to groin/finger jab to eyes etc.
- **IN EITHER** case move very fast (to maintain surprise).

SPLAT!

SPIRITUALITY....

....**VITAL TO THE USE of this unique weapon** -In ancient Japan was considered in 2 parts - 1) Inner peace & - 2) A nurtured belief that the weapon in use is an extension of the body (WITH A LIFE OF ITS OWN).

TRAINING....

....**REQUIRES EXTREME familiarity with the chain** (thru constant handling & practice) - Until its weight, length & characteristics (in motion of all kinds) .... BECOME SECOND NATURE.

THE SHOUT....

....IS A FIERCESOME yell uttered in combat with every aggressive strike (or counter).
- **WHAT DOES IT DO?** - **Solidifies** the body at the instant of impact - **Distracts** the opponent from your move - **Upsets** the opponent's spiritual equilibrium - **Strengthens** your spirituality (& confidence) by self-hypnosis.
- **HOW DO I DO IT?** - **Breathe in** thru nose (first sending air to belly, then chest) - **Then breathe out** thru mouth (the air from chest) - **Then forcibly expel** the air from belly (by contracting muscles) while letting forth your most fierce, single syllable, shout..... "YAAH!!!!"

THE WRIST..

.... movement is very critical for speed, power & technique.

"THE SNAKE STRIKE"

- **HAND** positions shown over.

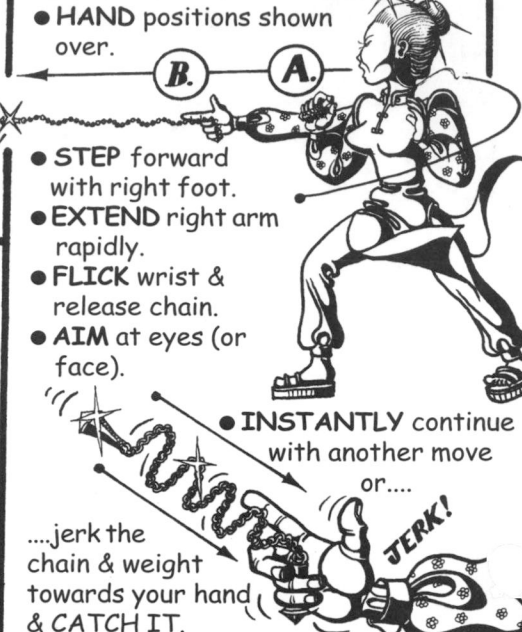

Ⓑ Ⓐ

- **STEP** forward with right foot.
- **EXTEND** right arm rapidly.
- **FLICK** wrist & release chain.
- **AIM** at eyes (or face).

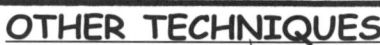

- **INSTANTLY** continue with another move or....

....jerk the chain & weight towards your hand & CATCH IT.

JERK!

WEAPON BLOCKS

CLINK!

- **COMBINE BLOCKING** techniques with rapid follow-up strikes (e.g. kicks [or release one end of chain & "whip strike" with other]).

WAK!

OTHER TECHNIQUES

- **SHORT** grip (doubled up) for close conflict.
- **LIMB** entanglement (on weapon hands/wrists &/or ankles) works well with practice.

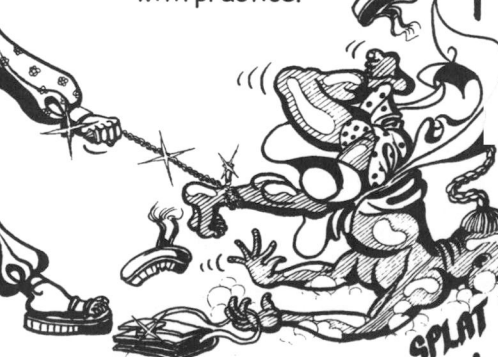

SPLAT

MANRIKIGUSARI DESIGN*

E. = CHAIN LENGTH (swivel to swivel)

B.

C.

A.

D.

NOTE: That both end weights are the same.

(DIMENSIONS IN INCHES)

	A	B	C	D	E
SMALL	2	3/4	3/8	3/16	18
MEDIUM	3	1	1/2	1/4	24
LARGE	4	1 1/4	5/8	5/16	30

- **MADE FROM** any semi-hard, high density metal (e.g. brass, iron [not aluminium]).

ALL KNOWN ASIAN EXERCISE & HEALTH PHILOSOPHIES PROMOTING LONGEVITY EXTOL CORRECT BREATHING AS A BASIS FOR SUCCESS.

WHAT IS IT?

A.

- **BREATH CONTROL is the simplest (& most effective) means of purifying & revitalizing body & mind** - In Asia its use is well-known for developing "Ching Chi" (or "Ki") your vital energy supply, which is traditionally centered in the kidneys &/or "Hara" (conception vessel #6 [3 fingers below belly button]).

- **WHERE?** - **It can be done anywhere** - WALKING, WORKING, SOCIALIZING, EVEN WHEN SLEEPING (WITH PRACTICE).

B.

- **ASIAN PHILOSOPHY holds that each life** (barring accidents) **has a set number of breaths** - & that by breathing more slowly(& deeply) that life is extended proportionally (in health & time).

- **POSITIONS** most often assumed for stationary formal breathing exercises (& meditation) are with hands (& body) as in "A" or "B" - But in any case KEEP BACK/NECK STRAIGHT.

BENEFITS

- **LOGIC:** As **all body parts** (the brain included) **need oxygen to function properly** - & as deep rhythmic breathing dramatically increases its availability (via the blood) some effects are:

- **INCREASED ENERGY** (because of MORE EFFICIENT NUTRIENT ASSIMILATION).

- **INCREASED WASTE ELIMINATION** (as mainly gases [e.g. carbon dioxide] but also **toxins** [such as uric acid] **are expelled via each breath**).

- **DRAMATIC RELAXATION** of mind (& body) EFFECTIVE WITHIN A FEW MINUTES OF STARTING EXERCISES.

- **VITAL FORCE ACCUMULATION** (Yogis call it "Prana") within body (& mind) which is absorbed (& stored) **for future use as energy & vitality** (rather like a bank account of life).

- **SLIMMING: A metabolism well supplied with oxygen is more efficient** (& energetic) resulting in fat deposits being used as body fuel.

- **INSOMNIA: Relax your muscles progressively** (from toes to scalp) - Then use rhythmic breathing (e.g.: inhale - 5 sec., hold - 5, exhale - 5).

- **REJUVENATION via increased flexibility of joints/muscles/tendons** - Reduction of fatigue, hard arteries & headaches - INCREASED LUNG & MENTAL CAPACITY.

- **ANGRY/SCARED/NERVOUS?** - Take a deep breath & hold it for 10 (or more) heartbeats - Then exhale slowly - THIS WILL CALM YOU IN A QUITE DRAMATIC WAY - **If still upset do it a few more times**.

HARA BREATHING

- **"HARA"** (3 fingers below belly button) is defined as the center of bodily vitality.
- **"HARA BREATH"** - **Inhale** (count of 5) thru nose (expanding "Hara") - **Hold** (count of 5) & accumulate "Ki" - **Exhale** (count of 5) thru mouth (contracting "Hara" & expel waste).
- **GENTLE** & controlled is the mode of breathing (**so that a feather in front of nose/mouth barely moves**).
- **TONGUE** should be on roof of mouth during inhale & hold.
- **VISUALIZE** the "Ki" in every breath flowing into your "Hara" (& every body part requiring it).
- **FILL LUNGS** completely with each breath - Starting with abdomen then lower (& upper) ribs - **Exhale completely in opposite order**.

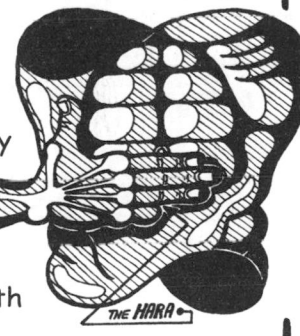

THE HARA

SEXUAL BREATHING

- **SIT** on bed/low seat with feet flat on floor - Keep a **STRAIGHT BACK** & cup parted knees with palms (index finger & thumb touch).
- **INHALE thru nose** & lean (45 degrees) forward.
- **FEEL ENERGY** flow thru soles of feet to conception vessel #1 (between sex organs & anus).
- **INHALE** 10% more & lean forward 10 degrees more - Send the energy to the tip of penis/uterus.
- **EXHALE** slowly **thru mouth** whilst sitting back vertically.
- **REPEAT** as required **to build up sexual desire & stamina**.

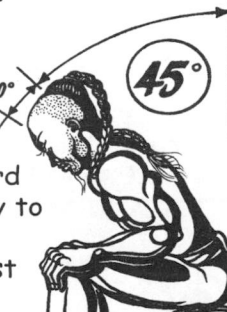

45°
10°

THE PRECIOUS SET OF MONKS' BREATHING EXERCISES I
Live Longer & Healthier With These Simple Techniques

Abdul demonstrates the "HELLO SUN" breathing exercises

- **WHERE?** - In a quiet (if possible beautiful) place, with good air, on an empty stomach, preferably facing the rising sun - Enjoy it. "_VERY THERAPUTIC & BENEFICIAL_"
- **YOU NEED** - Timing, breath control & perseverance for 4 - 16 minutes/day. "_EVERYDAY IS BEST_"
- **YOU GET** - _A rejuvenated metabolism_ with quite dramatic benefits via oxygenated blood supply, _increased flexibility/muscle tone/circulation, stimulated organs/glands & mental serenity._
- **HOW?** - INHALE & EXHALE _COMPLETELY (& SLOWLY)_ WITH EACH BREATH.

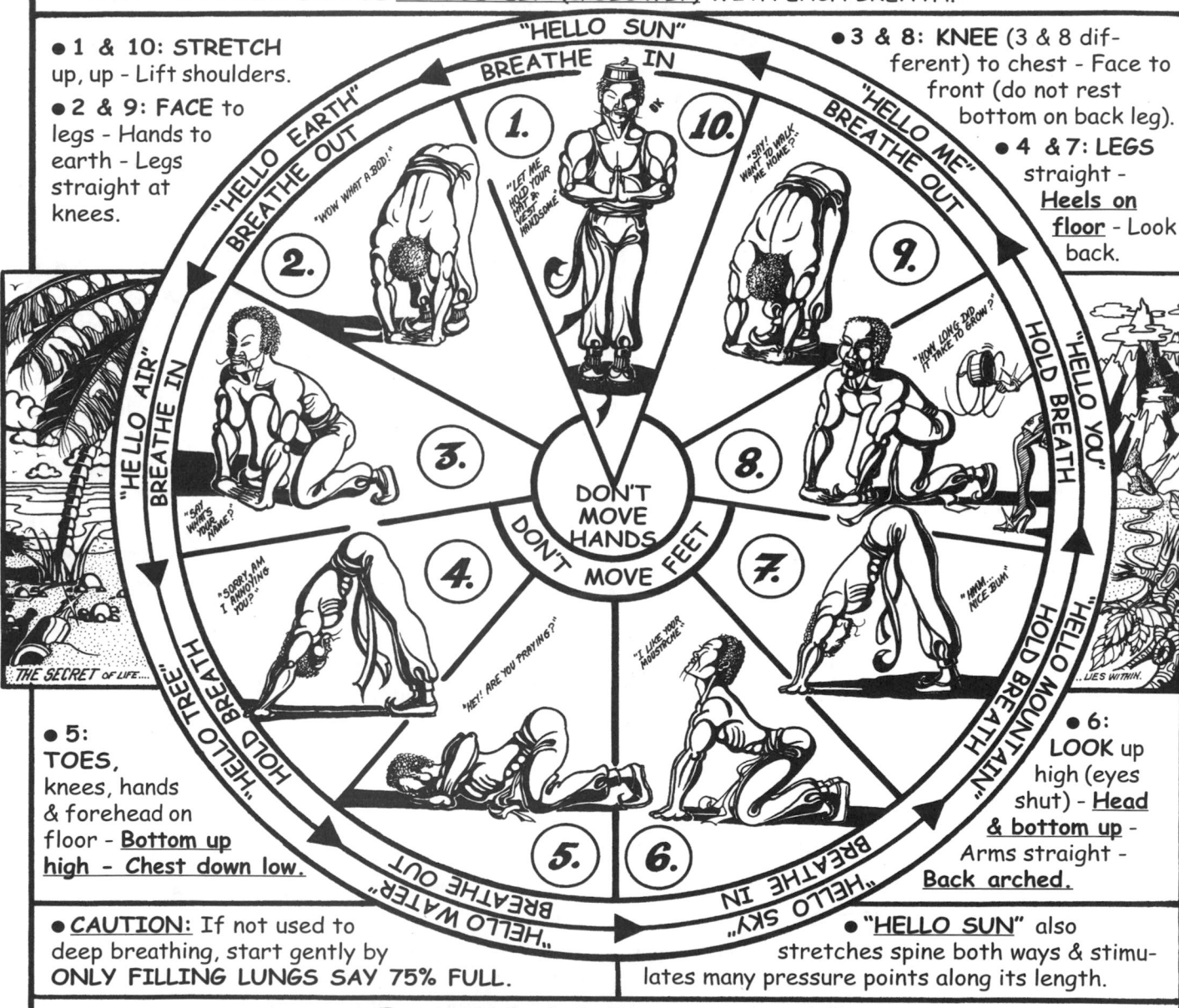

- **1 & 10: STRETCH** up, up - Lift shoulders.
- **2 & 9: FACE** to legs - Hands to earth - Legs straight at knees.

"HELLO SUN" BREATHE IN

"HELLO EARTH" BREATHE OUT

"WOW WHAT A BOD!"

"LET ME HOLD YOUR HAT & VEST HANDSOME"

"SAY! WANT TO WALK ME HOME?"

"HELLO ME" BREATHE OUT

- **3 & 8: KNEE** (3 & 8 different) to chest - Face to front (do not rest bottom on back leg).
- **4 & 7: LEGS** straight - _Heels on floor_ - Look back.

"HELLO AIR" BREATHE IN

"SAY! WHAT'S YOUR NAME?"

"SORRY! AM I ANNOYING YOU?"

DON'T MOVE HANDS

DON'T MOVE FEET

"HOW LONG DID IT TAKE TO GROW?"

"HELLO YOU" HOLD BREATH

"HMM. NICE BUM."

"HEY! ARE YOU PRAYING?"

"I LIKE YOUR MOUSTACHE"

"HELLO MOUNTAIN" HOLD BREATH

"HELLO ... LIES WITHIN."

"HELLO TREE" HOLD BREATH

"HELLO WATER" BREATHE OUT

"HELLO SKY" BREATHE IN

"HELLO SUN" also stretches spine both ways & stimulates many pressure points along its length.

THE SECRET of LIFE.....

- **5: TOES,** knees, hands & forehead on floor - _Bottom up high - Chest down low._
- **CAUTION:** If not used to deep breathing, start gently by **ONLY FILLING LUNGS SAY 75% FULL.**

- **6: LOOK** up high (eyes shut) - _Head & bottom up_ - Arms straight - _Back arched._

THE COMPLETE BREATH TECHNIQUE

- **EMPTY LUNGS** completely - **(I) INHALE** thru nose for 8 seconds filling abdomen then chest completely - **(II) HOLD FULL** for 32 seconds (try 16 at first) - **(III) EXHALE** gently & completely for 16 seconds thru mouth (in reverse order of "I") - **(IV) HOLD EMPTY** for 4 seconds.
- **REPEAT AS REQUIRED** (_ODD NUMBER OF TIMES FOR WOMEN - EVEN FOR MEN_).

THE ALTERNATE NOSTRIL TECHNIQUE

- **POSITION: RIGHT INDEX FINGER ON "IN DO"** (between eyebrows), **RIGHT THUMB ON RIGHT NOSTRIL & RIGHT MIDDLE FINGER ON LEFT NOSTRIL.**
- **TECHNIQUE: ALTERNATELY** (lifting middle finger/thumb) - Breathe In (L) - Hold - Breathe out (R) - Pause - In (R) - Hold - Out (L) - Pause etc. - Do it slowly. ● **A _VERY_ POWERFUL EXERCISE.**

CAUTION: THESE ANCIENT CHINESE EXERCISES ARE POWERFUL STIMULATORS of BODY & SOUL - START SLOWLY & CAREFULLY.

- **MEASURE** the circumference of your chest **& plot it (& your weight) on a monthly graph.**
- **PRE-TRAIN** for about a week prior to starting - Practice gently but completly - Empty & fill your lungs at intervals during each day - **Alternatively perform the exercise with only half full/empty lungs.**

- **WHEN YOU COME TO START** - **Do so before eating** & after visiting the bathroom - Wear **nothing** (or loose clothing) - **Pick clean air** (& pleasant surroundings) - **Perform a few loosening up exercises** - Then breathe slowly & deeply (in thru nose & out from mouth) - **Think only positive thoughts** - Then pause for 3 SECONDS (FEMALE) & 4 SECONDS (MALE) **at each complete exhale & inhale.**

CODE FOR PAGES 251/2: OUT = LUNGS EMPTY	IN = LUNGS FULL	PI = PALMS IN
PU = PALMS UP	PD = PALMS DOWN	T = TIP TOE	S = STRETCH

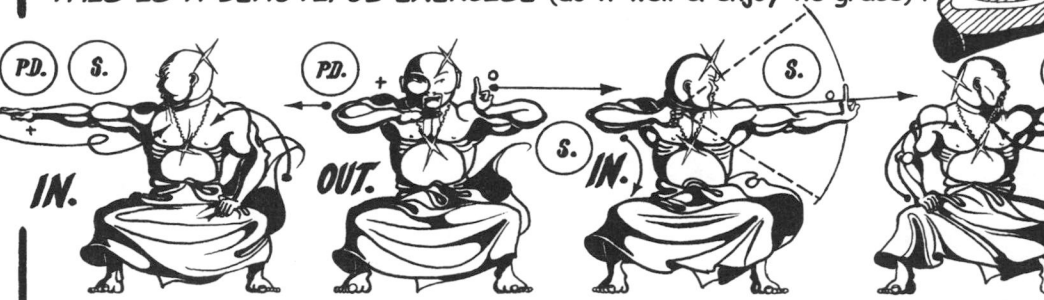

"SCOOP THE STREAM"

* AT THIS POSITION palm up changes to palm down.

● DON'T FORGET TO stretch hard at #2 & #4

"PUSH THE SKY"

●△ this hand grips the back of the thigh under the buttock.

"SHAOLIN ARCHER"

"THIS IS A BEAUTIFUL EXERCISE (do it well & enjoy its grace)".

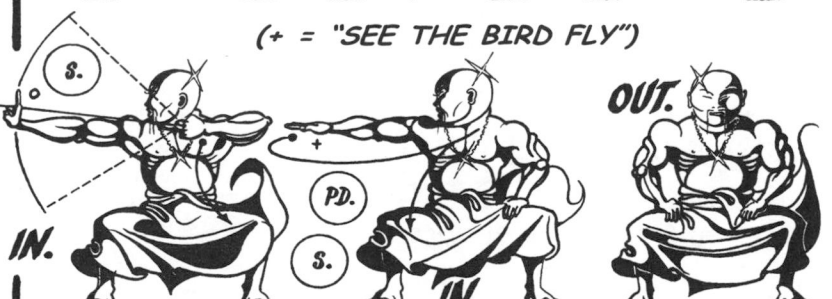

(+ = "SEE THE BIRD FLY")

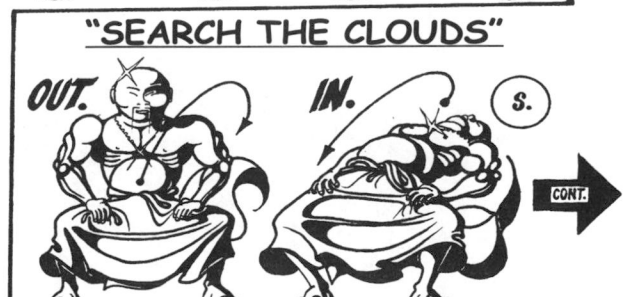

"SEARCH THE CLOUDS"

CONT.

THE PRECIOUS SET OF MONKS' BREATHING EXERCISES II

A Most Valuable 8-Part Sequence Demonstrated By The **SHORT MONK**

"SEARCH THE CLOUDS" (CONTINUED)

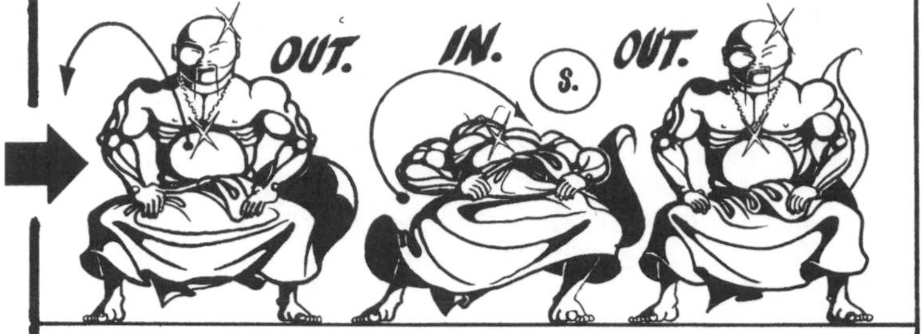
OUT.
IN.
S.
OUT.

"LIFT THE ROCK"

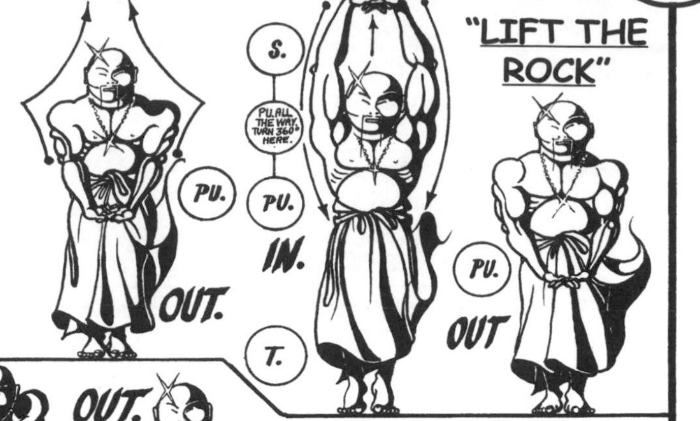
OUT.
S.
PU. ALL THE WAY. TURN 360° HERE.
PU.
PU.
IN.
T.
PU.
OUT

"TOUCH THE SKY — PRESS THE EARTH"

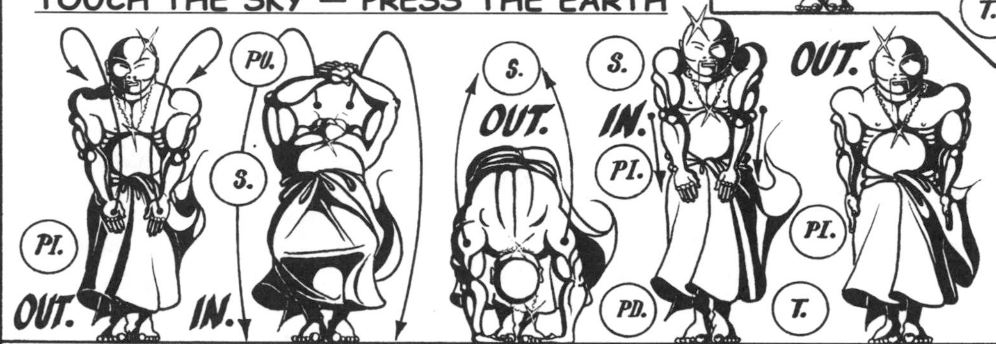
PI.
OUT.
PU.
S.
IN.
S.
OUT.
S.
IN.
PI.
PD.
OUT.
PI.
T.

● **In all eight exercises stretch as far as possible with each move.** (in this one: far back in #2, far forward (with legs straight) in #3 & high up in #4.)

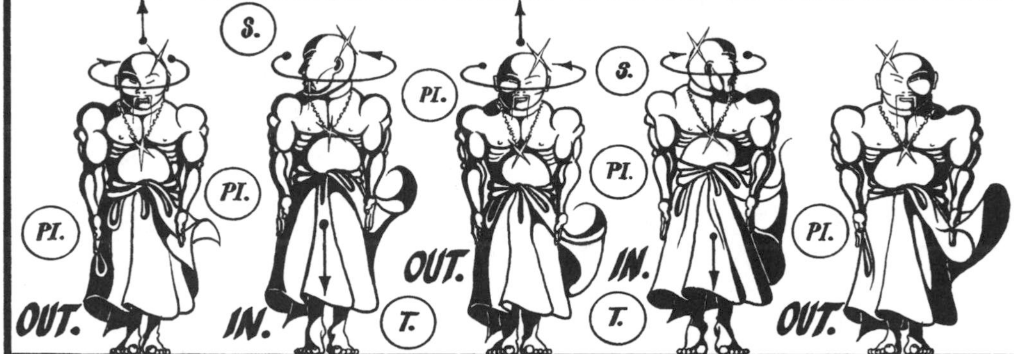
PI.
OUT.
S.
PI.
IN.
PI.
OUT.
T.
S.
PI.
IN.
T.
PI.
OUT.

"EYE OF THE TIGER"

● **In all eight exercises inhale & exhale as smoothly & completely as possible** (in this one rise on toes & turn eyes & head only (as far as possible) on each inhalation.

"GRIP THE BIRD EGG"

● In this exercise: Hold the hands as rigid fists but **with a small hollow in the middle**.

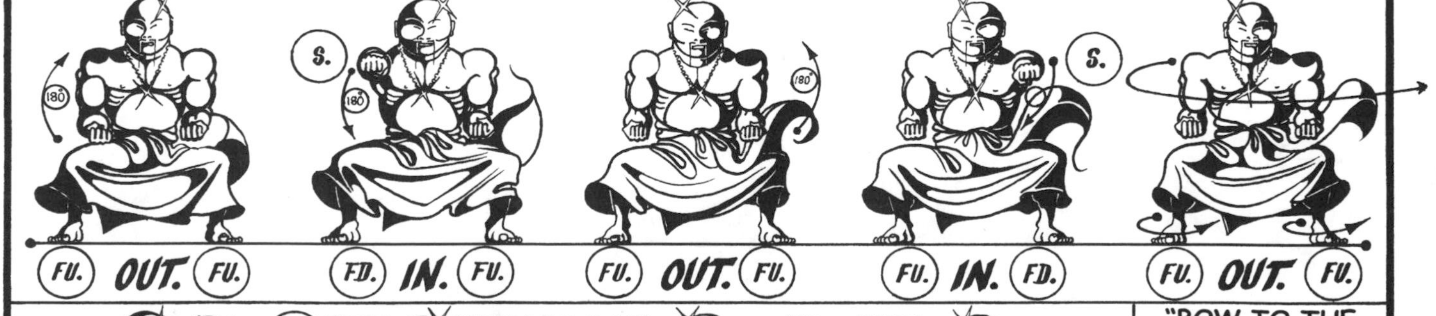
180°
S.
180°
180°
S.
FU. OUT. FU.
FD. IN. FU.
FU. OUT. FU.
FU. IN. FD.
FU. OUT. FU.

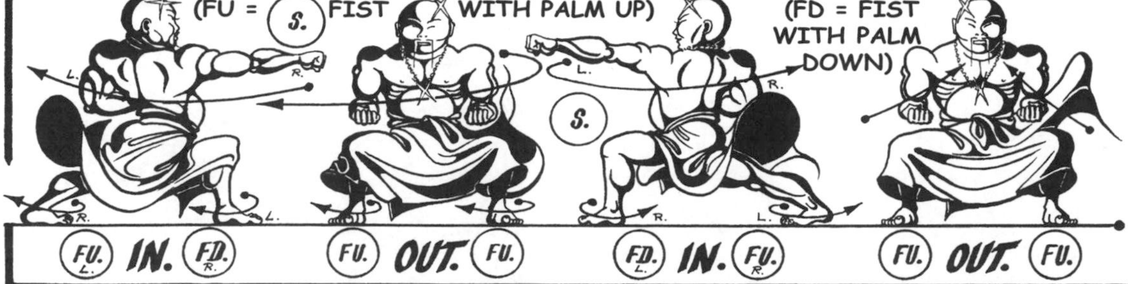
(FU = FIST WITH PALM UP)
(FD = FIST WITH PALM DOWN)
S.
S.
L.
R.
FU. L. IN. FD. R.
FU. OUT. FU.
FD. L. IN. FU. R.
FU. OUT. FU.

"BOW TO THE LIGHT WITHIN"

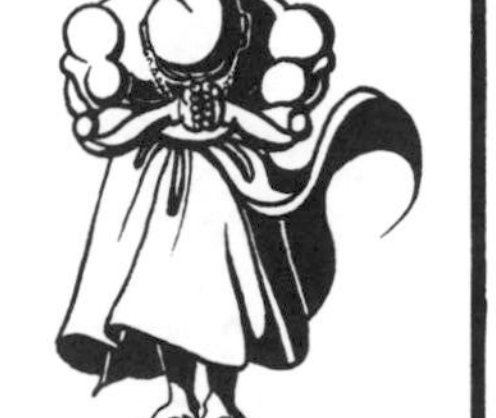

Repeat each of the preceding eight exercises from 1-8 times each, each day. When finished, don't sit for a few minutes.

The "Black Monk" Demonstrates How To Maintain Strength & Well-Being In Restrictive Situations

1.
BACK - BUTTOCKS - BACK OF LEGS

BALANCE on elbows & heels &....

....lift body high here.

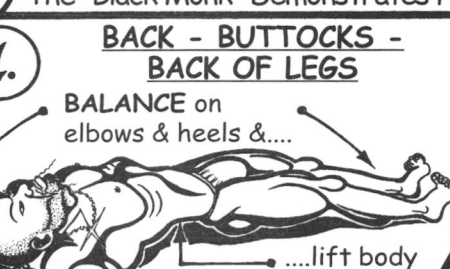

STOMACH - NECK - CHEST - FRONT OF THIGHS

2.

Press

Lift

Press

Lift

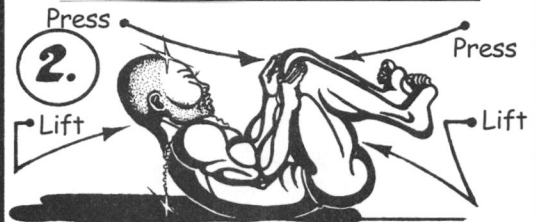

BACK OF ARMS - SHOULDERS - BACK

- LIE ON back with arms out - **Palms up** - Press down hard.
- **DON'T** forget breathing. **3.** x3.

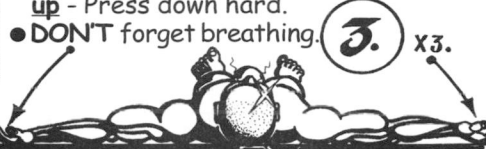

NOTE: NUMBERS 3 & 4 are each done in 3 positions as shown - **They are often exceuted consecutively & in rotation** (A, B, C, A, B, C etc.) & also without the usual intervening respiratory rest cycle.

A.

B.

C.

FRONT & INNER ARMS - CHEST - SHOULDERS

- LIE ON front with arms out - **Palms down** - Press down hard. **4.** x3.

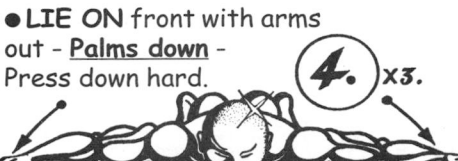

OUTER THIGHS - CHEST - SHOULDERS

- IN SITTING position - Push knees towards each other very hard with palms **(don't touch).** **5.**

- STOP - READ THIS FIRST

- **ISOMETRICS ARE** exercises in which the muscles are prevented from contracting by **tensing against a fixed object** (or another muscle).

- **MEALS REQUIRE** the bodies energy & attention for efficient digestion - **So don't exercise for 1-2 hours after eating**.

- **WARM UP** by other moderate activity for a few minutes **before starting** this exercise set.

- **SETS:** Each position is assumed & tensed - 2 times for **children** - 3 times for **women** - 4 times for **men**.

- **BREATHING: As you tense the muscle exhale (& count) slowly thru the mouth** - As you relax the muscle **inhale thru the nose** - Rest for 1 complete respiratory cycle before the next set (unless you are alternating the sets - e.g. to left then to right etc).

- **TIMING** of each tensing of the muscles (1 exhalation thru the mouth) is ideally - 7, 9, 11, 13 or 15 secs **for girls/women** - & 8, 10, 12, 14 or 16 secs **for boys/men**.

SHINS-KNEES -FRONT & BACK THIGHS

- CROSS ANKLES only - Push one leg forward & the other back - **Then swap.** **6.** x2.

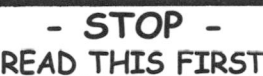

INNER THIGHS - GROIN - KNEES

- SIT DOWN - Put a pad between knees - Force them together **hard.** **7.**

BALL OR PAD

STOMACH - INNER ARMS - BACK - SHOULDERS - CHEST

- SIT ON floor - Bend knees - Push down **with semi-straight arms.** **8.**

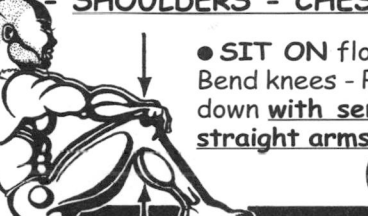

CHEST - INNER FOREARMS - SIDES - BICEPS

- PRESS palms together (at chest level) hard - **Don't forget breathing.** **9.**

UPPER BACK - SHOULDERS - FOREARMS - BICEPS

- HOOK fingers together **at level shown** - Pull hard. **10.**

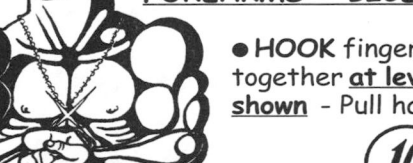

FRONT & BACK OF ARMS - CHEST - UPPER BACK - SHOULDERS

- CLASSIC muscle pose - One bent arm **palm up** (to side) - The other (**palm down**) pressing hard - Then swap. **11.** x2.

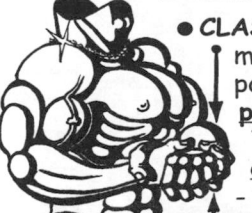

BACK OF UPPER ARMS - CHEST

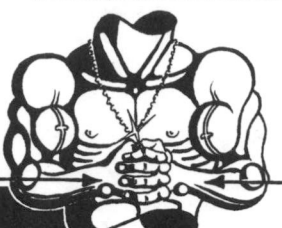

● PRESS one hand (fist) into the other (palm) <u>at waist level</u> - Hard. **12.**

CHEST - FRONT & BACK OF ARMS -UPPER BACK - SHOULDERS

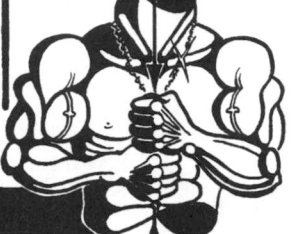

● FISTS on top of each other - Press up/down - **Then swap.** **13.** x2.

OUTER & INNER ARMS - ELBOWS - SHOULDERS

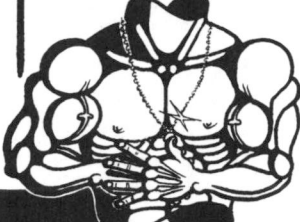

● "R" PRESS away from body - "L" press into body - **Then swap.** **14.** x2.

SHOULDERS - OUTER FOREARMS - UPPER BACK - CHEST

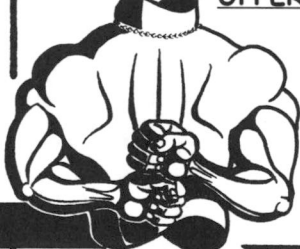

● PUT forearms (with clenched fists) behind back - **Press forward** - Hard. **15.**

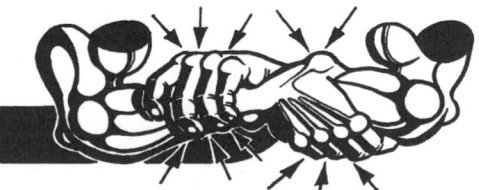

FOREARMS - HANDS - FINGERS

● GRIP both forearms (or legs) - Squeeze very hard. **16.**

FOREARMS - HANDS - WRISTS - FINGERS

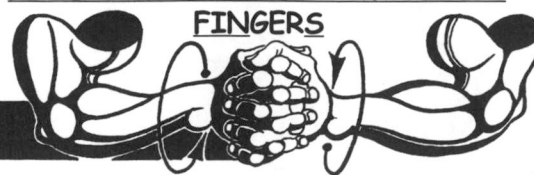

● INTERLINK fingers - Twist in opposite ways - **Then swap.** **17.** x2.

● FORCE LEVEL is naturally varied according to each individuals current status (& progress) by that person themselves - It should (<u>after one weeks graduated initiation</u>) be at your maximum strength level - <u>However use the first (& last) 2 seconds of each "tension period" (set) to increase & decrease the force</u> (to & from that maximum).

● ROTATION: For everyday use it is recommended that you either - <u>a) Concentrate on specific exercises only</u> according to your needs & perform them 6 days/week or - <u>b) Start at exercise #1 & go on consecutively</u> until circumstances dictate stopping - Then start the next day where you stopped off.

● NUTRITION: <u>For maximum benefit, strength & long life</u> - A simple yin/yang balanced diet of about 65% whole grains - 25% cooked vegetables - 10% low fat animal protein - 5% other (incl. fruit) is most recommended.

● HISTORY: This system is reputed to originate from ancient China (about 150 BC) - <u>It was developed (but kept secret) by 4 Buddhist monks</u> imprisoned in a tiny stone cell (& fed only rice) - They eventually escaped by applying nerve pressure on their guards thru the bars of the door....

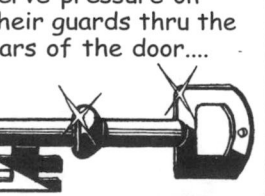

FINGERS - HANDS - FOREARMS

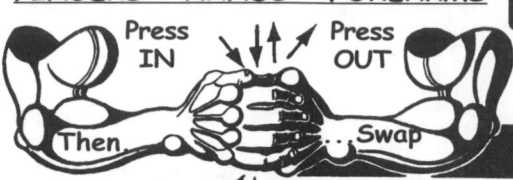

Press IN   Press OUT

Then   ...Swap

● WITH <u>fingers & thumbs straight</u> - "cage" those of one hand - Apply force in/out. **18.** x2.

FRONT OF NECK - ACU. POINTS

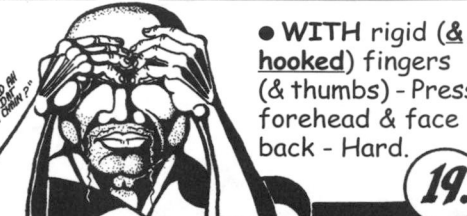

"WAT DID OH DO WIT DAT BUDDHA COMIN'?"

● WITH rigid (<u>& hooked</u>) fingers (& thumbs) - Press forehead & face back - Hard. **19.**

BACK OF NECK - UPPER CENTER BACK-ACU POINTS

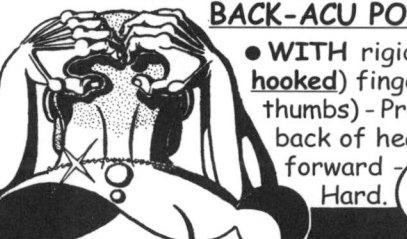

● WITH rigid (<u>& hooked</u>) fingers (& thumbs) - Press back of head forward - Hard. **20.**

SIDE OF NECK - ACU POINTS

● WITH rigid (<u>& hooked</u>) fingers - Press side of head hard - Then swap. **21.** x2.

ALL NECK - ACU POINTS

● WITH rigid fingers on back of head - & heel of other palm on chin - Twist head (<u>careful</u>) - Then swap. **22.** x2.

<u>NOTE:</u> CALF MUSCLES are difficult to exercise isometrically - The 4 monks reputedly performed "<u>Calf Raises</u>" from a semi "squat position" (roof only 53 ins high) - But you can do them standing up.

LOM PING was unfortunately, a sickly child. He had always been that way despite the efforts of his mother & "Fat Aunt Ho," who had fed him as much fresh goats milk & mung beans as his poor appetite would allow. Still, his frame was bony & his eyes lacked the sparkle of the other children in the village, who sometimes ran around him at school chanting "Mot Cha! Mot Cha!" ("Slow Ant"). Lom Ping did not like school & became even more moody. Claiming an ache in his sunken belly he just lay on the straw mat in the corner of the hut for most of the day, refusing even chicken wings in spicy sauce, made especially for him by "Fat Aunt Ho."

ABOUT THAT TIME, as fate would have it, there came to that village a wandering mystic, pushing a wooden cart decorated with strange foreign designs. He was very old & his clothes were ragged, yet his step was lively & his eyes beneath the wide straw hat, twinkled.

WHEN LOM PING'S MOTHER saw the old man rattling along the track by her house, on an impulse she rushed out & told him about Lom Ping. She begged him to give the boy some medicine. The old man listened without saying a word to her sad story, then, taking a small wooden hammer from his belt, struck one of four bells hanging from a plaited cord above his cart. "DING" went the little bell & the old man spoke for the first time in a quiet voice: "Bring me a cool drink, Dog Mai" (Lom Ping's mother twitched nervously, because that was her name & she had not told it to him) …. "& when I am finished, I will place the cup under that Bladoo tree with the little yellow flowers & continue on my way. Send your son to see me before that time & I will do what I can for him, on one condition." Dog Mai answered in a whisper because the old man made her nervous. He continued, "The boy must come alone …." he paused & gazed up at the top of the Bladoo tree "…. because to be free, the spirit must first wish to be so." Thanking the old man with a Wai (palms together) Dog Mai hurried back in to the house & shaking Lom Ping, told him to take this jar of cool water to the old man under the Bladoo tree.

LOM PING RELUCTANTLY approached the old man sitting cross-legged in the shade & bowing politely offered the water. He was about to turn away & hurry back, as the silent white bearded figure & peculiar cart with its carved sides made him even more ill at ease than usual, when the old man spoke:
"Sit down, Lom Ping, & wait …. so that you may return this jar to your mother when I am finished." Lom Ping cautiously squatted down a safe distance from the old man & gazed curiously at the mysterious cart. His eyes lingered on the four bells strung one above the other. Each was the size of a large duck egg, but unlike the rest of the old man's possessions, shone as though polished daily. The old man drank very slowly & Lom Ping felt a strange need to know the use of those bells. At last, in a faint voice, he inquired so, addressing the old man as "Sir" in order not to upset him.

THE OLD MAN DID NOT LOOK UP & Lom Ping thought he had fallen asleep, but then after a long pause, he asked:
"What do you wish for in your life, Lom Ping?" The boy was confused by this question but managed to reply in a small voice:
"Sir, I wish I was strong & clever, with friends & perhaps rich, to help my mother, but I am small & sickly." The old man continued to sip his water then said:
"That which you seek lies beyond the path marked by one of those 4 bells …. so, borrow this & strike one bell, once only" …. & he held out a small brassbound wooden hammer in his sinewy brown hand.

LOM PING HESITATED, then took the hammer:
"Which bell should I strike, Sir?" he stuttered….

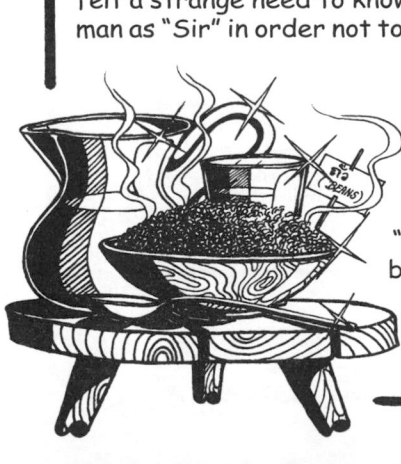

— cont.over —→

THE PRECIOUS RING

To That Village Came A Mystic, Whose Name It Was Better Not To Ask

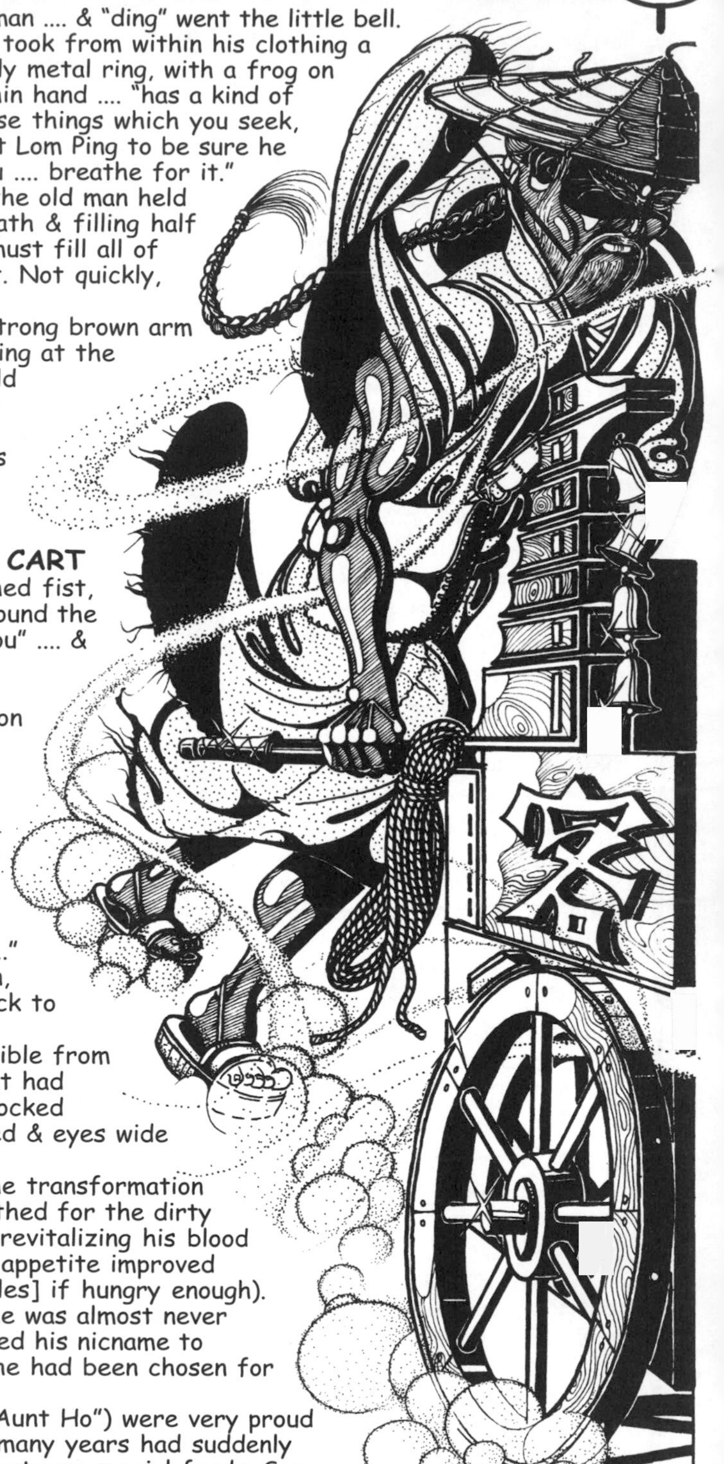

...."That one which your heart tells you to," replied the old man .... & "ding" went the little bell. "Now, come here & we will see what you have chosen." He took from within his clothing a small mottled green object, which Lom Ping saw was an ugly metal ring, with a frog on it .... "This ring" said the old man, placing it in the boy's thin hand .... "has a kind of magic in it, which can transform your life & bring you those things which you seek, BUT.... " & the old man stopped talking & peered intently at Lom Ping to be sure he was paying attention ".... it will only work for you when you .... breathe for it."

LOM PING WANTED to interrupt, but the old man held up his hand. "So, instead of taking your usual shallow breath & filling half of your lungs, if you want your dreams to come true you must fill all of your lungs, starting in your belly & ending with your chest. Not quickly, but slowly & completely .... enough for you & the frog."

THE OLD MAN REACHED OUT a strong brown arm & with one finger lifted the chin of the boy, who was staring at the ring, turning it & trying its large hole over each of his child fingers in turn. "Do you wish to do this thing or would you prefer to return to your life as it is now?" he asked in a gentle voice. A small tear trickled down each of Lom Ping's cheeks & he mumbled in a whisper, "I do want to breathe for the frog, but the ring is too big for me" & a sob escaped his throat.

THE OLD MAN TOOK FROM HIS CART a leather thong, which after prying open Lom Ping's clenched fist, he threaded thru the ring & deftly knotted, then hung it round the boy's neck. "Now let me see you breathe, as I have told you" .... & Lom Ping's scrawny chest began to rise & fall in a steady rhythm. One could almost hear the bones creaking & the tissues & sinews stretching with this unaccustomed exertion .... "You can wear it around your neck until your fingers grow big," said the old man after a few minutes, "& I would suggest you do not tell others of the true prupose of your frog. Unless prehaps, one day when you are grown up, you may give it to someone who needs it more than you."

FOR THE FIRST TIME Lom Ping looked directly in the old man's eyes & surprising himself with his bravery exclaimed .... "Thank you, thank you, Sir!..." & impulsively hugged the neck of the seated old man. Then, catching up the water jar ran (yes ran) back down the track to his house.

THE OLD BLADOO TREE was not visible from Dog Mai's house, so although curious she had not seen what had transpired thereunder & was thus amazed to be nearly knocked over by Lom Ping rushing thru the door with cheeks flushed & eyes wide .... because Lom Ping almost never ran.

EVEN MORE ASTONISHING was the transformation in the little boy over the coming days & weeks. As he breathed for the dirty green frog, the life-giving oxygen coursed thru his body, revitalizing his blood supply & tissue nutrition. He became alert & cheerful. His appetite improved dramatically (he would even eat Pak Dtom [boiled vegetables] if hungry enough). His skinny body started to fill out with flesh & muscle & he was almost never sick. At school the other kids stopped teasing him & changed his nicname to "Pung" (bee), because he was so busy. Within two months he had been chosen for the school football team & was top of his class in spelling!

HIS MOTHER DOG MAI (also "Fat Aunt Ho") were very proud of him & everyone wondered how the sad little boy of so many years had suddenly blossomed into such vibrant health. He took no medicine & ate no special foods. Sometimes he was asked about the green metal ring he wore on a leather thong round his neck & never took off, even in the bath .... but he just said it was a gift from a friend & as such could not be discarded, even if ugly.

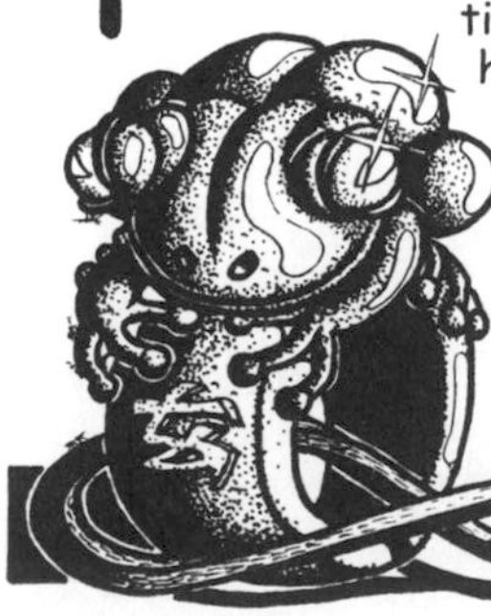

AND NO ONE except Lom Ping ever really thought of a strange wooden cart, with 4 shiny brass bells pushed by a ragged old man whose real name was BECOFYDW*

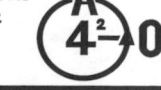

***CAUTION:** The real name of the old man has been encrypted to protect sensitive intellects (children/artists etc.) from shock &/or compulsions - Decoding should be carried out by the person seeking the old mans identity - Using the key:

A
$4^2 \rightarrow 0$

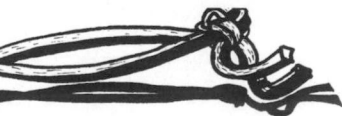

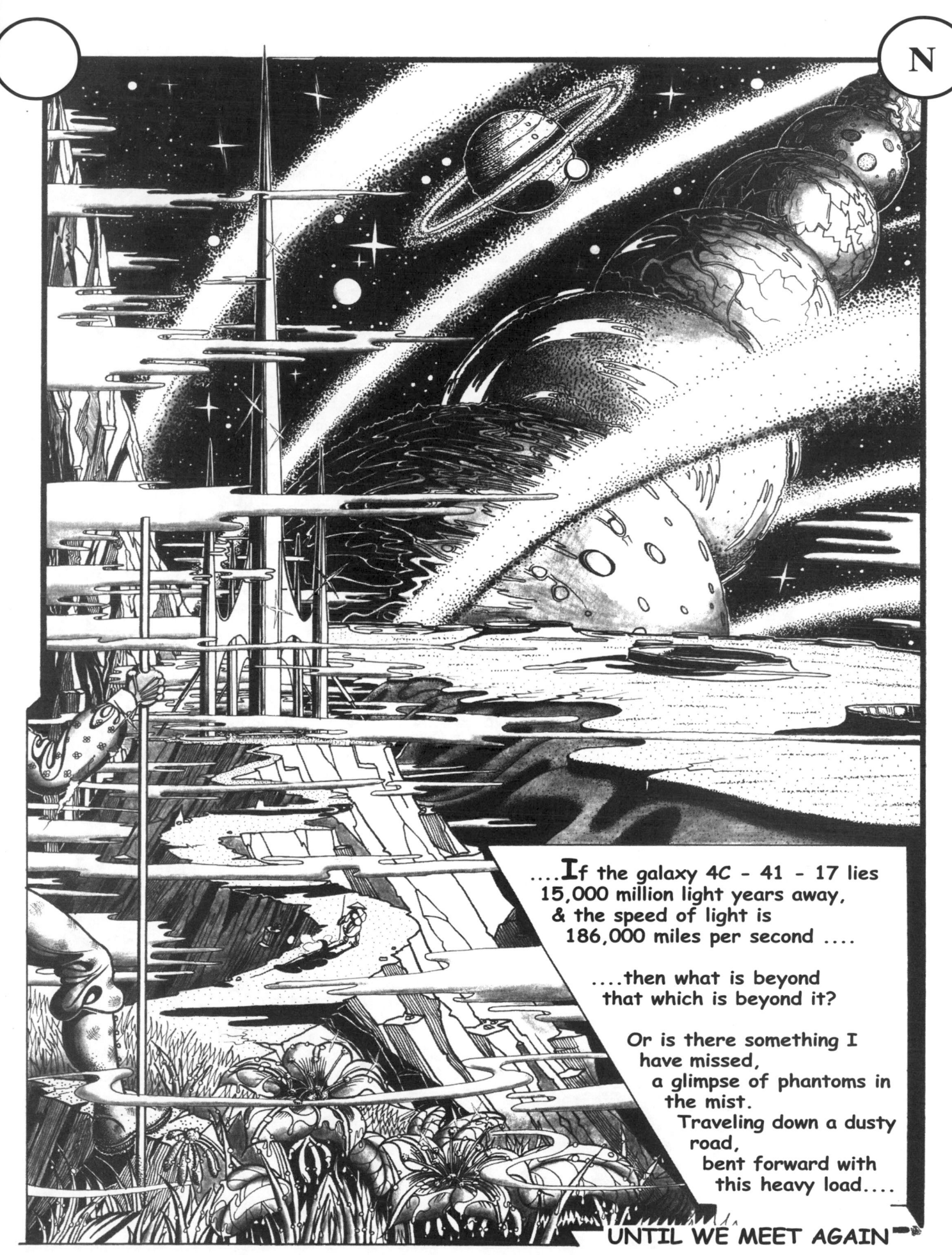

....If the galaxy 4C - 41 - 17 lies
15,000 million light years away,
& the speed of light is
186,000 miles per second ....

....then what is beyond
that which is beyond it?

Or is there something I
have missed,
a glimpse of phantoms in
the mist.
Traveling down a dusty
road,
bent forward with
this heavy load....

UNTIL WE MEET AGAIN

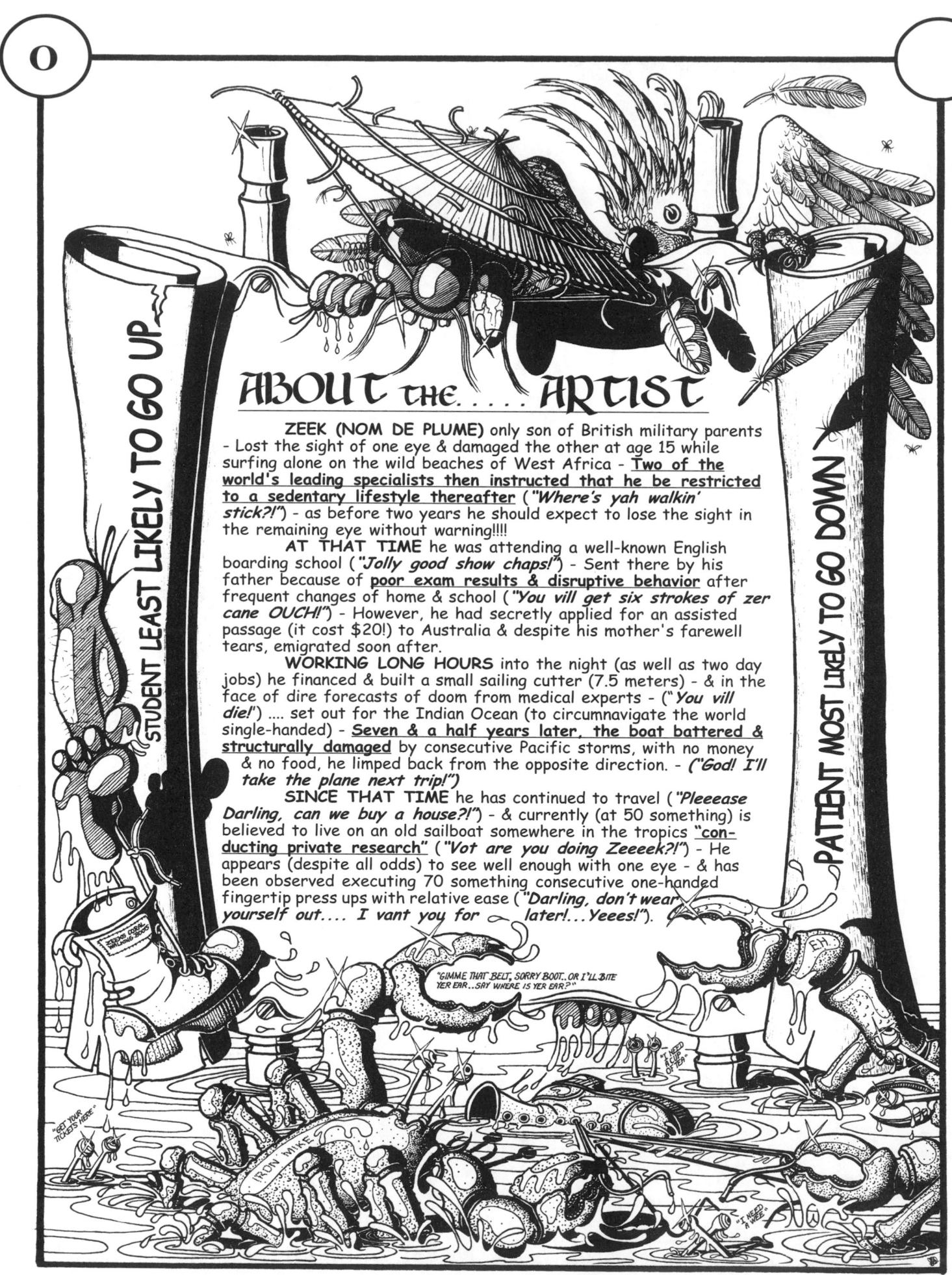

0

STUDENT LEAST LIKELY TO GO UP

PATIENT MOST LIKELY TO GO DOWN

ABOUT the..... ARTIST

ZEEK (NOM DE PLUME) only son of British military parents - Lost the sight of one eye & damaged the other at age 15 while surfing alone on the wild beaches of West Africa - <u>**Two of the world's leading specialists then instructed that he be restricted to a sedentary lifestyle thereafter**</u> (*"Where's yah walkin' stick?!"*) - as before two years he should expect to lose the sight in the remaining eye without warning!!!!

AT THAT TIME he was attending a well-known English boarding school (*"Jolly good show chaps!"*) - Sent there by his father because of <u>**poor exam results & disruptive behavior**</u> after frequent changes of home & school (*"You vill get six strokes of zer cane OUCH!"*) - However, he had secretly applied for an assisted passage (it cost $20!) to Australia & despite his mother's farewell tears, emigrated soon after.

WORKING LONG HOURS into the night (as well as two day jobs) he financed & built a small sailing cutter (7.5 meters) - & in the face of dire forecasts of doom from medical experts - (*"You vill die!"*) .... set out for the Indian Ocean (to circumnavigate the world single-handed) - <u>**Seven & a half years later, the boat battered & structurally damaged**</u> by consecutive Pacific storms, with no money & no food, he limped back from the opposite direction. - (*"God! I'll take the plane next trip!"*)

SINCE THAT TIME he has continued to travel (*"Pleeease Darling, can we buy a house?!"*) - & currently (at 50 something) is believed to live on an old sailboat somewhere in the tropics <u>**"conducting private research"**</u> (*"Vot are you doing Zeeeek?!"*) - He appears (despite all odds) to see well enough with one eye - & has been observed executing 70 something consecutive one-handed fingertip press ups with relative ease (*"Darling, don't wear yourself out.... I vant you for later!...Yeees!"*).

"GIMME THAT BELT, SORRY BOOT...OR I'LL BITE YER EAR...SAY WHERE IS YER EAR?"

INDEX NOTES

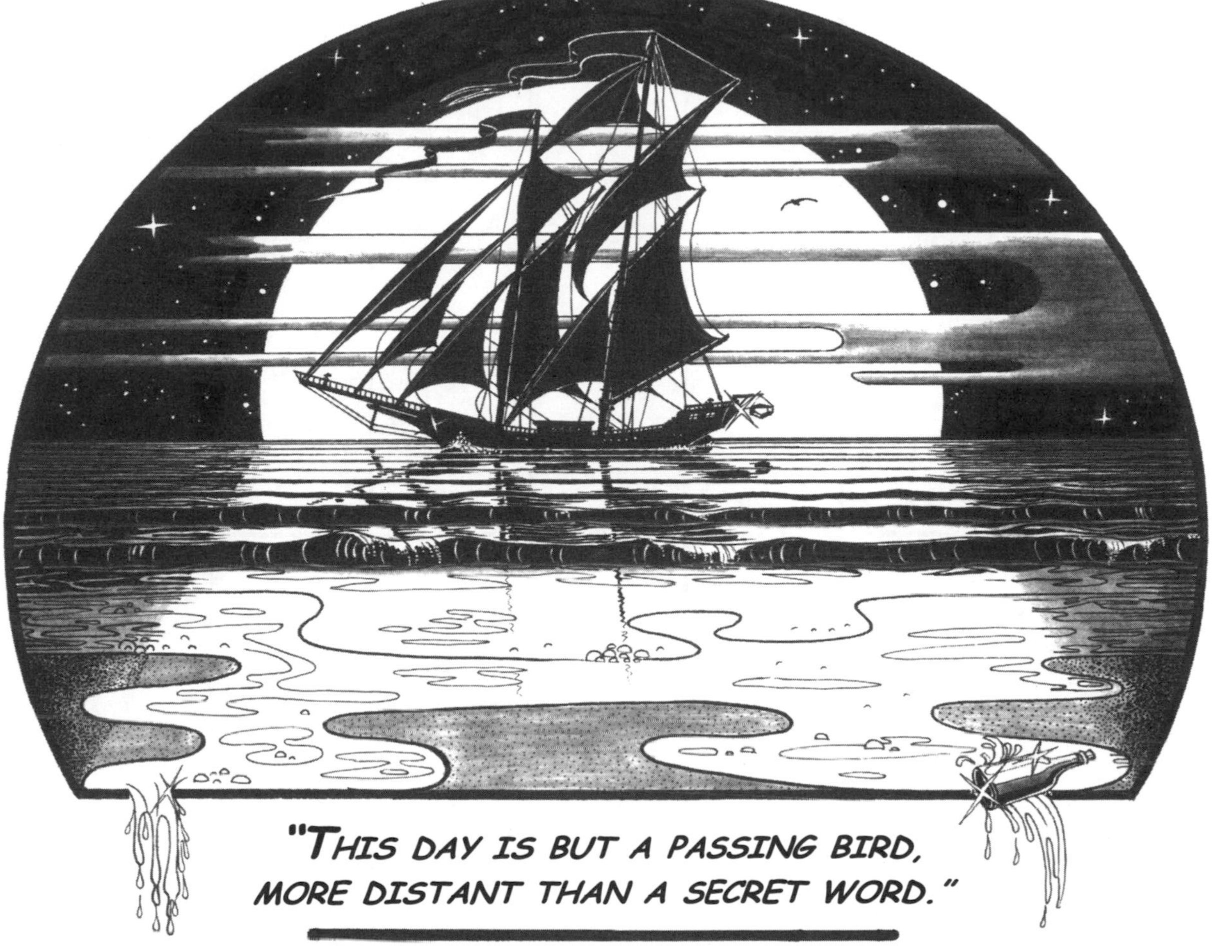

"THIS DAY IS BUT A PASSING BIRD,
MORE DISTANT THAN A SECRET WORD."

INDEX ACCESS

SHEN KU IS A HIGHLY CONDENSED "FORM" OF MULTIPLE SUBJECTS with a transgalactic logic spread - Therefore terminology & doctrine (even spelling) content are extensive & varied - So, enter this index with your enquiry from various angles (& with an open mind) - Example: For "stress" also look up: Anxiety - Fear - Worry - Temper - Nerves - Depression - Insomnia - Fatigue etc.

PLEASE BE ADVISED ALSO THAT in the experience of this researcher conclusions on situations may vary widely between individual "experts" - Example: The West says "Eat potatoes" - The East says "Don't" - Therefore examine progress in your chosen endeavour diagnostically (use graphs) but with a....***POSITIVE OUTLOOK***

IN CONCLUSION . . .

. . . SHEN KU is a "form" of which the logics are universally & timelessly applicable. It may *totally* "boggle" a vivid imagination - We are talking profound relevance to *any* "intelligent" life, in *any* galaxy, at *any* time (past, present or distant future) - THEREFORE fellow Traveler thru time & space, of *whatever* race, culture, or status as we are in existence on this microdot for only a millisecond our recognition of an eternally valid logic in this first intergalactic artform requires that it be . . . DEDICATED TO ALL LIFE IN ANY GALAXY suffering from illness, persecution, circumstance or despair — This work is for you . . . DON'T GIVE UP.

UNTIL WE MEET AGAIN.... ZEEK

A TRAVELER'S PERSONAL LOG PAGE #.......

SAMPLE: Photocopy This Page Only For A Record Of Your Journey

Q

| DEPARTED | | VIA | | ARRIVED | | STAYED | | | NOTES | CODE |
Date	Where	Carrier	Price	Date	Where	Name	Tel.	Price	CODE ENTRIES with a number & record longer comments on back.	

Q1

DEPARTED		VIA		ARRIVED		STAYED			NOTES	CODE
Date	Where	Carrier	Price	Date	Where	Name	Tel.	Price	CODE ENTRIES with a number & record longer comments on back.	

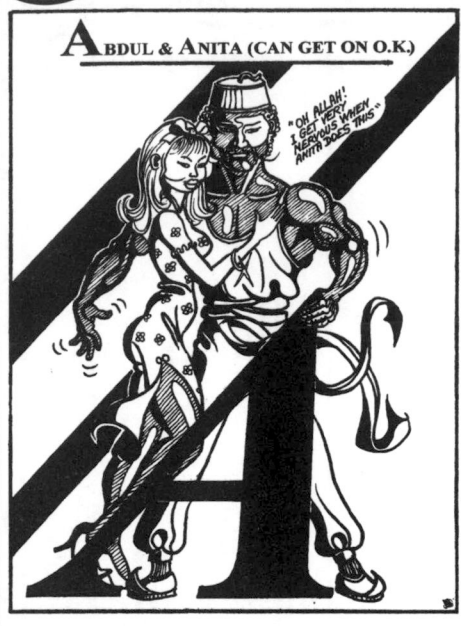

ABDUL & ANITA (CAN GET ON O.K.)

"OH ALLAH! I GET VERY NERVOUS WHEN ANITA DOES THIS"

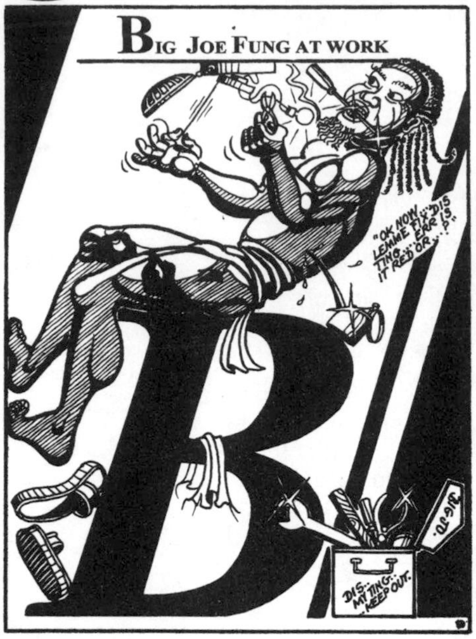
BIG JOE FUNG AT WORK
"OK NOW...DIS LEMME FIX ERR IS TING.... IT RED OR...?"
DIS.. MY TING.. KEEP OUT.

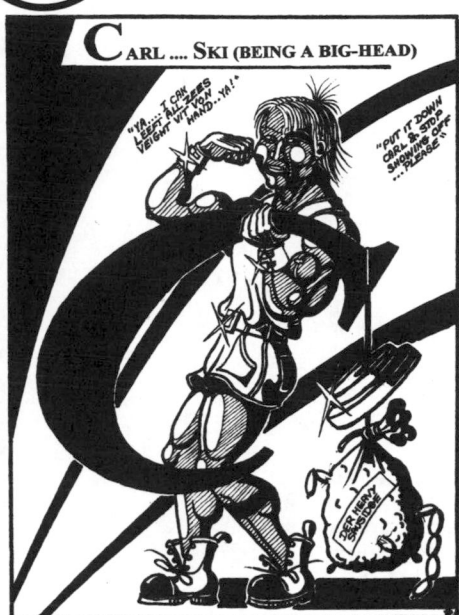

CARL .... SKI (BEING A BIG-HEAD)

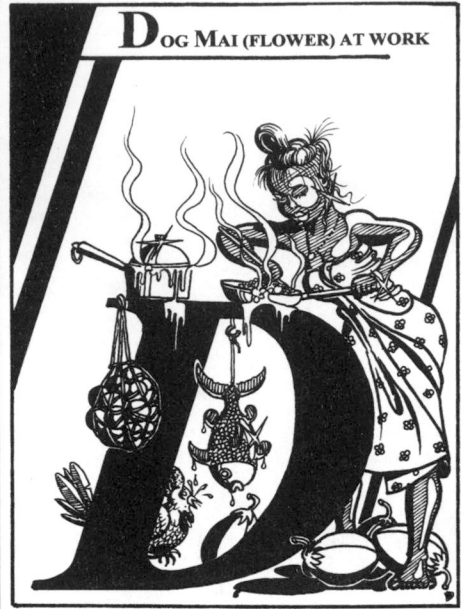

DOG MAI (FLOWER) AT WORK

FROM....
Deceptive (sign of)

INDEX

TO....
Drugs (and allergens)

P10

P11

FROM....

Drugs (and sex)

INDEX

TO....

Eucalyptus Oil

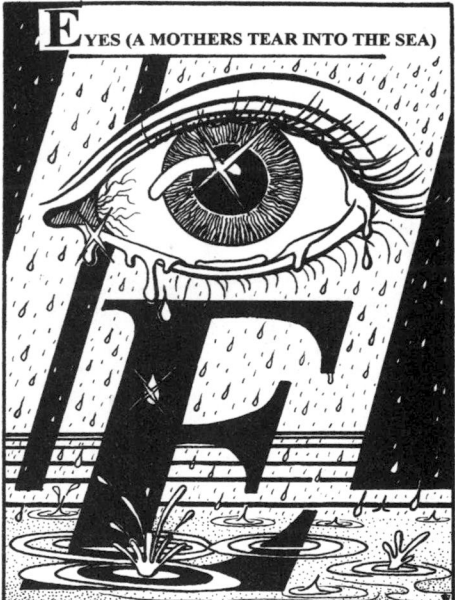

EYES (A MOTHERS TEAR INTO THE SEA)

FROM....
Eupatorium Purpureum

INDEX

TO....
Fallout (radiation)

P12

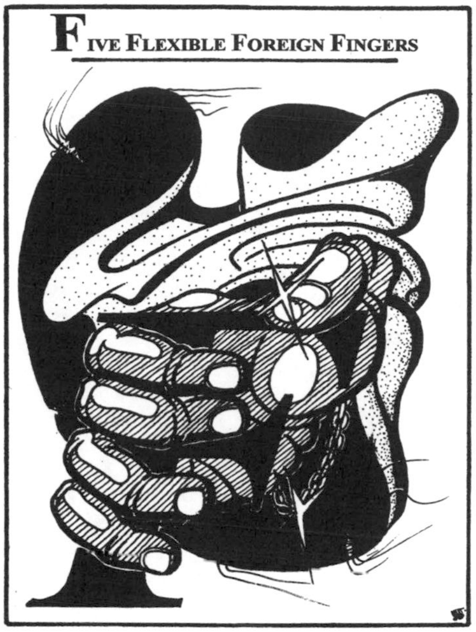

FIVE FLEXIBLE FOREIGN FINGERS

P13

FROM....
Falls (martial arts)

INDEX

TO....
Flexibility (and backache)

FROM....

Flexibility

INDEX

TO....

Garbage Cans (smell)

P14

P15

FROM....
Garbage Tips

INDEX

TO....
Grips (exercise)

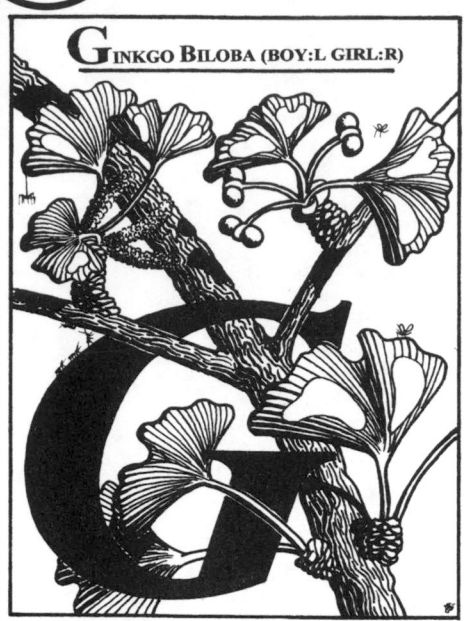

GINKGO BILOBA (BOY:L GIRL:R)

FROM....
Griseofulvin

INDEX

TO....
Headache (from stomach)

P16

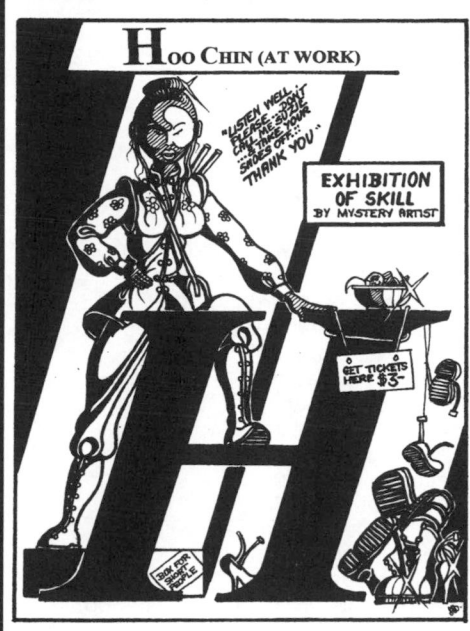

Hoo Chin (at work)

"LISTEN WELL... PLEASE SUPPLY CALL ME SUPPLY YOUR SHOES OFF... THANK YOU"

EXHIBITION OF SKILL BY MYSTERY ARTIST

GET TICKETS HERE $3

P17

FROM....
Headache (sinus)

INDEX

TO....
Hyperactive

FROM....
Hyperactive Kids

INDEX

TO....
Iron (rust and stains)

P18

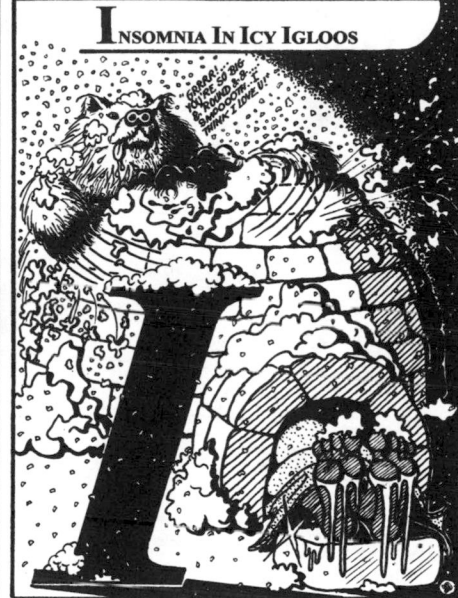

INSOMNIA IN ICY IGLOOS

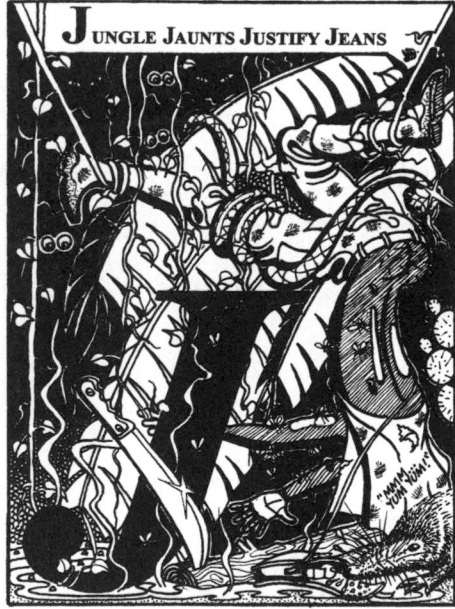

JUNGLE JAUNTS JUSTIFY JEANS

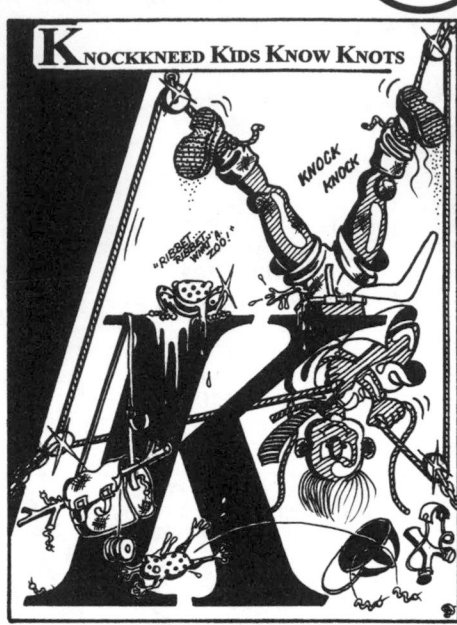

KNOCKKNEED KIDS KNOW KNOTS

FROM....
Kidneys (swollen)

INDEX

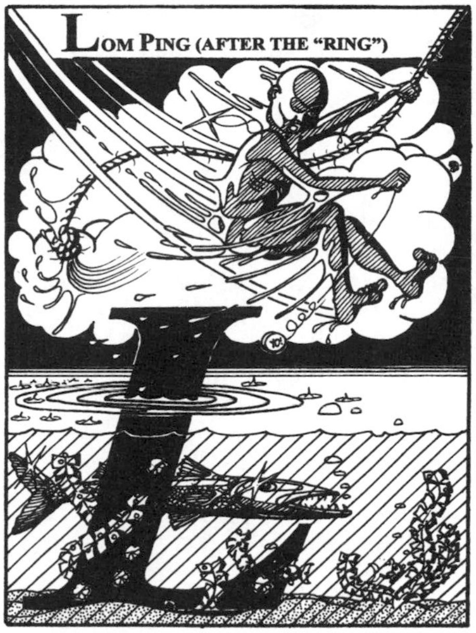

TO....
Life - good (sign of)

P20

LOM PING (AFTER THE "RING")

P21

FROM....
Life - long (sign of)

INDEX

TO....
Mackerel (storage)

FROM....
Mackerel

INDEX

TO....
Mentha (X) Peperita

P22

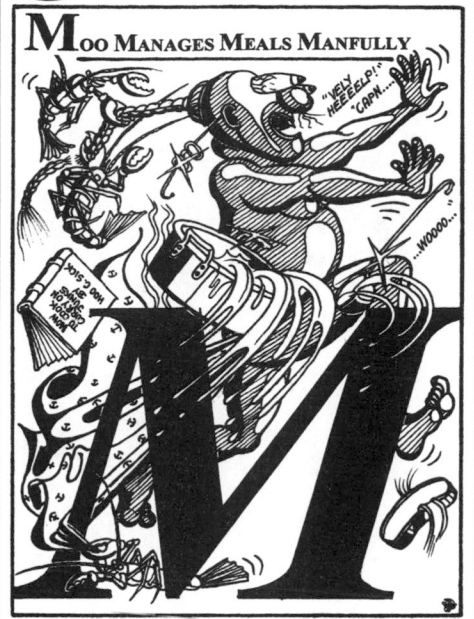

MOO **M**ANAGES **M**EALS **M**ANFULLY

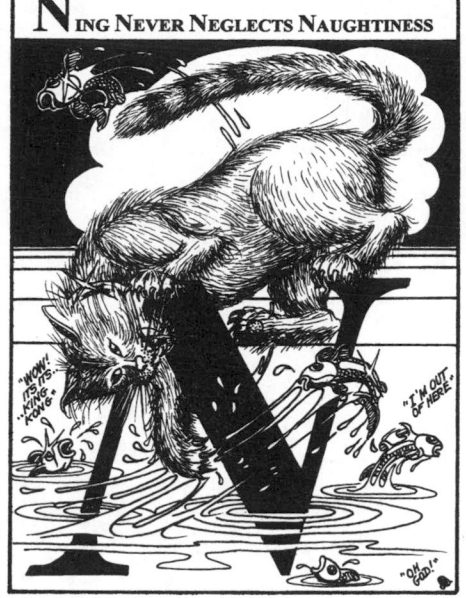

NING NEVER NEGLECTS NAUGHTINESS

P25

FROM....
Nettle Tea

INDEX

TO....
Organs (overburdened)

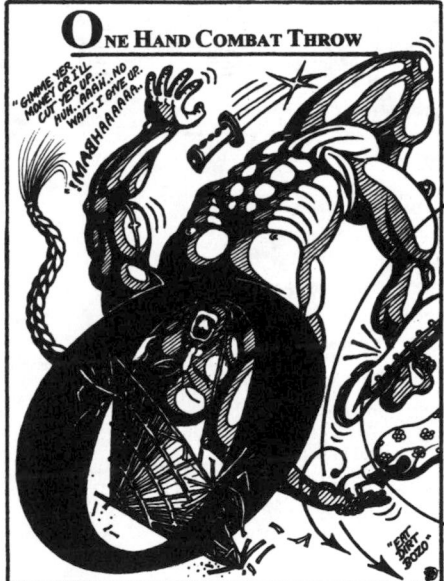

FROM....

Organs (pain in)

INDEX

TO....

Peach

P26

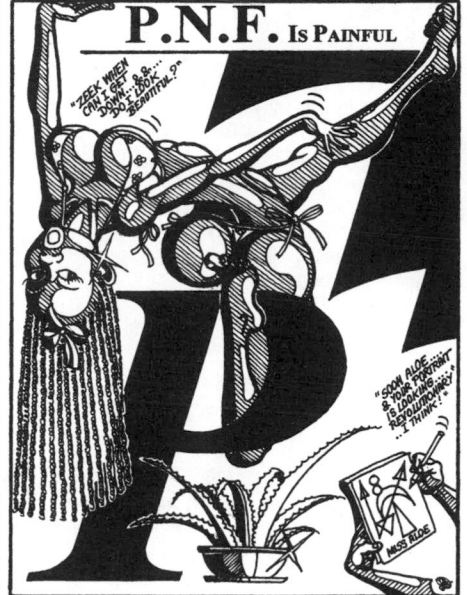

FROM....

Poles (and navigation)

INDEX

TO....

Pyrethrum (plant)

P28

P29

FROM....
Pyridoxine

INDEX

TO....
Ribs

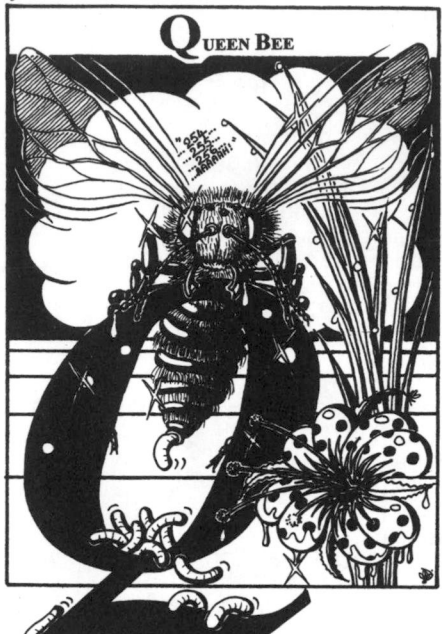

QUEEN BEE

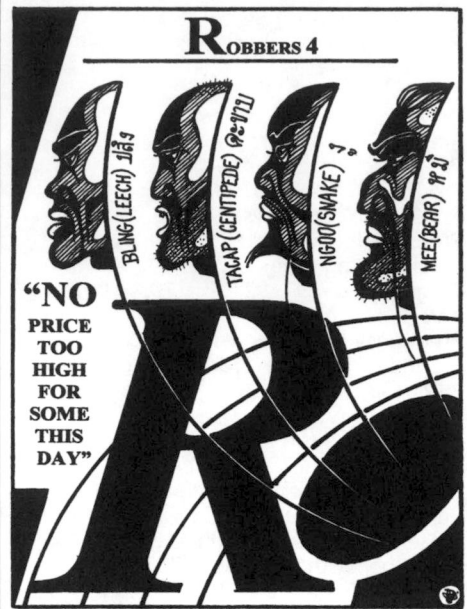

ROBBERS 4

"NO PRICE TOO HIGH FOR SOME THIS DAY"

FROM....
Rice

INDEX

TO....
Scabicide

P30

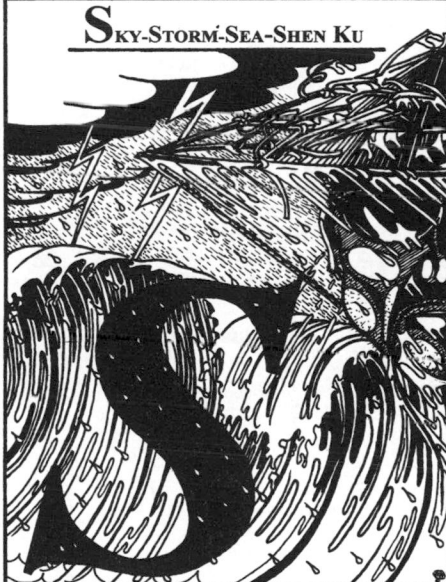

SKY-STORM-SEA-SHEN KU

FROM....
Shins (tsubos)

INDEX

TO....
Skin Cells (dead/remove)

P32

FROM....
Spikes (throwing)

INDEX

TO....
Stomach Throw

P34

P35

FROM....
Stomach Tsubos

INDEX

TO....
Symptoms (fish poisoning)

FROM....
Symptoms (quick guide)

INDEX

TO....
Tin (stains)

P36

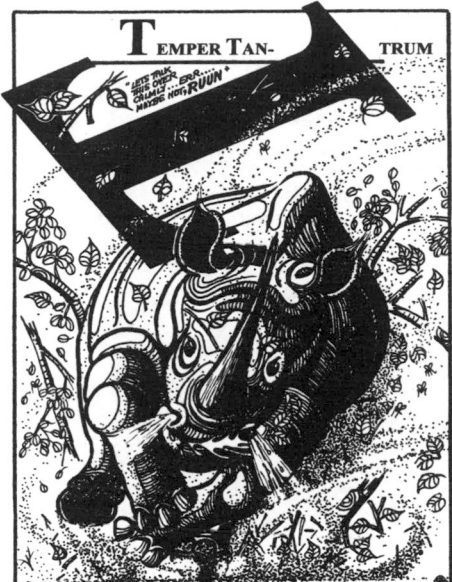

FROM....
Tummy (skin on)

INDEX

TO....
Vegetables (and yin/yang)

P38

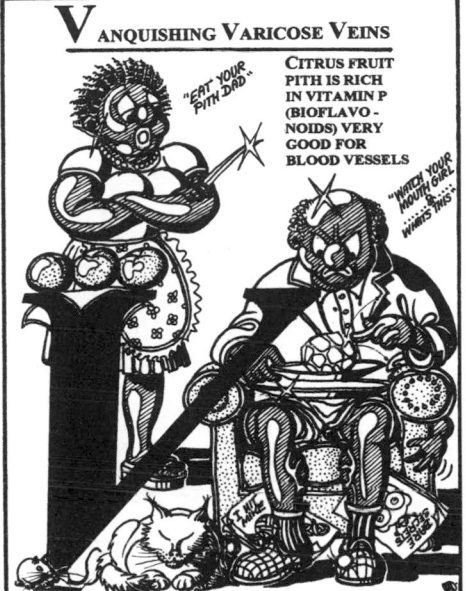

U NIDENTIFIED UNDERSTANDING

WHAT HAPPENED BEFORE TIME BEGAN?

WHAT LIES BEYOND THE END OF SPACE? OR IS THERE SOMETHING I HAVE MISSED?

V ANQUISHING VARICOSE VEINS

"EAT YOUR PITH DAD."

CITRUS FRUIT PITH IS RICH IN VITAMIN P (BIOFLAVO- NOIDS) VERY GOOD FOR BLOOD VESSELS

"WATCH YOUR MOUTH GIRL WHEN THIS."

P39

FROM....
Vegetables (boiled)

INDEX

TO....
Wasting Diseases

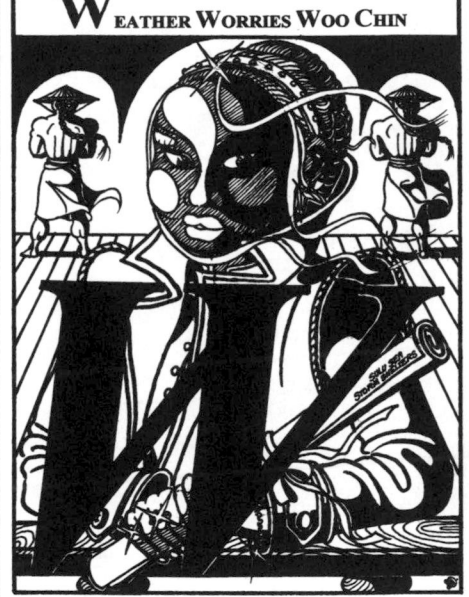

WEATHER WORRIES WOO CHIN

FROM....
Watch Strap (security)

INDEX

TO....
X-ray (damage/repair)

P40

P41

FROM....
X-rays (damage)

INDEX

TO....
Zucchini

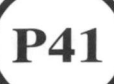

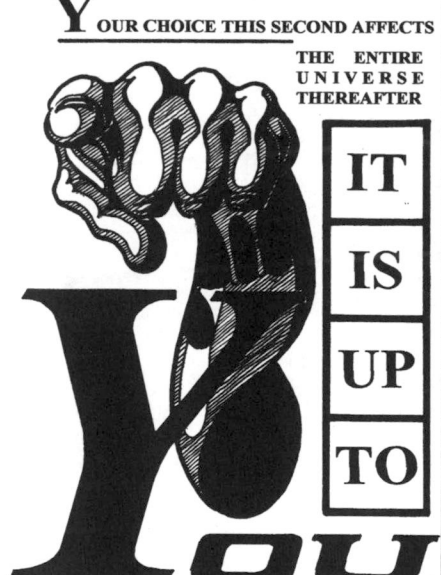

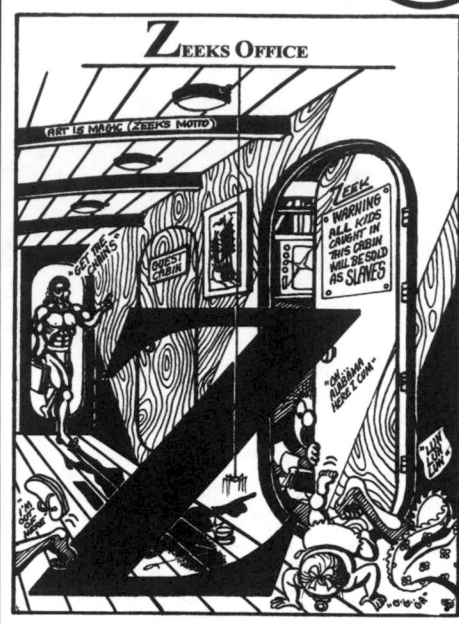